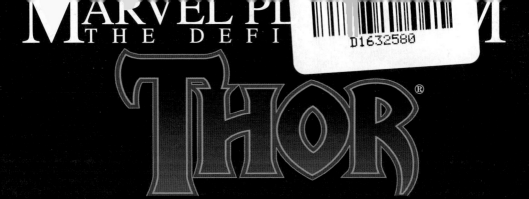

MARVEL PLATINUM
THE DEFINITIVE
THOR®

OURNEY INTO MYSTERY #83
DECEMBER 1962
WRITER: STAN LEE AND LARRY LEIBER
PENCILLER: JACK KIRBY
INKER: JOE SINOTT
LETTERS: ART SIMEK

THE MIGHTY THOR #159
DECEMBER 1968
WRITER: STAN LEE
PENCILLER: JACK KIRBY
INKER: VINCENT COLLETTA
LETTERS: SAMUEL ROSEN

THE MIGHTY THOR #200
JUNE 1972
WRITER: STAN LEE AND GERRY CONWAY
PENCILLER: JOHN BUSCEMA
INKER: JOHN VERPOORTEN
LETTERS: ART SIMEK

THE MIGHTY THOR #337
NOVEMBER 1983
WRITER: WALT SIMONSON
PENCILLER: WALT SIMONSON
INKS: WALT SIMONSON
LETTERS: JOHN E. WORKMAN JR.
COLOURS: GEORGE ROUSSOS

THE MIGHTY THOR #338
DECEMBER 1983
WRITER: WALT SIMONSON
PENCILLER: WALT SIMONSON
INKS: WALT SIMONSON
LETTERS: JOHN E. WORKMAN JR.
COLOURS: GEORGE ROUSSOS

THE MIGHTY THOR #339
JANUARY 1984
WRITER: WALT SIMONSON
PENCILLER: WALT SIMONSON
INKS: WALT SIMONSON
LETTERS: JOHN E. WORKMAN JR.
COLOURS: GEORGE ROUSSOS

THE MIGHTY THOR VOL. 2 #1
JULY 1998
WRITER: DAN JURGENS
PENCILLER: JOHN ROMITA JR.
INKS: KLAUS JANSON
LETTERS: RICHARD STARKINGS AND COMICRAFT'S DAVID LANPHEAR
COLOURS: GREGORY WRIGHT

THE MIGHTY THOR VOL. 2 #2
AUGUST 1998
WRITER: DAN JURGENS
PENCILLER: JOHN ROMITA JR.
INKS: KLAUS JANSON
LETTERS: RICHARD STARKINGS AND COMICRAFT'S DAVID LANPHEAR
COLOURS: GREGORY WRIGHT

THE MIGHTY THOR VOL. 2 #84
NOVEMBER 2004
WRITER: DANIEL BERMAN AND MICHAEL AVON OEMING
PENCILLER: ANDREA DI VITO
INKS: ANDREA DIVITO
LETTERS: CHRIS ELIOPOULOS
COLOURS: LAURA VILLARI

THE MIGHTY THOR VOL. 2 #85
DECEMBER 2004
WRITER: DANIEL BERMAN AND MICHAEL AVON OEMING
PENCILLER: ANDREA DI VITO
INKS: ANDREA DIVITO
LETTERS: VIRTUAL CALLIGRAPHY'S RANDY GENTILE
COLOURS: LAURA VILLARI

THOR VOL. 3 #3
NOVEMBER 2007
WRITER: J. MICHAEL STRACZYNSKI
PENCILLER: OLIVIER COIPEL
INKS: MARK MORALES
LETTERS: CHRIS ELIOPOULOS
COLOURS: LAURA MARTIN

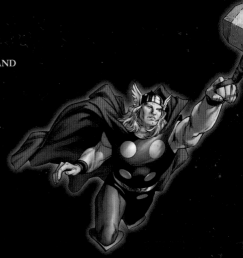

MARVEL® presents: MARVEL PLATINUM: THE DEFINITIVE THOR

MARVEL PLATINUM: THE DEFINITIVE THOR. Contains material originally published in magazine form as JOURNEY INTO MYSTERY #83, THOR VOLUME 1 #159, 200, 337-339, THOR VOLUME 3 #1-2 and 84-85, THOR VOLUME 3 #3. First printing 2011. Published by Panini Publishing, a division of Panini UK Limited. Mike Riddell, Managing Director. Alan O'Keefe, Managing Editor. Mark Irvine, Production Manager. Marco M. Lupoi, Publishing Director Europe. Brady Webb, Reprint Editor. Angela Gray, Will Lucas, Tim Warran-Smith, Designers. Office of publication: Brockbourne House, 77 Mount Ephraim, Tunbridge Wells, Kent TN4 8BS.

INTRODUCTION
BY STAN LEE

Hi, Fellow Asgardians!

Verily are ye blessed, for thou holdeth in thy grateful hands a truly tremendous tome! Yea, within yon hallowed pages thou shalt find the most time-honored Thor tales of all, each chronicling the Thunder God's greatest adventures and brought to thee by some of the most time-honored writers and artists in all of Marveldom. If e'er a collection deserveth the title **Marvel Platinum**, surely it be this! But spare me thy gratitude—thou ain't seen nothin' yet!

But what is it that makes the mighty Thunder God a favorite with fans throughout the world? Glad you asked!

One special and most obvious quality is the fact that, unlike his fellow superheroes, Thor's roots are set in ancient and classic mythology. And not just any old mythology, but the rich tapestry that is Norse mythology -- a world of frost giants, fire demons, dragons, dwarfs, warrior-maidens, bigger-than-life heroes and even bigger, viler villains, plus some of the most astounding, eye-popping, awe-inspiring locations in all the nine realms which provide a breathtaking backdrop to the ever-growing danger and drama!!

With such a wealth of source material is it any wonder that the Thunder God became an instant smash? Here is a hero who not only shares the same struggles as the rest of us – bills to pay, a regular job, family problems and, of course, his love life – but also has to contend with being the heroic heir to the throne of Asgard! You wonder how he ever finds time to get a haircut!

Also, as you know, the secret to a great heroic saga is conflict, and that's practically Thor's middle name. With two lives, one mortal and one godly, come two loves. One in the form of beautiful nurse Jane Foster and the other, of course, is the stunning Lady Sif. Add a jealous foster brother like the dangerous, dastardly, deadly Loki, god of evil, and Thor's overbearing, unpredictable father Odin, and you've got one heck of a rollercoaster ride for our poor hammer-wielding hero!

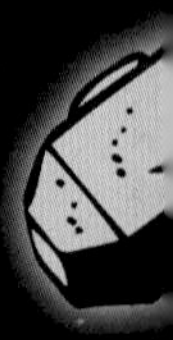

So what lays ahead, O truth seeker? Well, why not start at the beginning with Thor's début in **Journey Into Mystery #83**? It's a classic tale entitled **Thor The Mighty! And The Stone Men From Saturn!** T'was mightily scripted by my clever kid brother, **Larrapin' Larry Lieber** and majestically drawn by **Jack "King" Kirby!**

But if you think that initial tale is where our hero's origin begins, then you don't know Marvel! Why present one origin when we can keep playing with 'em? Let's rush forward to **The Mighty Thor #159** which we published after Thor's incredible first appearance and his instant popularity. You see, he quickly took over **Journey Into Mystery** and the mag was rechristened *The Mighty Thor*. So, in ish #159, we propel you into one of Thor's most startling tales, pandemoniously penned by yours truly and once again inimitably illustrated by **Jolly Jack Kirby**. In this saga we answer one of the thorniest questions that had been plaguing Marvel fans for six long years – 'if Doctor Don Blake is Thor then what happened to the original son of Odin?!!'

Once your mind stops spinning from those incredible revelations, before you have a chance to catch your breath, we plunge you headlong into a classic thriller whose title says it all-- *Beware! If This Be--Ragnarok!* This is where the Asgardians hear the prophesy of their own apocalypse! It's a tale so full of shocks it should come with a health warning! And, as an added bonus, it's illustrated by the truly great **John Buscema!**

Following that legendary tale we join Thor in a dazzling double-header--*Doom!*, *A Fool And His Hammer...* and *Something Old, Something New...*, as the Thunder God encounters an adversary who's as much a hero as Thor himself – and wait'll you see him!! **Wondrous Walt Simonson** takes the artistic helm as he propels our Odinson into the depths of space, where he faces the might of that unforgettable alien, Beta Ray Bill, as well as a challenge to his right to wield the mighty uru hammer, Mjolnir!

Next, the creative reins are passed to that rhapsodic writer **Dan Jurgens** and the powerful penciler **John Romita Jr.** in their wondrous stories *In Search Of The Gods* and *Deal with The Devil!* Together they weave a masterful tale of tragedy and heroism, as Thor and his fellow Avengers battle the Destroyer, one of the most powerful forces to bestride Midgard (that's good ol' Earth, in case you came in late, Bunky).

Believe it or not, there's still more – how lucky can you be? Thor's adventures reach new heights as, under the titanic team of **Michael Avon Oeming** and **Andrea DiVito**, Asgard falls to the ever-deceitful, ever-diabolical and always deadly Loki, as he finally brings about the unthinkable Ragnarok! How can Thor, now Lord of Asgard, save his people and his realm from the unstoppable forces of fate and prophesy? That's a rhetorical question, pilgrim,'cause you'll haveta read it yourself — and you won't believe how this one ends!

Speaking of which, all good legends must come to a conclusion, and what better way to end this collection than with a good old-fashioned hero-versus-hero slugfest! The title **Everything Old Is New Again** belies the pulse-pounding you can only find in an Asgardian classic such as this. After missing the now-classic Superhero Civil War, Thor is back, mad and spoilin' for a fight! So, in steps Iron Man, the one Avenger who ol' Goldilocks holds most responsible for that darkest of days, where friend fought friend and where Captain America, one of the few mortals to earn Thor's greatest respect, was killed!

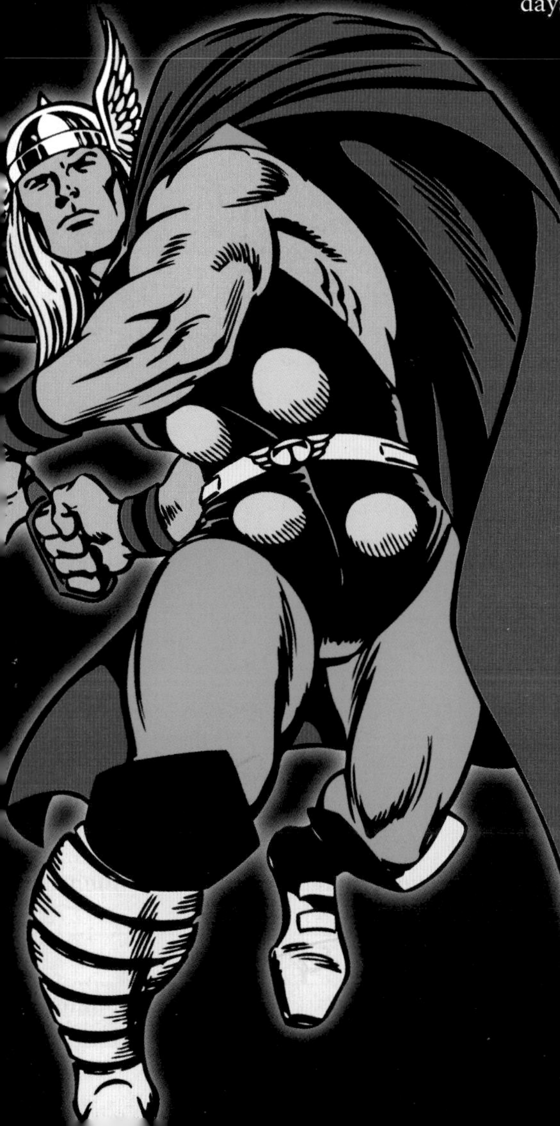

Now you'll finally get your wish as I start winding down so you can get to the good stuff. It isn't often I praise a mag that doesn't contain my own stories, but this one deserves all the plaudits and accolades we can give it. So wait no longer, for the Rainbow Bridge doth beckon and epic adventure lies in store. But you won't get rid of me that easily, 'cause I'll be following every hammer blow right there with you!

Excelsior!

Stan
2011

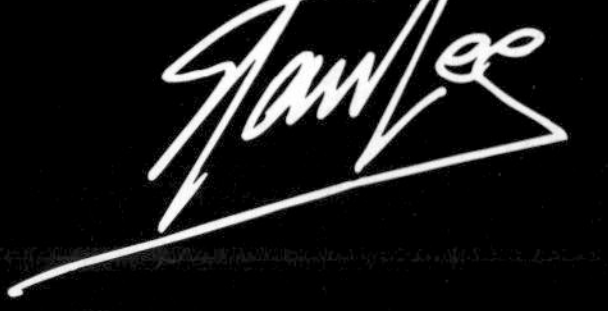

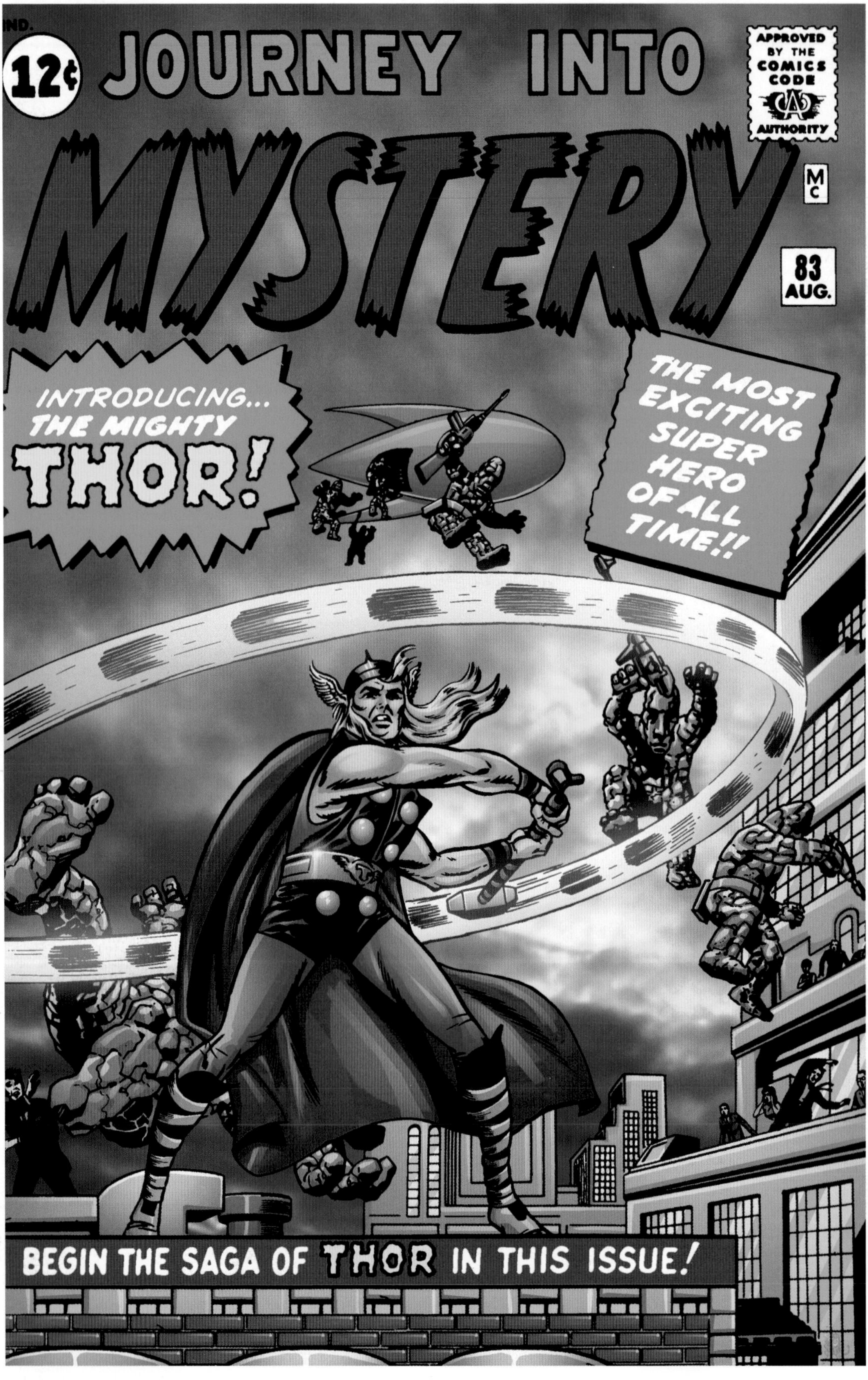
IND.
12¢
JOURNEY INTO
MYSTERY
MC
APPROVED BY THE COMICS CODE AUTHORITY
83 AUG.
INTRODUCING... THE MIGHTY THOR!
THE MOST EXCITING SUPER HERO OF ALL TIME!!
BEGIN THE SAGA OF THOR IN THIS ISSUE!

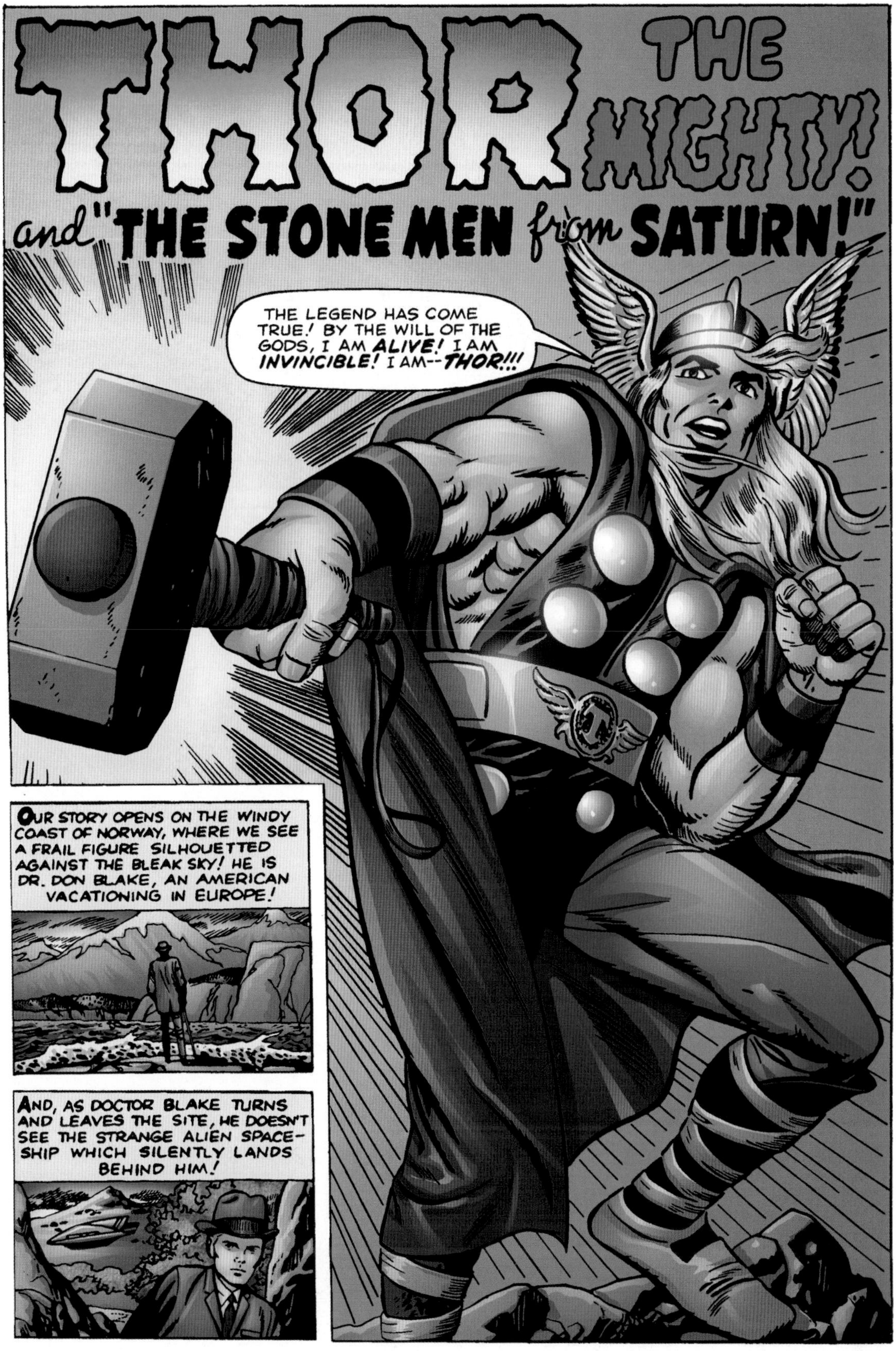
THOR THE MIGHTY!
and "THE STONE MEN from SATURN!"
THE LEGEND HAS COME TRUE! BY THE WILL OF THE GODS, I AM ALIVE! I AM INVINCIBLE! I AM--THOR!!!
OUR STORY OPENS ON THE WINDY COAST OF NORWAY, WHERE WE SEE A FRAIL FIGURE SILHOUETTED AGAINST THE BLEAK SKY! HE IS DR. DON BLAKE, AN AMERICAN VACATIONING IN EUROPE!
AND, AS DOCTOR BLAKE TURNS AND LEAVES THE SITE, HE DOESN'T SEE THE STRANGE ALIEN SPACE-SHIP WHICH SILENTLY LANDS BEHIND HIM!

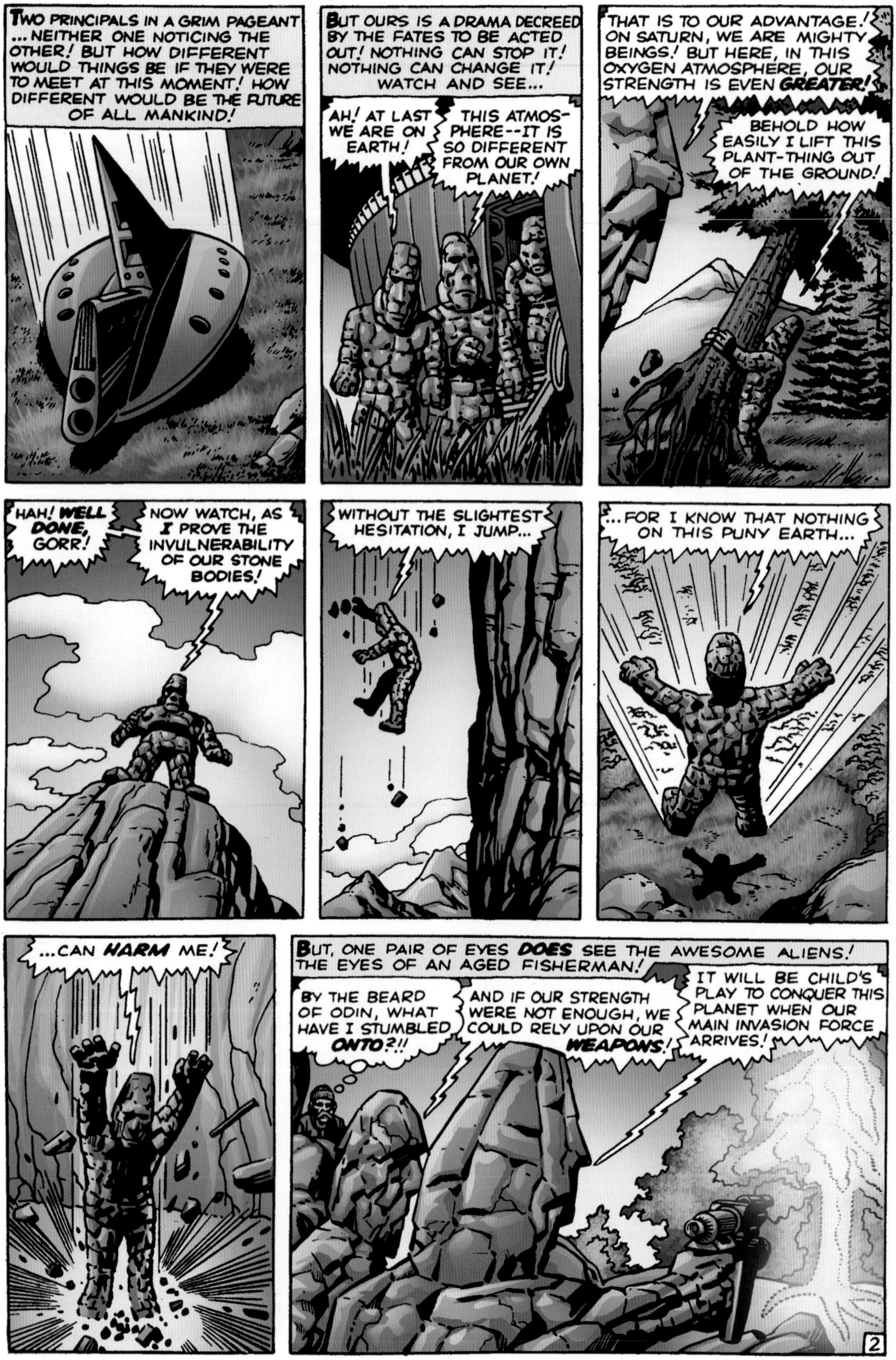
TWO PRINCIPALS IN A GRIM PAGEANT ... NEITHER ONE NOTICING THE OTHER! BUT HOW DIFFERENT WOULD THINGS BE IF THEY WERE TO MEET AT THIS MOMENT! HOW DIFFERENT WOULD BE THE FUTURE OF ALL MANKIND!
BUT OURS IS A DRAMA DECREED BY THE FATES TO BE ACTED OUT! NOTHING CAN STOP IT! NOTHING CAN CHANGE IT! WATCH AND SEE...
AH! AT LAST WE ARE ON EARTH!
THIS ATMOSPHERE--IT IS SO DIFFERENT FROM OUR OWN PLANET!
THAT IS TO OUR ADVANTAGE! ON SATURN, WE ARE MIGHTY BEINGS! BUT HERE, IN THIS OXYGEN ATMOSPHERE, OUR STRENGTH IS EVEN GREATER!
BEHOLD HOW EASILY I LIFT THIS PLANT-THING OUT OF THE GROUND!
HAH! WELL DONE, GORR!
NOW WATCH, AS I PROVE THE INVULNERABILITY OF OUR STONE BODIES!
WITHOUT THE SLIGHTEST HESITATION, I JUMP...
...FOR I KNOW THAT NOTHING ON THIS PUNY EARTH...
...CAN HARM ME!
BUT, ONE PAIR OF EYES DOES SEE THE AWESOME ALIENS! THE EYES OF AN AGED FISHERMAN!
BY THE BEARD OF ODIN, WHAT HAVE I STUMBLED ONTO?!!
AND IF OUR STRENGTH WERE NOT ENOUGH, WE COULD RELY UPON OUR WEAPONS!
IT WILL BE CHILD'S PLAY TO CONQUER THIS PLANET WHEN OUR MAIN INVASION FORCE ARRIVES!
2

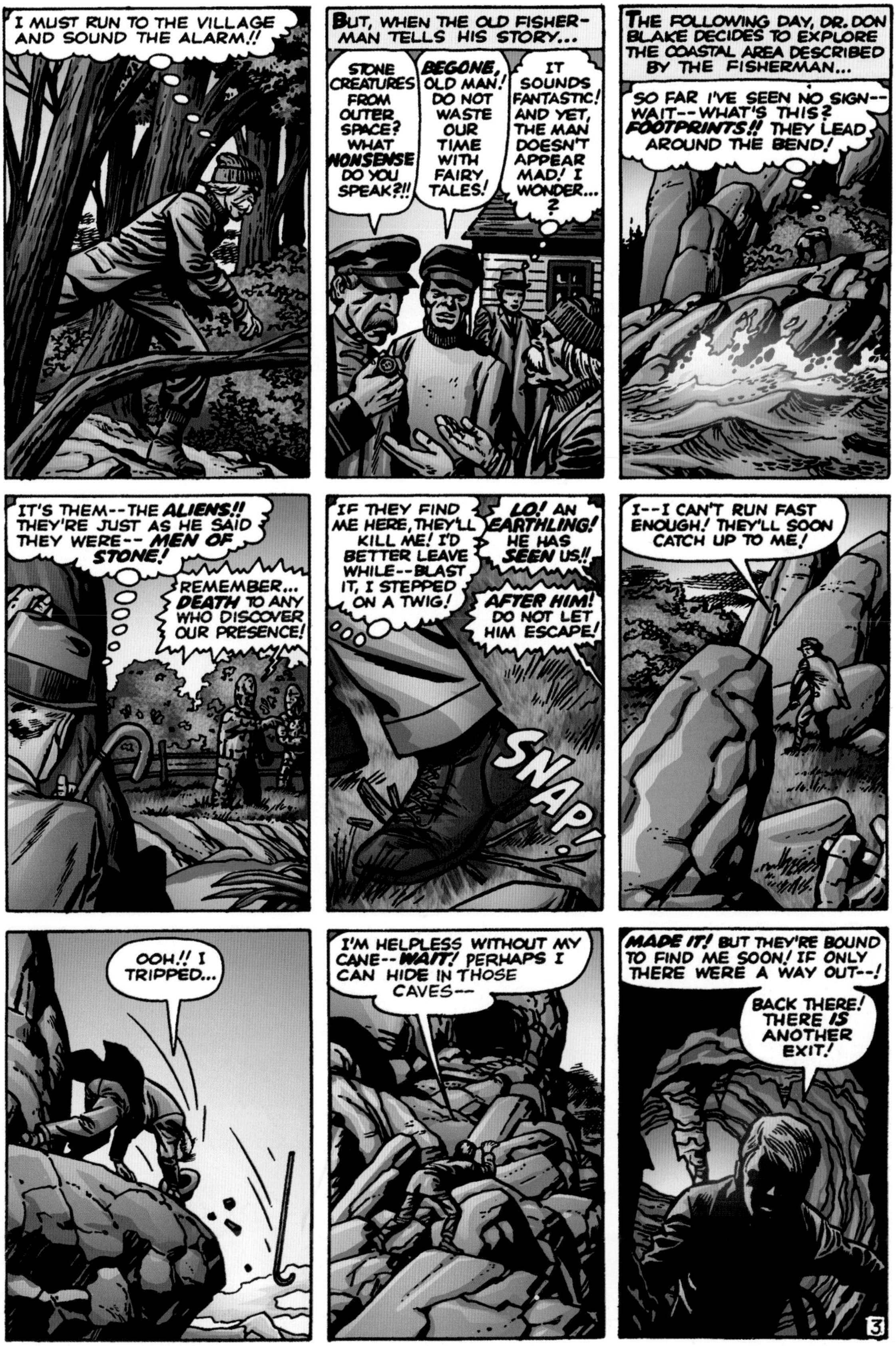

I MUST RUN TO THE VILLAGE AND SOUND THE ALARM!!
BUT, WHEN THE OLD FISHERMAN TELLS HIS STORY...
STONE CREATURES FROM OUTER SPACE? WHAT NONSENSE DO YOU SPEAK?!!
BEGONE, OLD MAN! DO NOT WASTE OUR TIME WITH FAIRY TALES!
IT SOUNDS FANTASTIC! AND YET, THE MAN DOESN'T APPEAR MAD! I WONDER...?
THE FOLLOWING DAY, DR. DON BLAKE DECIDES TO EXPLORE THE COASTAL AREA DESCRIBED BY THE FISHERMAN...
SO FAR I'VE SEEN NO SIGN-- WAIT--WHAT'S THIS? FOOTPRINTS!! THEY LEAD AROUND THE BEND!
IT'S THEM--THE ALIENS!! THEY'RE JUST AS HE SAID THEY WERE-- MEN OF STONE!
REMEMBER... DEATH TO ANY WHO DISCOVER OUR PRESENCE!
IF THEY FIND ME HERE, THEY'LL KILL ME! I'D BETTER LEAVE WHILE--BLAST IT, I STEPPED ON A TWIG!
LO! AN EARTHLING! HE HAS SEEN US!!
AFTER HIM! DO NOT LET HIM ESCAPE!
SNAP!
I--I CAN'T RUN FAST ENOUGH! THEY'LL SOON CATCH UP TO ME!
OOH!! I TRIPPED...
I'M HELPLESS WITHOUT MY CANE--WAIT! PERHAPS I CAN HIDE IN THOSE CAVES--
MADE IT! BUT THEY'RE BOUND TO FIND ME SOON! IF ONLY THERE WERE A WAY OUT--!
BACK THERE! THERE IS ANOTHER EXIT!
3

...BUT IT'S BLOCKED BY THIS BOULDER! UHHH-- IT'S HOPELESS! I CAN'T BUDGE IT AT ALL!

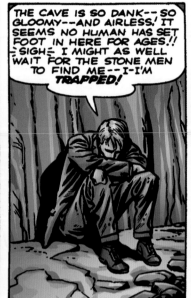

THE CAVE IS SO DANK-- SO GLOOMY--AND AIRLESS! IT SEEMS NO HUMAN HAS SET FOOT IN HERE FOR AGES!! -SIGH- I MIGHT AS WELL WAIT FOR THE STONE MEN TO FIND ME--I-I'M *TRAPPED!*

BUT, SUDDENLY...

THE WALL IS *OPENING!!* I MUST HAVE PRESSED SOME KIND OF HIDDEN LEVER WHEN I LEANED AGAINST IT!

IT'S A SECRET CHAMBER! BUT THERE'S NOTHING INSIDE... EXCEPT THAT GNARLED WOODEN STICK--LIKE AN ANCIENT CANE!

I WONDER? PERHAPS BY USING THIS AS A LEVER, I CAN *MOVE* THE BOULDER!

UHHH... I... I *STILL* CAN'T BUDGE IT! BUT I *MUST* KEEP TRYING... MUSTN'T GIVE UP... IT'S MY ONLY CHANCE TO ESCAPE!

NO! IT--IT'S *HOPELESS!* EVEN A *BULLDOZER* COULDN'T MOVE THAT GIANT ROCK!

IN HELPLESS ANGER, DON BLAKE STRIKES THE USELESS CANE AGAINST THE IMMOVABLE BOULDER, AND, AS HE DOES SO...

WHA--?!!

4

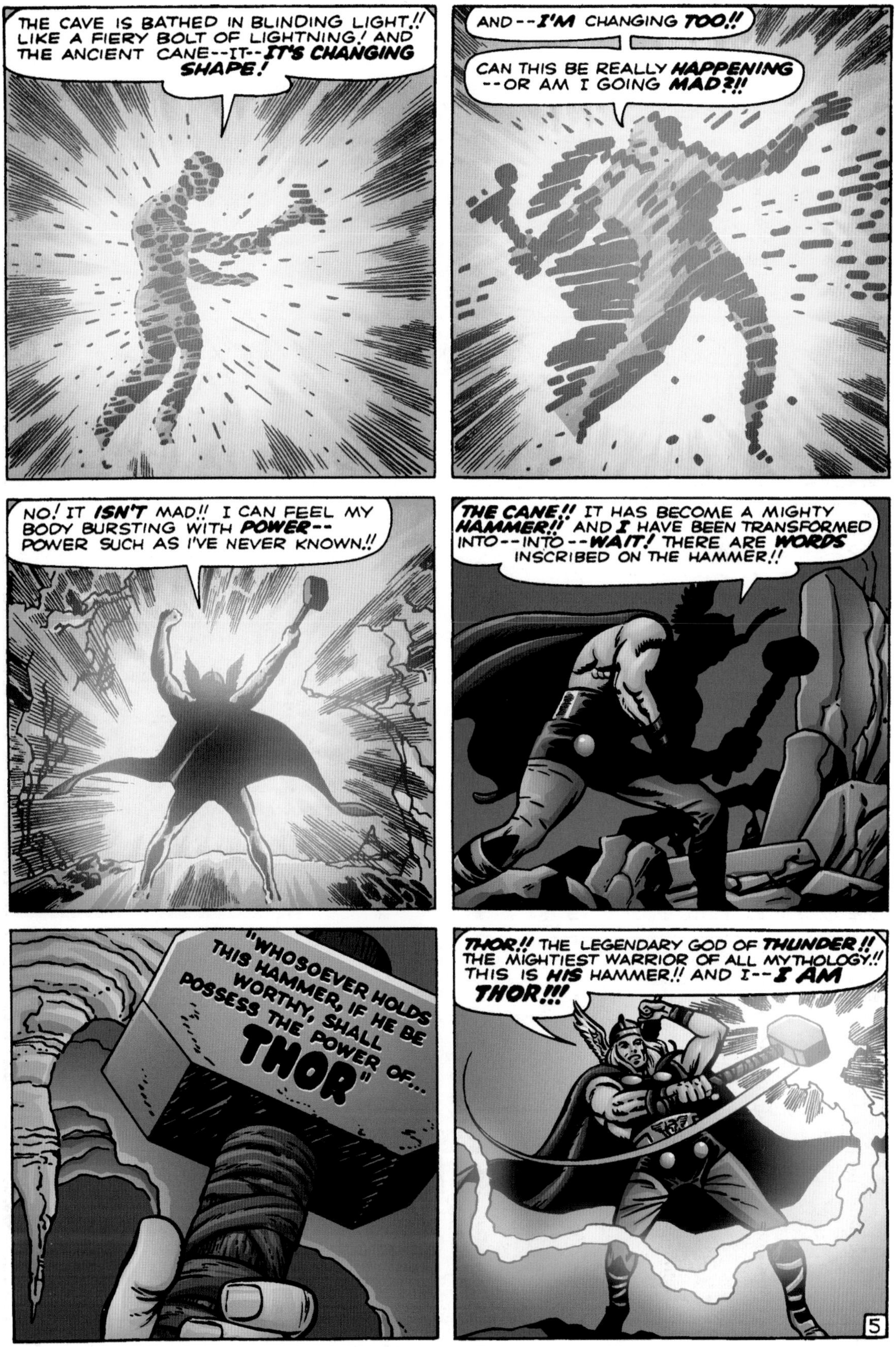
THE CAVE IS BATHED IN BLINDING LIGHT!! LIKE A FIERY BOLT OF LIGHTNING! AND THE ANCIENT CANE--IT--IT'S CHANGING SHAPE!
AND--I'M CHANGING TOO!!
CAN THIS BE REALLY HAPPENING --OR AM I GOING MAD?!!
NO! IT ISN'T MAD!! I CAN FEEL MY BODY BURSTING WITH POWER-- POWER SUCH AS I'VE NEVER KNOWN!!
THE CANE!! IT HAS BECOME A MIGHTY HAMMER!! AND I HAVE BEEN TRANSFORMED INTO--INTO--WAIT! THERE ARE WORDS INSCRIBED ON THE HAMMER!!
"WHOSOEVER HOLDS THIS HAMMER, IF HE BE WORTHY, SHALL POSSESS THE POWER OF... THOR"
THOR!! THE LEGENDARY GOD OF THUNDER!! THE MIGHTIEST WARRIOR OF ALL MYTHOLOGY!! THIS IS HIS HAMMER!! AND I--I AM THOR!!!
5

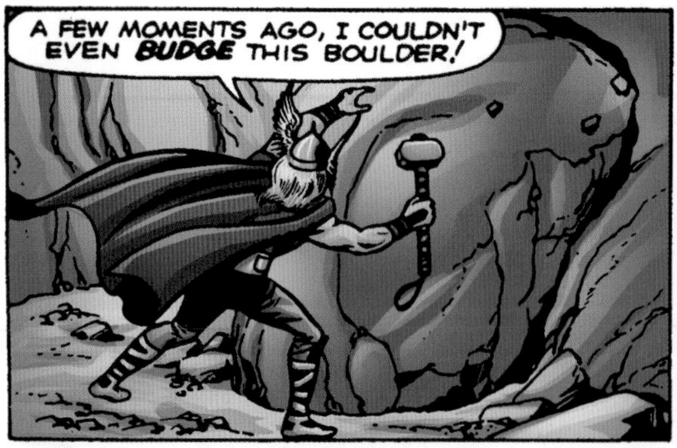
A FEW MOMENTS AGO, I COULDN'T EVEN BUDGE THIS BOULDER!

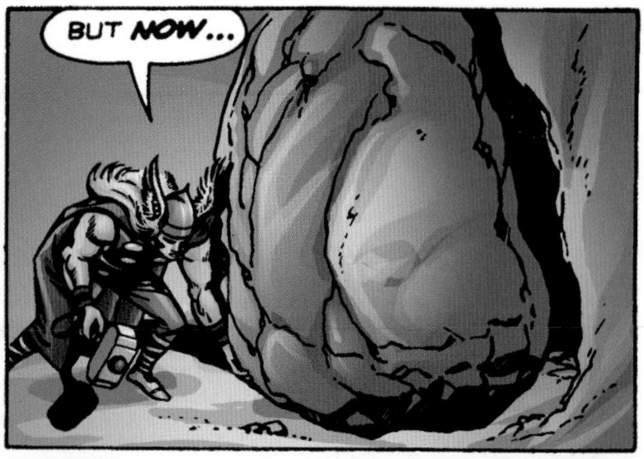
BUT NOW...

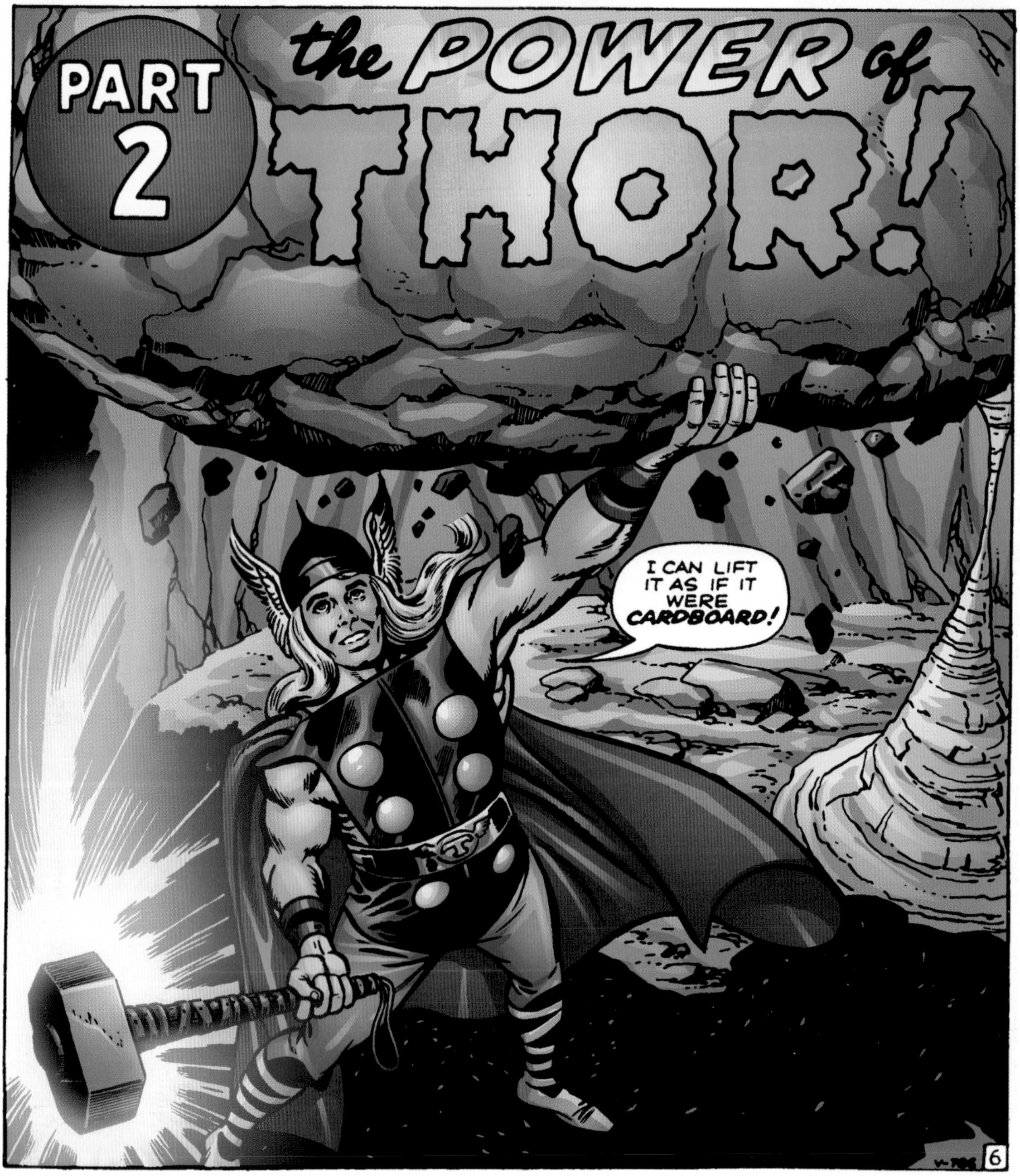
PART 2
the POWER of THOR!
I CAN LIFT IT AS IF IT WERE CARDBOARD!
6

THE STONE CREATURES WILL NEVER SUSPECT THAT THEIR FRAIL QUARRY ESCAPED THROUGH THIS REAR EXIT!

BUT WHAT HAPPENS *NOW?* DO I WALK AMIDST THE CIVILIZED WORLD AS A-MYTHOLOGICAL GOD?? OR--? IT IS TOO BEWILDERING! I MUST PAUSE...AND THINK THIS OUT!

THOR...THE GOD OF THUNDER! WHAT DO I REMEMBER OF HIM FROM MY SCHOOL DAYS? HE WAS THE NOBLEST AND STRONGEST OF ALL THE NORSE GODS!

THE FOURTH DAY OF THE WEEK, THURSDAY WAS NAMED IN HIS HONOR! HE WAS--*WHA*--? WHAT'S *HAPPENING* TO ME?? I'M -- I'M *CHANGING* AGAIN.!!

I'M BACK TO *NORMAL* ONCE MORE! BUT *HOW??* WHAT *CAUSED* IT?? WAIT-- THE INSCRIPTION ON THE HAMMER--

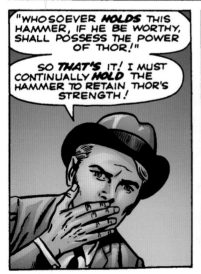

"WHOSOEVER *HOLDS* THIS HAMMER, IF HE BE WORTHY, SHALL POSSESS THE POWER OF THOR!"

SO *THAT'S* IT! I MUST CONTINUALLY *HOLD* THE HAMMER TO RETAIN THOR'S STRENGTH!

IF I LET *GO* OF IT, IN ABOUT SIXTY SECONDS I REVERT BACK TO MY NORMAL SELF!

ACCORDING TO THE LEGEND, THOR'S HAMMER HAD *OTHER* CHARACTERISTICS! ONE, IS THAT IT WAS SO *HEAVY,* NONE BUT MIGHTY THOR COULD *LIFT* IT!

7

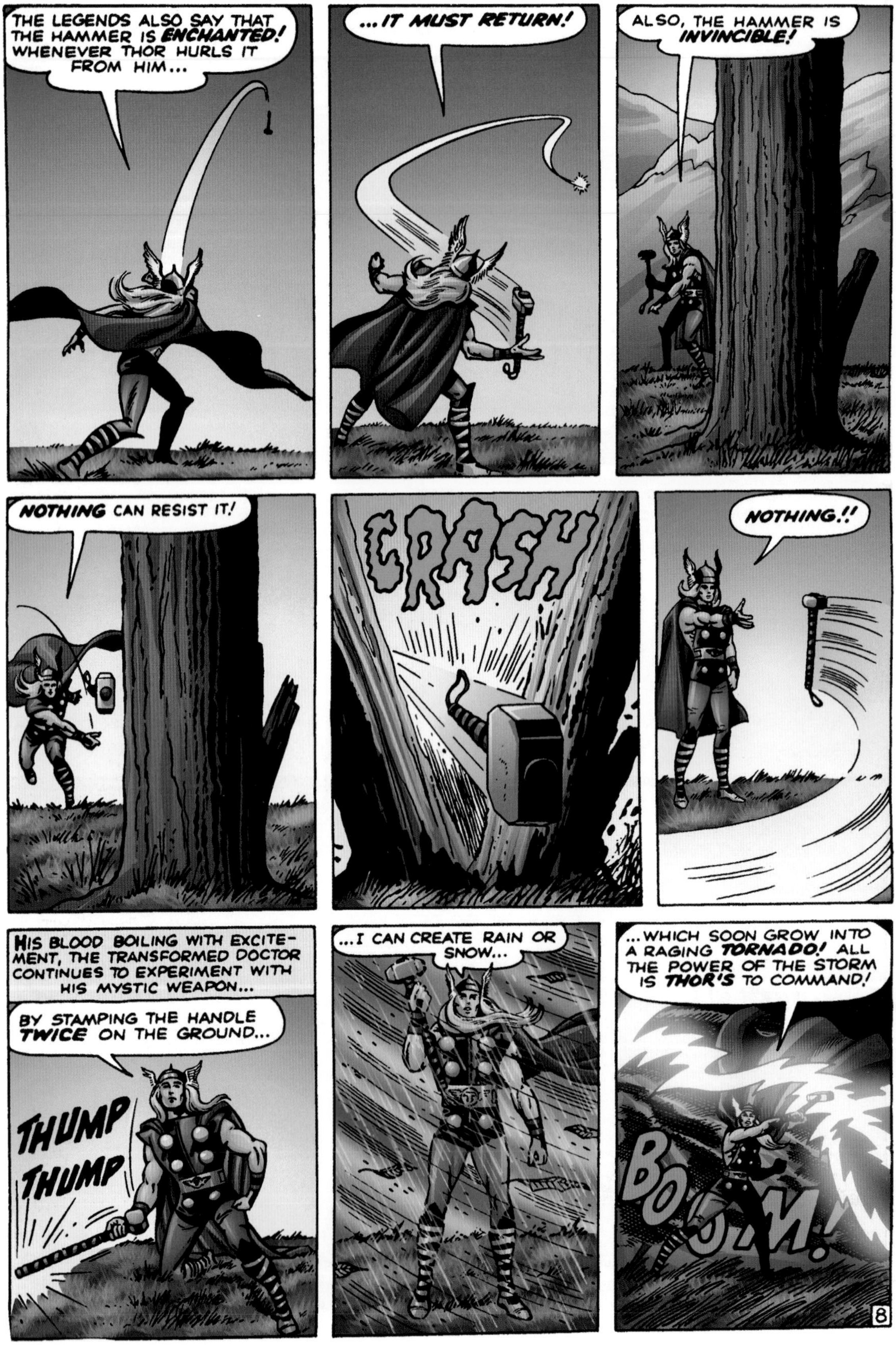
THE LEGENDS ALSO SAY THAT THE HAMMER IS ENCHANTED! WHENEVER THOR HURLS IT FROM HIM...
...IT MUST RETURN!
ALSO, THE HAMMER IS INVINCIBLE!
NOTHING CAN RESIST IT!
CRASH
NOTHING.!!
HIS BLOOD BOILING WITH EXCITEMENT, THE TRANSFORMED DOCTOR CONTINUES TO EXPERIMENT WITH HIS MYSTIC WEAPON...
BY STAMPING THE HANDLE TWICE ON THE GROUND...
THUMP
THUMP
...I CAN CREATE RAIN OR SNOW...
...WHICH SOON GROW INTO A RAGING TORNADO! ALL THE POWER OF THE STORM IS THOR'S TO COMMAND!
BOOM!
8

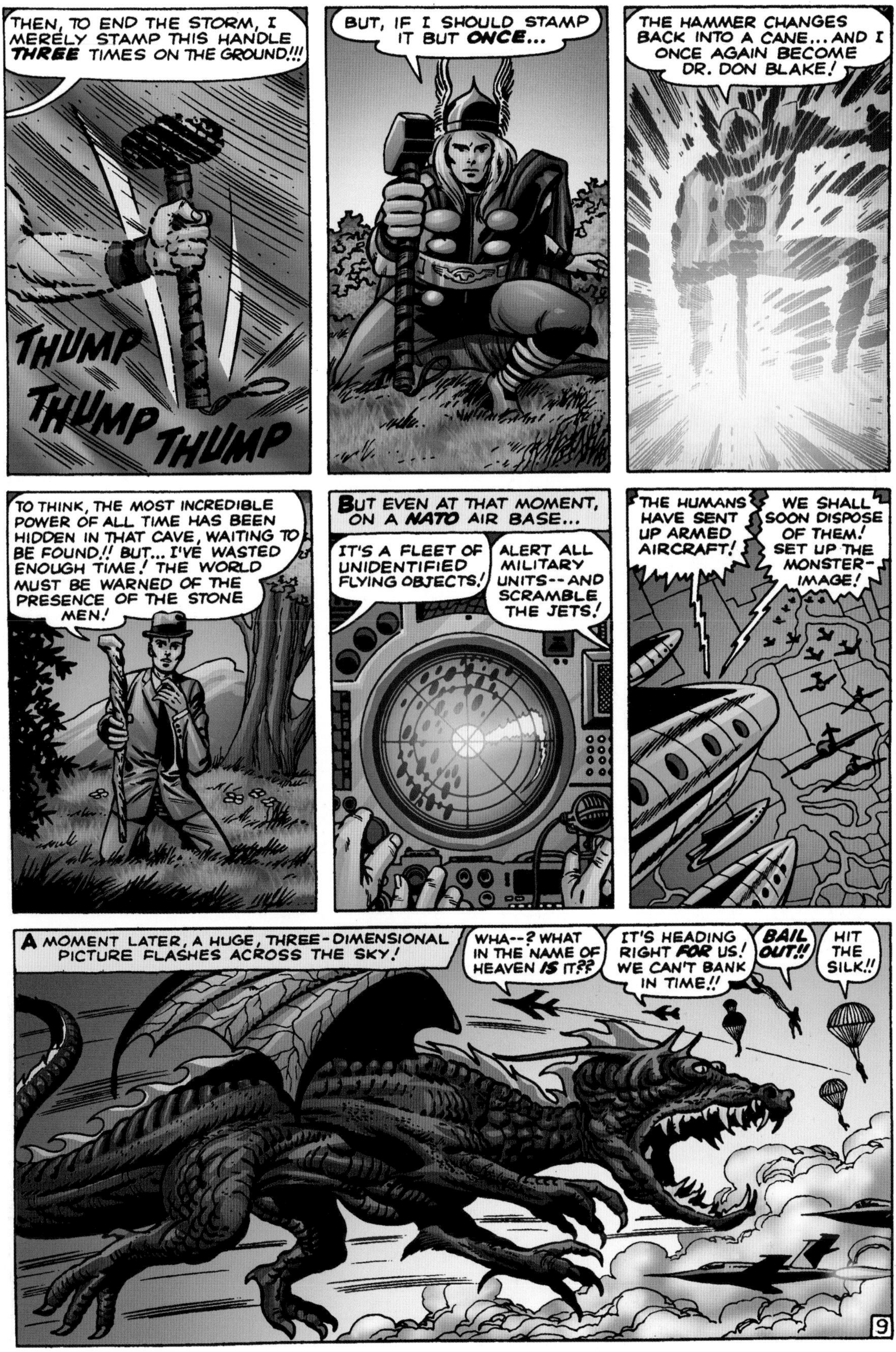
THEN, TO END THE STORM, I MERELY STAMP THIS HANDLE THREE TIMES ON THE GROUND!!!
THUMP
THUMP
THUMP
BUT, IF I SHOULD STAMP IT BUT ONCE...
THE HAMMER CHANGES BACK INTO A CANE... AND I ONCE AGAIN BECOME DR. DON BLAKE!
TO THINK, THE MOST INCREDIBLE POWER OF ALL TIME HAS BEEN HIDDEN IN THAT CAVE, WAITING TO BE FOUND!! BUT... I'VE WASTED ENOUGH TIME! THE WORLD MUST BE WARNED OF THE PRESENCE OF THE STONE MEN!
BUT EVEN AT THAT MOMENT, ON A NATO AIR BASE...
IT'S A FLEET OF UNIDENTIFIED FLYING OBJECTS!
ALERT ALL MILITARY UNITS--AND SCRAMBLE THE JETS!
THE HUMANS HAVE SENT UP ARMED AIRCRAFT!
WE SHALL SOON DISPOSE OF THEM! SET UP THE MONSTER-IMAGE!
A MOMENT LATER, A HUGE, THREE-DIMENSIONAL PICTURE FLASHES ACROSS THE SKY!
WHA--? WHAT IN THE NAME OF HEAVEN IS IT??
IT'S HEADING RIGHT FOR US! WE CAN'T BANK IN TIME!!
BAIL OUT!!
HIT THE SILK!!
9

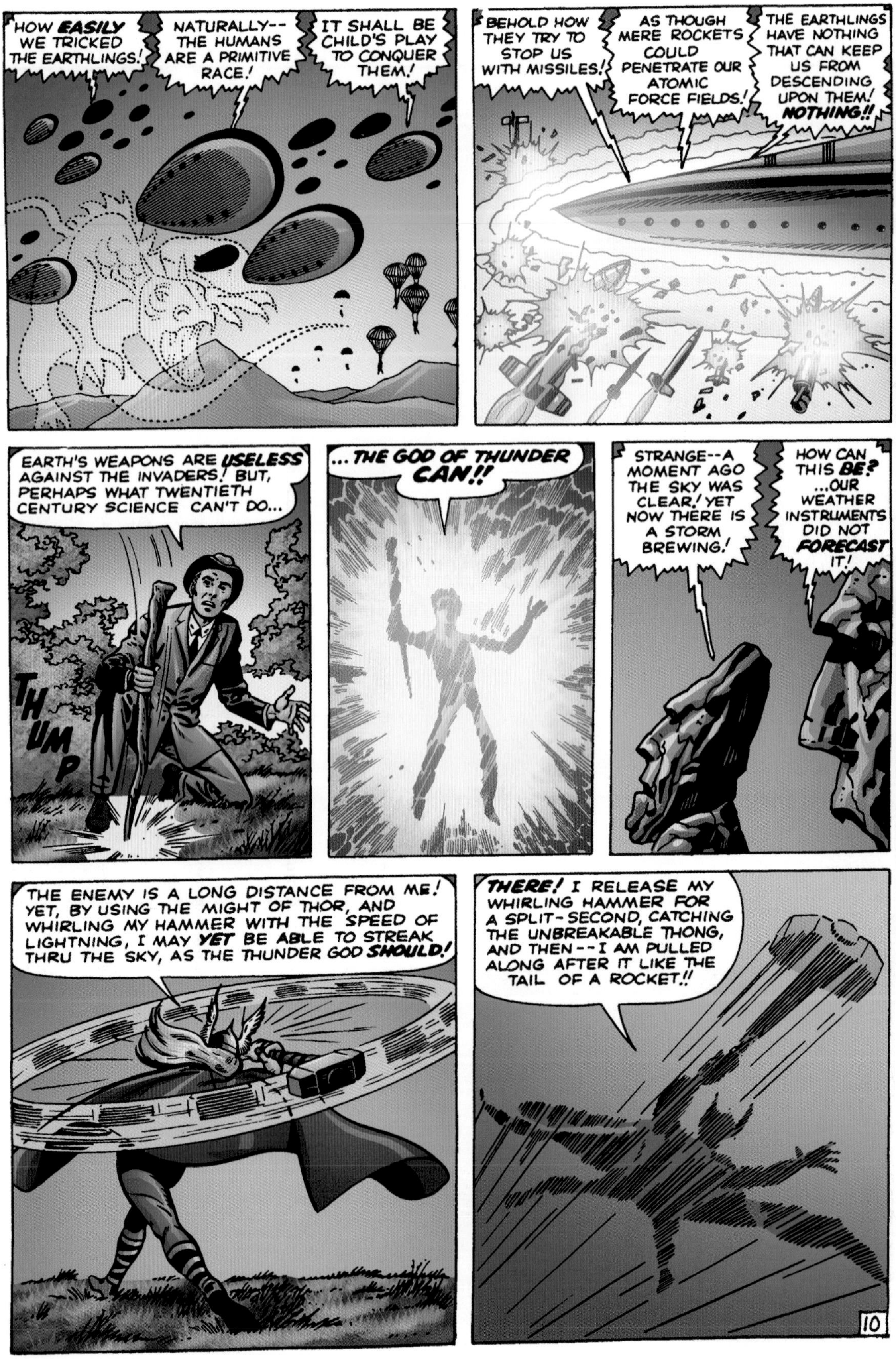
HOW EASILY WE TRICKED THE EARTHLINGS!
NATURALLY-- THE HUMANS ARE A PRIMITIVE RACE!
IT SHALL BE CHILD'S PLAY TO CONQUER THEM!
BEHOLD HOW THEY TRY TO STOP US WITH MISSILES!
AS THOUGH MERE ROCKETS COULD PENETRATE OUR ATOMIC FORCE FIELDS!
THE EARTHLINGS HAVE NOTHING THAT CAN KEEP US FROM DESCENDING UPON THEM! NOTHING!!
EARTH'S WEAPONS ARE USELESS AGAINST THE INVADERS! BUT, PERHAPS WHAT TWENTIETH CENTURY SCIENCE CAN'T DO...
THUMP
...THE GOD OF THUNDER CAN!!
STRANGE--A MOMENT AGO THE SKY WAS CLEAR! YET NOW THERE IS A STORM BREWING!
HOW CAN THIS BE? ...OUR WEATHER INSTRUMENTS DID NOT FORECAST IT!
THE ENEMY IS A LONG DISTANCE FROM ME! YET, BY USING THE MIGHT OF THOR, AND WHIRLING MY HAMMER WITH THE SPEED OF LIGHTNING, I MAY YET BE ABLE TO STREAK THRU THE SKY, AS THE THUNDER GOD SHOULD!
THERE! I RELEASE MY WHIRLING HAMMER FOR A SPLIT-SECOND, CATCHING THE UNBREAKABLE THONG, AND THEN--I AM PULLED ALONG AFTER IT LIKE THE TAIL OF A ROCKET!!
10

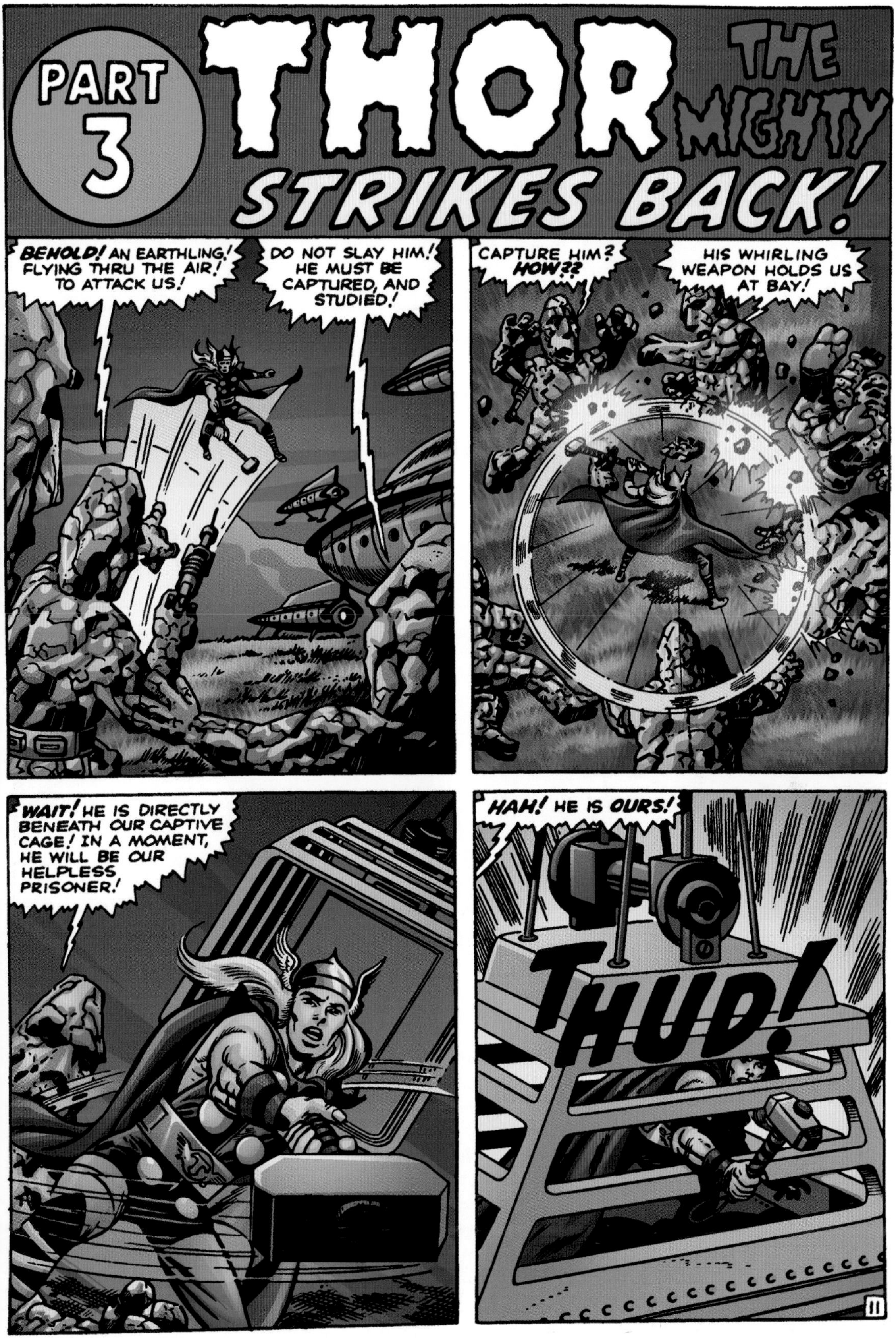
PART 3
THOR THE MIGHTY STRIKES BACK!
BEHOLD! AN EARTHLING! FLYING THRU THE AIR! TO ATTACK US!
DO NOT SLAY HIM! HE MUST BE CAPTURED, AND STUDIED!
CAPTURE HIM? HOW??
HIS WHIRLING WEAPON HOLDS US AT BAY!
WAIT! HE IS DIRECTLY BENEATH OUR CAPTIVE CAGE! IN A MOMENT, HE WILL BE OUR HELPLESS PRISONER!
HAH! HE IS OURS!
THUD!
11

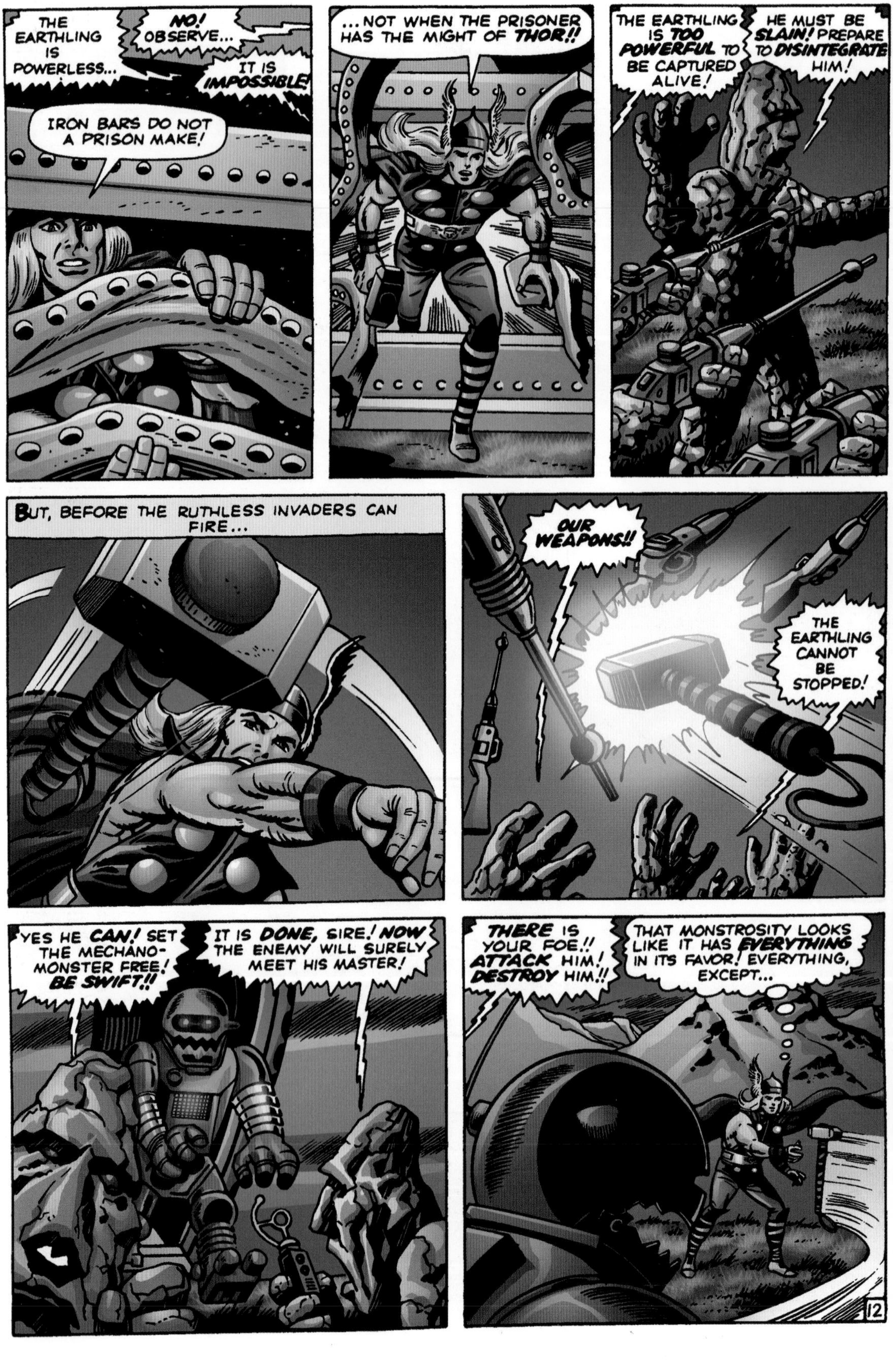
THE EARTHLING IS POWERLESS...
NO! OBSERVE...
IT IS IMPOSSIBLE!
IRON BARS DO NOT A PRISON MAKE!
...NOT WHEN THE PRISONER HAS THE MIGHT OF THOR!!
THE EARTHLING IS TOO POWERFUL TO BE CAPTURED ALIVE!
HE MUST BE SLAIN! PREPARE TO DISINTEGRATE HIM!
BUT, BEFORE THE RUTHLESS INVADERS CAN FIRE...
OUR WEAPONS!!
THE EARTHLING CANNOT BE STOPPED!
YES HE CAN! SET THE MECHANO-MONSTER FREE! BE SWIFT!!
IT IS DONE, SIRE! NOW THE ENEMY WILL SURELY MEET HIS MASTER!
THERE IS YOUR FOE!! ATTACK HIM! DESTROY HIM!!
THAT MONSTROSITY LOOKS LIKE IT HAS EVERYTHING IN ITS FAVOR! EVERYTHING, EXCEPT...
12

...THE HAMMER OF THOR.!

CLANG!

HE HAS VANQUISHED THE MECHANO-MONSTER!

THE HUMAN IS TOO MIGHTY --TOO SKILLED IN THE ART OF BATTLE!

AND WE KNOW NOT HOW MANY MORE THERE ARE LIKE HIM ON EARTH!

BACK!! BACK TO THE SHIPS AT ONCE!! WE MUST FLEE THIS ACCURSED PLANET!!

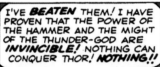

I'VE BEATEN THEM! I HAVE PROVEN THAT THE POWER OF THE HAMMER AND THE MIGHT OF THE THUNDER-GOD ARE INVINCIBLE! NOTHING CAN CONQUER THOR! NOTHING!!

HERE COMES THE INFANTRY! IF I REMAIN HERE, THEY'LL QUESTION ME!! THEY WON'T REST TILL THEY'VE LEARNED MY SECRET! I'LL BECOME AN INTERNATIONAL CURIOSITY!

BUT, ALL THAT CAN BE AVOIDED BY ONE GESTURE...

THUMP

LOOK! THE INVADERS ARE FLYING AWAY!

BUT WHY?? WHAT COULD HAVE DRIVEN THEM OFF??

I DON'T KNOW! THERE'S NO ONE IN SIGHT...

NATO

...EXCEPT THAT LAME PASSER-BY, WITH A GNARLED OLD CANE!

WELL, IT'S A CINCH THAT SKINNY GENT ISN'T EARTH'S SECRET WEAPON!

THE MENACE IS ENDED! NOW, IT'S TIME FOR ME TO GO BACK TO THE STATES... TAKING WITH ME THE GREATEST POWER EVER KNOWN TO MORTAL MAN!

EDITOR'S NOTE: THE MIGHTY THOR, THE GREATEST NEW SUPER HERO OF ALL TIME, WILL APPEAR REGULARLY IN JOURNEY INTO MYSTERY! RESERVE NEXT MONTH'S ISSUE AT YOUR NEWSDEALER NOW! IT'S SURE TO BE A SELLOUT!

the END

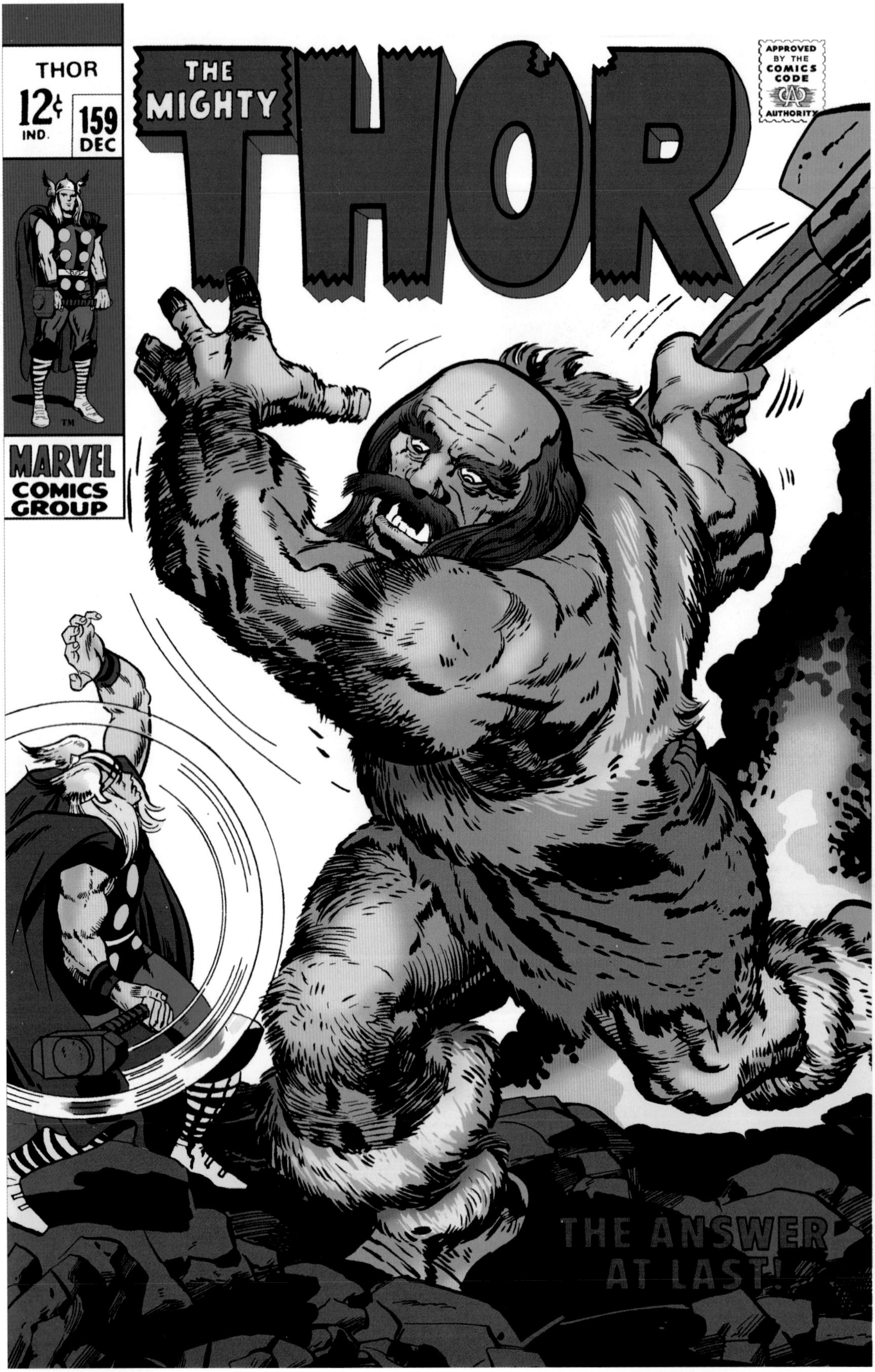
THOR
12¢
IND.
159
DEC
MARVEL
COMICS
GROUP
THE MIGHTY
THOR
APPROVED BY THE COMICS CODE AUTHORITY
THE ANSWER AT LAST!

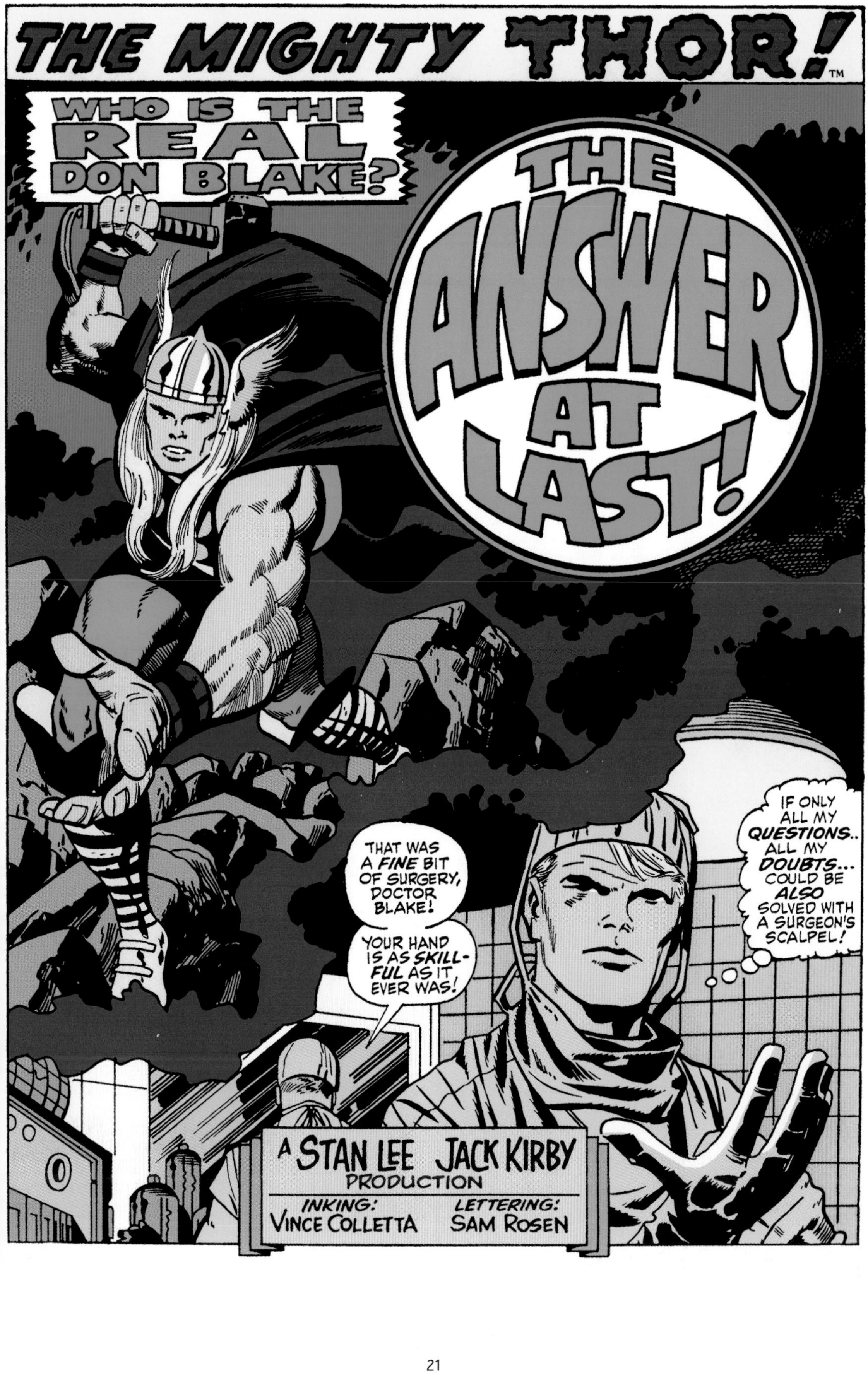
THE MIGHTY THOR!
WHO IS THE REAL DON BLAKE?
THE ANSWER AT LAST!
IF ONLY ALL MY QUESTIONS.. ALL MY DOUBTS... COULD BE ALSO SOLVED WITH A SURGEON'S SCALPEL!
THAT WAS A FINE BIT OF SURGERY, DOCTOR BLAKE!
YOUR HAND IS AS SKILL-FUL AS IT EVER WAS!
A STAN LEE JACK KIRBY PRODUCTION
INKING: VINCE COLLETTA
LETTERING: SAM ROSEN

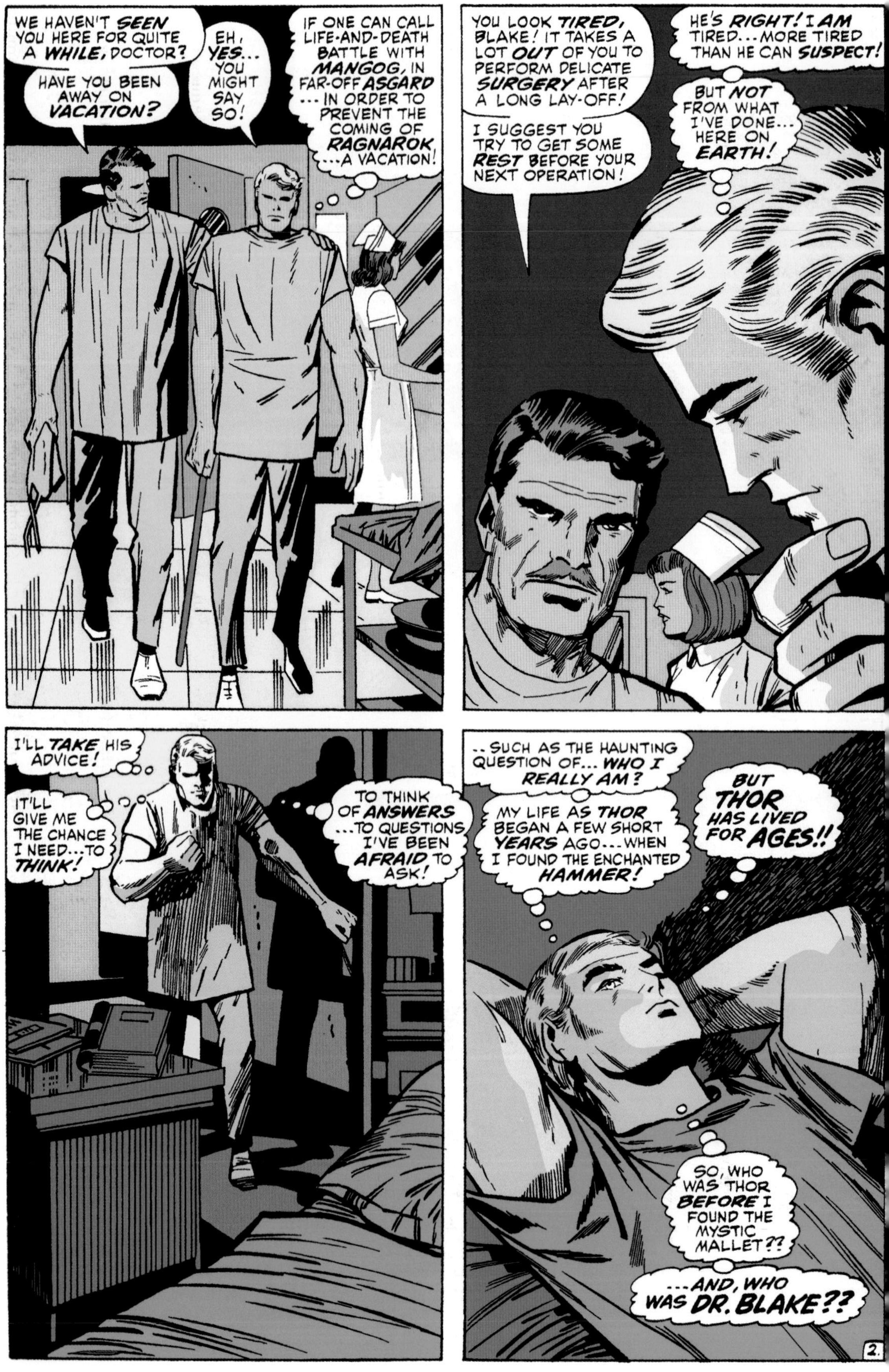
WE HAVEN'T SEEN YOU HERE FOR QUITE A WHILE, DOCTOR?
HAVE YOU BEEN AWAY ON VACATION?
EH, YES... YOU MIGHT SAY SO!
IF ONE CAN CALL LIFE-AND-DEATH BATTLE WITH MANGOG, IN FAR-OFF ASGARD ... IN ORDER TO PREVENT THE COMING OF RAGNAROK ...A VACATION!
YOU LOOK TIRED, BLAKE! IT TAKES A LOT OUT OF YOU TO PERFORM DELICATE SURGERY AFTER A LONG LAY-OFF!
I SUGGEST YOU TRY TO GET SOME REST BEFORE YOUR NEXT OPERATION!
HE'S RIGHT! I AM TIRED... MORE TIRED THAN HE CAN SUSPECT!
BUT NOT FROM WHAT I'VE DONE... HERE ON EARTH!
I'LL TAKE HIS ADVICE!
IT'LL GIVE ME THE CHANCE I NEED... TO THINK!
TO THINK OF ANSWERS ...TO QUESTIONS I'VE BEEN AFRAID TO ASK!
..SUCH AS THE HAUNTING QUESTION OF... WHO I REALLY AM?
MY LIFE AS THOR BEGAN A FEW SHORT YEARS AGO... WHEN I FOUND THE ENCHANTED HAMMER!
BUT THOR HAS LIVED FOR AGES!!
SO, WHO WAS THOR BEFORE I FOUND THE MYSTIC MALLET??
...AND, WHO WAS DR. BLAKE??
2.

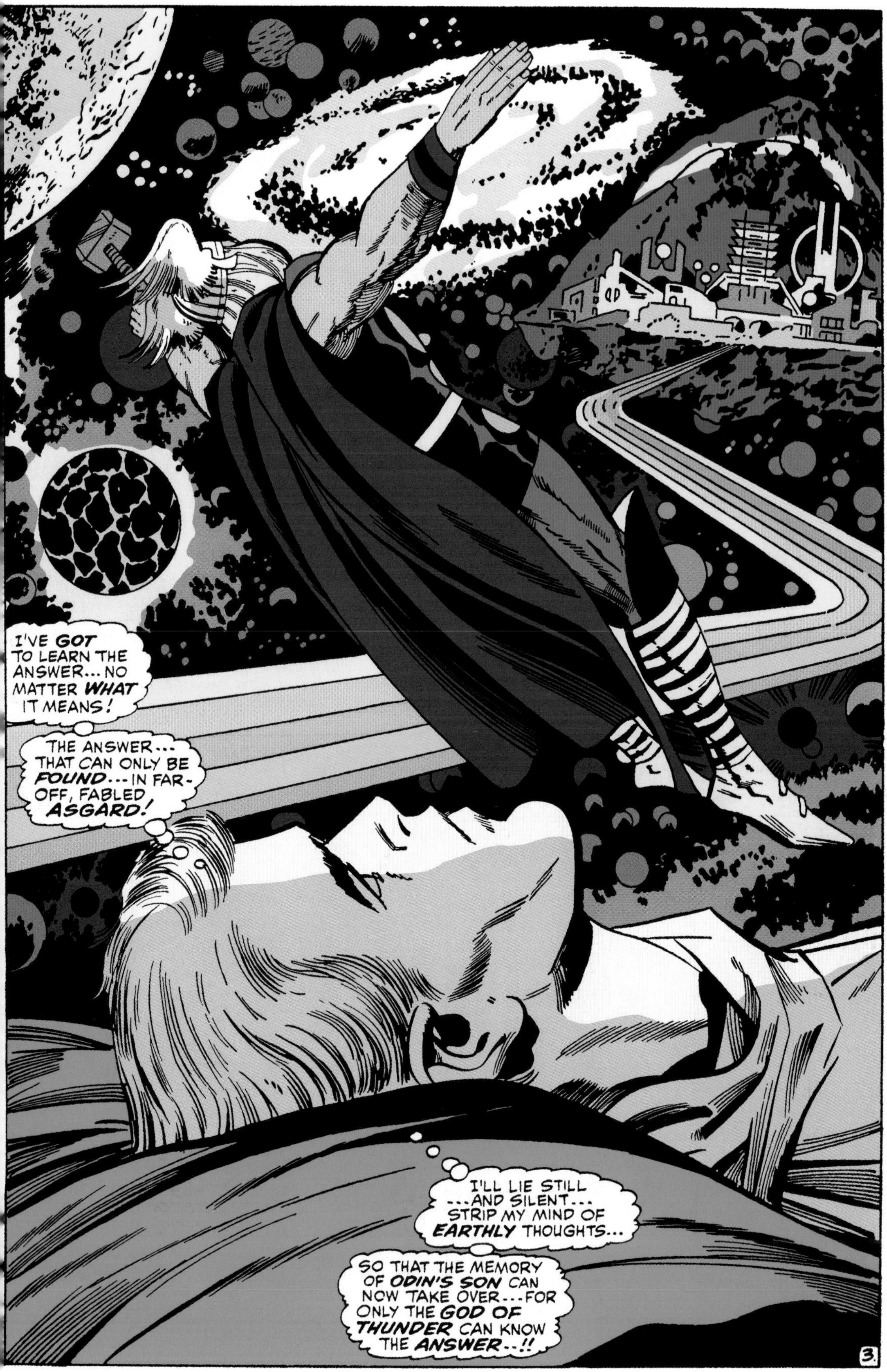
I'VE GOT TO LEARN THE ANSWER... NO MATTER WHAT IT MEANS!
THE ANSWER... THAT CAN ONLY BE FOUND... IN FAR-OFF, FABLED ASGARD!
I'LL LIE STILL ...AND SILENT... STRIP MY MIND OF EARTHLY THOUGHTS...
SO THAT THE MEMORY OF ODIN'S SON CAN NOW TAKE OVER... FOR ONLY THE GOD OF THUNDER CAN KNOW THE ANSWER--!!
3.

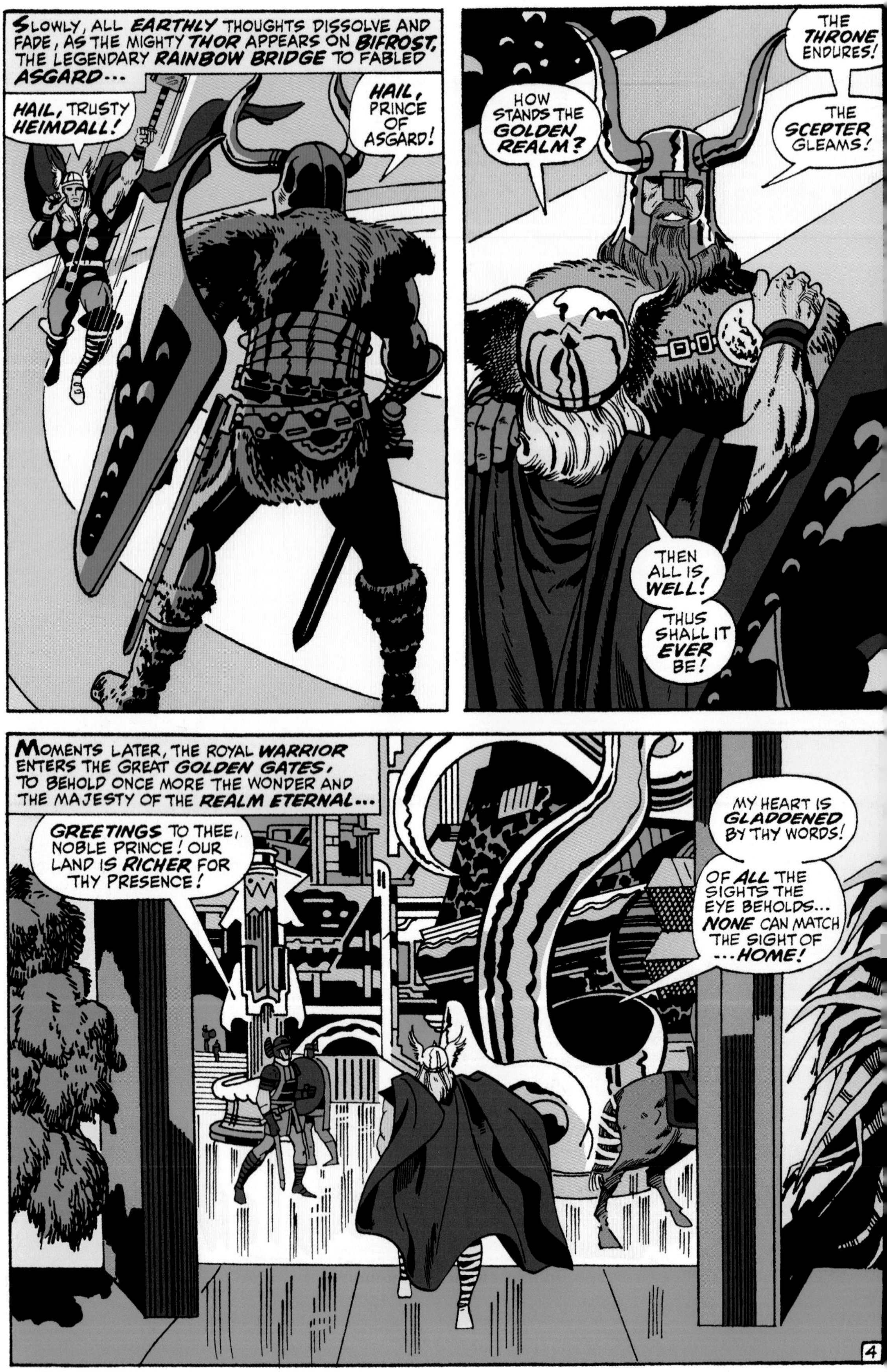
SLOWLY, ALL EARTHLY THOUGHTS DISSOLVE AND FADE, AS THE MIGHTY THOR APPEARS ON BIFROST, THE LEGENDARY RAINBOW BRIDGE TO FABLED ASGARD...
HAIL, TRUSTY HEIMDALL!
HAIL, PRINCE OF ASGARD!
HOW STANDS THE GOLDEN REALM?
THE THRONE ENDURES!
THE SCEPTER GLEAMS!
THEN ALL IS WELL!
THUS SHALL IT EVER BE!
MOMENTS LATER, THE ROYAL WARRIOR ENTERS THE GREAT GOLDEN GATES, TO BEHOLD ONCE MORE THE WONDER AND THE MAJESTY OF THE REALM ETERNAL...
GREETINGS TO THEE, NOBLE PRINCE! OUR LAND IS RICHER FOR THY PRESENCE!
MY HEART IS GLADDENED BY THY WORDS!
OF ALL THE SIGHTS THE EYE BEHOLDS... NONE CAN MATCH THE SIGHT OF ...HOME!
4

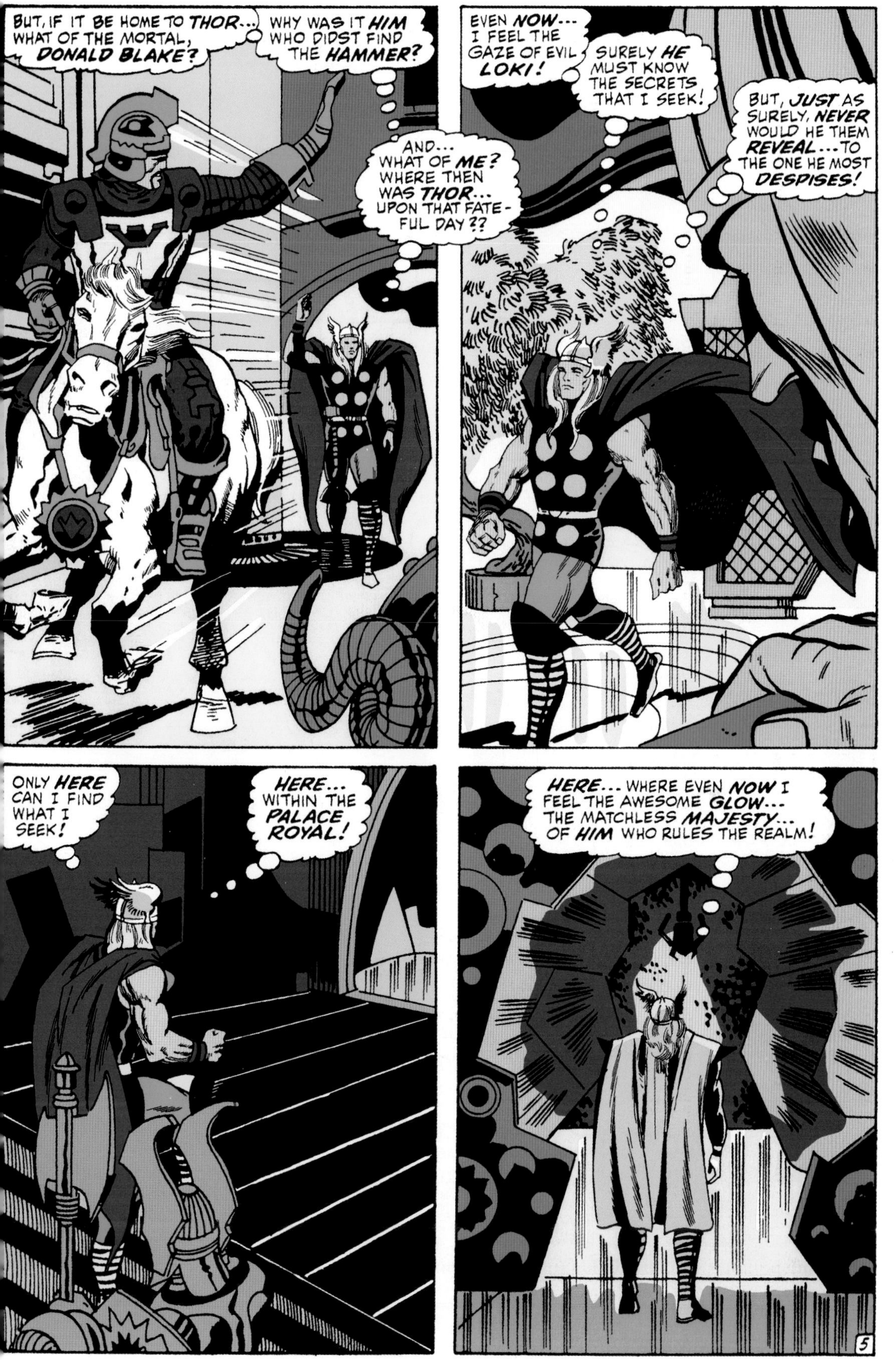
BUT, IF IT BE HOME TO THOR... WHAT OF THE MORTAL, DONALD BLAKE?
WHY WAS IT HIM WHO DIDST FIND THE HAMMER?
AND... WHAT OF ME? WHERE THEN WAS THOR... UPON THAT FATE-FUL DAY??
EVEN NOW... I FEEL THE GAZE OF EVIL LOKI!
SURELY HE MUST KNOW THE SECRETS THAT I SEEK!
BUT, JUST AS SURELY, NEVER WOULD HE THEM REVEAL... TO THE ONE HE MOST DESPISES!
ONLY HERE CAN I FIND WHAT I SEEK!
HERE... WITHIN THE PALACE ROYAL!
HERE... WHERE EVEN NOW I FEEL THE AWESOME GLOW... THE MATCHLESS MAJESTY... OF HIM WHO RULES THE REALM!
5

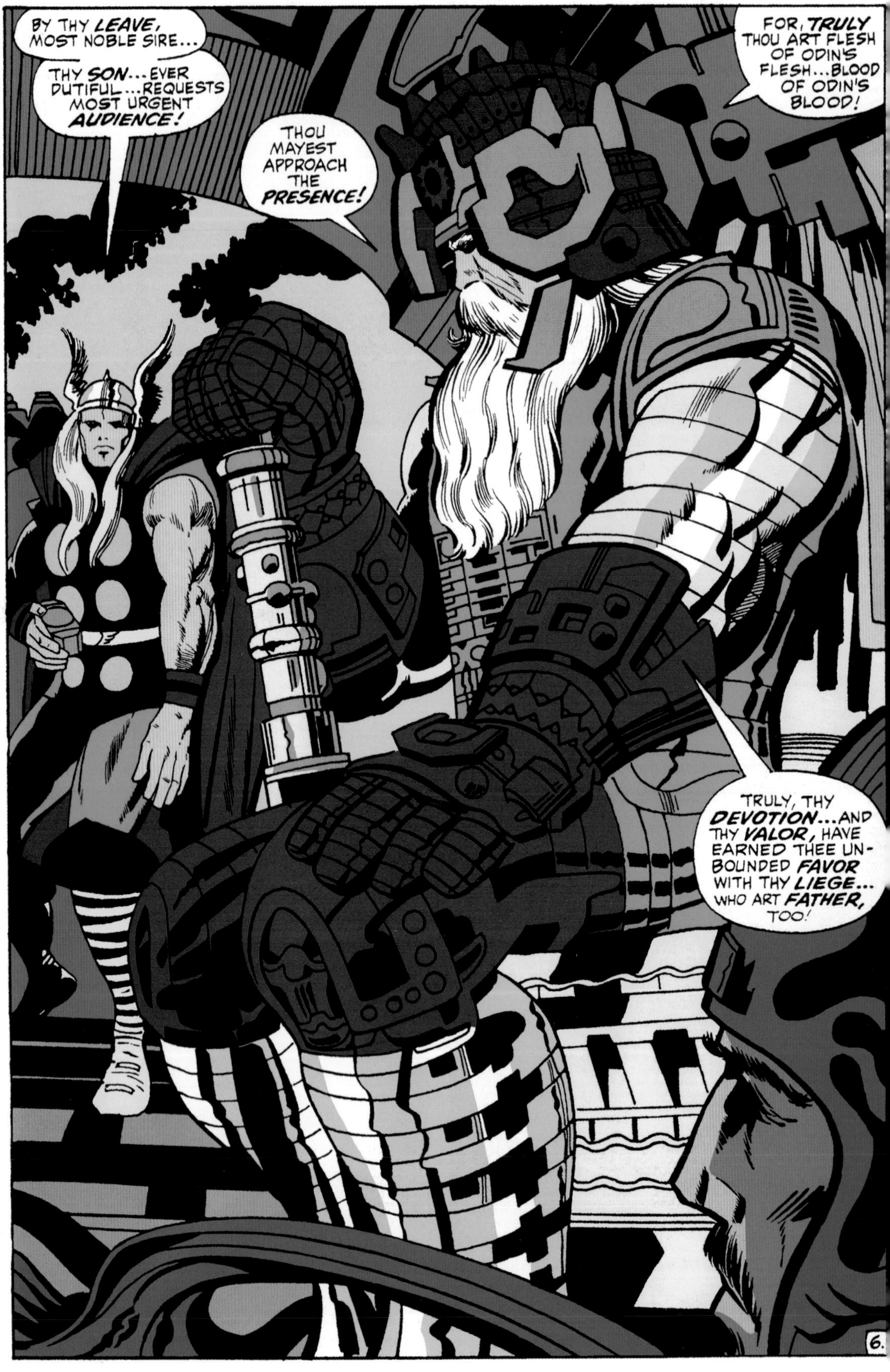
BY THY LEAVE, MOST NOBLE SIRE...
THY SON... EVER DUTIFUL... REQUESTS MOST URGENT AUDIENCE!
THOU MAYEST APPROACH THE PRESENCE!
FOR, TRULY THOU ART FLESH OF ODIN'S FLESH... BLOOD OF ODIN'S BLOOD!
TRULY, THY DEVOTION... AND THY VALOR, HAVE EARNED THEE UN-BOUNDED FAVOR WITH THY LIEGE... WHO ART FATHER, TOO!
6.

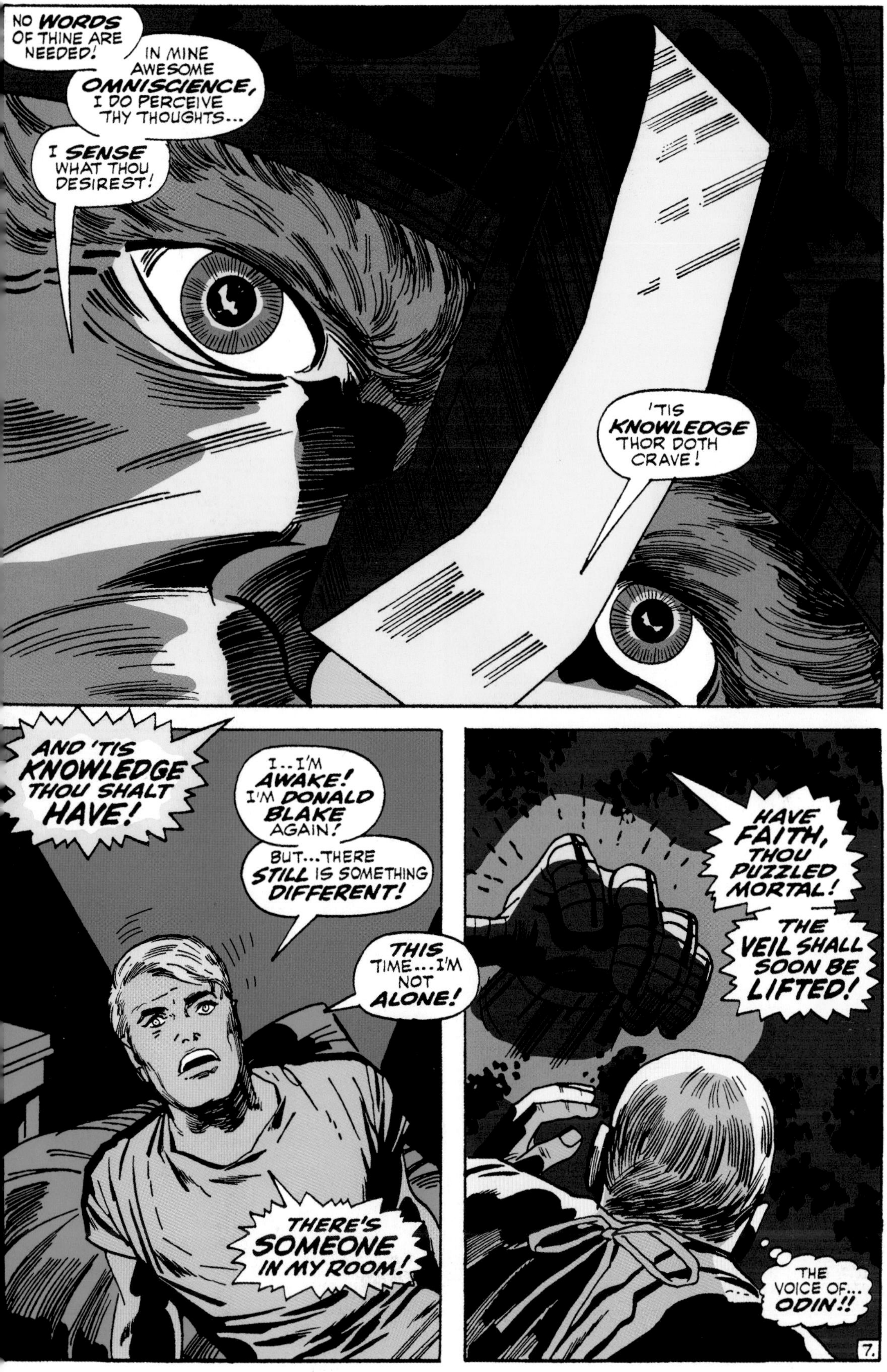
NO WORDS OF THINE ARE NEEDED!
IN MINE AWESOME OMNISCIENCE, I DO PERCEIVE THY THOUGHTS...
I SENSE WHAT THOU DESIREST!
'TIS KNOWLEDGE THOR DOTH CRAVE!
AND 'TIS KNOWLEDGE THOU SHALT HAVE!
I..I'M AWAKE! I'M DONALD BLAKE AGAIN!
BUT...THERE STILL IS SOMETHING DIFFERENT!
THIS TIME...I'M NOT ALONE!
THERE'S SOMEONE IN MY ROOM!
HAVE FAITH, THOU PUZZLED MORTAL!
THE VEIL SHALL SOON BE LIFTED!
THE VOICE OF... ODIN!!
7.

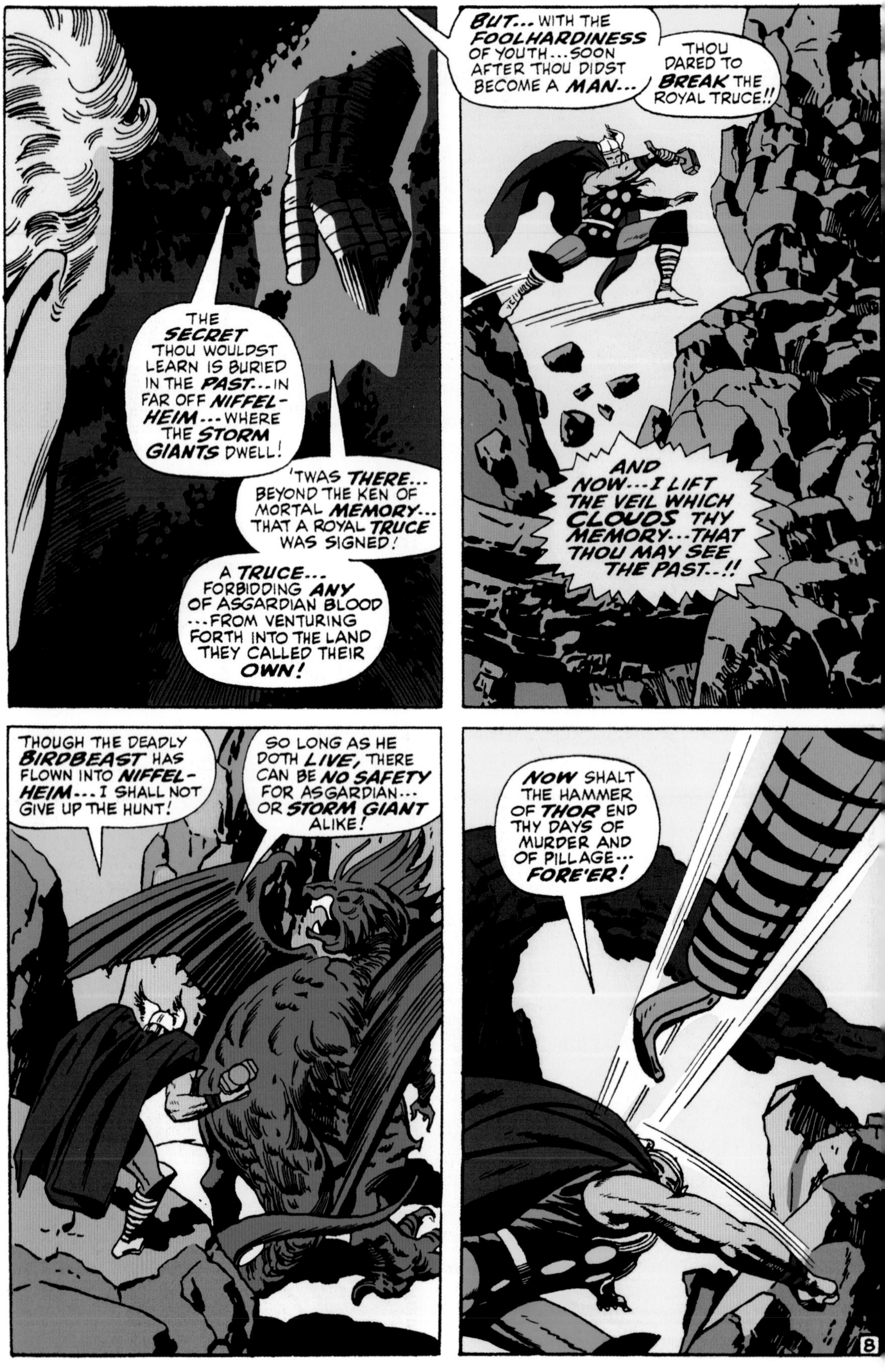
THE SECRET THOU WOULDST LEARN IS BURIED IN THE PAST...IN FAR OFF NIFFEL-HEIM...WHERE THE STORM GIANTS DWELL!
'TWAS THERE... BEYOND THE KEN OF MORTAL MEMORY... THAT A ROYAL TRUCE WAS SIGNED!
A TRUCE... FORBIDDING ANY OF ASGARDIAN BLOOD ...FROM VENTURING FORTH INTO THE LAND THEY CALLED THEIR OWN!
BUT... WITH THE FOOLHARDINESS OF YOUTH...SOON AFTER THOU DIDST BECOME A MAN...
THOU DARED TO BREAK THE ROYAL TRUCE!!
AND NOW...I LIFT THE VEIL WHICH CLOUDS THY MEMORY...THAT THOU MAY SEE THE PAST..!!
THOUGH THE DEADLY BIRDBEAST HAS FLOWN INTO NIFFEL-HEIM...I SHALL NOT GIVE UP THE HUNT!
SO LONG AS HE DOTH LIVE, THERE CAN BE NO SAFETY FOR ASGARDIAN... OR STORM GIANT ALIKE!
NOW SHALT THE HAMMER OF THOR END THY DAYS OF MURDER AND OF PILLAGE... FORE'ER!
8

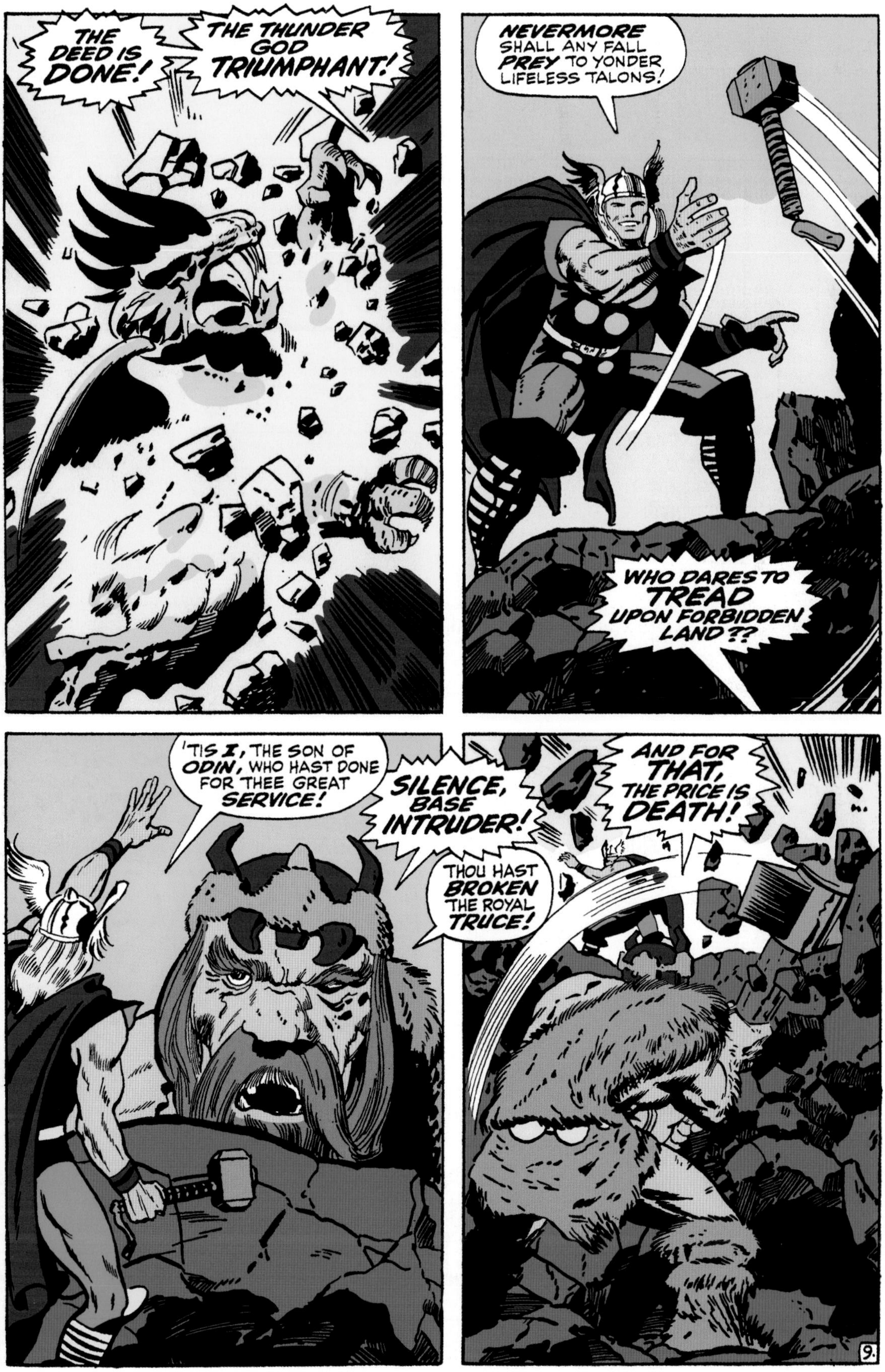
THE DEED IS DONE!
THE THUNDER GOD TRIUMPHANT!
NEVERMORE SHALL ANY FALL PREY TO YONDER LIFELESS TALONS!
WHO DARES TO TREAD UPON FORBIDDEN LAND??
'TIS I, THE SON OF ODIN, WHO HAST DONE FOR THEE GREAT SERVICE!
SILENCE, BASE INTRUDER!
THOU HAST BROKEN THE ROYAL TRUCE!
AND FOR THAT, THE PRICE IS DEATH!
9.

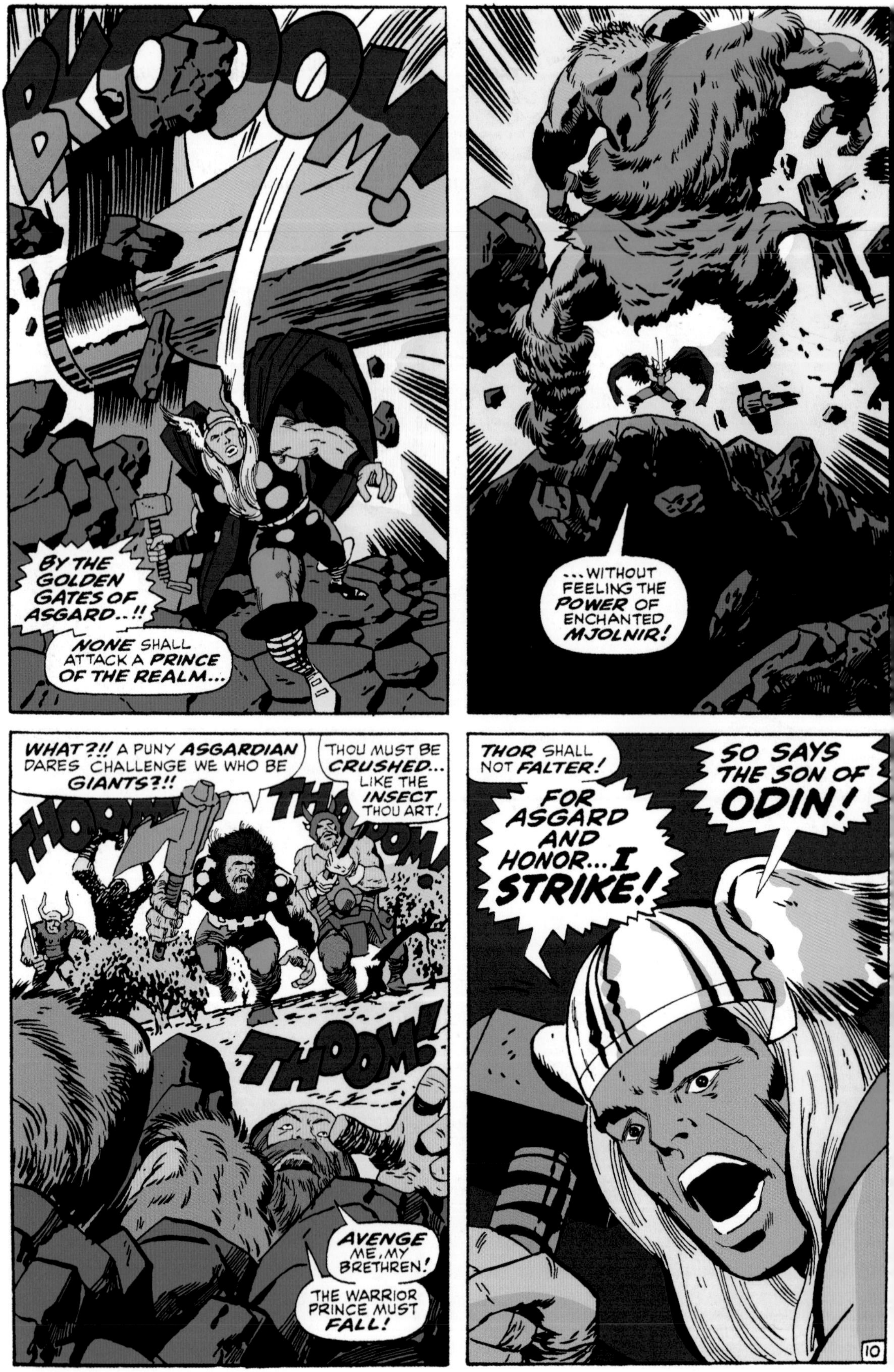
BADOOOM!
BY THE GOLDEN GATES OF ASGARD..!!
NONE SHALL ATTACK A PRINCE OF THE REALM...
...WITHOUT FEELING THE POWER OF ENCHANTED MJOLNIR!
WHAT?!! A PUNY ASGARDIAN DARES CHALLENGE WE WHO BE GIANTS?!!
THOU MUST BE CRUSHED... LIKE THE INSECT THOU ART!
THOOM!
THOOM!
THOOM!
AVENGE ME, MY BRETHREN!
THE WARRIOR PRINCE MUST FALL!
THOR SHALL NOT FALTER!
FOR ASGARD AND HONOR... I STRIKE!
SO SAYS THE SON OF ODIN!
10

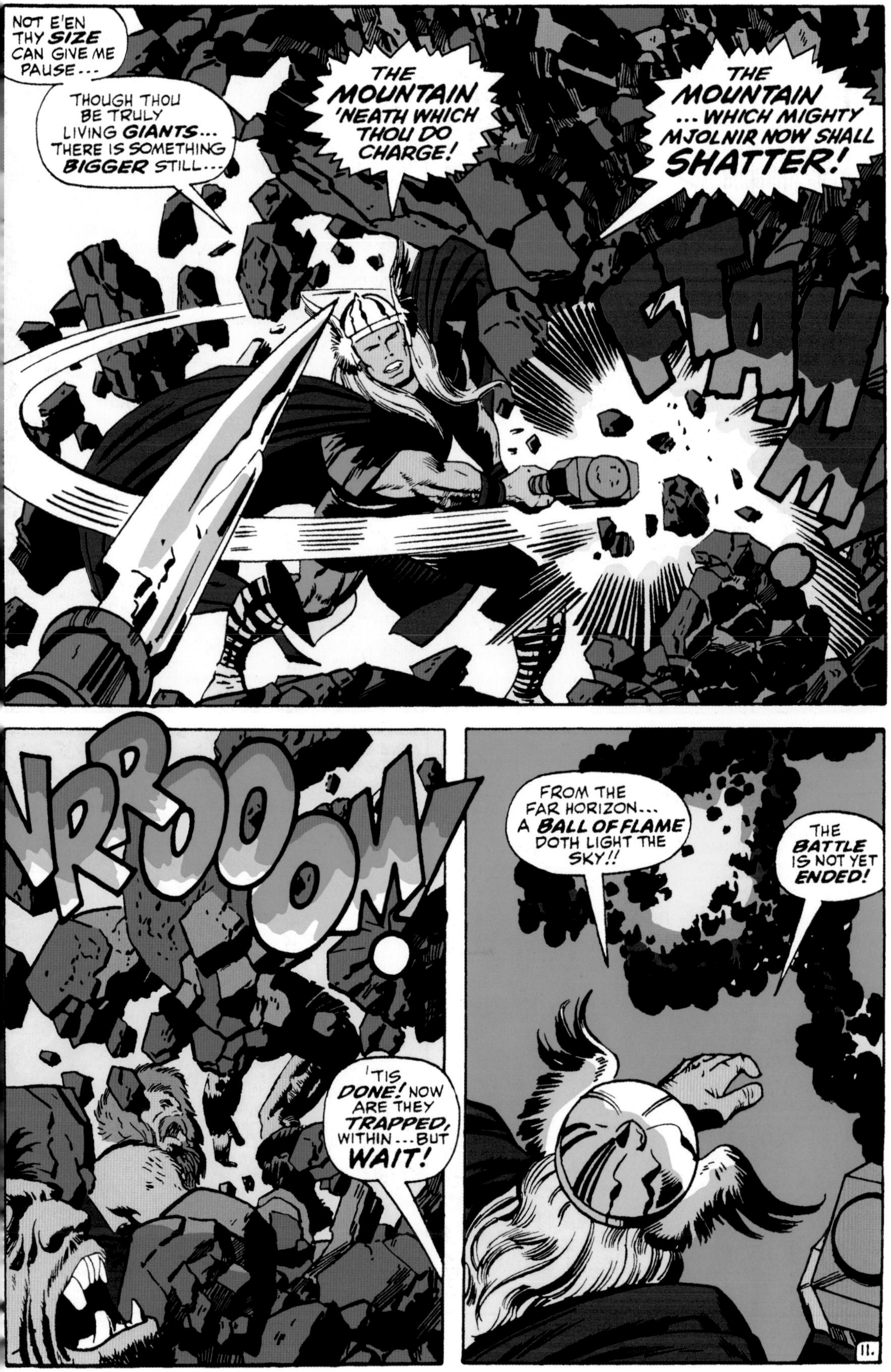
NOT E'EN THY SIZE CAN GIVE ME PAUSE---
THOUGH THOU BE TRULY LIVING GIANTS... THERE IS SOMETHING BIGGER STILL...
THE MOUNTAIN 'NEATH WHICH THOU DO CHARGE!
THE MOUNTAIN ... WHICH MIGHTY MJOLNIR NOW SHALL SHATTER!
'TIS DONE! NOW ARE THEY TRAPPED, WITHIN ... BUT WAIT!
FROM THE FAR HORIZON... A BALL OF FLAME DOTH LIGHT THE SKY!!
THE BATTLE IS NOT YET ENDED!
11.

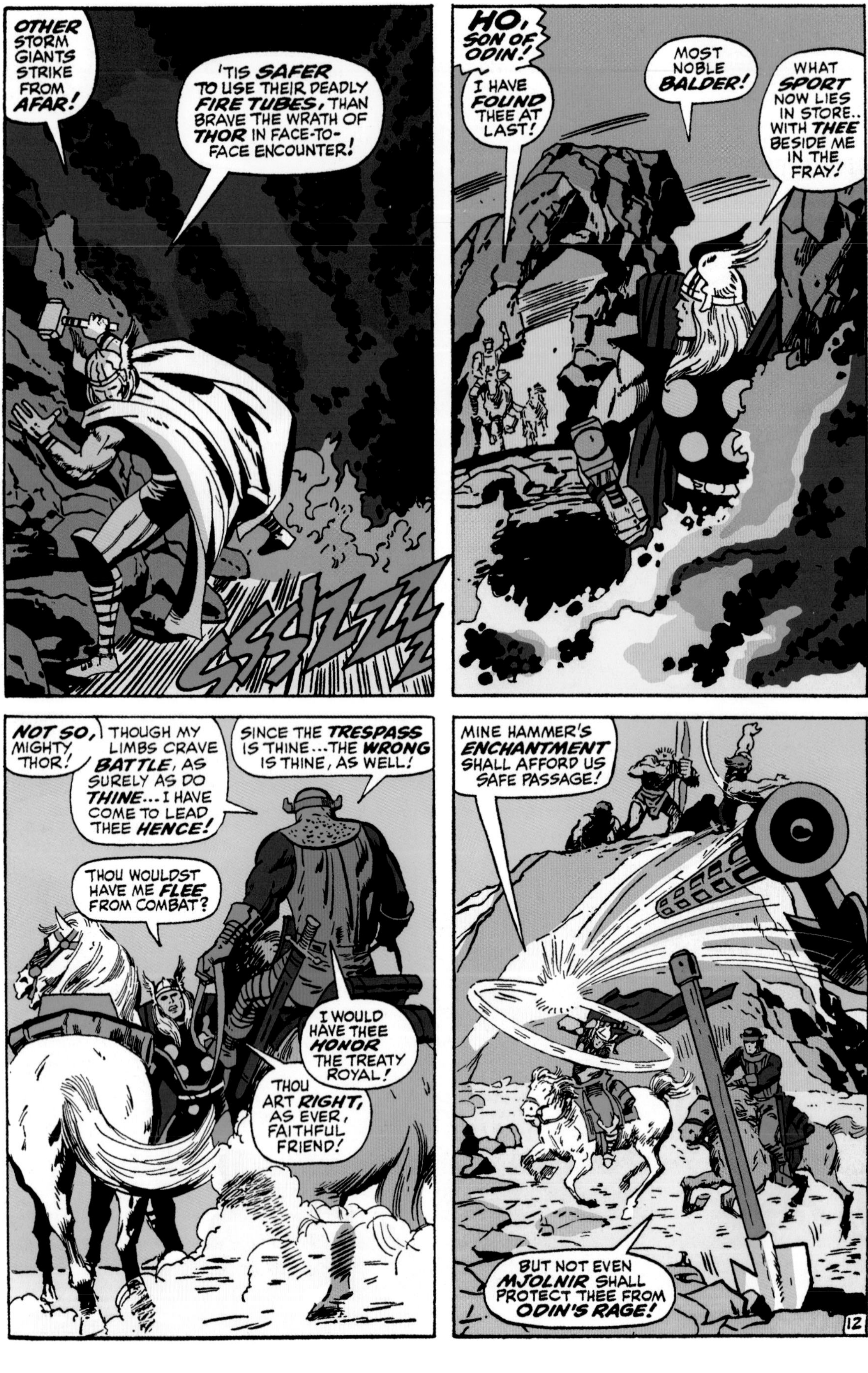
OTHER STORM GIANTS STRIKE FROM AFAR!
'TIS SAFER TO USE THEIR DEADLY FIRE TUBES, THAN BRAVE THE WRATH OF THOR IN FACE-TO-FACE ENCOUNTER!
SSSIZZZZ
HO, SON OF ODIN!
I HAVE FOUND THEE AT LAST!
MOST NOBLE BALDER!
WHAT SPORT NOW LIES IN STORE.. WITH THEE BESIDE ME IN THE FRAY!
NOT SO, MIGHTY THOR!
THOUGH MY LIMBS CRAVE BATTLE, AS SURELY AS DO THINE... I HAVE COME TO LEAD THEE HENCE!
SINCE THE TRESPASS IS THINE... THE WRONG IS THINE, AS WELL!
THOU WOULDST HAVE ME FLEE FROM COMBAT?
I WOULD HAVE THEE HONOR THE TREATY ROYAL!
THOU ART RIGHT, AS EVER, FAITHFUL FRIEND!
MINE HAMMER'S ENCHANTMENT SHALL AFFORD US SAFE PASSAGE!
BUT NOT EVEN MJOLNIR SHALL PROTECT THEE FROM ODIN'S RAGE!
12

YOU HAVE SHOWN THAT THOR WAS *YOUNG*... *HEADSTRONG*... SUPREMELY *CONFIDENT* OF HIS OWN GODLIKE *POWER!*

BUT, WHAT HAS THAT TO DO WITH *ME?*

CANST THOU NOT *SEE? THY* FATE... AND *HIS*... ARE *ONE AND THE SAME!*

BUT *STILL* YOU SPEAK IN RIDDLES!

HOW DID *I* ENTER THE PICTURE? AND WHERE WAS *HE?* WHERE WAS THE *ORIGINAL* THOR, WHEN I CAME ON THE SCENE??

ONLY *YOU* CAN TELL ME... FOR I HAVE *NO MEMORY* OF THOSE EVENTS!

AYE! 'TIS AS ODIN *PLANNED* IT!

'TWAS NOT *SEEMLY* FOR THEE TO KNOW... TILL *NOW!*

THEREFORE, CLEAR THY *MIND* OF EVERY THOUGHT... AS I TAKE THEE TO THE *PAST* ONCE MORE...!

FOR THOU MUST *RETURN* TO ASGARD... TO THE MEMORY OF YON LUSTY, BRAWLING ERA..!

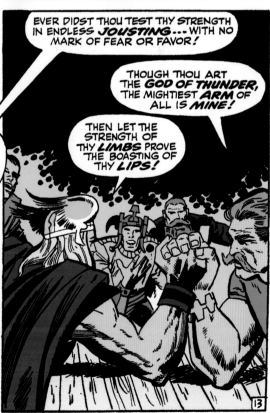

EVER DIDST THOU TEST THY STRENGTH IN ENDLESS *JOUSTING*... WITH NO MARK OF FEAR OR FAVOR!

THOUGH THOU ART THE *GOD OF THUNDER*, THE MIGHTIEST *ARM* OF ALL IS *MINE!*

THEN LET THE STRENGTH OF THY *LIMBS* PROVE THE BOASTING OF THY *LIPS!*

13

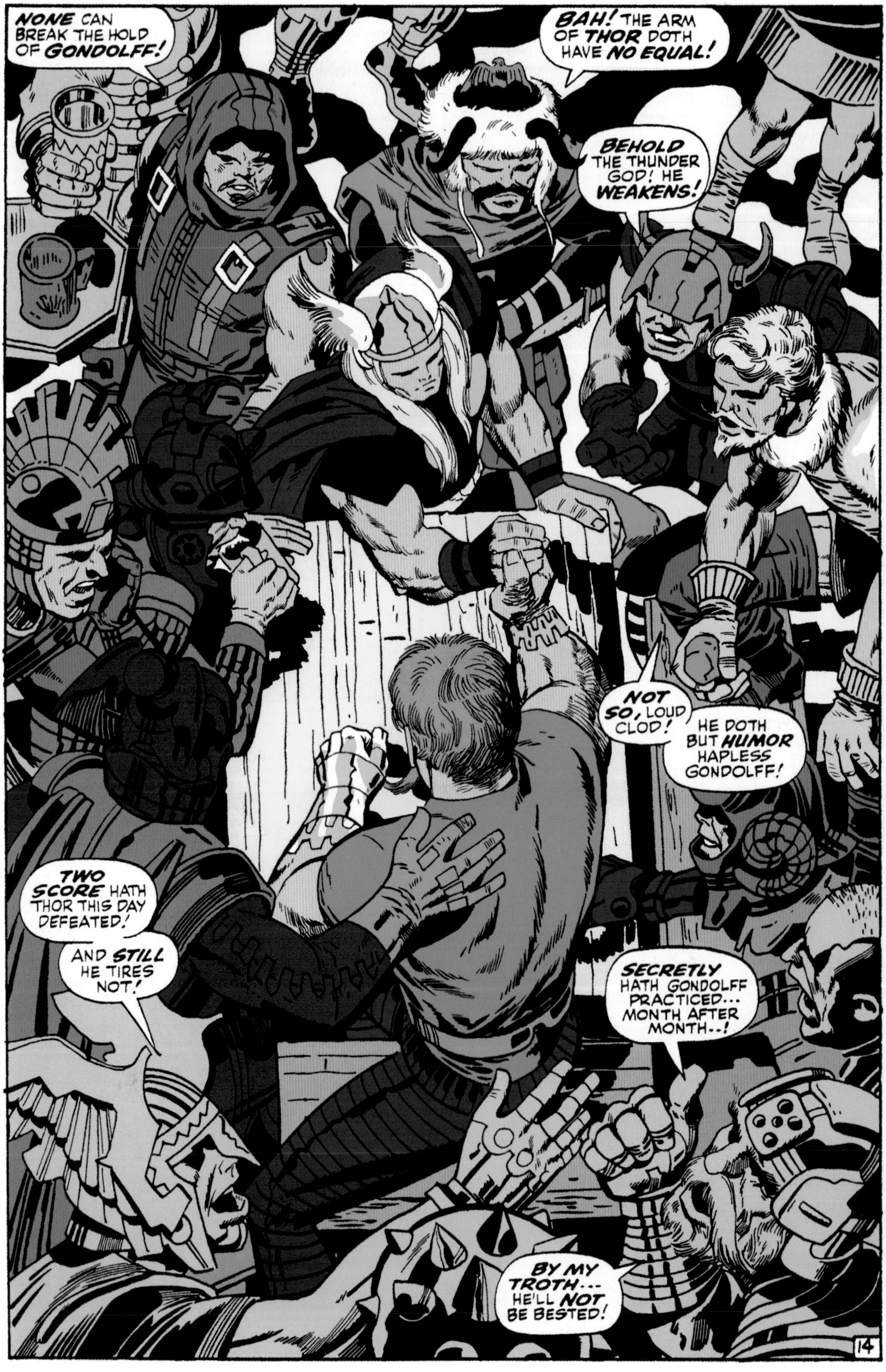
NONE CAN BREAK THE HOLD OF GONDOLFF!
BAH! THE ARM OF THOR DOTH HAVE NO EQUAL!
BEHOLD THE THUNDER GOD! HE WEAKENS!
NOT SO, LOUD CLOD!
HE DOTH BUT HUMOR HAPLESS GONDOLFF!
TWO SCORE HATH THOR THIS DAY DEFEATED!
AND STILL HE TIRES NOT!
SECRETLY HATH GONDOLFF PRACTICED... MONTH AFTER MONTH..!
BY MY TROTH... HE'LL NOT BE BESTED!
14

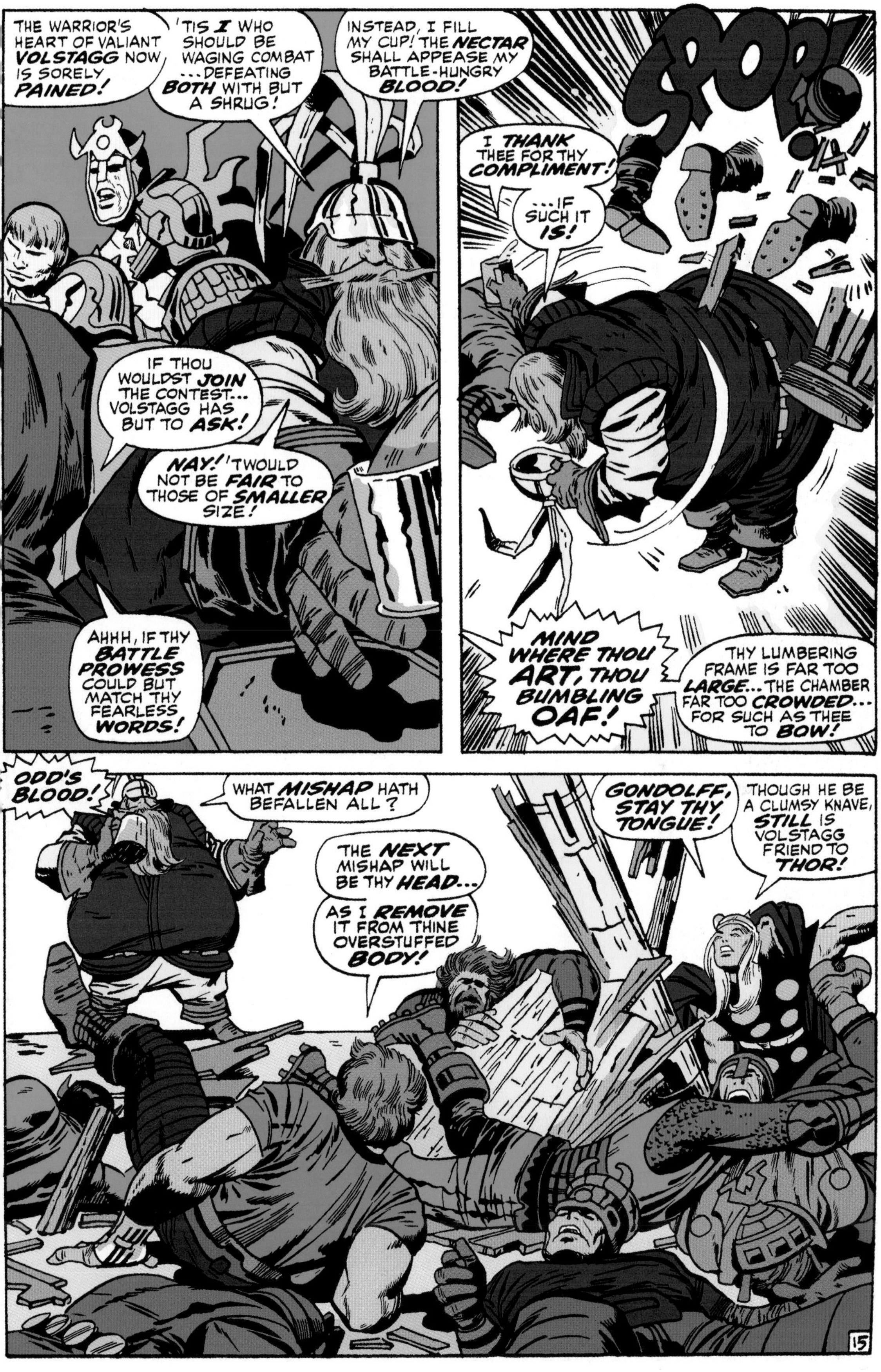
THE WARRIOR'S HEART OF VALIANT VOLSTAGG NOW IS SORELY PAINED!
'TIS I WHO SHOULD BE WAGING COMBAT ...DEFEATING BOTH WITH BUT A SHRUG!
INSTEAD, I FILL MY CUP! THE NECTAR SHALL APPEASE MY BATTLE-HUNGRY BLOOD!
IF THOU WOULDST JOIN THE CONTEST... VOLSTAGG HAS BUT TO ASK!
NAY! 'TWOULD NOT BE FAIR TO THOSE OF SMALLER SIZE!
AHHH, IF THY BATTLE PROWESS COULD BUT MATCH THY FEARLESS WORDS!
SPOP!
I THANK THEE FOR THY COMPLIMENT!
...IF SUCH IT IS!
MIND WHERE THOU ART, THOU BUMBLING OAF!
THY LUMBERING FRAME IS FAR TOO LARGE... THE CHAMBER FAR TOO CROWDED... FOR SUCH AS THEE TO BOW!
ODD'S BLOOD!
WHAT MISHAP HATH BEFALLEN ALL?
THE NEXT MISHAP WILL BE THY HEAD...
AS I REMOVE IT FROM THINE OVERSTUFFED BODY!
GONDOLFF, STAY THY TONGUE!
THOUGH HE BE A CLUMSY KNAVE, STILL IS VOLSTAGG FRIEND TO THOR!
15

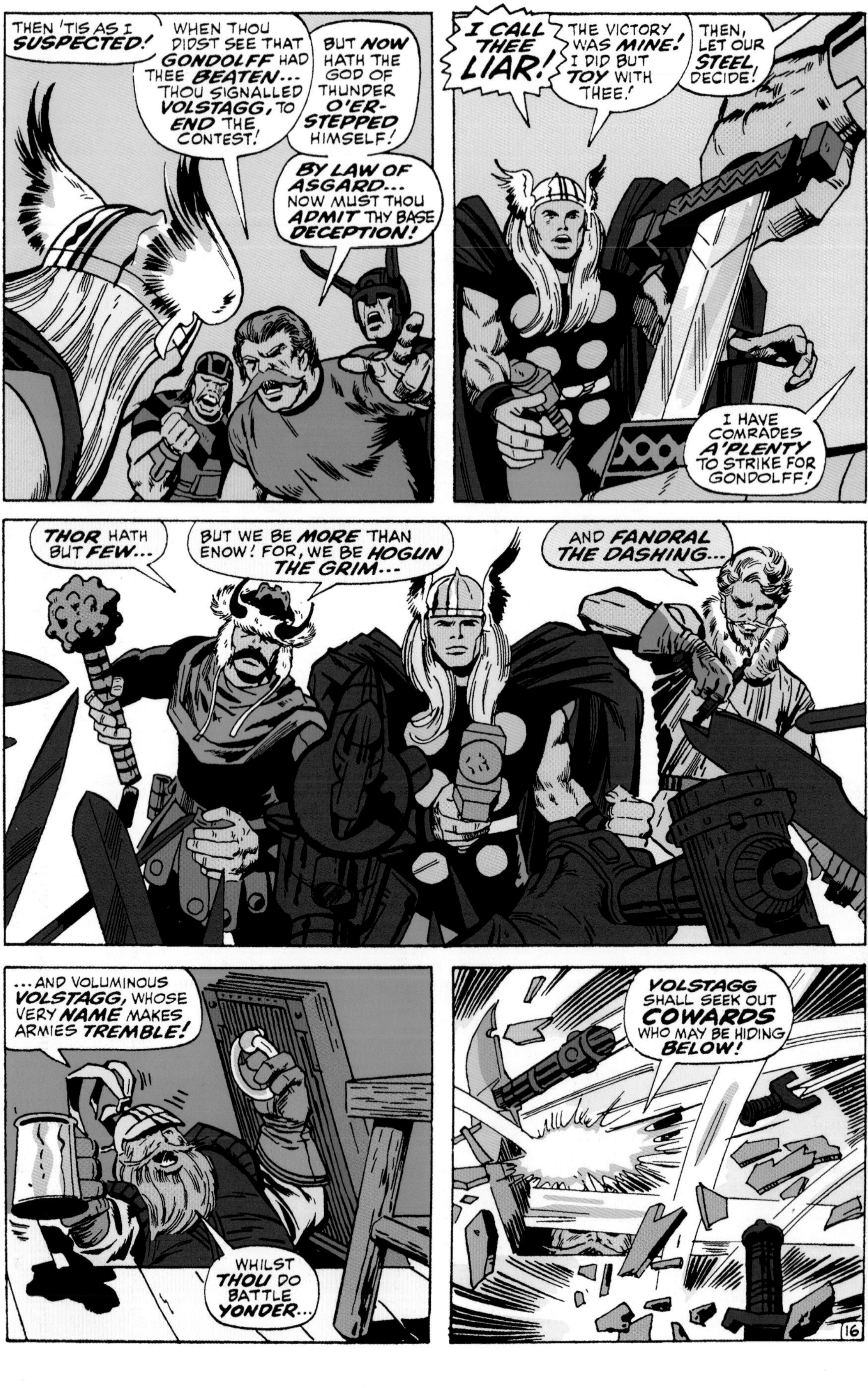
THEN 'TIS AS I SUSPECTED!
WHEN THOU DIDST SEE THAT GONDOLFF HAD THEE BEATEN... THOU SIGNALLED VOLSTAGG, TO END THE CONTEST!
BUT NOW HATH THE GOD OF THUNDER O'ER-STEPPED HIMSELF!
BY LAW OF ASGARD... NOW MUST THOU ADMIT THY BASE DECEPTION!
I CALL THEE LIAR!
THE VICTORY WAS MINE! I DID BUT TOY WITH THEE!
THEN, LET OUR STEEL DECIDE!
I HAVE COMRADES A'PLENTY TO STRIKE FOR GONDOLFF!
THOR HATH BUT FEW...
BUT WE BE MORE THAN ENOW! FOR, WE BE HOGUN THE GRIM...
AND FANDRAL THE DASHING...
...AND VOLUMINOUS VOLSTAGG, WHOSE VERY NAME MAKES ARMIES TREMBLE!
WHILST THOU DO BATTLE YONDER...
VOLSTAGG SHALL SEEK OUT COWARDS WHO MAY BE HIDING BELOW!
16

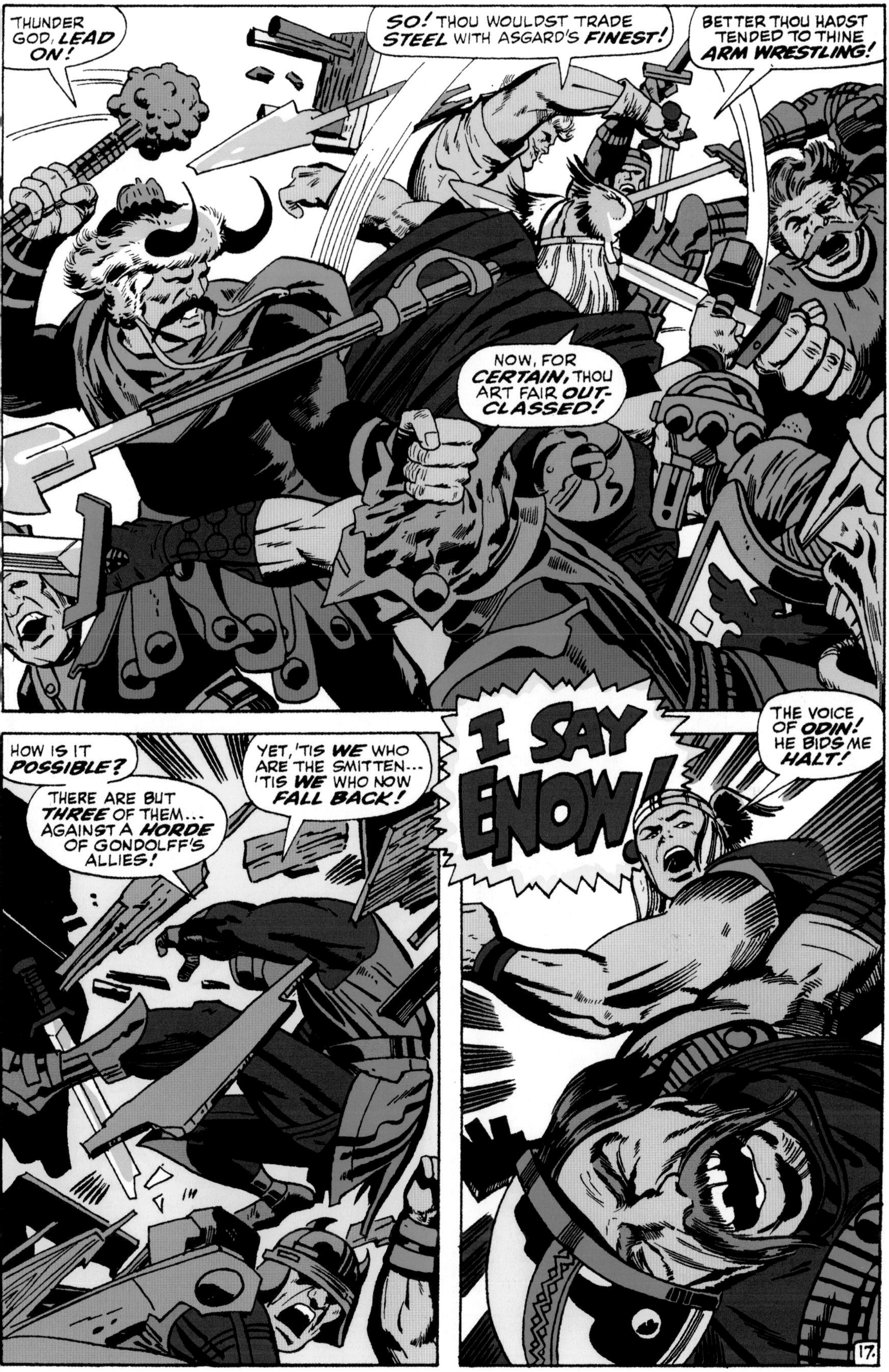
THUNDER GOD, LEAD ON!
SO! THOU WOULDST TRADE STEEL WITH ASGARD'S FINEST!
BETTER THOU HADST TENDED TO THINE ARM WRESTLING!
NOW, FOR CERTAIN, THOU ART FAIR OUT-CLASSED!
HOW IS IT POSSIBLE?
THERE ARE BUT THREE OF THEM... AGAINST A HORDE OF GONDOLFF'S ALLIES!
YET, 'TIS WE WHO ARE THE SMITTEN... 'TIS WE WHO NOW FALL BACK!
I SAY ENOW!
THE VOICE OF ODIN! HE BIDS ME HALT!
17.

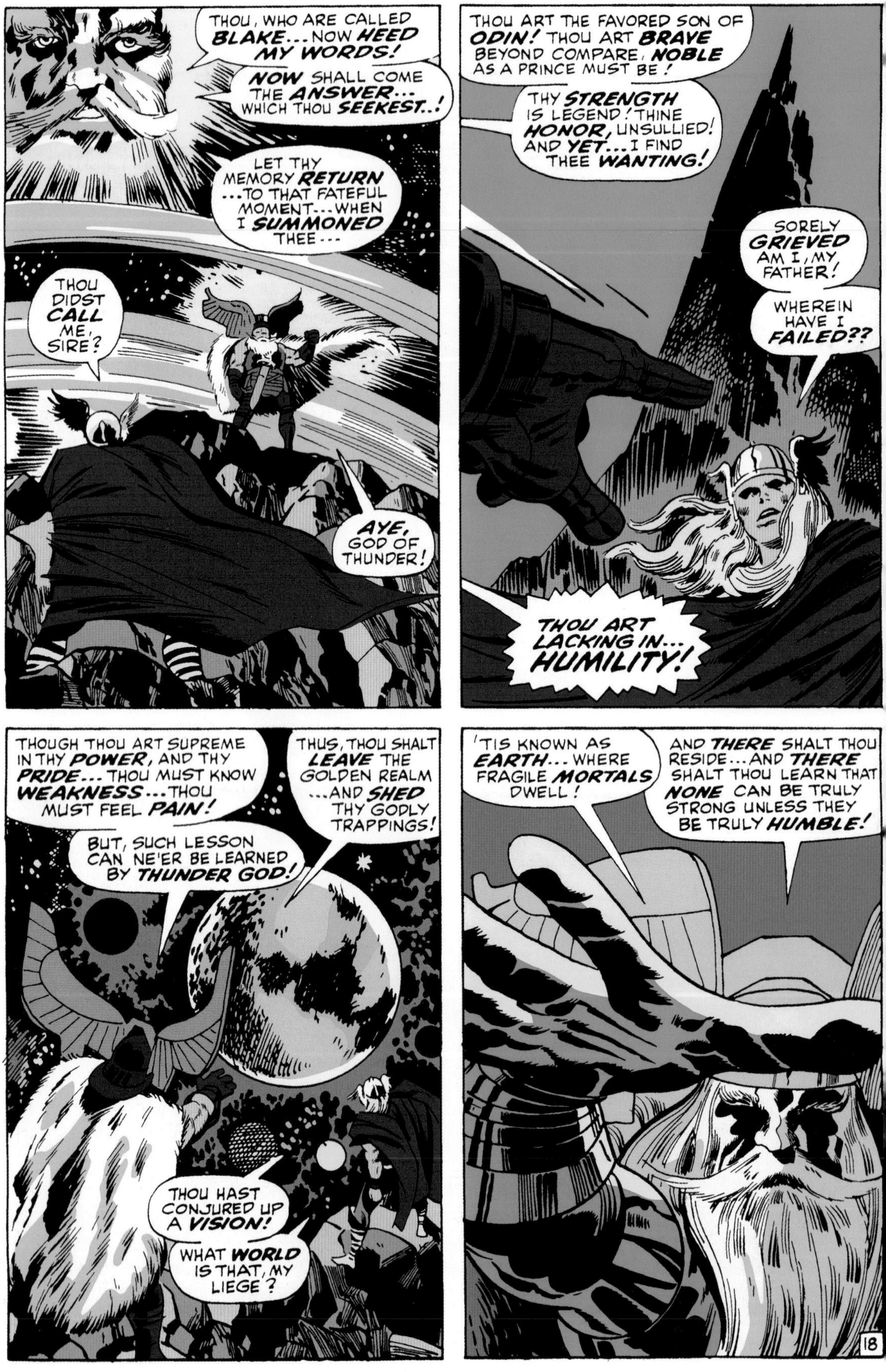
THOU, WHO ARE CALLED BLAKE... NOW HEED MY WORDS!
NOW SHALL COME THE ANSWER... WHICH THOU SEEKEST..!
LET THY MEMORY RETURN ...TO THAT FATEFUL MOMENT... WHEN I SUMMONED THEE---
THOU DIDST CALL ME, SIRE?
AYE, GOD OF THUNDER!
THOU ART THE FAVORED SON OF ODIN! THOU ART BRAVE BEYOND COMPARE, NOBLE AS A PRINCE MUST BE!
THY STRENGTH IS LEGEND! THINE HONOR, UNSULLIED! AND YET... I FIND THEE WANTING!
SORELY GRIEVED AM I, MY FATHER!
WHEREIN HAVE I FAILED??
THOU ART LACKING IN... HUMILITY!
THOUGH THOU ART SUPREME IN THY POWER, AND THY PRIDE... THOU MUST KNOW WEAKNESS... THOU MUST FEEL PAIN!
BUT, SUCH LESSON CAN NE'ER BE LEARNED BY THUNDER GOD!
THUS, THOU SHALT LEAVE THE GOLDEN REALM ...AND SHED THY GODLY TRAPPINGS!
THOU HAST CONJURED UP A VISION!
WHAT WORLD IS THAT, MY LIEGE?
'TIS KNOWN AS EARTH... WHERE FRAGILE MORTALS DWELL!
AND THERE SHALT THOU RESIDE... AND THERE SHALT THOU LEARN THAT NONE CAN BE TRULY STRONG UNLESS THEY BE TRULY HUMBLE!
18

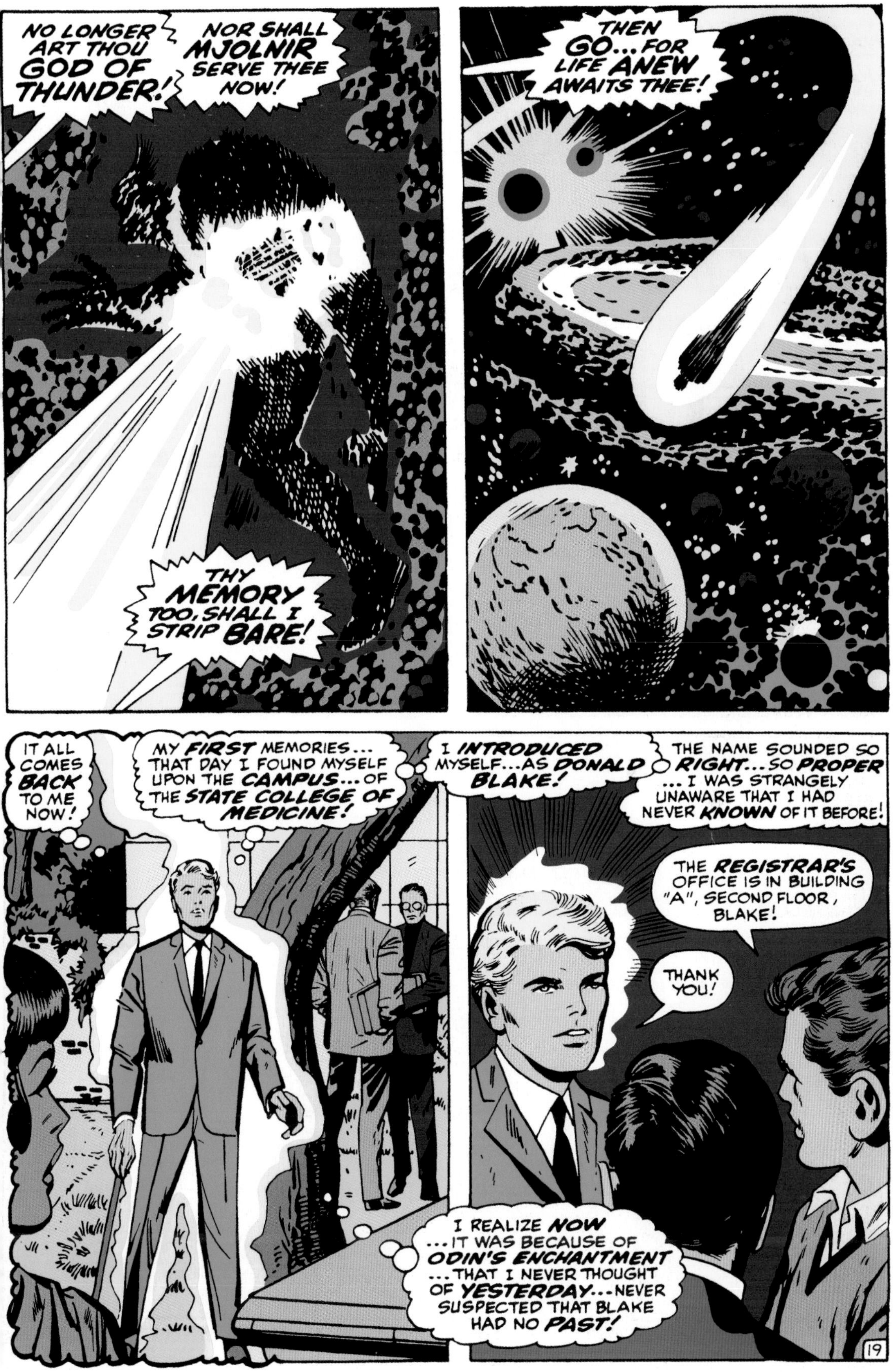

NO LONGER ART THOU GOD OF THUNDER!
NOR SHALL MJOLNIR SERVE THEE NOW!
THY MEMORY TOO, SHALL I STRIP BARE!
THEN GO...FOR LIFE ANEW AWAITS THEE!
IT ALL COMES BACK TO ME NOW!
MY FIRST MEMORIES... THAT DAY I FOUND MYSELF UPON THE CAMPUS...OF THE STATE COLLEGE OF MEDICINE!
I INTRODUCED MYSELF...AS DONALD BLAKE!
THE NAME SOUNDED SO RIGHT...SO PROPER ...I WAS STRANGELY UNAWARE THAT I HAD NEVER KNOWN OF IT BEFORE!
THE REGISTRAR'S OFFICE IS IN BUILDING "A", SECOND FLOOR, BLAKE!
THANK YOU!
I REALIZE NOW ...IT WAS BECAUSE OF ODIN'S ENCHANTMENT ...THAT I NEVER THOUGHT OF YESTERDAY...NEVER SUSPECTED THAT BLAKE HAD NO PAST!
19

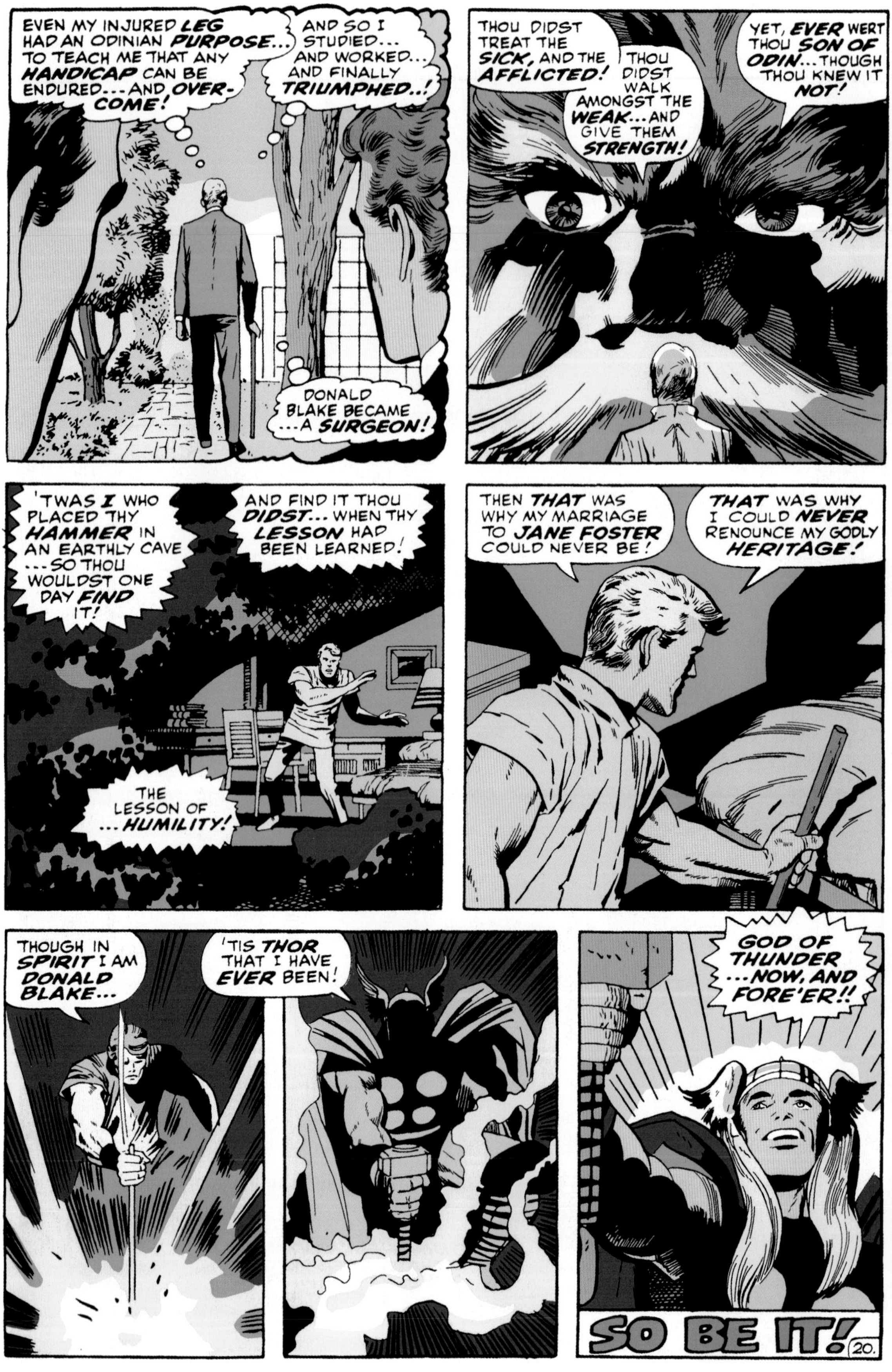
EVEN MY INJURED LEG HAD AN ODINIAN PURPOSE... TO TEACH ME THAT ANY HANDICAP CAN BE ENDURED... AND OVER-COME!
AND SO I STUDIED... AND WORKED... AND FINALLY TRIUMPHED..!
DONALD BLAKE BECAME ...A SURGEON!
THOU DIDST TREAT THE SICK, AND THE AFFLICTED!
THOU DIDST WALK AMONGST THE WEAK... AND GIVE THEM STRENGTH!
YET, EVER WERT THOU SON OF ODIN... THOUGH THOU KNEW IT NOT!
'TWAS I WHO PLACED THY HAMMER IN AN EARTHLY CAVE ...SO THOU WOULDST ONE DAY FIND IT!
AND FIND IT THOU DIDST... WHEN THY LESSON HAD BEEN LEARNED!
THE LESSON OF ...HUMILITY!
THEN THAT WAS WHY MY MARRIAGE TO JANE FOSTER COULD NEVER BE!
THAT WAS WHY I COULD NEVER RENOUNCE MY GODLY HERITAGE!
THOUGH IN SPIRIT I AM DONALD BLAKE...
'TIS THOR THAT I HAVE EVER BEEN!
GOD OF THUNDER ...NOW, AND FORE'ER!!
SO BE IT!
20.

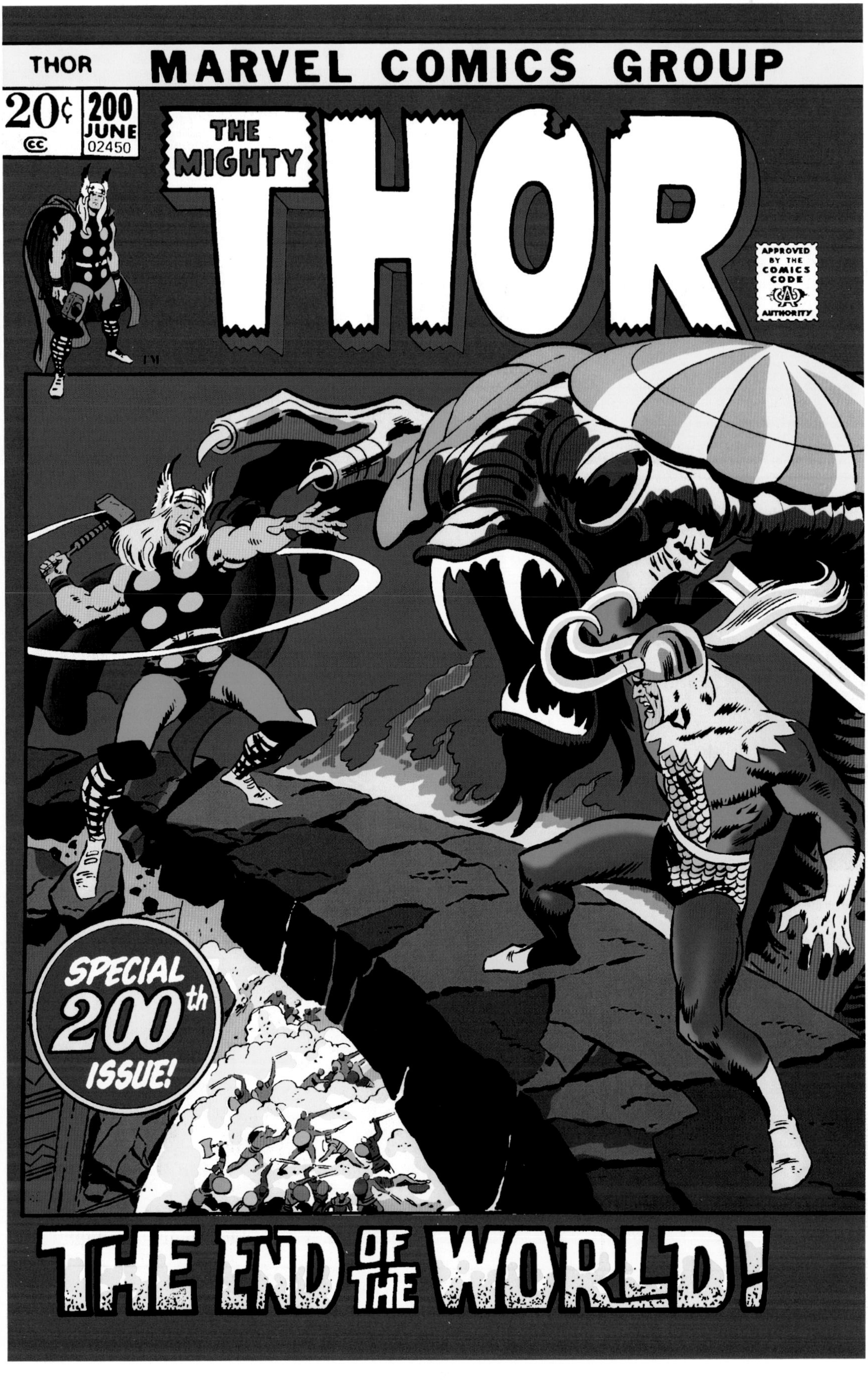
THOR
MARVEL COMICS GROUP
20¢
200
JUNE
02450
THE MIGHTY
THOR
APPROVED BY THE COMICS CODE AUTHORITY
SPECIAL 200th ISSUE!
THE END OF THE WORLD!

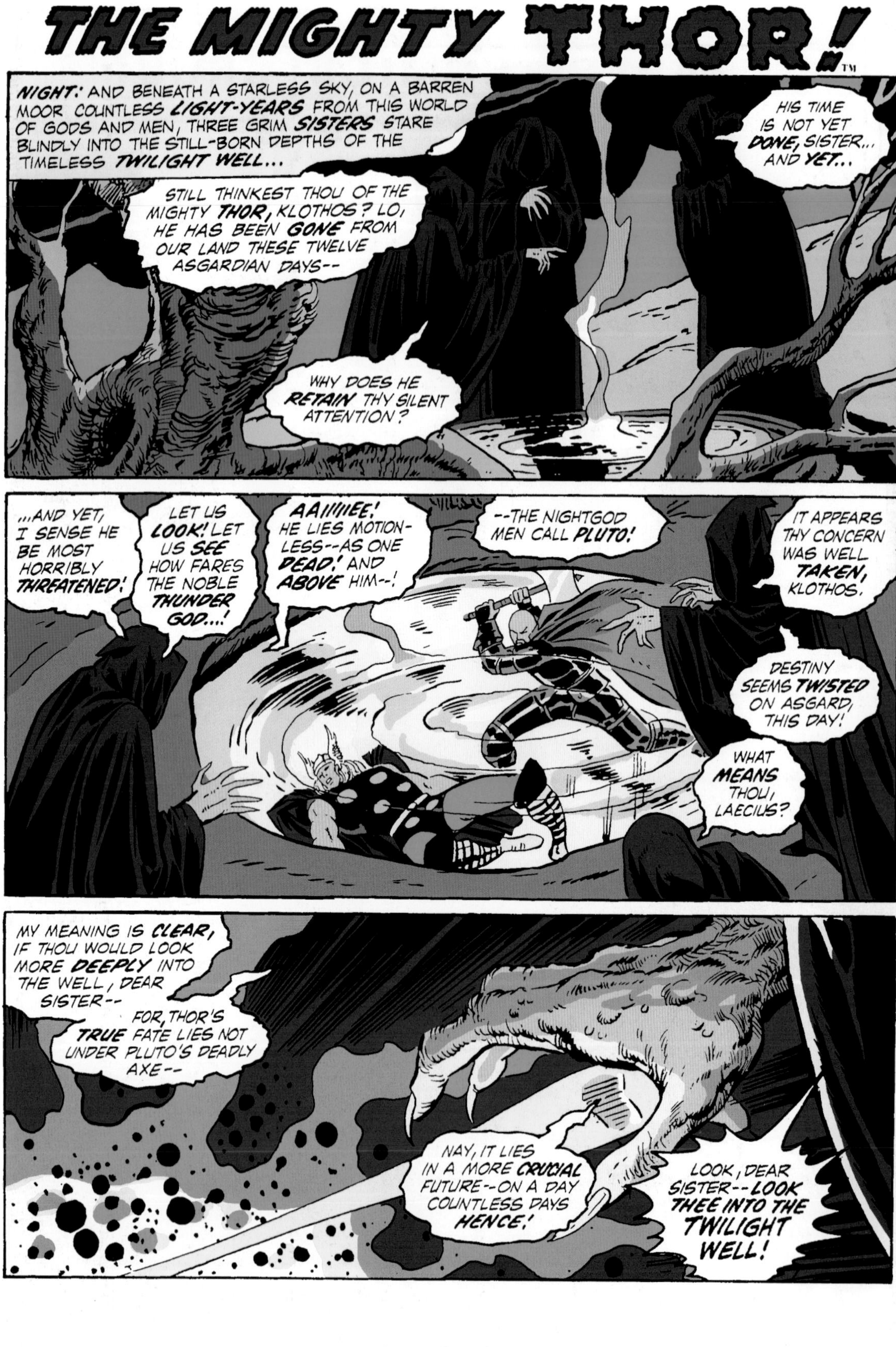
THE MIGHTY THOR!™
NIGHT: AND BENEATH A STARLESS SKY, ON A BARREN MOOR COUNTLESS LIGHT-YEARS FROM THIS WORLD OF GODS AND MEN, THREE GRIM SISTERS STARE BLINDLY INTO THE STILL-BORN DEPTHS OF THE TIMELESS TWILIGHT WELL...
HIS TIME IS NOT YET DONE, SISTER... AND YET...
STILL THINKEST THOU OF THE MIGHTY THOR, KLOTHOS? LO, HE HAS BEEN GONE FROM OUR LAND THESE TWELVE ASGARDIAN DAYS--
WHY DOES HE RETAIN THY SILENT ATTENTION?
...AND YET, I SENSE HE BE MOST HORRIBLY THREATENED!
LET US LOOK! LET US SEE HOW FARES THE NOBLE THUNDER GOD...!
AAIIIIEE! HE LIES MOTION-LESS--AS ONE DEAD! AND ABOVE HIM--!
--THE NIGHTGOD MEN CALL PLUTO!
IT APPEARS THY CONCERN WAS WELL TAKEN, KLOTHOS.
DESTINY SEEMS TWISTED ON ASGARD, THIS DAY!
WHAT MEANS THOU, LAECIUS?
MY MEANING IS CLEAR, IF THOU WOULD LOOK MORE DEEPLY INTO THE WELL, DEAR SISTER--
FOR, THOR'S TRUE FATE LIES NOT UNDER PLUTO'S DEADLY AXE--
NAY, IT LIES IN A MORE CRUCIAL FUTURE--ON A DAY COUNTLESS DAYS HENCE!
LOOK, DEAR SISTER--LOOK THEE INTO THE TWILIGHT WELL!

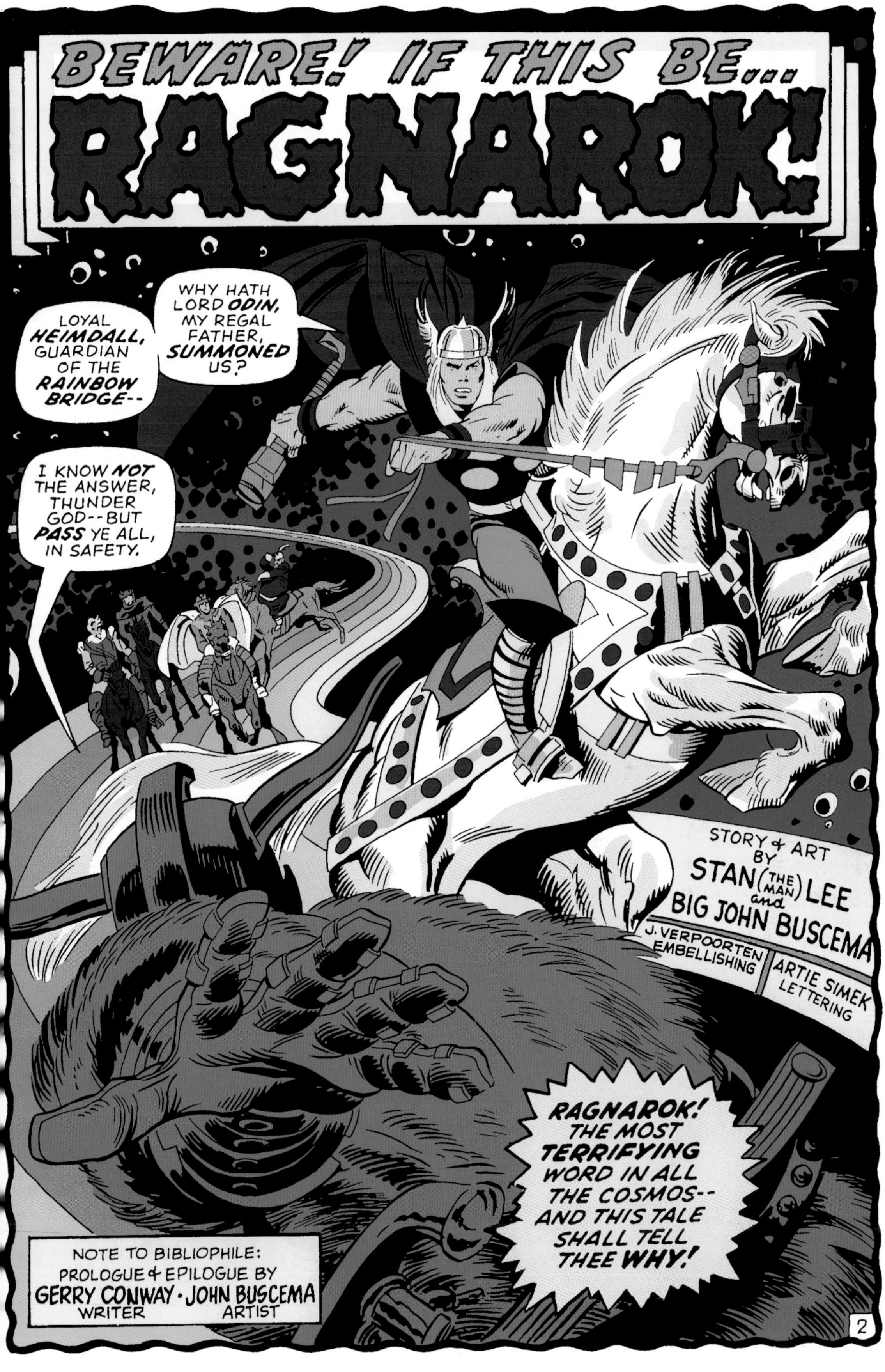
BEWARE! IF THIS BE...
RAGNAROK!
WHY HATH LORD ODIN, MY REGAL FATHER, SUMMONED US?
LOYAL HEIMDALL, GUARDIAN OF THE RAINBOW BRIDGE--
I KNOW NOT THE ANSWER, THUNDER GOD--BUT PASS YE ALL, IN SAFETY.
STORY & ART BY
STAN (THE MAN) LEE
and
BIG JOHN BUSCEMA
J. VERPOORTEN EMBELLISHING
ARTIE SIMEK LETTERING
RAGNAROK! THE MOST TERRIFYING WORD IN ALL THE COSMOS-- AND THIS TALE SHALL TELL THEE WHY!
NOTE TO BIBLIOPHILE: PROLOGUE & EPILOGUE BY
GERRY CONWAY · JOHN BUSCEMA
WRITER ARTIST
2

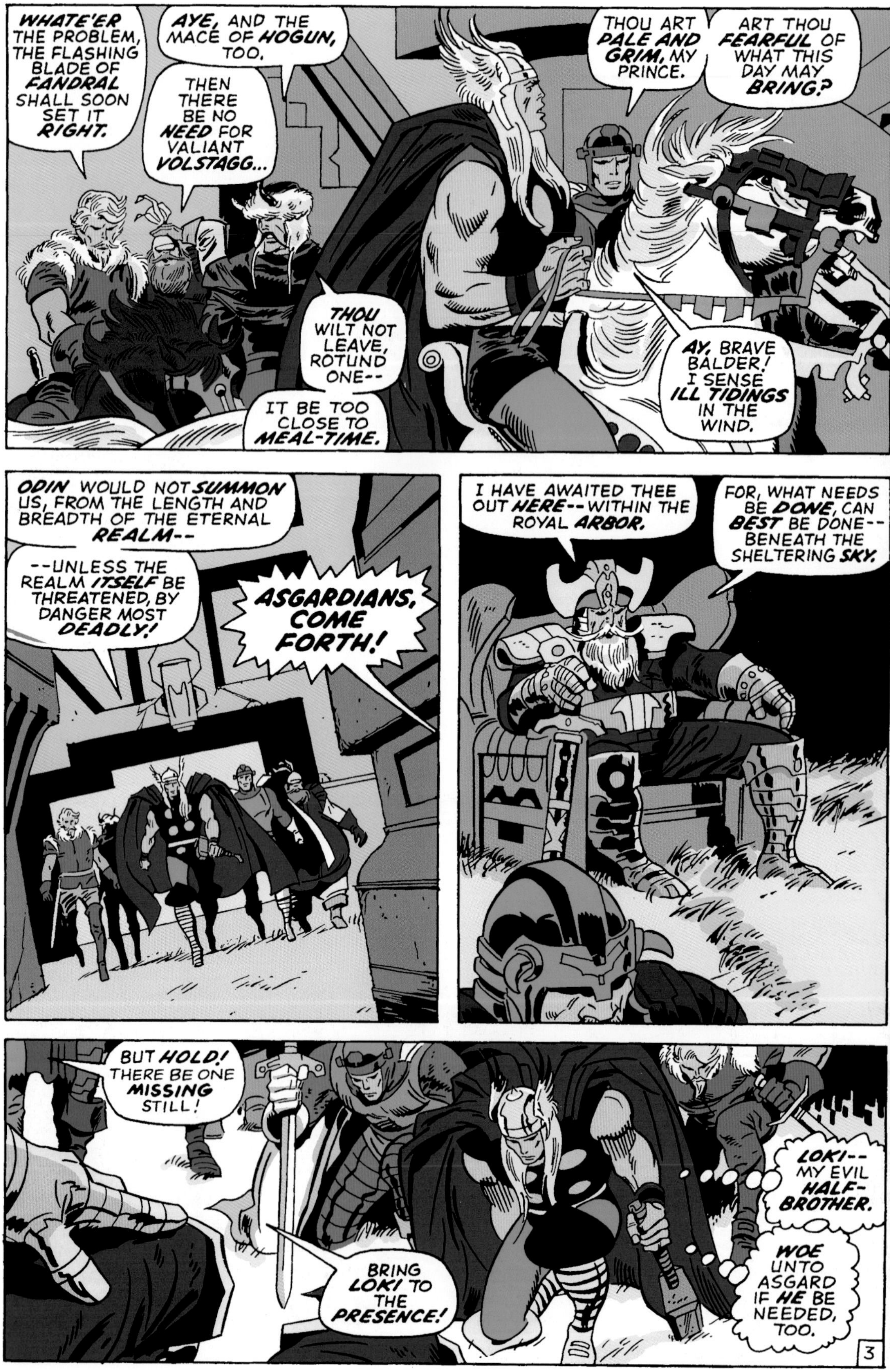
WHATE'ER THE PROBLEM, THE FLASHING BLADE OF FANDRAL SHALL SOON SET IT RIGHT.
AYE, AND THE MACE OF HOGUN, TOO.
THEN THERE BE NO NEED FOR VALIANT VOLSTAGG...
THOU WILT NOT LEAVE, ROTUND ONE--
IT BE TOO CLOSE TO MEAL-TIME.
THOU ART PALE AND GRIM, MY PRINCE.
ART THOU FEARFUL OF WHAT THIS DAY MAY BRING?
AY, BRAVE BALDER! I SENSE ILL TIDINGS IN THE WIND.
ODIN WOULD NOT SUMMON US, FROM THE LENGTH AND BREADTH OF THE ETERNAL REALM--
--UNLESS THE REALM ITSELF BE THREATENED, BY DANGER MOST DEADLY!
ASGARDIANS, COME FORTH!
I HAVE AWAITED THEE OUT HERE-- WITHIN THE ROYAL ARBOR.
FOR, WHAT NEEDS BE DONE, CAN BEST BE DONE-- BENEATH THE SHELTERING SKY.
BUT HOLD! THERE BE ONE MISSING STILL!
BRING LOKI TO THE PRESENCE!
LOKI-- MY EVIL HALF-BROTHER.
WOE UNTO ASGARD IF HE BE NEEDED, TOO.
3

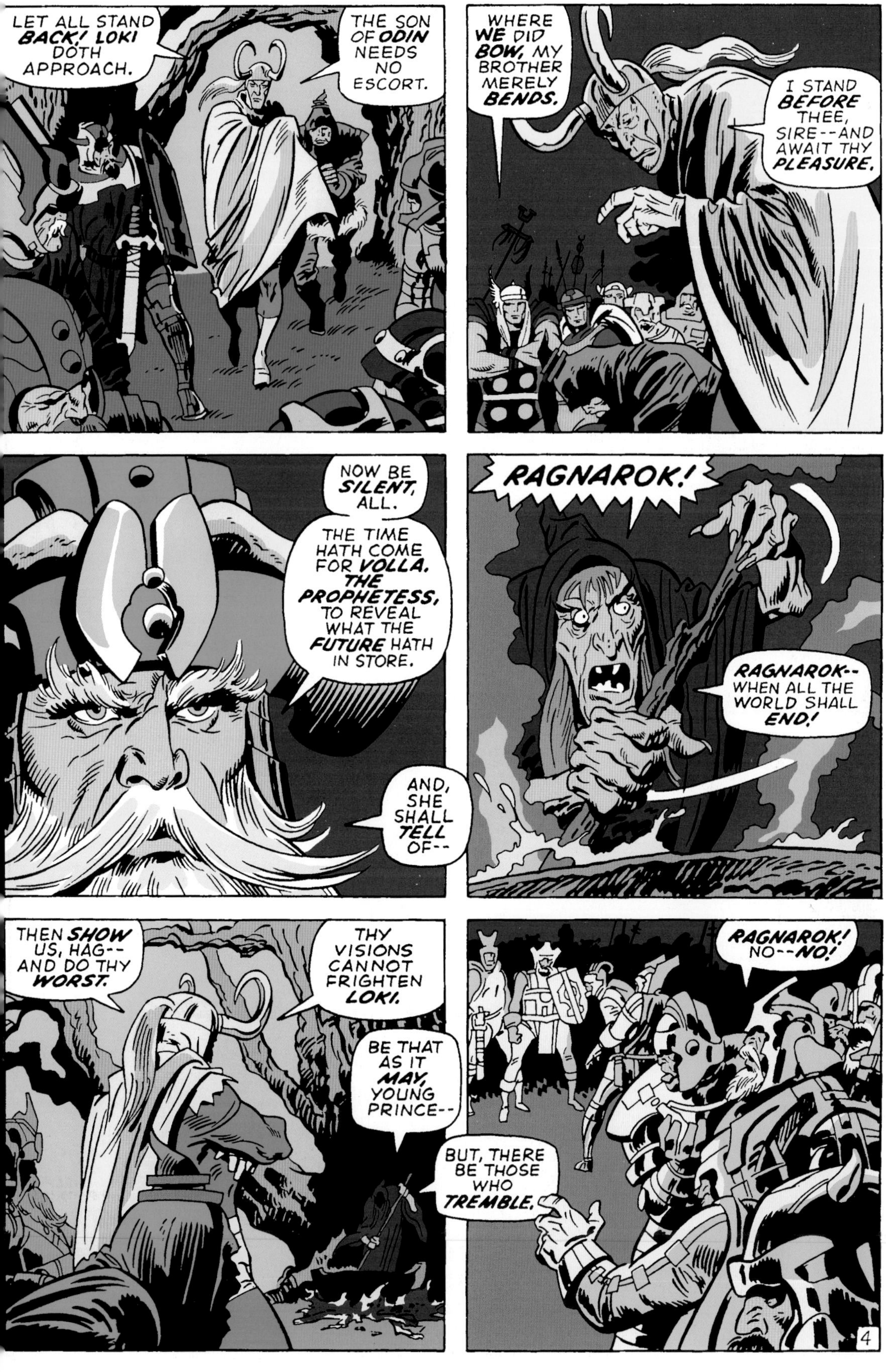
LET ALL STAND BACK! LOKI DOTH APPROACH.
THE SON OF ODIN NEEDS NO ESCORT.
WHERE WE DID BOW, MY BROTHER MERELY BENDS.
I STAND BEFORE THEE, SIRE--AND AWAIT THY PLEASURE.
NOW BE SILENT, ALL.
THE TIME HATH COME FOR VOLLA, THE PROPHETESS, TO REVEAL WHAT THE FUTURE HATH IN STORE.
AND, SHE SHALL TELL OF--
RAGNAROK!
RAGNAROK--WHEN ALL THE WORLD SHALL END!
THEN SHOW US, HAG--AND DO THY WORST.
THY VISIONS CANNOT FRIGHTEN LOKI.
BE THAT AS IT MAY, YOUNG PRINCE--
BUT, THERE BE THOSE WHO TREMBLE.
RAGNAROK! NO--NO!
4

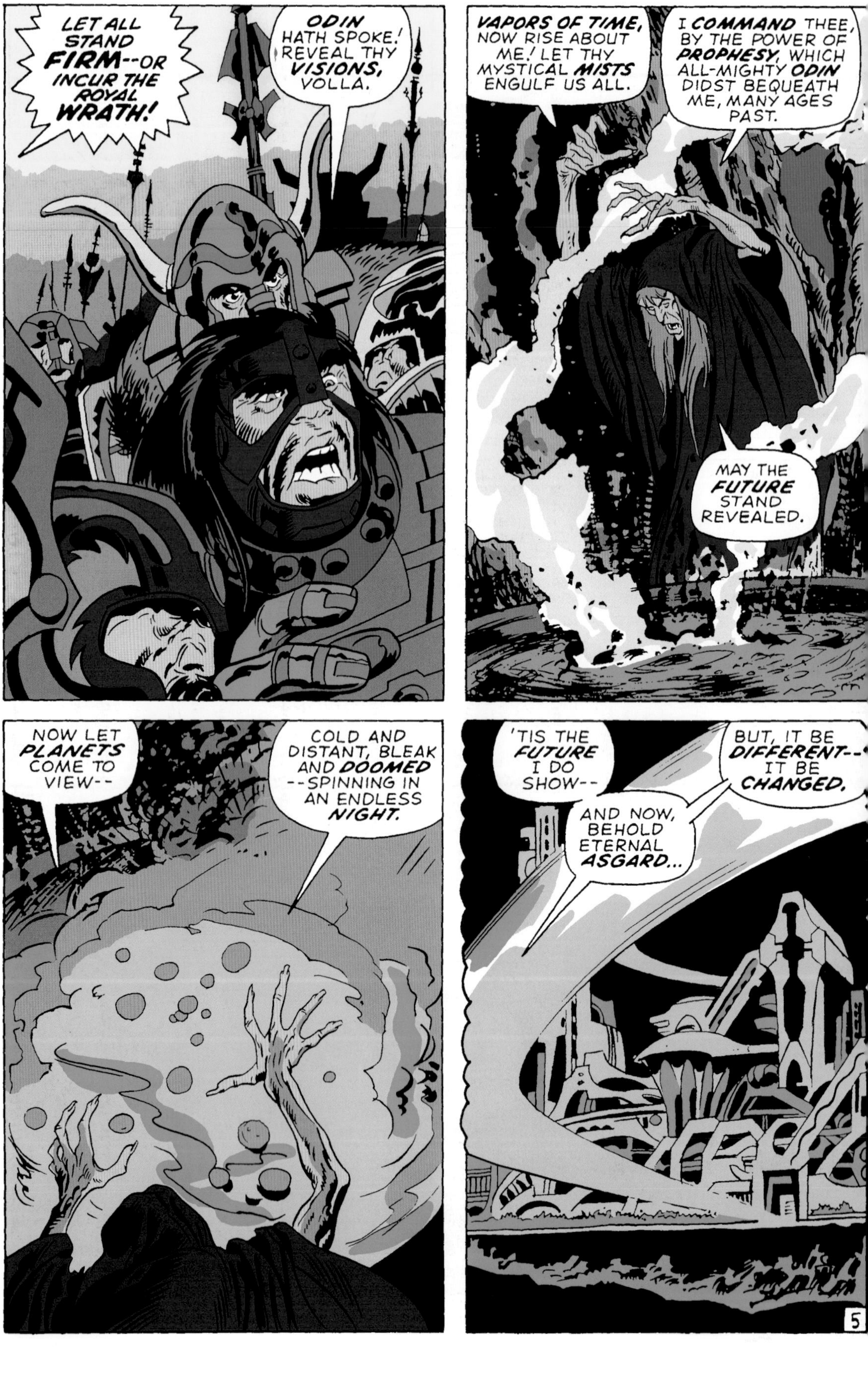
LET ALL STAND FIRM--OR INCUR THE ROYAL WRATH!
ODIN HATH SPOKE! REVEAL THY VISIONS, VOLLA.
VAPORS OF TIME, NOW RISE ABOUT ME! LET THY MYSTICAL MISTS ENGULF US ALL.
I COMMAND THEE, BY THE POWER OF PROPHESY, WHICH ALL-MIGHTY ODIN DIDST BEQUEATH ME, MANY AGES PAST.
MAY THE FUTURE STAND REVEALED.
NOW LET PLANETS COME TO VIEW--
COLD AND DISTANT, BLEAK AND DOOMED --SPINNING IN AN ENDLESS NIGHT.
'TIS THE FUTURE I DO SHOW--
BUT, IT BE DIFFERENT-- IT BE CHANGED.
AND NOW, BEHOLD ETERNAL ASGARD...
5

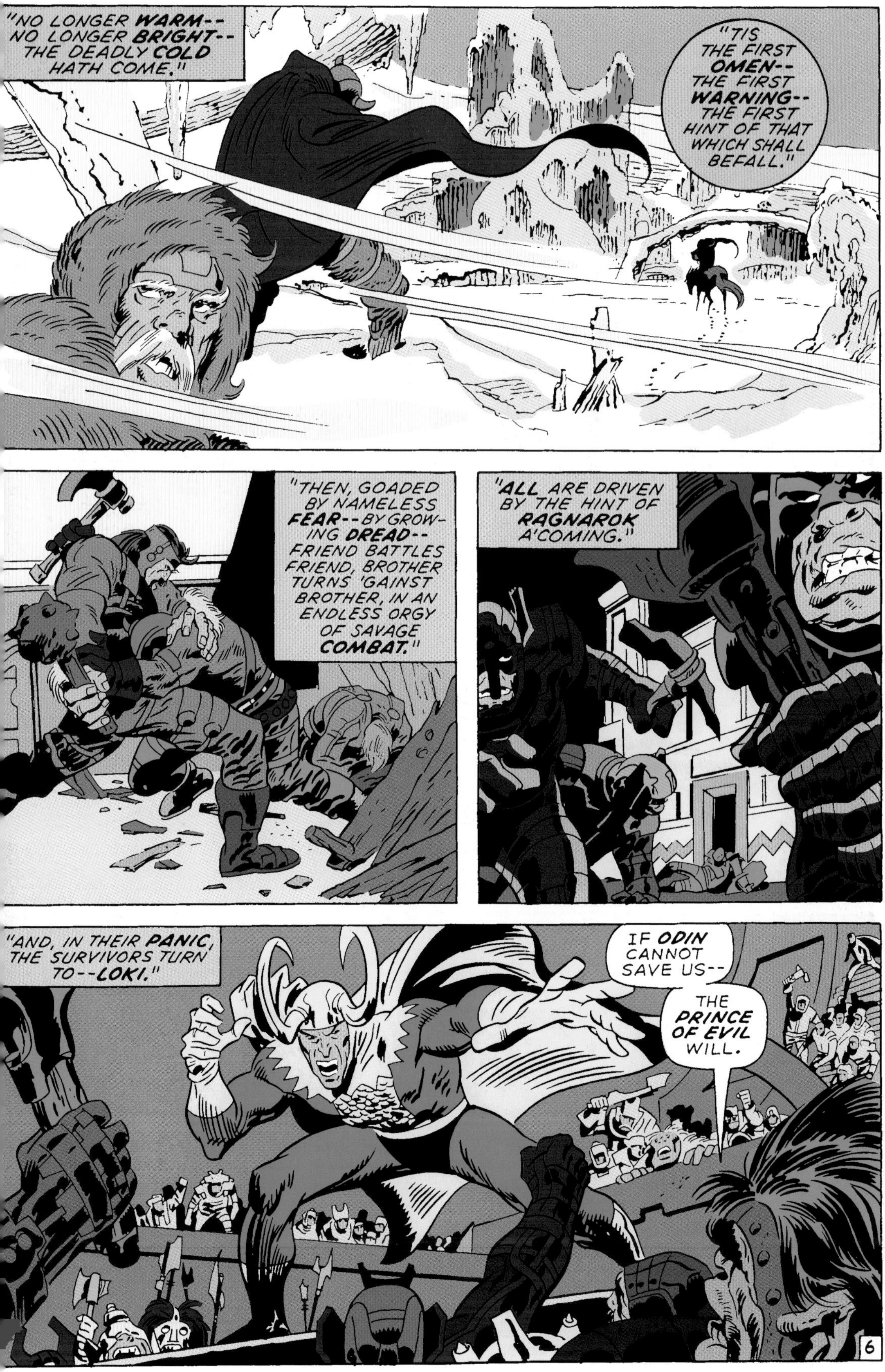
"NO LONGER WARM-- NO LONGER BRIGHT-- THE DEADLY COLD HATH COME."
"TIS THE FIRST OMEN-- THE FIRST WARNING-- THE FIRST HINT OF THAT WHICH SHALL BEFALL."
"THEN, GOADED BY NAMELESS FEAR--BY GROWING DREAD-- FRIEND BATTLES FRIEND, BROTHER TURNS 'GAINST BROTHER, IN AN ENDLESS ORGY OF SAVAGE COMBAT."
"ALL ARE DRIVEN BY THE HINT OF RAGNAROK A'COMING."
"AND, IN THEIR PANIC, THE SURVIVORS TURN TO--LOKI."
IF ODIN CANNOT SAVE US--
THE PRINCE OF EVIL WILL.
6

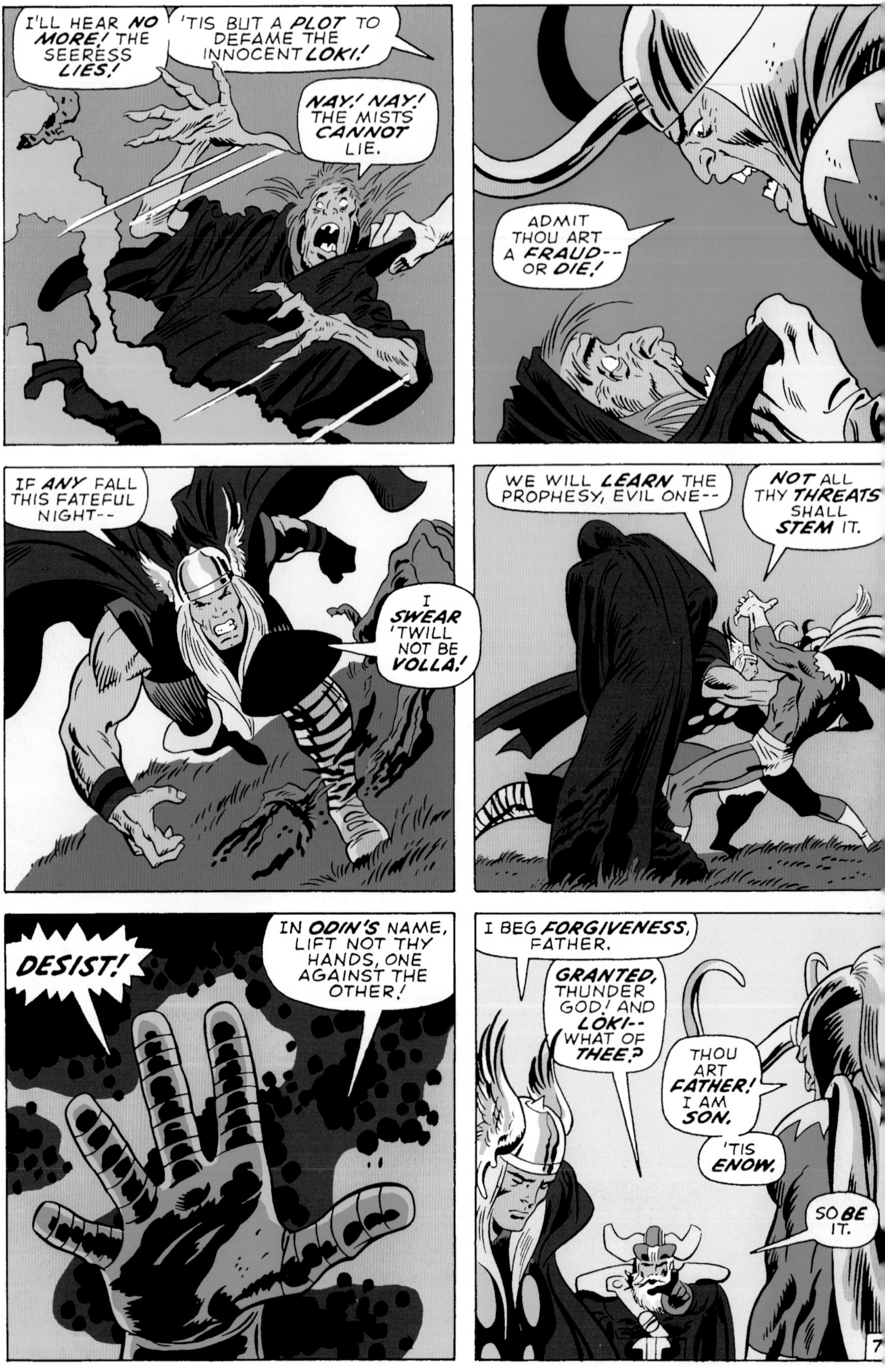
I'LL HEAR NO MORE! THE SEERESS LIES!
'TIS BUT A PLOT TO DEFAME THE INNOCENT LOKI!
NAY! NAY! THE MISTS CANNOT LIE.
ADMIT THOU ART A FRAUD-- OR DIE!
IF ANY FALL THIS FATEFUL NIGHT--
I SWEAR 'TWILL NOT BE VOLLA!
WE WILL LEARN THE PROPHESY, EVIL ONE--
NOT ALL THY THREATS SHALL STEM IT.
DESIST!
IN ODIN'S NAME, LIFT NOT THY HANDS, ONE AGAINST THE OTHER!
I BEG FORGIVENESS, FATHER.
GRANTED, THUNDER GOD! AND LOKI-- WHAT OF THEE?
THOU ART FATHER! I AM SON.
'TIS ENOW.
SO BE IT.
7

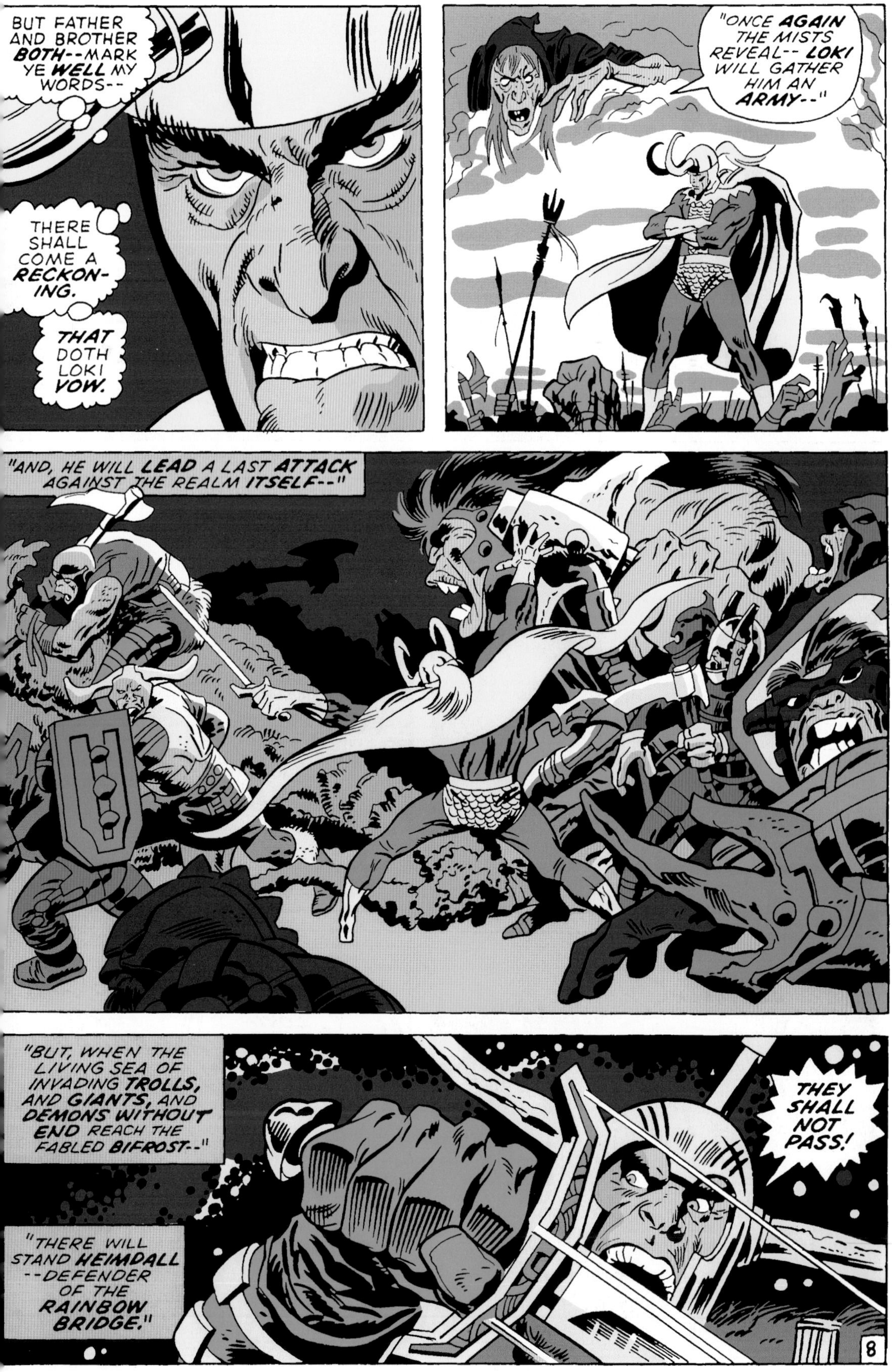

BUT FATHER AND BROTHER BOTH--MARK YE WELL MY WORDS--
THERE SHALL COME A RECKONING.
THAT DOTH LOKI VOW.
"ONCE AGAIN THE MISTS REVEAL-- LOKI WILL GATHER HIM AN ARMY--"
"AND, HE WILL LEAD A LAST ATTACK AGAINST THE REALM ITSELF--"
"BUT, WHEN THE LIVING SEA OF INVADING TROLLS, AND GIANTS, AND DEMONS WITHOUT END REACH THE FABLED BIFROST--"
THEY SHALL NOT PASS!
"THERE WILL STAND HEIMDALL --DEFENDER OF THE RAINBOW BRIDGE."
8

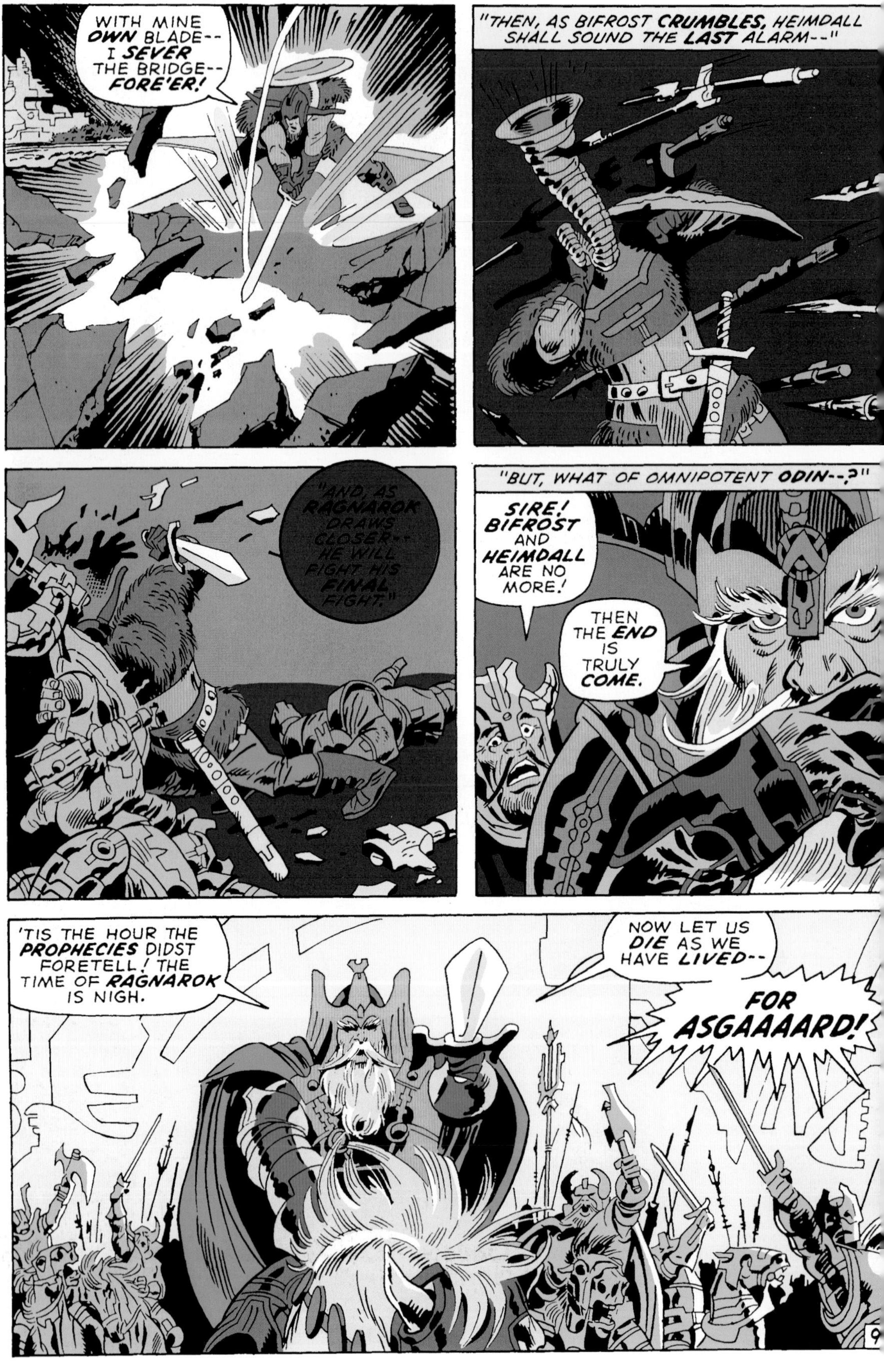
WITH MINE OWN BLADE-- I SEVER THE BRIDGE-- FORE'ER!
"THEN, AS BIFROST CRUMBLES, HEIMDALL SHALL SOUND THE LAST ALARM--"
"AND, AS RAGNAROK DRAWS CLOSER-- HE WILL FIGHT HIS FINAL FIGHT."
"BUT, WHAT OF OMNIPOTENT ODIN--?"
SIRE! BIFROST AND HEIMDALL ARE NO MORE!
THEN THE END IS TRULY COME.
'TIS THE HOUR THE PROPHECIES DIDST FORETELL! THE TIME OF RAGNAROK IS NIGH.
NOW LET US DIE AS WE HAVE LIVED--
FOR ASGAAAARD!
9

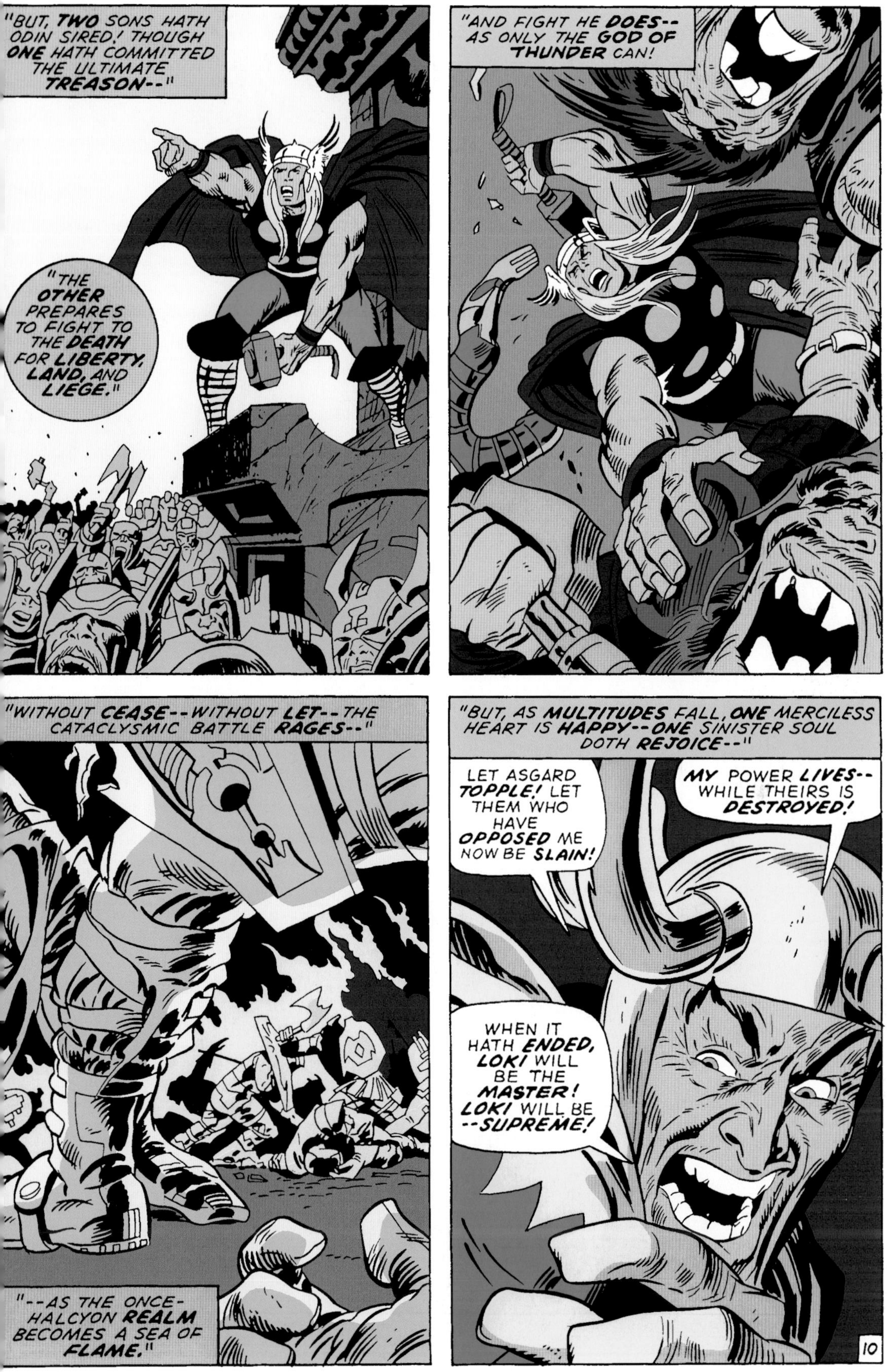
"BUT, TWO SONS HATH ODIN SIRED! THOUGH ONE HATH COMMITTED THE ULTIMATE TREASON--"
"THE OTHER PREPARES TO FIGHT TO THE DEATH FOR LIBERTY, LAND, AND LIEGE."
"AND FIGHT HE DOES--AS ONLY THE GOD OF THUNDER CAN!
"WITHOUT CEASE--WITHOUT LET--THE CATACLYSMIC BATTLE RAGES--"
"--AS THE ONCE-HALCYON REALM BECOMES A SEA OF FLAME."
"BUT, AS MULTITUDES FALL, ONE MERCILESS HEART IS HAPPY--ONE SINISTER SOUL DOTH REJOICE--"
LET ASGARD TOPPLE! LET THEM WHO HAVE OPPOSED ME NOW BE SLAIN!
MY POWER LIVES--WHILE THEIRS IS DESTROYED!
WHEN IT HATH ENDED, LOKI WILL BE THE MASTER! LOKI WILL BE --SUPREME!
10

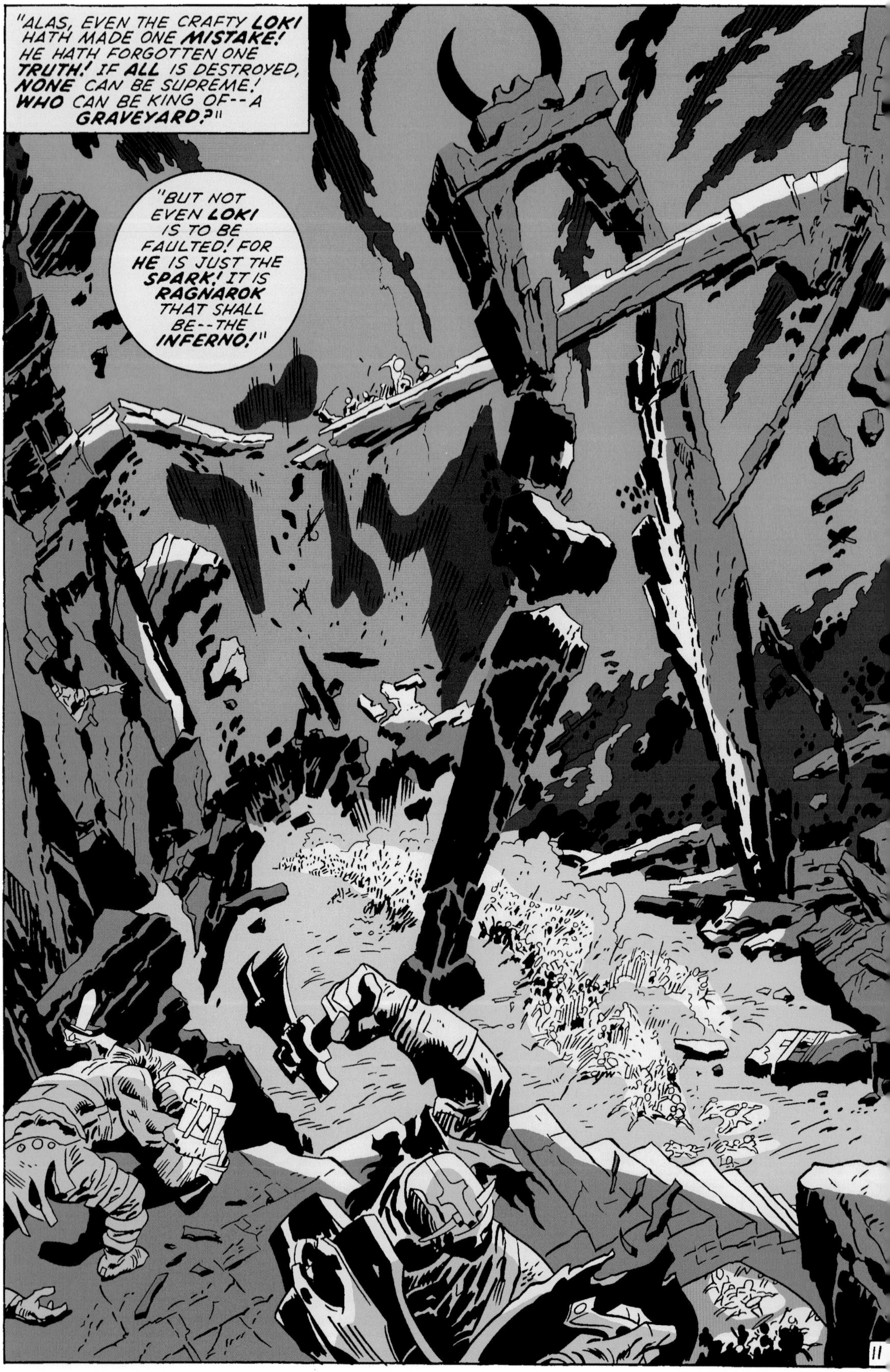
"ALAS, EVEN THE CRAFTY LOKI HATH MADE ONE MISTAKE! HE HATH FORGOTTEN ONE TRUTH! IF ALL IS DESTROYED, NONE CAN BE SUPREME! WHO CAN BE KING OF--A GRAVEYARD?"
"BUT NOT EVEN LOKI IS TO BE FAULTED! FOR HE IS JUST THE SPARK! IT IS RAGNAROK THAT SHALL BE--THE INFERNO!"
11

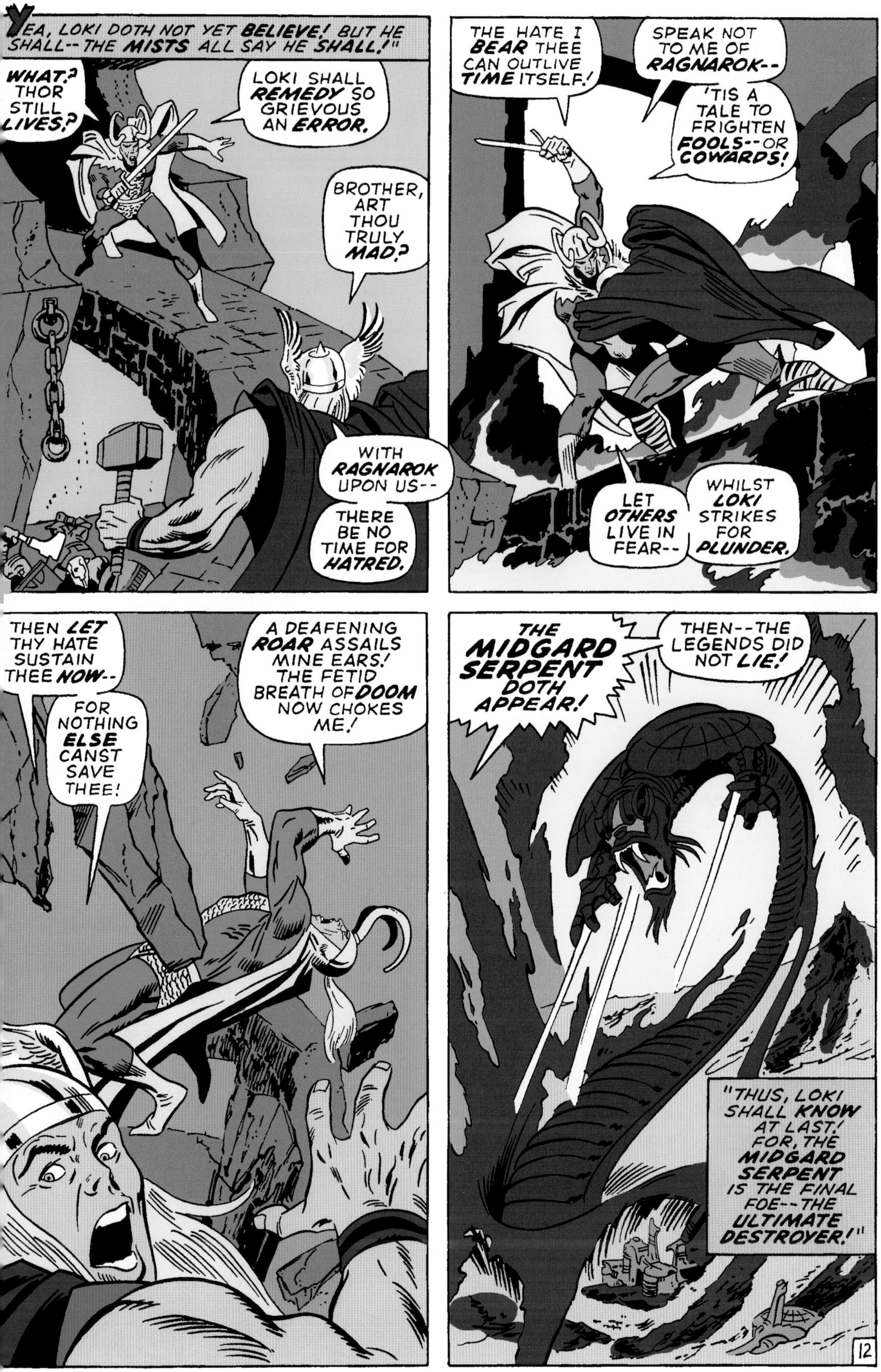
YEA, LOKI DOTH NOT YET BELIEVE! BUT HE SHALL--THE MISTS ALL SAY HE SHALL!"
WHAT? THOR STILL LIVES?
LOKI SHALL REMEDY SO GRIEVOUS AN ERROR.
BROTHER, ART THOU TRULY MAD?
WITH RAGNAROK UPON US--
THERE BE NO TIME FOR HATRED.
THE HATE I BEAR THEE CAN OUTLIVE TIME ITSELF!
SPEAK NOT TO ME OF RAGNAROK--
'TIS A TALE TO FRIGHTEN FOOLS--OR COWARDS!
LET OTHERS LIVE IN FEAR--
WHILST LOKI STRIKES FOR PLUNDER.
THEN LET THY HATE SUSTAIN THEE NOW--
FOR NOTHING ELSE CANST SAVE THEE!
A DEAFENING ROAR ASSAILS MINE EARS! THE FETID BREATH OF DOOM NOW CHOKES ME!
THE MIDGARD SERPENT DOTH APPEAR!
THEN--THE LEGENDS DID NOT LIE!
"THUS, LOKI SHALL KNOW AT LAST! FOR, THE MIDGARD SERPENT IS THE FINAL FOE--THE ULTIMATE DESTROYER!"
12

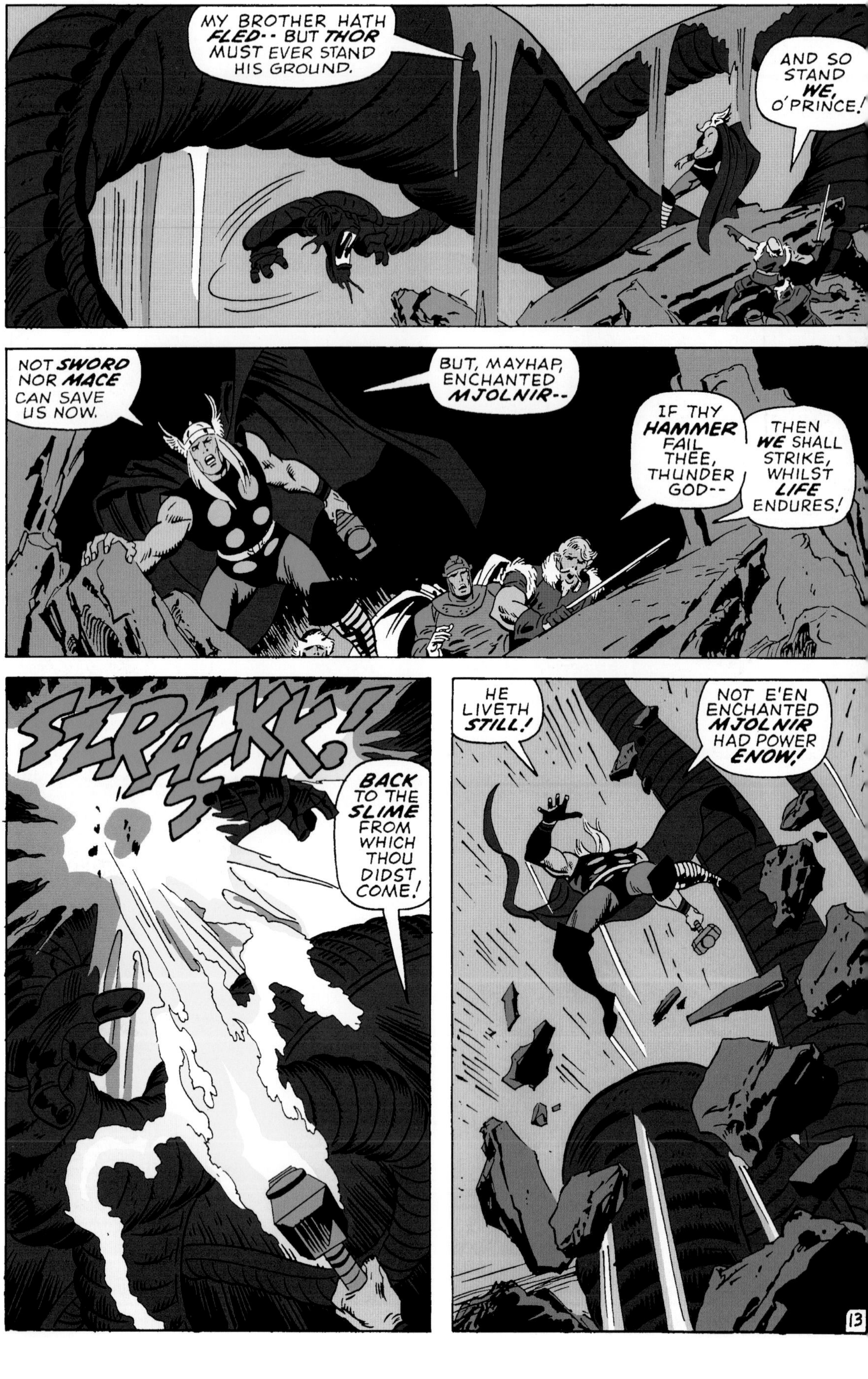

MY BROTHER HATH FLED-- BUT THOR MUST EVER STAND HIS GROUND.
AND SO STAND WE, O'PRINCE!
NOT SWORD NOR MACE CAN SAVE US NOW.
BUT, MAYHAP, ENCHANTED MJOLNIR--
IF THY HAMMER FAIL THEE, THUNDER GOD--
THEN WE SHALL STRIKE, WHILST LIFE ENDURES!
SZRAKK!
BACK TO THE SLIME FROM WHICH THOU DIDST COME!
HE LIVETH STILL!
NOT E'EN ENCHANTED MJOLNIR HAD POWER ENOW!
13

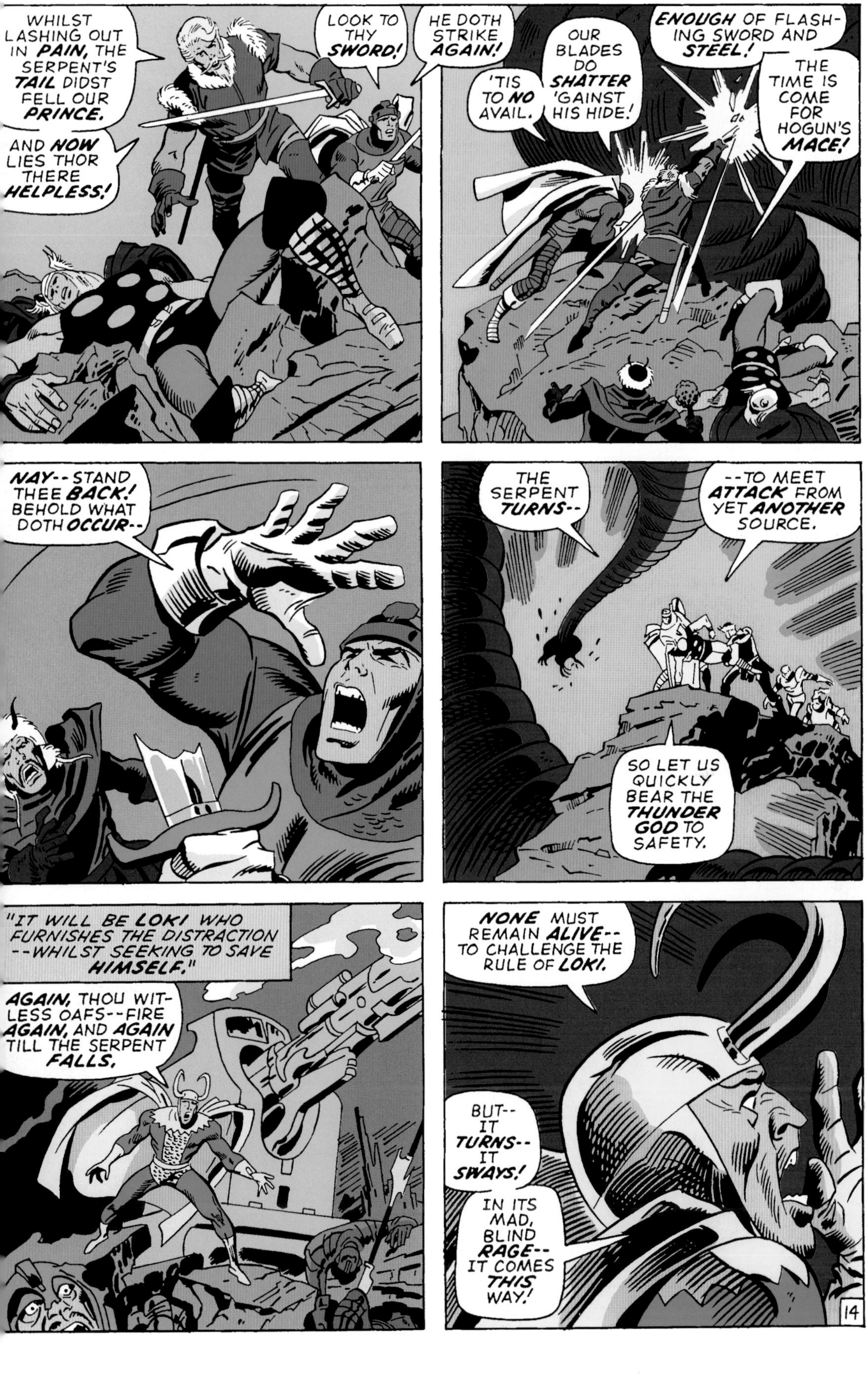
WHILST LASHING OUT IN PAIN, THE SERPENT'S TAIL DIDST FELL OUR PRINCE.
AND NOW LIES THOR THERE HELPLESS!
LOOK TO THY SWORD!
HE DOTH STRIKE AGAIN!
'TIS TO NO AVAIL.
OUR BLADES DO SHATTER 'GAINST HIS HIDE!
ENOUGH OF FLASHING SWORD AND STEEL!
THE TIME IS COME FOR HOGUN'S MACE!
NAY--STAND THEE BACK! BEHOLD WHAT DOTH OCCUR--
THE SERPENT TURNS--
--TO MEET ATTACK FROM YET ANOTHER SOURCE.
SO LET US QUICKLY BEAR THE THUNDER GOD TO SAFETY.
"IT WILL BE LOKI WHO FURNISHES THE DISTRACTION --WHILST SEEKING TO SAVE HIMSELF."
AGAIN, THOU WITLESS OAFS--FIRE AGAIN, AND AGAIN TILL THE SERPENT FALLS.
NONE MUST REMAIN ALIVE--TO CHALLENGE THE RULE OF LOKI.
BUT--IT TURNS--IT SWAYS!
IN ITS MAD, BLIND RAGE--IT COMES THIS WAY!
14

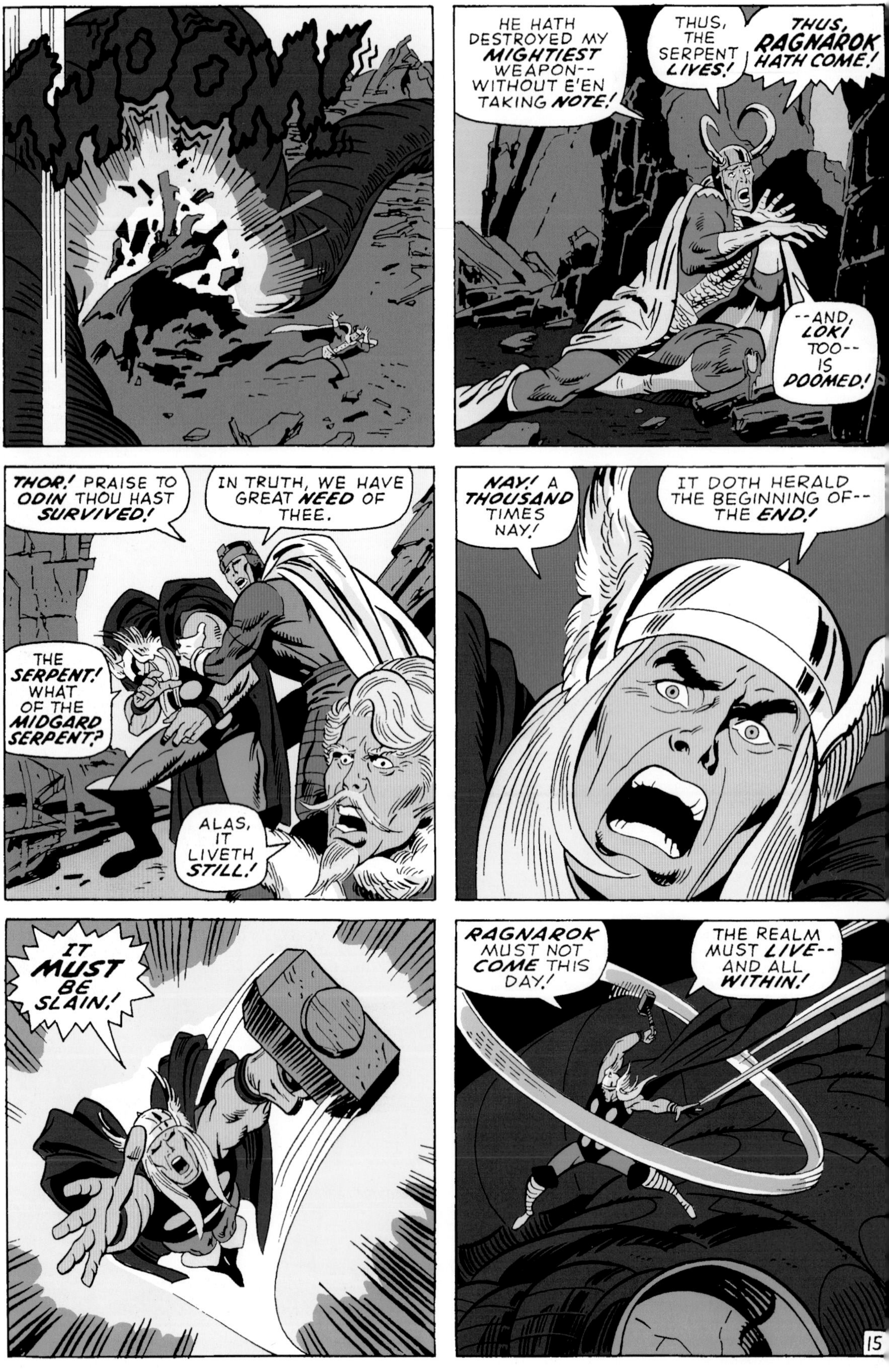

THOOM!
HE HATH DESTROYED MY MIGHTIEST WEAPON--WITHOUT E'EN TAKING NOTE!
THUS, THE SERPENT LIVES!
THUS, RAGNAROK HATH COME!
--AND, LOKI TOO--IS DOOMED!
THOR! PRAISE TO ODIN THOU HAST SURVIVED!
IN TRUTH, WE HAVE GREAT NEED OF THEE.
THE SERPENT! WHAT OF THE MIDGARD SERPENT?
ALAS, IT LIVETH STILL!
NAY! A THOUSAND TIMES NAY!
IT DOTH HERALD THE BEGINNING OF--THE END!
IT MUST BE SLAIN!
RAGNAROK MUST NOT COME THIS DAY!
THE REALM MUST LIVE--AND ALL WITHIN!
15

AND LIVE IT **WILL!**

"BUT, THOUGH HE SHALL FIGHT AS **NO** MAN HATH EVER FOUGHT **BEFORE**--WHEN THE SERPENT FINALLY **FALLS**--"

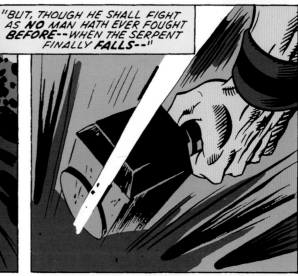

"--THE REALM **ENTIRE** SHALL BE RENT **ASUNDER**--AND ALL WILL KNOW THE **END** HATH COME."

16

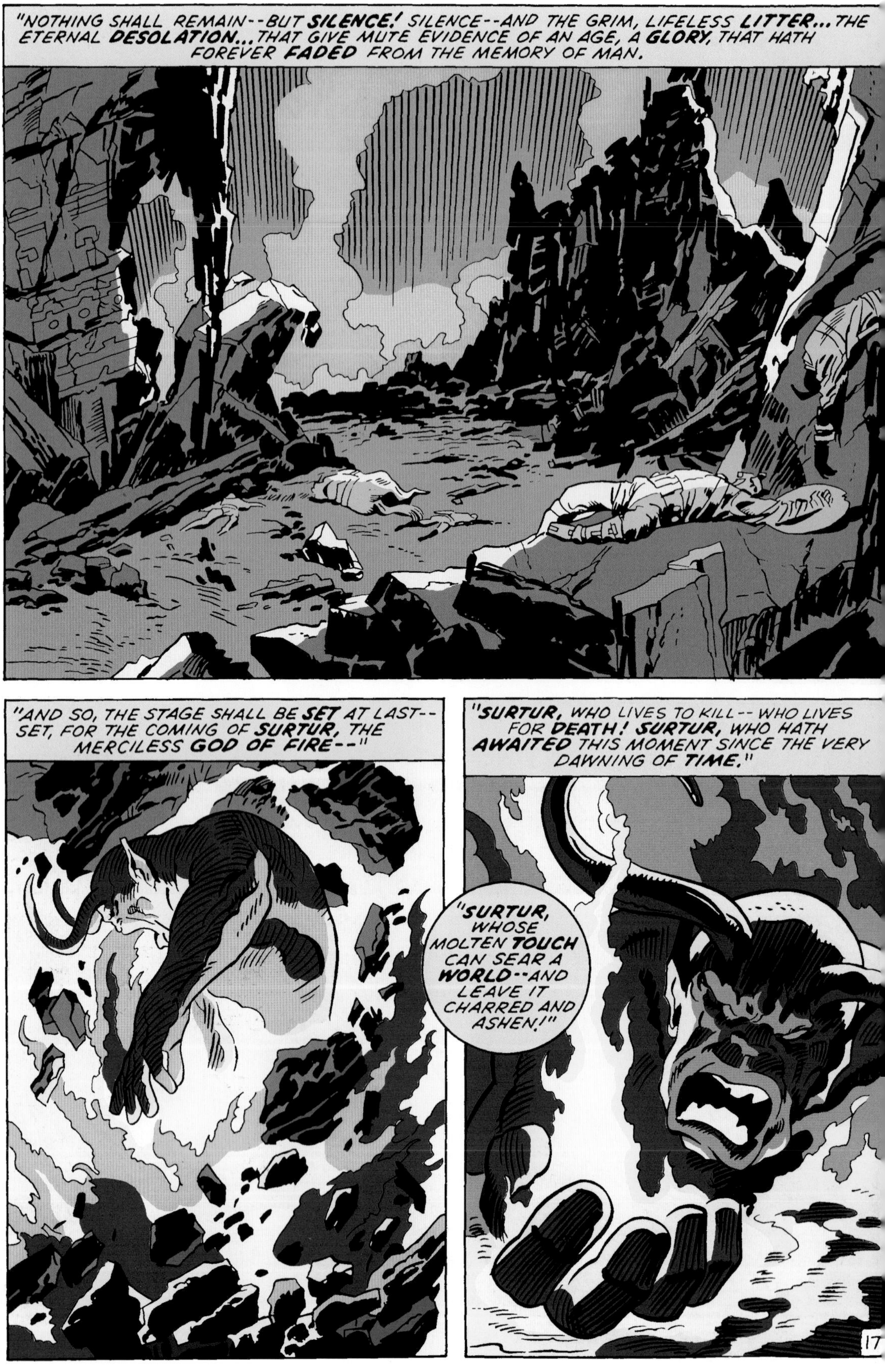
"NOTHING SHALL REMAIN--BUT SILENCE! SILENCE--AND THE GRIM, LIFELESS LITTER...THE ETERNAL DESOLATION...THAT GIVE MUTE EVIDENCE OF AN AGE, A GLORY, THAT HATH FOREVER FADED FROM THE MEMORY OF MAN.
"AND SO, THE STAGE SHALL BE SET AT LAST--SET, FOR THE COMING OF SURTUR, THE MERCILESS GOD OF FIRE--"
"SURTUR, WHO LIVES TO KILL--WHO LIVES FOR DEATH! SURTUR, WHO HATH AWAITED THIS MOMENT SINCE THE VERY DAWNING OF TIME."
"SURTUR, WHOSE MOLTEN TOUCH CAN SEAR A WORLD--AND LEAVE IT CHARRED AND ASHEN!"
17

"*THIS* DO THE MISTS REVEAL!"

"*THIS* DO THE PROPHECIES FORETELL!*"

"AND THEN, AT LAST-- *NAUGHT* SHALL REMAIN OF THE GOLDEN REALM, SAVE A FIERY, FLAMING *EMBER*--A SMOLDERING, CELESTIAL *CINDER* IN THE FABRIC OF *ETERNITY.*"

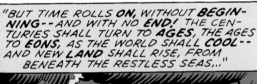

"BUT TIME ROLLS *ON,* WITHOUT *BEGINNING*--AND WITH NO *END!* THE CENTURIES SHALL TURN TO *AGES,* THE AGES TO *EONS,* AS THE WORLD SHALL *COOL*--AND NEW *LAND* SHALL RISE, FROM BENEATH THE RESTLESS SEAS..."

"AND, AS IT EVER *WAS*--AND AS EVER IT MUST *BE*--NEW *LIFE* SHALL COME A'BORNING-- AND *GODS* SHALL RISE AGAIN!*"

18

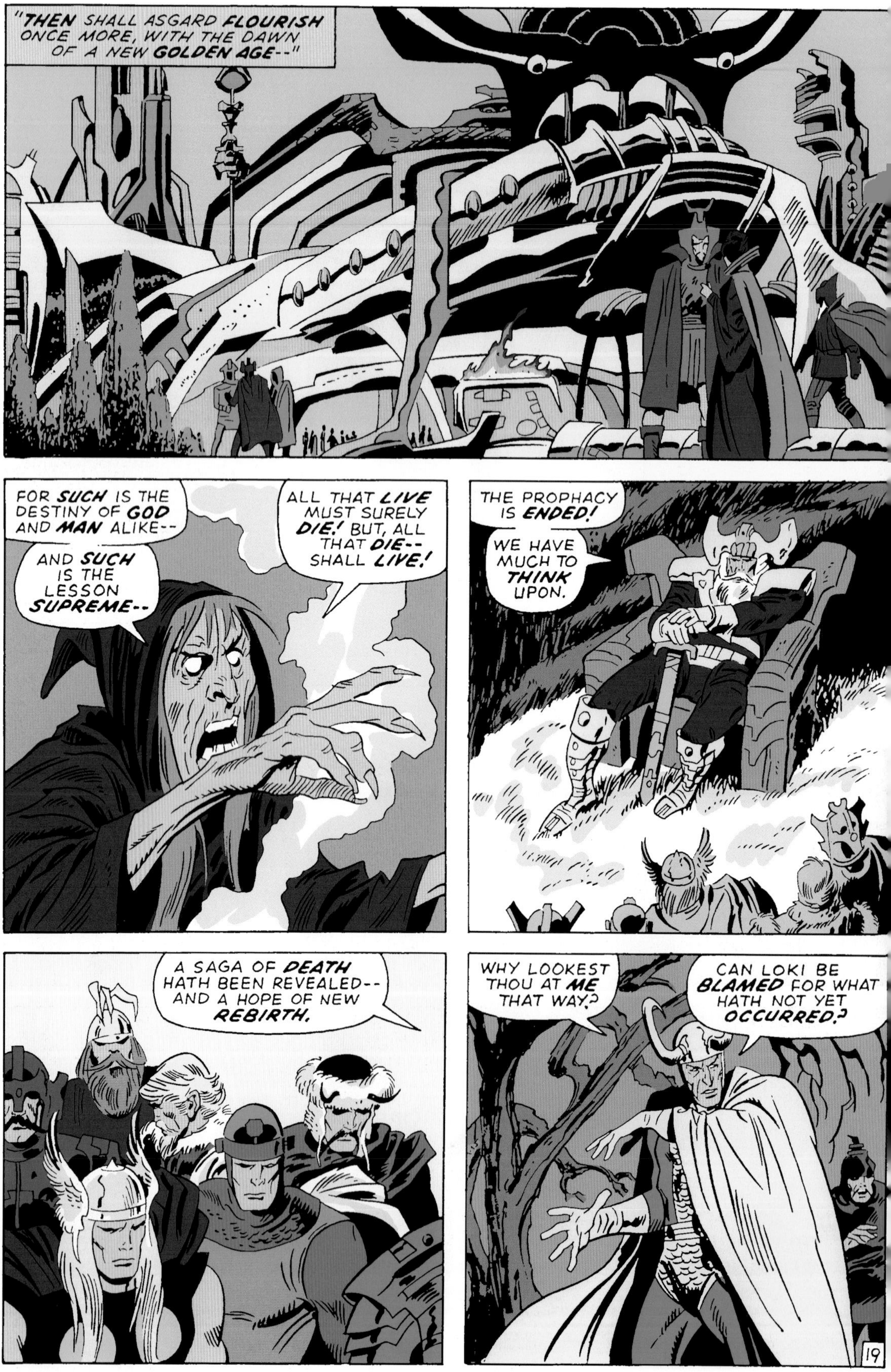
"THEN SHALL ASGARD FLOURISH ONCE MORE, WITH THE DAWN OF A NEW GOLDEN AGE--"
FOR SUCH IS THE DESTINY OF GOD AND MAN ALIKE--
AND SUCH IS THE LESSON SUPREME--
ALL THAT LIVE MUST SURELY DIE! BUT, ALL THAT DIE-- SHALL LIVE!
THE PROPHACY IS ENDED!
WE HAVE MUCH TO THINK UPON.
A SAGA OF DEATH HATH BEEN REVEALED-- AND A HOPE OF NEW REBIRTH.
WHY LOOKEST THOU AT ME THAT WAY?
CAN LOKI BE BLAMED FOR WHAT HATH NOT YET OCCURRED?
19

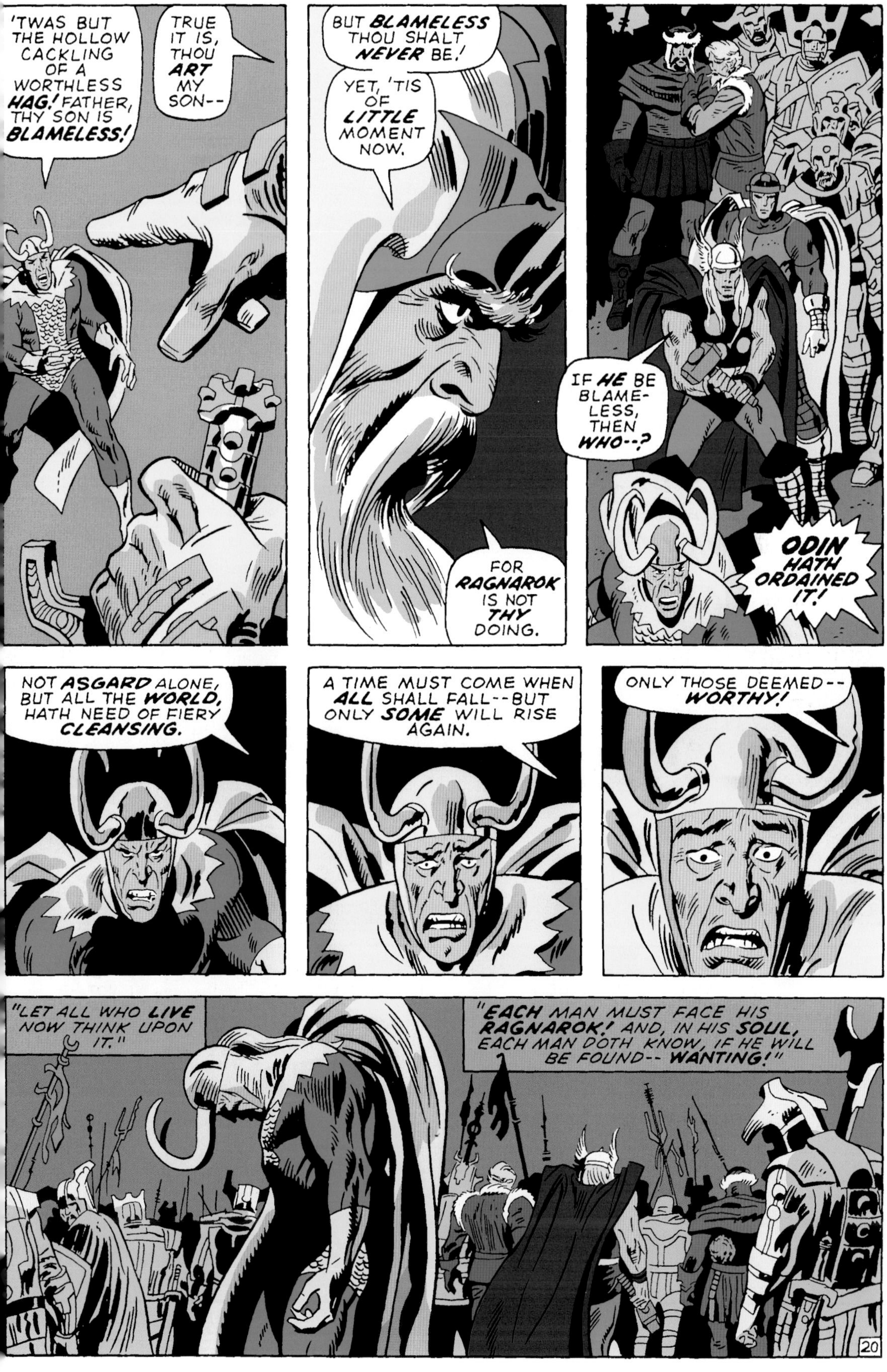
'TWAS BUT THE HOLLOW CACKLING OF A WORTHLESS HAG! FATHER, THY SON IS BLAMELESS!
TRUE IT IS, THOU ART MY SON--
BUT BLAMELESS THOU SHALT NEVER BE!
YET, 'TIS OF LITTLE MOMENT NOW.
FOR RAGNAROK IS NOT THY DOING.
IF HE BE BLAMELESS, THEN WHO--?
ODIN HATH ORDAINED IT!
NOT ASGARD ALONE, BUT ALL THE WORLD, HATH NEED OF FIERY CLEANSING.
A TIME MUST COME WHEN ALL SHALL FALL--BUT ONLY SOME WILL RISE AGAIN.
ONLY THOSE DEEMED-- WORTHY!
"LET ALL WHO LIVE NOW THINK UPON IT."
"EACH MAN MUST FACE HIS RAGNAROK! AND, IN HIS SOUL, EACH MAN DOTH KNOW, IF HE WILL BE FOUND-- WANTING!"
20

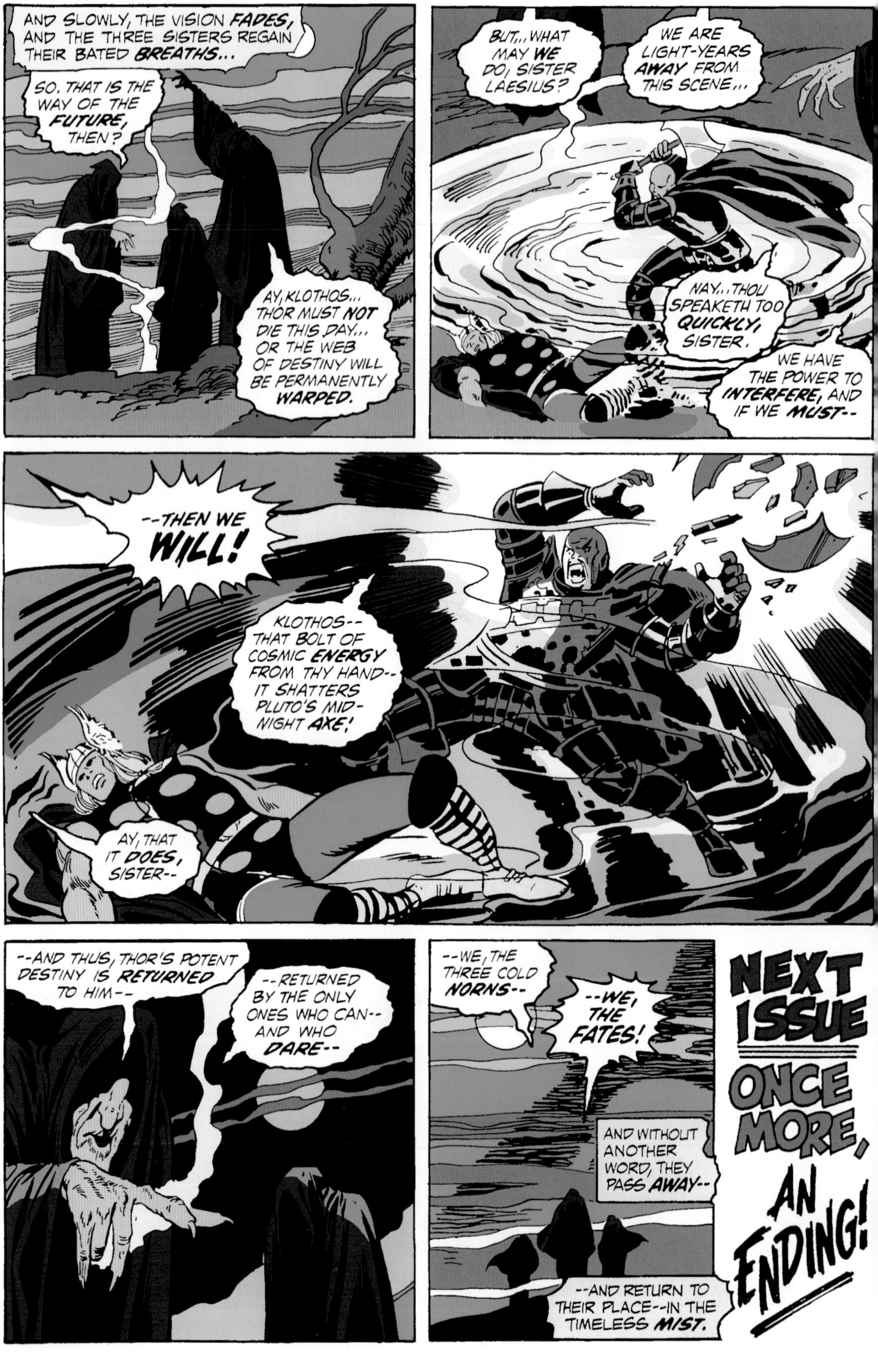
AND SLOWLY, THE VISION FADES, AND THE THREE SISTERS REGAIN THEIR BATED BREATHS...
SO. THAT IS THE WAY OF THE FUTURE, THEN?
AY, KLOTHOS... THOR MUST NOT DIE THIS DAY... OR THE WEB OF DESTINY WILL BE PERMANENTLY WARPED.
BUT,.. WHAT MAY WE DO, SISTER LAESIUS?
WE ARE LIGHT-YEARS AWAY FROM THIS SCENE,..
NAY,.. THOU SPEAKETH TOO QUICKLY, SISTER.
WE HAVE THE POWER TO INTERFERE, AND IF WE MUST--
--THEN WE WILL!
KLOTHOS-- THAT BOLT OF COSMIC ENERGY FROM THY HAND-- IT SHATTERS PLUTO'S MID-NIGHT AXE!
AY, THAT IT DOES, SISTER--
--AND THUS, THOR'S POTENT DESTINY IS RETURNED TO HIM--
--RETURNED BY THE ONLY ONES WHO CAN-- AND WHO DARE--
--WE, THE THREE COLD NORNS--
--WE, THE FATES!
AND WITHOUT ANOTHER WORD, THEY PASS AWAY--
--AND RETURN TO THEIR PLACE--IN THE TIMELESS MIST.
NEXT ISSUE
ONCE MORE, AN ENDING!

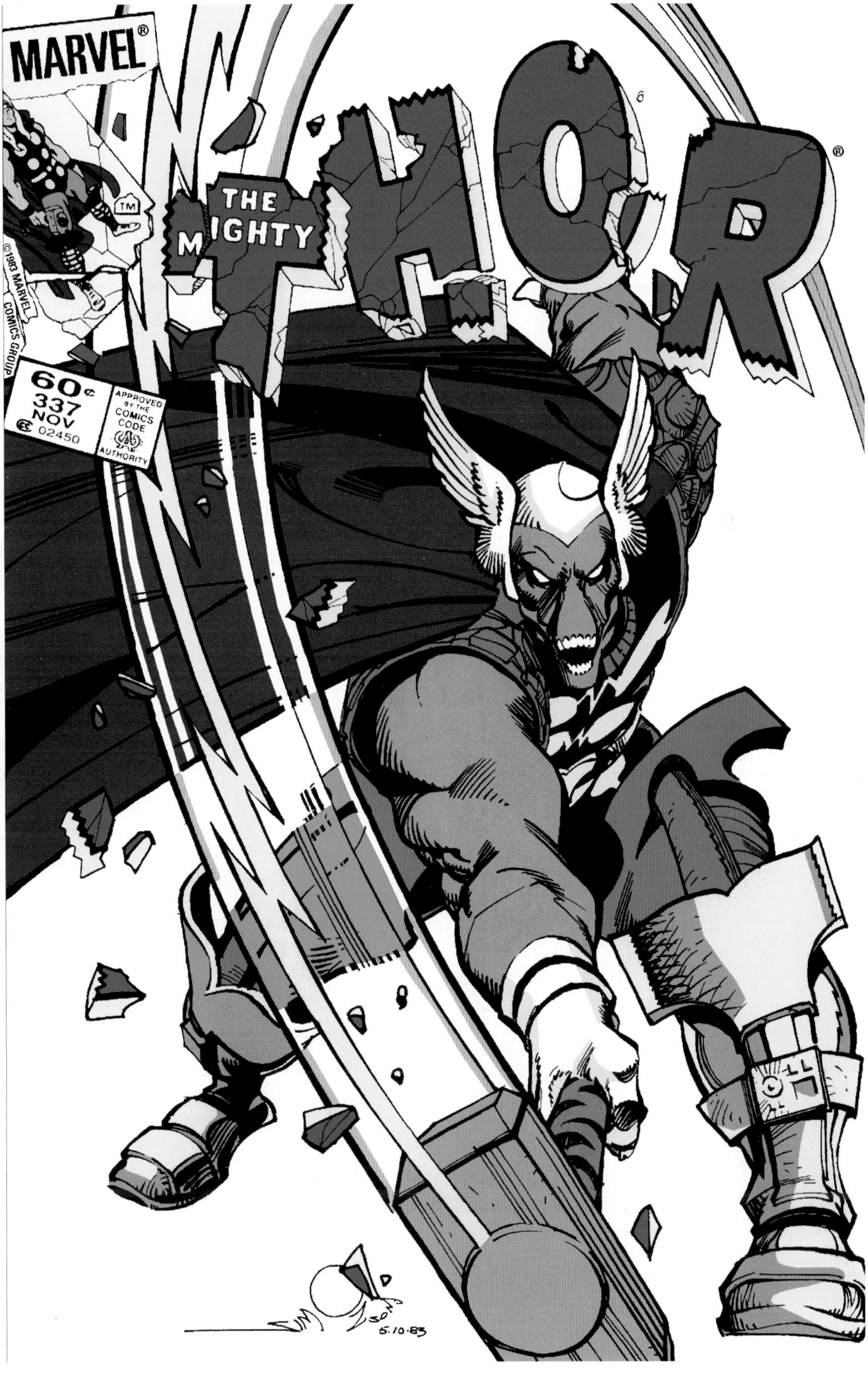
MARVEL®
THE MIGHTY THOR®
©1983 MARVEL COMICS GROUP
60¢
337
NOV
02450
APPROVED BY THE COMICS CODE AUTHORITY
5.10.83

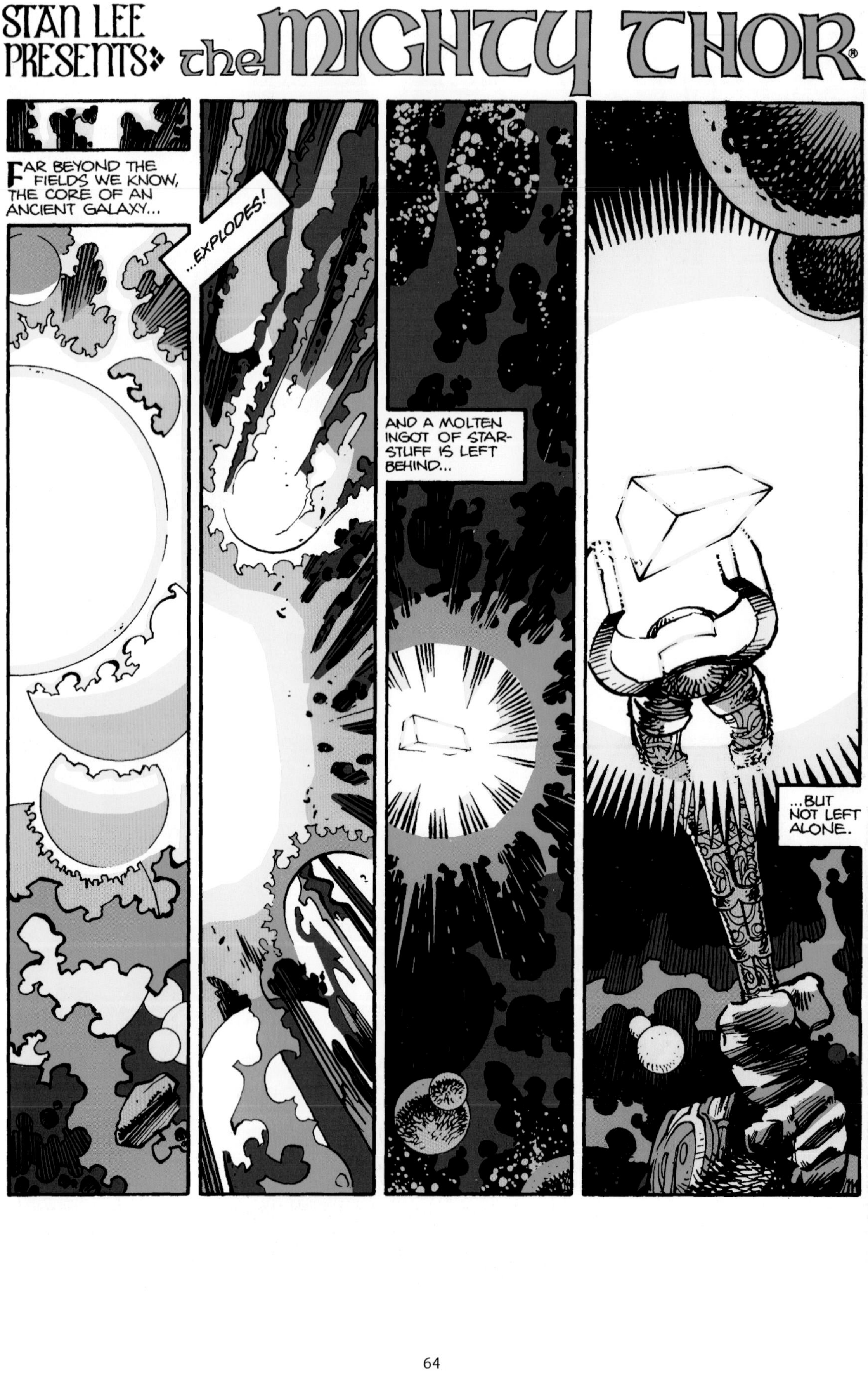
STAN LEE PRESENTS: the MIGHTY THOR®
FAR BEYOND THE FIELDS WE KNOW, THE CORE OF AN ANCIENT GALAXY...
...EXPLODES!
AND A MOLTEN INGOT OF STAR-STUFF IS LEFT BEHIND...
...BUT NOT LEFT ALONE.

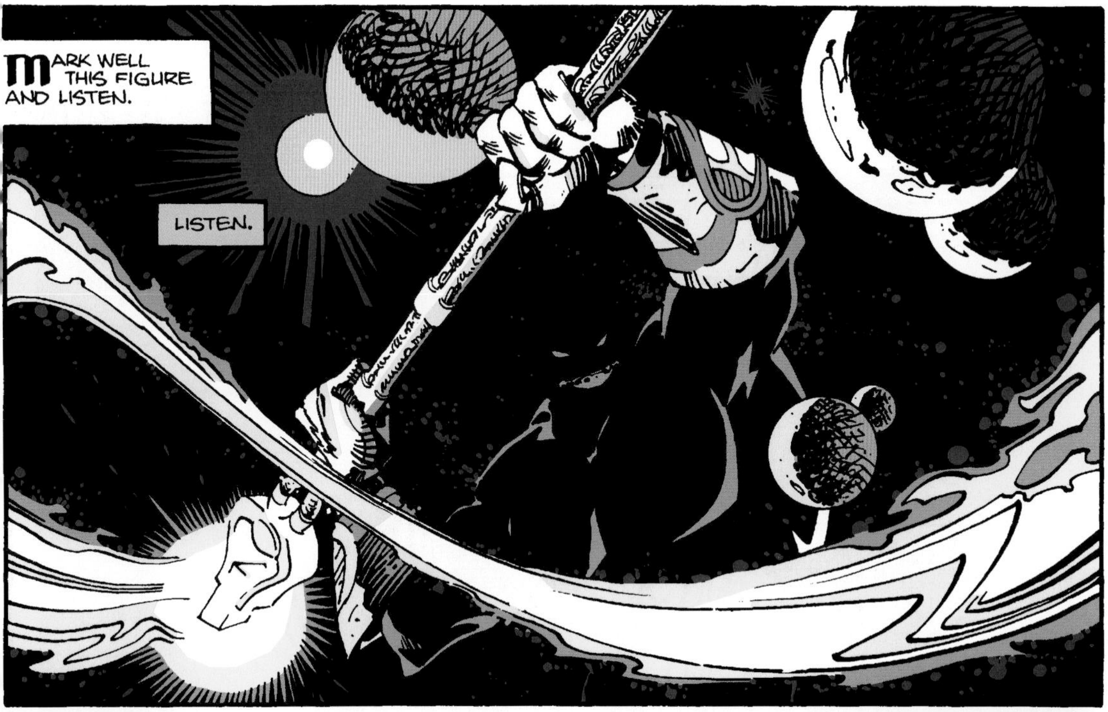
MARK WELL THIS FIGURE AND LISTEN.
LISTEN.

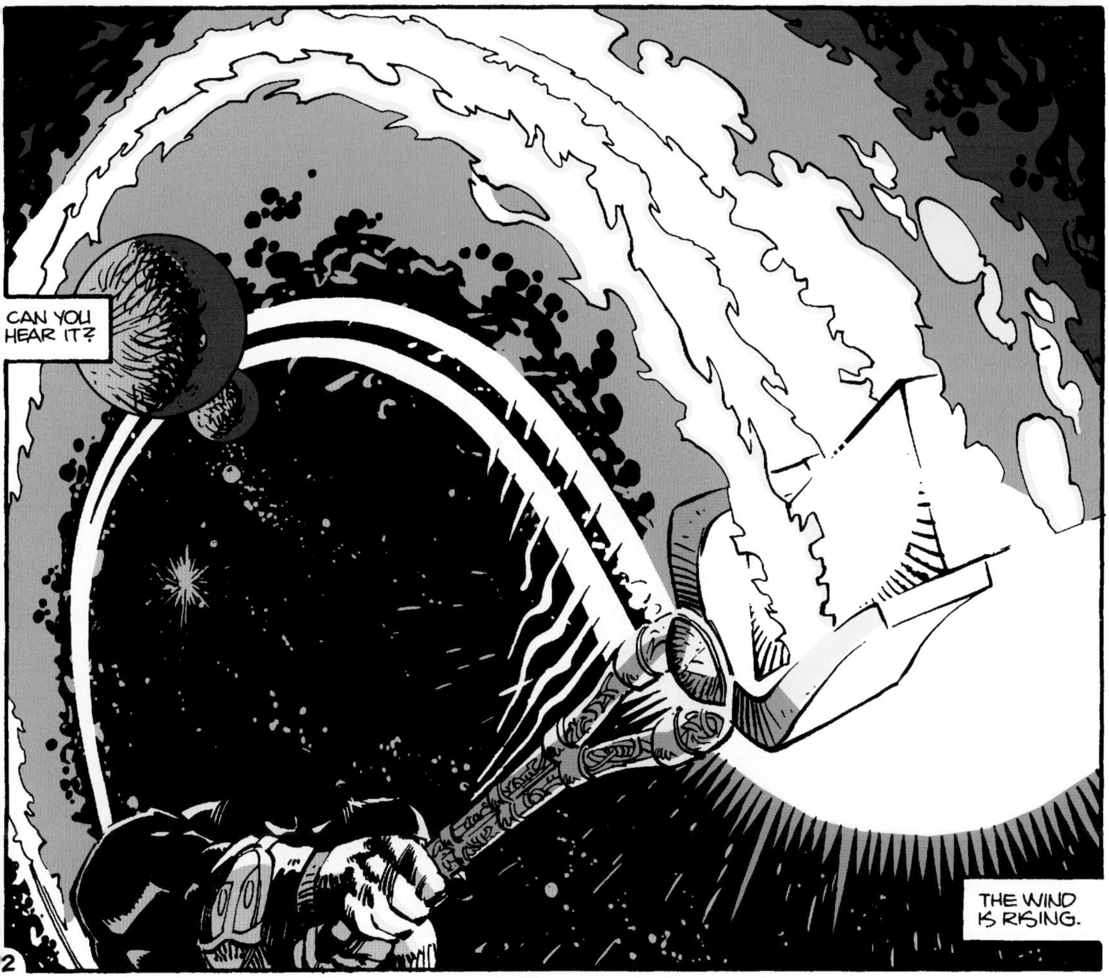
CAN YOU HEAR IT?
THE WIND IS RISING.
2

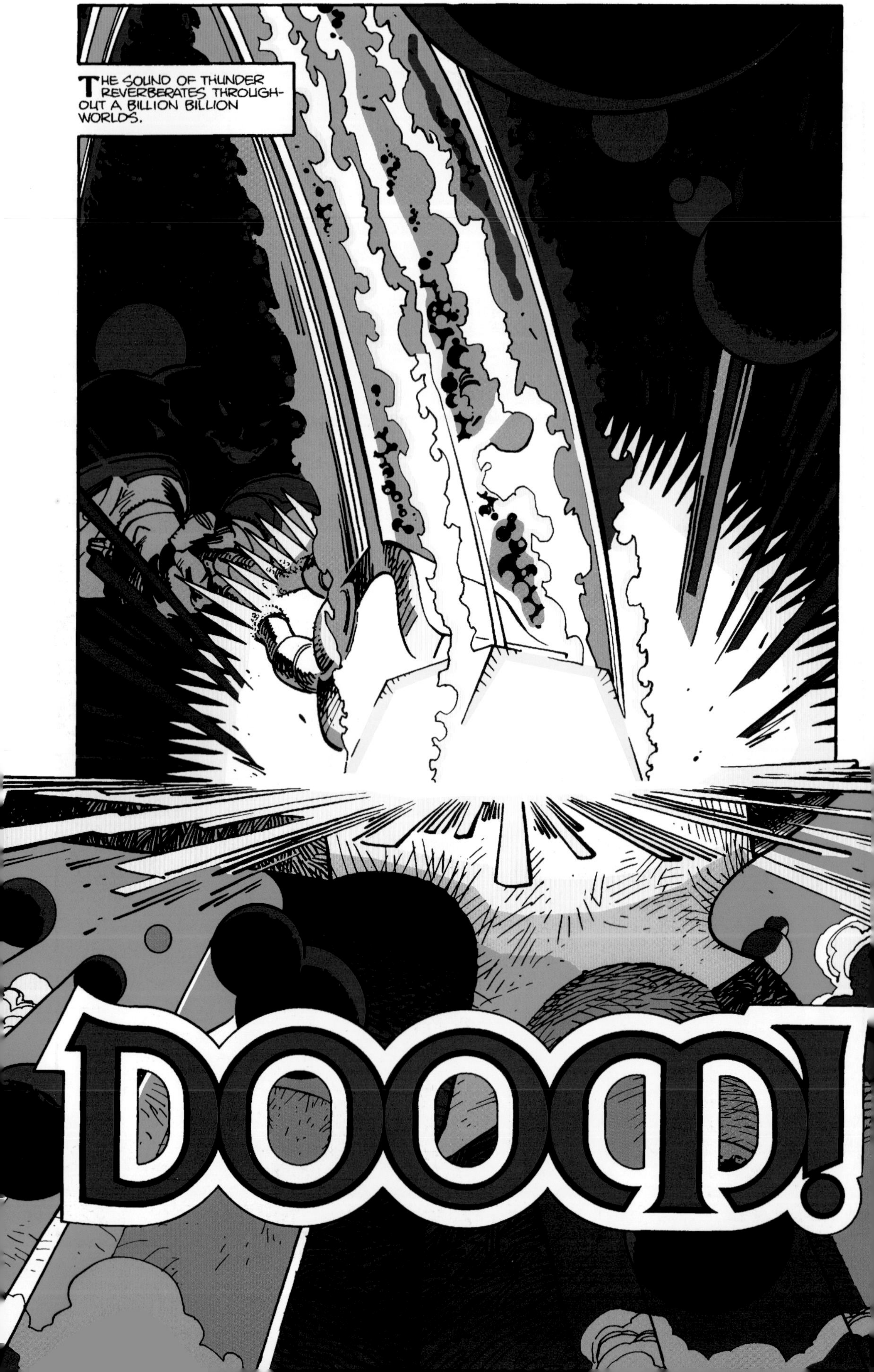
THE SOUND OF THUNDER REVERBERATES THROUGHOUT A BILLION BILLION WORLDS.
DOOM!

YET HERE ON EARTH, THE ECHOES ARE BURIED BENEATH THE SOUNDS OF THE CITY, AS CHICAGO BASKS IN A SUMMER AFTERNOON, AND DR. DONALD BLAKE STROLLS THROUGH GRANT PARK...

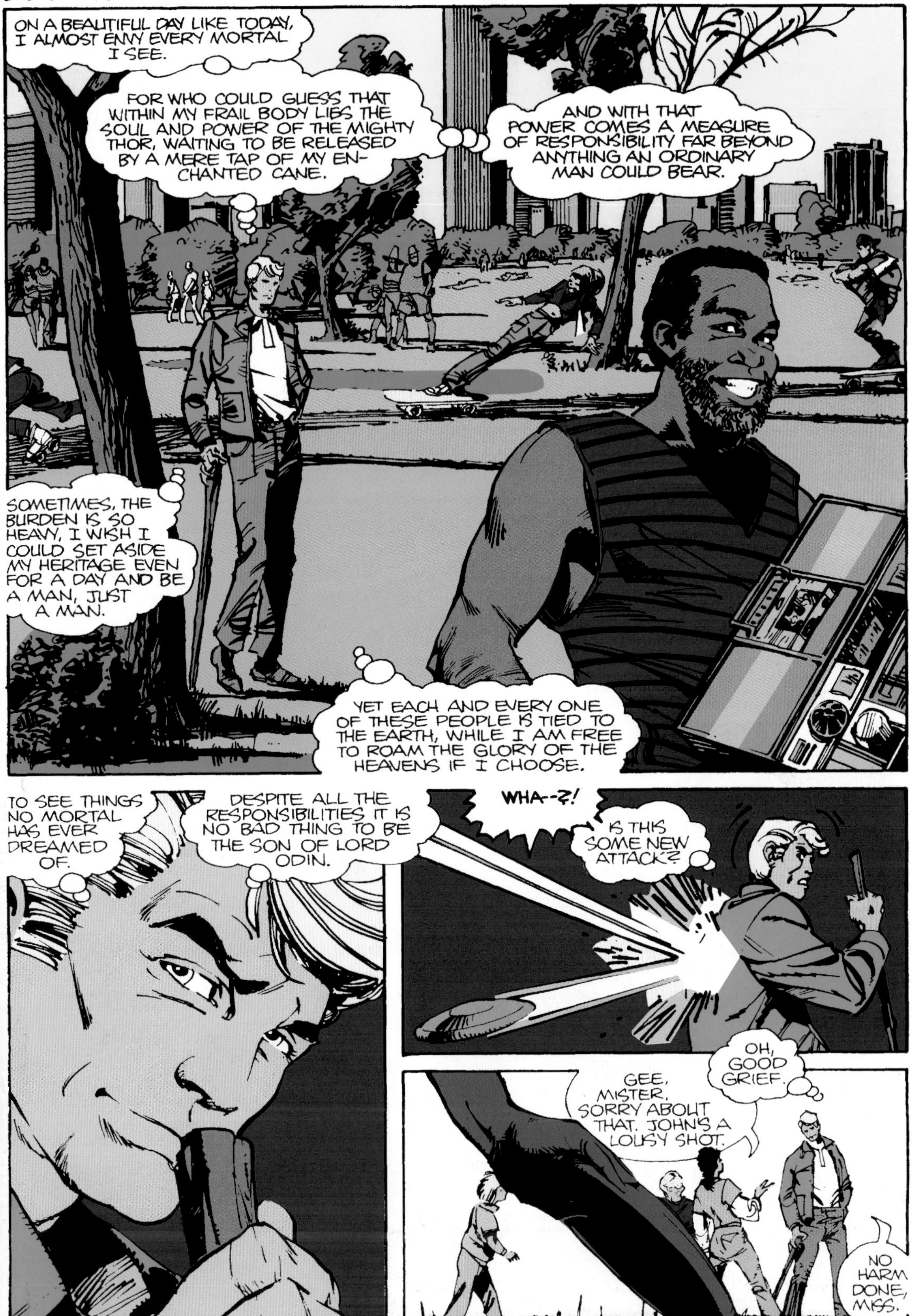
ON A BEAUTIFUL DAY LIKE TODAY, I ALMOST ENVY EVERY MORTAL I SEE.
FOR WHO COULD GUESS THAT WITHIN MY FRAIL BODY LIES THE SOUL AND POWER OF THE MIGHTY THOR, WAITING TO BE RELEASED BY A MERE TAP OF MY EN-CHANTED CANE.
AND WITH THAT POWER COMES A MEASURE OF RESPONSIBILITY FAR BEYOND ANYTHING AN ORDINARY MAN COULD BEAR.
SOMETIMES, THE BURDEN IS SO HEAVY, I WISH I COULD SET ASIDE MY HERITAGE EVEN FOR A DAY AND BE A MAN, JUST A MAN.
YET EACH AND EVERY ONE OF THESE PEOPLE IS TIED TO THE EARTH, WHILE I AM FREE TO ROAM THE GLORY OF THE HEAVENS IF I CHOOSE.
TO SEE THINGS NO MORTAL HAS EVER DREAMED OF.
DESPITE ALL THE RESPONSIBILITIES IT IS NO BAD THING TO BE THE SON OF LORD ODIN.
WHA--?!
IS THIS SOME NEW ATTACK?
OH, GOOD GRIEF.
GEE, MISTER, SORRY ABOUT THAT. JOHN'S A LOUSY SHOT.
NO HARM DONE, MISS.
4

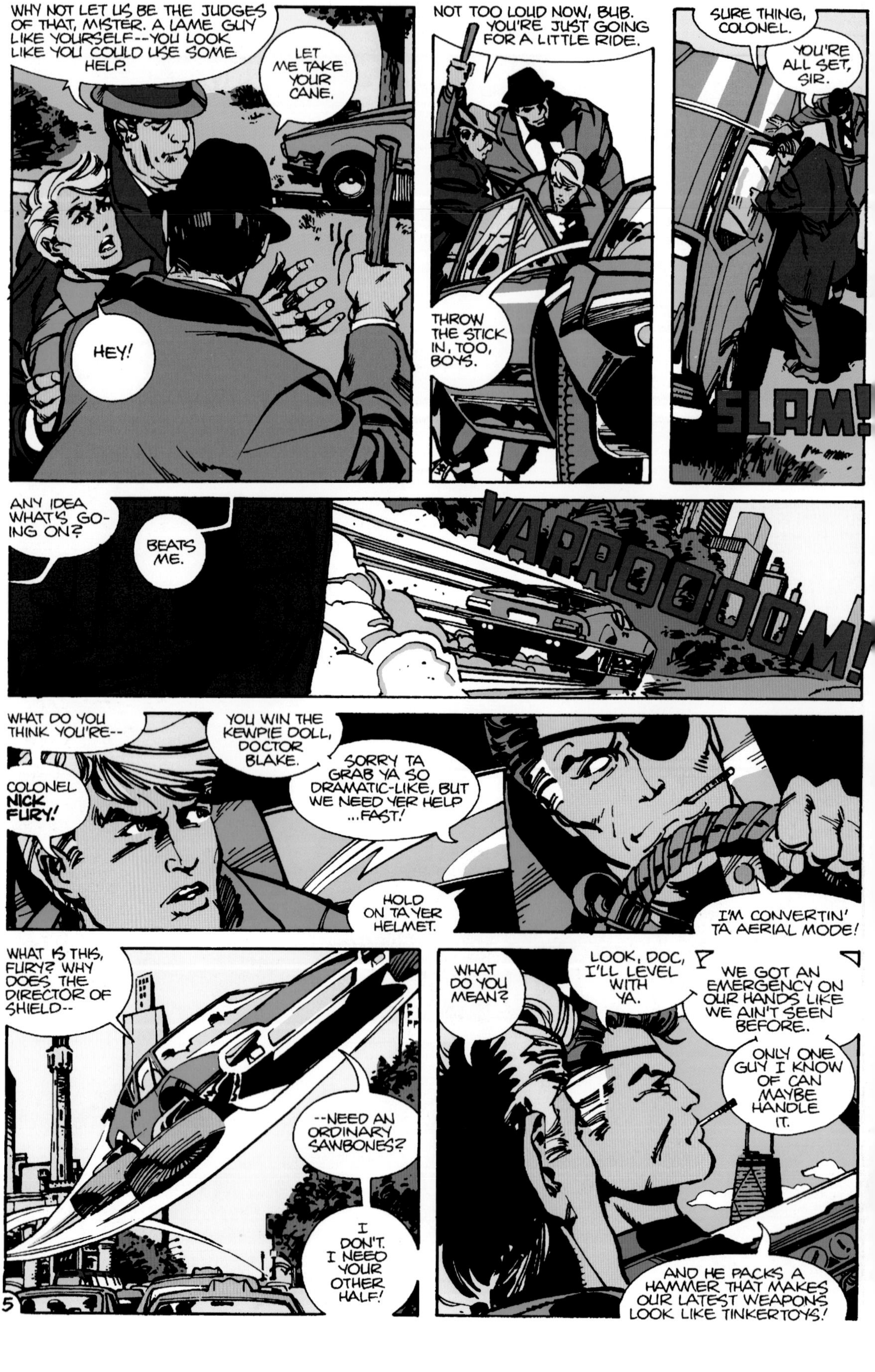
WHY NOT LET US BE THE JUDGES OF THAT, MISTER. A LAME GUY LIKE YOURSELF--YOU LOOK LIKE YOU COULD USE SOME HELP.
LET ME TAKE YOUR CANE.
HEY!
NOT TOO LOUD NOW, BUB. YOU'RE JUST GOING FOR A LITTLE RIDE.
THROW THE STICK IN, TOO, BOYS.
SURE THING, COLONEL.
YOU'RE ALL SET, SIR.
SLAM!
ANY IDEA WHAT'S GO-ING ON?
BEATS ME.
VARROOOOOM!
WHAT DO YOU THINK YOU'RE--
COLONEL NICK FURY!
YOU WIN THE KEWPIE DOLL, DOCTOR BLAKE.
SORRY TA GRAB YA SO DRAMATIC-LIKE, BUT WE NEED YER HELP ...FAST!
HOLD ON TA YER HELMET.
I'M CONVERTIN' TA AERIAL MODE!
WHAT IS THIS, FURY? WHY DOES THE DIRECTOR OF SHIELD--
--NEED AN ORDINARY SAWBONES?
I DON'T. I NEED YOUR OTHER HALF!
5
WHAT DO YOU MEAN?
LOOK, DOC, I'LL LEVEL WITH YA.
WE GOT AN EMERGENCY ON OUR HANDS LIKE WE AIN'T SEEN BEFORE.
ONLY ONE GUY I KNOW OF CAN MAYBE HANDLE IT.
AND HE PACKS A HAMMER THAT MAKES OUR LATEST WEAPONS LOOK LIKE TINKERTOYS!

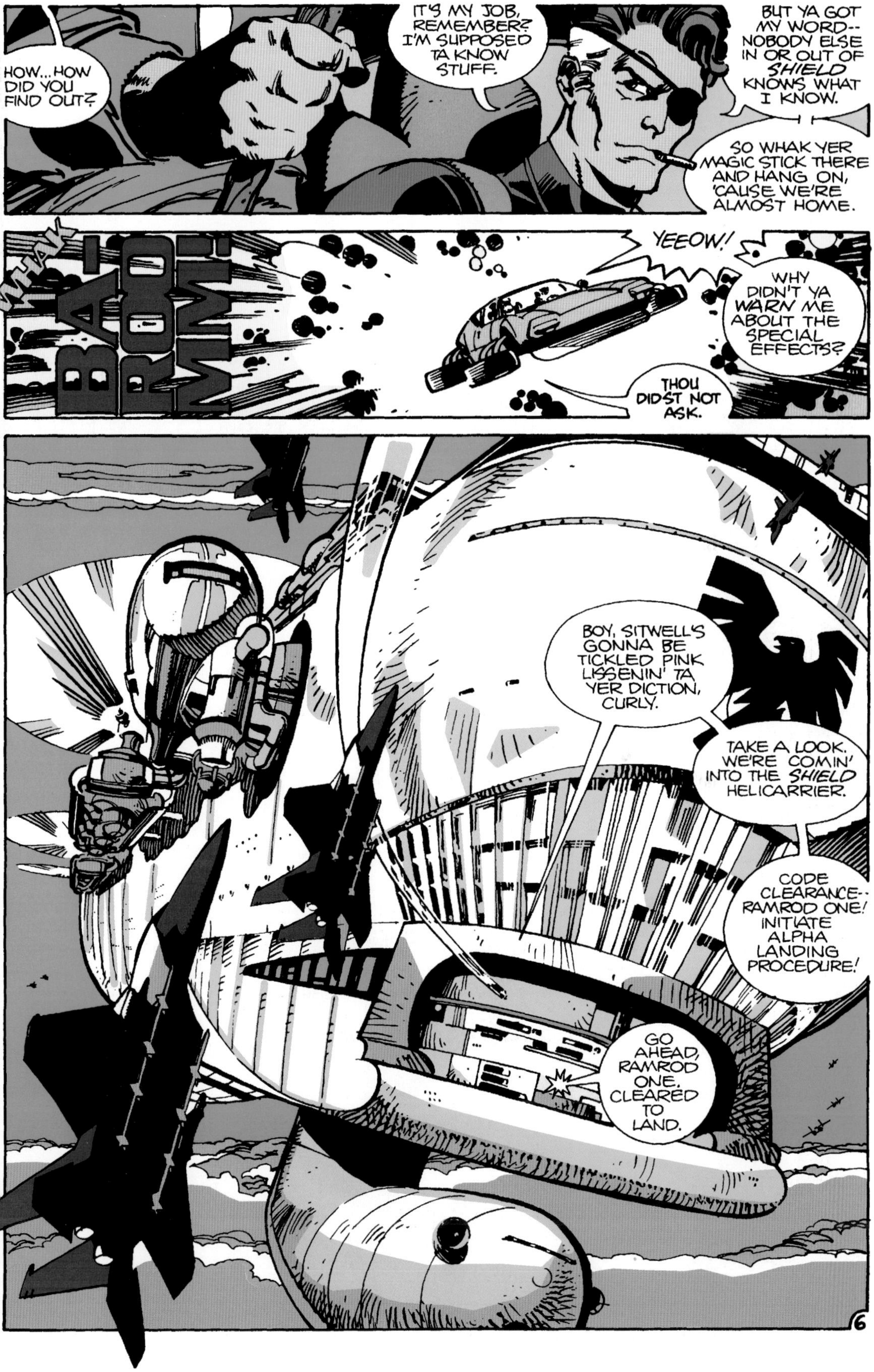
HOW...HOW DID YOU FIND OUT?
IT'S MY JOB, REMEMBER? I'M SUPPOSED TA KNOW STUFF.
BUT YA GOT MY WORD-- NOBODY ELSE IN OR OUT OF SHIELD KNOWS WHAT I KNOW.
SO WHAK YER MAGIC STICK THERE AND HANG ON, 'CAUSE WE'RE ALMOST HOME.
WHAK
BA-ROOMM!
YEEOW!
WHY DIDN'T YA WARN ME ABOUT THE SPECIAL EFFECTS?
THOU DIDST NOT ASK.
BOY, SITWELL'S GONNA BE TICKLED PINK LISSENIN' TA YER DICTION, CURLY.
TAKE A LOOK. WE'RE COMIN' INTO THE SHIELD HELICARRIER.
CODE CLEARANCE-- RAMROD ONE! INITIATE ALPHA LANDING PROCEDURE!
GO AHEAD, RAMROD ONE. CLEARED TO LAND.
6

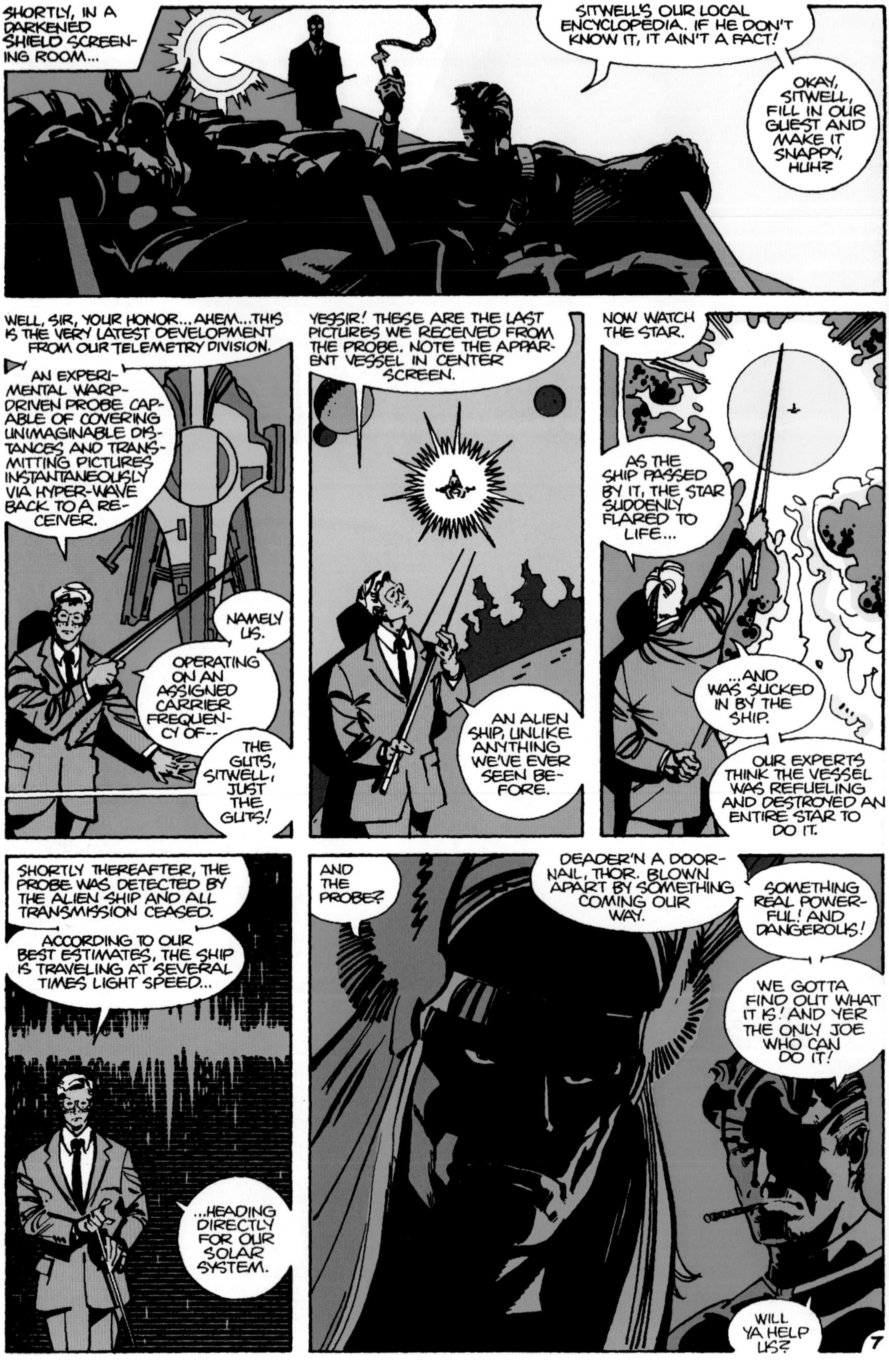
SHORTLY, IN A DARKENED SHIELD SCREENING ROOM...
SITWELL'S OUR LOCAL ENCYCLOPEDIA. IF HE DON'T KNOW IT, IT AIN'T A FACT!
OKAY, SITWELL, FILL IN OUR GUEST AND MAKE IT SNAPPY, HUH?
WELL, SIR, YOUR HONOR...AHEM...THIS IS THE VERY LATEST DEVELOPMENT FROM OUR TELEMETRY DIVISION.
AN EXPERIMENTAL WARP-DRIVEN PROBE CAPABLE OF COVERING UNIMAGINABLE DISTANCES AND TRANSMITTING PICTURES INSTANTANEOUSLY VIA HYPER-WAVE BACK TO A RECEIVER.
NAMELY US.
OPERATING ON AN ASSIGNED CARRIER FREQUENCY OF--
THE GUTS, SITWELL, JUST THE GUTS!
YESSIR! THESE ARE THE LAST PICTURES WE RECEIVED FROM THE PROBE. NOTE THE APPARENT VESSEL IN CENTER SCREEN.
AN ALIEN SHIP, UNLIKE ANYTHING WE'VE EVER SEEN BEFORE.
NOW WATCH THE STAR.
AS THE SHIP PASSED BY IT, THE STAR SUDDENLY FLARED TO LIFE...
...AND WAS SUCKED IN BY THE SHIP.
OUR EXPERTS THINK THE VESSEL WAS REFUELING AND DESTROYED AN ENTIRE STAR TO DO IT.
SHORTLY THEREAFTER, THE PROBE WAS DETECTED BY THE ALIEN SHIP AND ALL TRANSMISSION CEASED.
ACCORDING TO OUR BEST ESTIMATES, THE SHIP IS TRAVELING AT SEVERAL TIMES LIGHT SPEED...
...HEADING DIRECTLY FOR OUR SOLAR SYSTEM.
AND THE PROBE?
DEADER'N A DOORNAIL, THOR. BLOWN APART BY SOMETHING COMING OUR WAY.
SOMETHING REAL POWERFUL! AND DANGEROUS!
WE GOTTA FIND OUT WHAT IT IS! AND YER THE ONLY JOE WHO CAN DO IT!
WILL YA HELP US?
7

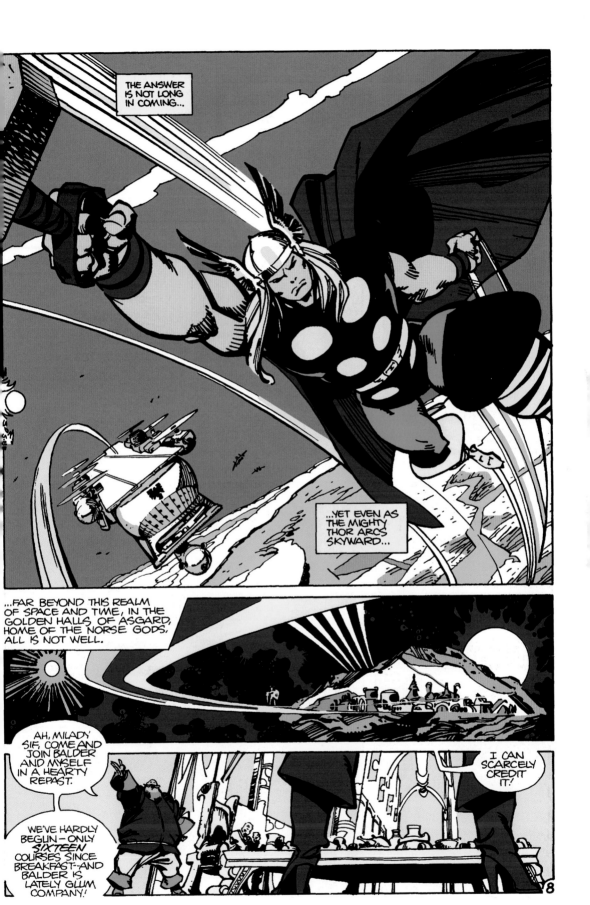

THE ANSWER IS NOT LONG IN COMING...

...YET EVEN AS THE MIGHTY THOR ARCS SKYWARD...

...FAR BEYOND THIS REALM OF SPACE AND TIME, IN THE GOLDEN HALLS OF ASGARD, HOME OF THE NORSE GODS, ALL IS NOT WELL.

AH, MILADY SIF, COME AND JOIN BALDER AND MYSELF IN A HEARTY REPAST.

WE'VE HARDLY BEGUN—ONLY *SIXTEEN* COURSES SINCE BREAKFAST--AND BALDER IS LATELY GLUM COMPANY!

I CAN SCARCELY CREDIT IT!

8

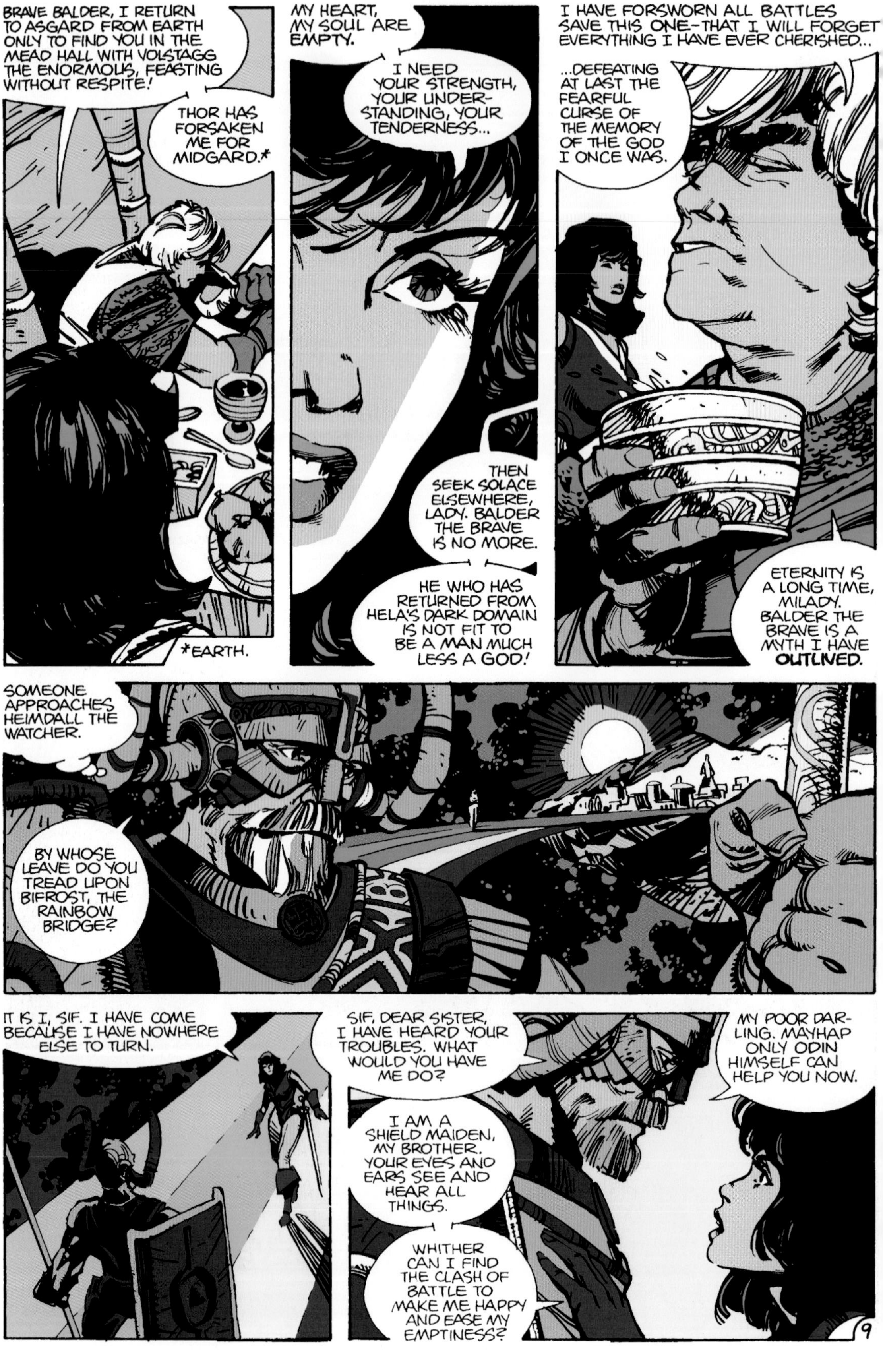
BRAVE BALDER, I RETURN TO ASGARD FROM EARTH ONLY TO FIND YOU IN THE MEAD HALL WITH VOLSTAGG THE ENORMOUS, FEASTING WITHOUT RESPITE!
THOR HAS FORSAKEN ME FOR MIDGARD.*
*EARTH.
MY HEART, MY SOUL ARE EMPTY.
I NEED YOUR STRENGTH, YOUR UNDERSTANDING, YOUR TENDERNESS...
THEN SEEK SOLACE ELSEWHERE, LADY. BALDER THE BRAVE IS NO MORE.
HE WHO HAS RETURNED FROM HELA'S DARK DOMAIN IS NOT FIT TO BE A MAN MUCH LESS A GOD!
I HAVE FORSWORN ALL BATTLES SAVE THIS ONE--THAT I WILL FORGET EVERYTHING I HAVE EVER CHERISHED...
...DEFEATING AT LAST THE FEARFUL CURSE OF THE MEMORY OF THE GOD I ONCE WAS.
ETERNITY IS A LONG TIME, MILADY. BALDER THE BRAVE IS A MYTH I HAVE OUTLIVED.
SOMEONE APPROACHES HEIMDALL THE WATCHER.
BY WHOSE LEAVE DO YOU TREAD UPON BIFROST, THE RAINBOW BRIDGE?
IT IS I, SIF. I HAVE COME BECAUSE I HAVE NOWHERE ELSE TO TURN.
SIF, DEAR SISTER, I HAVE HEARD YOUR TROUBLES. WHAT WOULD YOU HAVE ME DO?
I AM A SHIELD MAIDEN, MY BROTHER. YOUR EYES AND EARS SEE AND HEAR ALL THINGS.
WHITHER CAN I FIND THE CLASH OF BATTLE TO MAKE ME HAPPY AND EASE MY EMPTINESS?
MY POOR DARLING. MAYHAP ONLY ODIN HIMSELF CAN HELP YOU NOW.
9

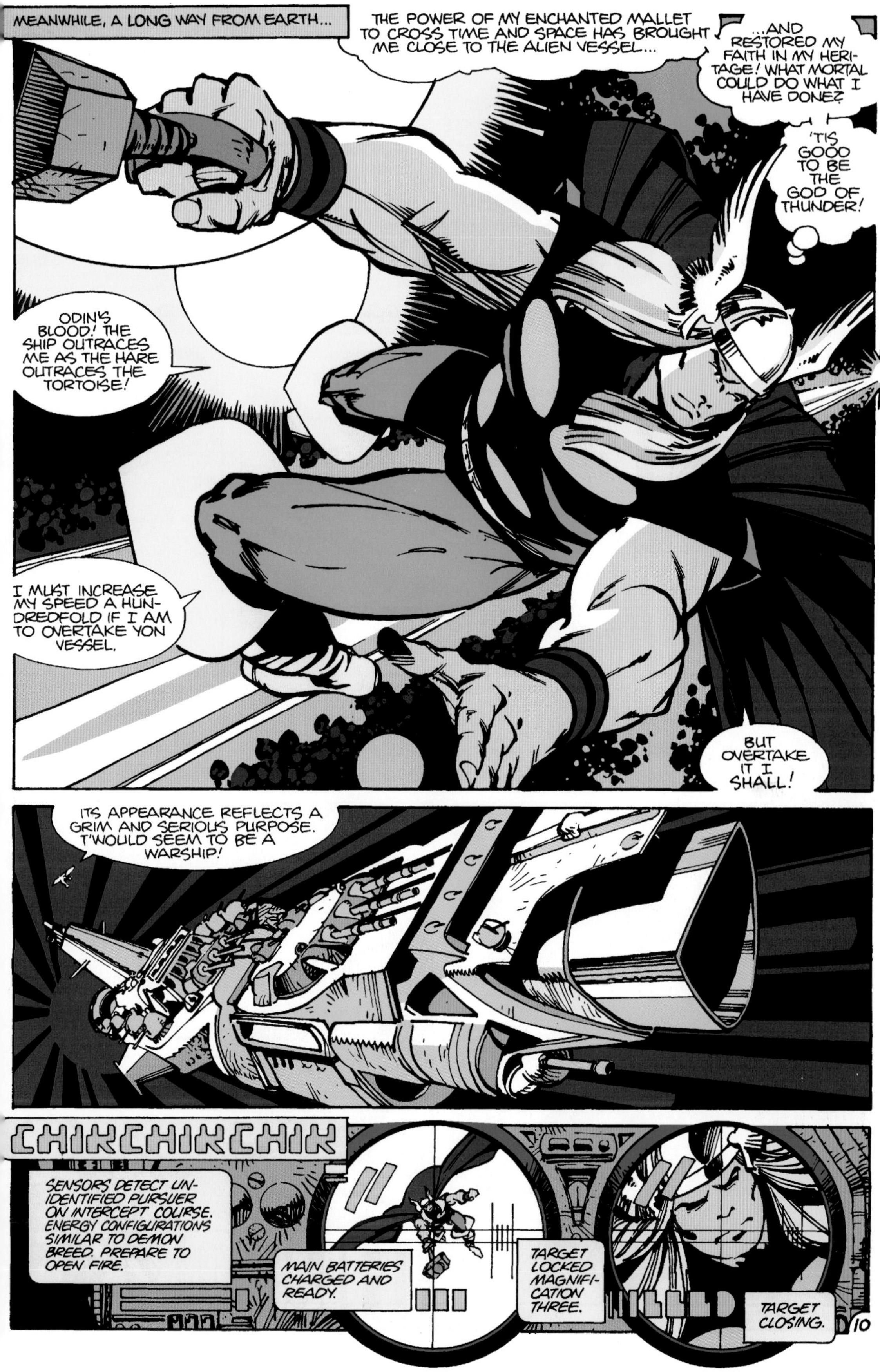
MEANWHILE, A LONG WAY FROM EARTH...
THE POWER OF MY ENCHANTED MALLET TO CROSS TIME AND SPACE HAS BROUGHT ME CLOSE TO THE ALIEN VESSEL...
...AND RESTORED MY FAITH IN MY HERITAGE! WHAT MORTAL COULD DO WHAT I HAVE DONE?
'TIS GOOD TO BE THE GOD OF THUNDER!
ODIN'S BLOOD! THE SHIP OUTRACES ME AS THE HARE OUTRACES THE TORTOISE!
I MUST INCREASE MY SPEED A HUNDREDFOLD IF I AM TO OVERTAKE YON VESSEL.
BUT OVERTAKE IT I SHALL!
ITS APPEARANCE REFLECTS A GRIM AND SERIOUS PURPOSE. T'WOULD SEEM TO BE A WARSHIP!
CHIKCHIKCHIK
SENSORS DETECT UNIDENTIFIED PURSUER ON INTERCEPT COURSE. ENERGY CONFIGURATIONS SIMILAR TO DEMON BREED. PREPARE TO OPEN FIRE.
MAIN BATTERIES CHARGED AND READY.
TARGET LOCKED MAGNIFICATION THREE.
TARGET CLOSING.
10

FIRE!

BY THE GOLDEN SPIRES OF ASGARD!

AN ENERGY BOLT OF PURE FORCE!

CLIKCLIK

THIS DEMON IS MUCH STRONGER THAN PREVIOUS INTRUDERS!

ALL BATTERIES OPEN FIRE!

AGAIN THE VESSEL DIRECTS AN UNPROVOKED ATTACK AT ME!

SO BE IT!

LET THE HAMMER OF THOR SPEAK FOR ME NOW!

THRAAKKT

AS EVER, MY HAMMER RETURNS TO ME...

...AND NOW, BEFORE A FURTHER ATTACK CAN BEGIN...

...I SHALL AVOID THE DEADLY WEAPONRY AND ENTER THE SHIP AS ONLY THE GOD OF THUNDER CAN!

PERHAPS INSIDE I CAN DISCOVER THE PURPOSE OF THIS DEADLY VESSEL.

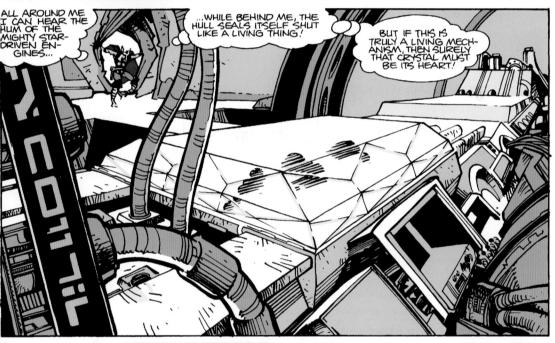

ALL AROUND ME I CAN HEAR THE HUM OF THE MIGHTY STAR-DRIVEN EN-GINES...

...WHILE BEHIND ME, THE HULL SEALS ITSELF SHUT LIKE A LIVING THING!

BUT IF THIS IS TRULY A LIVING MECH-ANISM, THEN SURELY THAT CRYSTAL MUST BE ITS HEART!

YET WHAT LIES HERE AT ITS VERY CENTER?

A FIGURE OF SOME SIZE.

PERHAPS-- EH?

CHIKCHIK

DANGER! DANGER!

INTRUDER HAS BREACHED THE HULL!

ULTIMATE DEFENSE PROCEDURE!

RELEASE COLDSLEEP DEFENSE!

KRASH!

UGGH!

12

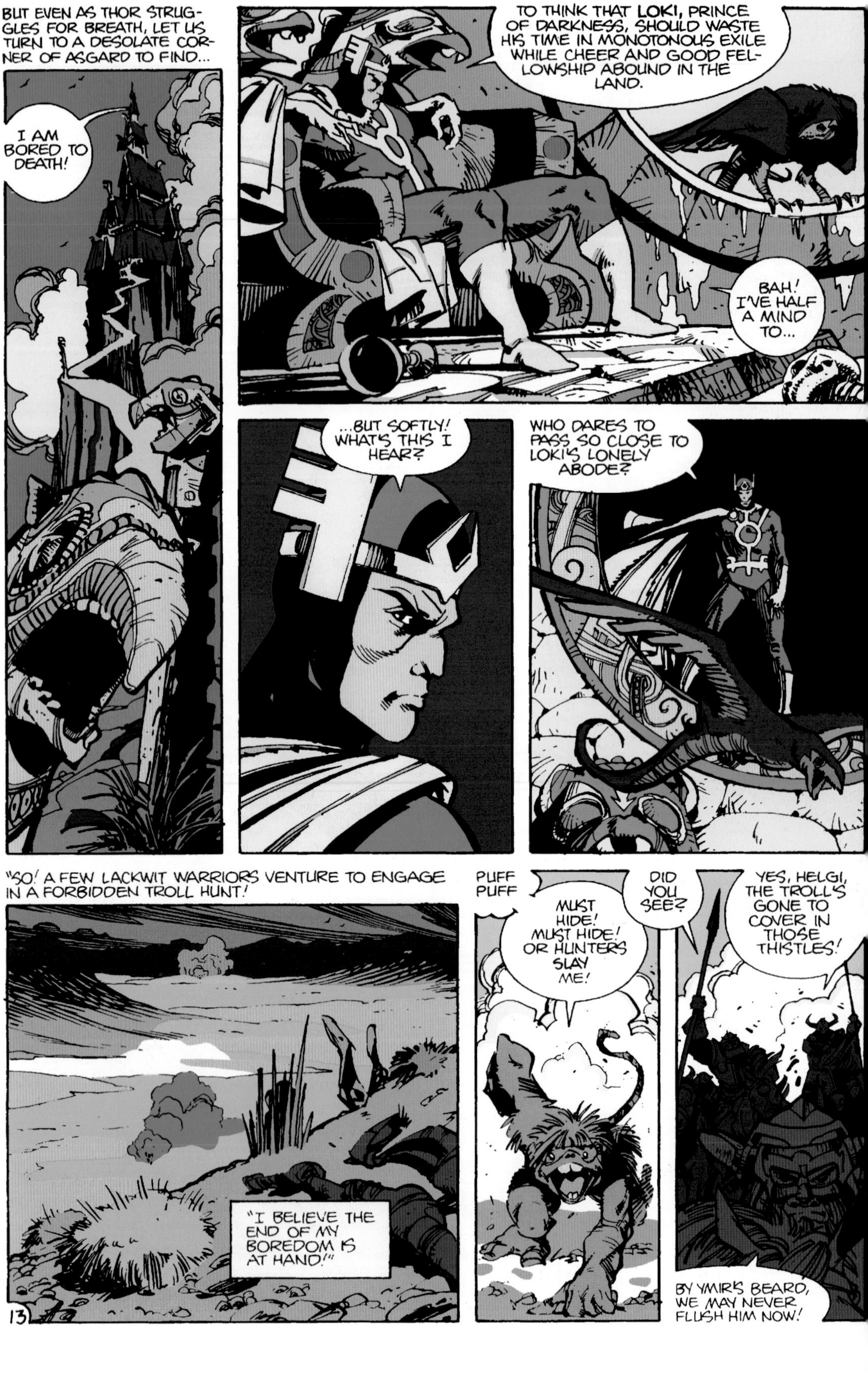
BUT EVEN AS THOR STRUGGLES FOR BREATH, LET US TURN TO A DESOLATE CORNER OF ASGARD TO FIND...
I AM BORED TO DEATH!
TO THINK THAT LOKI, PRINCE OF DARKNESS, SHOULD WASTE HIS TIME IN MONOTONOUS EXILE WHILE CHEER AND GOOD FELLOWSHIP ABOUND IN THE LAND.
BAH! I'VE HALF A MIND TO...
...BUT SOFTLY! WHAT'S THIS I HEAR?
WHO DARES TO PASS SO CLOSE TO LOKI'S LONELY ABODE?
"SO! A FEW LACKWIT WARRIORS VENTURE TO ENGAGE IN A FORBIDDEN TROLL HUNT!
"I BELIEVE THE END OF MY BOREDOM IS AT HAND!"
13
PUFF PUFF
MUST HIDE! MUST HIDE! OR HUNTERS SLAY ME!
DID YOU SEE?
YES, HELGI, THE TROLL'S GONE TO COVER IN THOSE THISTLES!
BY YMIR'S BEARD, WE MAY NEVER FLUSH HIM NOW!

LITTLE ONE! PSST! LITTLE ONE!

HUH?

IT GIRL! SHE...SHE BEAUTIFUL!

DO NOT BE AFRAID, LITTLE TROLL. I CAN HELP YOU. I CAN HIDE YOU.

COME. LOOK AT ME. GIVE ME YOUR HAND...

...AND FEAR NOTHING.

LOOK AT ME.

I...

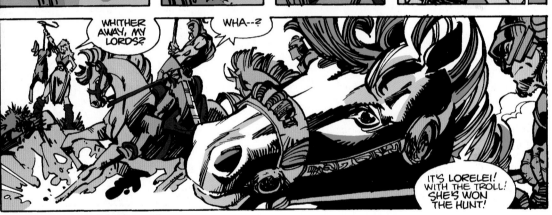

WHITHER AWAY, MY LORDS?

WHA--?

IT'S LORELEI! WITH THE TROLL! SHE'S WON THE HUNT!

JUST AS I FORETOLD YOU!

WEAPONS AND STRENGTH ARE NOT EVERYTHING, MY LORDS.

INDEED, MILADY. AS NONE KNOW BETTER THAN I.

I THINK WE SHOULD DISCUSS THIS FURTHER. WILL YOU NOT ACCOMPANY ME BACK TO MY HUMBLE DWELLING?

PERHAPS I SHALL, MY LORD.

LORELEI, YOU'D BEST LEAVE WITH US. THE OPEN HAND OF LOKI IS NOT SAFE!

NOR WILL YOU BE SAFE IF ODIN LEARNS OF THIS HUNT! LEAVE US AND FORGET WHAT HAS HAPPENED HERE...

...OR THE NEXT HAND OF LOKI YOU SEE WILL BE FILLED WITH MENACE.

14

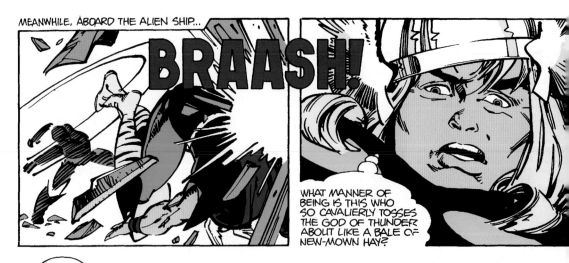

MEANWHILE, ABOARD THE ALIEN SHIP...

BRAASH!

WHAT MANNER OF BEING IS THIS WHO SO CAVALIERLY TOSSES THE GOD OF THUNDER ABOUT LIKE A BALE OF NEW-MOWN HAY?

RISE UP, DEMON!

YOU HAVE PURSUED ME ONLY TO FIND DEATH!

AND WHEN I AM THROUGH WITH YOU, YOU WILL WELCOME IT!

I AM CALLED BILL--*BETA RAY BILL!*

15

BUT DO NOT TROUBLE YOUR-SELF TO REMEMBER IT!

YOU SHOULD HAVE WAITED FOR YOUR FELLOWS TO ARRIVE RATHER THAN FACE ME ALONE!

I DO NOT KNOW WHAT YOU MEAN, CREATURE...

...BUT NONE MAY TOUCH THE MIGHTY THOR SO WITHOUT PAYING THE PRICE!

YET HOW IS IT YOU SPEAK MY TONGUE?

AAGGH!

THE SHIP WAS RIGHT! YOU ARE MUCH STRONGER THAN YOUR PREDECESSORS!

APPARENTLY THE BREED IS IMPROVING!

BUT IT WILL NOT SAVE YOU!

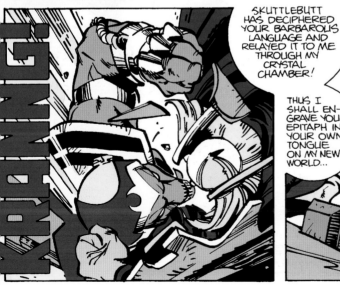

KRANNG!

SKUTTLEBUTT HAS DECIPHERED YOUR BARBAROUS LANGUAGE AND RELAYED IT TO ME THROUGH MY CRYSTAL CHAMBER!

THUS I SHALL EN-GRAVE YOUR EPITAPH IN YOUR OWN TONGUE ON MY NEW WORLD...

...ON THE MEMORIAL CELEBRATING MY VICTORY OVER YOU AND ALL OF DEMONKIND!

16

YOU STILL SPEAK IN RIDDLES, WARRIOR...

...BUT IT IS CLEAR TO ME THAT I CAN NEVER PERMIT SUCH A DANGEROUS ENTITY TO REACH EARTH...

...EVEN IF I MUST DESTROY THIS SHIP FROM WITHIN TO STOP YOU!

CHIKCHIK

INTERNAL MONITORS INDICATE GRAVE DAMAGE TO SURVIVAL AND WEAPONS SYSTEMS.

IMMEDIATE LANDING NECESSARY TO EFFECT REPAIRS. BEGIN INSTRUMENT SEARCH FOR POTENTIAL SITES!

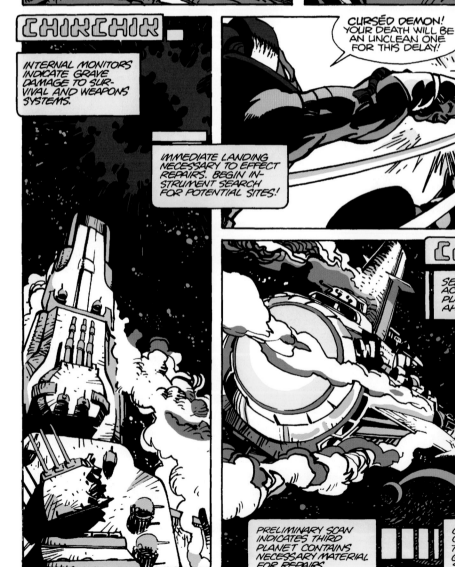

CURSÉD DEMON! YOUR DEATH WILL BE AN UNCLEAN ONE FOR THIS DELAY!

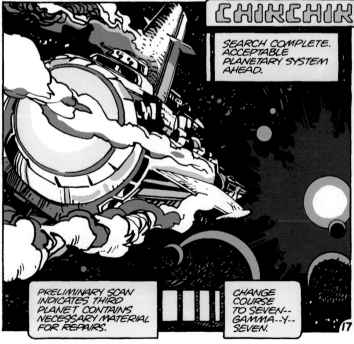

CHIKCHIK

SEARCH COMPLETE. ACCEPTABLE PLANETARY SYSTEM AHEAD.

PRELIMINARY SCAN INDICATES THIRD PLANET CONTAINS NECESSARY MATERIAL FOR REPAIRS.

CHANGE COURSE TO SEVEN-- GAMMA--Y-- SEVEN.

17

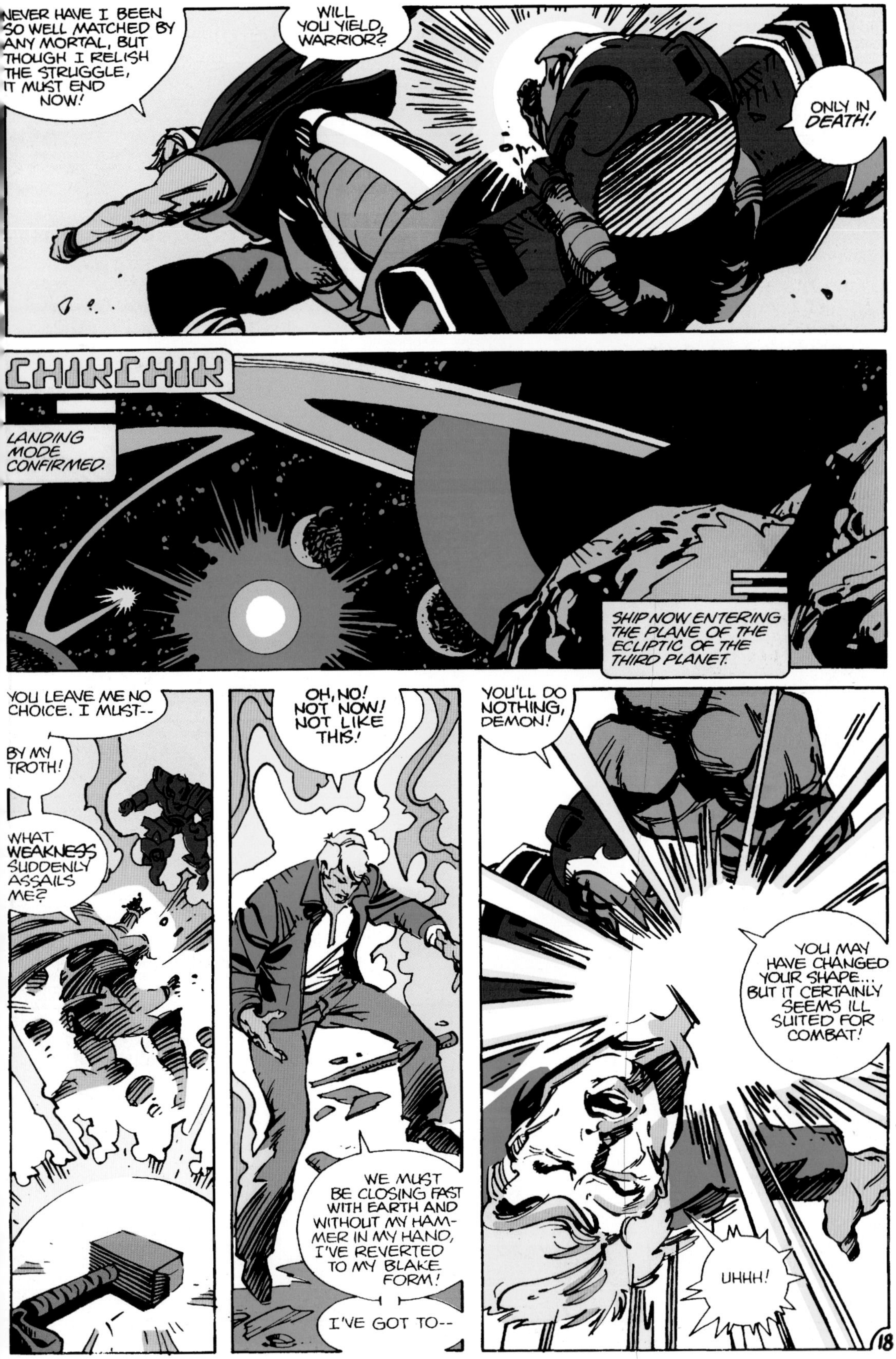
NEVER HAVE I BEEN SO WELL MATCHED BY ANY MORTAL, BUT THOUGH I RELISH THE STRUGGLE, IT MUST END NOW!
WILL YOU YIELD, WARRIOR?
ONLY IN DEATH!
CHKCHK
LANDING MODE CONFIRMED.
SHIP NOW ENTERING THE PLANE OF THE ECLIPTIC OF THE THIRD PLANET.
YOU LEAVE ME NO CHOICE. I MUST--
BY MY TROTH!
WHAT WEAKNESS SUDDENLY ASSAILS ME?
OH, NO! NOT NOW! NOT LIKE THIS!
WE MUST BE CLOSING FAST WITH EARTH AND WITHOUT MY HAMMER IN MY HAND, I'VE REVERTED TO MY BLAKE FORM!
I'VE GOT TO--
YOU'LL DO NOTHING, DEMON!
YOU MAY HAVE CHANGED YOUR SHAPE... BUT IT CERTAINLY SEEMS ILL SUITED FOR COMBAT!
UHHH!
18

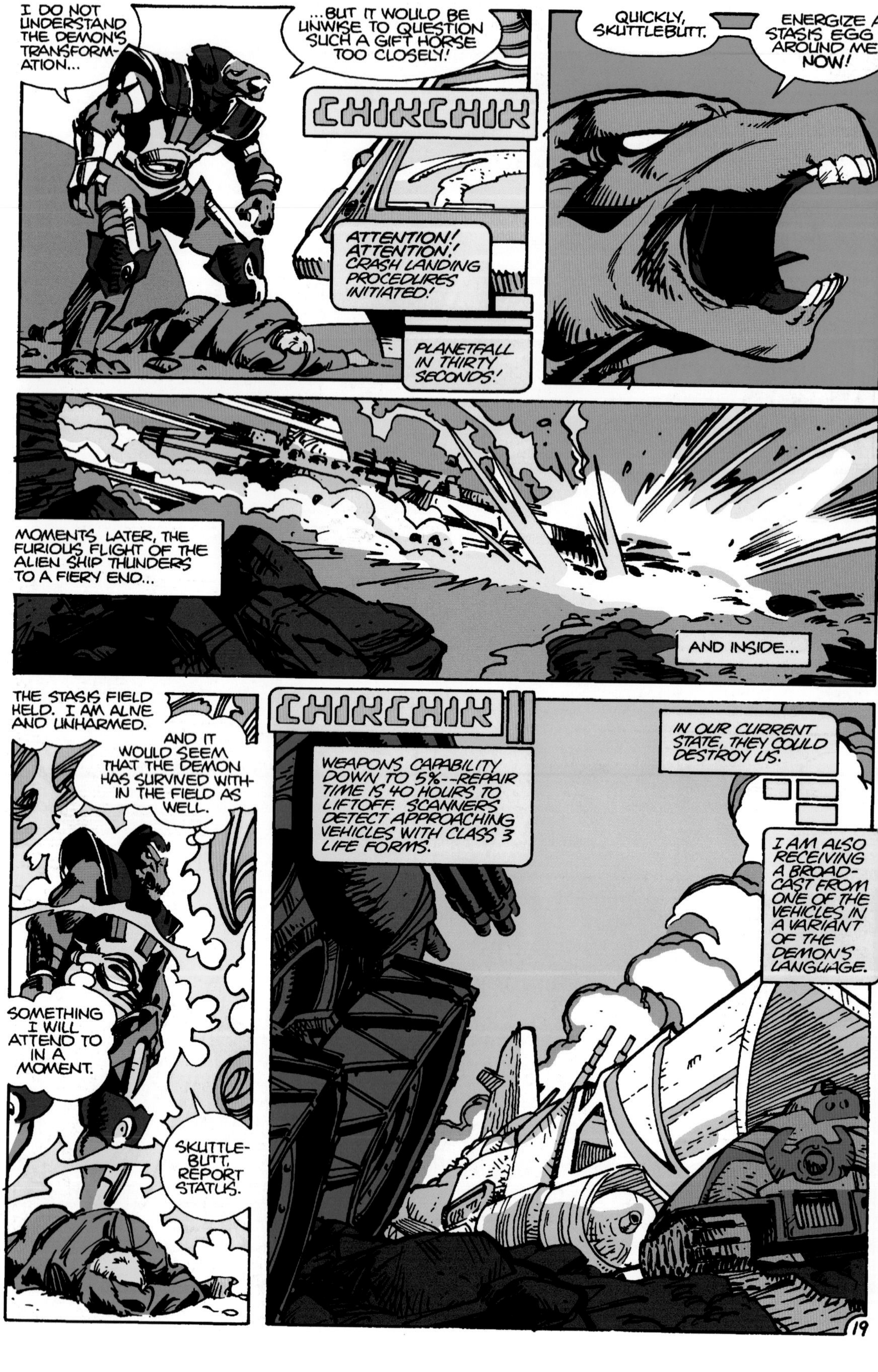
I DO NOT UNDERSTAND THE DEMON'S TRANSFORM-ATION...
...BUT IT WOULD BE UNWISE TO QUESTION SUCH A GIFT HORSE TOO CLOSELY!
CHIRCHIR
ATTENTION! ATTENTION! CRASH LANDING PROCEDURES INITIATED!
PLANETFALL IN THIRTY SECONDS!
QUICKLY, SKUTTLEBUTT.
ENERGIZE A STASIS EGG AROUND ME NOW!
MOMENTS LATER, THE FURIOUS FLIGHT OF THE ALIEN SHIP THUNDERS TO A FIERY END...
AND INSIDE...
THE STASIS FIELD HELD. I AM ALNE AND UNHARMED.
AND IT WOULD SEEM THAT THE DEMON HAS SURVIVED WITH-IN THE FIELD AS WELL.
SOMETHING I WILL ATTEND TO IN A MOMENT.
SKUTTLE-BUTT, REPORT STATUS.
CHIRCHIR
WEAPONS CAPABILITY DOWN TO 5%--REPAIR TIME IS 40 HOURS TO LIFTOFF. SCANNERS DETECT APPROACHING VEHICLES WITH CLASS 3 LIFE FORMS.
IN OUR CURRENT STATE, THEY COULD DESTROY US.
I AM ALSO RECEIVING A BROAD-CAST FROM ONE OF THE VEHICLES IN A VARIANT OF THE DEMON'S LANGUAGE.
19

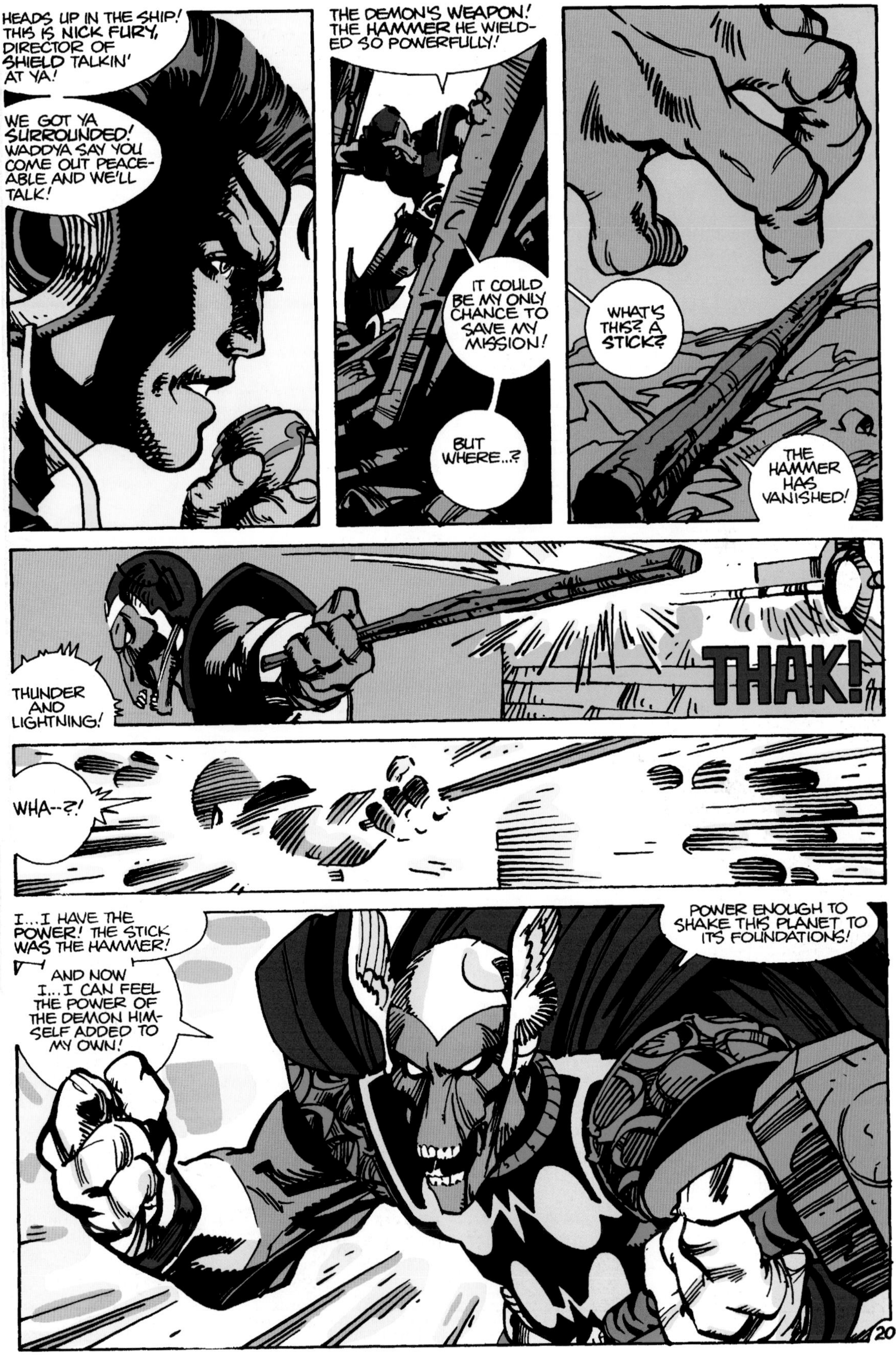
HEADS UP IN THE SHIP! THIS IS NICK FURY, DIRECTOR OF SHIELD TALKIN' AT YA!
WE GOT YA SURROUNDED! WADDYA SAY YOU COME OUT PEACEABLE AND WE'LL TALK!
THE DEMON'S WEAPON! THE HAMMER HE WIELDED SO POWERFULLY!
IT COULD BE MY ONLY CHANCE TO SAVE MY MISSION!
BUT WHERE...?
WHAT'S THIS? A STICK?
THE HAMMER HAS VANISHED!
THUNDER AND LIGHTNING!
THAK!
WHA--?!
I...I HAVE THE POWER! THE STICK WAS THE HAMMER!
AND NOW I...I CAN FEEL THE POWER OF THE DEMON HIMSELF ADDED TO MY OWN!
POWER ENOUGH TO SHAKE THIS PLANET TO ITS FOUNDATIONS!
20

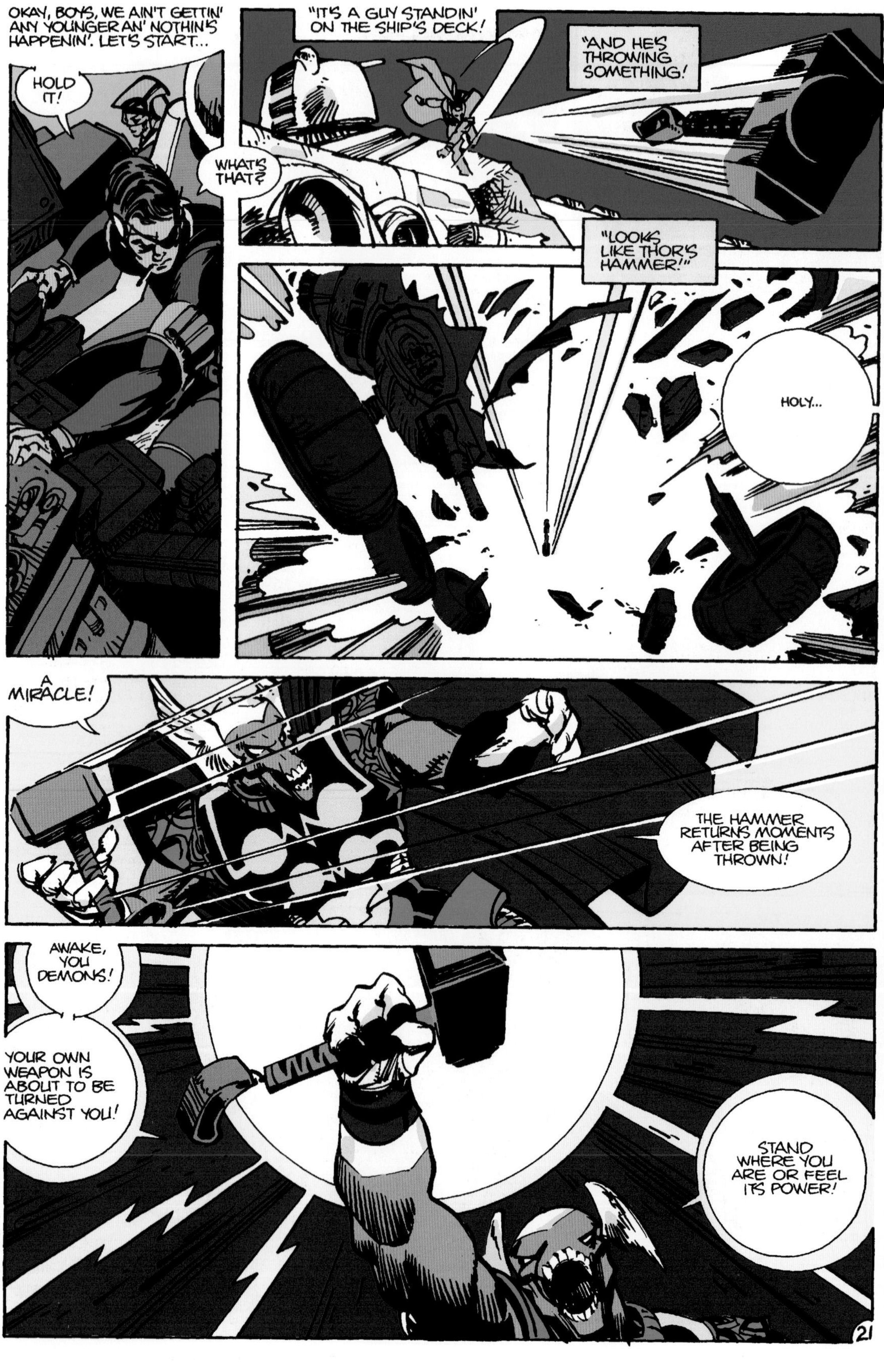
OKAY, BOYS, WE AIN'T GETTIN' ANY YOUNGER AN' NOTHIN'S HAPPENIN'. LET'S START...
HOLD IT!
WHAT'S THAT?
"IT'S A GUY STANDIN' ON THE SHIP'S DECK!
"AND HE'S THROWING SOMETHING!
"LOOKS LIKE THOR'S HAMMER!"
HOLY...
A MIRACLE!
THE HAMMER RETURNS MOMENTS AFTER BEING THROWN!
AWAKE, YOU DEMONS!
YOUR OWN WEAPON IS ABOUT TO BE TURNED AGAINST YOU!
STAND WHERE YOU ARE OR FEEL ITS POWER!
21

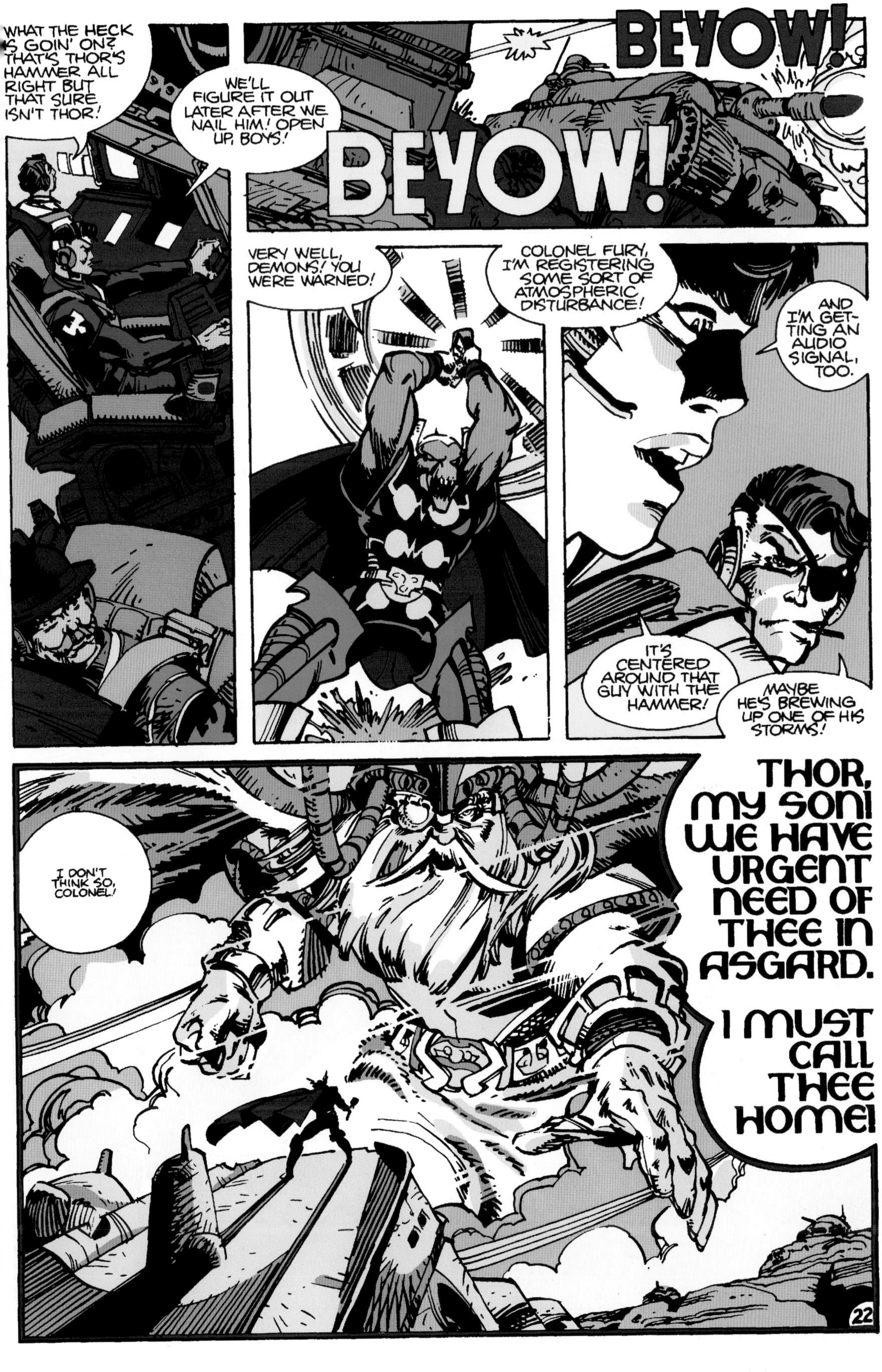

WHAT THE HECK IS GOIN' ON? THAT'S THOR'S HAMMER ALL RIGHT BUT THAT SURE ISN'T THOR!
WE'LL FIGURE IT OUT LATER AFTER WE NAIL HIM! OPEN UP, BOYS!
BEYOW!
BEYOW!
VERY WELL, DEMONS! YOU WERE WARNED!
COLONEL FURY, I'M REGISTERING SOME SORT OF ATMOSPHERIC DISTURBANCE!
AND I'M GETTING AN AUDIO SIGNAL, TOO.
IT'S CENTERED AROUND THAT GUY WITH THE HAMMER!
MAYBE HE'S BREWING UP ONE OF HIS STORMS!
I DON'T THINK SO, COLONEL!
THOR, MY SON! WE HAVE URGENT NEED OF THEE IN ASGARD.
I MUST CALL THEE HOME!
22

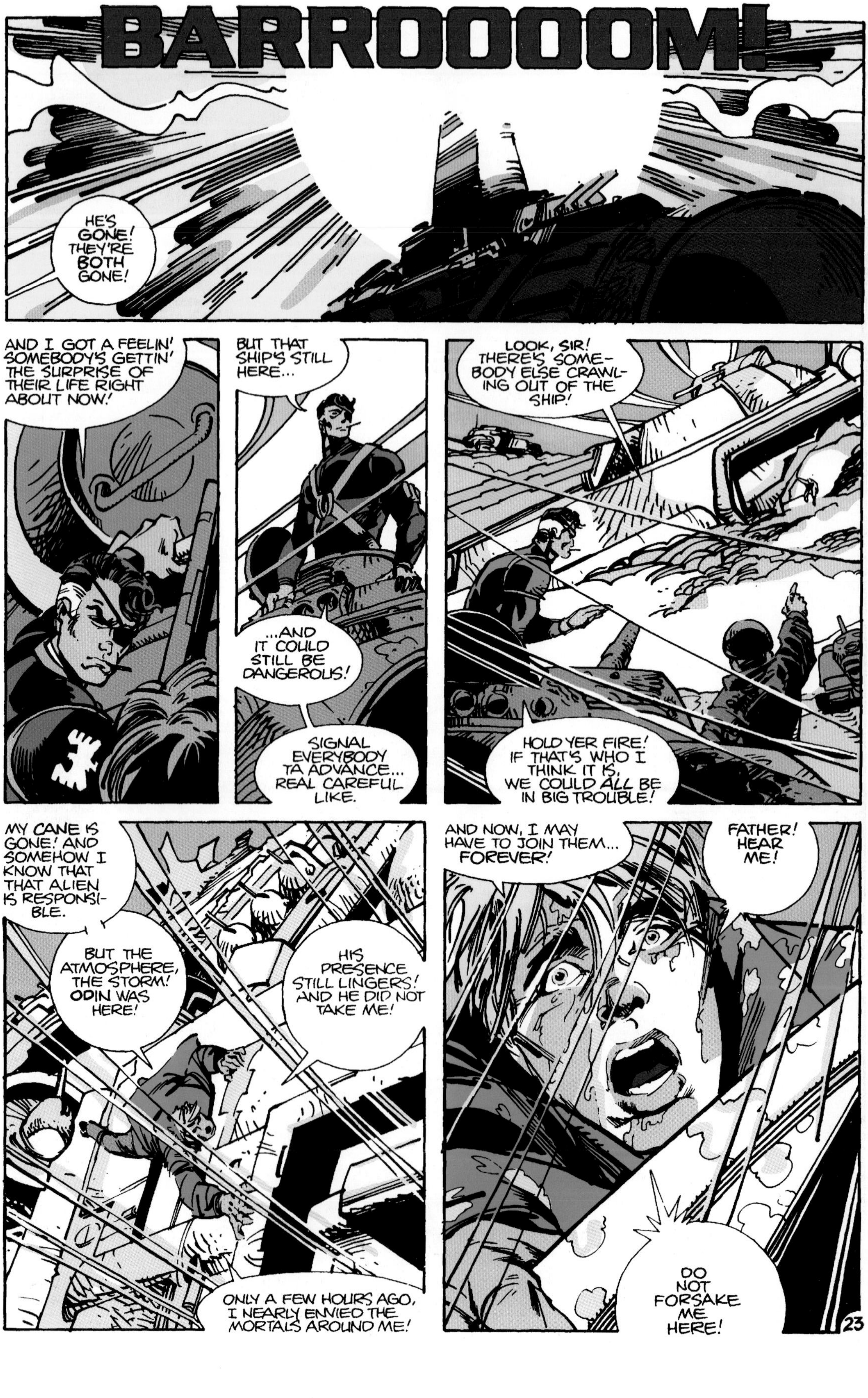
BARROOOOM!
HE'S GONE! THEY'RE BOTH GONE!
AND I GOT A FEELIN' SOMEBODY'S GETTIN' THE SURPRISE OF THEIR LIFE RIGHT ABOUT NOW!
BUT THAT SHIP'S STILL HERE...
...AND IT COULD STILL BE DANGEROUS!
SIGNAL EVERYBODY TA ADVANCE... REAL CAREFUL LIKE.
LOOK, SIR! THERE'S SOME-BODY ELSE CRAWL-ING OUT OF THE SHIP!
HOLD YER FIRE! IF THAT'S WHO I THINK IT IS, WE COULD ALL BE IN BIG TROUBLE!
MY CANE IS GONE! AND SOMEHOW I KNOW THAT THAT ALIEN IS RESPONSI-BLE.
BUT THE ATMOSPHERE, THE STORM! ODIN WAS HERE!
HIS PRESENCE STILL LINGERS! AND HE DID NOT TAKE ME!
ONLY A FEW HOURS AGO, I NEARLY ENVIED THE MORTALS AROUND ME!
AND NOW, I MAY HAVE TO JOIN THEM... FOREVER!
FATHER! HEAR ME!
DO NOT FORSAKE ME HERE!
23

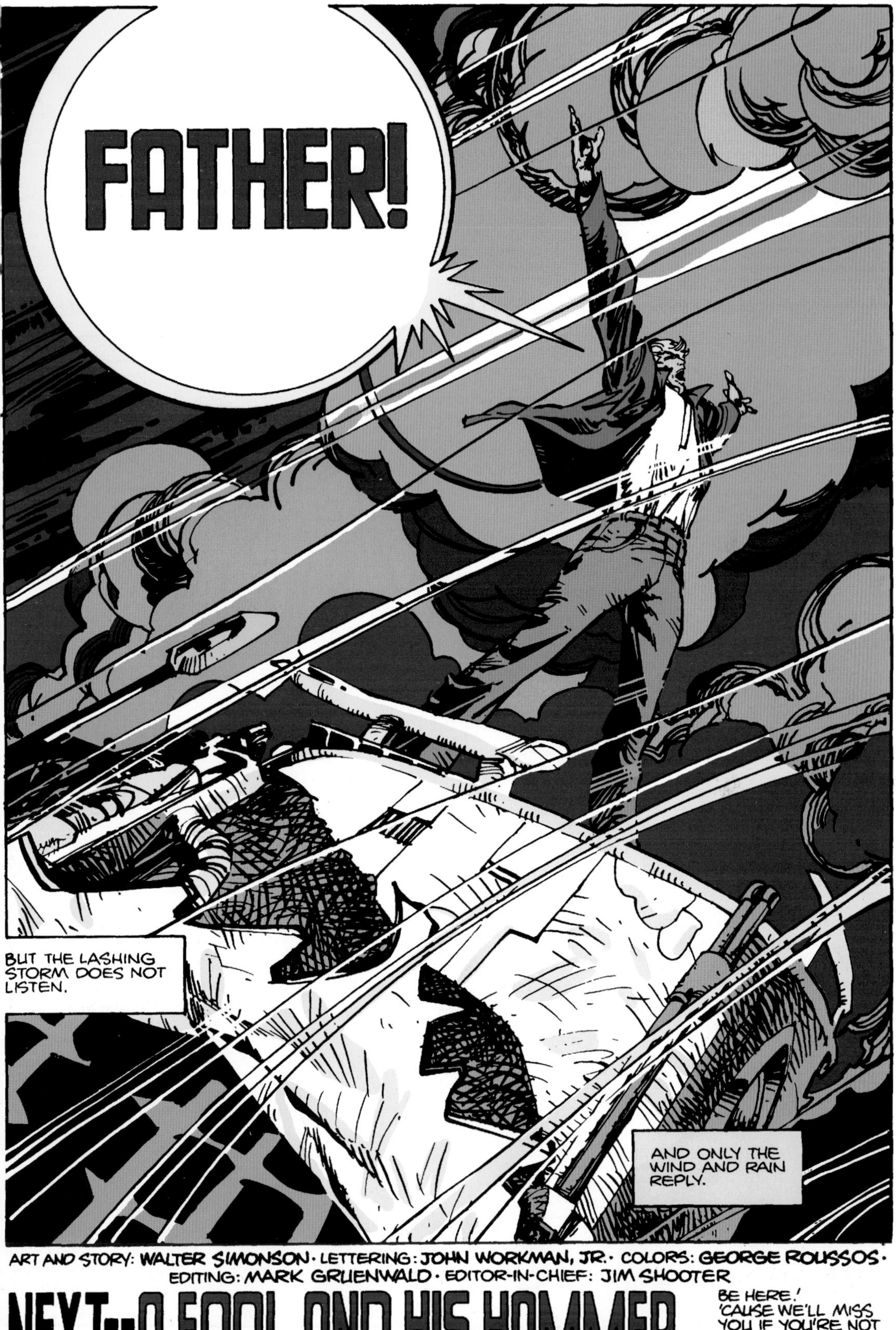
FATHER!
BUT THE LASHING STORM DOES NOT LISTEN.
AND ONLY THE WIND AND RAIN REPLY.

ART AND STORY: WALTER SIMONSON · LETTERING: JOHN WORKMAN, JR. · COLORS: GEORGE ROUSSOS · EDITING: MARK GRUENWALD · EDITOR-IN-CHIEF: JIM SHOOTER

NEXT--A FOOL AND HIS HAMMER...

BE HERE! 'CAUSE WE'LL MISS YOU IF YOU'RE NOT AROUND.

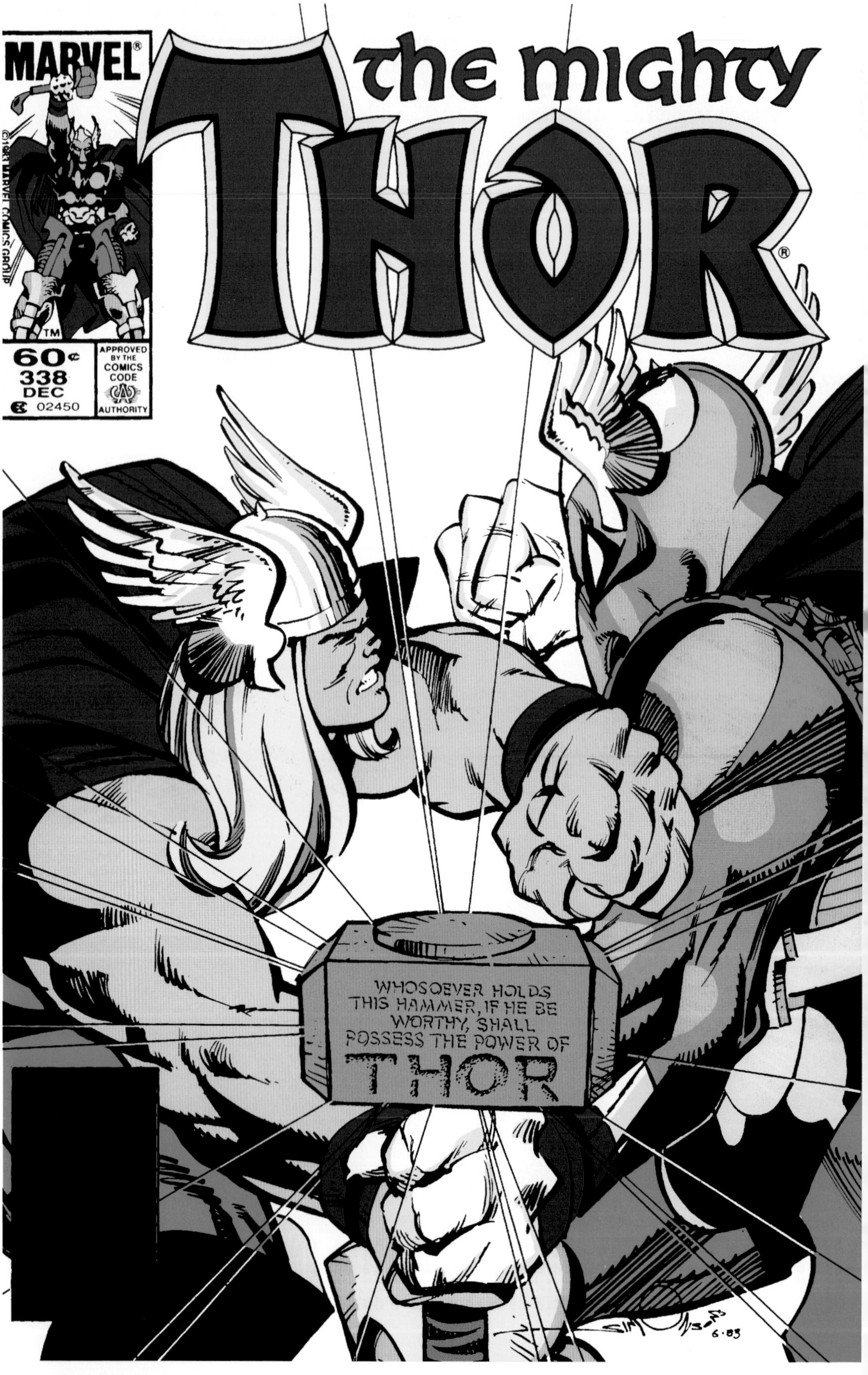
MARVEL
the mighty THOR
60¢
338
DEC
02450
APPROVED BY THE COMICS CODE AUTHORITY
WHOSOEVER HOLDS THIS HAMMER, IF HE BE WORTHY, SHALL POSSESS THE POWER OF
THOR

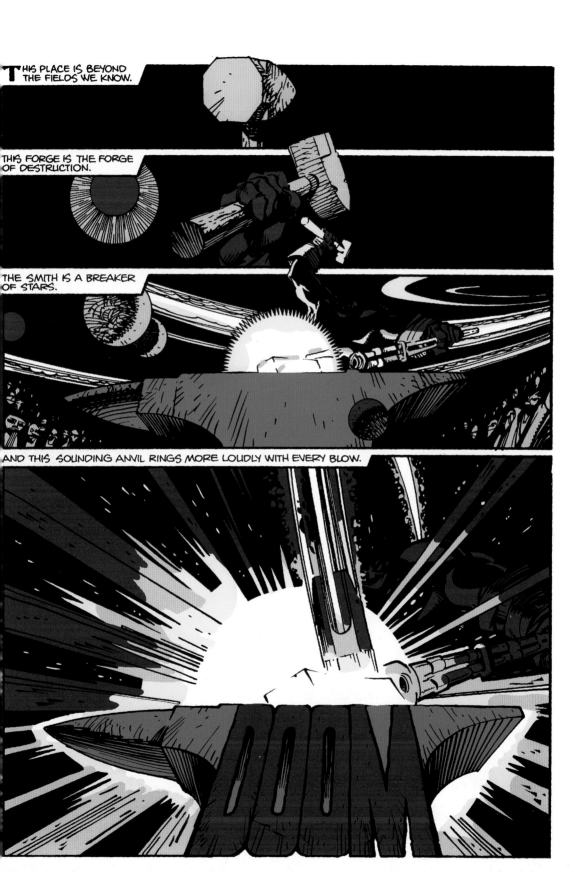

THIS PLACE IS BEYOND THE FIELDS WE KNOW.

THIS FORGE IS THE FORGE OF DESTRUCTION.

THE SMITH IS A BREAKER OF STARS.

AND THIS SOUNDING ANVIL RINGS MORE LOUDLY WITH EVERY BLOW.

DOOM

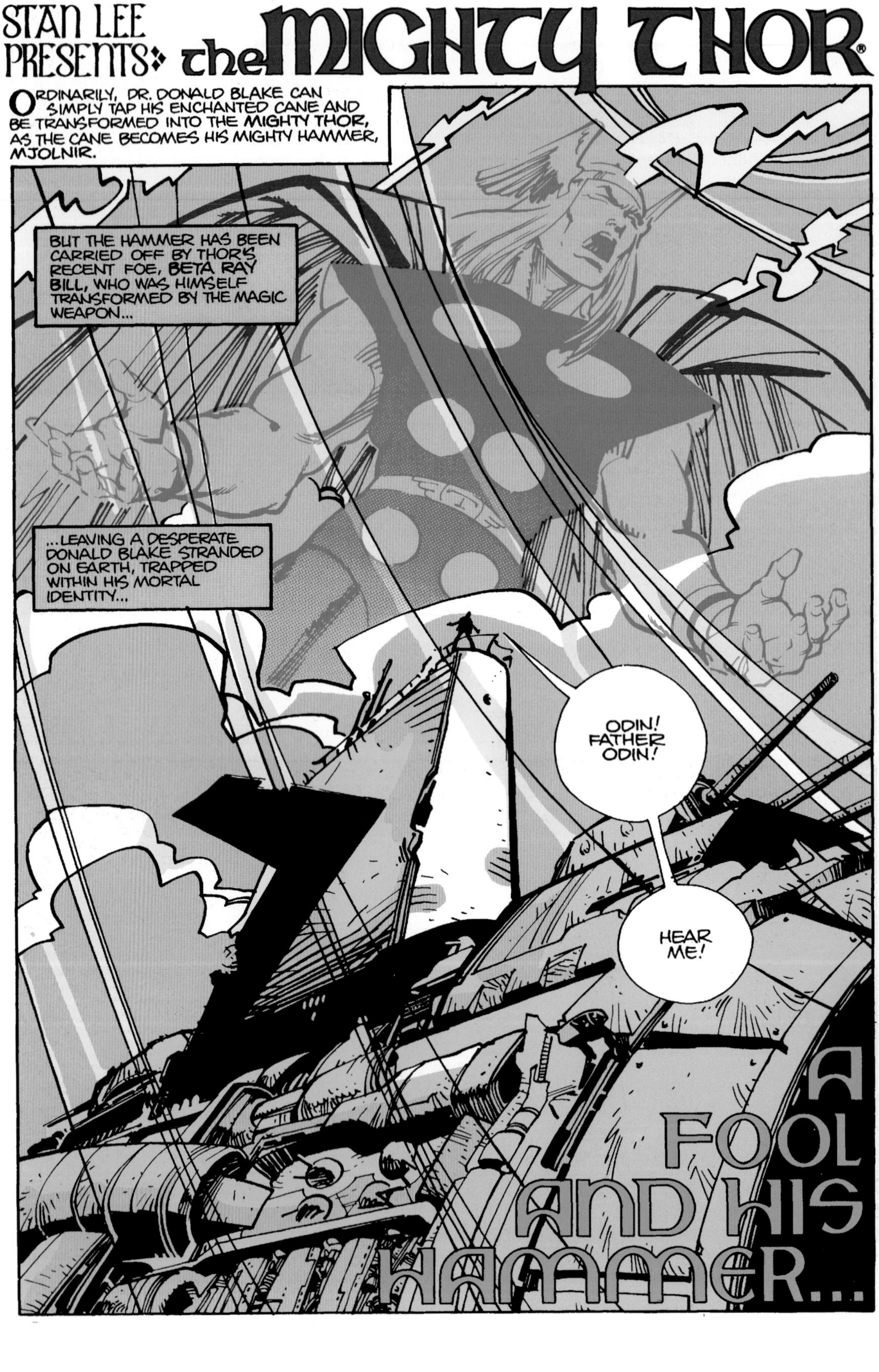

STAN LEE PRESENTS: the MIGHTY THOR®
ORDINARILY, DR. DONALD BLAKE CAN SIMPLY TAP HIS ENCHANTED CANE AND BE TRANSFORMED INTO THE MIGHTY THOR, AS THE CANE BECOMES HIS MIGHTY HAMMER, MJOLNIR.
BUT THE HAMMER HAS BEEN CARRIED OFF BY THOR'S RECENT FOE, BETA RAY BILL, WHO WAS HIMSELF TRANSFORMED BY THE MAGIC WEAPON...
...LEAVING A DESPERATE DONALD BLAKE STRANDED ON EARTH, TRAPPED WITHIN HIS MORTAL IDENTITY...
ODIN! FATHER ODIN!
HEAR ME!
A FOOL AND HIS HAMMER...

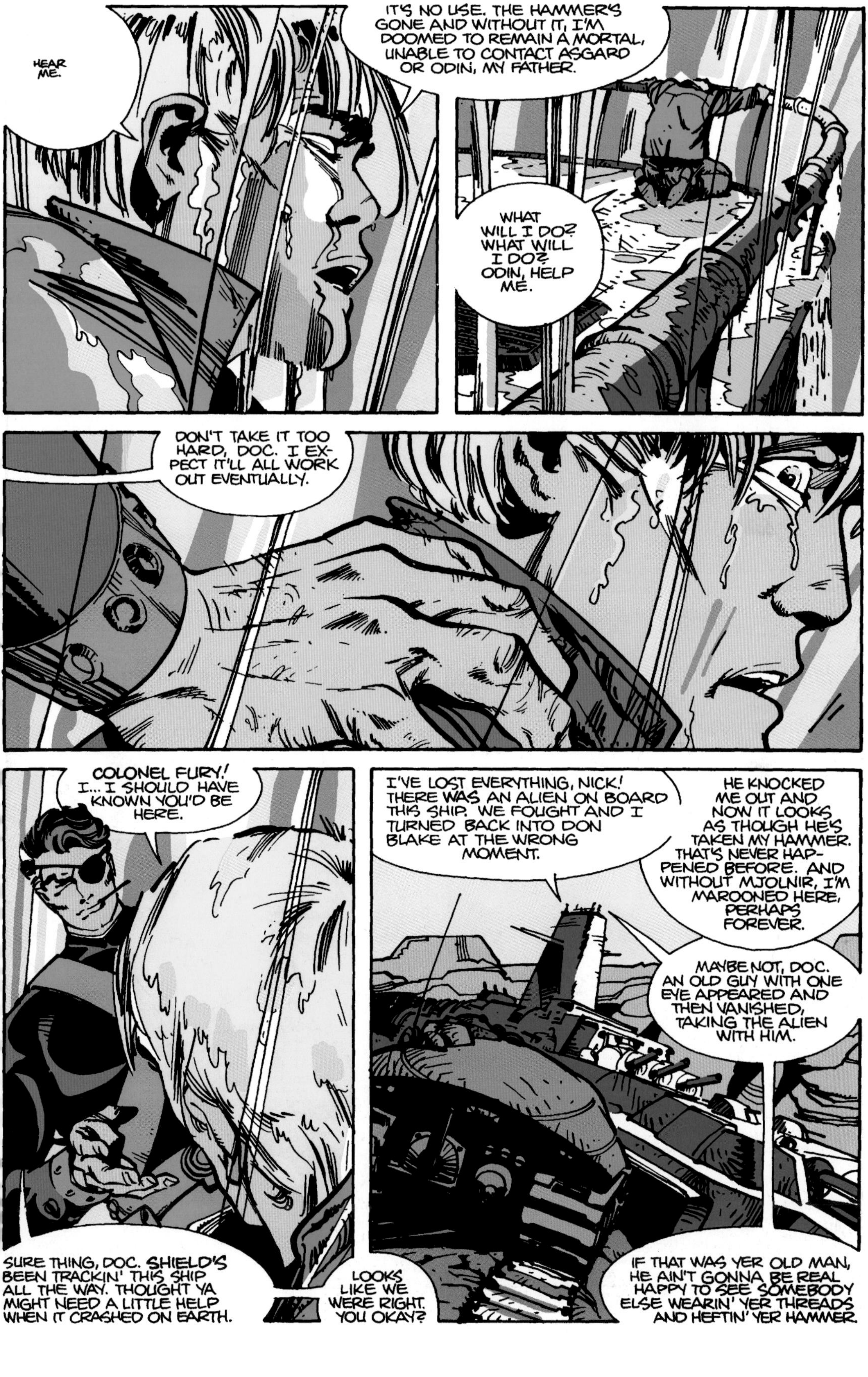
HEAR ME.
IT'S NO USE. THE HAMMER'S GONE AND WITHOUT IT, I'M DOOMED TO REMAIN A MORTAL, UNABLE TO CONTACT ASGARD OR ODIN, MY FATHER.
WHAT WILL I DO? WHAT WILL I DO? ODIN, HELP ME.
DON'T TAKE IT TOO HARD, DOC. I EXPECT IT'LL ALL WORK OUT EVENTUALLY.
COLONEL FURY! I... I SHOULD HAVE KNOWN YOU'D BE HERE.
SURE THING, DOC. SHIELD'S BEEN TRACKIN' THIS SHIP ALL THE WAY. THOUGHT YA MIGHT NEED A LITTLE HELP WHEN IT CRASHED ON EARTH.
LOOKS LIKE WE WERE RIGHT. YOU OKAY?
I'VE LOST EVERYTHING, NICK! THERE WAS AN ALIEN ON BOARD THIS SHIP. WE FOUGHT AND I TURNED BACK INTO DON BLAKE AT THE WRONG MOMENT.
HE KNOCKED ME OUT AND NOW IT LOOKS AS THOUGH HE'S TAKEN MY HAMMER. THAT'S NEVER HAPPENED BEFORE. AND WITHOUT MJOLNIR, I'M MAROONED HERE, PERHAPS FOREVER.
MAYBE NOT, DOC. AN OLD GUY WITH ONE EYE APPEARED AND THEN VANISHED, TAKING THE ALIEN WITH HIM.
IF THAT WAS YER OLD MAN, HE AIN'T GONNA BE REAL HAPPY TO SEE SOMEBODY ELSE WEARIN' YER THREADS AND HEFTIN' YER HAMMER.

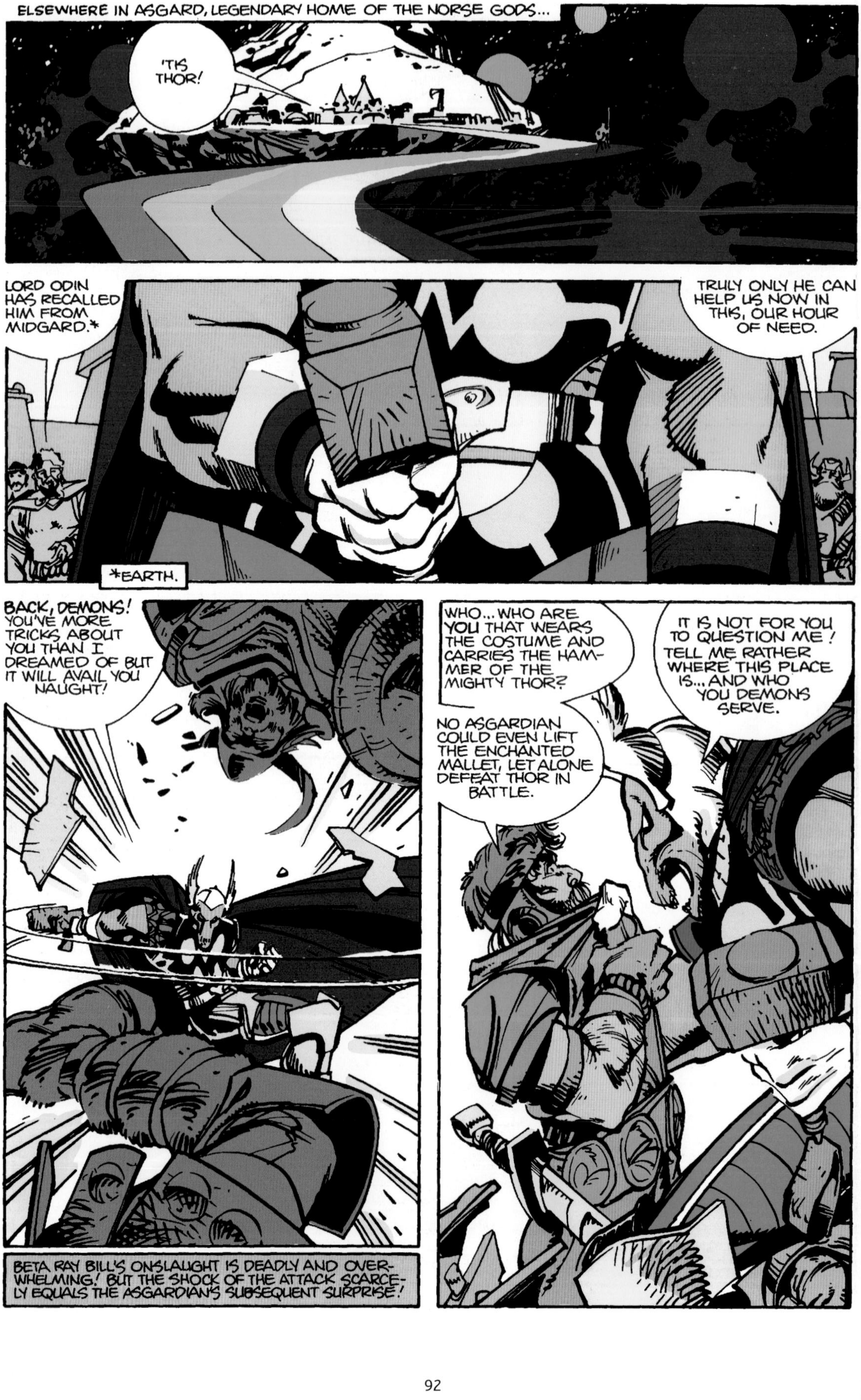
ELSEWHERE IN ASGARD, LEGENDARY HOME OF THE NORSE GODS...
'TIS THOR!
LORD ODIN HAS RECALLED HIM FROM MIDGARD.*
TRULY ONLY HE CAN HELP US NOW IN THIS, OUR HOUR OF NEED.
*EARTH.
BACK, DEMONS! YOU'VE MORE TRICKS ABOUT YOU THAN I DREAMED OF BUT IT WILL AVAIL YOU NAUGHT!
BETA RAY BILL'S ONSLAUGHT IS DEADLY AND OVERWHELMING! BUT THE SHOCK OF THE ATTACK SCARCELY EQUALS THE ASGARDIAN'S SUBSEQUENT SURPRISE!
WHO... WHO ARE YOU THAT WEARS THE COSTUME AND CARRIES THE HAMMER OF THE MIGHTY THOR?
NO ASGARDIAN COULD EVEN LIFT THE ENCHANTED MALLET, LET ALONE DEFEAT THOR IN BATTLE.
IT IS NOT FOR YOU TO QUESTION ME! TELL ME RATHER WHERE THIS PLACE IS... AND WHO YOU DEMONS SERVE.

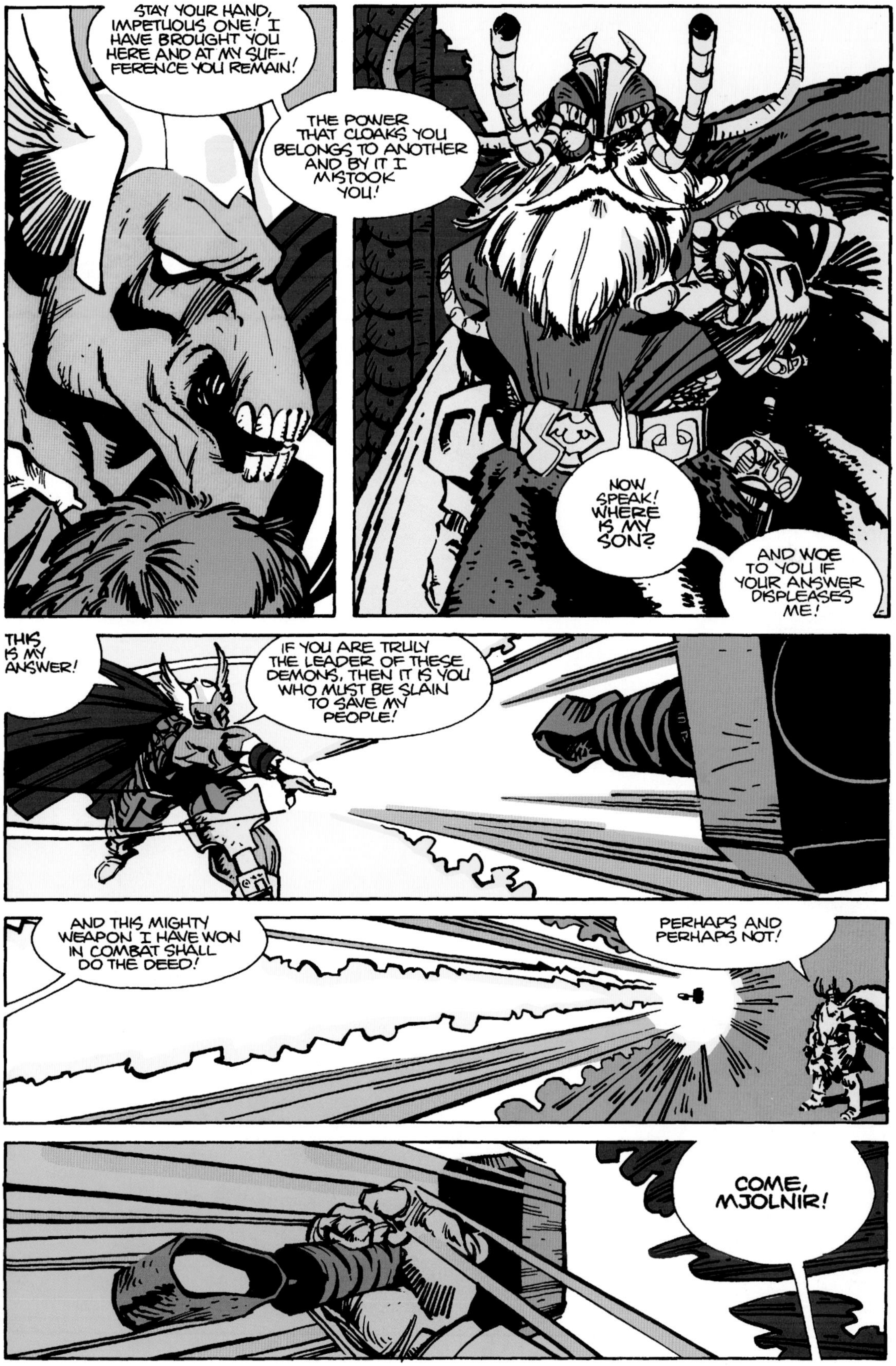
STAY YOUR HAND, IMPETUOUS ONE! I HAVE BROUGHT YOU HERE AND AT MY SUFFERENCE YOU REMAIN!
THE POWER THAT CLOAKS YOU BELONGS TO ANOTHER AND BY IT I MISTOOK YOU!
NOW SPEAK! WHERE IS MY SON?
AND WOE TO YOU IF YOUR ANSWER DISPLEASES ME!
THIS IS MY ANSWER!
IF YOU ARE TRULY THE LEADER OF THESE DEMONS, THEN IT IS YOU WHO MUST BE SLAIN TO SAVE MY PEOPLE!
AND THIS MIGHTY WEAPON I HAVE WON IN COMBAT SHALL DO THE DEED!
PERHAPS AND PERHAPS NOT!
COME, MJOLNIR!

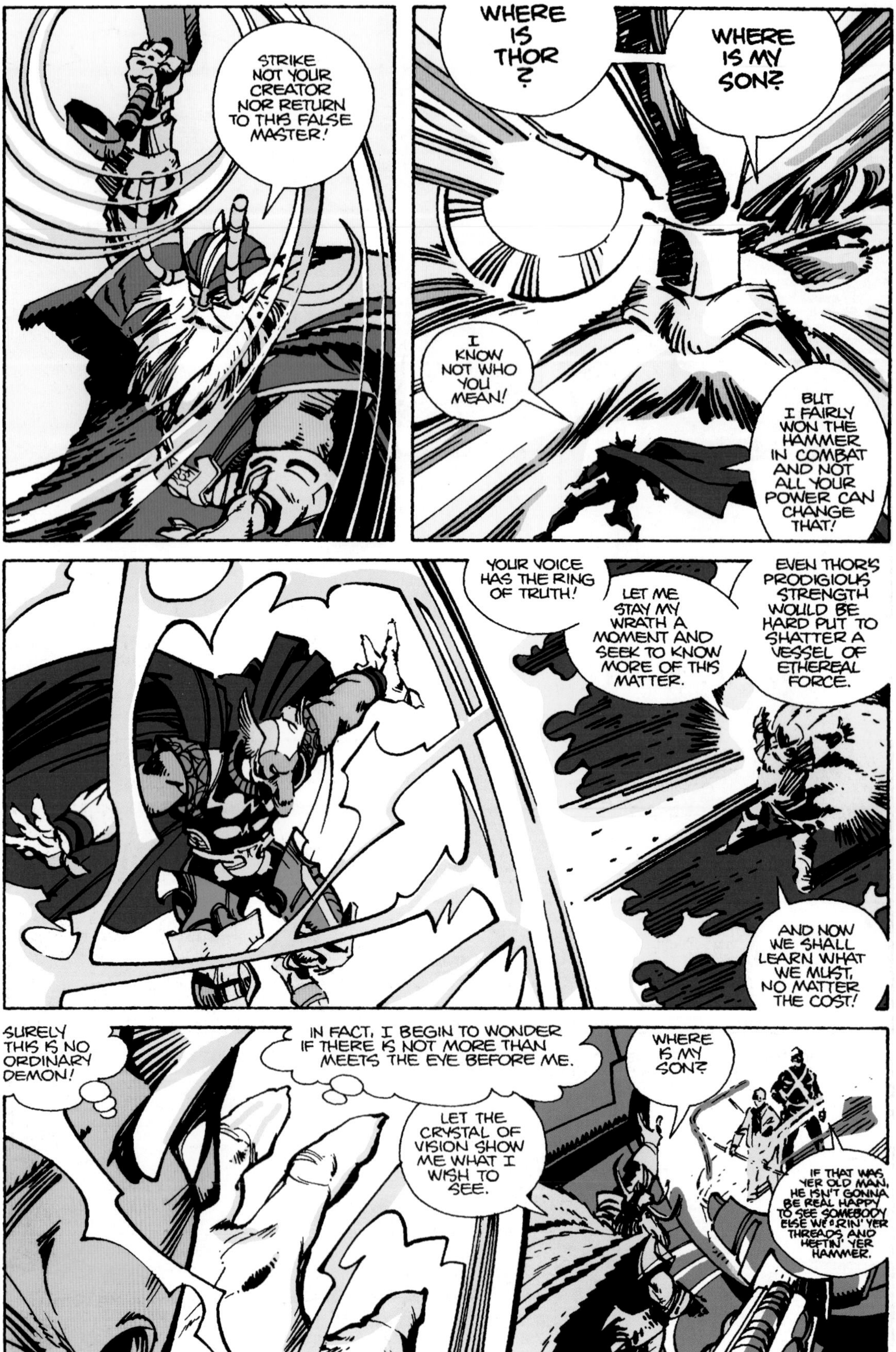
STRIKE NOT YOUR CREATOR NOR RETURN TO THIS FALSE MASTER!
WHERE IS THOR?
WHERE IS MY SON?
I KNOW NOT WHO YOU MEAN!
BUT I FAIRLY WON THE HAMMER IN COMBAT AND NOT ALL YOUR POWER CAN CHANGE THAT!
YOUR VOICE HAS THE RING OF TRUTH!
LET ME STAY MY WRATH A MOMENT AND SEEK TO KNOW MORE OF THIS MATTER.
EVEN THOR'S PRODIGIOUS STRENGTH WOULD BE HARD PUT TO SHATTER A VESSEL OF ETHEREAL FORCE.
AND NOW WE SHALL LEARN WHAT WE MUST, NO MATTER THE COST!
SURELY THIS IS NO ORDINARY DEMON!
IN FACT, I BEGIN TO WONDER IF THERE IS NOT MORE THAN MEETS THE EYE BEFORE ME.
LET THE CRYSTAL OF VISION SHOW ME WHAT I WISH TO SEE.
WHERE IS MY SON?
IF THAT WAS YER OLD MAN, HE ISN'T GONNA BE REAL HAPPY TO SEE SOMEBODY ELSE WE'RIN' YER THREADS AND HEFTIN' YER HAMMER.

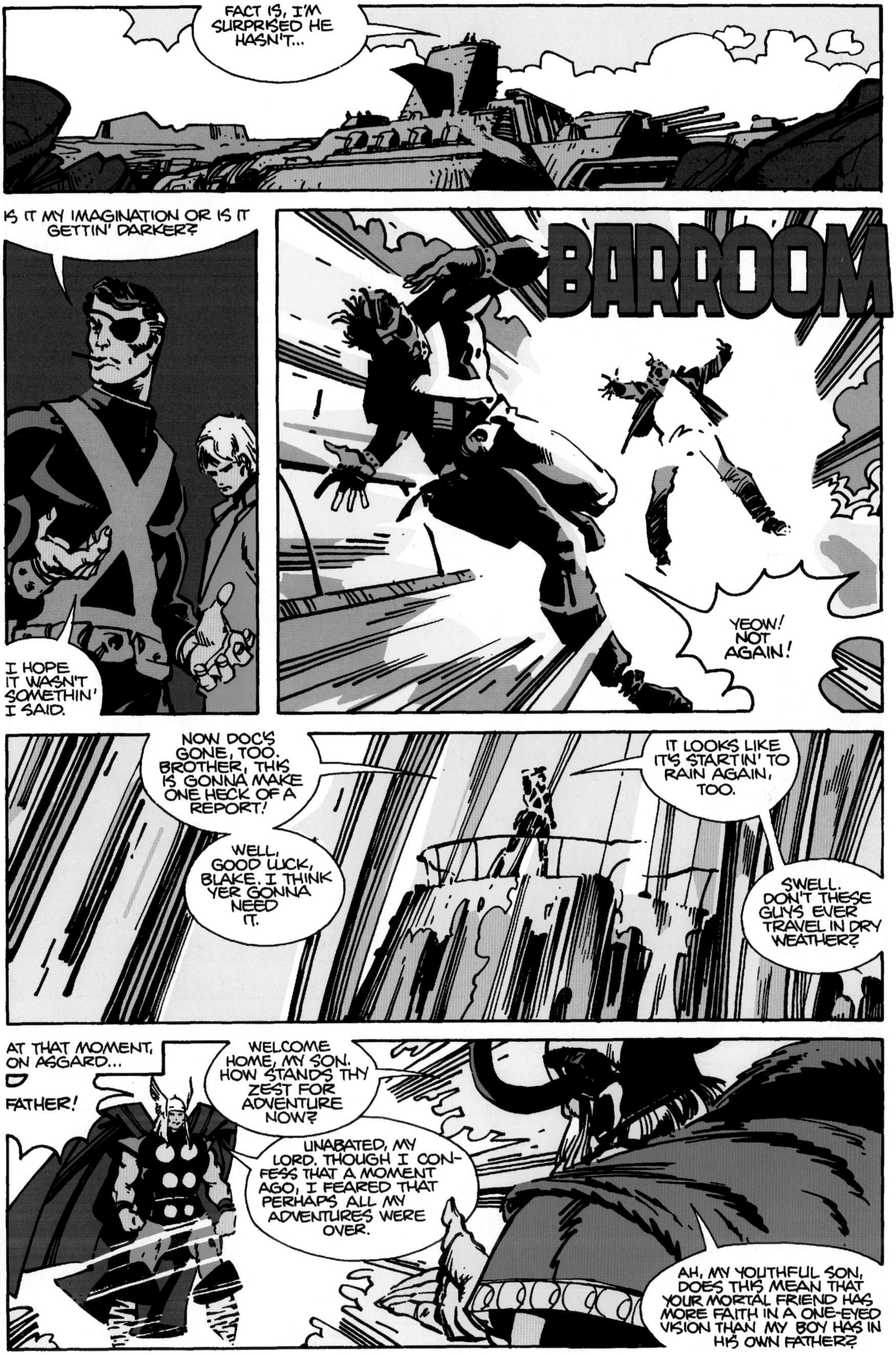
FACT IS, I'M SURPRISED HE HASN'T...
IS IT MY IMAGINATION OR IS IT GETTIN' DARKER?
I HOPE IT WASN'T SOMETHIN' I SAID.
BARROOM
YEOW! NOT AGAIN!
NOW DOC'S GONE, TOO. BROTHER, THIS IS GONNA MAKE ONE HECK OF A REPORT!
WELL, GOOD LUCK, BLAKE. I THINK YER GONNA NEED IT.
IT LOOKS LIKE IT'S STARTIN' TO RAIN AGAIN, TOO.
SWELL. DON'T THESE GUYS EVER TRAVEL IN DRY WEATHER?
AT THAT MOMENT, ON ASGARD...
FATHER!
WELCOME HOME, MY SON. HOW STANDS THY ZEST FOR ADVENTURE NOW?
UNABATED, MY LORD. THOUGH I CONFESS THAT A MOMENT AGO, I FEARED THAT PERHAPS ALL MY ADVENTURES WERE OVER.
AH, MY YOUTHFUL SON, DOES THIS MEAN THAT YOUR MORTAL FRIEND HAS MORE FAITH IN A ONE-EYED VISION THAN MY BOY HAS IN HIS OWN FATHER?

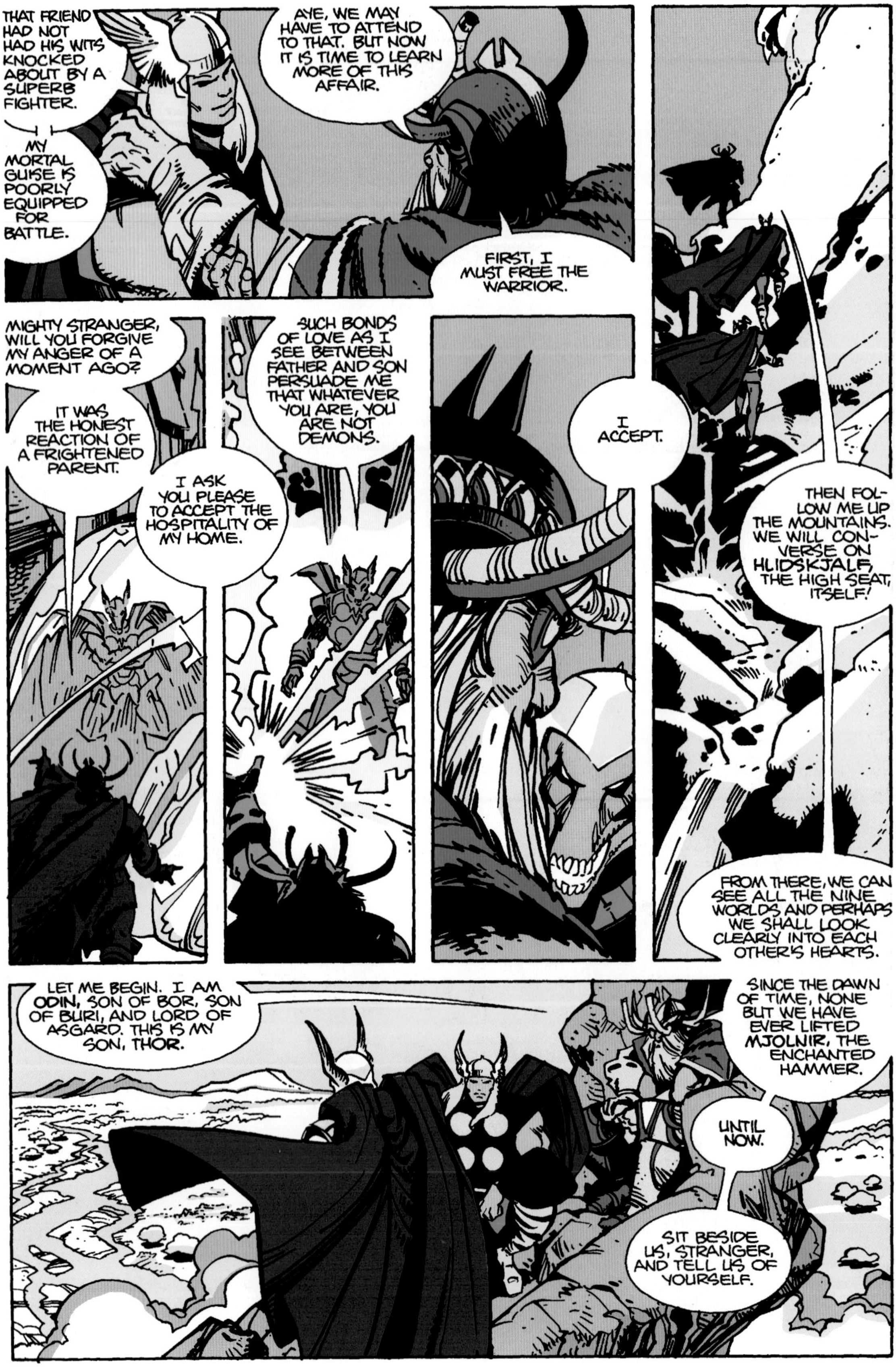
THAT FRIEND HAD NOT HAD HIS WITS KNOCKED ABOUT BY A SUPERB FIGHTER.
MY MORTAL GUISE IS POORLY EQUIPPED FOR BATTLE.
AYE, WE MAY HAVE TO ATTEND TO THAT. BUT NOW IT IS TIME TO LEARN MORE OF THIS AFFAIR.
FIRST, I MUST FREE THE WARRIOR.
MIGHTY STRANGER, WILL YOU FORGIVE MY ANGER OF A MOMENT AGO?
IT WAS THE HONEST REACTION OF A FRIGHTENED PARENT.
SUCH BONDS OF LOVE AS I SEE BETWEEN FATHER AND SON PERSUADE ME THAT WHATEVER YOU ARE, YOU ARE NOT DEMONS.
I ASK YOU PLEASE TO ACCEPT THE HOSPITALITY OF MY HOME.
I ACCEPT.
THEN FOLLOW ME UP THE MOUNTAINS. WE WILL CONVERSE ON HLIDSKJALF, THE HIGH SEAT, ITSELF!
FROM THERE, WE CAN SEE ALL THE NINE WORLDS AND PERHAPS WE SHALL LOOK CLEARLY INTO EACH OTHER'S HEARTS.
LET ME BEGIN. I AM ODIN, SON OF BOR, SON OF BURI, AND LORD OF ASGARD. THIS IS MY SON, THOR.
SINCE THE DAWN OF TIME, NONE BUT WE HAVE EVER LIFTED MJOLNIR, THE ENCHANTED HAMMER.
UNTIL NOW.
SIT BESIDE US, STRANGER, AND TELL US OF YOURSELF.

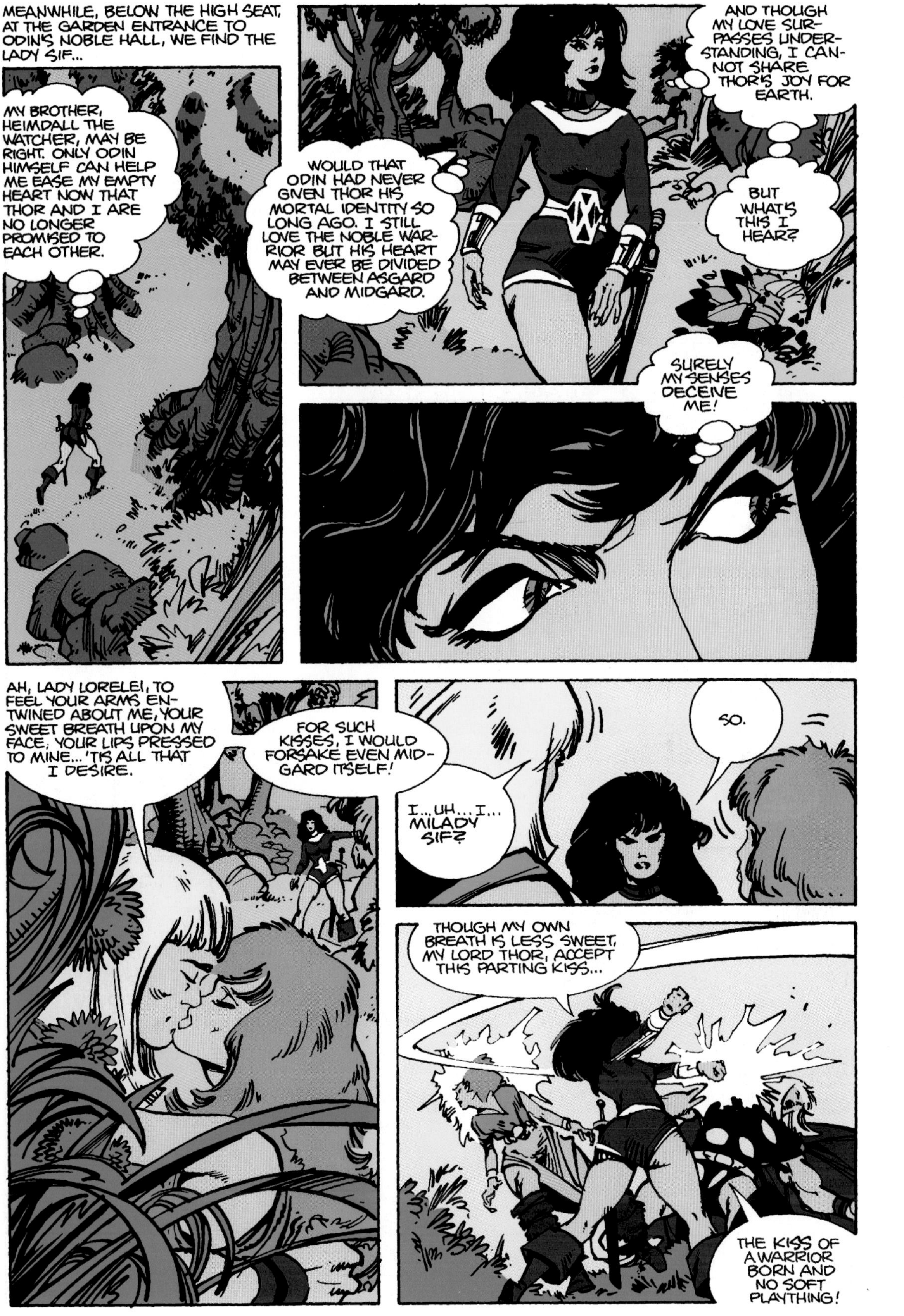
MEANWHILE, BELOW THE HIGH SEAT, AT THE GARDEN ENTRANCE TO ODIN'S NOBLE HALL, WE FIND THE LADY SIF...
MY BROTHER, HEIMDALL THE WATCHER, MAY BE RIGHT. ONLY ODIN HIMSELF CAN HELP ME EASE MY EMPTY HEART NOW THAT THOR AND I ARE NO LONGER PROMISED TO EACH OTHER.
WOULD THAT ODIN HAD NEVER GIVEN THOR HIS MORTAL IDENTITY SO LONG AGO. I STILL LOVE THE NOBLE WARRIOR BUT HIS HEART MAY EVER BE DIVIDED BETWEEN ASGARD AND MIDGARD.
AND THOUGH MY LOVE SURPASSES UNDERSTANDING, I CANNOT SHARE THOR'S JOY FOR EARTH.
BUT WHAT'S THIS I HEAR?
SURELY MY SENSES DECEIVE ME!
AH, LADY LORELEI, TO FEEL YOUR ARMS ENTWINED ABOUT ME, YOUR SWEET BREATH UPON MY FACE, YOUR LIPS PRESSED TO MINE... 'TIS ALL THAT I DESIRE.
FOR SUCH KISSES, I WOULD FORSAKE EVEN MIDGARD ITSELF!
SO.
I... UH... I... MILADY SIF?
THOUGH MY OWN BREATH IS LESS SWEET, MY LORD THOR, ACCEPT THIS PARTING KISS...
THE KISS OF A WARRIOR BORN AND NO SOFT PLAYTHING!

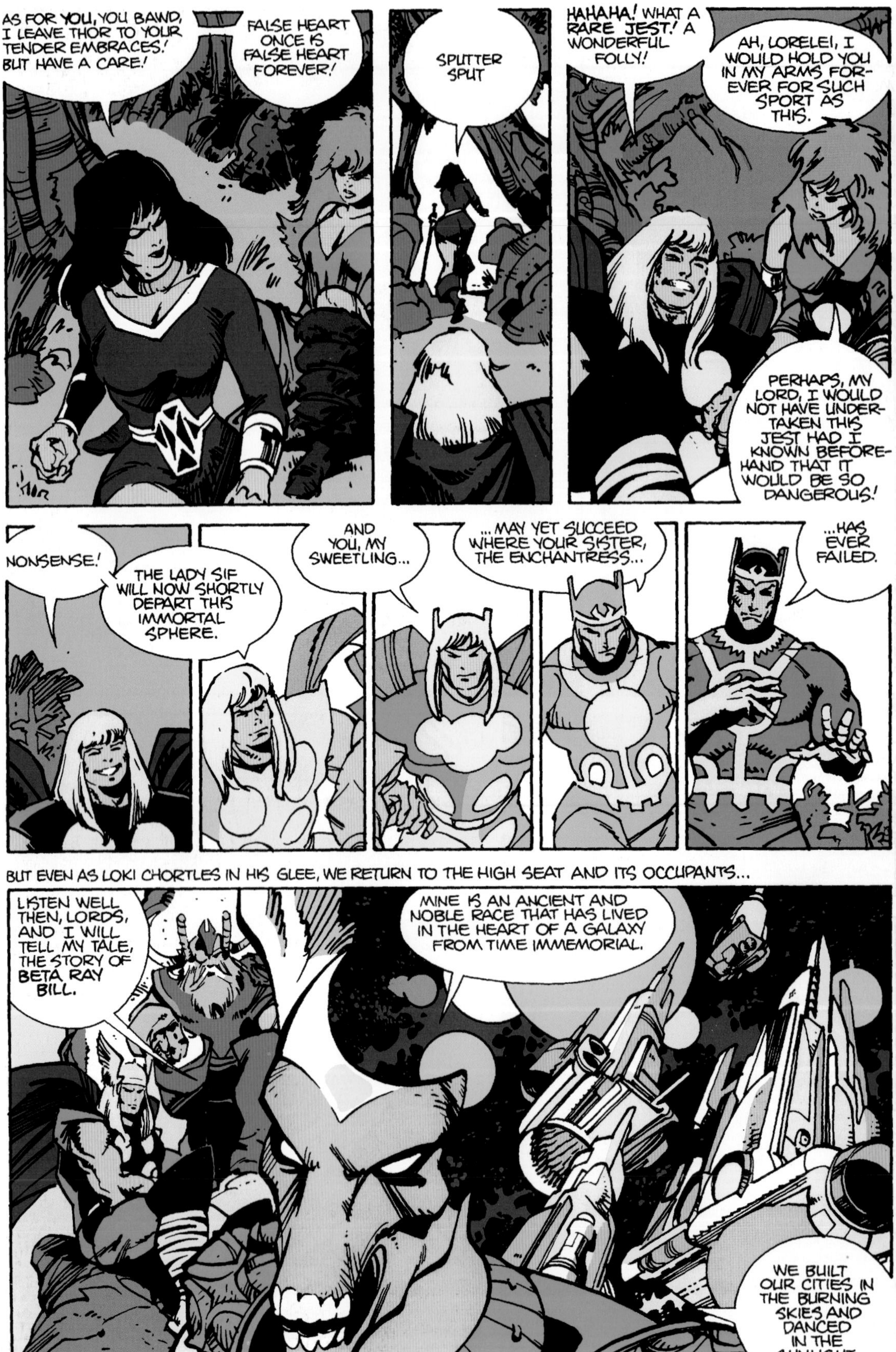

AS FOR YOU, YOU BAWD, I LEAVE THOR TO YOUR TENDER EMBRACES! BUT HAVE A CARE!
FALSE HEART ONCE IS FALSE HEART FOREVER!
SPUTTER SPUT
HAHAHA! WHAT A RARE JEST! A WONDERFUL FOLLY!
AH, LORELEI, I WOULD HOLD YOU IN MY ARMS FOREVER FOR SUCH SPORT AS THIS.
PERHAPS, MY LORD, I WOULD NOT HAVE UNDERTAKEN THIS JEST HAD I KNOWN BEFOREHAND THAT IT WOULD BE SO DANGEROUS!
NONSENSE!
THE LADY SIF WILL NOW SHORTLY DEPART THIS IMMORTAL SPHERE.
AND YOU, MY SWEETLING...
...MAY YET SUCCEED WHERE YOUR SISTER, THE ENCHANTRESS...
...HAS EVER FAILED.
BUT EVEN AS LOKI CHORTLES IN HIS GLEE, WE RETURN TO THE HIGH SEAT AND ITS OCCUPANTS...
LISTEN WELL THEN, LORDS, AND I WILL TELL MY TALE, THE STORY OF BETA RAY BILL.
MINE IS AN ANCIENT AND NOBLE RACE THAT HAS LIVED IN THE HEART OF A GALAXY FROM TIME IMMEMORIAL.
WE BUILT OUR CITIES IN THE BURNING SKIES AND DANCED IN THE SUNLIGHT.

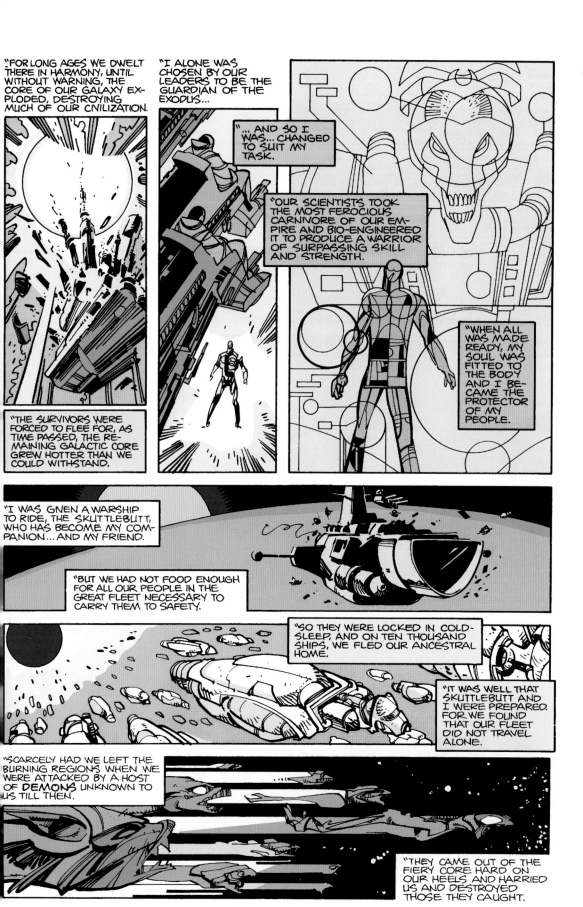

"FOR LONG AGES WE DWELT THERE IN HARMONY, UNTIL WITHOUT WARNING, THE CORE OF OUR GALAXY EXPLODED, DESTROYING MUCH OF OUR CIVILIZATION.

"I ALONE WAS CHOSEN BY OUR LEADERS TO BE THE GUARDIAN OF THE EXODUS...

"... AND SO I WAS... CHANGED TO SUIT MY TASK.

"OUR SCIENTISTS TOOK THE MOST FEROCIOUS CARNIVORE OF OUR EMPIRE AND BIO-ENGINEERED IT TO PRODUCE A WARRIOR OF SURPASSING SKILL AND STRENGTH.

"WHEN ALL WAS MADE READY, MY SOUL WAS FITTED TO THE BODY AND I BECAME THE PROTECTOR OF MY PEOPLE.

"THE SURVIVORS WERE FORCED TO FLEE FOR, AS TIME PASSED, THE REMAINING GALACTIC CORE GREW HOTTER THAN WE COULD WITHSTAND.

"I WAS GIVEN A WARSHIP TO RIDE, THE SKUTTLEBUTT, WHO HAS BECOME MY COMPANION... AND MY FRIEND.

"BUT WE HAD NOT FOOD ENOUGH FOR ALL OUR PEOPLE IN THE GREAT FLEET NECESSARY TO CARRY THEM TO SAFETY.

"SO THEY WERE LOCKED IN COLD-SLEEP, AND ON TEN THOUSAND SHIPS, WE FLED OUR ANCESTRAL HOME.

"IT WAS WELL THAT SKUTTLEBUTT AND I WERE PREPARED, FOR WE FOUND THAT OUR FLEET DID NOT TRAVEL ALONE.

"SCARCELY HAD WE LEFT THE BURNING REGIONS WHEN WE WERE ATTACKED BY A HOST OF **DEMONS** UNKNOWN TO US TILL THEN.

"THEY CAME OUT OF THE FIERY CORE HARD ON OUR HEELS AND HARRIED US AND DESTROYED THOSE THEY CAUGHT.

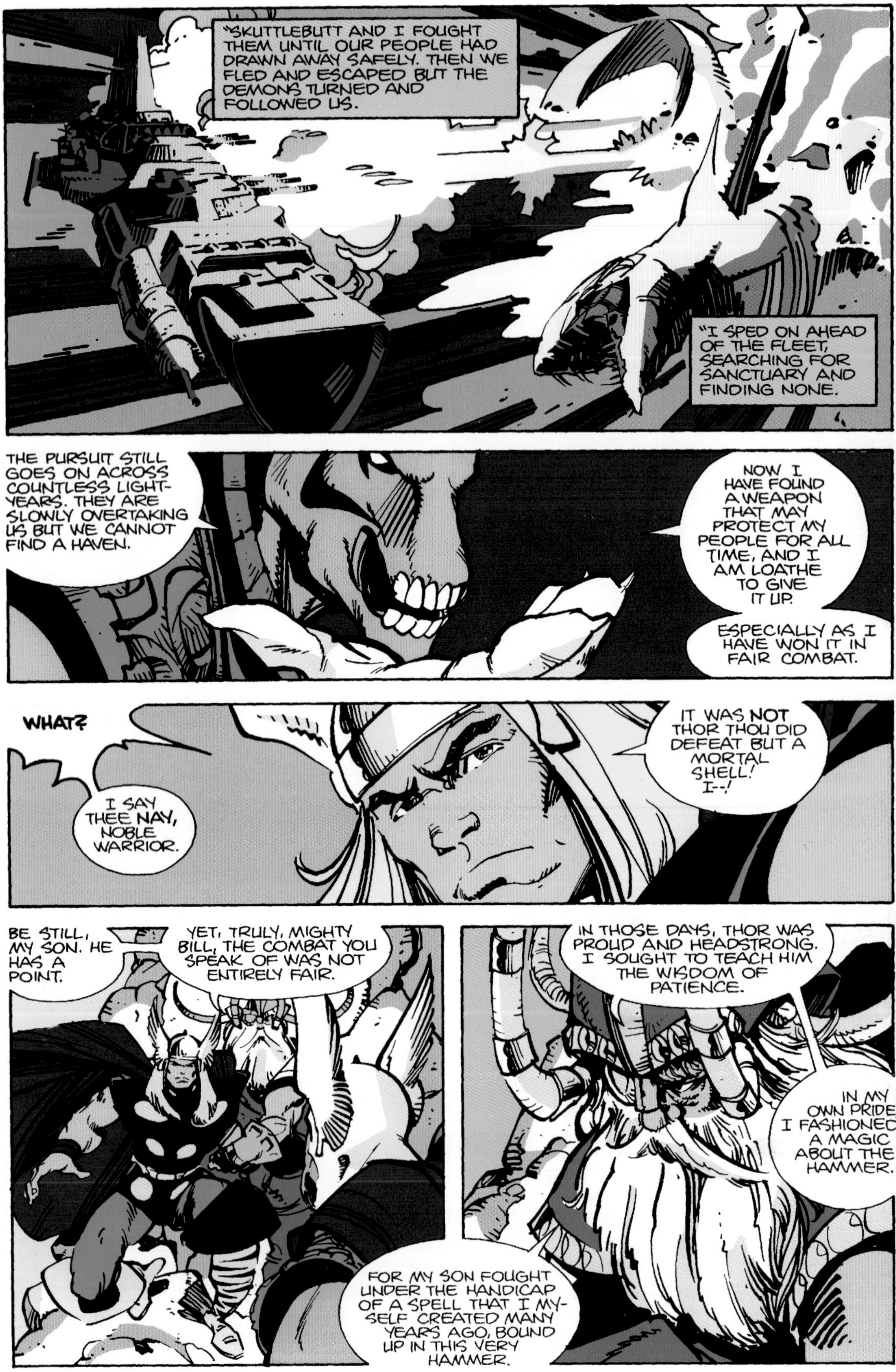
"SKUTTLEBUTT AND I FOUGHT THEM UNTIL OUR PEOPLE HAD DRAWN AWAY SAFELY. THEN WE FLED AND ESCAPED BUT THE DEMONS TURNED AND FOLLOWED US.
"I SPED ON AHEAD OF THE FLEET, SEARCHING FOR SANCTUARY AND FINDING NONE.
THE PURSUIT STILL GOES ON ACROSS COUNTLESS LIGHT-YEARS. THEY ARE SLOWLY OVERTAKING US BUT WE CANNOT FIND A HAVEN.
NOW I HAVE FOUND A WEAPON THAT MAY PROTECT MY PEOPLE FOR ALL TIME, AND I AM LOATHE TO GIVE IT UP.
ESPECIALLY AS I HAVE WON IT IN FAIR COMBAT.
WHAT?
I SAY THEE NAY, NOBLE WARRIOR.
IT WAS NOT THOR THOU DID DEFEAT BUT A MORTAL SHELL! I--!
BE STILL, MY SON. HE HAS A POINT.
YET, TRULY, MIGHTY BILL, THE COMBAT YOU SPEAK OF WAS NOT ENTIRELY FAIR.
FOR MY SON FOUGHT UNDER THE HANDICAP OF A SPELL THAT I MY-SELF CREATED MANY YEARS AGO, BOUND UP IN THIS VERY HAMMER.
IN THOSE DAYS, THOR WAS PROUD AND HEADSTRONG. I SOUGHT TO TEACH HIM THE WISDOM OF PATIENCE.
IN MY OWN PRIDE, I FASHIONED A MAGIC ABOUT THE HAMMER.

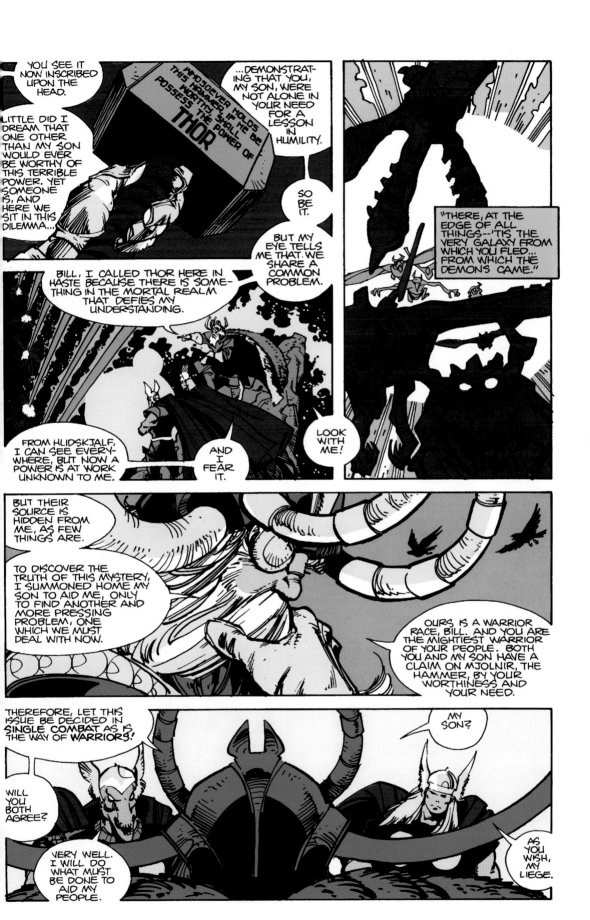

YOU SEE IT NOW INSCRIBED UPON THE HEAD.

WHOSOEVER HOLDS THIS HAMMER, IF HE BE WORTHY, SHALL POSSESS THE POWER OF **THOR**

LITTLE DID I DREAM THAT ONE OTHER THAN MY SON WOULD EVER BE WORTHY OF THIS TERRIBLE POWER. YET SOMEONE IS, AND HERE WE SIT IN THIS DILEMMA...

...DEMONSTRATING THAT YOU, MY SON, WERE NOT ALONE IN YOUR NEED FOR A LESSON IN HUMILITY.

SO BE IT.

BUT MY EYE TELLS ME THAT WE SHARE A COMMON PROBLEM.

BILL, I CALLED THOR HERE IN HASTE BECAUSE THERE IS SOMETHING IN THE MORTAL REALM THAT DEFIES MY UNDERSTANDING.

"THERE, AT THE EDGE OF ALL THINGS--'TIS THE VERY GALAXY FROM WHICH YOU FLED... FROM WHICH THE DEMONS CAME."

FROM HLIDSKJALF, I CAN SEE EVERYWHERE, BUT NOW A POWER IS AT WORK UNKNOWN TO ME.

AND I FEAR IT.

LOOK WITH ME!

BUT THEIR SOURCE IS HIDDEN FROM ME, AS FEW THINGS ARE.

TO DISCOVER THE TRUTH OF THIS MYSTERY, I SUMMONED HOME MY SON TO AID ME, ONLY TO FIND ANOTHER AND MORE PRESSING PROBLEM, ONE WHICH WE MUST DEAL WITH NOW.

OURS IS A WARRIOR RACE, BILL. AND YOU ARE THE MIGHTIEST WARRIOR OF YOUR PEOPLE. BOTH YOU AND MY SON HAVE A CLAIM ON MJOLNIR, THE HAMMER, BY YOUR WORTHINESS AND YOUR NEED.

THEREFORE, LET THIS ISSUE BE DECIDED IN SINGLE COMBAT AS IS THE WAY OF **WARRIORS!**

MY SON?

WILL YOU BOTH AGREE?

VERY WELL. I WILL DO WHAT MUST BE DONE TO AID MY PEOPLE.

AS YOU WISH, MY LIEGE.

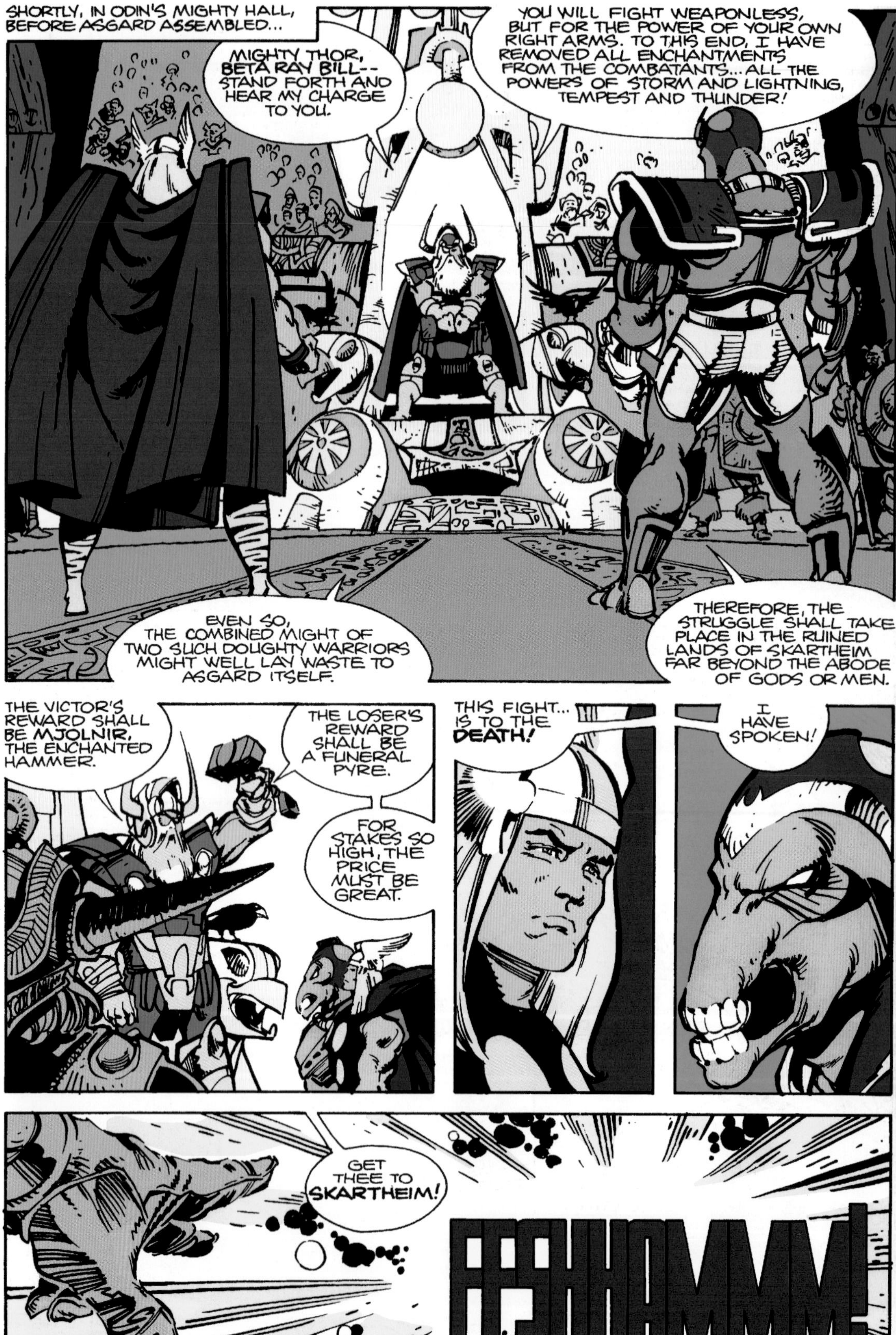
SHORTLY, IN ODIN'S MIGHTY HALL, BEFORE ASGARD ASSEMBLED...
MIGHTY THOR, BETA RAY BILL-- STAND FORTH AND HEAR MY CHARGE TO YOU.
YOU WILL FIGHT WEAPONLESS, BUT FOR THE POWER OF YOUR OWN RIGHT ARMS. TO THIS END, I HAVE REMOVED ALL ENCHANTMENTS FROM THE COMBATANTS... ALL THE POWERS OF STORM AND LIGHTNING, TEMPEST AND THUNDER!
EVEN SO, THE COMBINED MIGHT OF TWO SUCH DOUGHTY WARRIORS MIGHT WELL LAY WASTE TO ASGARD ITSELF.
THEREFORE, THE STRUGGLE SHALL TAKE PLACE IN THE RUINED LANDS OF SKARTHEIM FAR BEYOND THE ABODE OF GODS OR MEN.
THE VICTOR'S REWARD SHALL BE MJOLNIR, THE ENCHANTED HAMMER.
THE LOSER'S REWARD SHALL BE A FUNERAL PYRE.
FOR STAKES SO HIGH, THE PRICE MUST BE GREAT.
THIS FIGHT... IS TO THE DEATH!
I HAVE SPOKEN!
GET THEE TO SKARTHEIM!
FFSHHAMMM!

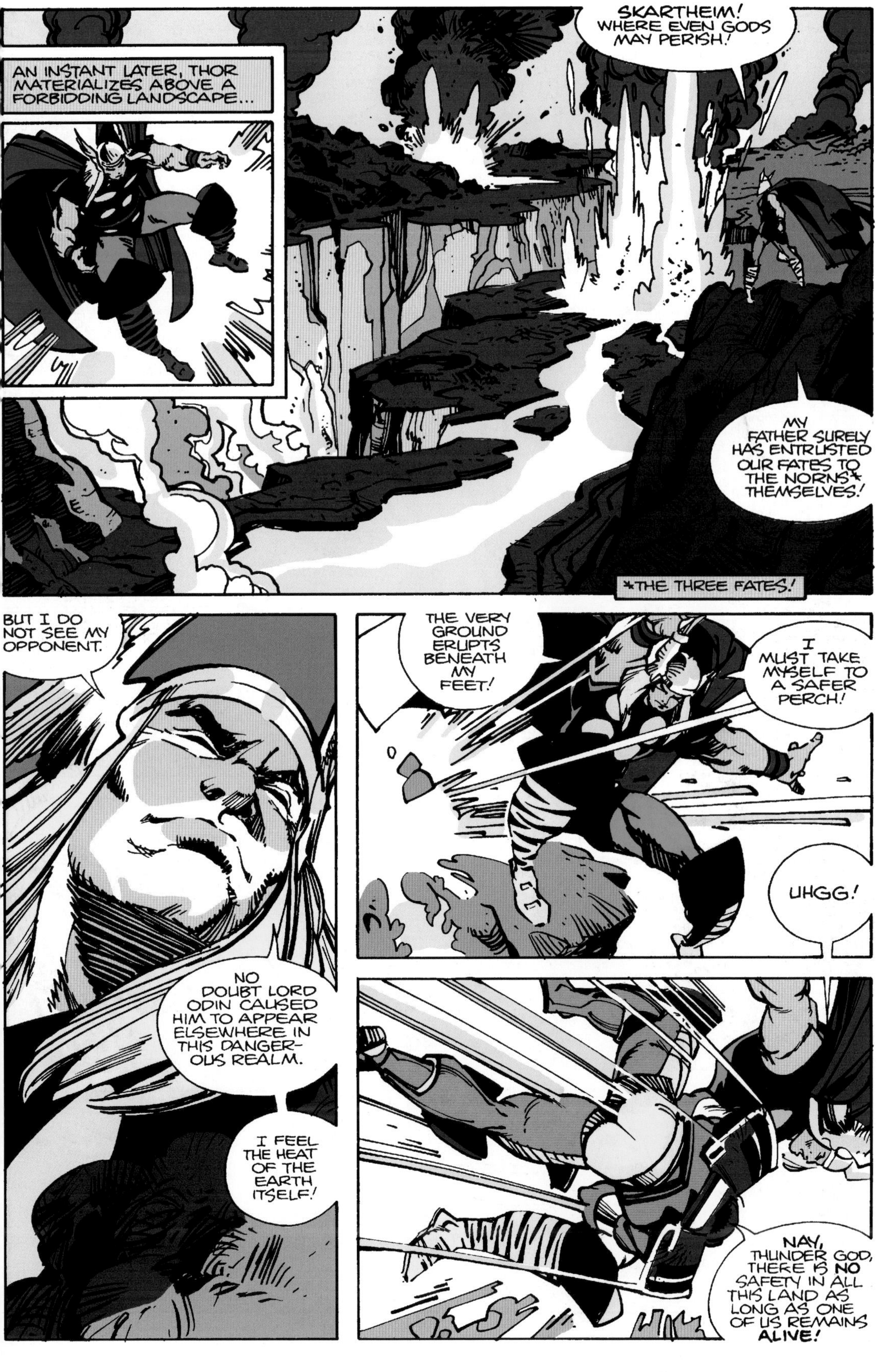

AN INSTANT LATER, THOR MATERIALIZES ABOVE A FORBIDDING LANDSCAPE...
SKARTHEIM! WHERE EVEN GODS MAY PERISH!
MY FATHER SURELY HAS ENTRUSTED OUR FATES TO THE NORNS* THEMSELVES!
*THE THREE FATES!
BUT I DO NOT SEE MY OPPONENT.
NO DOUBT LORD ODIN CAUSED HIM TO APPEAR ELSEWHERE IN THIS DANGER-OUS REALM.
I FEEL THE HEAT OF THE EARTH ITSELF!
THE VERY GROUND ERUPTS BENEATH MY FEET!
I MUST TAKE MYSELF TO A SAFER PERCH!
UHGG!
NAY, THUNDER GOD, THERE IS NO SAFETY IN ALL THIS LAND AS LONG AS ONE OF US REMAINS ALIVE!

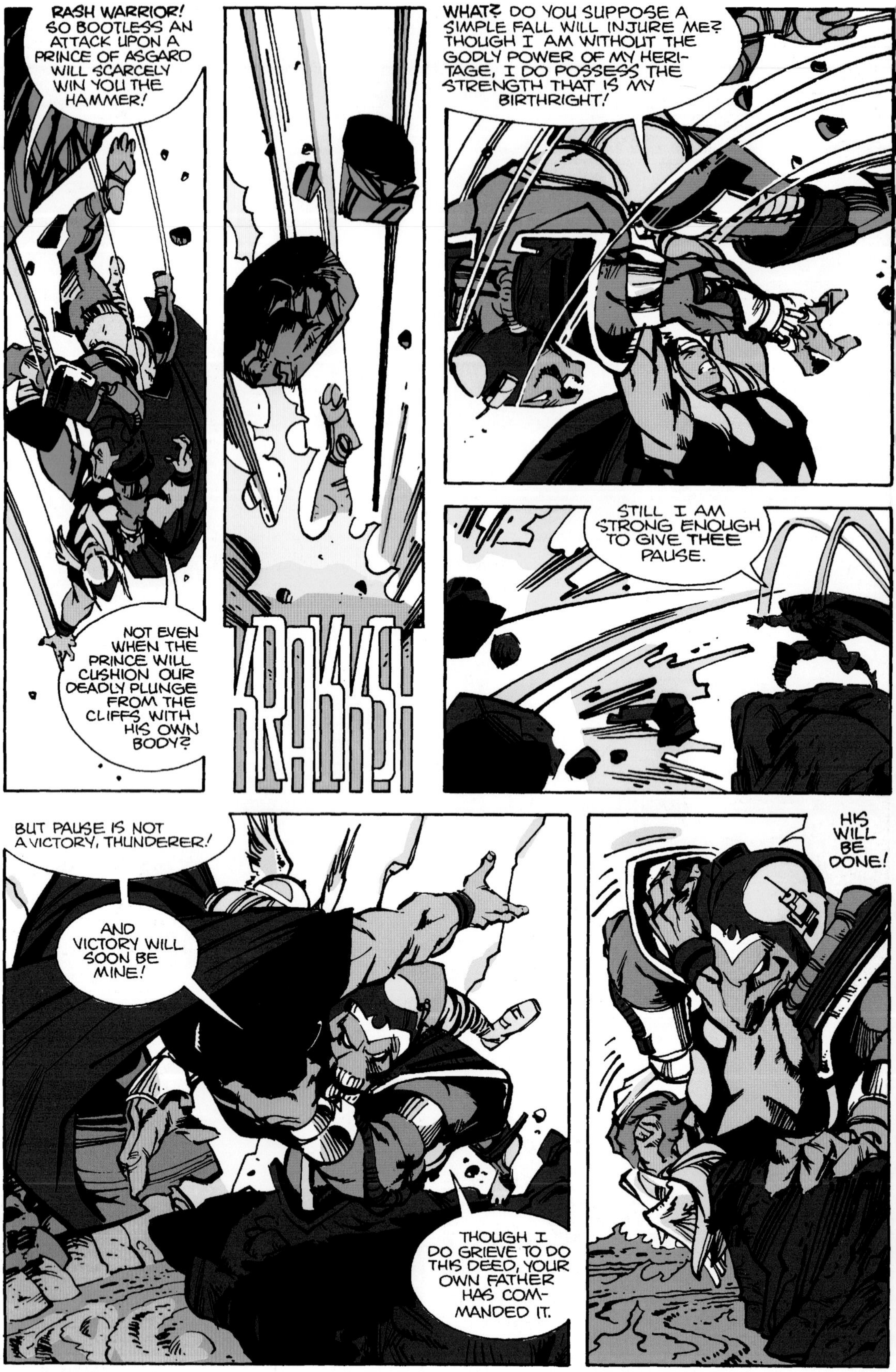
RASH WARRIOR! SO BOOTLESS AN ATTACK UPON A PRINCE OF ASGARD WILL SCARCELY WIN YOU THE HAMMER!
NOT EVEN WHEN THE PRINCE WILL CUSHION OUR DEADLY PLUNGE FROM THE CLIFFS WITH HIS OWN BODY?
KRAKKSH
WHAT? DO YOU SUPPOSE A SIMPLE FALL WILL INJURE ME? THOUGH I AM WITHOUT THE GODLY POWER OF MY HERITAGE, I DO POSSESS THE STRENGTH THAT IS MY BIRTHRIGHT!
STILL I AM STRONG ENOUGH TO GIVE THEE PAUSE.
BUT PAUSE IS NOT A VICTORY, THUNDERER!
AND VICTORY WILL SOON BE MINE!
THOUGH I DO GRIEVE TO DO THIS DEED, YOUR OWN FATHER HAS COMMANDED IT.
HIS WILL BE DONE!

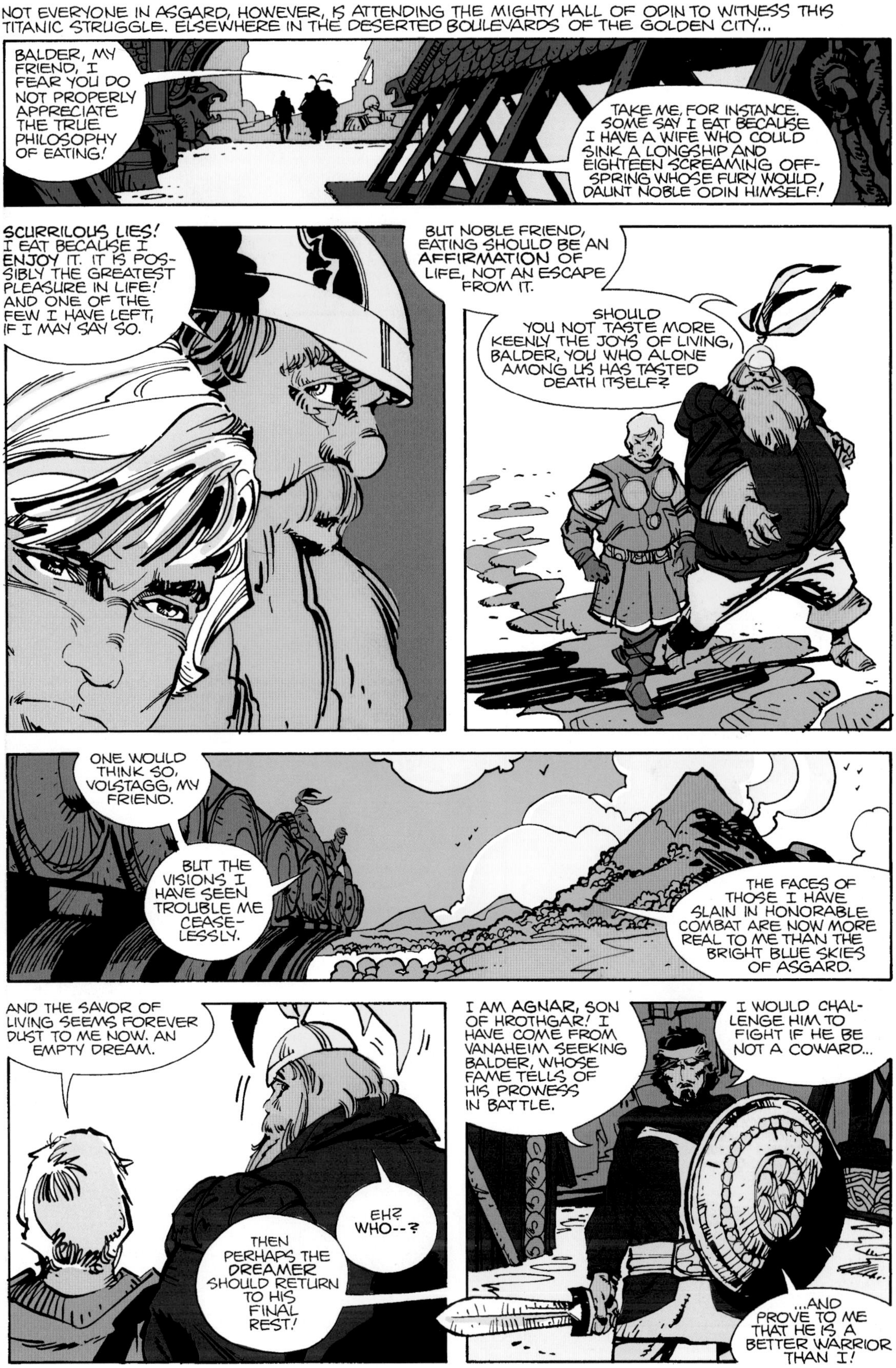
NOT EVERYONE IN ASGARD, HOWEVER, IS ATTENDING THE MIGHTY HALL OF ODIN TO WITNESS THIS TITANIC STRUGGLE. ELSEWHERE IN THE DESERTED BOULEVARDS OF THE GOLDEN CITY...
BALDER, MY FRIEND, I FEAR YOU DO NOT PROPERLY APPRECIATE THE TRUE PHILOSOPHY OF EATING!
TAKE ME, FOR INSTANCE. SOME SAY I EAT BECAUSE I HAVE A WIFE WHO COULD SINK A LONGSHIP AND EIGHTEEN SCREAMING OFF-SPRING WHOSE FURY WOULD DAUNT NOBLE ODIN HIMSELF!
SCURRILOUS LIES! I EAT BECAUSE I ENJOY IT. IT IS POS-SIBLY THE GREATEST PLEASURE IN LIFE! AND ONE OF THE FEW I HAVE LEFT, IF I MAY SAY SO.
BUT NOBLE FRIEND, EATING SHOULD BE AN AFFIRMATION OF LIFE, NOT AN ESCAPE FROM IT.
SHOULD YOU NOT TASTE MORE KEENLY THE JOYS OF LIVING, BALDER, YOU WHO ALONE AMONG US HAS TASTED DEATH ITSELF?
ONE WOULD THINK SO, VOLSTAGG, MY FRIEND.
BUT THE VISIONS I HAVE SEEN TROUBLE ME CEASE-LESSLY.
THE FACES OF THOSE I HAVE SLAIN IN HONORABLE COMBAT ARE NOW MORE REAL TO ME THAN THE BRIGHT BLUE SKIES OF ASGARD.
AND THE SAVOR OF LIVING SEEMS FOREVER DUST TO ME NOW. AN EMPTY DREAM.
EH? WHO--?
THEN PERHAPS THE DREAMER SHOULD RETURN TO HIS FINAL REST!
I AM AGNAR, SON OF HROTHGAR! I HAVE COME FROM VANAHEIM SEEKING BALDER, WHOSE FAME TELLS OF HIS PROWESS IN BATTLE.
I WOULD CHAL-LENGE HIM TO FIGHT IF HE BE NOT A COWARD...
...AND PROVE TO ME THAT HE IS A BETTER WARRIOR THAN I!

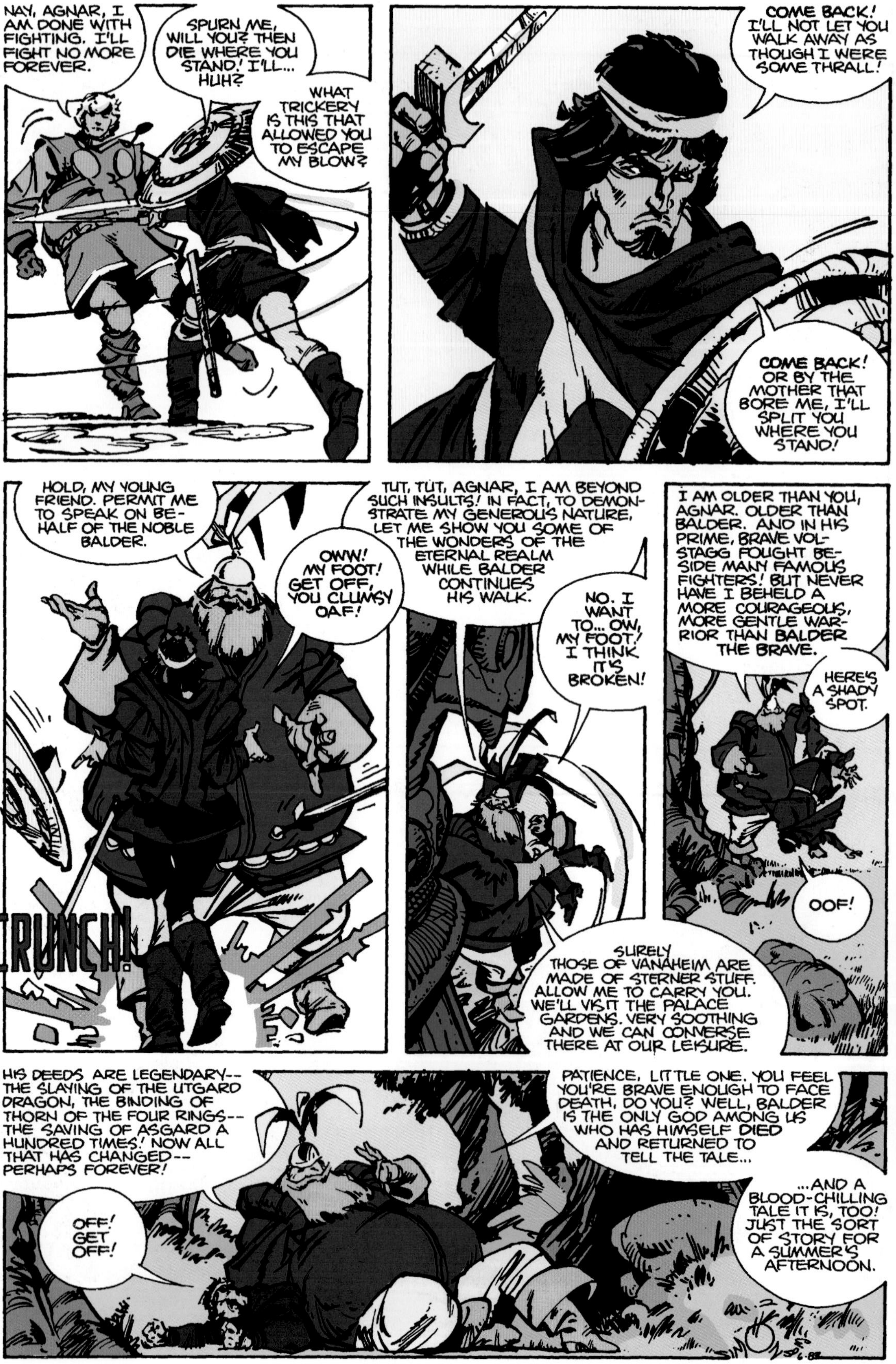
NAY, AGNAR, I AM DONE WITH FIGHTING. I'LL FIGHT NO MORE FOREVER.
SPURN ME, WILL YOU? THEN DIE WHERE YOU STAND! I'LL... HUH?
WHAT TRICKERY IS THIS THAT ALLOWED YOU TO ESCAPE MY BLOW?
COME BACK! I'LL NOT LET YOU WALK AWAY AS THOUGH I WERE SOME THRALL!
COME BACK! OR BY THE MOTHER THAT BORE ME, I'LL SPLIT YOU WHERE YOU STAND!
HOLD, MY YOUNG FRIEND. PERMIT ME TO SPEAK ON BE-HALF OF THE NOBLE BALDER.
OWW! MY FOOT! GET OFF, YOU CLUMSY OAF!
CRUNCH!
TUT, TUT, AGNAR, I AM BEYOND SUCH INSULTS! IN FACT, TO DEMON-STRATE MY GENEROUS NATURE, LET ME SHOW YOU SOME OF THE WONDERS OF THE ETERNAL REALM WHILE BALDER CONTINUES HIS WALK.
NO. I WANT TO... OW, MY FOOT! I THINK IT'S BROKEN!
SURELY THOSE OF VANAHEIM ARE MADE OF STERNER STUFF. ALLOW ME TO CARRY YOU. WE'LL VISIT THE PALACE GARDENS. VERY SOOTHING AND WE CAN CONVERSE THERE AT OUR LEISURE.
I AM OLDER THAN YOU, AGNAR. OLDER THAN BALDER. AND IN HIS PRIME, BRAVE VOL-STAGG FOUGHT BE-SIDE MANY FAMOUS FIGHTERS! BUT NEVER HAVE I BEHELD A MORE COURAGEOUS, MORE GENTLE WAR-RIOR THAN BALDER THE BRAVE.
HERE'S A SHADY SPOT.
OOF!
HIS DEEDS ARE LEGENDARY-- THE SLAYING OF THE UTGARD DRAGON, THE BINDING OF THORN OF THE FOUR RINGS-- THE SAVING OF ASGARD A HUNDRED TIMES! NOW ALL THAT HAS CHANGED-- PERHAPS FOREVER!
OFF! GET OFF!
PATIENCE, LITTLE ONE. YOU FEEL YOU'RE BRAVE ENOUGH TO FACE DEATH, DO YOU? WELL, BALDER IS THE ONLY GOD AMONG US WHO HAS HIMSELF DIED AND RETURNED TO TELL THE TALE...
...AND A BLOOD-CHILLING TALE IT IS, TOO! JUST THE SORT OF STORY FOR A SUMMER'S AFTERNOON.

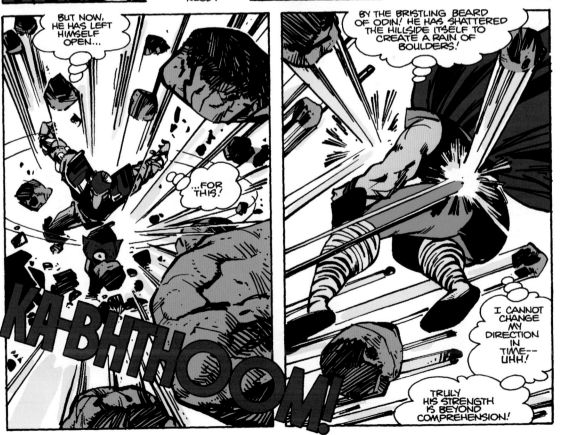

IT IS, HOWEVER, A TALE WE WILL HEAR ANOTHER TIME, FOR IN THE REMOTE LAND OF SKARTHEIM, WE FIND...

BACK, WARRIOR! THE HAMMER IS NOT YET THINE!

NEVER BEFORE HAVE I FOUGHT ONE SO WORTHY OR NOBLE! BUT IF I FAIL...

NEITHER HERO SURRENDERS AN INCH AS THE BATTLE RAGES ACROSS THE ANCIENT LAND, TEARING THE VERY MOUNTAINS FROM THEIR ROOTS UNTIL...

SHAKK!!!

...WHAT OF MY GUARDIANSHIP OF EARTH? WHO SHALL BE HER CHAMPION IN TIME OF NEED?

I SENSE THAT MY FOE IS TIRING EVEN AS I! THE MOMENT OF DECISION IS UPON US!

WILL THE THUNDER GOD NEVER BREAK? AGAIN HE LEAPS TO DO BATTLE WITH UNDIMINISHED FERVOR!

BUT NOW, HE HAS LEFT HIMSELF OPEN...

...FOR THIS!

KA-BHTHOOM!

BY THE BRISTLING BEARD OF ODIN! HE HAS SHATTERED THE HILLSIDE ITSELF TO CREATE A RAIN OF BOULDERS!

I CANNOT CHANGE MY DIRECTION IN TIME-- UHH!

TRULY HIS STRENGTH IS BEYOND COMPREHENSION!

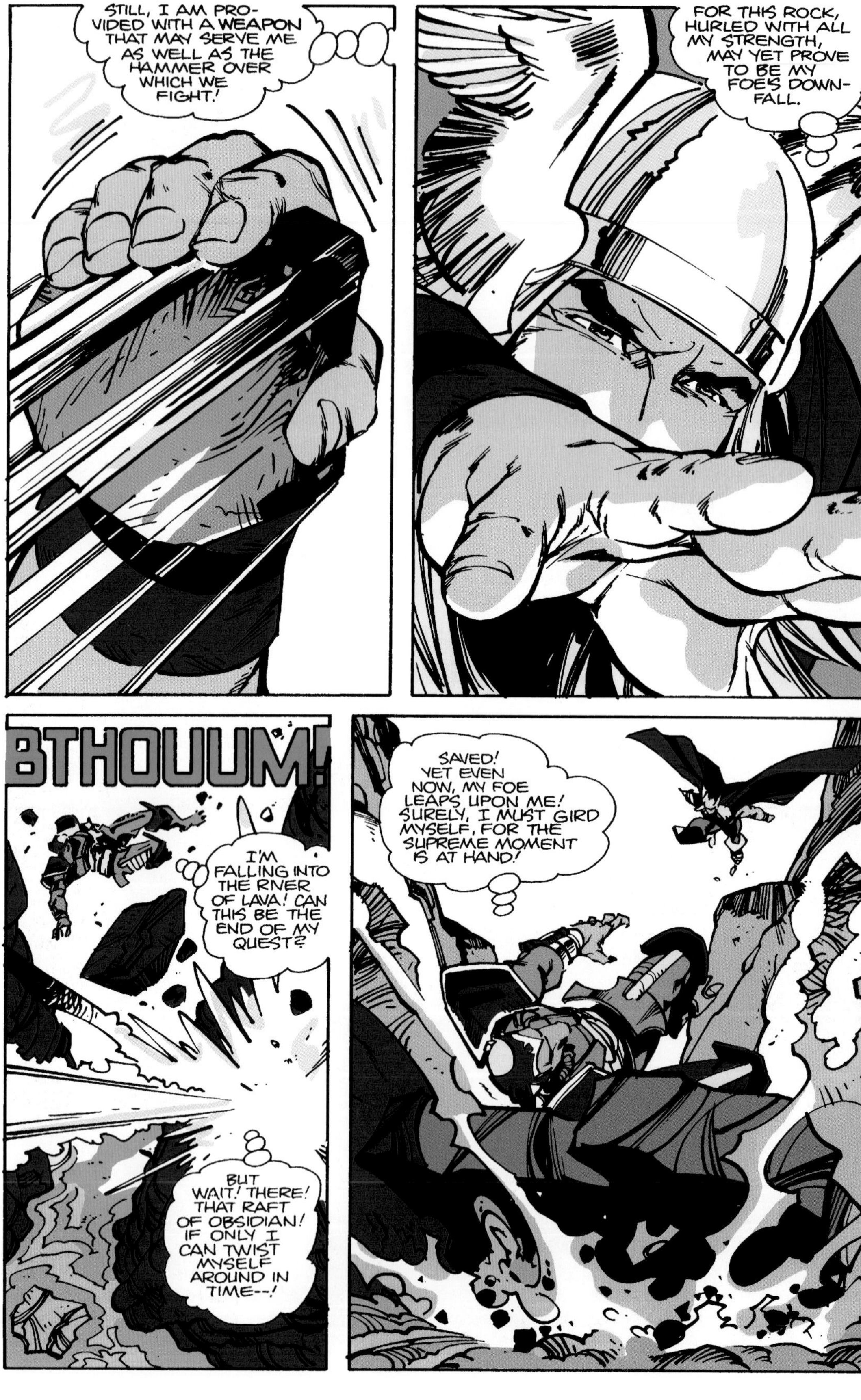

STILL, I AM PROVIDED WITH A WEAPON THAT MAY SERVE ME AS WELL AS THE HAMMER OVER WHICH WE FIGHT!
FOR THIS ROCK, HURLED WITH ALL MY STRENGTH, MAY YET PROVE TO BE MY FOE'S DOWNFALL.
BTHOUUM!
I'M FALLING INTO THE RIVER OF LAVA! CAN THIS BE THE END OF MY QUEST?
BUT WAIT! THERE! THAT RAFT OF OBSIDIAN! IF ONLY I CAN TWIST MYSELF AROUND IN TIME--!
SAVED! YET EVEN NOW, MY FOE LEAPS UPON ME! SURELY, I MUST GIRD MYSELF, FOR THE SUPREME MOMENT IS AT HAND!

MERE WORDS CANNOT DESCRIBE THE POWER OF THE BLOWS AS BOTH COMBATANTS UNLEASH THEIR FULL FURY IN ONE FINAL CATACLYSMIC EFFORT!

THE BLAST LEVELS THE SURROUNDING COUNTRYSIDE...

...TIME IS FROZEN IN THE INSTANT...

...AND ALL OF NATURE SEEMS TO HOLD ITS BREATH...

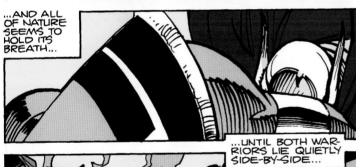

...UNTIL BOTH WARRIORS LIE QUIETLY SIDE-BY-SIDE...

...AS THEIR OBSIDIAN RAFT FLOATS DOWN THE RIVER OF LAVA TOWARD A SPECTACULAR DESTRUCTION!

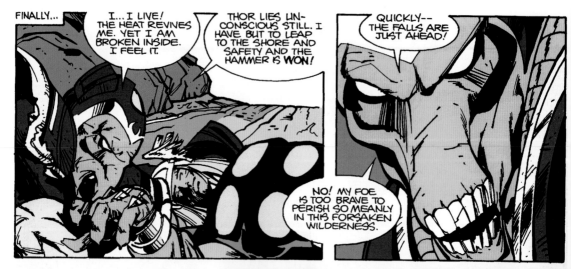

FINALLY...

I...I LIVE! THE HEAT REVIVES ME. YET I AM BROKEN INSIDE. I FEEL IT.

THOR LIES UN-CONSCIOUS STILL. I HAVE BUT TO LEAP TO THE SHORE AND SAFETY AND THE HAMMER IS WON!

QUICKLY-- THE FALLS ARE JUST AHEAD!

NO! MY FOE IS TOO BRAVE TO PERISH SO MEANLY IN THIS FORSAKEN WILDERNESS.

I...UGH...I MUST CARRY US BOTH TO SAFETY.

TOO LATE! THE RAFT AL-READY PLUNGES O'ER THE FIERY BRINK! BUT I MUST TRY!

AND WITH A FINAL GROAN, BETA RAY BILL LEAPS FOR THE SHORE...

...ONLY TO BE ENVELOPED BY A BLINDING FLASH OF ENERGY...

...THAT TRANSPORTS HIM IN THE WINK OF AN EYE TO THE GLEAMING HALLS OF ASGARD BEFORE A SHOCKED AND SILENT GATHERING.

LORD ODIN, YOUR SON YET LIVES. THE FINEST FOE I HAVE EVER FOUGHT. BUT I HAVE BESTED HIM.

THE HAMMER... IS MINE!

NEXT: **SOMETHING OLD, SOMETHING NEW...!**

BETTER STOCK UP ON COPIES, KIDS! THIS ONE'LL BE A COLLECTOR'S ITEM FOR SURE!

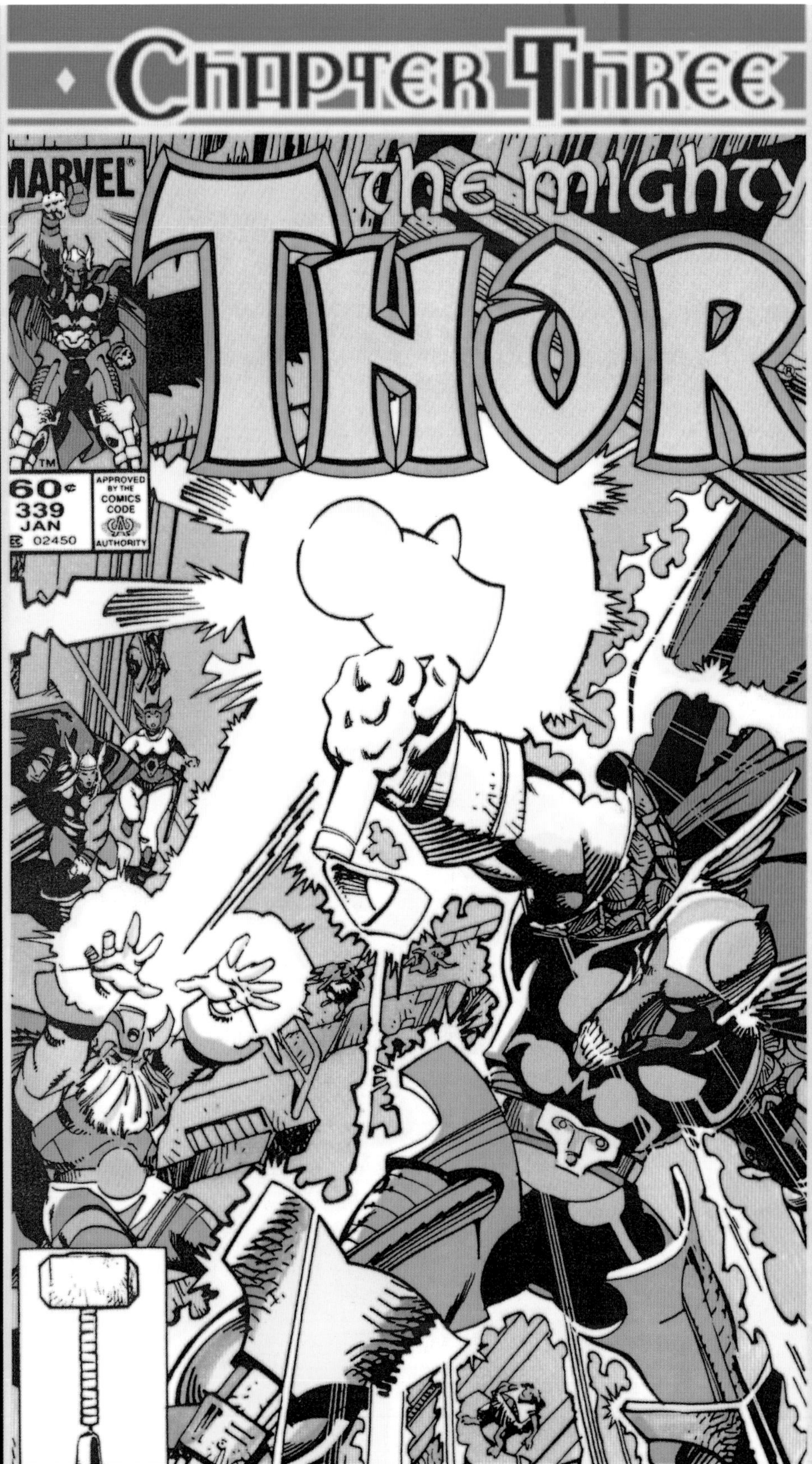
Chapter Three
MARVEL
the mighty
THOR
60¢
339
JAN
02450
APPROVED BY THE COMICS CODE AUTHORITY

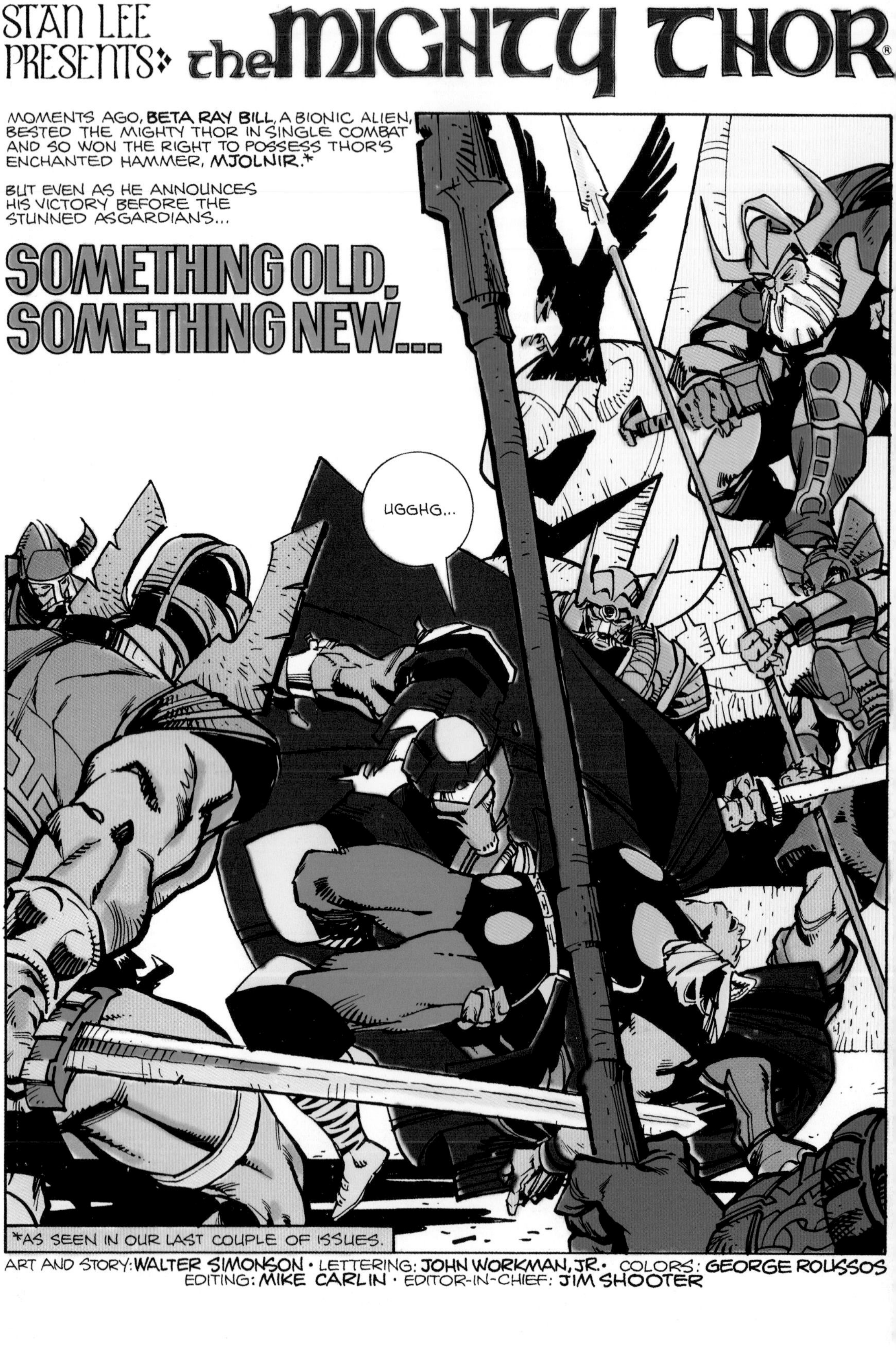
STAN LEE PRESENTS: the MIGHTY THOR®
MOMENTS AGO, BETA RAY BILL, A BIONIC ALIEN, BESTED THE MIGHTY THOR IN SINGLE COMBAT AND SO WON THE RIGHT TO POSSESS THOR'S ENCHANTED HAMMER, MJOLNIR.*
BUT EVEN AS HE ANNOUNCES HIS VICTORY BEFORE THE STUNNED ASGARDIANS...
SOMETHING OLD, SOMETHING NEW...
UGGHG...
*AS SEEN IN OUR LAST COUPLE OF ISSUES.
ART AND STORY: WALTER SIMONSON • LETTERING: JOHN WORKMAN, JR. • COLORS: GEORGE ROUSSOS
EDITING: MIKE CARLIN • EDITOR-IN-CHIEF: JIM SHOOTER

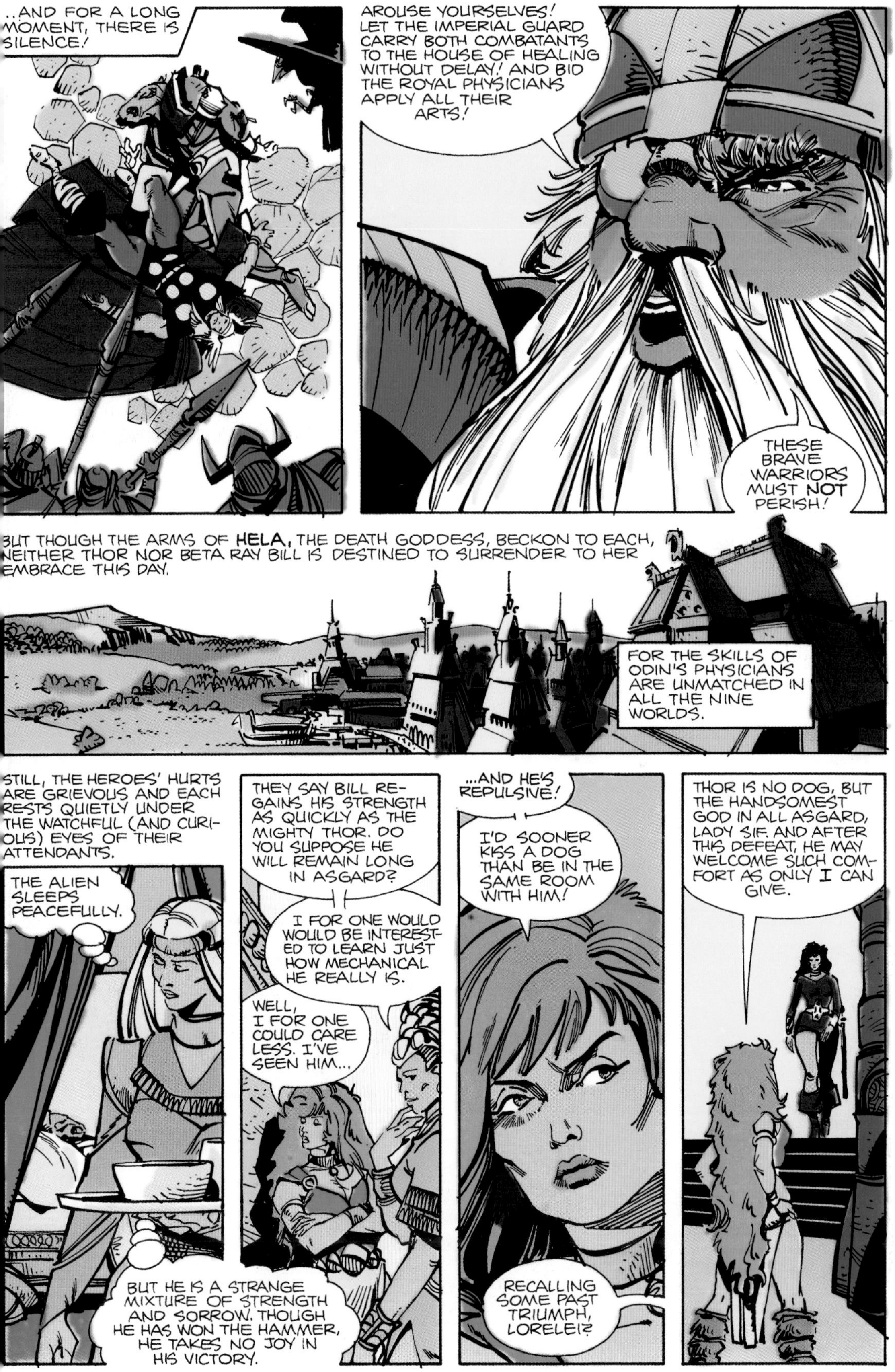
..AND FOR A LONG MOMENT, THERE IS SILENCE!
AROUSE YOURSELVES! LET THE IMPERIAL GUARD CARRY BOTH COMBATANTS TO THE HOUSE OF HEALING WITHOUT DELAY! AND BID THE ROYAL PHYSICIANS APPLY ALL THEIR ARTS!
THESE BRAVE WARRIORS MUST NOT PERISH!
BUT THOUGH THE ARMS OF HELA, THE DEATH GODDESS, BECKON TO EACH, NEITHER THOR NOR BETA RAY BILL IS DESTINED TO SURRENDER TO HER EMBRACE THIS DAY.
FOR THE SKILLS OF ODIN'S PHYSICIANS ARE UNMATCHED IN ALL THE NINE WORLDS.
STILL, THE HEROES' HURTS ARE GRIEVOUS AND EACH RESTS QUIETLY UNDER THE WATCHFUL (AND CURIOUS) EYES OF THEIR ATTENDANTS.
THE ALIEN SLEEPS PEACEFULLY.
BUT HE IS A STRANGE MIXTURE OF STRENGTH AND SORROW. THOUGH HE HAS WON THE HAMMER, HE TAKES NO JOY IN HIS VICTORY.
THEY SAY BILL REGAINS HIS STRENGTH AS QUICKLY AS THE MIGHTY THOR. DO YOU SUPPOSE HE WILL REMAIN LONG IN ASGARD?
I FOR ONE WOULD WOULD BE INTERESTED TO LEARN JUST HOW MECHANICAL HE REALLY IS.
WELL, I FOR ONE COULD CARE LESS. I'VE SEEN HIM...
...AND HE'S REPULSIVE!
I'D SOONER KISS A DOG THAN BE IN THE SAME ROOM WITH HIM!
RECALLING SOME PAST TRIUMPH, LORELEI?
THOR IS NO DOG, BUT THE HANDSOMEST GOD IN ALL ASGARD, LADY SIF. AND AFTER THIS DEFEAT, HE MAY WELCOME SUCH COMFORT AS ONLY I CAN GIVE.

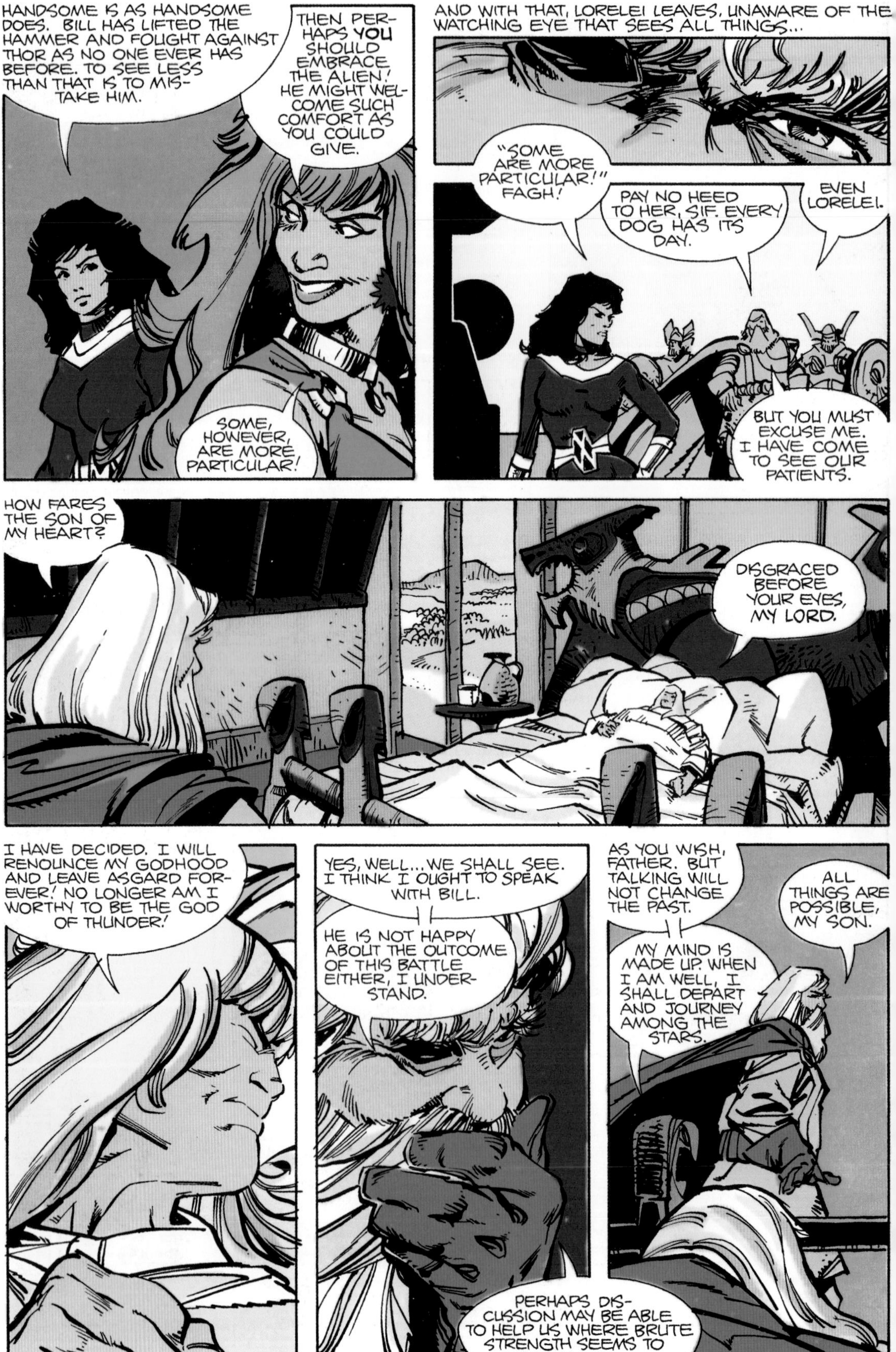
HANDSOME IS AS HANDSOME DOES. BILL HAS LIFTED THE HAMMER AND FOUGHT AGAINST THOR AS NO ONE EVER HAS BEFORE. TO SEE LESS THAN THAT IS TO MISTAKE HIM.
THEN PERHAPS YOU SHOULD EMBRACE THE ALIEN! HE MIGHT WELCOME SUCH COMFORT AS YOU COULD GIVE.
SOME, HOWEVER, ARE MORE PARTICULAR!
AND WITH THAT, LORELEI LEAVES, UNAWARE OF THE WATCHING EYE THAT SEES ALL THINGS...
"SOME ARE MORE PARTICULAR!" FAGH!
PAY NO HEED TO HER, SIF. EVERY DOG HAS ITS DAY.
EVEN LORELEI.
BUT YOU MUST EXCUSE ME. I HAVE COME TO SEE OUR PATIENTS.
HOW FARES THE SON OF MY HEART?
DISGRACED BEFORE YOUR EYES, MY LORD.
I HAVE DECIDED. I WILL RENOUNCE MY GODHOOD AND LEAVE ASGARD FOREVER! NO LONGER AM I WORTHY TO BE THE GOD OF THUNDER!
YES, WELL... WE SHALL SEE. I THINK I OUGHT TO SPEAK WITH BILL.
HE IS NOT HAPPY ABOUT THE OUTCOME OF THIS BATTLE EITHER, I UNDERSTAND.
PERHAPS DISCUSSION MAY BE ABLE TO HELP US WHERE BRUTE STRENGTH SEEMS TO HAVE FAILED.
AS YOU WISH, FATHER. BUT TALKING WILL NOT CHANGE THE PAST.
MY MIND IS MADE UP. WHEN I AM WELL, I SHALL DEPART AND JOURNEY AMONG THE STARS.
ALL THINGS ARE POSSIBLE, MY SON.

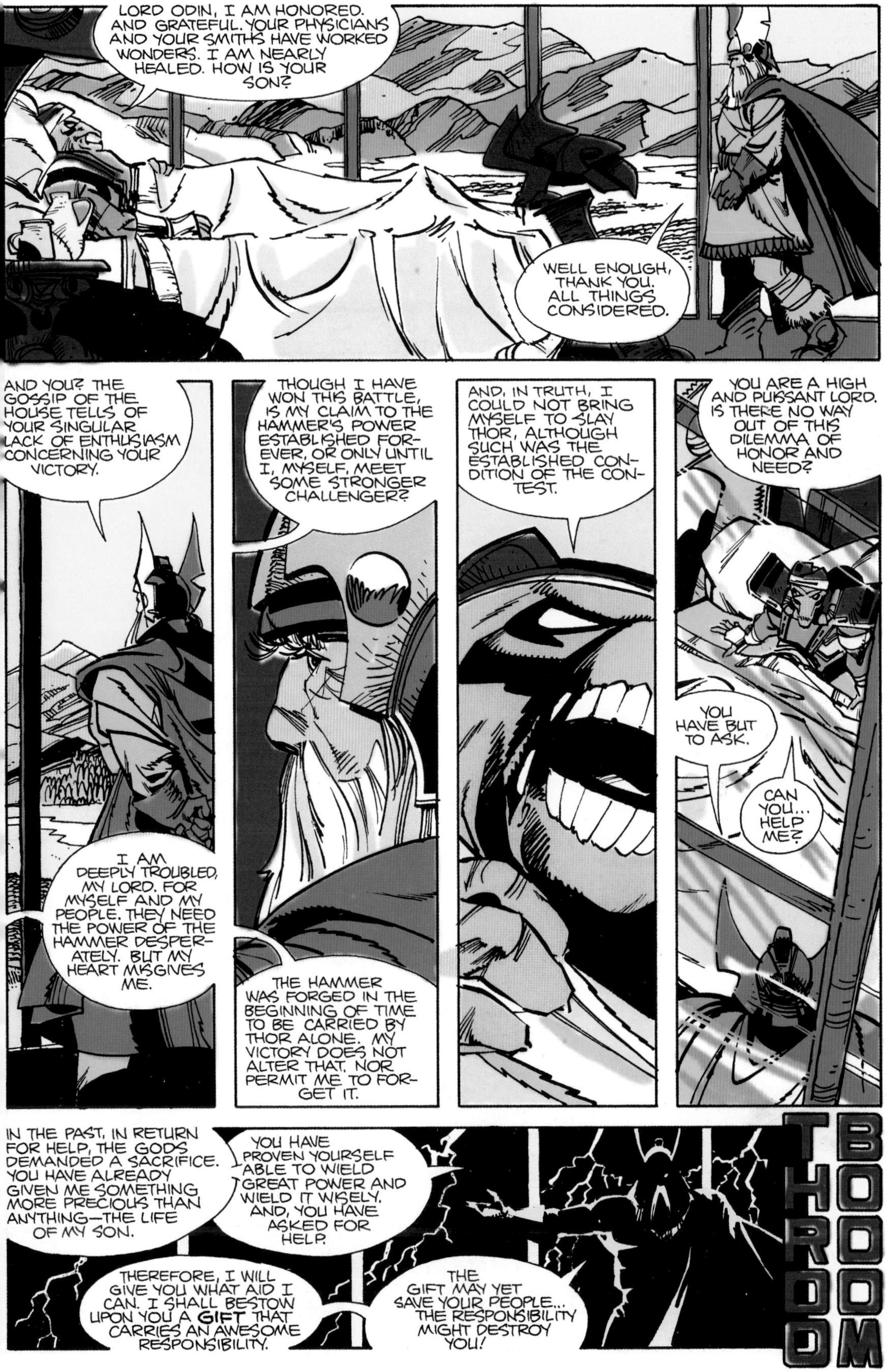

LORD ODIN, I AM HONORED. AND GRATEFUL. YOUR PHYSICIANS AND YOUR SMITHS HAVE WORKED WONDERS. I AM NEARLY HEALED. HOW IS YOUR SON?
WELL ENOUGH, THANK YOU. ALL THINGS CONSIDERED.
AND YOU? THE GOSSIP OF THE HOUSE TELLS OF YOUR SINGULAR LACK OF ENTHUSIASM CONCERNING YOUR VICTORY.
I AM DEEPLY TROUBLED, MY LORD. FOR MYSELF AND MY PEOPLE. THEY NEED THE POWER OF THE HAMMER DESPERATELY. BUT MY HEART MISGIVES ME.
THOUGH I HAVE WON THIS BATTLE, IS MY CLAIM TO THE HAMMER'S POWER ESTABLISHED FOREVER, OR ONLY UNTIL I, MYSELF, MEET SOME STRONGER CHALLENGER?
THE HAMMER WAS FORGED IN THE BEGINNING OF TIME TO BE CARRIED BY THOR ALONE. MY VICTORY DOES NOT ALTER THAT. NOR PERMIT ME TO FORGET IT.
AND, IN TRUTH, I COULD NOT BRING MYSELF TO SLAY THOR, ALTHOUGH SUCH WAS THE ESTABLISHED CONDITION OF THE CONTEST.
YOU ARE A HIGH AND PUISSANT LORD. IS THERE NO WAY OUT OF THIS DILEMMA OF HONOR AND NEED?
YOU HAVE BUT TO ASK.
CAN YOU... HELP ME?
IN THE PAST, IN RETURN FOR HELP, THE GODS DEMANDED A SACRIFICE. YOU HAVE ALREADY GIVEN ME SOMETHING MORE PRECIOUS THAN ANYTHING—THE LIFE OF MY SON.
YOU HAVE PROVEN YOURSELF ABLE TO WIELD GREAT POWER AND WIELD IT WISELY. AND, YOU HAVE ASKED FOR HELP.
THEREFORE, I WILL GIVE YOU WHAT AID I CAN. I SHALL BESTOW UPON YOU A GIFT THAT CARRIES AN AWESOME RESPONSIBILITY.
THE GIFT MAY YET SAVE YOUR PEOPLE... THE RESPONSIBILITY MIGHT DESTROY YOU!
THROOD
BOOOOM

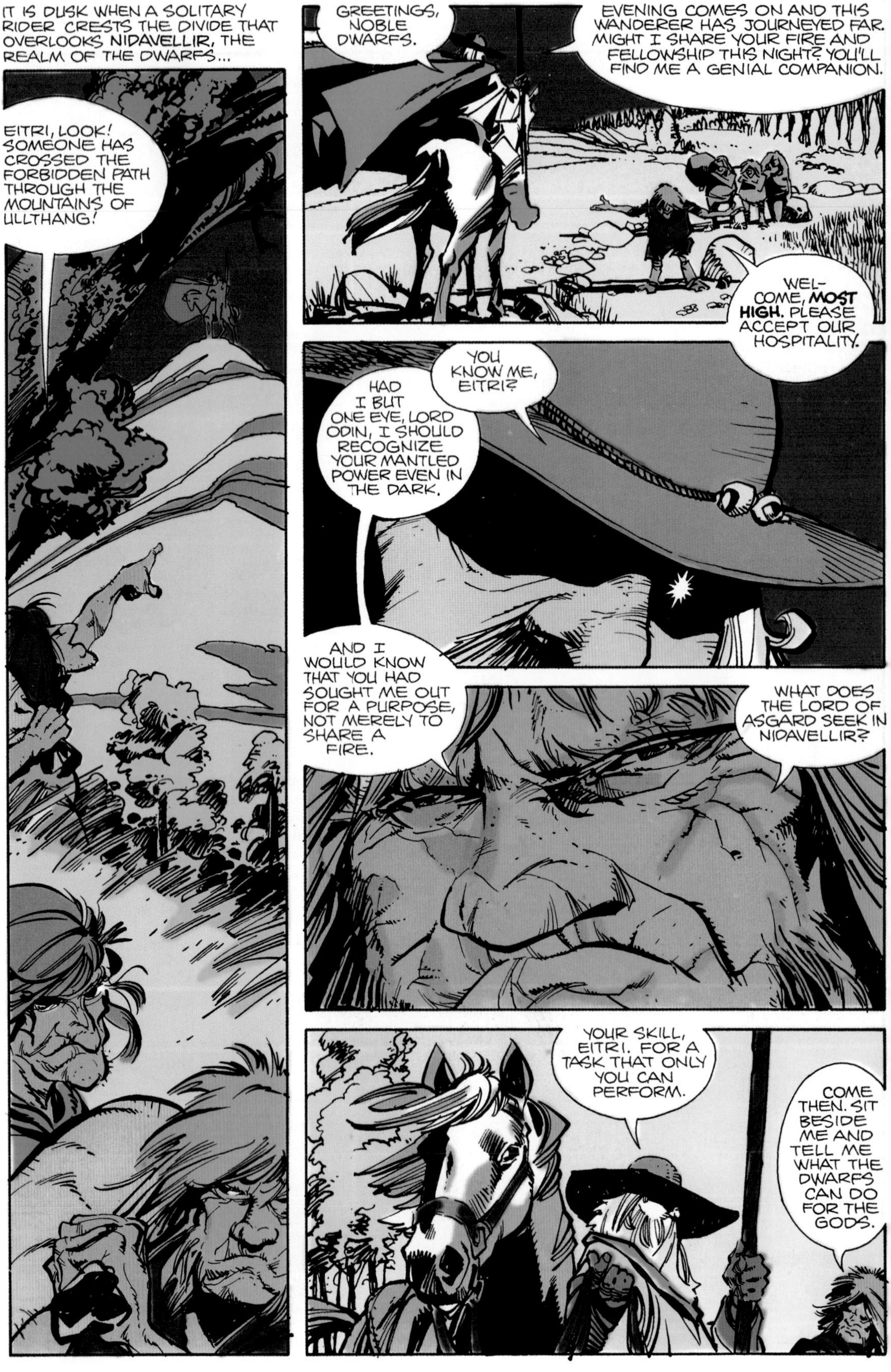
IT IS DUSK WHEN A SOLITARY RIDER CRESTS THE DIVIDE THAT OVERLOOKS NIDAVELLIR, THE REALM OF THE DWARFS...
EITRI, LOOK! SOMEONE HAS CROSSED THE FORBIDDEN PATH THROUGH THE MOUNTAINS OF ULLTHANG!
GREETINGS, NOBLE DWARFS.
EVENING COMES ON AND THIS WANDERER HAS JOURNEYED FAR. MIGHT I SHARE YOUR FIRE AND FELLOWSHIP THIS NIGHT? YOU'LL FIND ME A GENIAL COMPANION.
WEL-COME, MOST HIGH. PLEASE ACCEPT OUR HOSPITALITY.
YOU KNOW ME, EITRI?
HAD I BUT ONE EYE, LORD ODIN, I SHOULD RECOGNIZE YOUR MANTLED POWER EVEN IN THE DARK.
AND I WOULD KNOW THAT YOU HAD SOUGHT ME OUT FOR A PURPOSE, NOT MERELY TO SHARE A FIRE.
WHAT DOES THE LORD OF ASGARD SEEK IN NIDAVELLIR?
YOUR SKILL, EITRI. FOR A TASK THAT ONLY YOU CAN PERFORM.
COME THEN. SIT BESIDE ME AND TELL ME WHAT THE DWARFS CAN DO FOR THE GODS.

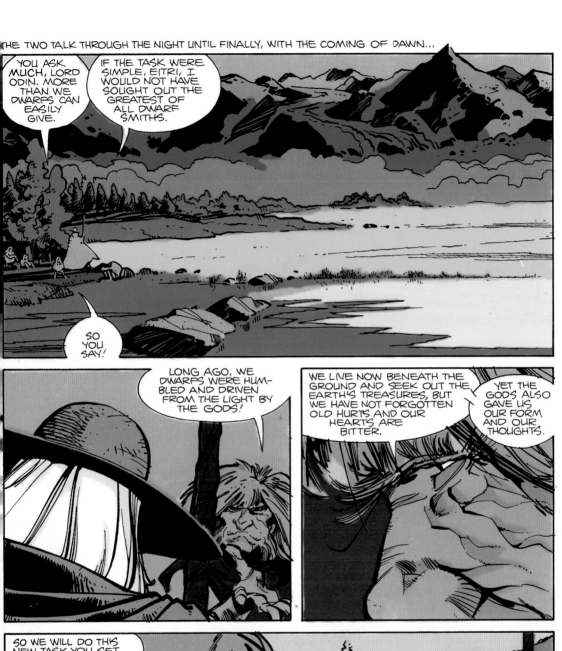

THE TWO TALK THROUGH THE NIGHT UNTIL FINALLY, WITH THE COMING OF DAWN...

YOU ASK MUCH, LORD ODIN. MORE THAN WE DWARFS CAN EASILY GIVE.

IF THE TASK WERE SIMPLE, EITRI, I WOULD NOT HAVE SOUGHT OUT THE GREATEST OF ALL DWARF SMITHS.

SO YOU SAY!

LONG AGO, WE DWARFS WERE HUMBLED AND DRIVEN FROM THE LIGHT BY THE GODS!

WE LIVE NOW BENEATH THE GROUND AND SEEK OUT THE EARTH'S TREASURES, BUT WE HAVE NOT FORGOTTEN OLD HURTS AND OUR HEARTS ARE BITTER.

YET THE GODS ALSO GAVE US OUR FORM AND OUR THOUGHTS.

SO WE WILL DO THIS NEW TASK YOU SET US BUT ON ONE CONDITION AND ONE CONDITION ONLY.

WE HAVE A CHAMPION AMONG US NOW, A MIGHTY FIGHTER.

SEND US A WOMAN WHO CAN DEFEAT HIM AND WE WILL DO THIS THING YOU ASK. BUT IF SHE LOSES, SHE MUST REMAIN WITH THE DWARFS FOREVER, TO SERVE OUR CHAMPION AS HIS CHATTEL!

THUS DO WE REPAY THE GODS FOR ANCIENT WRONGS!

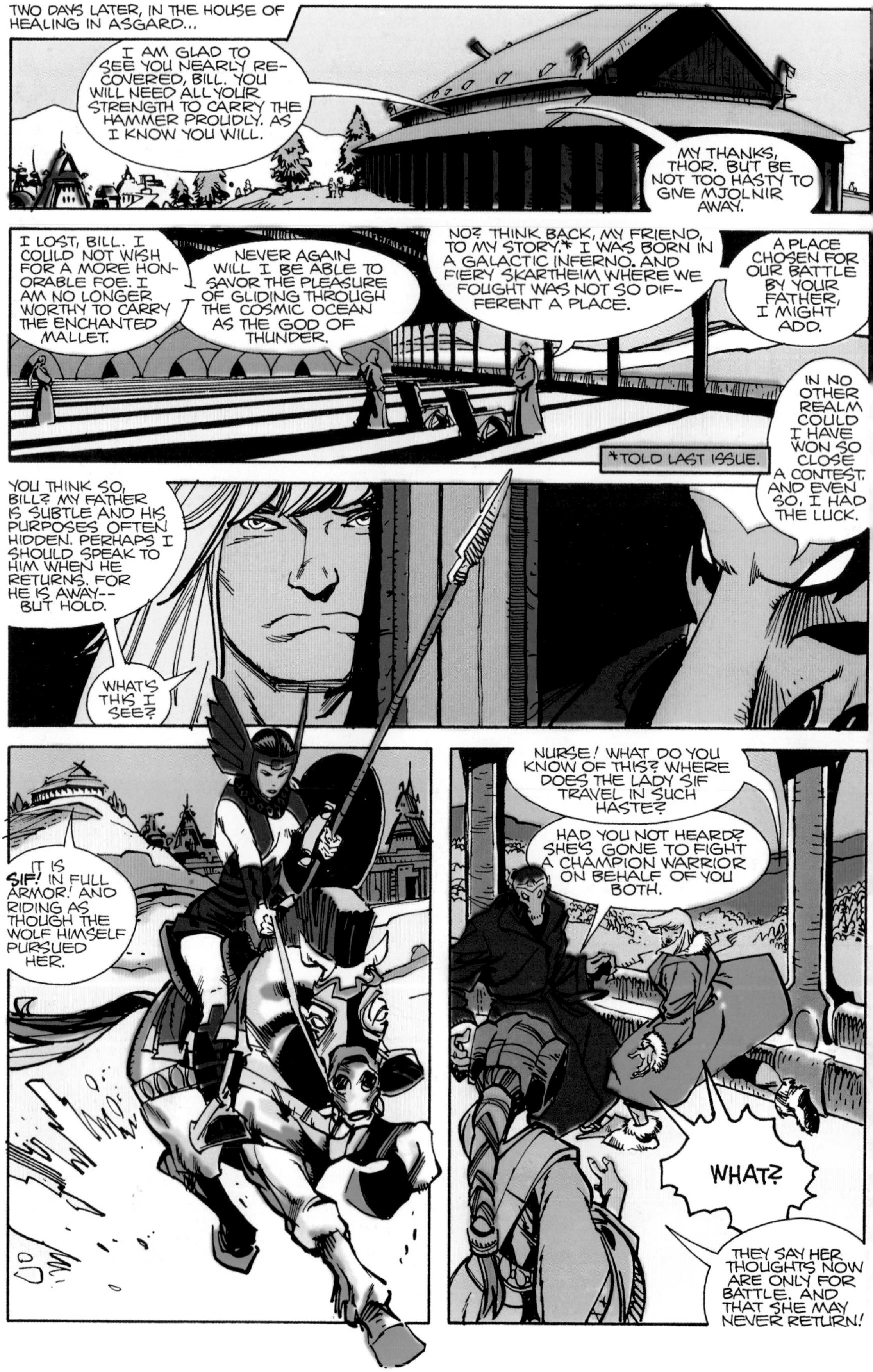
TWO DAYS LATER, IN THE HOUSE OF HEALING IN ASGARD...
I AM GLAD TO SEE YOU NEARLY RECOVERED, BILL. YOU WILL NEED ALL YOUR STRENGTH TO CARRY THE HAMMER PROUDLY. AS I KNOW YOU WILL.
MY THANKS, THOR. BUT BE NOT TOO HASTY TO GIVE MJOLNIR AWAY.
I LOST, BILL. I COULD NOT WISH FOR A MORE HONORABLE FOE. I AM NO LONGER WORTHY TO CARRY THE ENCHANTED MALLET.
NEVER AGAIN WILL I BE ABLE TO SAVOR THE PLEASURE OF GLIDING THROUGH THE COSMIC OCEAN AS THE GOD OF THUNDER.
NO? THINK BACK, MY FRIEND, TO MY STORY.* I WAS BORN IN A GALACTIC INFERNO. AND FIERY SKARTHEIM WHERE WE FOUGHT WAS NOT SO DIFFERENT A PLACE.
A PLACE CHOSEN FOR OUR BATTLE BY YOUR FATHER, I MIGHT ADD.
*TOLD LAST ISSUE.
IN NO OTHER REALM COULD I HAVE WON SO CLOSE A CONTEST. AND EVEN SO, I HAD THE LUCK.
YOU THINK SO, BILL? MY FATHER IS SUBTLE AND HIS PURPOSES OFTEN HIDDEN. PERHAPS I SHOULD SPEAK TO HIM WHEN HE RETURNS. FOR HE IS AWAY-- BUT HOLD.
WHAT'S THIS I SEE?
IT IS SIF! IN FULL ARMOR! AND RIDING AS THOUGH THE WOLF HIMSELF PURSUED HER.
NURSE! WHAT DO YOU KNOW OF THIS? WHERE DOES THE LADY SIF TRAVEL IN SUCH HASTE?
HAD YOU NOT HEARD? SHE'S GONE TO FIGHT A CHAMPION WARRIOR ON BEHALF OF YOU BOTH.
WHAT?
THEY SAY HER THOUGHTS NOW ARE ONLY FOR BATTLE. AND THAT SHE MAY NEVER RETURN!

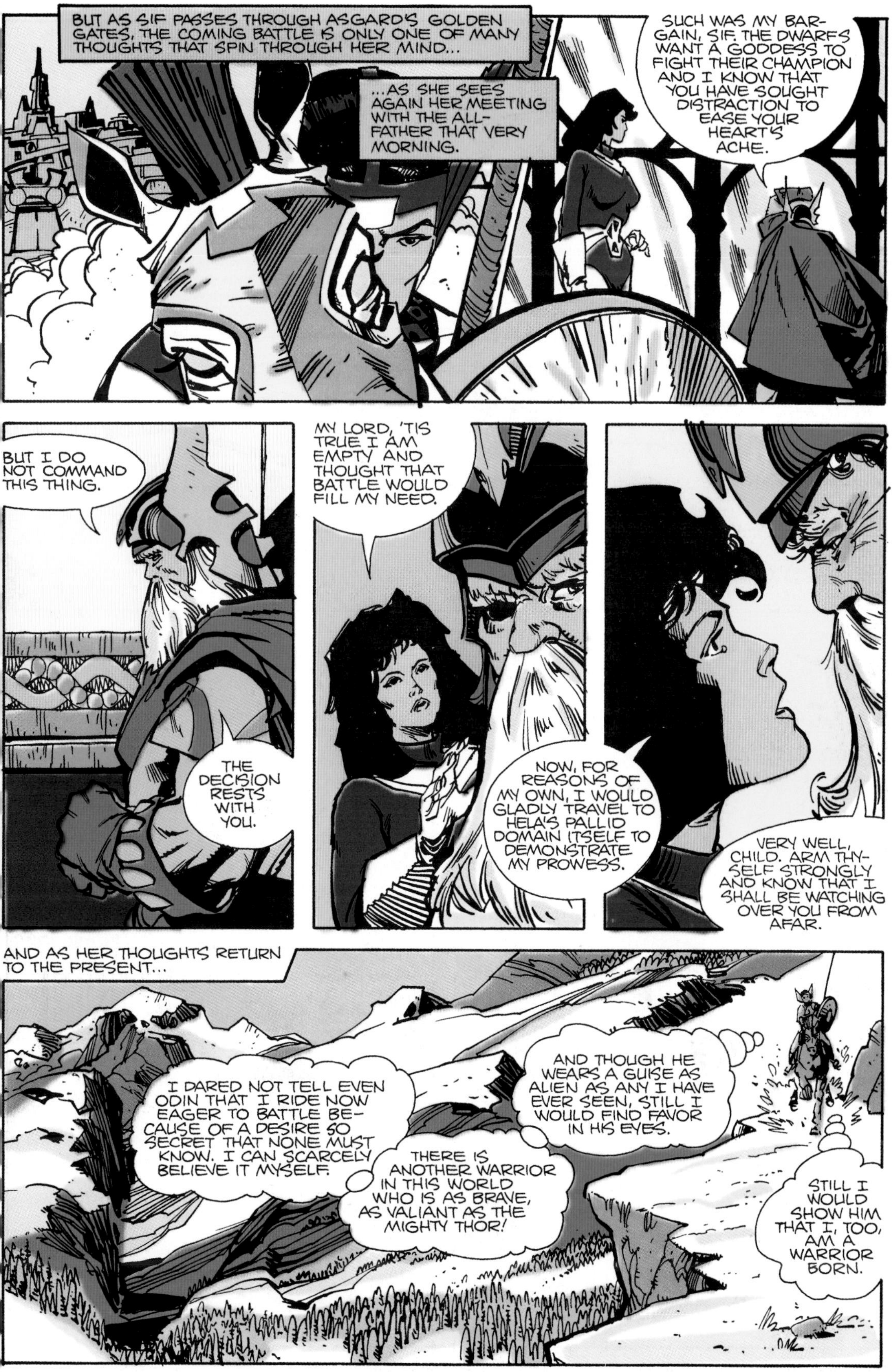
BUT AS SIF PASSES THROUGH ASGARD'S GOLDEN GATES, THE COMING BATTLE IS ONLY ONE OF MANY THOUGHTS THAT SPIN THROUGH HER MIND...
...AS SHE SEES AGAIN HER MEETING WITH THE ALL-FATHER THAT VERY MORNING.
SUCH WAS MY BARGAIN, SIF. THE DWARFS WANT A GODDESS TO FIGHT THEIR CHAMPION AND I KNOW THAT YOU HAVE SOUGHT DISTRACTION TO EASE YOUR HEART'S ACHE.
BUT I DO NOT COMMAND THIS THING.
THE DECISION RESTS WITH YOU.
MY LORD, 'TIS TRUE I AM EMPTY AND THOUGHT THAT BATTLE WOULD FILL MY NEED.
NOW, FOR REASONS OF MY OWN, I WOULD GLADLY TRAVEL TO HELA'S PALLID DOMAIN ITSELF TO DEMONSTRATE MY PROWESS.
VERY WELL, CHILD. ARM THYSELF STRONGLY AND KNOW THAT I SHALL BE WATCHING OVER YOU FROM AFAR.
AND AS HER THOUGHTS RETURN TO THE PRESENT...
I DARED NOT TELL EVEN ODIN THAT I RIDE NOW EAGER TO BATTLE BECAUSE OF A DESIRE SO SECRET THAT NONE MUST KNOW. I CAN SCARCELY BELIEVE IT MYSELF.
THERE IS ANOTHER WARRIOR IN THIS WORLD WHO IS AS BRAVE, AS VALIANT AS THE MIGHTY THOR!
AND THOUGH HE WEARS A GUISE AS ALIEN AS ANY I HAVE EVER SEEN, STILL I WOULD FIND FAVOR IN HIS EYES.
STILL I WOULD SHOW HIM THAT I, TOO, AM A WARRIOR BORN.

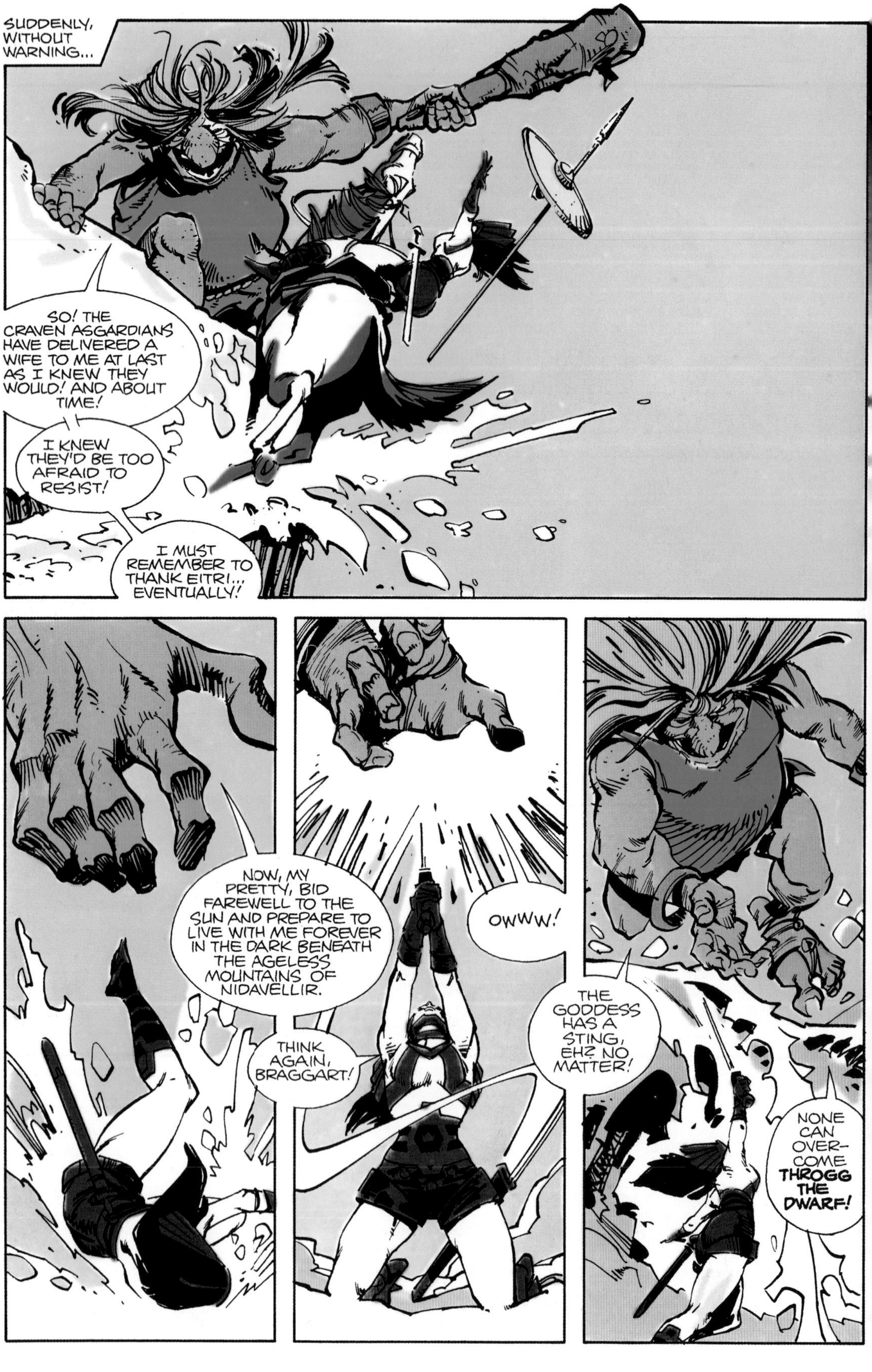
SUDDENLY, WITHOUT WARNING...
SO! THE CRAVEN ASGARDIANS HAVE DELIVERED A WIFE TO ME AT LAST AS I KNEW THEY WOULD! AND ABOUT TIME!
I KNEW THEY'D BE TOO AFRAID TO RESIST!
I MUST REMEMBER TO THANK EITRI... EVENTUALLY!
NOW, MY PRETTY, BID FAREWELL TO THE SUN AND PREPARE TO LIVE WITH ME FOREVER IN THE DARK BENEATH THE AGELESS MOUNTAINS OF NIDAVELLIR.
THINK AGAIN, BRAGGART!
OWWW!
THE GODDESS HAS A STING, EH? NO MATTER!
NONE CAN OVER-COME THROGG THE DWARF!

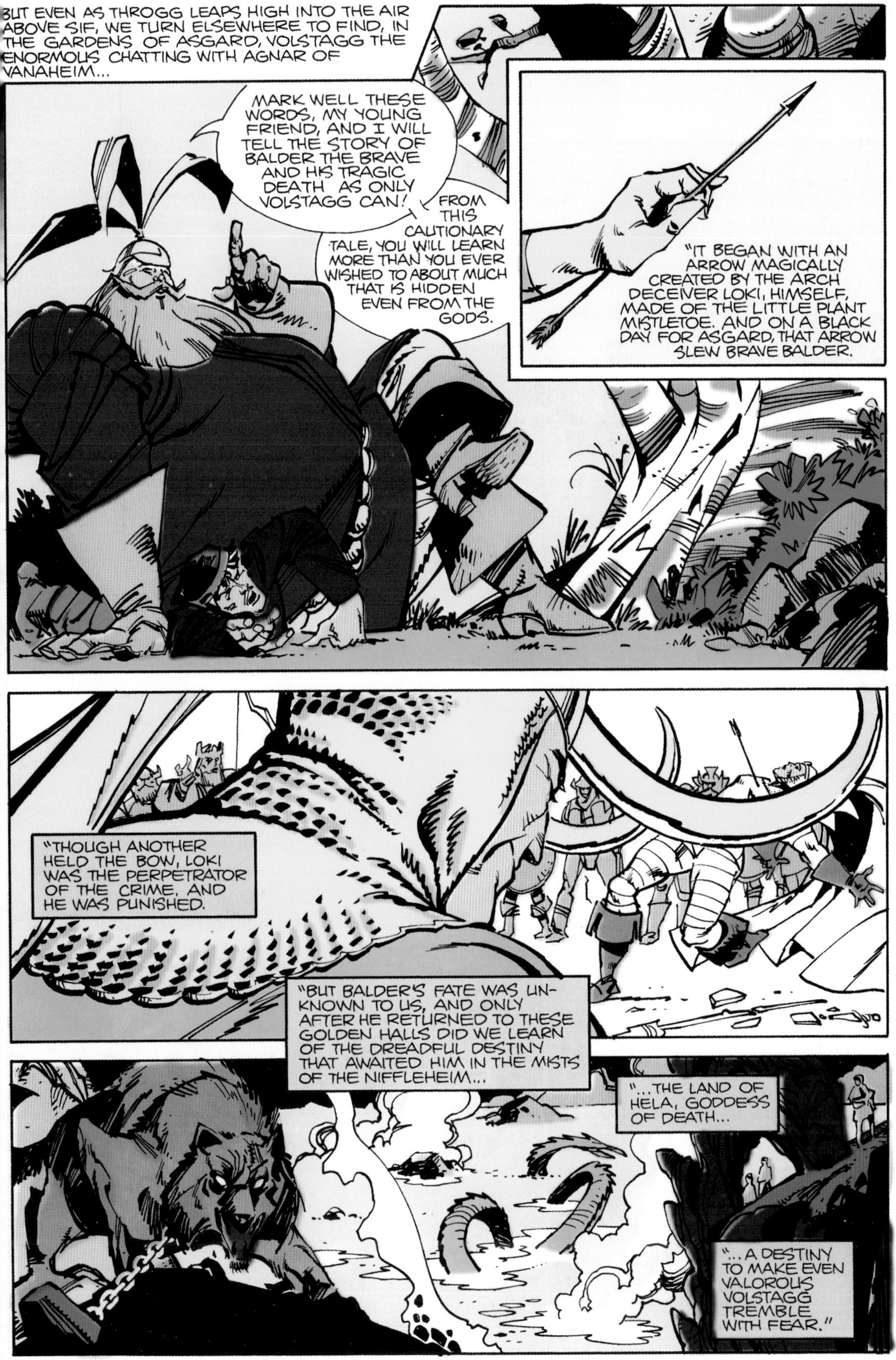

BUT EVEN AS THROGG LEAPS HIGH INTO THE AIR ABOVE SIF, WE TURN ELSEWHERE TO FIND, IN THE GARDENS OF ASGARD, VOLSTAGG THE ENORMOUS CHATTING WITH AGNAR OF VANAHEIM...
MARK WELL THESE WORDS, MY YOUNG FRIEND, AND I WILL TELL THE STORY OF BALDER THE BRAVE AND HIS TRAGIC DEATH AS ONLY VOLSTAGG CAN!
FROM THIS CAUTIONARY TALE, YOU WILL LEARN MORE THAN YOU EVER WISHED TO ABOUT MUCH THAT IS HIDDEN EVEN FROM THE GODS.
"IT BEGAN WITH AN ARROW MAGICALLY CREATED BY THE ARCH DECEIVER LOKI, HIMSELF, MADE OF THE LITTLE PLANT MISTLETOE. AND ON A BLACK DAY FOR ASGARD, THAT ARROW SLEW BRAVE BALDER.
"THOUGH ANOTHER HELD THE BOW, LOKI WAS THE PERPETRATOR OF THE CRIME, AND HE WAS PUNISHED.
"BUT BALDER'S FATE WAS UNKNOWN TO US, AND ONLY AFTER HE RETURNED TO THESE GOLDEN HALLS DID WE LEARN OF THE DREADFUL DESTINY THAT AWAITED HIM IN THE MISTS OF THE NIFFLEHEIM...
"...THE LAND OF HELA, GODDESS OF DEATH...
"...A DESTINY TO MAKE EVEN VALOROUS VOLSTAGG TREMBLE WITH FEAR."

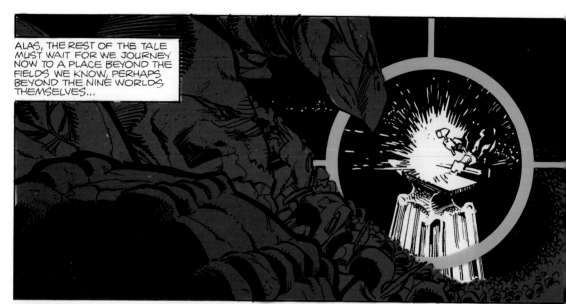

ALAS, THE REST OF THE TALE MUST WAIT FOR WE JOURNEY NOW TO A PLACE BEYOND THE FIELDS WE KNOW, PERHAPS BEYOND THE NINE WORLDS THEMSELVES...

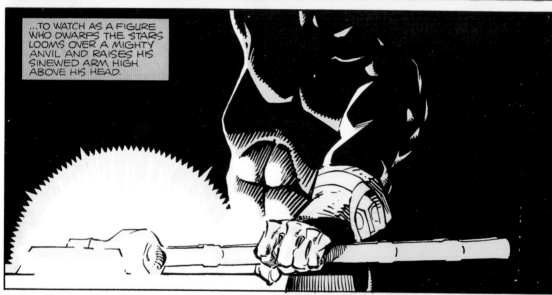

...TO WATCH AS A FIGURE WHO DWARFS THE STARS LOOMS OVER A MIGHTY ANVIL AND RAISES HIS SINEWED ARM HIGH ABOVE HIS HEAD.

AND EVEN OVER THE THUNDER OF HIS HAMMER, IF YOU LISTEN CAREFULLY, YOU CAN HEAR THE MURMUR OF THE HOST. AND THE MURMUR SAYS, "THE SWORD! THE SWORD!"

THE STORM IS RISING...

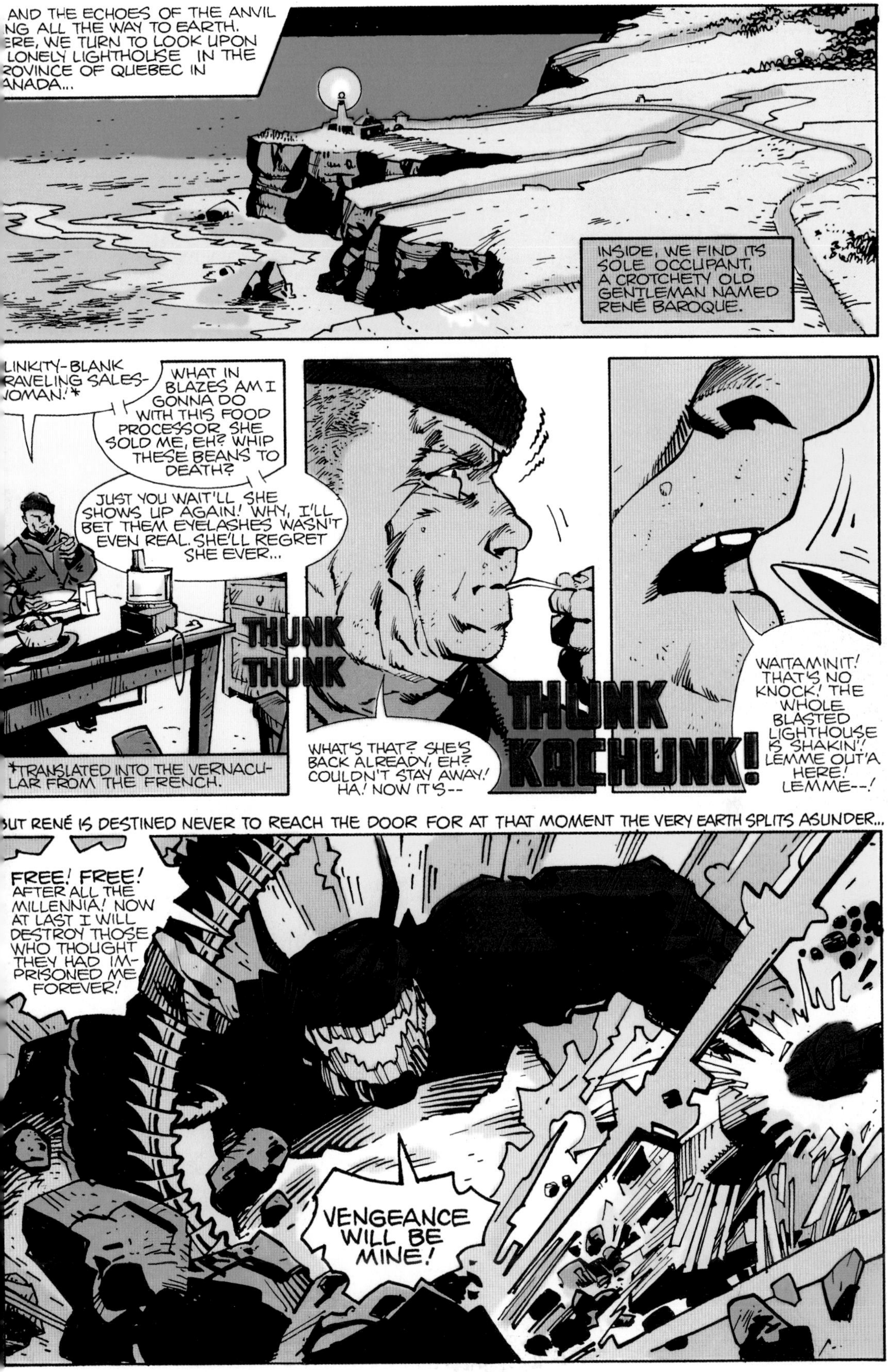

AND THE ECHOES OF THE ANVIL
NG ALL THE WAY TO EARTH.
ERE, WE TURN TO LOOK UPON
LONELY LIGHTHOUSE IN THE
ROVINCE OF QUEBEC IN
ANADA...
INSIDE, WE FIND ITS SOLE OCCUPANT, A CROTCHETY OLD GENTLEMAN NAMED RENÉ BAROQUE.
LINKITY-BLANK RAVELING SALES-WOMAN! *
WHAT IN BLAZES AM I GONNA DO WITH THIS FOOD PROCESSOR SHE SOLD ME, EH? WHIP THESE BEANS TO DEATH?
JUST YOU WAIT'LL SHE SHOWS UP AGAIN! WHY, I'LL BET THEM EYELASHES WASN'T EVEN REAL. SHE'LL REGRET SHE EVER...
THUNK
THUNK
*TRANSLATED INTO THE VERNACULAR FROM THE FRENCH.
WHAT'S THAT? SHE'S BACK ALREADY, EH? COULDN'T STAY AWAY! HA! NOW IT'S--
THUNK
KACHUNK!
WAITAMINIT! THAT'S NO KNOCK! THE WHOLE BLASTED LIGHTHOUSE IS SHAKIN'! LEMME OUT'A HERE! LEMME--!
UT RENÉ IS DESTINED NEVER TO REACH THE DOOR FOR AT THAT MOMENT THE VERY EARTH SPLITS ASUNDER...
FREE! FREE! AFTER ALL THE MILLENNIA! NOW AT LAST I WILL DESTROY THOSE WHO THOUGHT THEY HAD IMPRISONED ME FOREVER!
VENGEANCE WILL BE MINE!

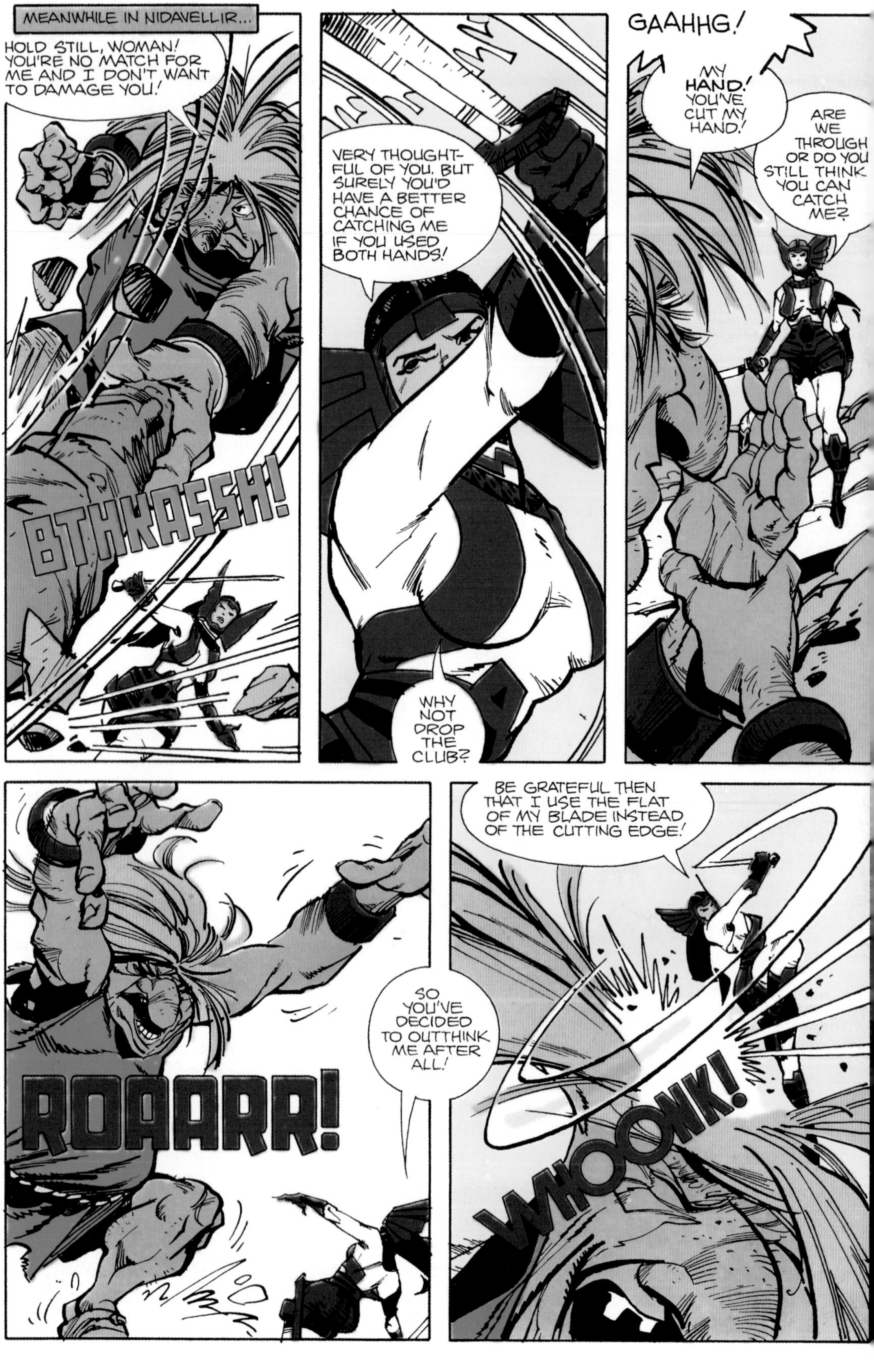
MEANWHILE IN NIDAVELLIR...
HOLD STILL, WOMAN! YOU'RE NO MATCH FOR ME AND I DON'T WANT TO DAMAGE YOU!
BTHKASSH!
VERY THOUGHTFUL OF YOU. BUT SURELY YOU'D HAVE A BETTER CHANCE OF CATCHING ME IF YOU USED BOTH HANDS!
WHY NOT DROP THE CLUB?
GAAHHG!
MY HAND! YOU'VE CUT MY HAND!
ARE WE THROUGH OR DO YOU STILL THINK YOU CAN CATCH ME?
ROAARR!
SO YOU'VE DECIDED TO OUTTHINK ME AFTER ALL!
BE GRATEFUL THEN THAT I USE THE FLAT OF MY BLADE INSTEAD OF THE CUTTING EDGE!
WHOONK!

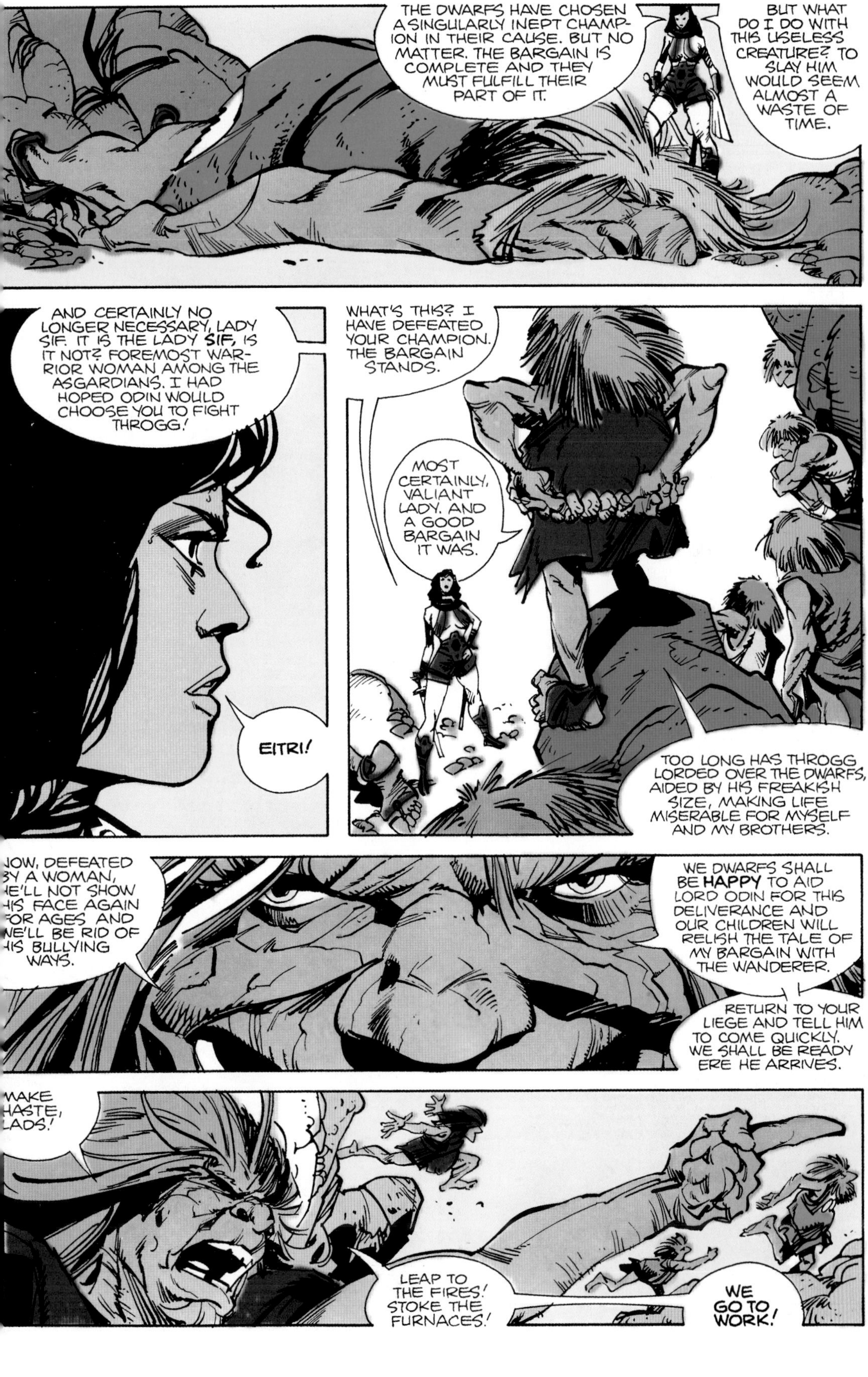
THE DWARFS HAVE CHOSEN A SINGULARLY INEPT CHAMPION IN THEIR CAUSE. BUT NO MATTER. THE BARGAIN IS COMPLETE AND THEY MUST FULFILL THEIR PART OF IT.
BUT WHAT DO I DO WITH THIS USELESS CREATURE? TO SLAY HIM WOULD SEEM ALMOST A WASTE OF TIME.
AND CERTAINLY NO LONGER NECESSARY, LADY SIF. IT IS THE LADY SIF, IS IT NOT? FOREMOST WARRIOR WOMAN AMONG THE ASGARDIANS. I HAD HOPED ODIN WOULD CHOOSE YOU TO FIGHT THROGG!
EITRI!
WHAT'S THIS? I HAVE DEFEATED YOUR CHAMPION. THE BARGAIN STANDS.
MOST CERTAINLY, VALIANT LADY. AND A GOOD BARGAIN IT WAS.
TOO LONG HAS THROGG LORDED OVER THE DWARFS, AIDED BY HIS FREAKISH SIZE, MAKING LIFE MISERABLE FOR MYSELF AND MY BROTHERS.
NOW, DEFEATED BY A WOMAN, HE'LL NOT SHOW HIS FACE AGAIN FOR AGES AND WE'LL BE RID OF HIS BULLYING WAYS.
WE DWARFS SHALL BE HAPPY TO AID LORD ODIN FOR THIS DELIVERANCE AND OUR CHILDREN WILL RELISH THE TALE OF MY BARGAIN WITH THE WANDERER.
RETURN TO YOUR LIEGE AND TELL HIM TO COME QUICKLY. WE SHALL BE READY ERE HE ARRIVES.
MAKE HASTE, LADS!
LEAP TO THE FIRES! STOKE THE FURNACES!
WE GO TO WORK!

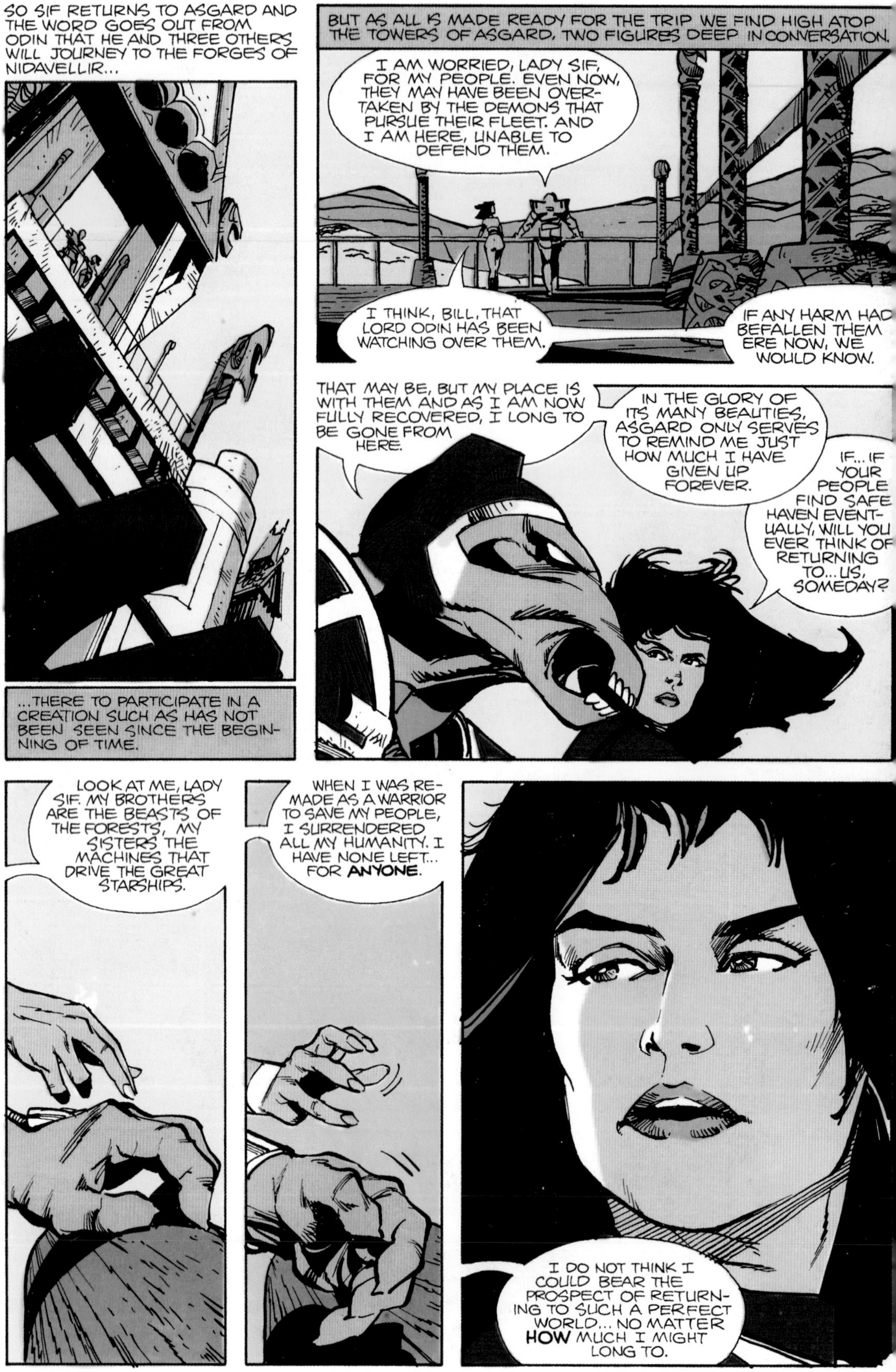
SO SIF RETURNS TO ASGARD AND THE WORD GOES OUT FROM ODIN THAT HE AND THREE OTHERS WILL JOURNEY TO THE FORGES OF NIDAVELLIR...
...THERE TO PARTICIPATE IN A CREATION SUCH AS HAS NOT BEEN SEEN SINCE THE BEGINNING OF TIME.
BUT AS ALL IS MADE READY FOR THE TRIP WE FIND HIGH ATOP THE TOWERS OF ASGARD, TWO FIGURES DEEP IN CONVERSATION.
I AM WORRIED, LADY SIF, FOR MY PEOPLE. EVEN NOW, THEY MAY HAVE BEEN OVERTAKEN BY THE DEMONS THAT PURSUE THEIR FLEET. AND I AM HERE, UNABLE TO DEFEND THEM.
I THINK, BILL, THAT LORD ODIN HAS BEEN WATCHING OVER THEM.
IF ANY HARM HAD BEFALLEN THEM ERE NOW, WE WOULD KNOW.
THAT MAY BE, BUT MY PLACE IS WITH THEM AND AS I AM NOW FULLY RECOVERED, I LONG TO BE GONE FROM HERE.
IN THE GLORY OF ITS MANY BEAUTIES, ASGARD ONLY SERVES TO REMIND ME JUST HOW MUCH I HAVE GIVEN UP FOREVER.
IF... IF YOUR PEOPLE FIND SAFE HAVEN EVENTUALLY, WILL YOU EVER THINK OF RETURNING TO... US, SOMEDAY?
LOOK AT ME, LADY SIF. MY BROTHERS ARE THE BEASTS OF THE FORESTS, MY SISTERS THE MACHINES THAT DRIVE THE GREAT STARSHIPS.
WHEN I WAS REMADE AS A WARRIOR TO SAVE MY PEOPLE, I SURRENDERED ALL MY HUMANITY. I HAVE NONE LEFT... FOR ANYONE.
I DO NOT THINK I COULD BEAR THE PROSPECT OF RETURNING TO SUCH A PERFECT WORLD... NO MATTER HOW MUCH I MIGHT LONG TO.

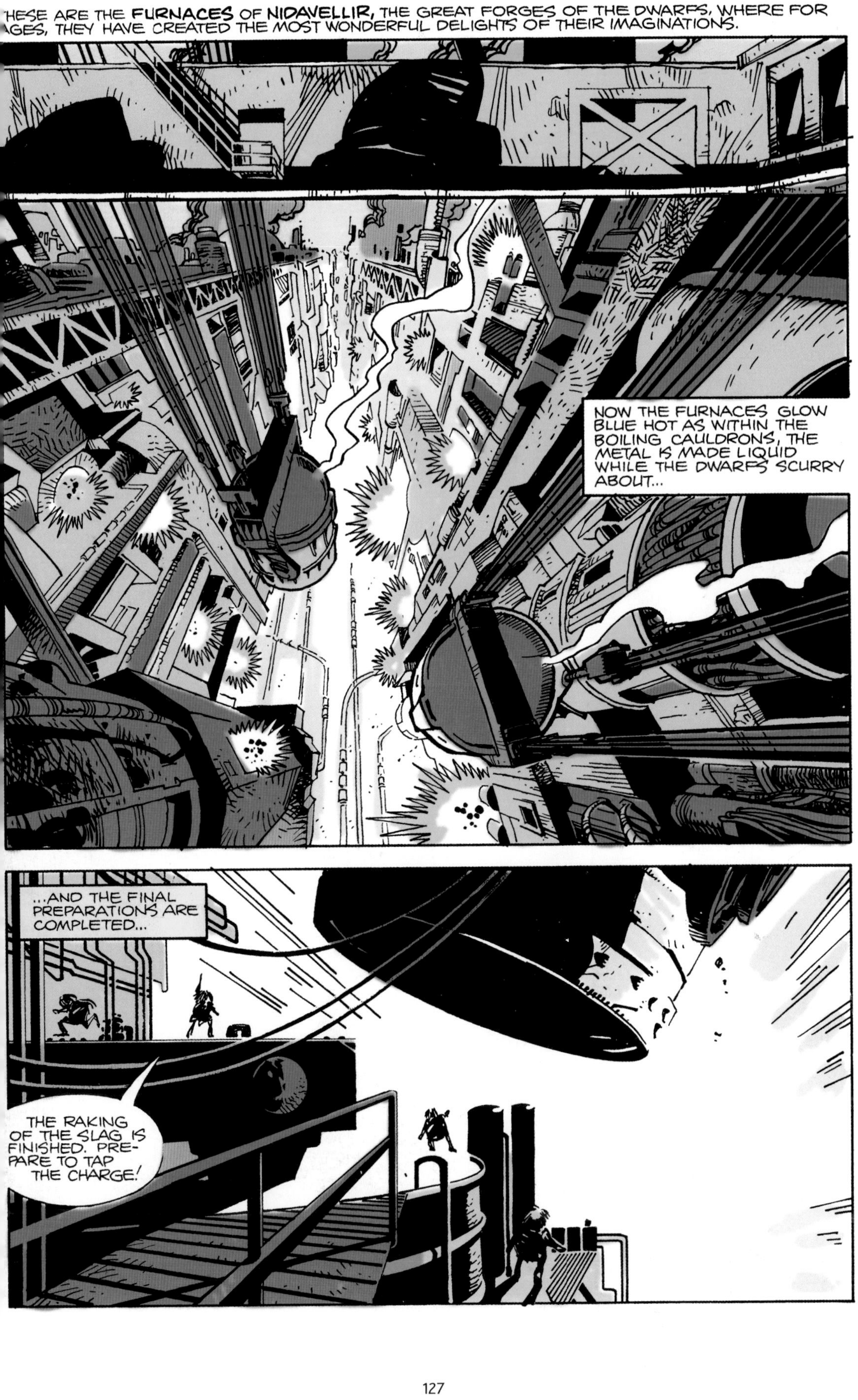
HESE ARE THE FURNACES OF NIDAVELLIR, THE GREAT FORGES OF THE DWARFS, WHERE FOR GES, THEY HAVE CREATED THE MOST WONDERFUL DELIGHTS OF THEIR IMAGINATIONS.
NOW THE FURNACES GLOW BLUE HOT AS WITHIN THE BOILING CAULDRONS, THE METAL IS MADE LIQUID WHILE THE DWARFS SCURRY ABOUT...
...AND THE FINAL PREPARATIONS ARE COMPLETED...
THE RAKING OF THE SLAG IS FINISHED. PREPARE TO TAP THE CHARGE!

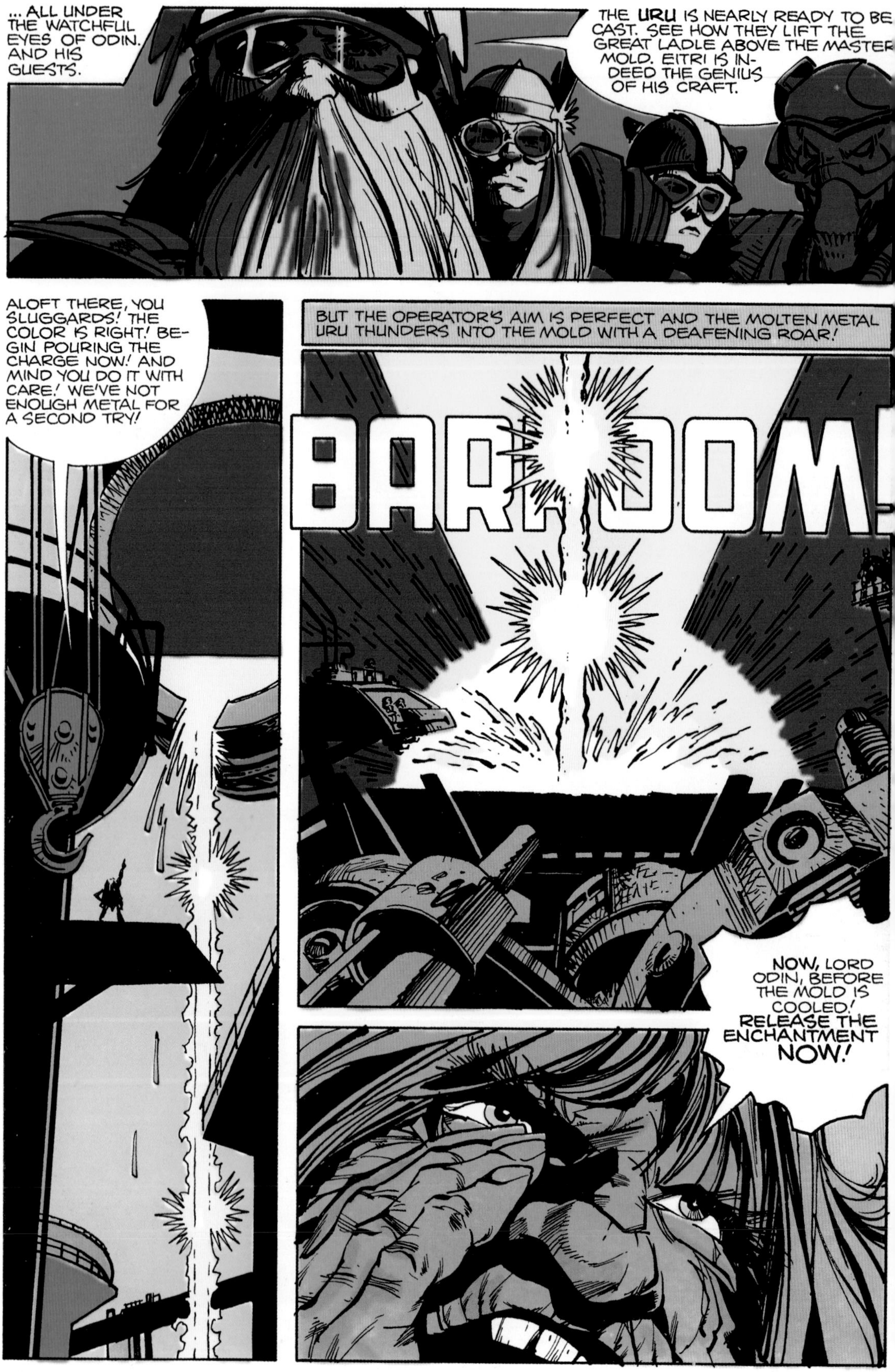
...ALL UNDER THE WATCHFUL EYES OF ODIN. AND HIS GUESTS.
THE URU IS NEARLY READY TO BE CAST. SEE HOW THEY LIFT THE GREAT LADLE ABOVE THE MASTER MOLD. EITRI IS INDEED THE GENIUS OF HIS CRAFT.
ALOFT THERE, YOU SLUGGARDS! THE COLOR IS RIGHT! BEGIN POURING THE CHARGE NOW! AND MIND YOU DO IT WITH CARE! WE'VE NOT ENOUGH METAL FOR A SECOND TRY!
BUT THE OPERATOR'S AIM IS PERFECT AND THE MOLTEN METAL URU THUNDERS INTO THE MOLD WITH A DEAFENING ROAR!
NOW, LORD ODIN, BEFORE THE MOLD IS COOLED! RELEASE THE ENCHANTMENT NOW!

STAND BACK! THIS IS THE MOMENT WHEN WE SUCCEED OR FAIL! I MUST STRIKE WITH THE FULL FORCE OF THE **ODIN POWER** TO ACHIEVE OUR PURPOSE!

ONLY THUS CAN THE MAGIKS WE DESIRE BE LOCKED WITHIN THE URU METAL **FOREVER!**

SO BE IT!

KA THOOM!

QUICKLY NOW, BILL. DON THIS GAUNTLET AND STEP FORWARD. FOR YOU THIS MAGIC IS PERFORMED AND TO YOU THIS MAGIC SHALL BE BOUND!

EITRI WILL INSTRUCT YOU!

WHAT MUST I DO, EITRI?

AS I RAISE THE DOOR, YOU MUST REACH INTO THE MOLTEN POOL WITHIN AND REMOVE THAT WHICH YOU FIND THERE. THE GAUNTLET WILL PROTECT YOU! MAKE **HASTE** OR THE MOMENT IS **LOST!**

NOW!

I...I FEEL **NOTHING--** HOLD! I HAVE IT! THE WEIGHT IS **ENORMOUS!** BUT IT GROWS LIGHTER EVEN AS I PULL IT FROM THE FIRE!

THE **POWER!** IT FLOWS INTO ME! I... I'M **CHANGING!**

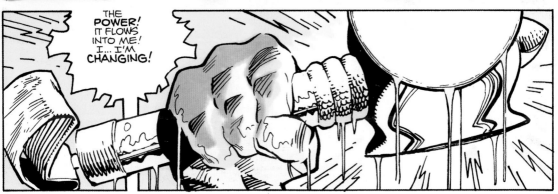

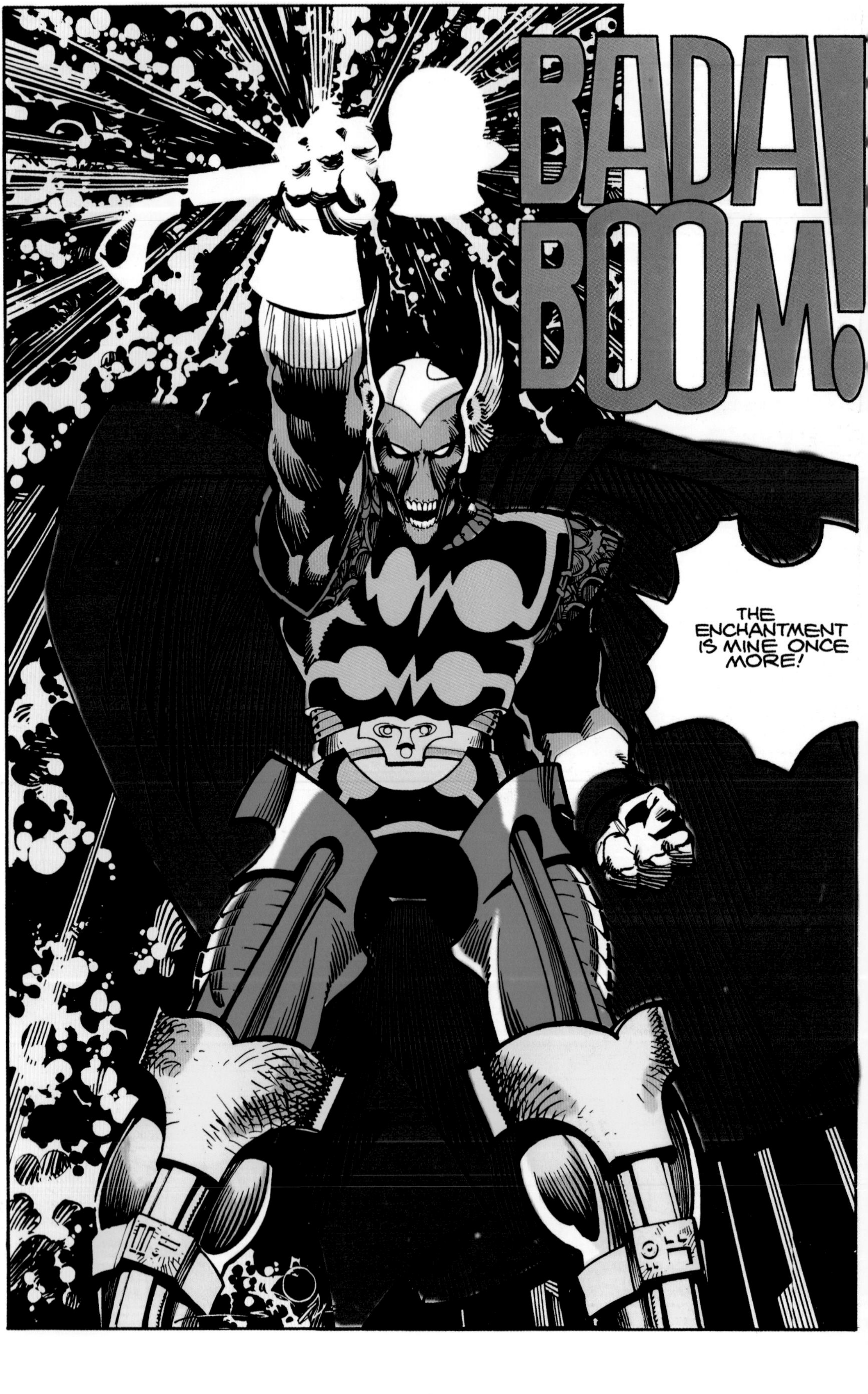
BADA BOOM!
THE ENCHANTMENT IS MINE ONCE MORE!

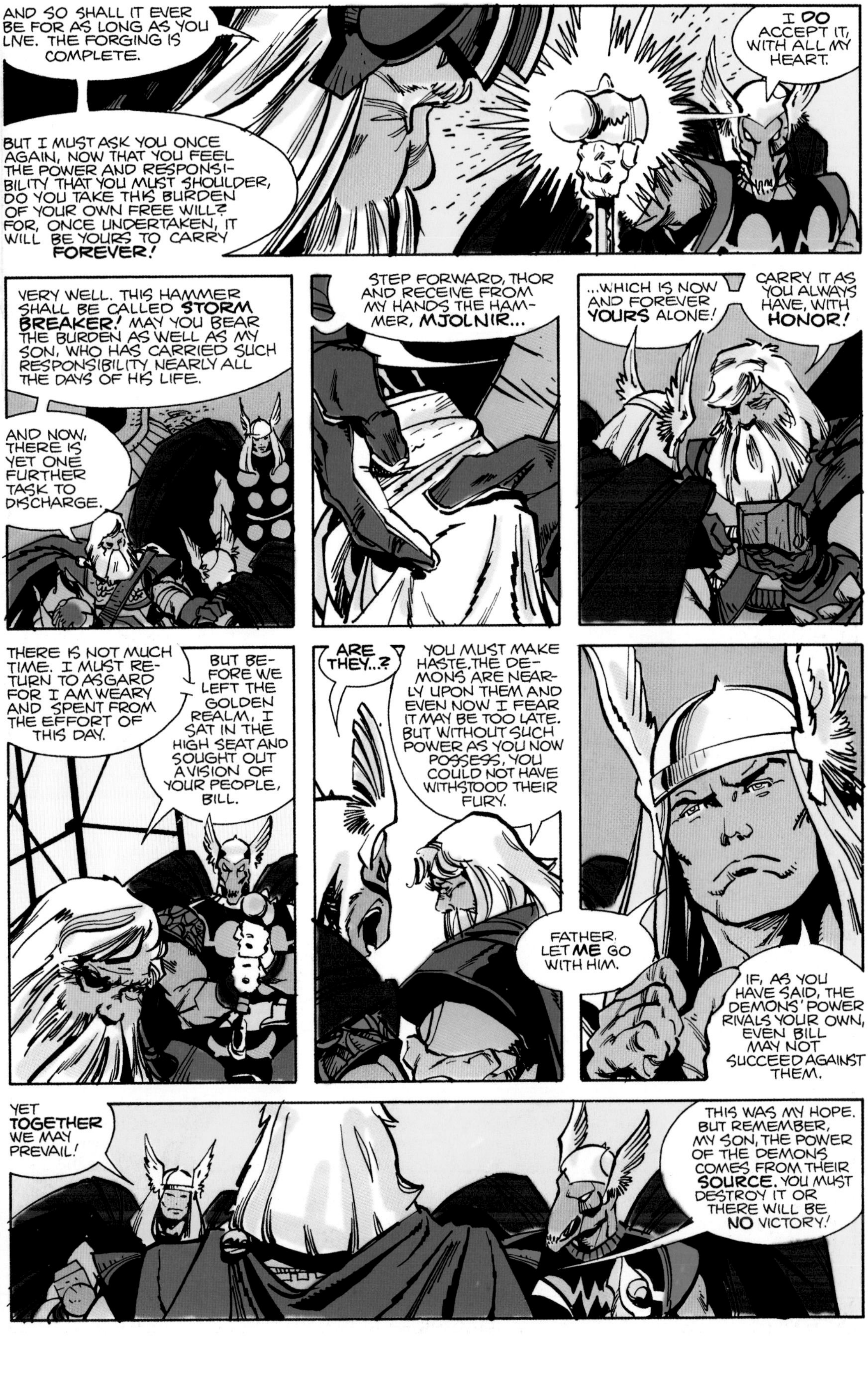

AND SO SHALL IT EVER BE FOR AS LONG AS YOU LIVE. THE FORGING IS COMPLETE.
BUT I MUST ASK YOU ONCE AGAIN, NOW THAT YOU FEEL THE POWER AND RESPONSIBILITY THAT YOU MUST SHOULDER, DO YOU TAKE THIS BURDEN OF YOUR OWN FREE WILL? FOR, ONCE UNDERTAKEN, IT WILL BE YOURS TO CARRY **FOREVER!**
I **DO** ACCEPT IT, WITH ALL MY HEART.
VERY WELL. THIS HAMMER SHALL BE CALLED **STORM BREAKER!** MAY YOU BEAR THE BURDEN AS WELL AS MY SON, WHO HAS CARRIED SUCH RESPONSIBILITY NEARLY ALL THE DAYS OF HIS LIFE.
AND NOW, THERE IS YET ONE FURTHER TASK TO DISCHARGE.
STEP FORWARD, THOR AND RECEIVE FROM MY HANDS THE HAMMER, **MJOLNIR**...
...WHICH IS NOW AND FOREVER **YOURS** ALONE!
CARRY IT AS YOU ALWAYS HAVE, WITH **HONOR!**
THERE IS NOT MUCH TIME. I MUST RETURN TO ASGARD FOR I AM WEARY AND SPENT FROM THE EFFORT OF THIS DAY.
BUT BEFORE WE LEFT THE GOLDEN REALM, I SAT IN THE HIGH SEAT AND SOUGHT OUT A VISION OF YOUR PEOPLE, BILL.
ARE THEY...?
YOU MUST MAKE HASTE, THE DEMONS ARE NEARLY UPON THEM AND EVEN NOW I FEAR IT MAY BE TOO LATE. BUT WITHOUT SUCH POWER AS YOU NOW POSSESS, YOU COULD NOT HAVE WITHSTOOD THEIR FURY.
FATHER. LET **ME** GO WITH HIM.
IF, AS YOU HAVE SAID, THE DEMONS' POWER RIVALS YOUR OWN, EVEN BILL MAY NOT SUCCEED AGAINST THEM.
YET **TOGETHER** WE MAY PREVAIL!
THIS WAS MY HOPE. BUT REMEMBER, MY SON, THE POWER OF THE DEMONS COMES FROM THEIR **SOURCE.** YOU MUST DESTROY IT OR THERE WILL BE **NO** VICTORY!

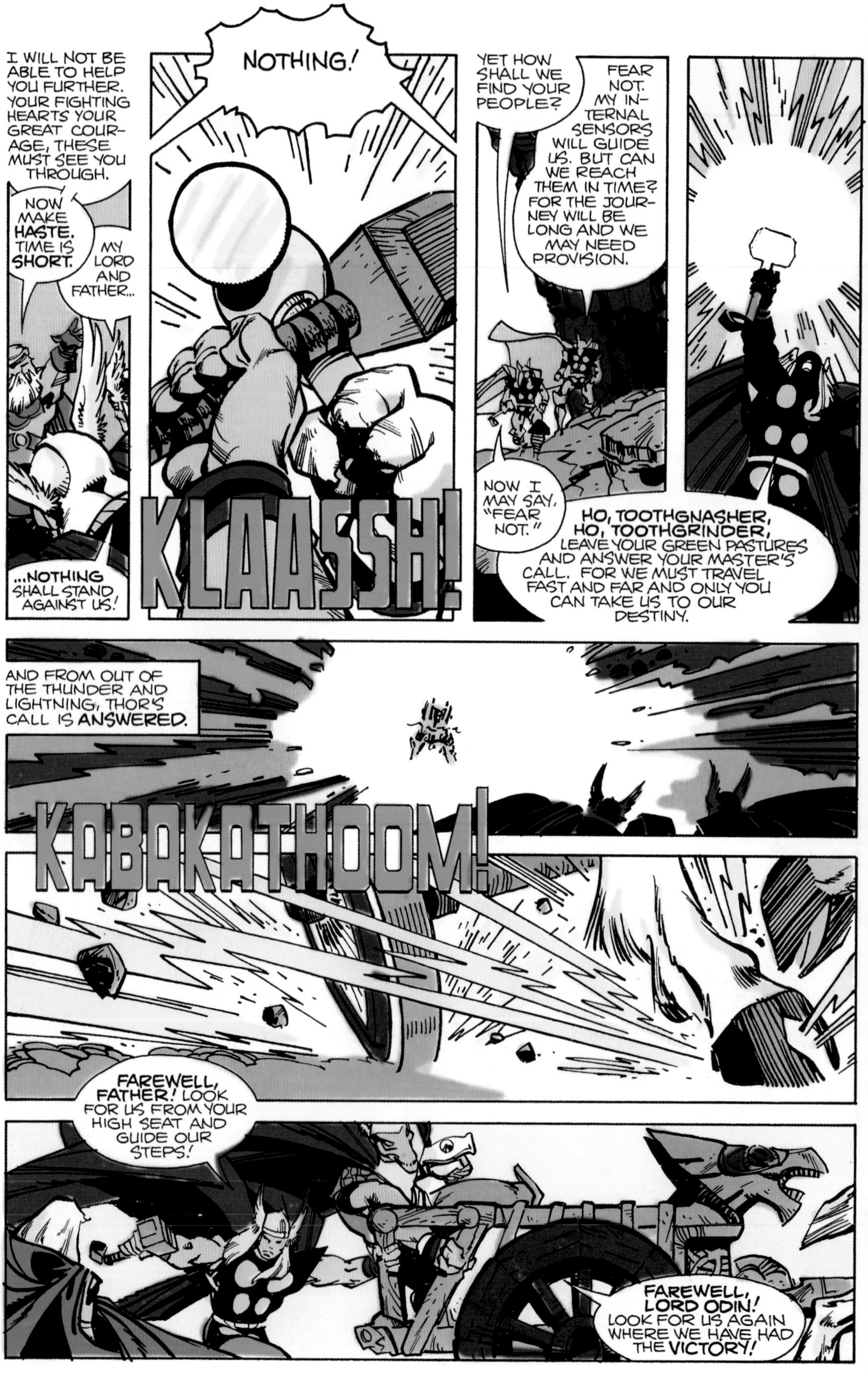

I WILL NOT BE ABLE TO HELP YOU FURTHER. YOUR FIGHTING HEARTS YOUR GREAT COURAGE, THESE MUST SEE YOU THROUGH.
NOW MAKE HASTE. TIME IS SHORT.
MY LORD AND FATHER...
...NOTHING SHALL STAND AGAINST US!
NOTHING!
KLAASSH!
YET HOW SHALL WE FIND YOUR PEOPLE?
FEAR NOT. MY INTERNAL SENSORS WILL GUIDE US. BUT CAN WE REACH THEM IN TIME? FOR THE JOURNEY WILL BE LONG AND WE MAY NEED PROVISION.
NOW I MAY SAY, "FEAR NOT."
HO, TOOTHGNASHER, HO, TOOTHGRINDER, LEAVE YOUR GREEN PASTURES AND ANSWER YOUR MASTER'S CALL. FOR WE MUST TRAVEL FAST AND FAR AND ONLY YOU CAN TAKE US TO OUR DESTINY.
AND FROM OUT OF THE THUNDER AND LIGHTNING, THOR'S CALL IS ANSWERED.
KABAKATHOOM!
FAREWELL, FATHER! LOOK FOR US FROM YOUR HIGH SEAT AND GUIDE OUR STEPS!
FAREWELL, LORD ODIN! LOOK FOR US AGAIN WHERE WE HAVE HAD THE VICTORY!

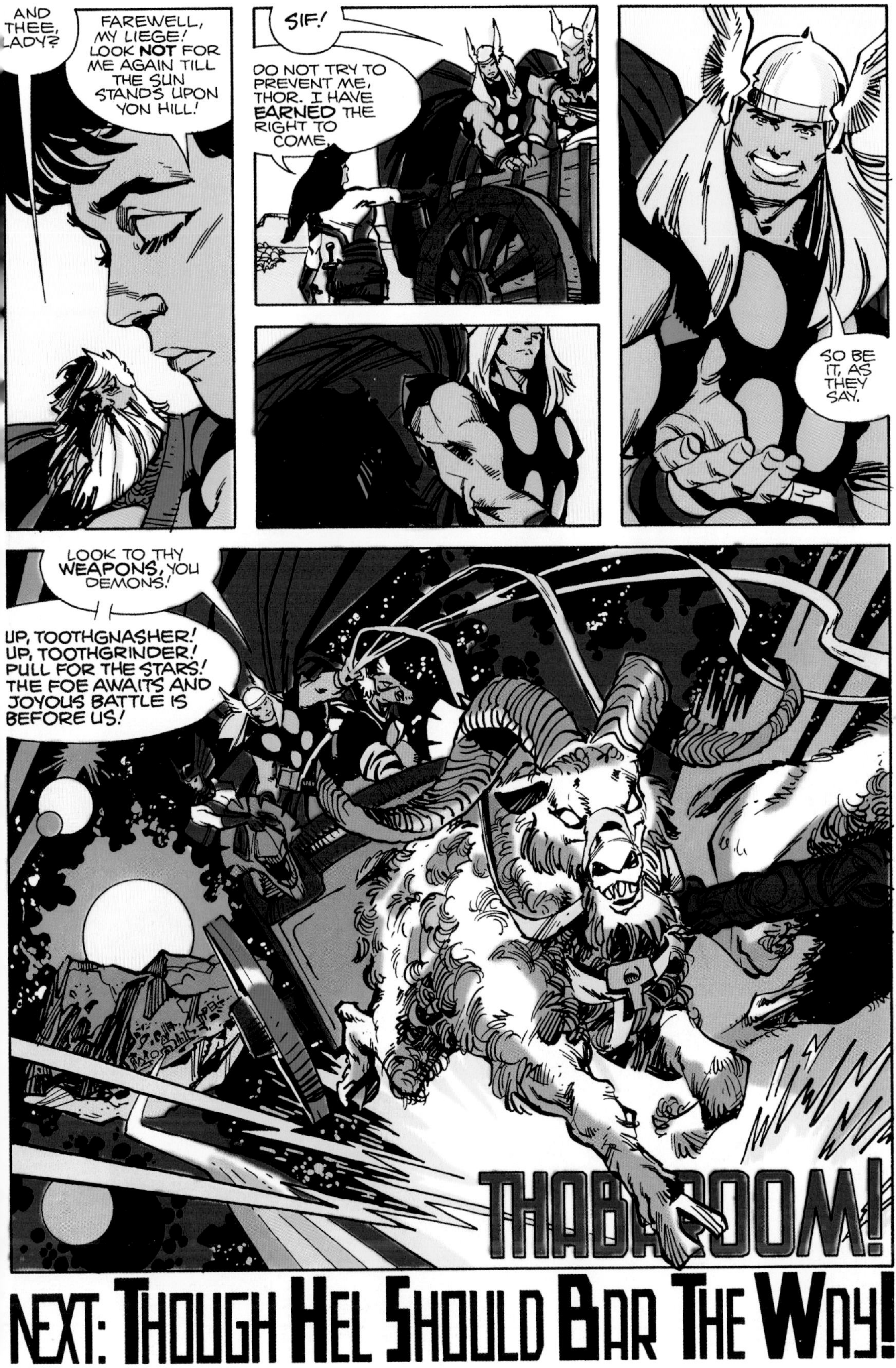

AND THEE, LADY?
FAREWELL, MY LIEGE! LOOK NOT FOR ME AGAIN TILL THE SUN STANDS UPON YON HILL!
SIF!
DO NOT TRY TO PREVENT ME, THOR. I HAVE EARNED THE RIGHT TO COME.
SO BE IT, AS THEY SAY.
LOOK TO THY WEAPONS, YOU DEMONS!
UP, TOOTHGNASHER! UP, TOOTHGRINDER! PULL FOR THE STARS! THE FOE AWAITS AND JOYOUS BATTLE IS BEFORE US!
THABAROOM!

NEXT: THOUGH HEL SHOULD BAR THE WAY!

MARVEL® GRAPHIC NOVEL

THE MIGHTY THOR VOLUME 2 #1

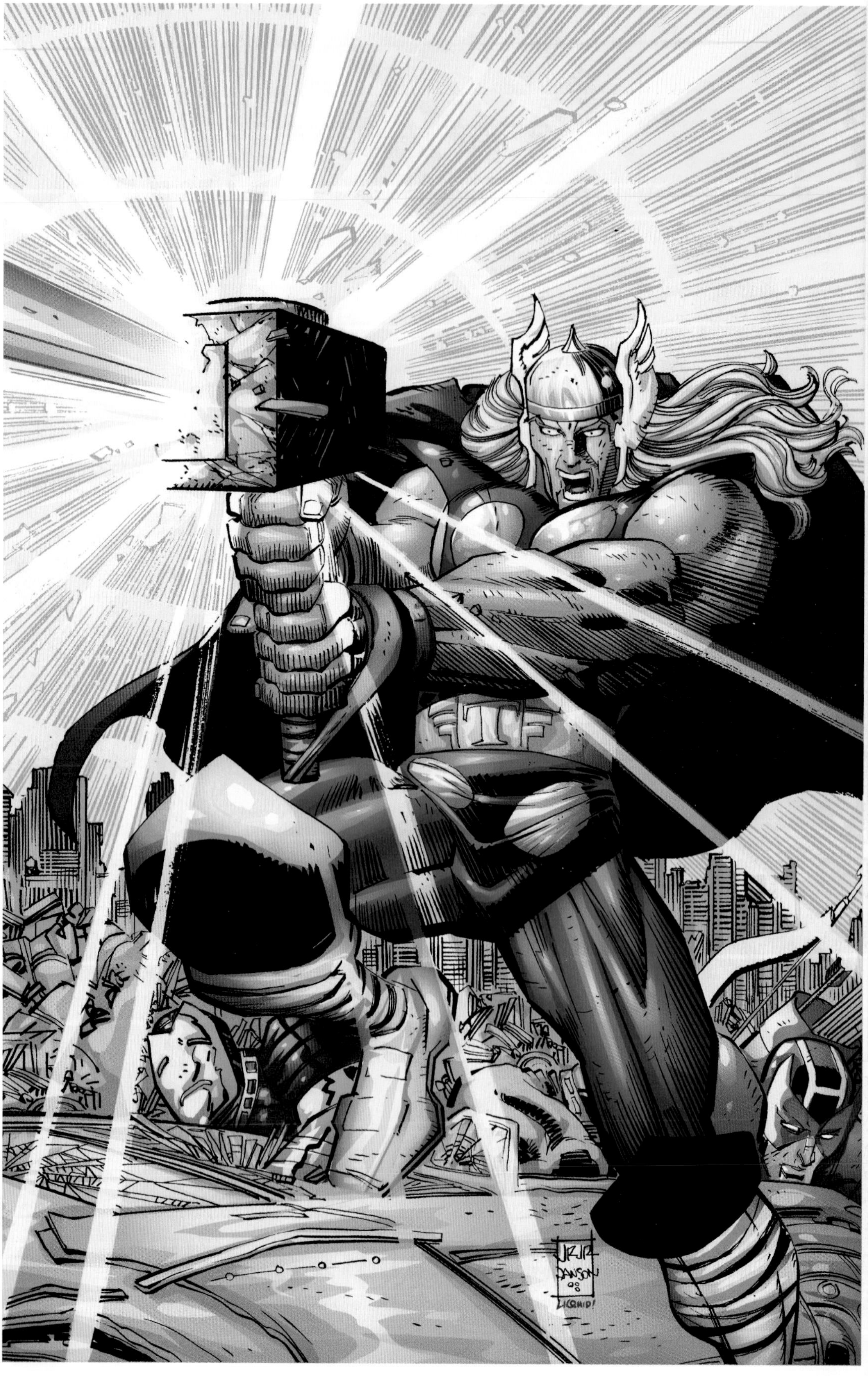

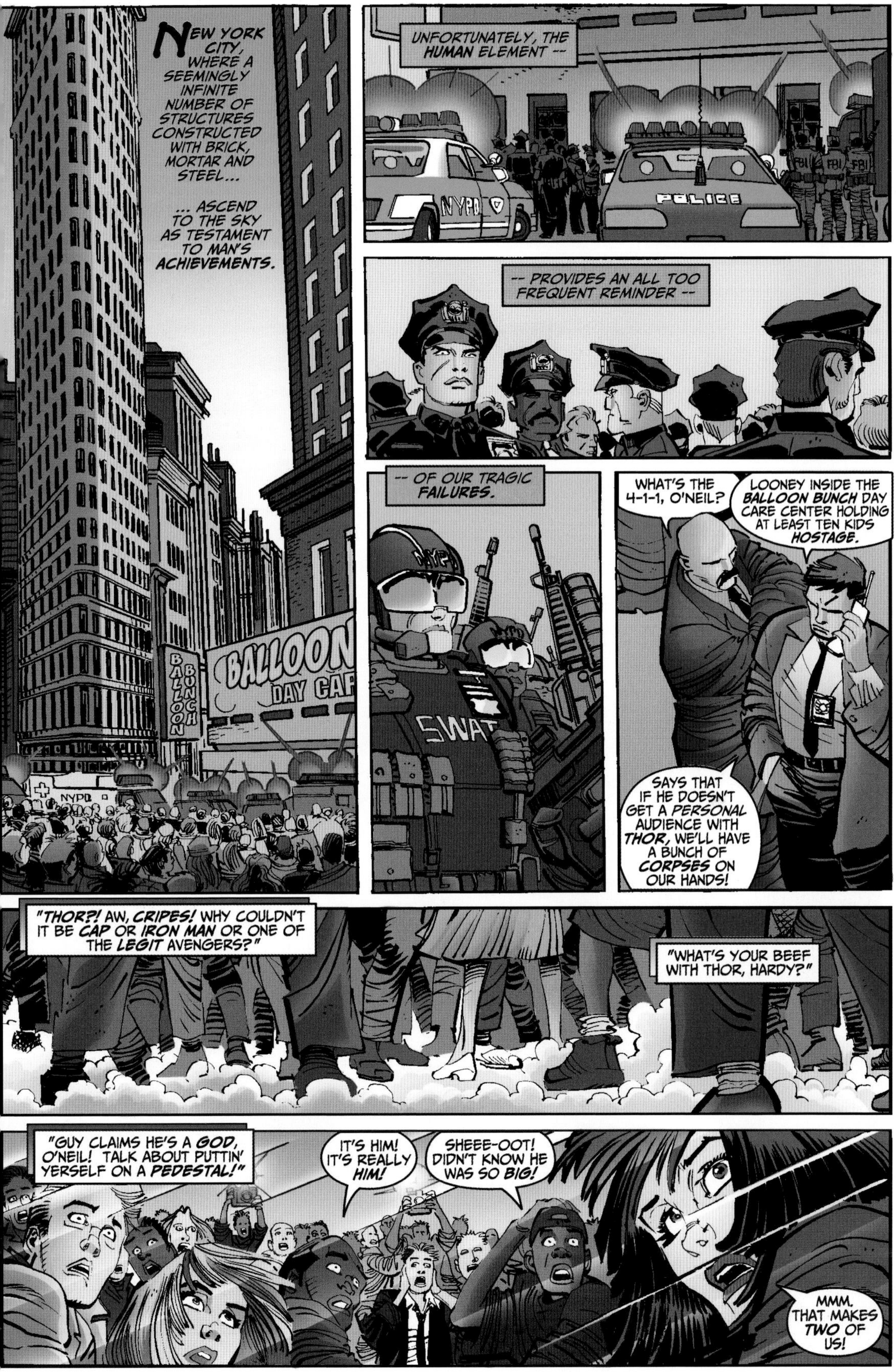

NEW YORK CITY, WHERE A SEEMINGLY INFINITE NUMBER OF STRUCTURES CONSTRUCTED WITH BRICK, MORTAR AND STEEL...
... ASCEND TO THE SKY AS TESTAMENT TO MAN'S ACHIEVEMENTS.
BALLOON BUNCH
BALLOON DAY CAR
NYPD
UNFORTUNATELY, THE HUMAN ELEMENT --
NYPD
POLICE
FBI
-- PROVIDES AN ALL TOO FREQUENT REMINDER --
-- OF OUR TRAGIC FAILURES.
SWAT
WHAT'S THE 4-1-1, O'NEIL?
LOONEY INSIDE THE BALLOON BUNCH DAY CARE CENTER HOLDING AT LEAST TEN KIDS HOSTAGE.
SAYS THAT IF HE DOESN'T GET A PERSONAL AUDIENCE WITH THOR, WE'LL HAVE A BUNCH OF CORPSES ON OUR HANDS!
"THOR?! AW, CRIPES! WHY COULDN'T IT BE CAP OR IRON MAN OR ONE OF THE LEGIT AVENGERS?"
"WHAT'S YOUR BEEF WITH THOR, HARDY?"
"GUY CLAIMS HE'S A GOD, O'NEIL! TALK ABOUT PUTTIN' YERSELF ON A PEDESTAL!"
IT'S HIM! IT'S REALLY HIM!
SHEEE-OOT! DIDN'T KNOW HE WAS SO BIG!
MMM. THAT MAKES TWO OF US!

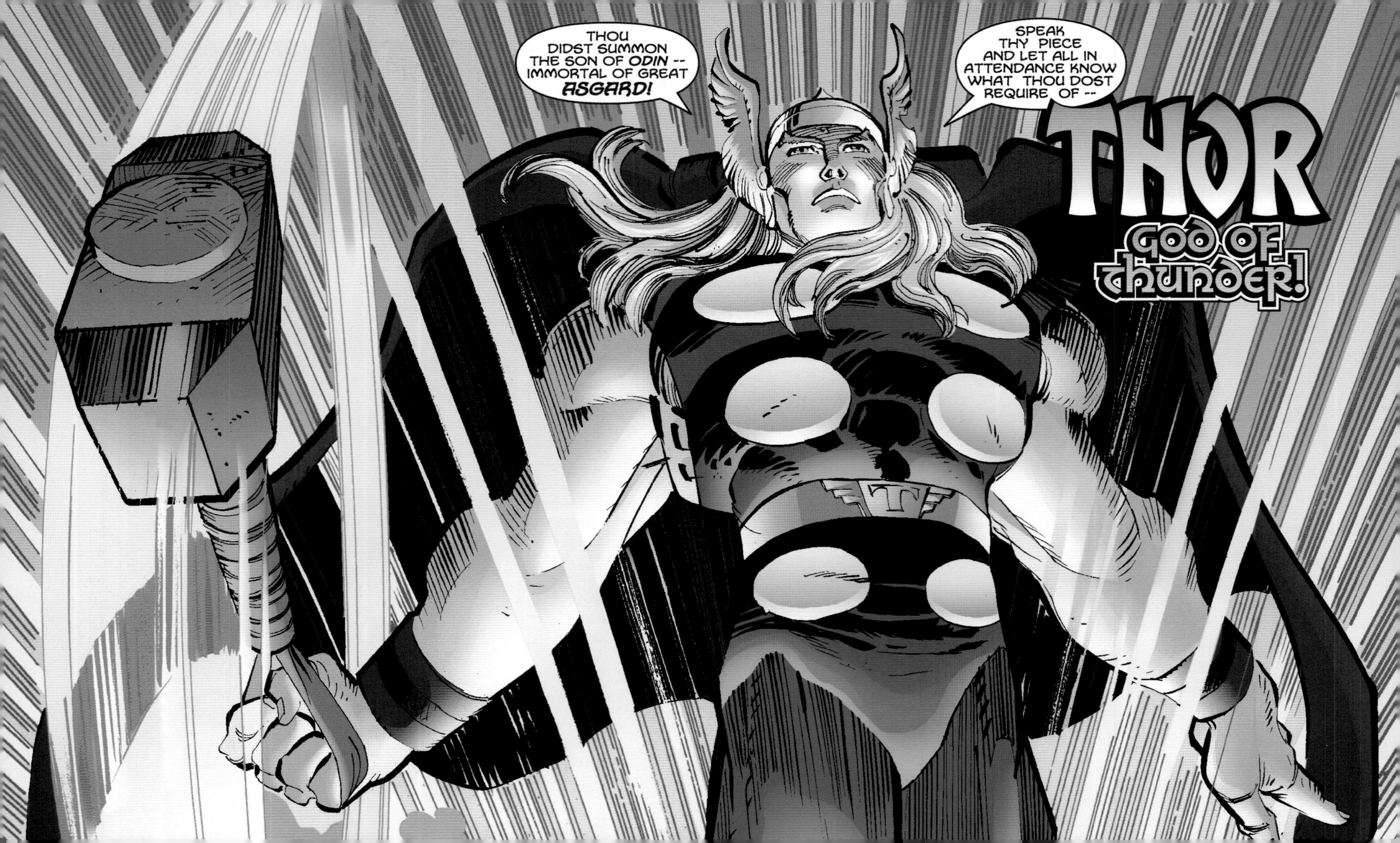
THOU DIDST SUMMON THE SON OF ODIN -- IMMORTAL OF GREAT ASGARD!
SPEAK THY PIECE AND LET ALL IN ATTENDANCE KNOW WHAT THOU DOST REQUIRE OF --
THOR
GOD OF THUNDER!

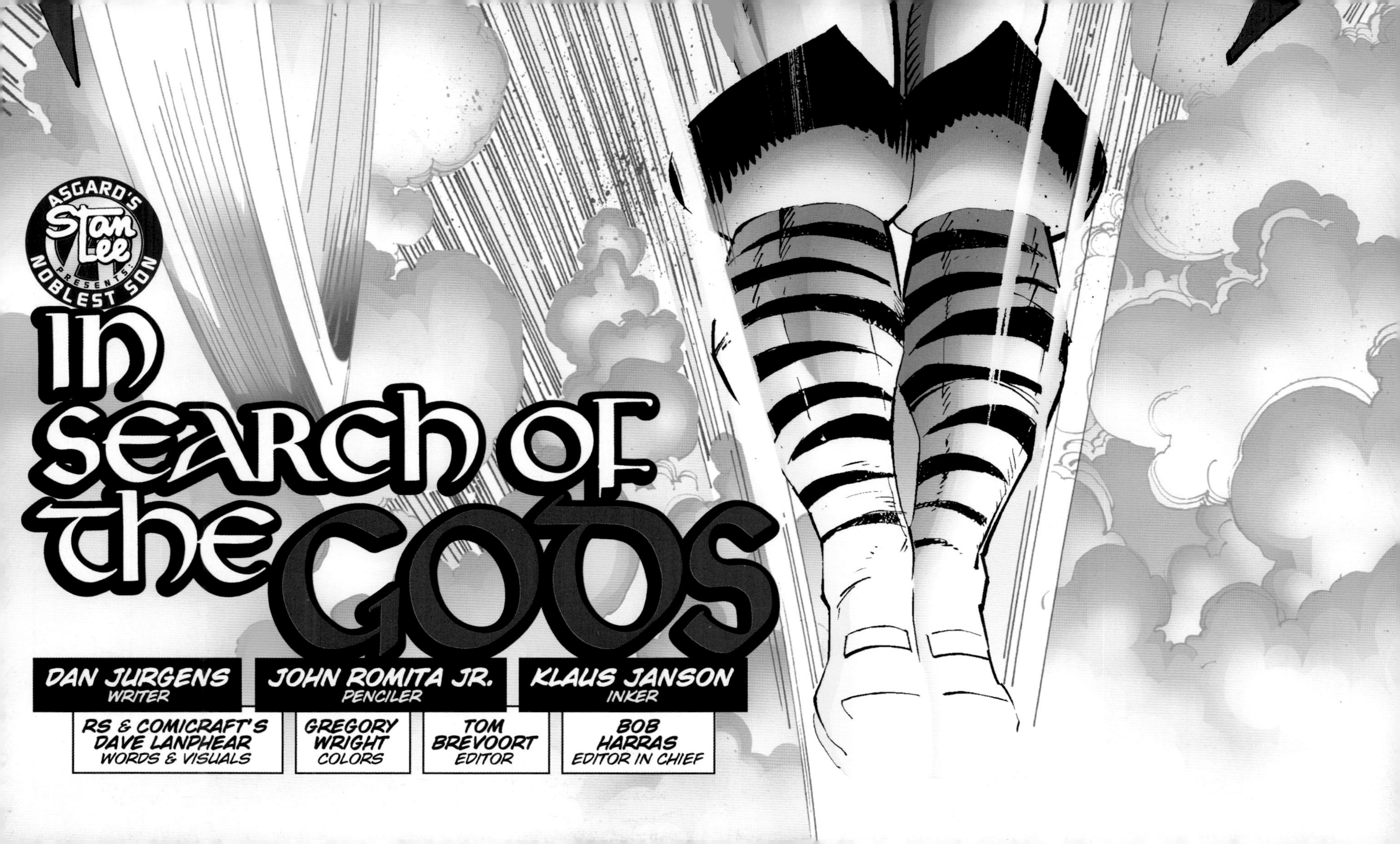
ASGARD'S NOBLEST SON
STAN LEE PRESENTS:
IN SEARCH OF THE GODS
DAN JURGENS WRITER
JOHN ROMITA JR. PENCILER
KLAUS JANSON INKER
RS & COMICRAFT'S DAVE LANPHEAR WORDS & VISUALS
GREGORY WRIGHT COLORS
TOM BREVOORT EDITOR
BOB HARRAS EDITOR IN CHIEF

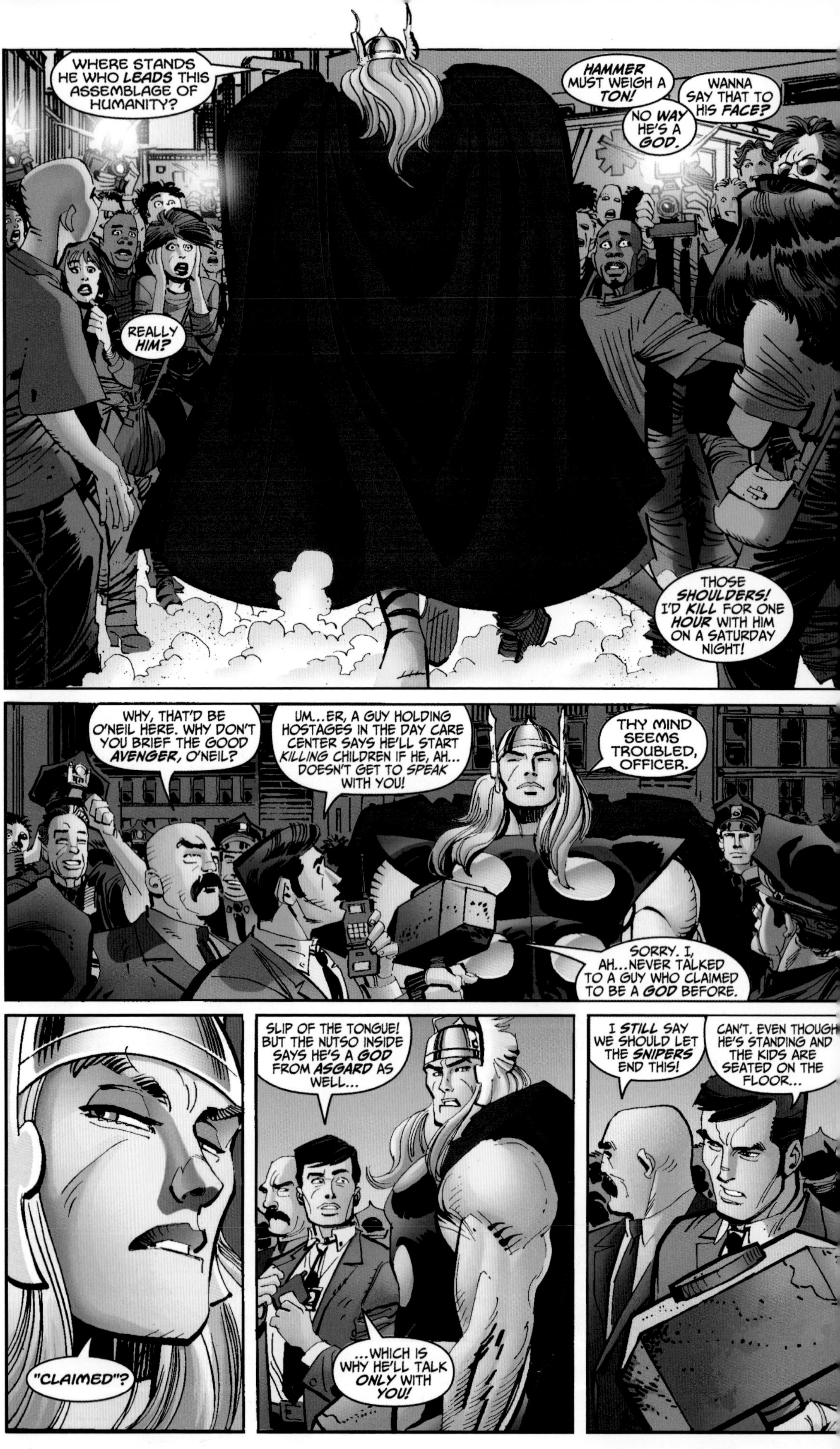
WHERE STANDS HE WHO LEADS THIS ASSEMBLAGE OF HUMANITY?
HAMMER MUST WEIGH A TON!
NO WAY HE'S A GOD.
WANNA SAY THAT TO HIS FACE?
REALLY HIM?
THOSE SHOULDERS! I'D KILL FOR ONE HOUR WITH HIM ON A SATURDAY NIGHT!
WHY, THAT'D BE O'NEIL HERE. WHY DON'T YOU BRIEF THE GOOD AVENGER, O'NEIL?
UM...ER, A GUY HOLDING HOSTAGES IN THE DAY CARE CENTER SAYS HE'LL START KILLING CHILDREN IF HE, AH... DOESN'T GET TO SPEAK WITH YOU!
THY MIND SEEMS TROUBLED, OFFICER.
SORRY. I, AH...NEVER TALKED TO A GUY WHO CLAIMED TO BE A GOD BEFORE.
"CLAIMED"?
SLIP OF THE TONGUE! BUT THE NUTSO INSIDE SAYS HE'S A GOD FROM ASGARD AS WELL...
...WHICH IS WHY HE'LL TALK ONLY WITH YOU!
I STILL SAY WE SHOULD LET THE SNIPERS END THIS!
CAN'T. EVEN THOUGH HE'S STANDING AND THE KIDS ARE SEATED ON THE FLOOR...

"...WE CAN'T BE SURE A RICOCHET WON'T HARM AN INNOCENT!"

BALLOON BUNC[H]
DAY CARE

STAY THY WEAPONS.

I KNOW NOT WHO THIS NE'ER-DO-WELL MAY BE -- -- BUT THE SCOURGE'S INFLICTION OF TERROR IS ABOUT TO END!

HEY! I CAN'T LET YOU GO MARCHING IN THERE WITHOUT KNOWING WHAT YOU PLAN TO-- HEY!

FORGET IT. YOU WANT HIM TO LISTEN -- GET ON YOUR KNEES.

BETTER GET YOUR AMBULANCE READY, OLSON! THINK WE'RE GONNA NEED IT!

Y'THINK THOR WOULD LET THOSE KIDS GET HURT?

I DON'T KNOW WHAT TO THINK.

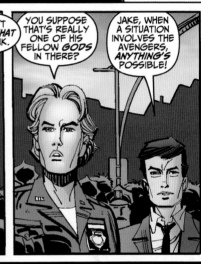

YOU SUPPOSE THAT'S REALLY ONE OF HIS FELLOW GODS IN THERE?

JAKE, WHEN A SITUATION INVOLVES THE AVENGERS, ANYTHING'S POSSIBLE!

IF IT BE A CONVERSATION WITH THOR THE SCOUNDREL WITHIN DESIRES--

-- 'TIS A CONVERSATION WITH THOR HE SHALL HAVE!

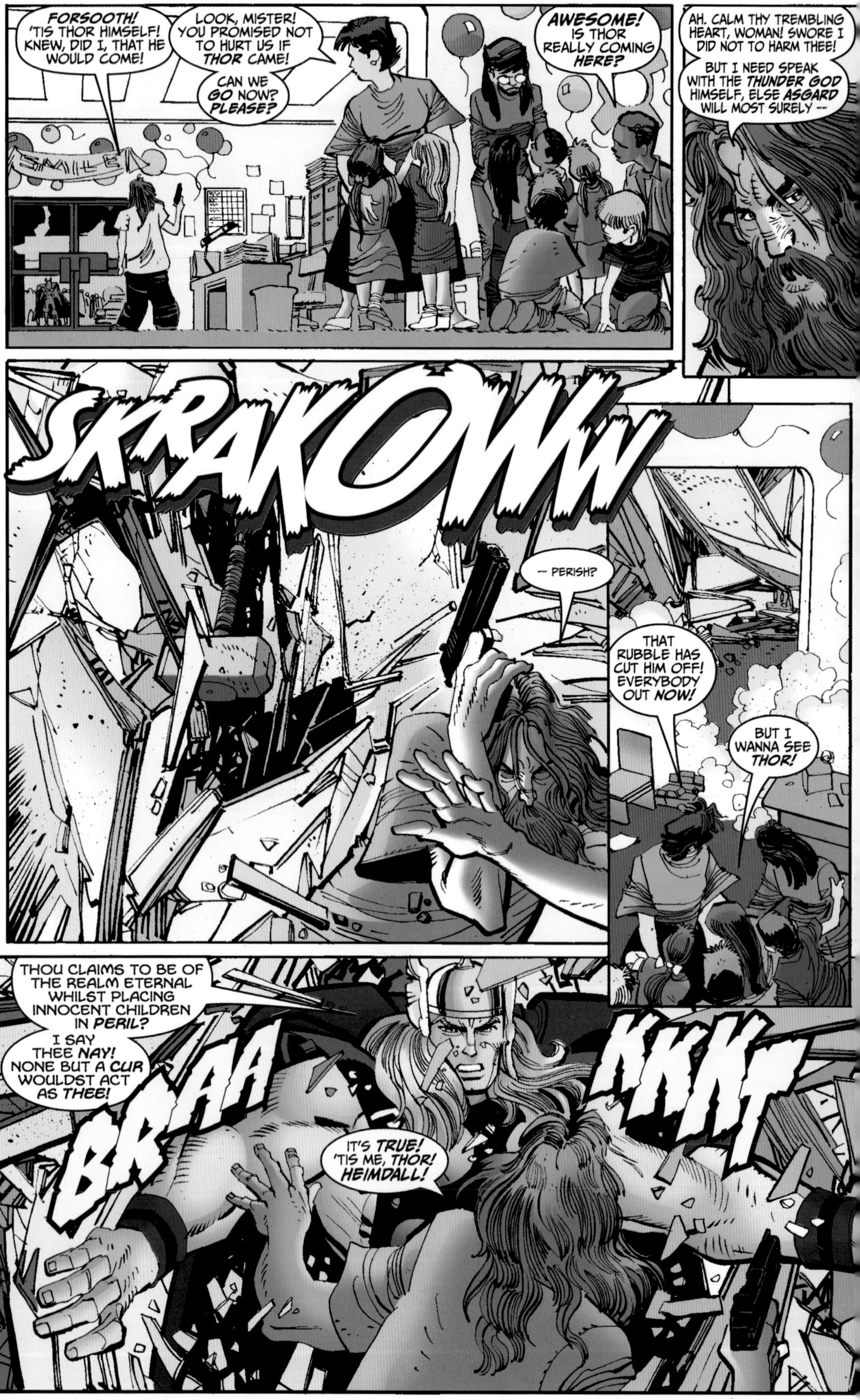
FORSOOTH! 'TIS THOR HIMSELF! KNEW, DID I, THAT HE WOULD COME!
LOOK, MISTER! YOU PROMISED NOT TO HURT US IF THOR CAME!
CAN WE GO NOW? PLEASE?
AWESOME! IS THOR REALLY COMING HERE?
AH. CALM THY TREMBLING HEART, WOMAN! SWORE I DID NOT TO HARM THEE!
BUT I NEED SPEAK WITH THE THUNDER GOD HIMSELF, ELSE ASGARD WILL MOST SURELY --
SKRAKOWW
-- PERISH?
THAT RUBBLE HAS CUT HIM OFF! EVERYBODY OUT NOW!
BUT I WANNA SEE THOR!
THOU CLAIMS TO BE OF THE REALM ETERNAL WHILST PLACING INNOCENT CHILDREN IN PERIL?
I SAY THEE NAY! NONE BUT A CUR WOULDST ACT AS THEE!
BRAAKKK
IT'S TRUE! 'TIS ME, THOR! HEIMDALL!

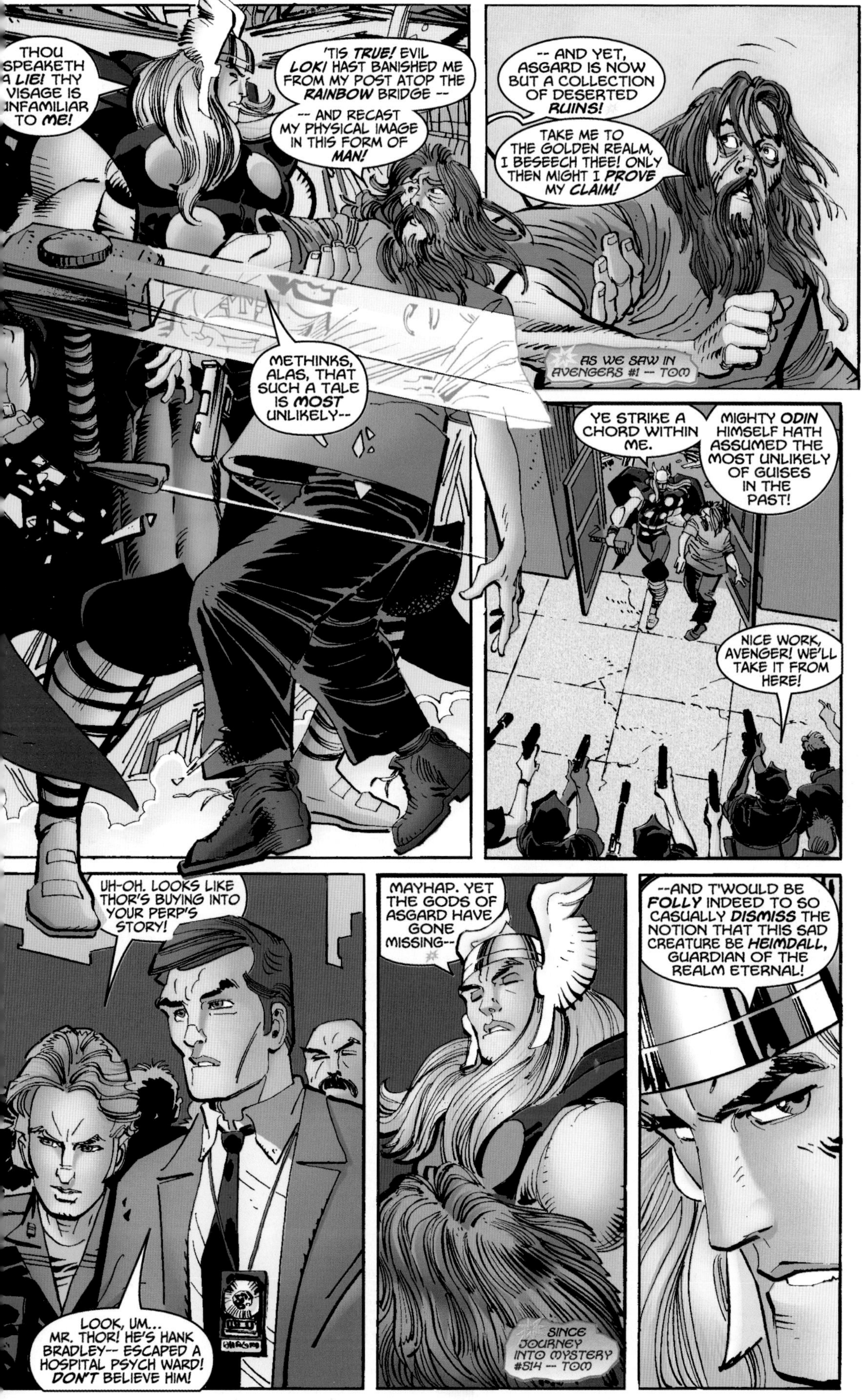

THOU SPEAKETH A LIE! THY VISAGE IS UNFAMILIAR TO ME!
'TIS TRUE! EVIL LOKI HAST BANISHED ME FROM MY POST ATOP THE RAINBOW BRIDGE --
-- AND RECAST MY PHYSICAL IMAGE IN THIS FORM OF MAN!
-- AND YET, ASGARD IS NOW BUT A COLLECTION OF DESERTED RUINS!
TAKE ME TO THE GOLDEN REALM, I BESEECH THEE! ONLY THEN MIGHT I PROVE MY CLAIM!
METHINKS, ALAS, THAT SUCH A TALE IS MOST UNLIKELY--
AS WE SAW IN AVENGERS #1 -- TOM
YE STRIKE A CHORD WITHIN ME.
MIGHTY ODIN HIMSELF HATH ASSUMED THE MOST UNLIKELY OF GUISES IN THE PAST!
NICE WORK, AVENGER! WE'LL TAKE IT FROM HERE!
UH-OH. LOOKS LIKE THOR'S BUYING INTO YOUR PERP'S STORY!
LOOK, UM... MR. THOR! HE'S HANK BRADLEY-- ESCAPED A HOSPITAL PSYCH WARD! DON'T BELIEVE HIM!
MAYHAP. YET THE GODS OF ASGARD HAVE GONE MISSING--
SINCE JOURNEY INTO MYSTERY #514 -- TOM
--AND T'WOULD BE FOLLY INDEED TO SO CASUALLY DISMISS THE NOTION THAT THIS SAD CREATURE BE HEIMDALL, GUARDIAN OF THE REALM ETERNAL!

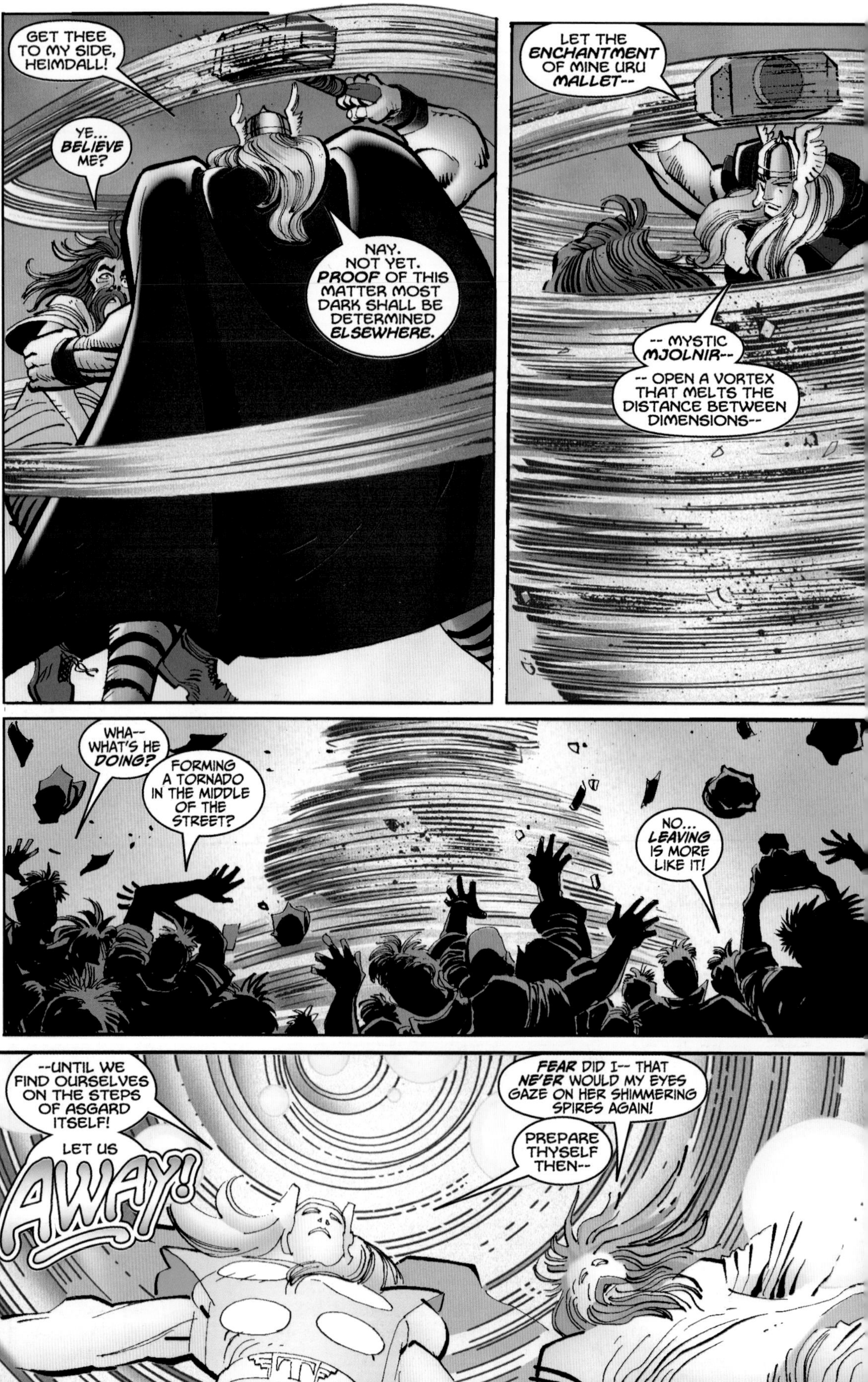
GET THEE TO MY SIDE, HEIMDALL!
YE... BELIEVE ME?
NAY. NOT YET. PROOF OF THIS MATTER MOST DARK SHALL BE DETERMINED ELSEWHERE.
LET THE ENCHANTMENT OF MINE URU MALLET--
-- MYSTIC MJOLNIR--
-- OPEN A VORTEX THAT MELTS THE DISTANCE BETWEEN DIMENSIONS--
WHA-- WHAT'S HE DOING?
FORMING A TORNADO IN THE MIDDLE OF THE STREET?
NO... LEAVING IS MORE LIKE IT!
--UNTIL WE FIND OURSELVES ON THE STEPS OF ASGARD ITSELF!
LET US
AWAY!
FEAR DID I-- THAT NE'ER WOULD MY EYES GAZE ON HER SHIMMERING SPIRES AGAIN!
PREPARE THYSELF THEN--

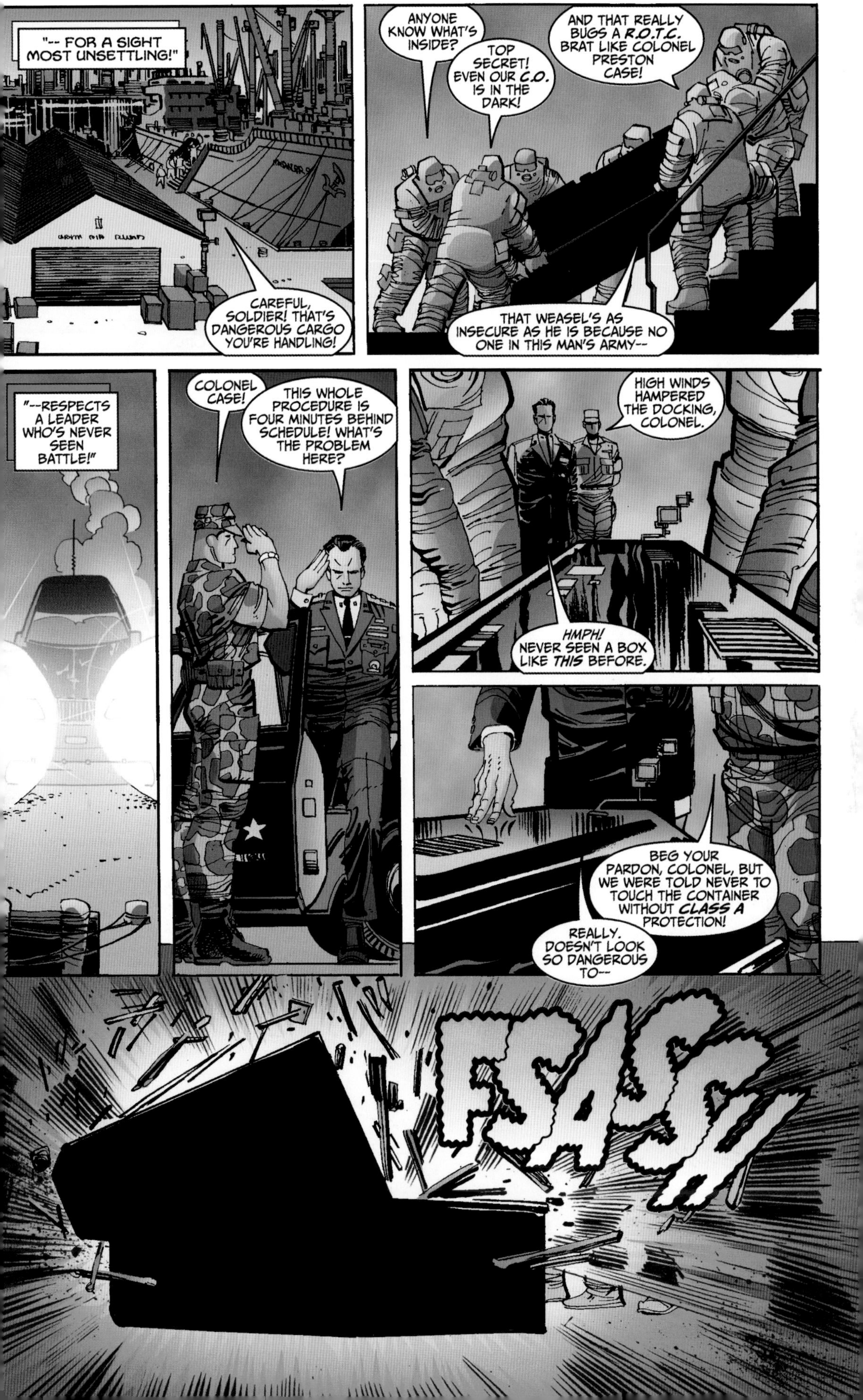
"-- FOR A SIGHT MOST UNSETTLING!"
CAREFUL, SOLDIER! THAT'S DANGEROUS CARGO YOU'RE HANDLING!
ANYONE KNOW WHAT'S INSIDE?
TOP SECRET! EVEN OUR C.O. IS IN THE DARK!
AND THAT REALLY BUGS A R.O.T.C. BRAT LIKE COLONEL PRESTON CASE!
THAT WEASEL'S AS INSECURE AS HE IS BECAUSE NO ONE IN THIS MAN'S ARMY--
"--RESPECTS A LEADER WHO'S NEVER SEEN BATTLE!"
COLONEL CASE!
THIS WHOLE PROCEDURE IS FOUR MINUTES BEHIND SCHEDULE! WHAT'S THE PROBLEM HERE?
HIGH WINDS HAMPERED THE DOCKING, COLONEL.
HMPH! NEVER SEEN A BOX LIKE THIS BEFORE.
BEG YOUR PARDON, COLONEL, BUT WE WERE TOLD NEVER TO TOUCH THE CONTAINER WITHOUT CLASS A PROTECTION!
REALLY. DOESN'T LOOK SO DANGEROUS TO--
FZAP

KIDS ARE *FINE*, JAKE! YOU AND HANNAH *WILL* GET YOUR DATE IN TONIGHT!

SCORE ONE FOR THE GOOD GUYS, DEMITRIUS! I'VE HAD TO STIFF HANNAH SO MANY TIMES THAT I'M *AMAZED* SHE'S AGREED TO MARRY ME!

YOU TWO LOVEBIRDS SET THE DATE YET?

JUST A FEW MONTHS FROM NOW, D!

UNLESS SHE COMES TO HER SENSES *FIRST*, THAT IS!

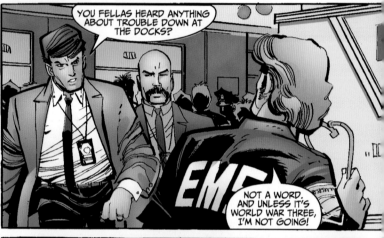

YOU FELLAS HEARD ANYTHING ABOUT TROUBLE DOWN AT THE DOCKS?

NOT A WORD. AND UNLESS IT'S WORLD WAR THREE, I'M NOT GOING!

BREEEP

BREEEP

SORRY, *LOVER BOY.* GOT ME A FEELING WE'RE GOING *OVERTIME!*

OH, NO...

OLSON HERE. AS IN *'ABOUT-TO-BE OFF-DUTY'* OLSON--

NOT YET, JAKE! PROCEED TO THE DOCKS A.S.A.P!

IS IT *WORLD WAR THREE?*

WORSE!

OH, MAN! WHEN HANNAH HEARS ABOUT THIS, I WON'T LIVE TO SEE THE MORNING!

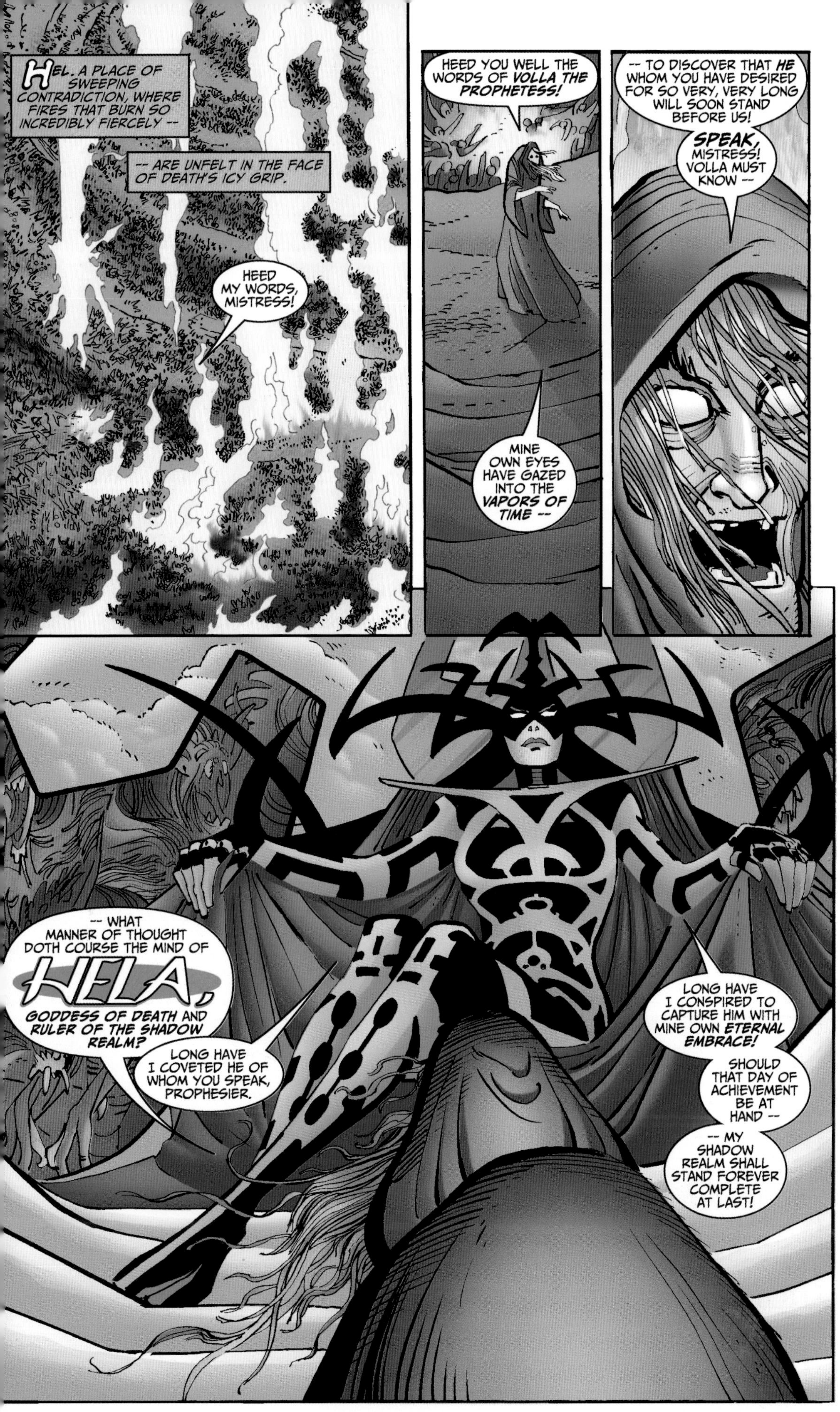
HEL. A PLACE OF SWEEPING CONTRADICTION, WHERE FIRES THAT BURN SO INCREDIBLY FIERCELY --
-- ARE UNFELT IN THE FACE OF DEATH'S ICY GRIP.
HEED MY WORDS, MISTRESS!
HEED YOU WELL THE WORDS OF VOLLA THE PROPHETESS!
MINE OWN EYES HAVE GAZED INTO THE VAPORS OF TIME --
-- TO DISCOVER THAT HE WHOM YOU HAVE DESIRED FOR SO VERY, VERY LONG WILL SOON STAND BEFORE US!
SPEAK, MISTRESS! VOLLA MUST KNOW --
-- WHAT MANNER OF THOUGHT DOTH COURSE THE MIND OF HELA, GODDESS OF DEATH AND RULER OF THE SHADOW REALM?
LONG HAVE I COVETED HE OF WHOM YOU SPEAK, PROPHESIER.
LONG HAVE I CONSPIRED TO CAPTURE HIM WITH MINE OWN ETERNAL EMBRACE!
SHOULD THAT DAY OF ACHIEVEMENT BE AT HAND --
-- MY SHADOW REALM SHALL STAND FOREVER COMPLETE AT LAST!

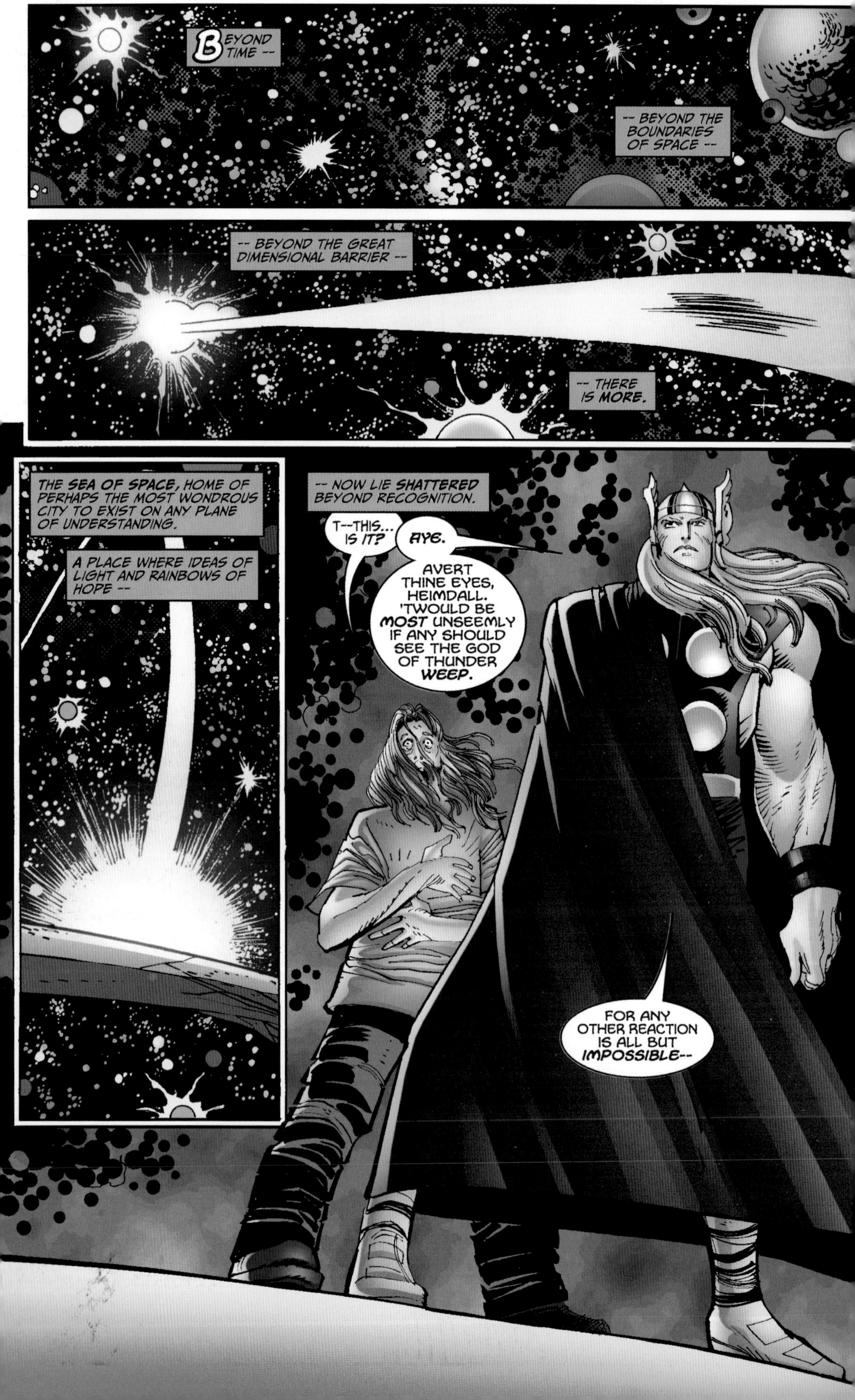
BEYOND TIME --
-- BEYOND THE BOUNDARIES OF SPACE --
-- BEYOND THE GREAT DIMENSIONAL BARRIER --
-- THERE IS MORE.
THE SEA OF SPACE, HOME OF PERHAPS THE MOST WONDROUS CITY TO EXIST ON ANY PLANE OF UNDERSTANDING.
A PLACE WHERE IDEAS OF LIGHT AND RAINBOWS OF HOPE --
-- NOW LIE SHATTERED BEYOND RECOGNITION.
T--THIS... IS IT?
AYE.
AVERT THINE EYES, HEIMDALL. 'TWOULD BE MOST UNSEEMLY IF ANY SHOULD SEE THE GOD OF THUNDER WEEP.
FOR ANY OTHER REACTION IS ALL BUT IMPOSSIBLE--

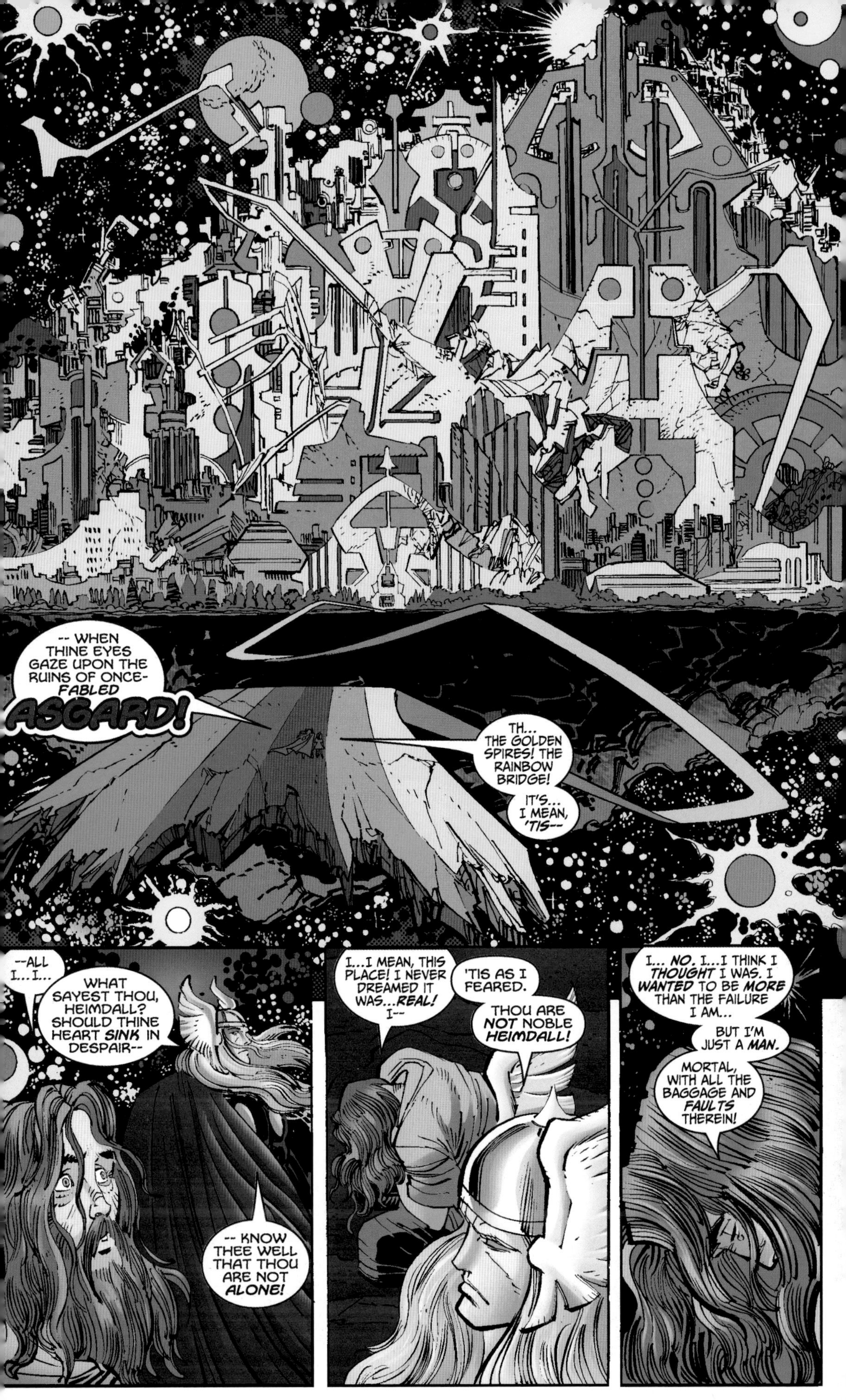
-- WHEN THINE EYES GAZE UPON THE RUINS OF ONCE-FABLED ASGARD!
TH... THE GOLDEN SPIRES! THE RAINBOW BRIDGE!
IT'S... I MEAN, 'TIS--
--ALL I... I...
WHAT SAYEST THOU, HEIMDALL? SHOULD THINE HEART SINK IN DESPAIR--
-- KNOW THEE WELL THAT THOU ARE NOT ALONE!
I...I MEAN, THIS PLACE! I NEVER DREAMED IT WAS...REAL! I--
'TIS AS I FEARED.
THOU ARE NOT NOBLE HEIMDALL!
I... NO. I...I THINK I THOUGHT I WAS. I WANTED TO BE MORE THAN THE FAILURE I AM...
BUT I'M JUST A MAN.
MORTAL, WITH ALL THE BAGGAGE AND FAULTS THEREIN!

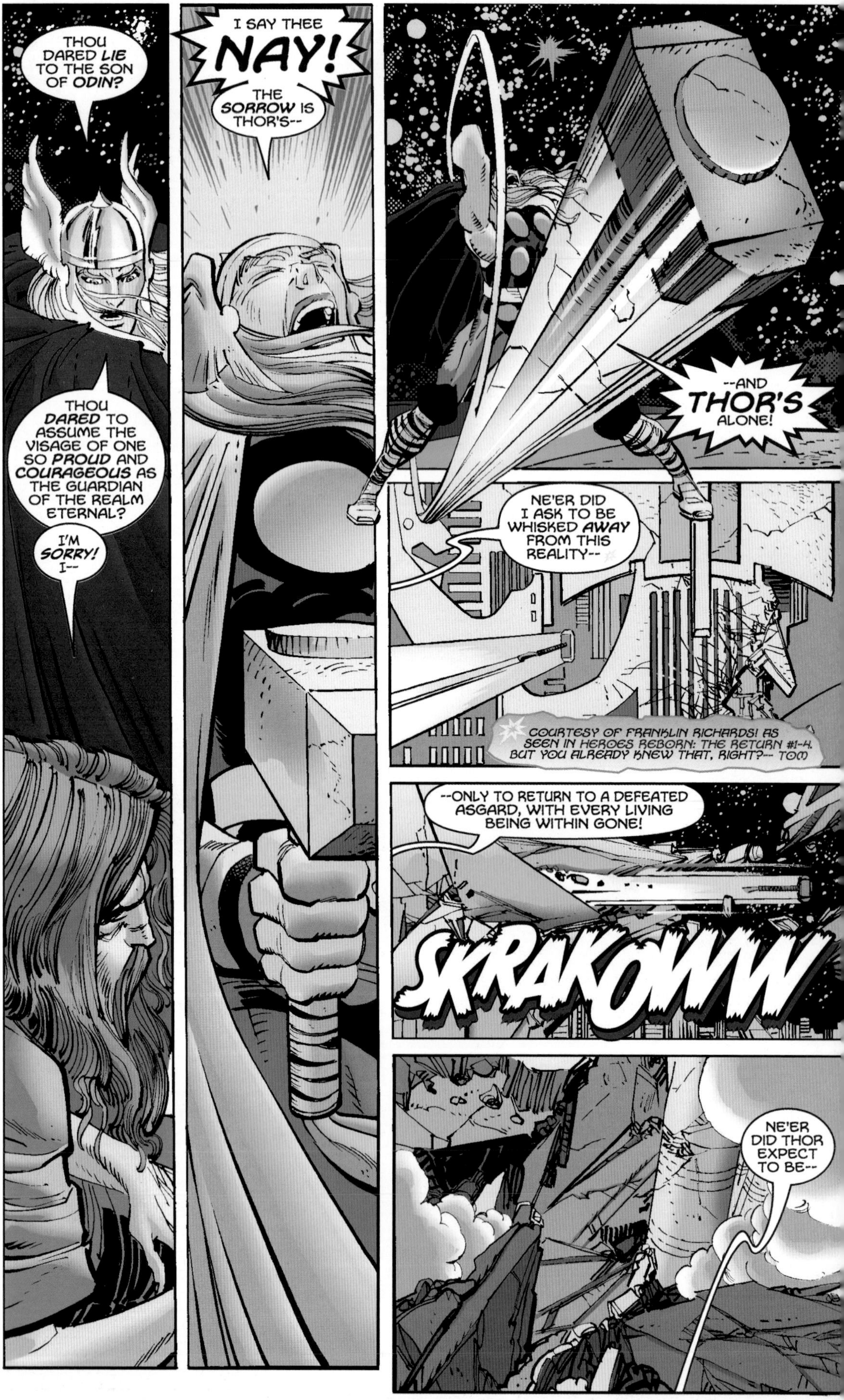
THOU DARED LIE TO THE SON OF ODIN?
THOU DARED TO ASSUME THE VISAGE OF ONE SO PROUD AND COURAGEOUS AS THE GUARDIAN OF THE REALM ETERNAL?
I'M SORRY! I--
I SAY THEE NAY!
THE SORROW IS THOR'S--
--AND THOR'S ALONE!
NE'ER DID I ASK TO BE WHISKED AWAY FROM THIS REALITY--
COURTESY OF FRANKLIN RICHARDS! AS SEEN IN HEROES REBORN: THE RETURN #1-4. BUT YOU ALREADY KNEW THAT, RIGHT?-- TOM
--ONLY TO RETURN TO A DEFEATED ASGARD, WITH EVERY LIVING BEING WITHIN GONE!
SKRAKOWW
NE'ER DID THOR EXPECT TO BE--

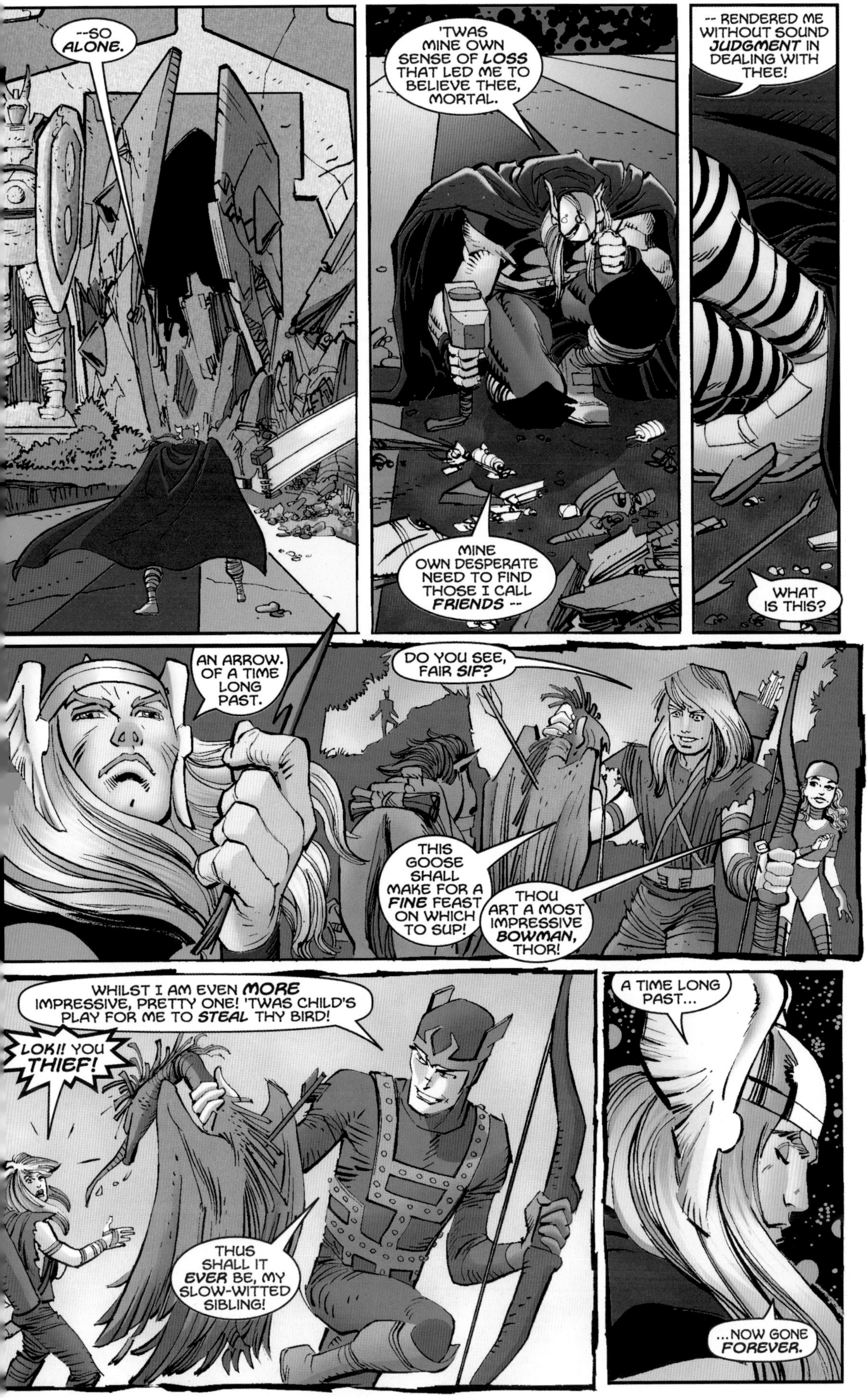
--SO ALONE.
'TWAS MINE OWN SENSE OF LOSS THAT LED ME TO BELIEVE THEE, MORTAL.
MINE OWN DESPERATE NEED TO FIND THOSE I CALL FRIENDS --
-- RENDERED ME WITHOUT SOUND JUDGMENT IN DEALING WITH THEE!
WHAT IS THIS?
AN ARROW. OF A TIME LONG PAST.
DO YOU SEE, FAIR SIF?
THIS GOOSE SHALL MAKE FOR A FINE FEAST ON WHICH TO SUP!
THOU ART A MOST IMPRESSIVE BOWMAN, THOR!
WHILST I AM EVEN MORE IMPRESSIVE, PRETTY ONE! 'TWAS CHILD'S PLAY FOR ME TO STEAL THY BIRD!
LOKI! YOU THIEF!
THUS SHALL IT EVER BE, MY SLOW-WITTED SIBLING!
A TIME LONG PAST...
...NOW GONE FOREVER.

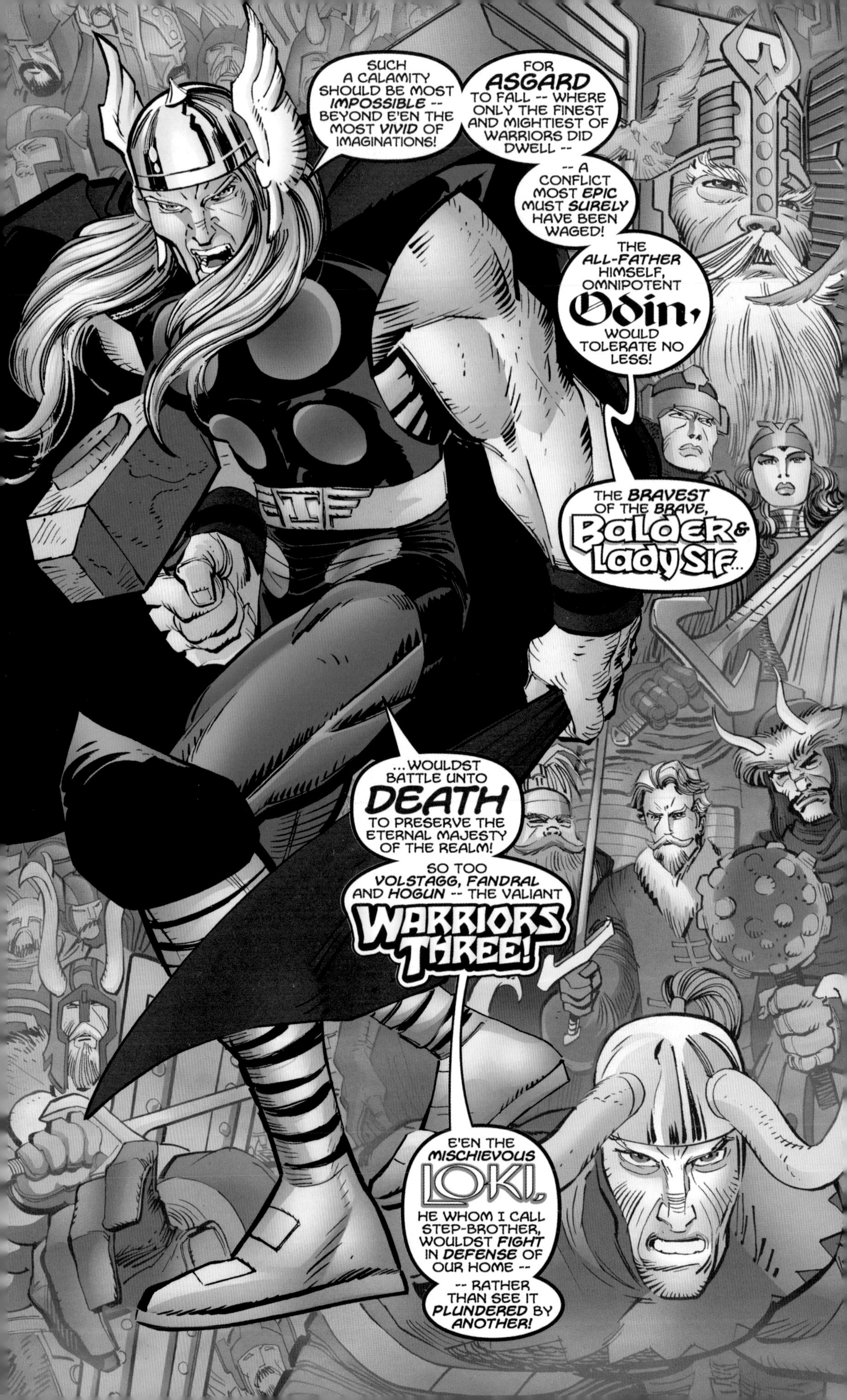

SUCH A CALAMITY SHOULD BE MOST IMPOSSIBLE -- BEYOND E'EN THE MOST VIVID OF IMAGINATIONS!
FOR ASGARD TO FALL -- WHERE ONLY THE FINEST AND MIGHTIEST OF WARRIORS DID DWELL --
-- A CONFLICT MOST EPIC MUST SURELY HAVE BEEN WAGED!
THE ALL-FATHER HIMSELF, OMNIPOTENT ODIN, WOULD TOLERATE NO LESS!
THE BRAVEST OF THE BRAVE, BALDER & LADY SIF...
...WOULDST BATTLE UNTO DEATH TO PRESERVE THE ETERNAL MAJESTY OF THE REALM!
SO TOO VOLSTAGG, FANDRAL AND HOGUN -- THE VALIANT WARRIORS THREE!
E'EN THE MISCHIEVOUS LOKI, HE WHOM I CALL STEP-BROTHER, WOULDST FIGHT IN DEFENSE OF OUR HOME --
-- RATHER THAN SEE IT PLUNDERED BY ANOTHER!

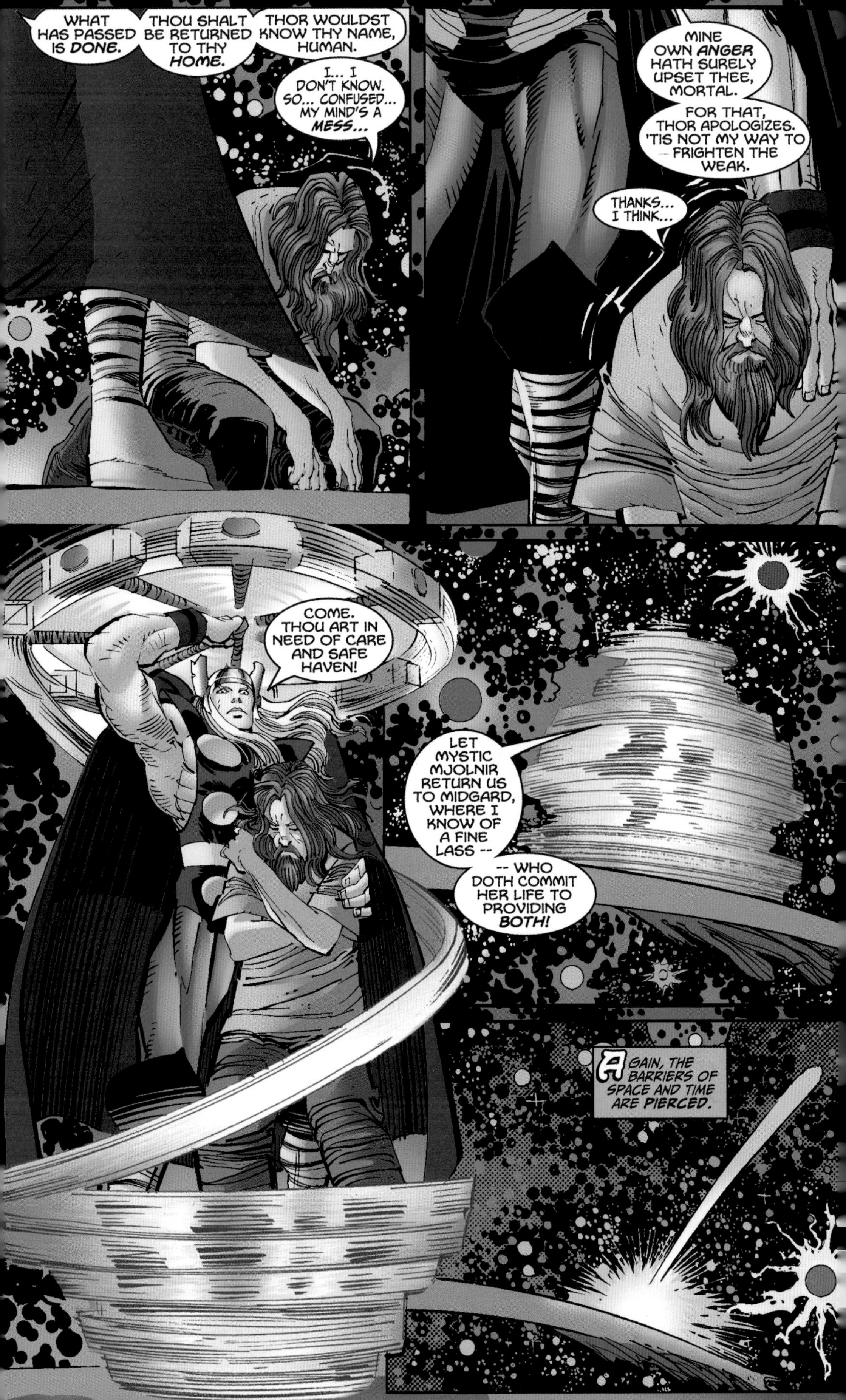
WHAT HAS PASSED IS DONE.
THOU SHALT BE RETURNED TO THY HOME.
THOR WOULDST KNOW THY NAME, HUMAN.
I... I DON'T KNOW. SO... CONFUSED... MY MIND'S A MESS...
MINE OWN ANGER HATH SURELY UPSET THEE, MORTAL.
FOR THAT, THOR APOLOGIZES. 'TIS NOT MY WAY TO FRIGHTEN THE WEAK.
THANKS... I THINK...
COME. THOU ART IN NEED OF CARE AND SAFE HAVEN!
LET MYSTIC MJOLNIR RETURN US TO MIDGARD, WHERE I KNOW OF A FINE LASS --
-- WHO DOTH COMMIT HER LIFE TO PROVIDING BOTH!
AGAIN, THE BARRIERS OF SPACE AND TIME ARE PIERCED.

BUT THIS TIME, DEEP IN THE RUINS OF ASGARD --

-- WHERE THE THUNDER GOD'S HAMMER MJOLNIR SHATTERED THE REMAINS OF A BUILDING --

-- THERE IS A WITNESS.

SHRAKKT

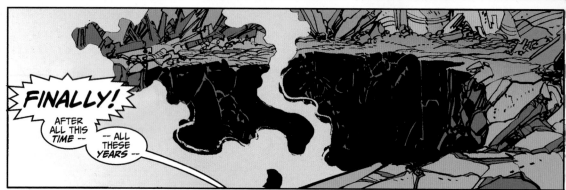

FINALLY!

AFTER ALL THIS TIME --

-- ALL THESE YEARS --

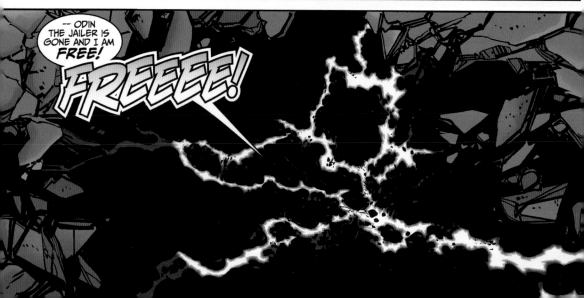

-- ODIN THE JAILER IS GONE AND I AM FREE!

FREEEE!

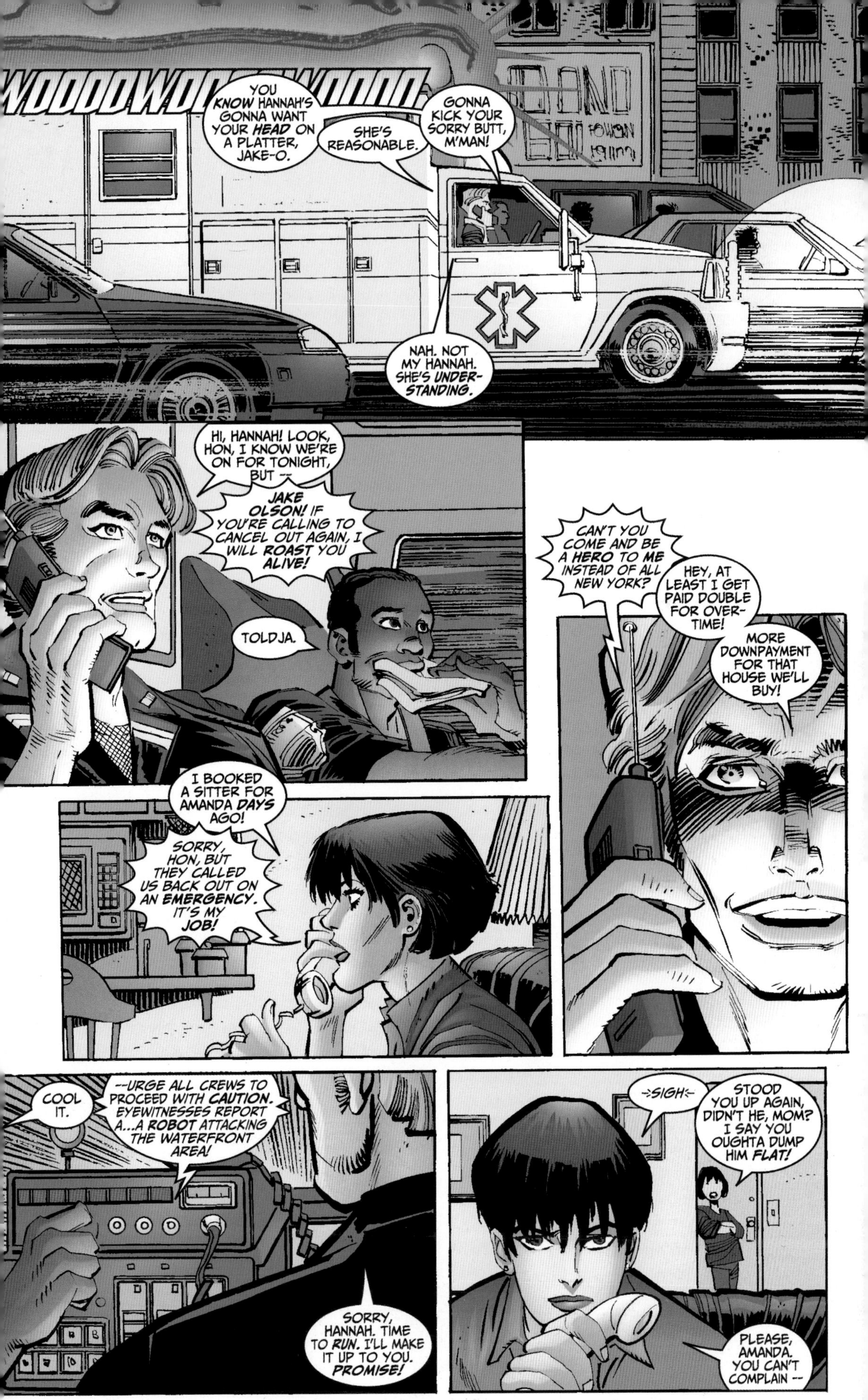
WOOOOWOOOOWOOOO
YOU KNOW HANNAH'S GONNA WANT YOUR HEAD ON A PLATTER, JAKE-O.
SHE'S REASONABLE.
GONNA KICK YOUR SORRY BUTT, M'MAN!
NAH. NOT MY HANNAH. SHE'S UNDER-STANDING.
HI, HANNAH! LOOK, HON, I KNOW WE'RE ON FOR TONIGHT, BUT --
JAKE OLSON! IF YOU'RE CALLING TO CANCEL OUT AGAIN, I WILL ROAST YOU ALIVE!
TOLDJA.
CAN'T YOU COME AND BE A HERO TO ME INSTEAD OF ALL NEW YORK?
HEY, AT LEAST I GET PAID DOUBLE FOR OVER-TIME!
MORE DOWNPAYMENT FOR THAT HOUSE WE'LL BUY!
I BOOKED A SITTER FOR AMANDA DAYS AGO!
SORRY, HON, BUT THEY CALLED US BACK OUT ON AN EMERGENCY. IT'S MY JOB!
COOL IT.
--URGE ALL CREWS TO PROCEED WITH CAUTION. EYEWITNESSES REPORT A...A ROBOT ATTACKING THE WATERFRONT AREA!
SORRY, HANNAH. TIME TO RUN. I'LL MAKE IT UP TO YOU. PROMISE!
-SIGH-
STOOD YOU UP AGAIN, DIDN'T HE, MOM? I SAY YOU OUGHTA DUMP HIM FLAT!
PLEASE, AMANDA. YOU CAN'T COMPLAIN --

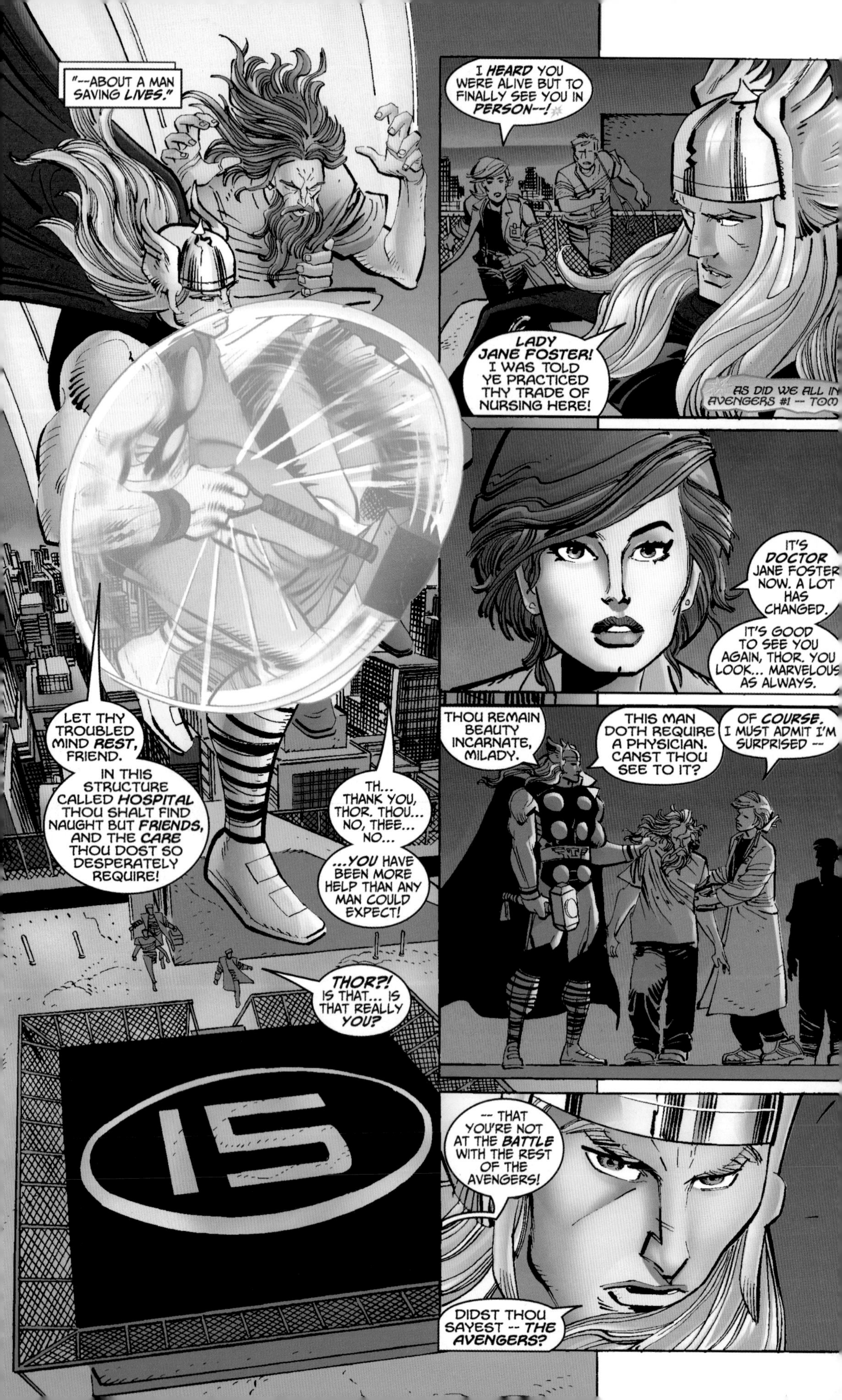
"--ABOUT A MAN SAVING LIVES."
LET THY TROUBLED MIND REST, FRIEND.
IN THIS STRUCTURE CALLED HOSPITAL THOU SHALT FIND NAUGHT BUT FRIENDS, AND THE CARE THOU DOST SO DESPERATELY REQUIRE!
TH... THANK YOU, THOR. THOU... NO, THEE... NO...
...YOU HAVE BEEN MORE HELP THAN ANY MAN COULD EXPECT!
THOR?! IS THAT... IS THAT REALLY YOU?
15
I HEARD YOU WERE ALIVE BUT TO FINALLY SEE YOU IN PERSON--!
LADY JANE FOSTER! I WAS TOLD YE PRACTICED THY TRADE OF NURSING HERE!
AS DID WE ALL IN AVENGERS #1 -- TOM
IT'S DOCTOR JANE FOSTER NOW. A LOT HAS CHANGED.
IT'S GOOD TO SEE YOU AGAIN, THOR. YOU LOOK... MARVELOUS AS ALWAYS.
THOU REMAIN BEAUTY INCARNATE, MILADY.
THIS MAN DOTH REQUIRE A PHYSICIAN. CANST THOU SEE TO IT?
OF COURSE. I MUST ADMIT I'M SURPRISED --
-- THAT YOU'RE NOT AT THE BATTLE WITH THE REST OF THE AVENGERS!
DIDST THOU SAYEST -- THE AVENGERS?

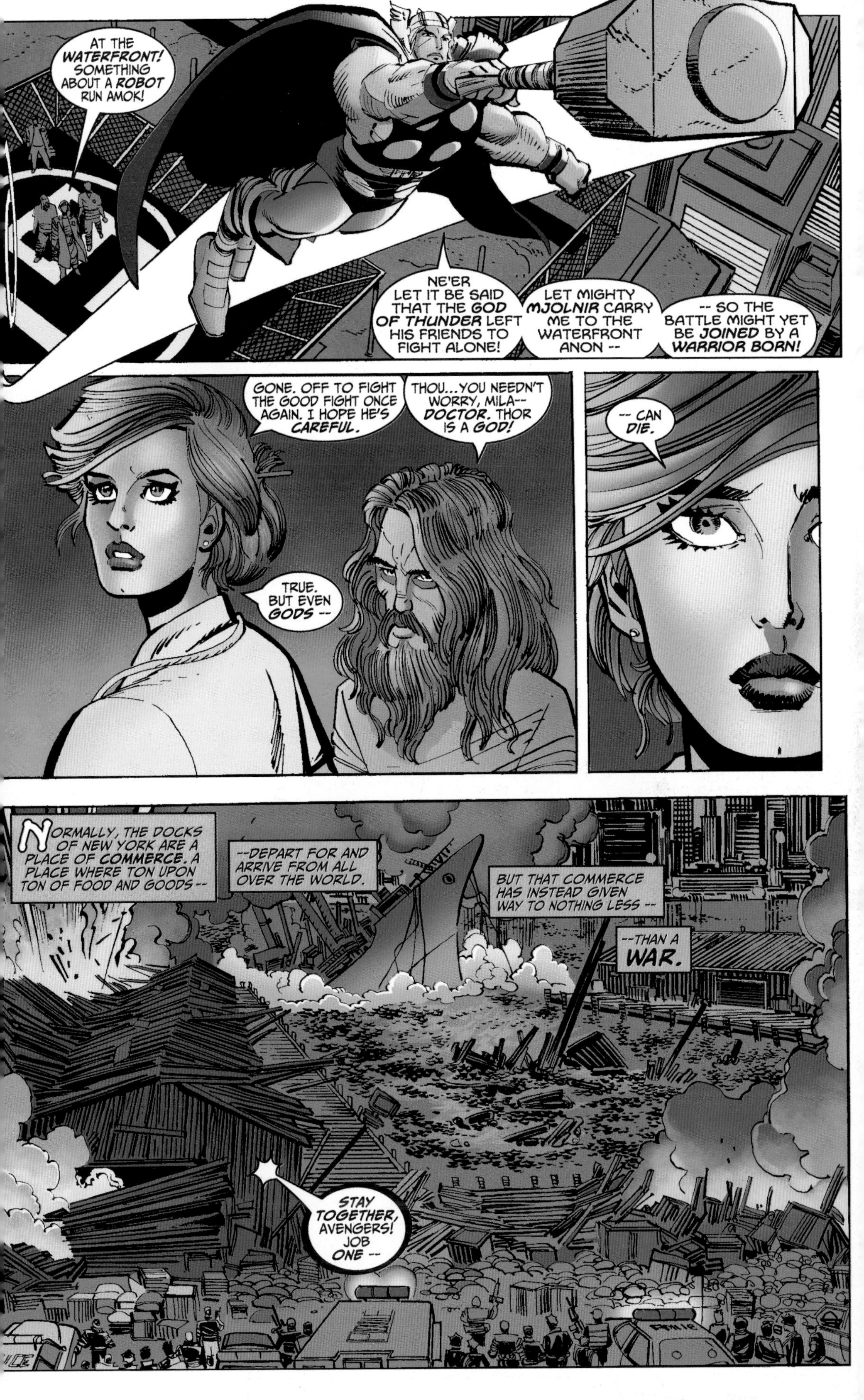
AT THE WATERFRONT! SOMETHING ABOUT A ROBOT RUN AMOK!
NE'ER LET IT BE SAID THAT THE GOD OF THUNDER LEFT HIS FRIENDS TO FIGHT ALONE!
LET MIGHTY MJOLNIR CARRY ME TO THE WATERFRONT ANON --
-- SO THE BATTLE MIGHT YET BE JOINED BY A WARRIOR BORN!
GONE. OFF TO FIGHT THE GOOD FIGHT ONCE AGAIN. I HOPE HE'S CAREFUL.
THOU...YOU NEEDN'T WORRY, MILA-- DOCTOR. THOR IS A GOD!
TRUE. BUT EVEN GODS --
-- CAN DIE.
NORMALLY, THE DOCKS OF NEW YORK ARE A PLACE OF COMMERCE. A PLACE WHERE TON UPON TON OF FOOD AND GOODS --
--DEPART FOR AND ARRIVE FROM ALL OVER THE WORLD.
BUT THAT COMMERCE HAS INSTEAD GIVEN WAY TO NOTHING LESS --
--THAN A WAR.
STAY TOGETHER, AVENGERS! JOB ONE --

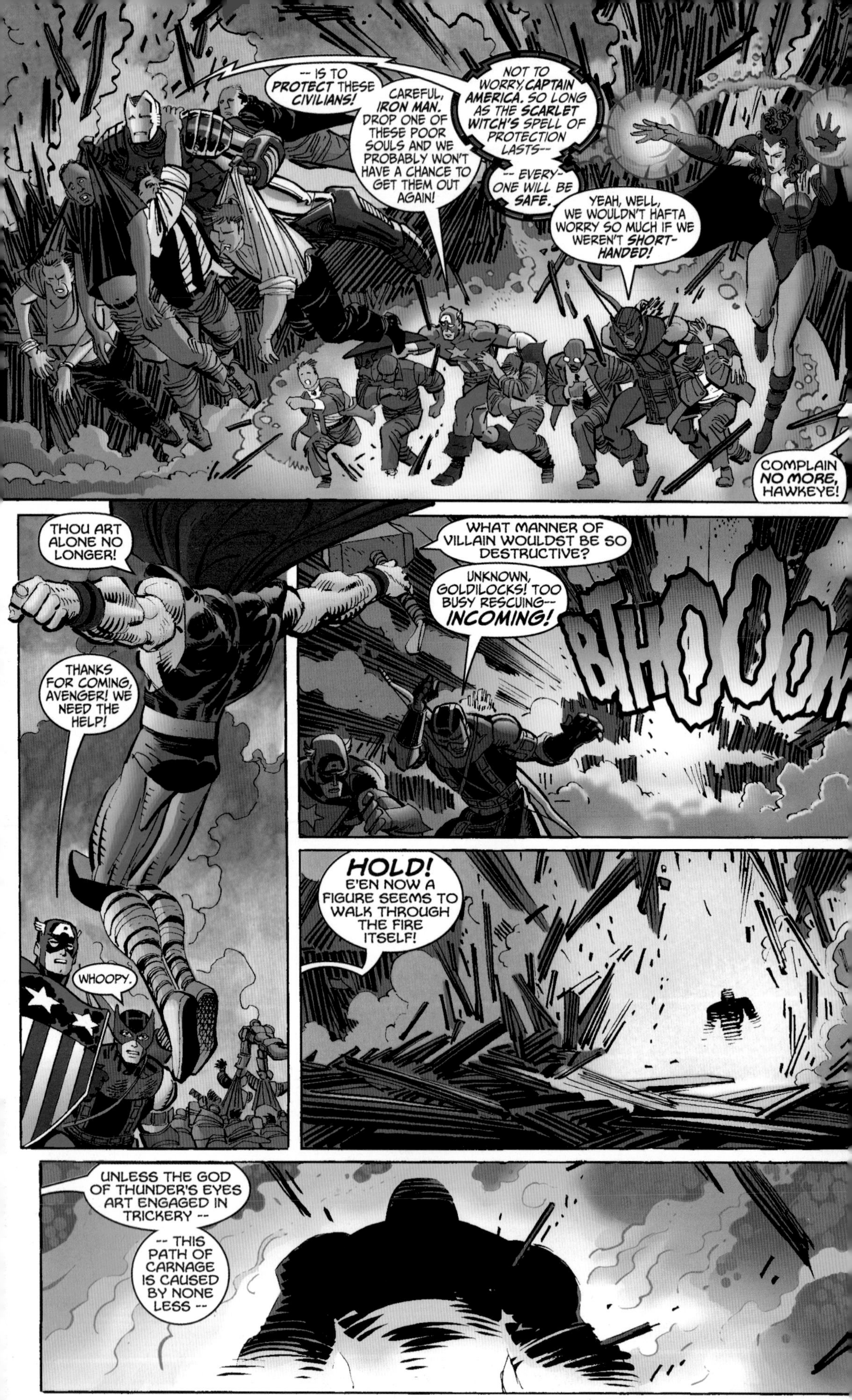

-- IS TO PROTECT THESE CIVILIANS!
CAREFUL, IRON MAN. DROP ONE OF THESE POOR SOULS AND WE PROBABLY WON'T HAVE A CHANCE TO GET THEM OUT AGAIN!
NOT TO WORRY, CAPTAIN AMERICA. SO LONG AS THE SCARLET WITCH'S SPELL OF PROTECTION LASTS--
-- EVERY-ONE WILL BE SAFE.
YEAH, WELL, WE WOULDN'T HAFTA WORRY SO MUCH IF WE WEREN'T SHORT-HANDED!
COMPLAIN NO MORE, HAWKEYE!
THOU ART ALONE NO LONGER!
THANKS FOR COMING, AVENGER! WE NEED THE HELP!
WHOOPY.
WHAT MANNER OF VILLAIN WOULDST BE SO DESTRUCTIVE?
UNKNOWN, GOLDILOCKS! TOO BUSY RESCUING-- INCOMING!
BHOOO
HOLD! E'EN NOW A FIGURE SEEMS TO WALK THROUGH THE FIRE ITSELF!
UNLESS THE GOD OF THUNDER'S EYES ART ENGAGED IN TRICKERY --
-- THIS PATH OF CARNAGE IS CAUSED BY NONE LESS --

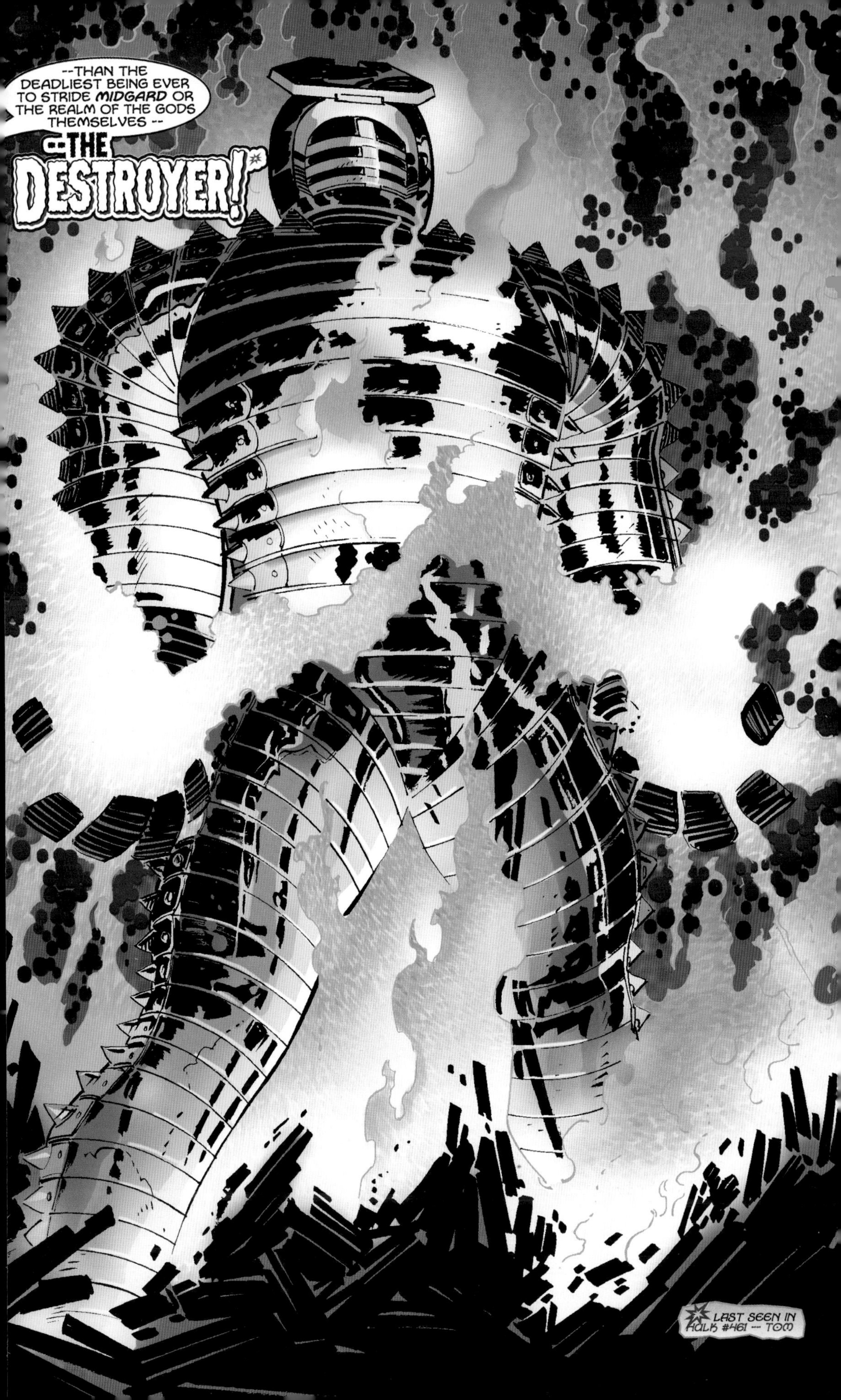
--THAN THE DEADLIEST BEING EVER TO STRIDE MIDGARD OR THE REALM OF THE GODS THEMSELVES --
--THE DESTROYER!
LAST SEEN IN HULK #461 -- TOM

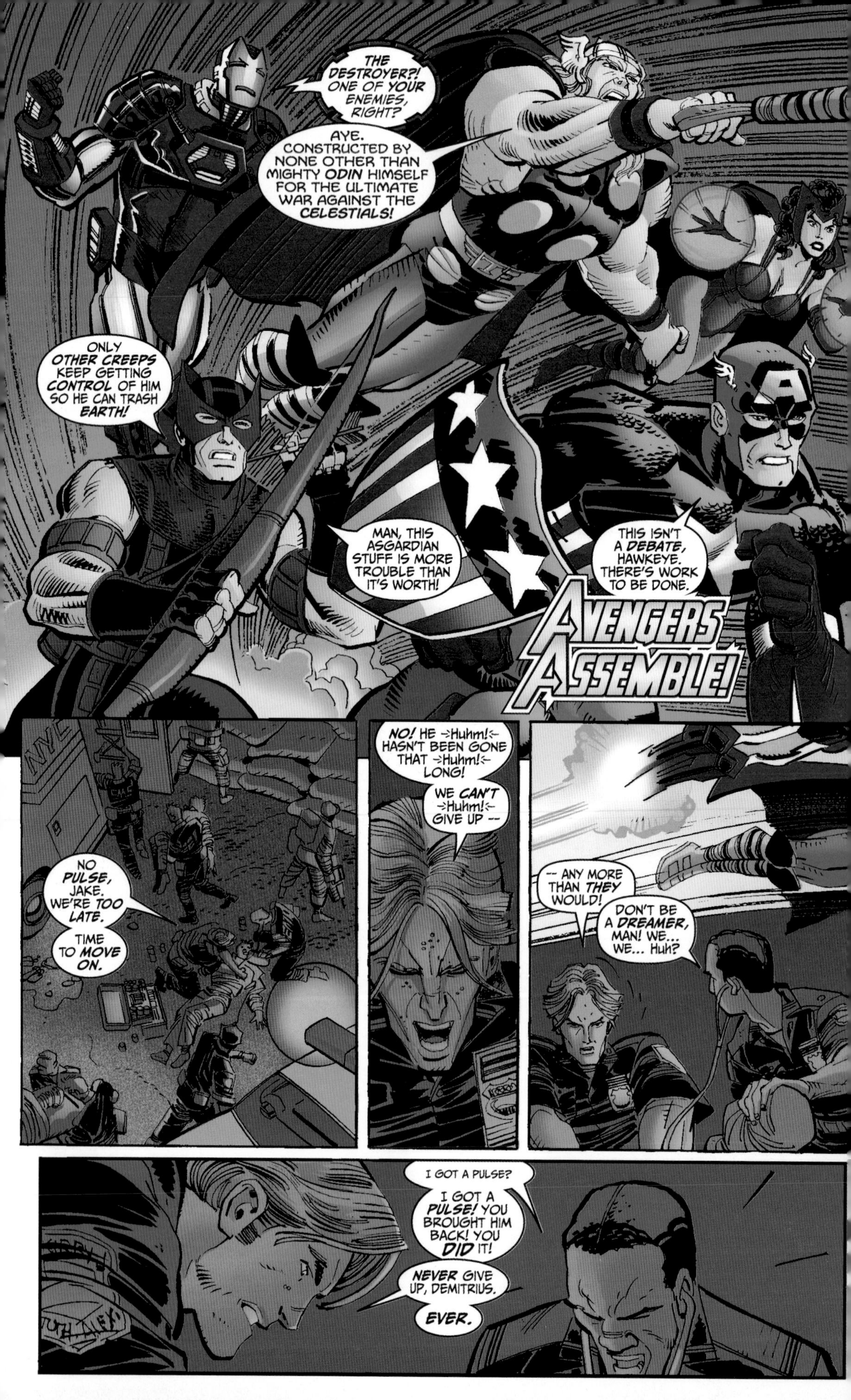
THE DESTROYER?! ONE OF YOUR ENEMIES, RIGHT?
AYE. CONSTRUCTED BY NONE OTHER THAN MIGHTY ODIN HIMSELF FOR THE ULTIMATE WAR AGAINST THE CELESTIALS!
ONLY OTHER CREEPS KEEP GETTING CONTROL OF HIM SO HE CAN TRASH EARTH!
MAN, THIS ASGARDIAN STUFF IS MORE TROUBLE THAN IT'S WORTH!
THIS ISN'T A DEBATE, HAWKEYE. THERE'S WORK TO BE DONE.
AVENGERS ASSEMBLE!
NO PULSE, JAKE. WE'RE TOO LATE.
TIME TO MOVE ON.
NO! HE -Huhm!- HASN'T BEEN GONE THAT -Huhm!- LONG!
WE CAN'T -Huhm!- GIVE UP --
-- ANY MORE THAN THEY WOULD!
DON'T BE A DREAMER, MAN! WE... WE... Huh?
I GOT A PULSE?
I GOT A PULSE! YOU BROUGHT HIM BACK! YOU DID IT!
NEVER GIVE UP, DEMITRIUS.
EVER.

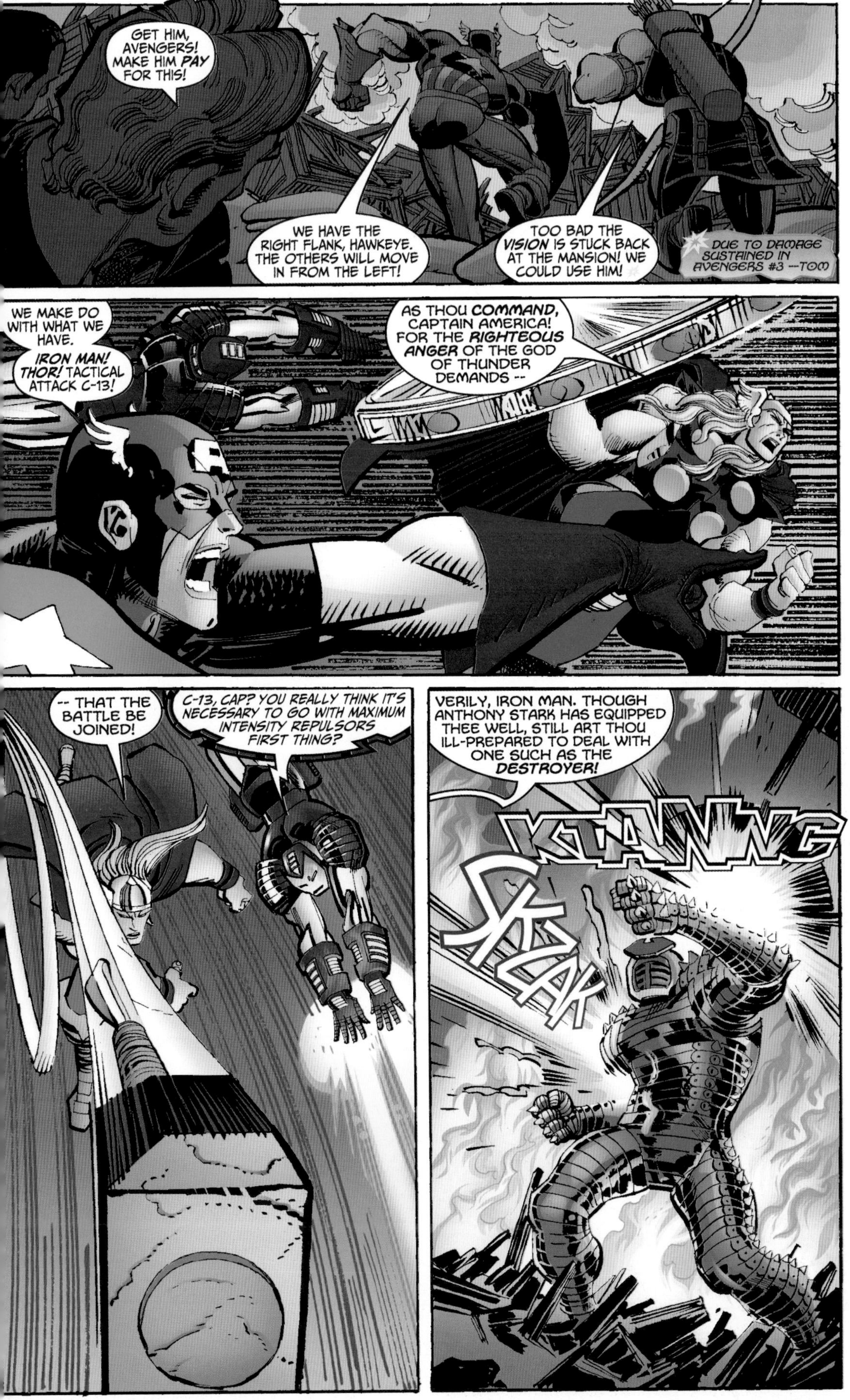
GET HIM, AVENGERS! MAKE HIM PAY FOR THIS!
WE HAVE THE RIGHT FLANK, HAWKEYE. THE OTHERS WILL MOVE IN FROM THE LEFT!
TOO BAD THE VISION IS STUCK BACK AT THE MANSION! WE COULD USE HIM!
DUE TO DAMAGE SUSTAINED IN AVENGERS #3 --TOM
WE MAKE DO WITH WHAT WE HAVE. IRON MAN! THOR! TACTICAL ATTACK C-13!
AS THOU COMMAND, CAPTAIN AMERICA! FOR THE RIGHTEOUS ANGER OF THE GOD OF THUNDER DEMANDS --
-- THAT THE BATTLE BE JOINED!
C-13, CAP? YOU REALLY THINK IT'S NECESSARY TO GO WITH MAXIMUM INTENSITY REPULSORS FIRST THING?
VERILY, IRON MAN. THOUGH ANTHONY STARK HAS EQUIPPED THEE WELL, STILL ART THOU ILL-PREPARED TO DEAL WITH ONE SUCH AS THE DESTROYER!
KTANNG
SKZAK

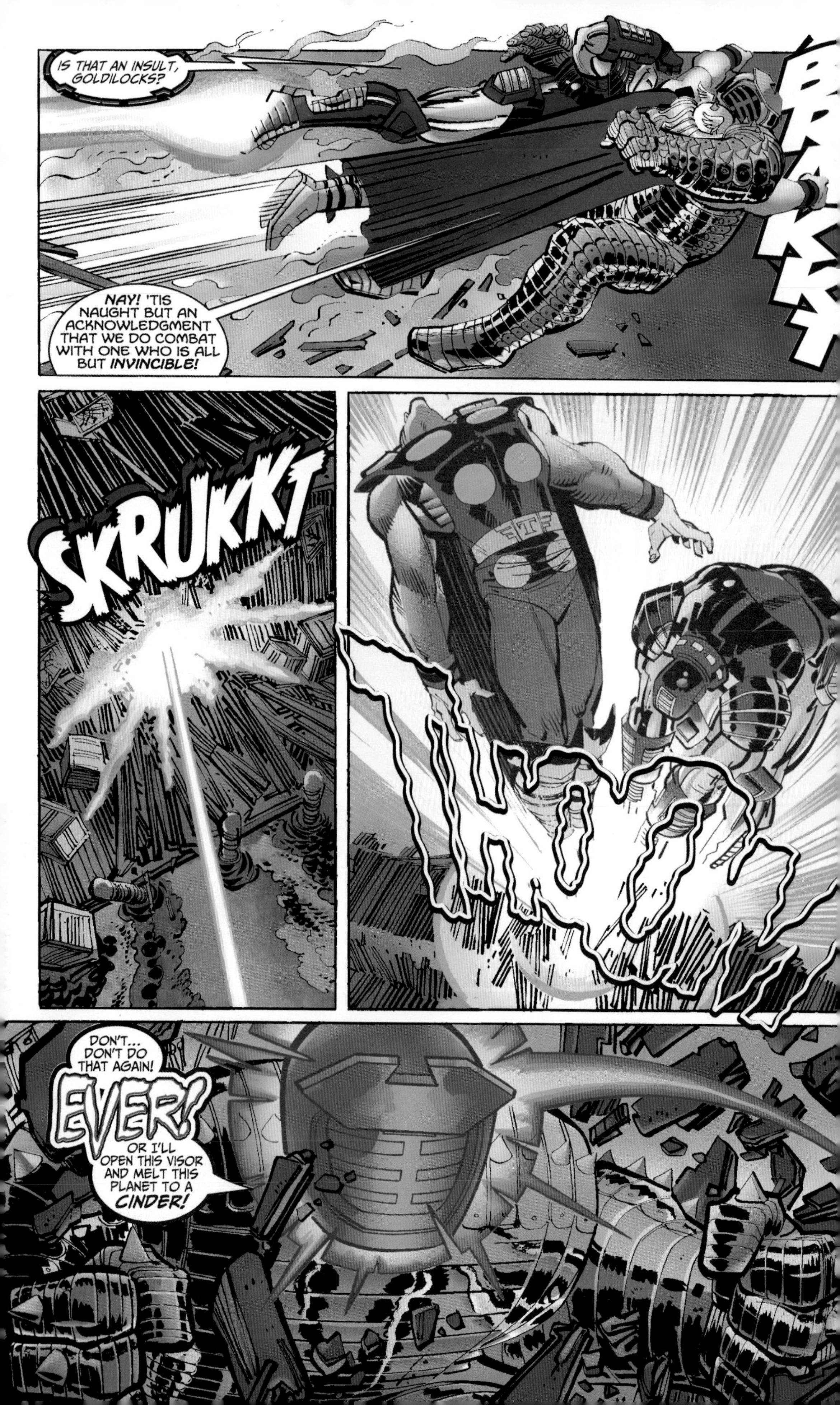

IS THAT AN INSULT, GOLDILOCKS?
BRAKKT
NAY! 'TIS NAUGHT BUT AN ACKNOWLEDGMENT THAT WE DO COMBAT WITH ONE WHO IS ALL BUT INVINCIBLE!
SKRUKKT
DON'T... DON'T DO THAT AGAIN!
EVER!
OR I'LL OPEN THIS VISOR AND MELT THIS PLANET TO A CINDER!

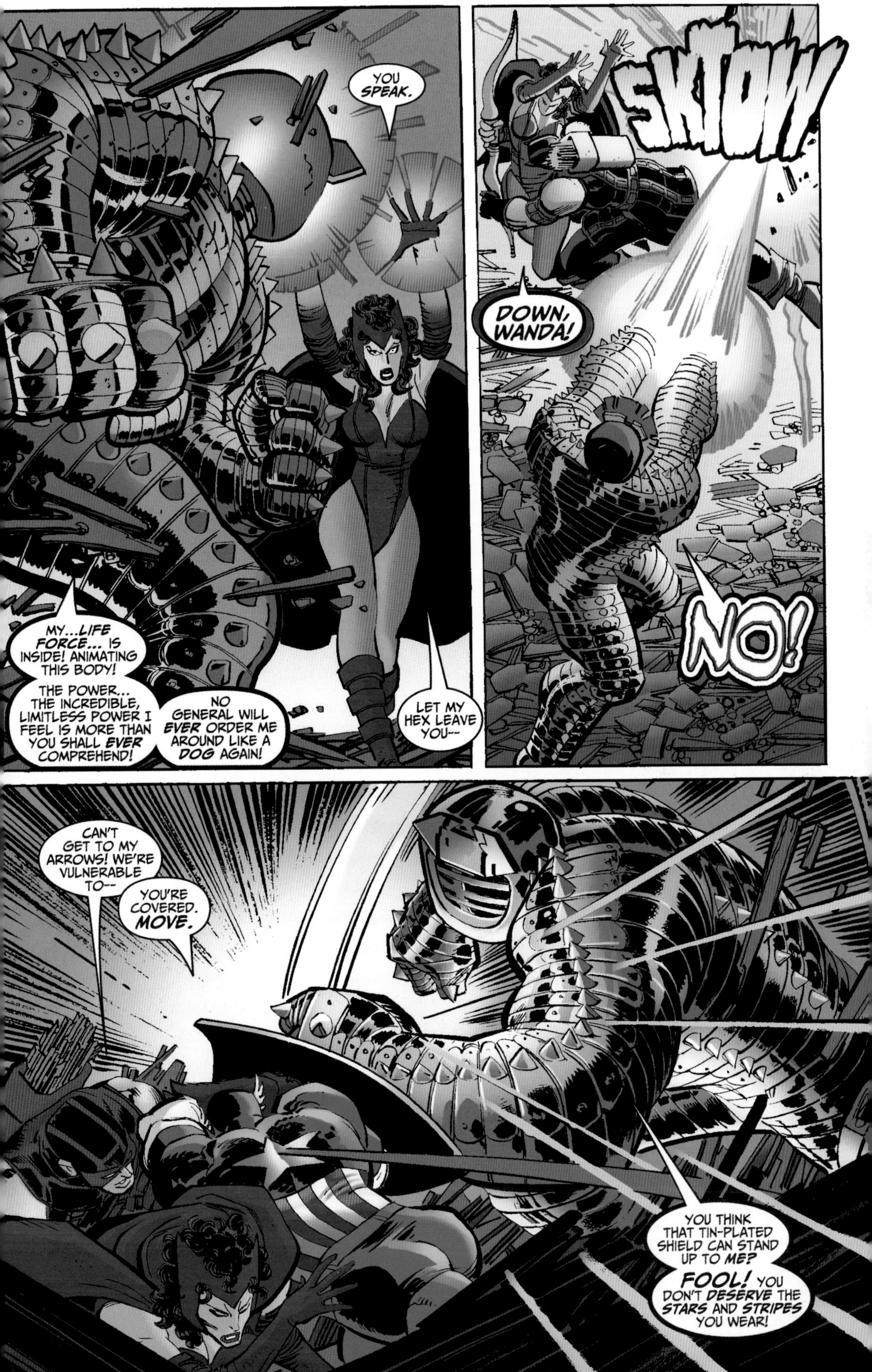
YOU SPEAK.
MY...LIFE FORCE... IS INSIDE! ANIMATING THIS BODY!
THE POWER... THE INCREDIBLE, LIMITLESS POWER I FEEL IS MORE THAN YOU SHALL EVER COMPREHEND!
NO GENERAL WILL EVER ORDER ME AROUND LIKE A DOG AGAIN!
LET MY HEX LEAVE YOU--
SKTOW
DOWN, WANDA!
NO!
CAN'T GET TO MY ARROWS! WE'RE VULNERABLE TO--
YOU'RE COVERED. MOVE.
YOU THINK THAT TIN-PLATED SHIELD CAN STAND UP TO ME?
FOOL! YOU DON'T DESERVE THE STARS AND STRIPES YOU WEAR!

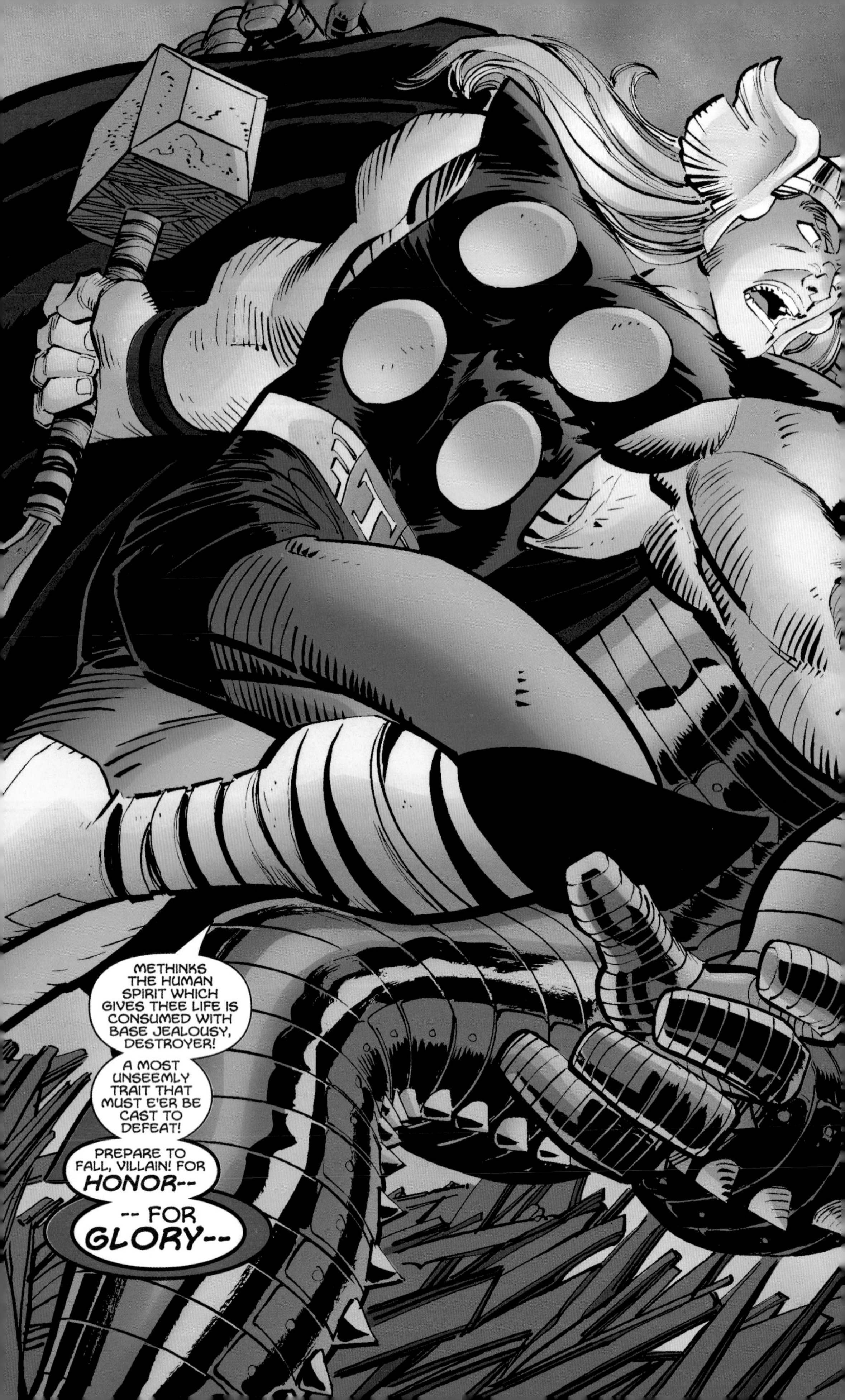
METHINKS THE HUMAN SPIRIT WHICH GIVES THEE LIFE IS CONSUMED WITH BASE JEALOUSY, DESTROYER!
A MOST UNSEEMLY TRAIT THAT MUST E'ER BE CAST TO DEFEAT!
PREPARE TO FALL, VILLAIN! FOR HONOR--
-- FOR GLORY--

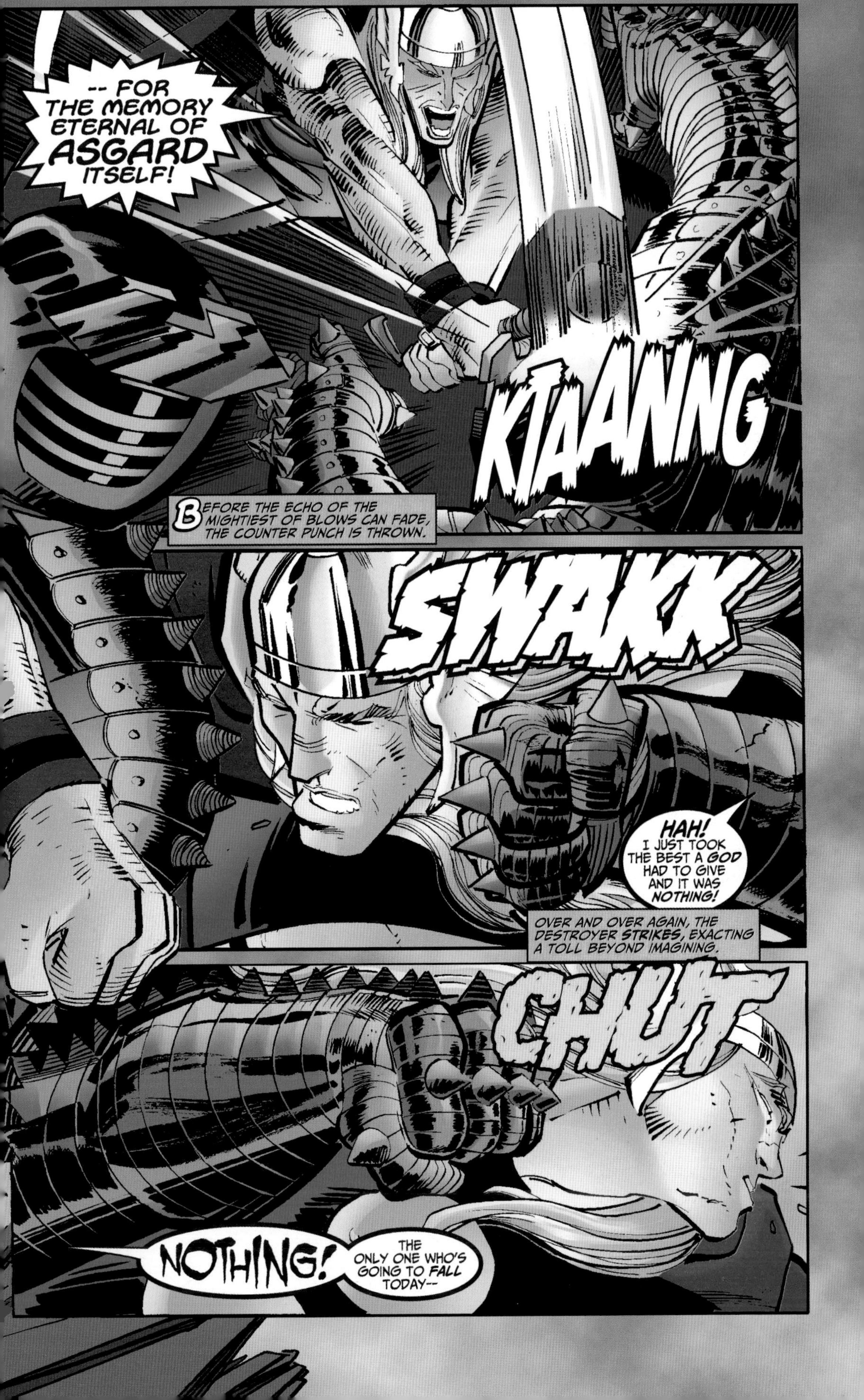

-- FOR THE MEMORY ETERNAL OF ASGARD ITSELF!
KTAANNG
BEFORE THE ECHO OF THE MIGHTIEST OF BLOWS CAN FADE, THE COUNTER PUNCH IS THROWN.
SWAKK
HAH! I JUST TOOK THE BEST A GOD HAD TO GIVE AND IT WAS NOTHING!
OVER AND OVER AGAIN, THE DESTROYER STRIKES, EXACTING A TOLL BEYOND IMAGINING.
CHUT
NOTHING!
THE ONLY ONE WHO'S GOING TO FALL TODAY--

"-- IS YOU!"

HOLY --! AN ADAMANTIUM SLAB COULDN'T TAKE THAT KINDA BEATING!

IT'S INTENTIONAL! THOR'S BUYING TIME SO WE CAN GET THE REMAINING CIVILIANS OUT OF THE WAY!

BUT -- EVEN THOR CANNOT WITHSTAND SUCH RELENTLESS PUNISHMENT FOR LONG!

THE EAST FLANK IS SECURE, COMMANDER! SHOULD WE OPEN FIRE?

YOU KIDDIN' ME, DEPAOLIS? WE CAN'T FIRE NOW! THAT'S AN AVENGER IN THERE --

"-- AND HE'S FIGHTIN' FOR US ALL!"

THOU ART EVIL COME TO LIFE, DESTROYER! AN EVIL THAT MUST BE VANQUISHED --

-- TO THE FIERY PITS OF HEL ITSELF!

SHRRRAKK

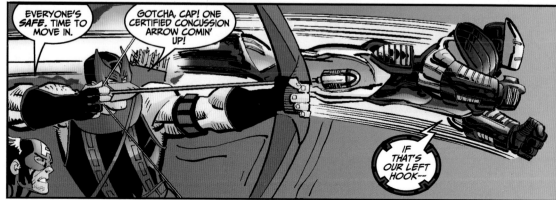

EVERYONE'S SAFE. TIME TO MOVE IN.

GOTCHA, CAP! ONE CERTIFIED CONCUSSION ARROW COMIN' UP!

IF THAT'S OUR LEFT HOOK --

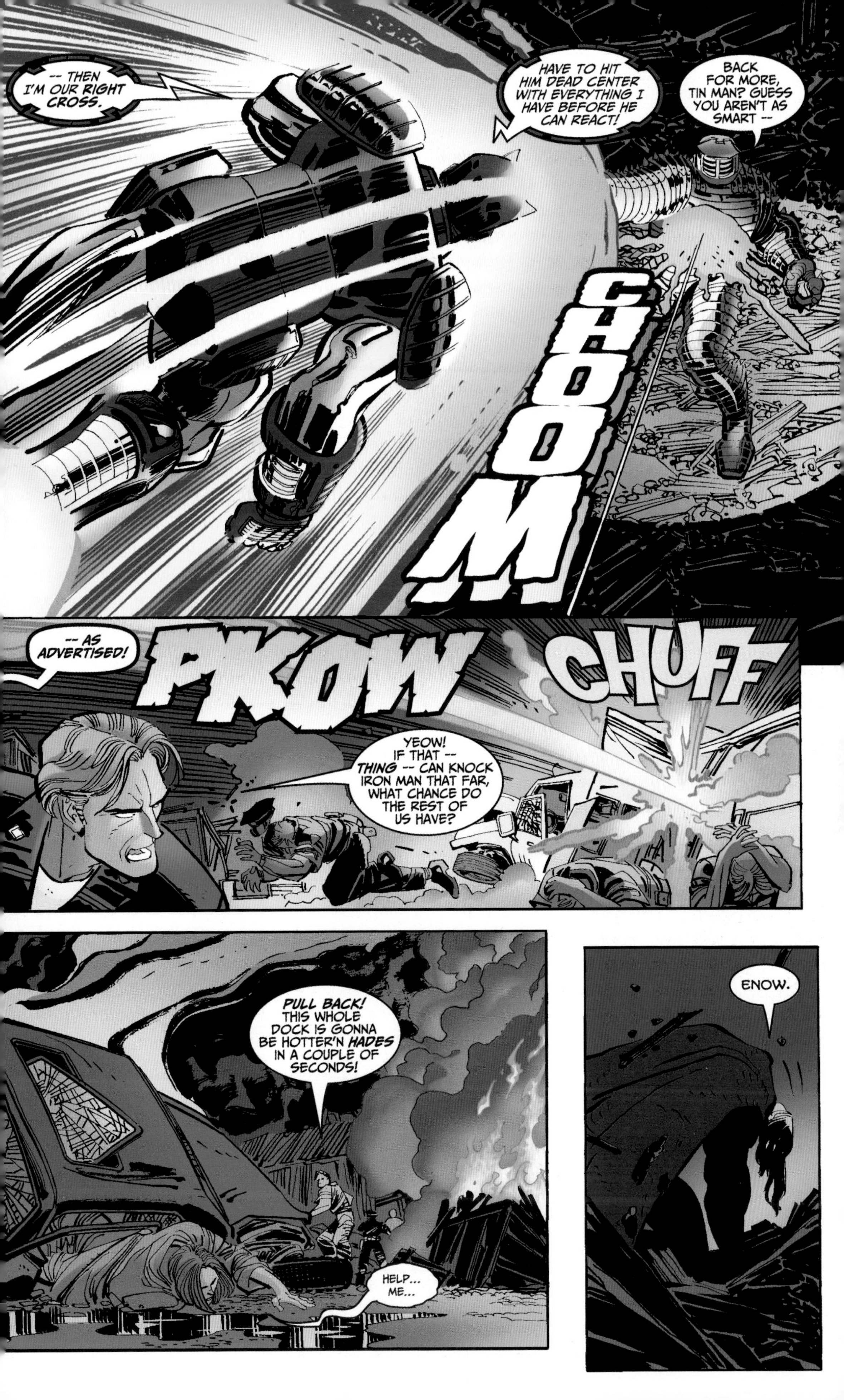
-- THEN I'M OUR RIGHT CROSS.
HAVE TO HIT HIM DEAD CENTER WITH EVERYTHING I HAVE BEFORE HE CAN REACT!
BACK FOR MORE, TIN MAN? GUESS YOU AREN'T AS SMART --
CHOOM
-- AS ADVERTISED!
PKOW
CHUFF
YEOW! IF THAT -- THING -- CAN KNOCK IRON MAN THAT FAR, WHAT CHANCE DO THE REST OF US HAVE?
PULL BACK! THIS WHOLE DOCK IS GONNA BE HOTTER'N HADES IN A COUPLE OF SECONDS!
HELP... ME...
ENOW.

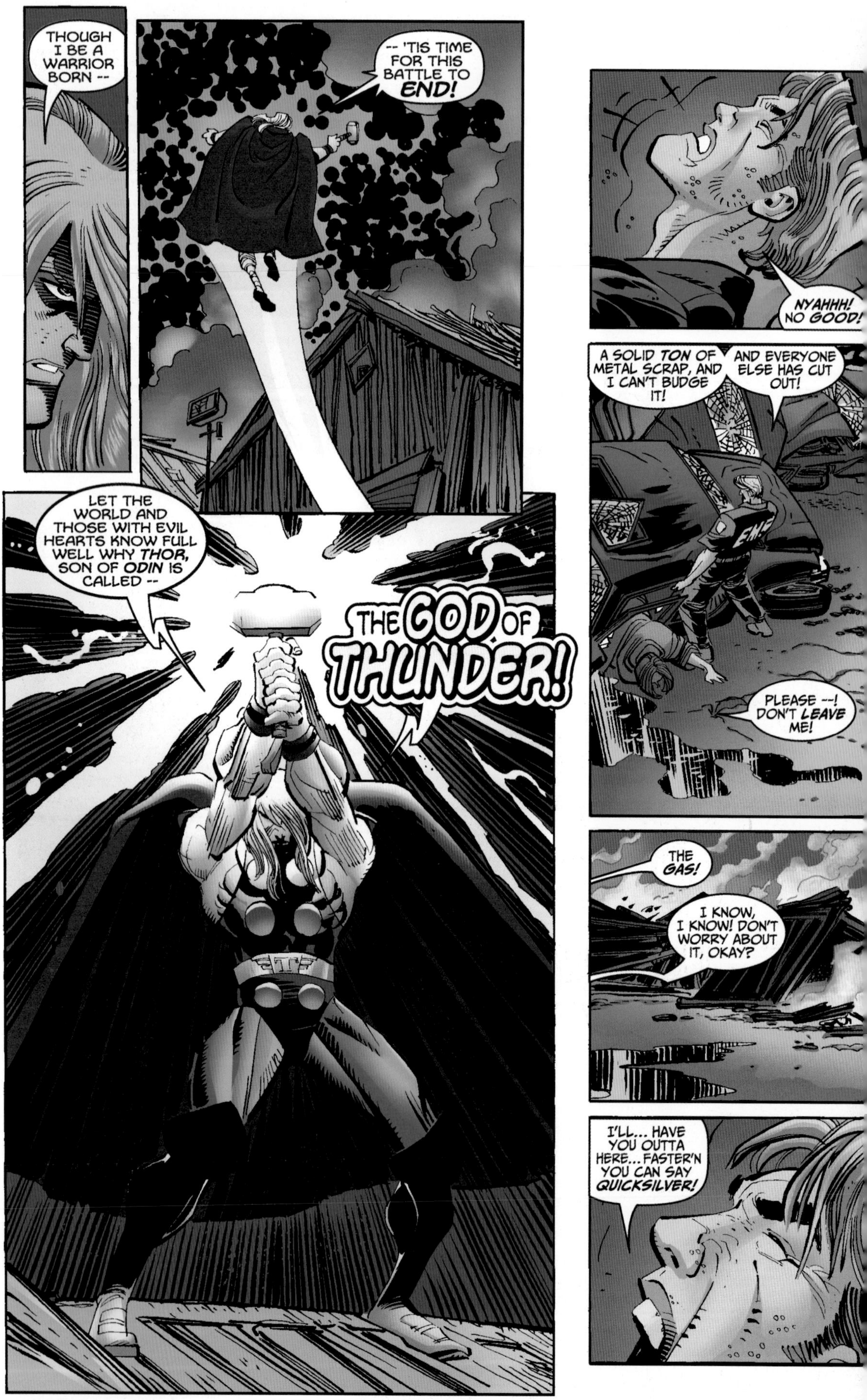
THOUGH I BE A WARRIOR BORN --
-- 'TIS TIME FOR THIS BATTLE TO END!
LET THE WORLD AND THOSE WITH EVIL HEARTS KNOW FULL WELL WHY THOR, SON OF ODIN IS CALLED --
THE GOD OF THUNDER!
NYAHHH! NO GOOD!
A SOLID TON OF METAL SCRAP, AND I CAN'T BUDGE IT!
AND EVERYONE ELSE HAS CUT OUT!
PLEASE --! DON'T LEAVE ME!
THE GAS!
I KNOW, I KNOW! DON'T WORRY ABOUT IT, OKAY?
I'LL... HAVE YOU OUTTA HERE... FASTER'N YOU CAN SAY QUICKSILVER!

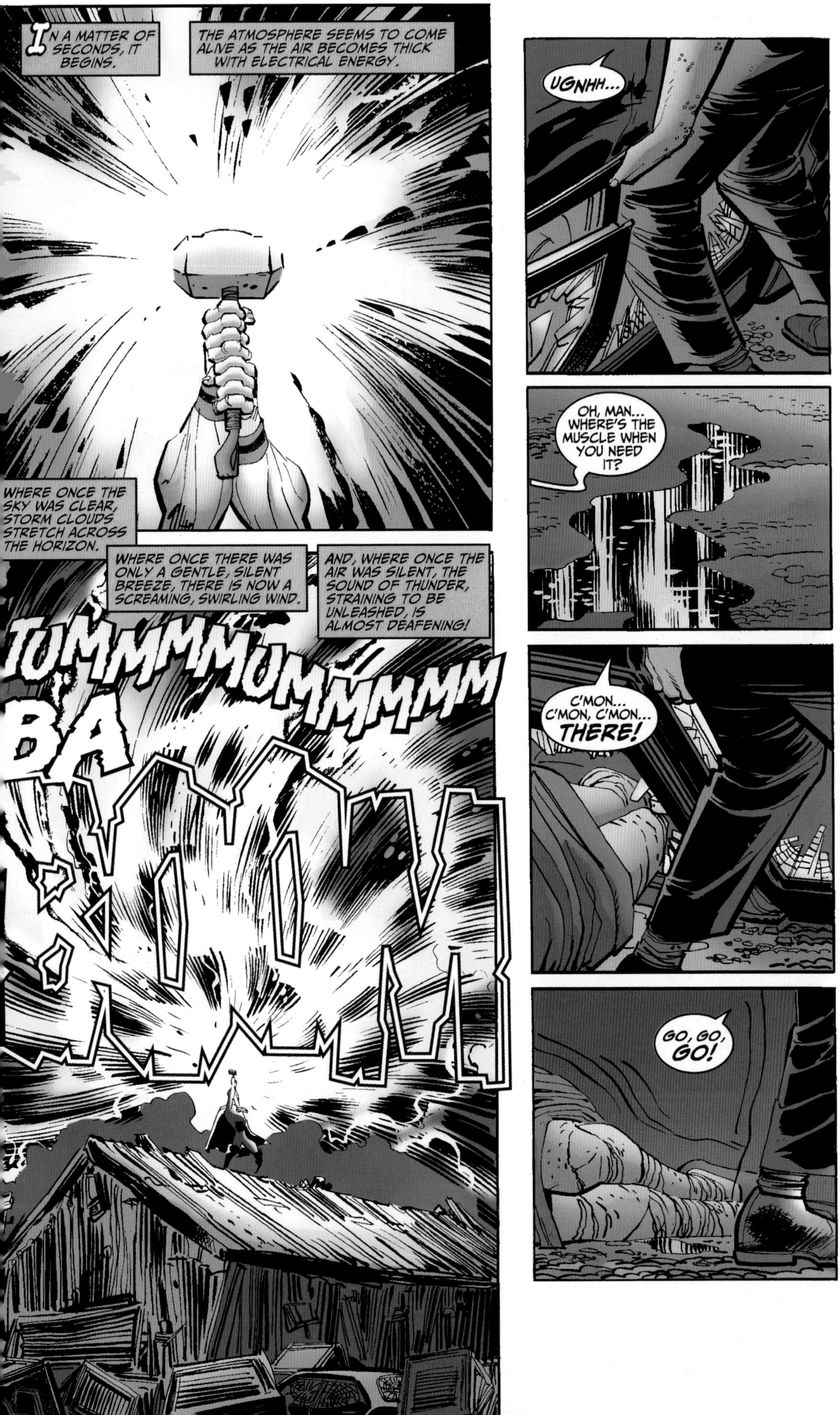
IN A MATTER OF SECONDS, IT BEGINS.
THE ATMOSPHERE SEEMS TO COME ALIVE AS THE AIR BECOMES THICK WITH ELECTRICAL ENERGY.
WHERE ONCE THE SKY WAS CLEAR, STORM CLOUDS STRETCH ACROSS THE HORIZON.
WHERE ONCE THERE WAS ONLY A GENTLE, SILENT BREEZE, THERE IS NOW A SCREAMING, SWIRLING WIND.
AND, WHERE ONCE THE AIR WAS SILENT, THE SOUND OF THUNDER, STRAINING TO BE UNLEASHED, IS ALMOST DEAFENING!
TUMMMMUMMMMM
BA
UGNHH...
OH, MAN... WHERE'S THE MUSCLE WHEN YOU NEED IT?
C'MON... C'MON, C'MON... THERE!
GO, GO, GO!

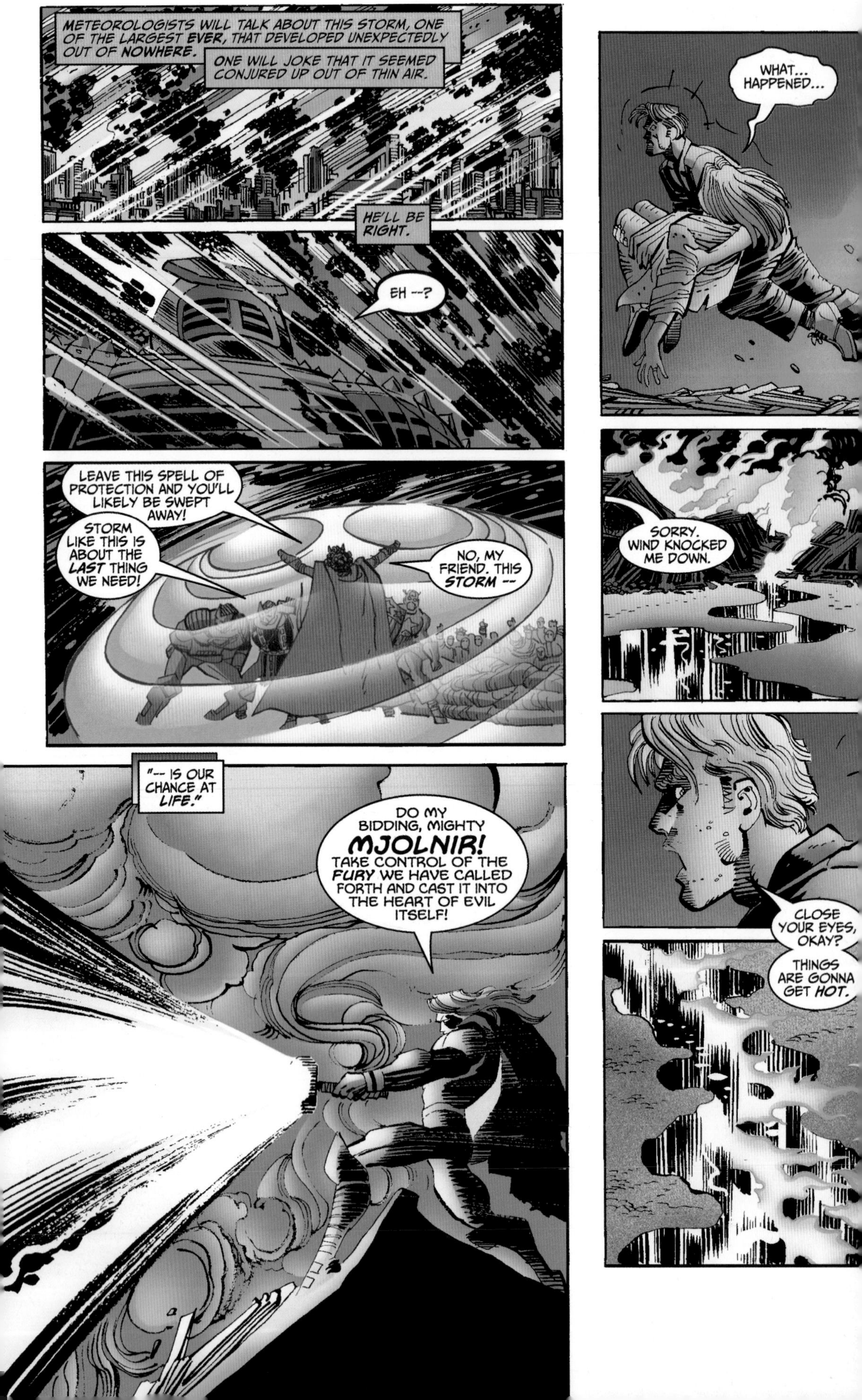

METEOROLOGISTS WILL TALK ABOUT THIS STORM, ONE OF THE LARGEST EVER, THAT DEVELOPED UNEXPECTEDLY OUT OF NOWHERE.
ONE WILL JOKE THAT IT SEEMED CONJURED UP OUT OF THIN AIR.
HE'LL BE RIGHT.
EH --?
LEAVE THIS SPELL OF PROTECTION AND YOU'LL LIKELY BE SWEPT AWAY!
STORM LIKE THIS IS ABOUT THE LAST THING WE NEED!
NO, MY FRIEND. THIS STORM --
"-- IS OUR CHANCE AT LIFE."
DO MY BIDDING, MIGHTY MJOLNIR! TAKE CONTROL OF THE FURY WE HAVE CALLED FORTH AND CAST IT INTO THE HEART OF EVIL ITSELF!
WHAT... HAPPENED...
SORRY. WIND KNOCKED ME DOWN.
CLOSE YOUR EYES, OKAY?
THINGS ARE GONNA GET HOT.

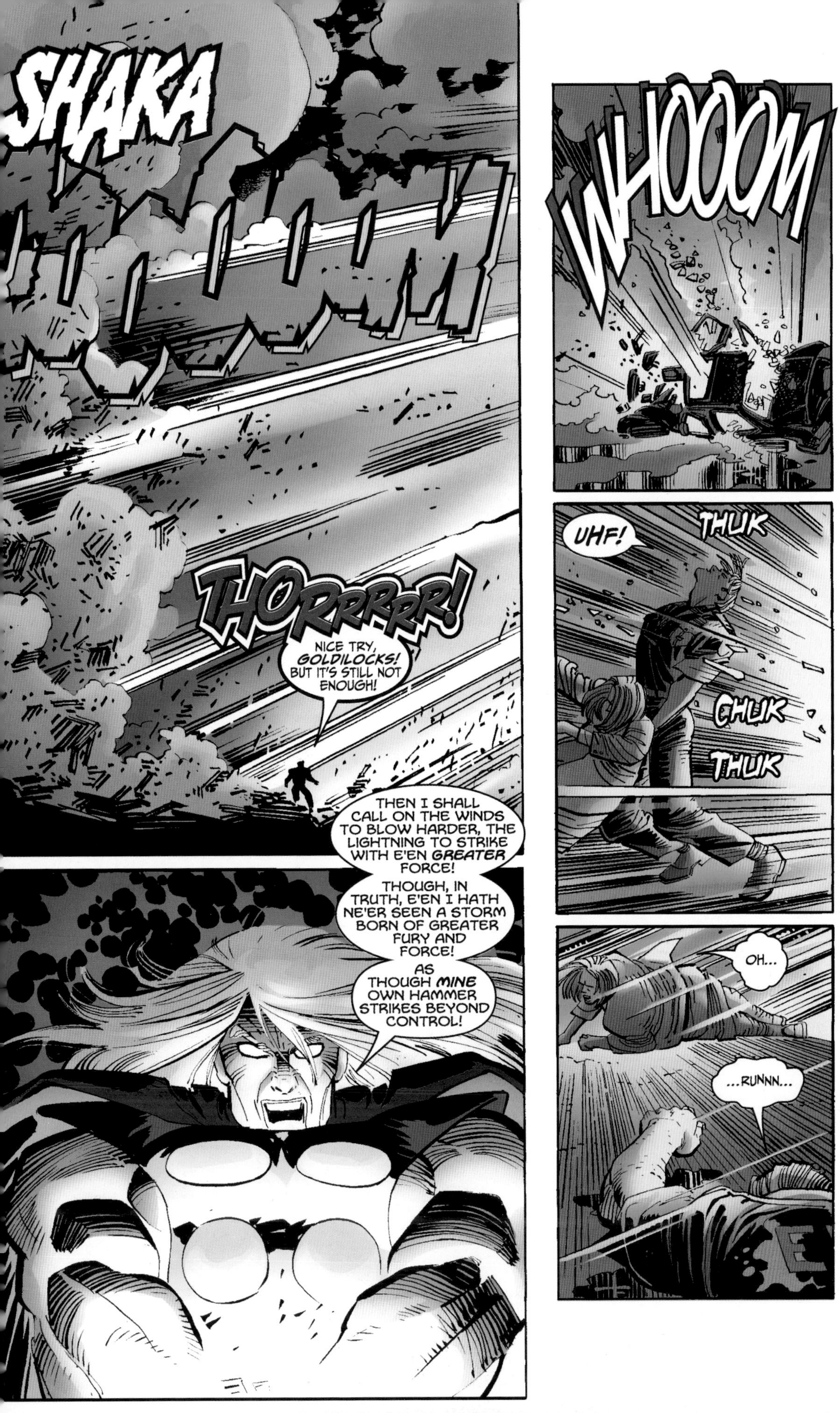
SHAKA
THOOOM
THORRRRR!
NICE TRY, GOLDILOCKS! BUT IT'S STILL NOT ENOUGH!
THEN I SHALL CALL ON THE WINDS TO BLOW HARDER, THE LIGHTNING TO STRIKE WITH E'EN GREATER FORCE!
THOUGH, IN TRUTH, E'EN I HATH NE'ER SEEN A STORM BORN OF GREATER FURY AND FORCE!
AS THOUGH MINE OWN HAMMER STRIKES BEYOND CONTROL!
WHOOOM
UHF!
THUK
CHUK
THUK
OH...
...RUNNN...

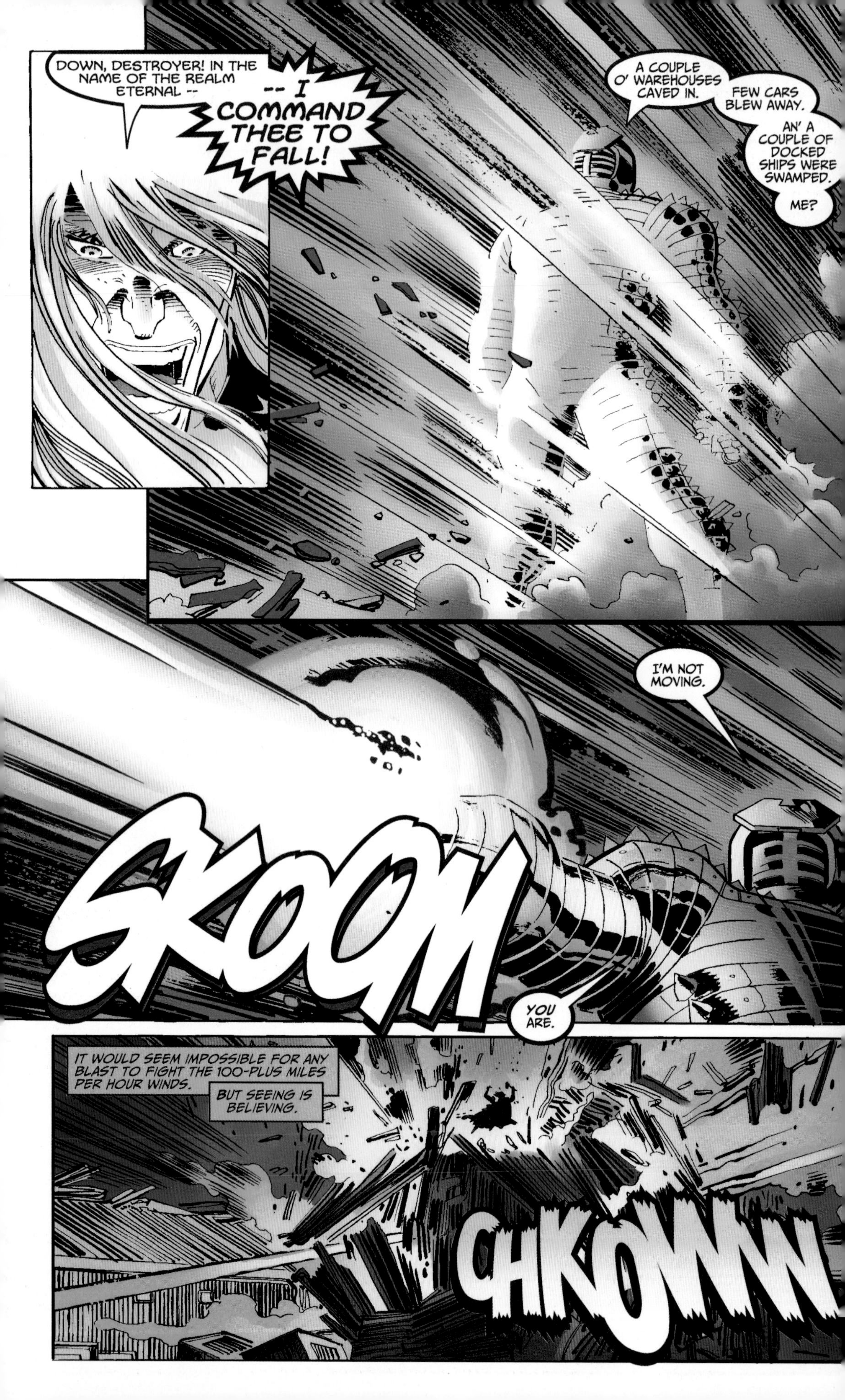
DOWN, DESTROYER! IN THE NAME OF THE REALM ETERNAL --
-- I COMMAND THEE TO FALL!
A COUPLE O' WAREHOUSES CAVED IN.
FEW CARS BLEW AWAY.
AN' A COUPLE OF DOCKED SHIPS WERE SWAMPED.
ME?
I'M NOT MOVING.
SKOOM
YOU ARE.
IT WOULD SEEM IMPOSSIBLE FOR ANY BLAST TO FIGHT THE 100-PLUS MILES PER HOUR WINDS.
BUT SEEING IS BELIEVING.
CHKOWWW

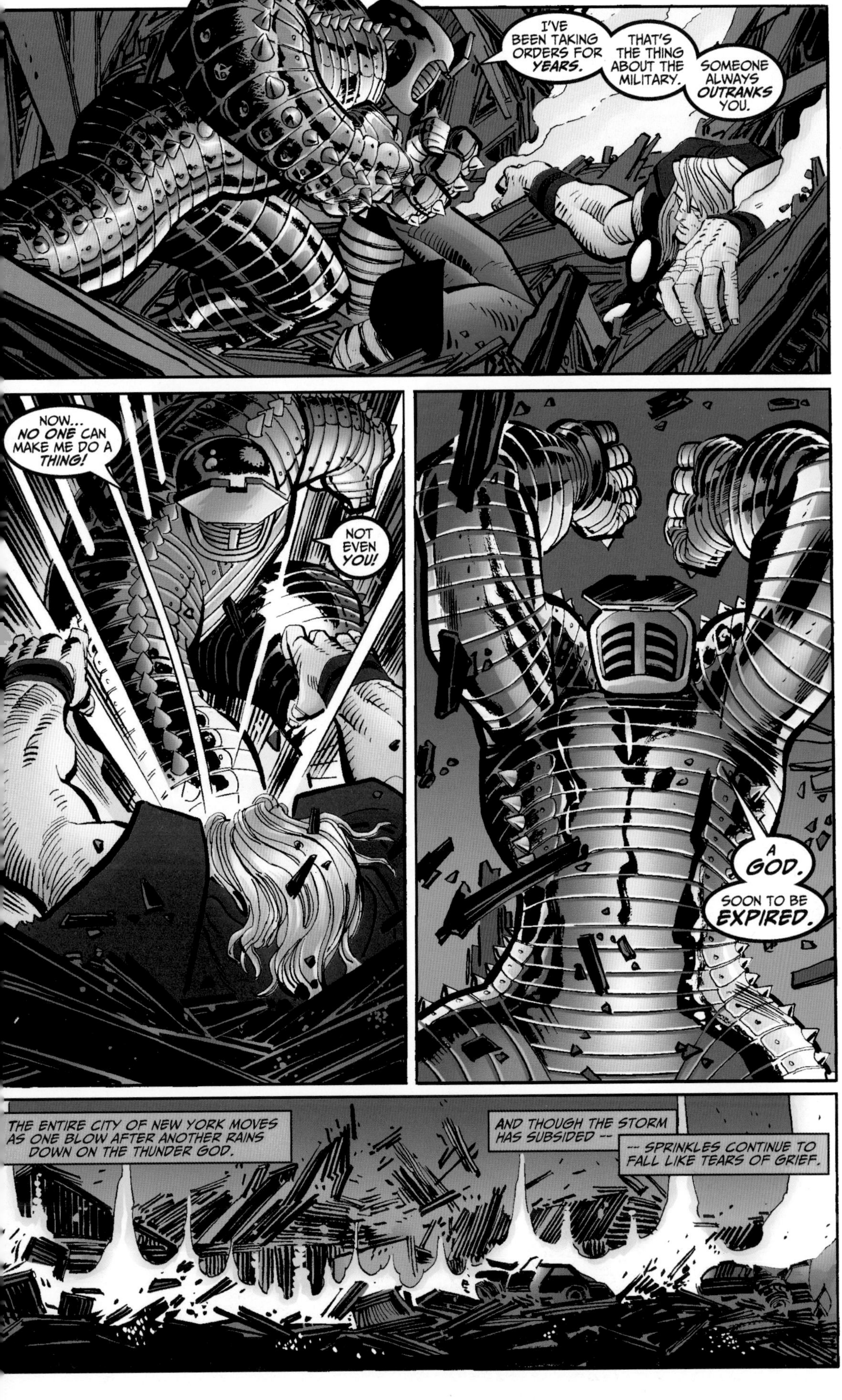
I'VE BEEN TAKING ORDERS FOR YEARS.
THAT'S THE THING ABOUT THE MILITARY.
SOMEONE ALWAYS OUTRANKS YOU.
NOW... NO ONE CAN MAKE ME DO A THING!
NOT EVEN YOU!
A GOD.
SOON TO BE EXPIRED.
THE ENTIRE CITY OF NEW YORK MOVES AS ONE BLOW AFTER ANOTHER RAINS DOWN ON THE THUNDER GOD.
AND THOUGH THE STORM HAS SUBSIDED --
-- SPRINKLES CONTINUE TO FALL LIKE TEARS OF GRIEF.

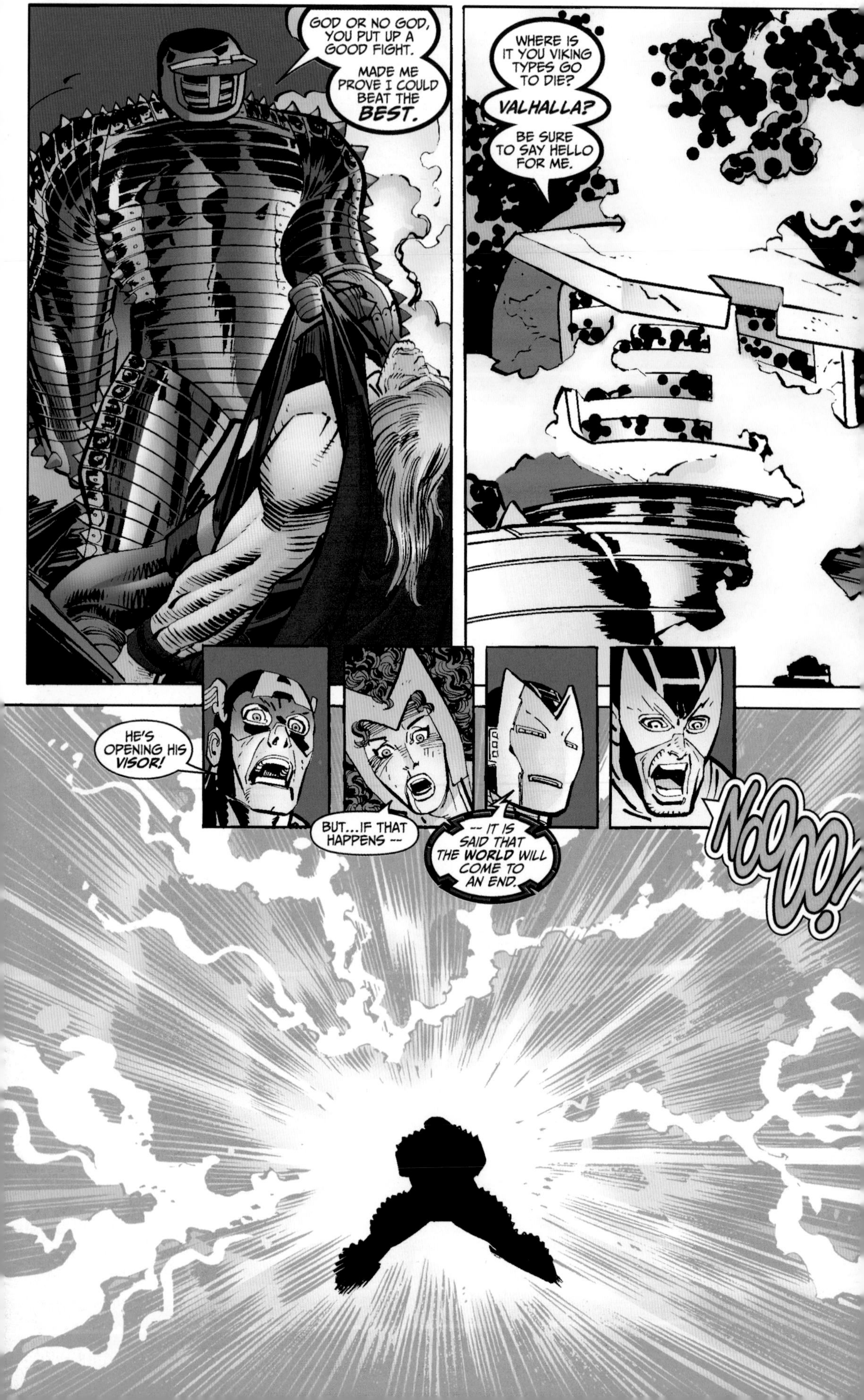
GOD OR NO GOD, YOU PUT UP A GOOD FIGHT.
MADE ME PROVE I COULD BEAT THE BEST.
WHERE IS IT YOU VIKING TYPES GO TO DIE?
VALHALLA?
BE SURE TO SAY HELLO FOR ME.
HE'S OPENING HIS VISOR!
BUT...IF THAT HAPPENS --
-- IT IS SAID THAT THE WORLD WILL COME TO AN END.
NOOOO!

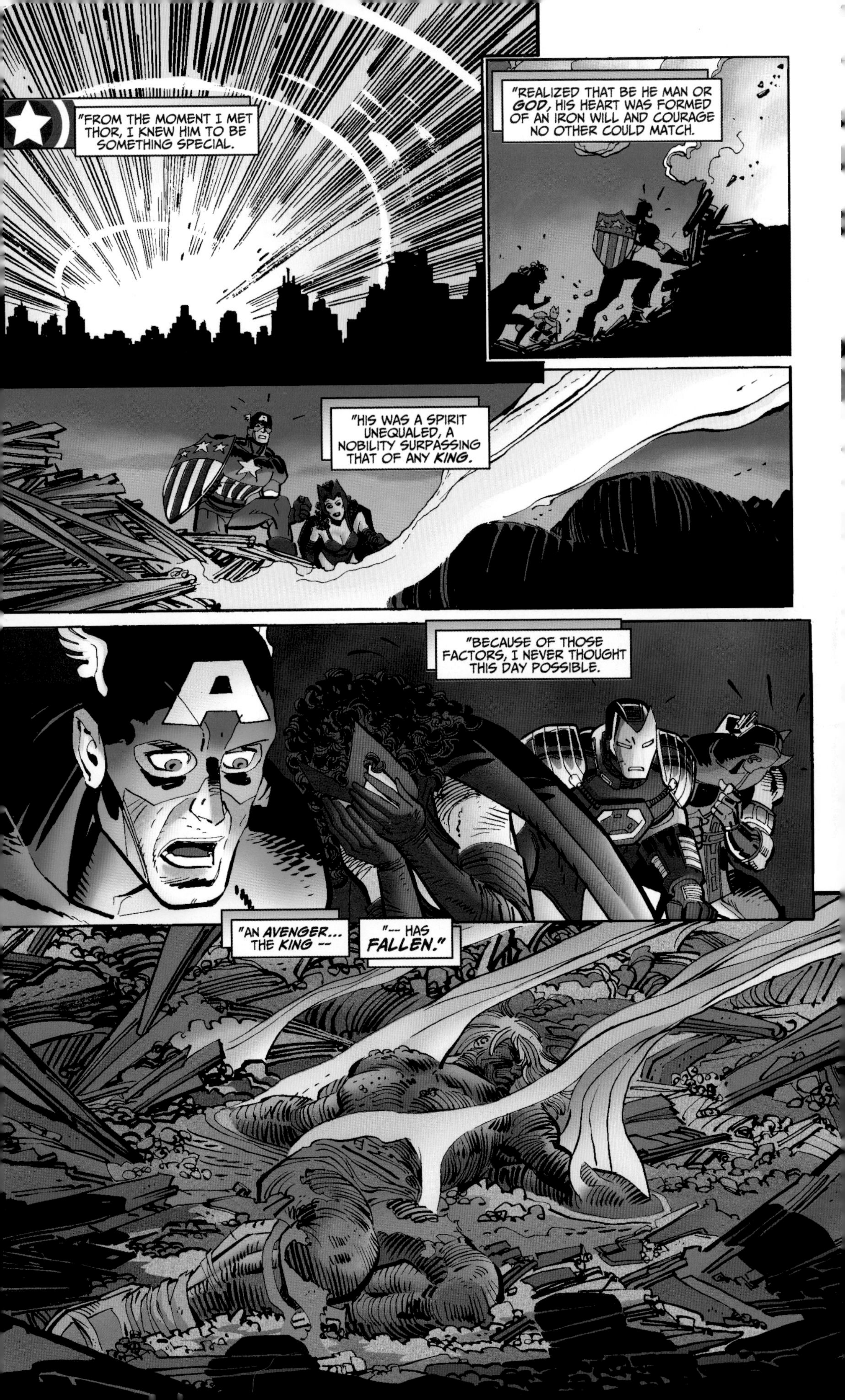
"FROM THE MOMENT I MET THOR, I KNEW HIM TO BE SOMETHING SPECIAL.
"REALIZED THAT BE HE MAN OR GOD, HIS HEART WAS FORMED OF AN IRON WILL AND COURAGE NO OTHER COULD MATCH.
"HIS WAS A SPIRIT UNEQUALED, A NOBILITY SURPASSING THAT OF ANY KING.
"BECAUSE OF THOSE FACTORS, I NEVER THOUGHT THIS DAY POSSIBLE.
"AN AVENGER... THE KING --
"-- HAS FALLEN."

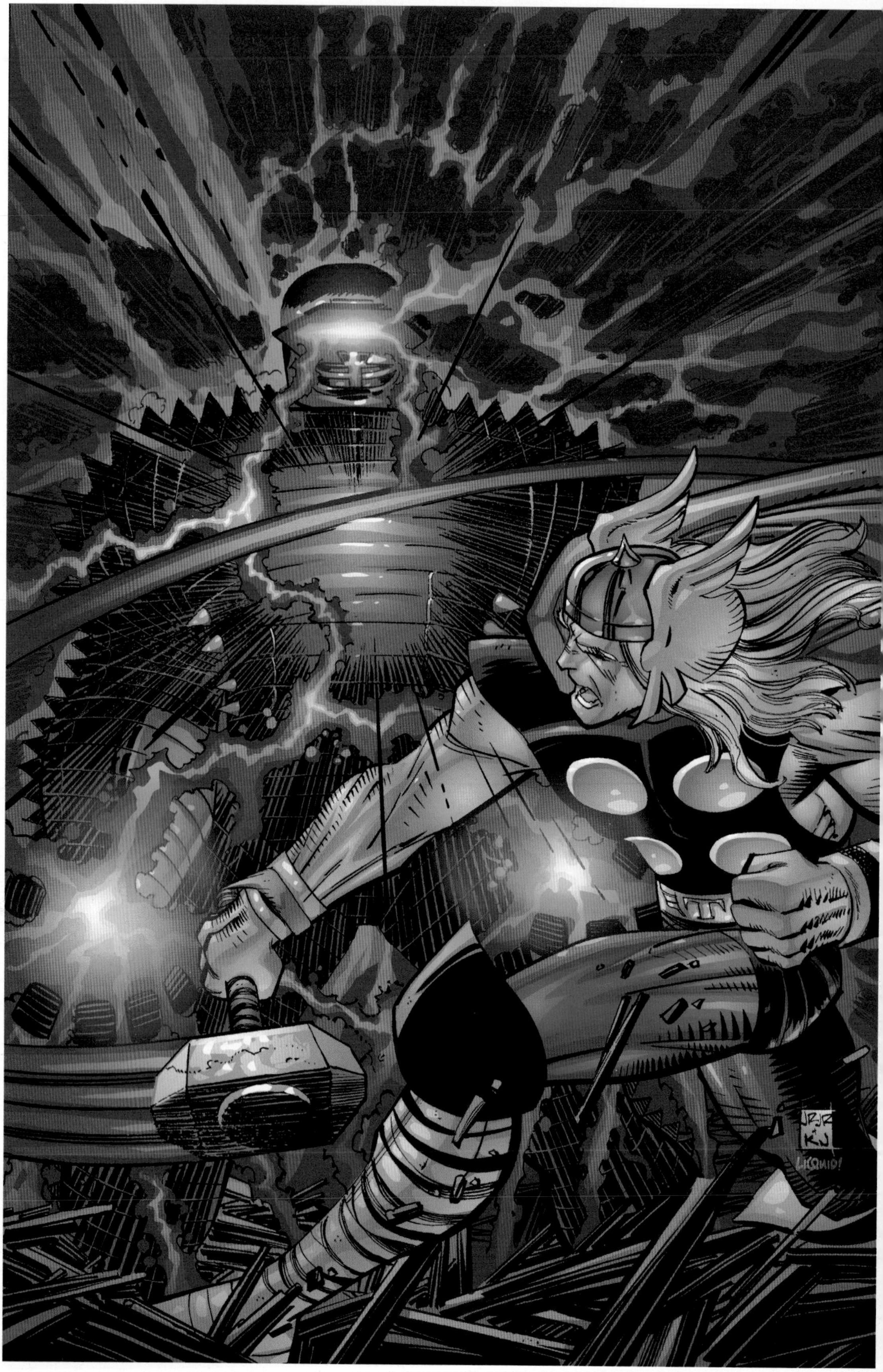
JRJR
KJ
LIQUID!

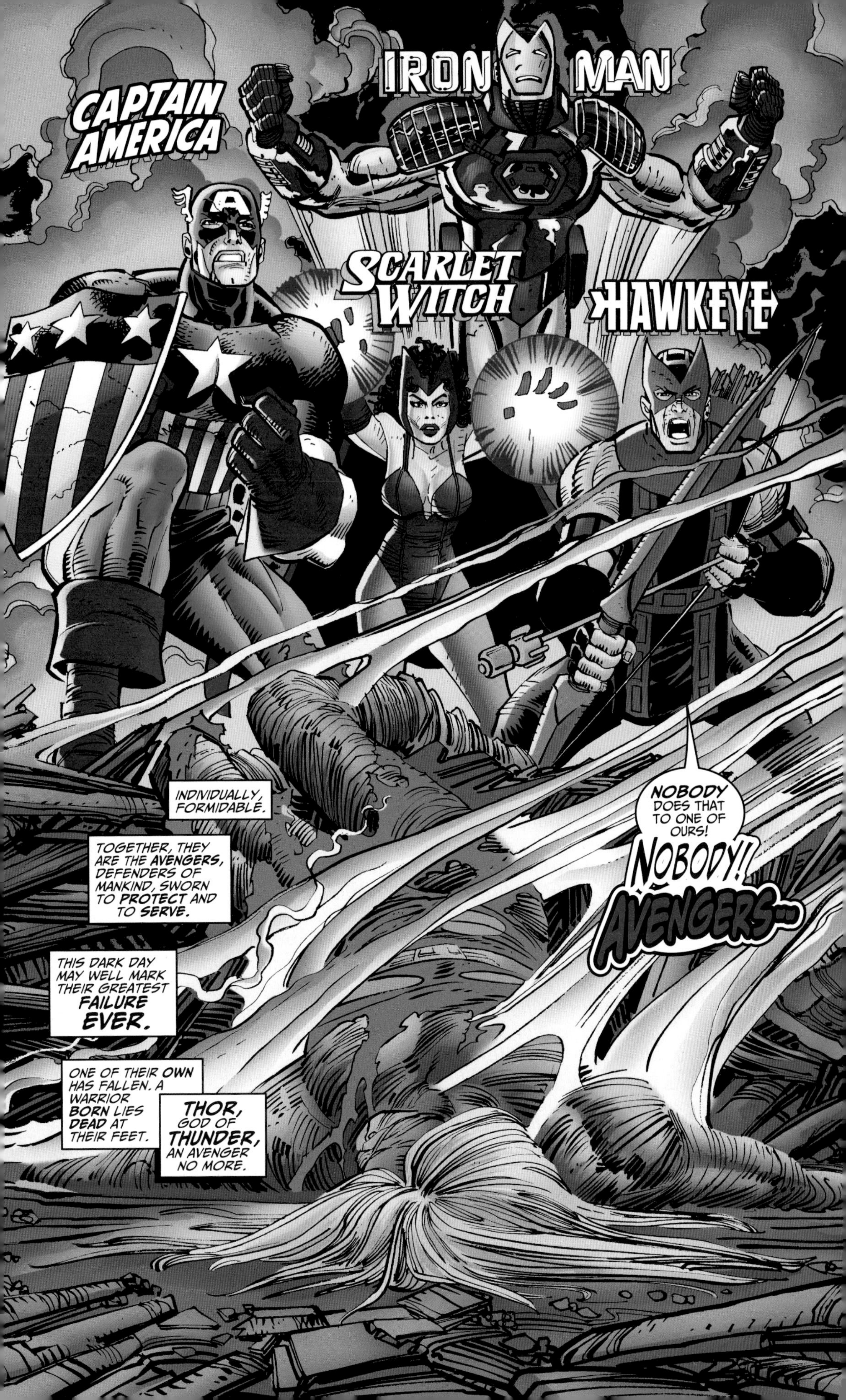
CAPTAIN AMERICA
IRON MAN
SCARLET WITCH
HAWKEYE
INDIVIDUALLY, FORMIDABLE.
TOGETHER, THEY ARE THE AVENGERS, DEFENDERS OF MANKIND, SWORN TO PROTECT AND TO SERVE.
THIS DARK DAY MAY WELL MARK THEIR GREATEST FAILURE EVER.
ONE OF THEIR OWN HAS FALLEN. A WARRIOR BORN LIES DEAD AT THEIR FEET.
THOR, GOD OF THUNDER, AN AVENGER NO MORE.
NOBODY DOES THAT TO ONE OF OURS!
NOBODY!!
AVENGERS--

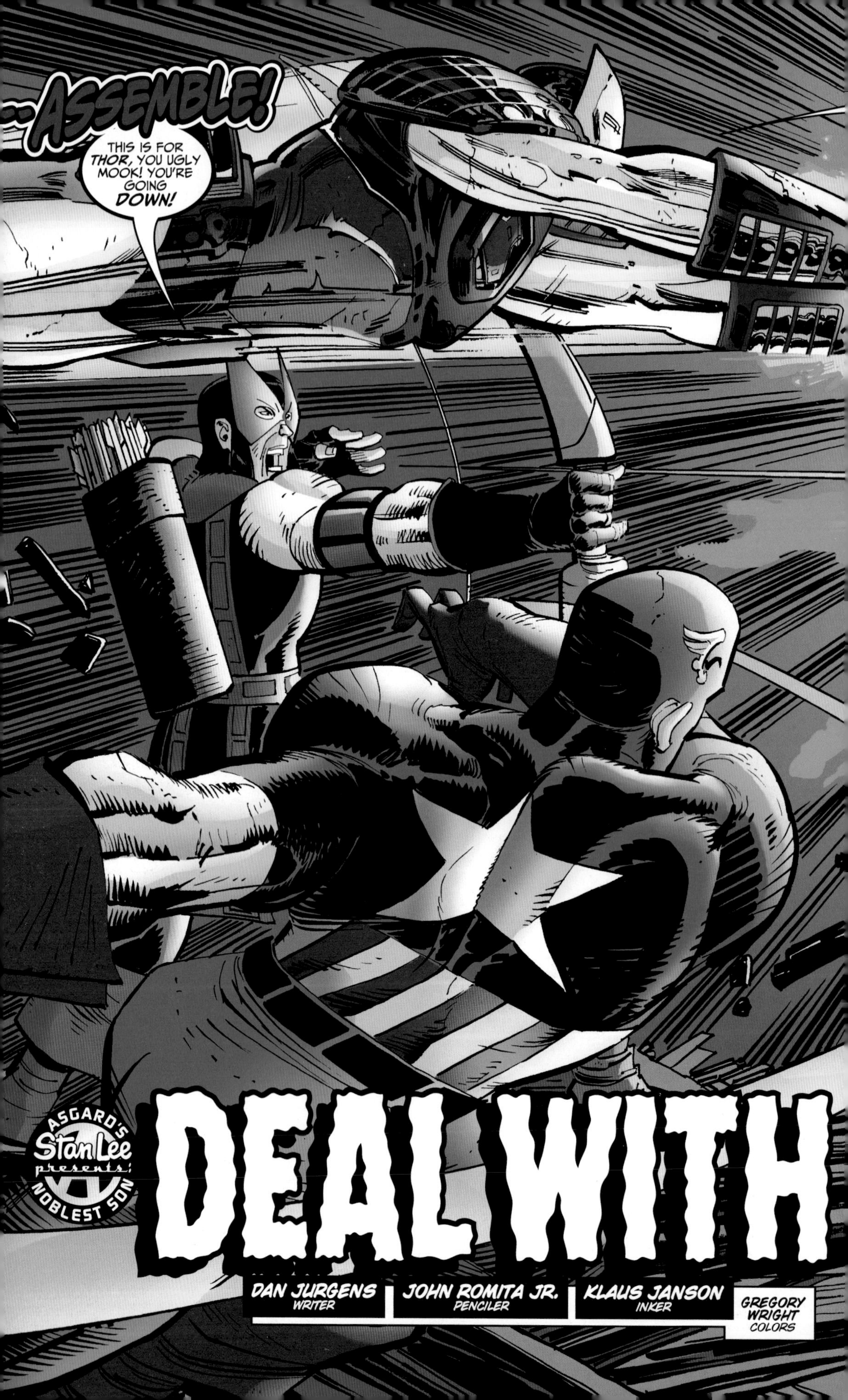

...ASSEMBLE!
THIS IS FOR THOR, YOU UGLY MOOK! YOU'RE GOING DOWN!
ASGARD'S NOBLEST SON
Stan Lee presents:
DEAL WITH
DAN JURGENS WRITER
JOHN ROMITA JR. PENCILER
KLAUS JANSON INKER
GREGORY WRIGHT COLORS

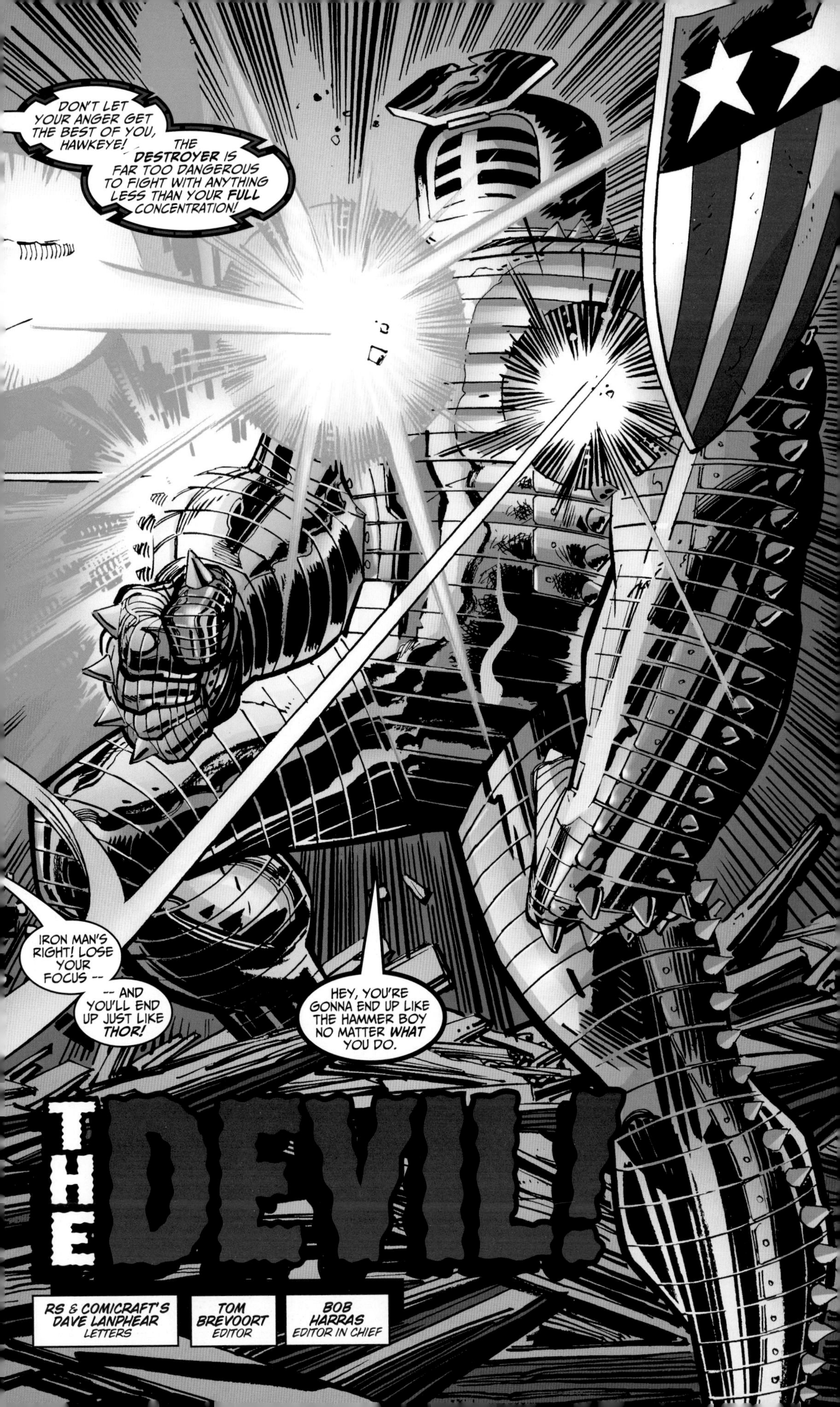
DON'T LET YOUR ANGER GET THE BEST OF YOU, HAWKEYE!
THE DESTROYER IS FAR TOO DANGEROUS TO FIGHT WITH ANYTHING LESS THAN YOUR FULL CONCENTRATION!
IRON MAN'S RIGHT! LOSE YOUR FOCUS --
-- AND YOU'LL END UP JUST LIKE THOR!
HEY, YOU'RE GONNA END UP LIKE THE HAMMER BOY NO MATTER WHAT YOU DO.
THE DEVIL!
RS & COMICRAFT'S DAVE LANPHEAR LETTERS
TOM BREVOORT EDITOR
BOB HARRAS EDITOR IN CHIEF

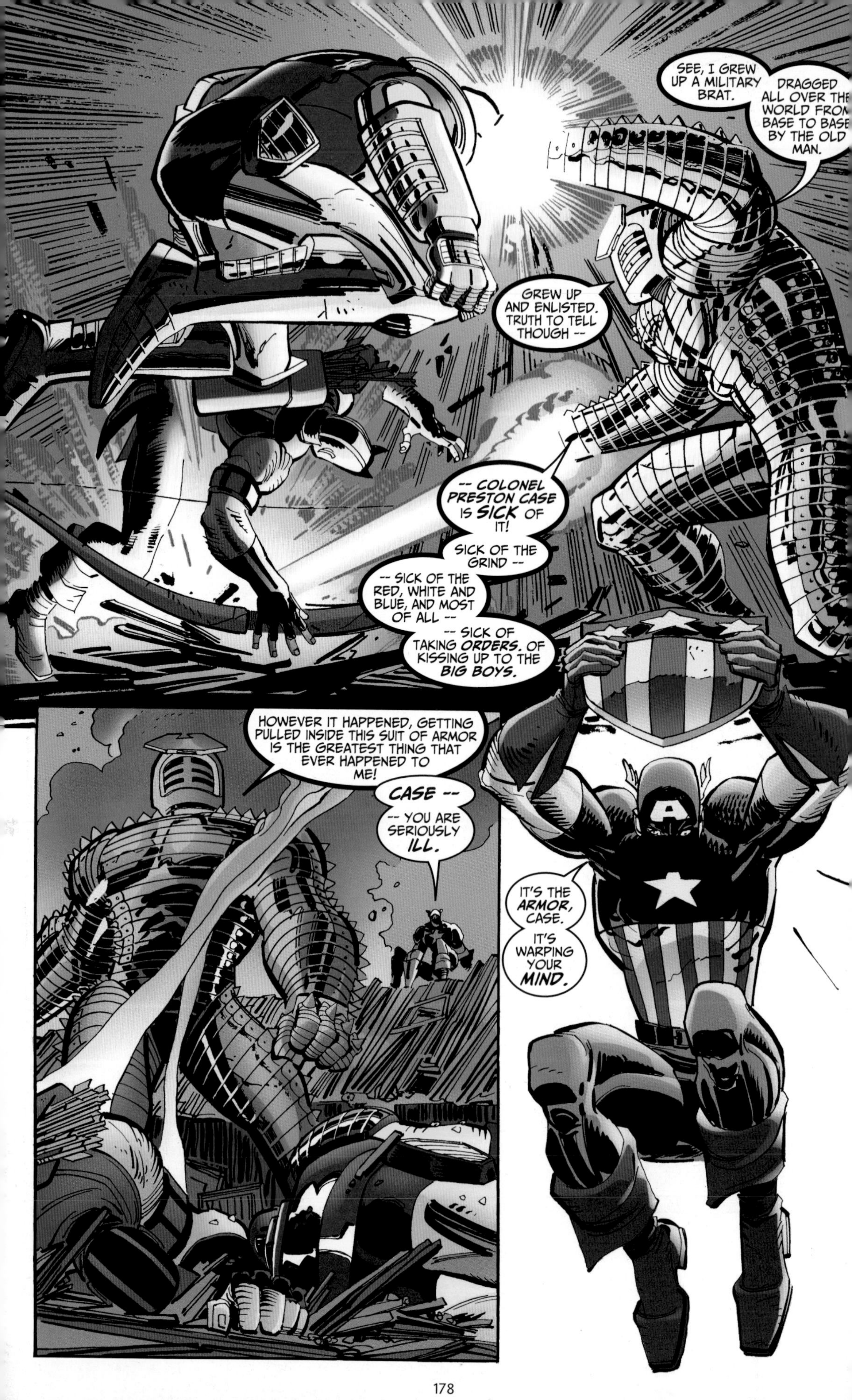
SEE, I GREW UP A MILITARY BRAT.
DRAGGED ALL OVER THE WORLD FROM BASE TO BASE BY THE OLD MAN.
GREW UP AND ENLISTED. TRUTH TO TELL THOUGH --
-- COLONEL PRESTON CASE IS SICK OF IT!
SICK OF THE GRIND --
-- SICK OF THE RED, WHITE AND BLUE, AND MOST OF ALL --
-- SICK OF TAKING ORDERS. OF KISSING UP TO THE BIG BOYS.
HOWEVER IT HAPPENED, GETTING PULLED INSIDE THIS SUIT OF ARMOR IS THE GREATEST THING THAT EVER HAPPENED TO ME!
CASE --
-- YOU ARE SERIOUSLY ILL.
IT'S THE ARMOR, CASE.
IT'S WARPING YOUR MIND.

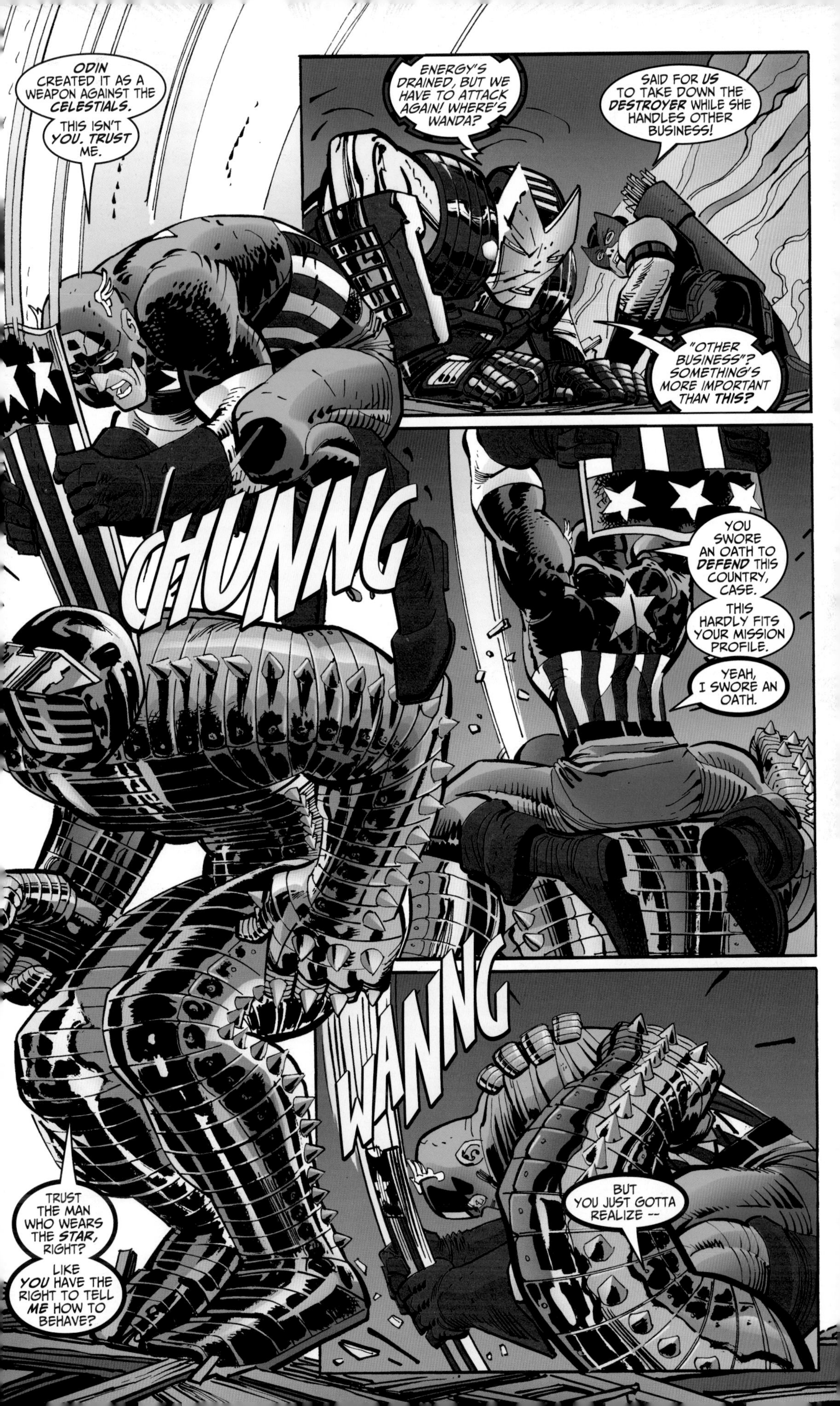

ODIN CREATED IT AS A WEAPON AGAINST THE CELESTIALS.
THIS ISN'T YOU. TRUST ME.
ENERGY'S DRAINED, BUT WE HAVE TO ATTACK AGAIN! WHERE'S WANDA?
SAID FOR US TO TAKE DOWN THE DESTROYER WHILE SHE HANDLES OTHER BUSINESS!
"OTHER BUSINESS"? SOMETHING'S MORE IMPORTANT THAN THIS?
CHUNNG
YOU SWORE AN OATH TO DEFEND THIS COUNTRY, CASE.
THIS HARDLY FITS YOUR MISSION PROFILE.
YEAH, I SWORE AN OATH.
TRUST THE MAN WHO WEARS THE STAR, RIGHT?
LIKE YOU HAVE THE RIGHT TO TELL ME HOW TO BEHAVE?
WANNG
BUT YOU JUST GOTTA REALIZE --

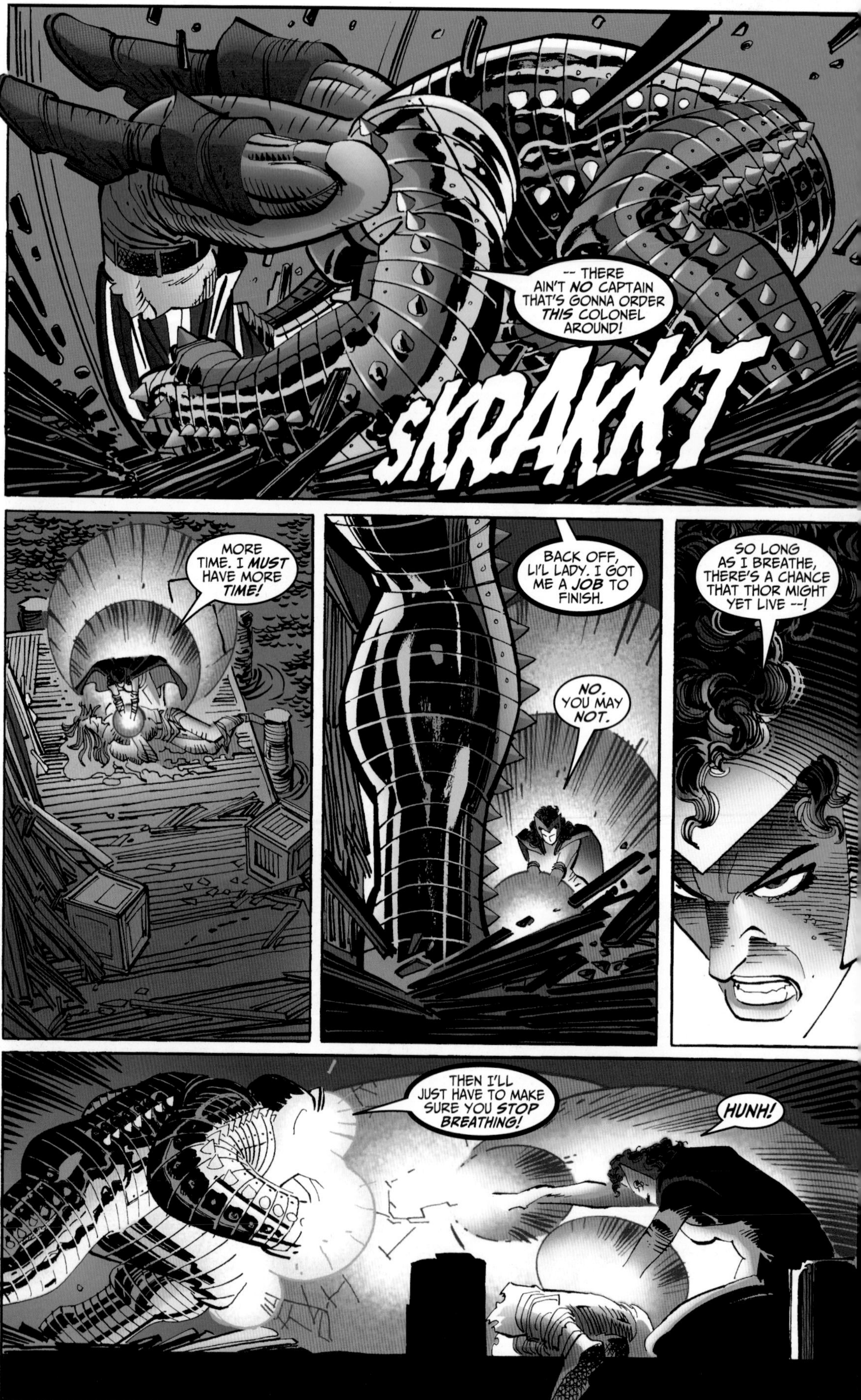

-- THERE AIN'T NO CAPTAIN THAT'S GONNA ORDER THIS COLONEL AROUND!
SKRAKKT
MORE TIME. I MUST HAVE MORE TIME!
BACK OFF, LI'L LADY. I GOT ME A JOB TO FINISH.
NO. YOU MAY NOT.
SO LONG AS I BREATHE, THERE'S A CHANCE THAT THOR MIGHT YET LIVE --!
THEN I'LL JUST HAVE TO MAKE SURE YOU STOP BREATHING!
HUNH!

YOU AND THE THUNDER GOD **BOTH!**

SHLAK

HE IS THE SON OF ALMIGHTY ODIN.

THE HEIR TO THE THRONE OF ETERNAL ASGARD ITSELF.

A GOD FOR WHOM EARTH WAS HOME.

POWER
BIRTHRI
NOBILIT
ESSENC
HIS SO

THE BE
VALIAN
IN HOR
KNOW

THOSE WHO ARE BORN TO EVIL HAVE TREMBLED BEFORE HIS MIGHT.

THOSE WHO WOULD HARM THE INNOCENT HAVE FALLEN TO HIS JUSTICE.

HIS IS THE POWER TO CALL FORTH THE WRATH OF THE HEAVENS, FORCING THE LIGHTNING AND THE WIND TO DO HIS BIDDING.

HE IS THE GOD OF *THUNDER*, A WARRIOR BORN.

AND AT LONG LAST, AFTER BATTLES TOO NUMEROUS TO COUNT --

-- DEATH ENVELOPS HIM.

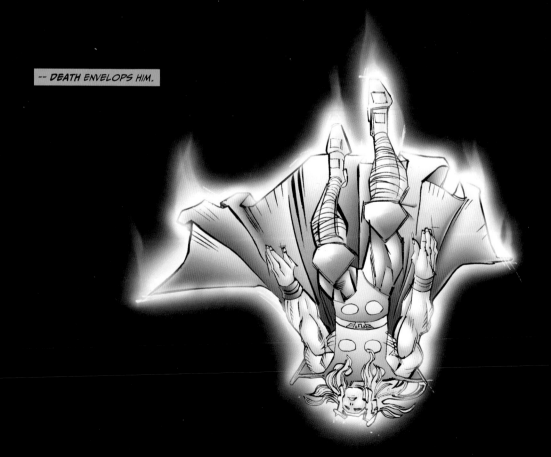

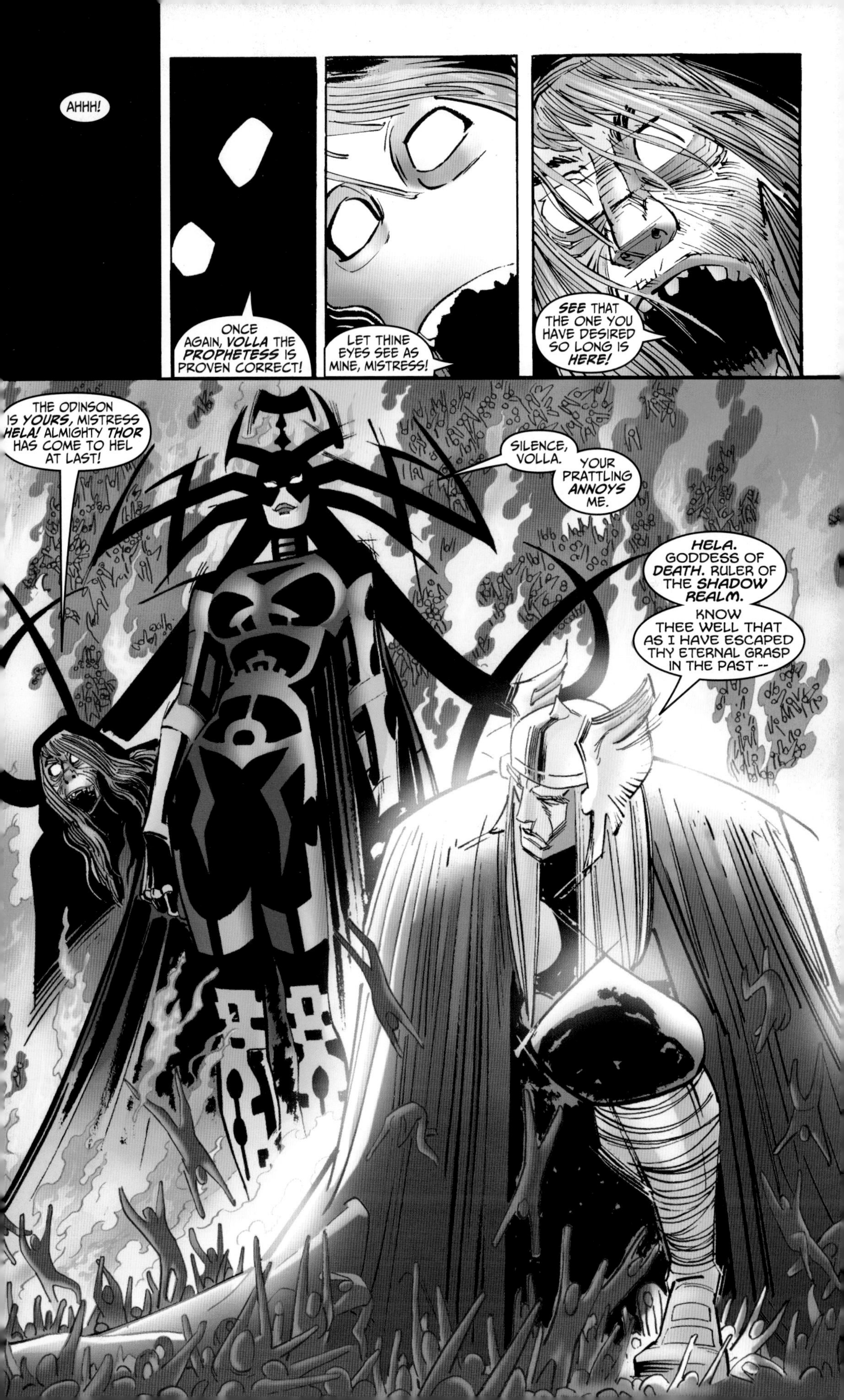
AHHH!
ONCE AGAIN, VOLLA THE PROPHETESS IS PROVEN CORRECT!
LET THINE EYES SEE AS MINE, MISTRESS!
SEE THAT THE ONE YOU HAVE DESIRED SO LONG IS HERE!
THE ODINSON IS YOURS, MISTRESS HELA! ALMIGHTY THOR HAS COME TO HEL AT LAST!
SILENCE, VOLLA.
YOUR PRATTLING ANNOYS ME.
HELA. GODDESS OF DEATH. RULER OF THE SHADOW REALM.
KNOW THEE WELL THAT AS I HAVE ESCAPED THY ETERNAL GRASP IN THE PAST --

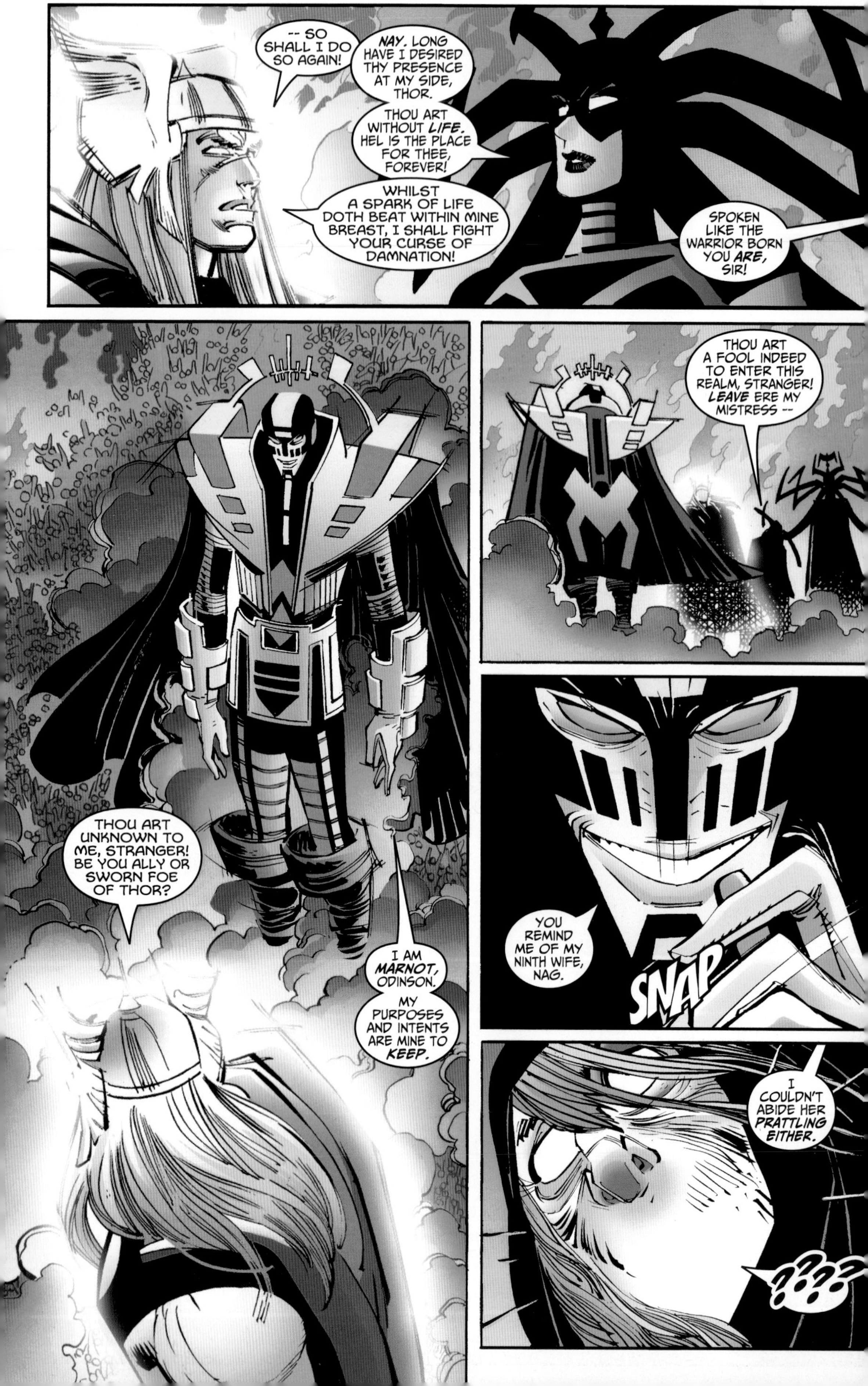
-- SO SHALL I DO SO AGAIN!
NAY. LONG HAVE I DESIRED THY PRESENCE AT MY SIDE, THOR.
THOU ART WITHOUT LIFE. HEL IS THE PLACE FOR THEE, FOREVER!
WHILST A SPARK OF LIFE DOTH BEAT WITHIN MINE BREAST, I SHALL FIGHT YOUR CURSE OF DAMNATION!
SPOKEN LIKE THE WARRIOR BORN YOU ARE, SIR!
THOU ART UNKNOWN TO ME, STRANGER! BE YOU ALLY OR SWORN FOE OF THOR?
I AM MARNOT, ODINSON.
MY PURPOSES AND INTENTS ARE MINE TO KEEP.
THOU ART A FOOL INDEED TO ENTER THIS REALM, STRANGER! LEAVE ERE MY MISTRESS --
YOU REMIND ME OF MY NINTH WIFE, NAG.
SNAP
I COULDN'T ABIDE HER PRATTLING EITHER.
???

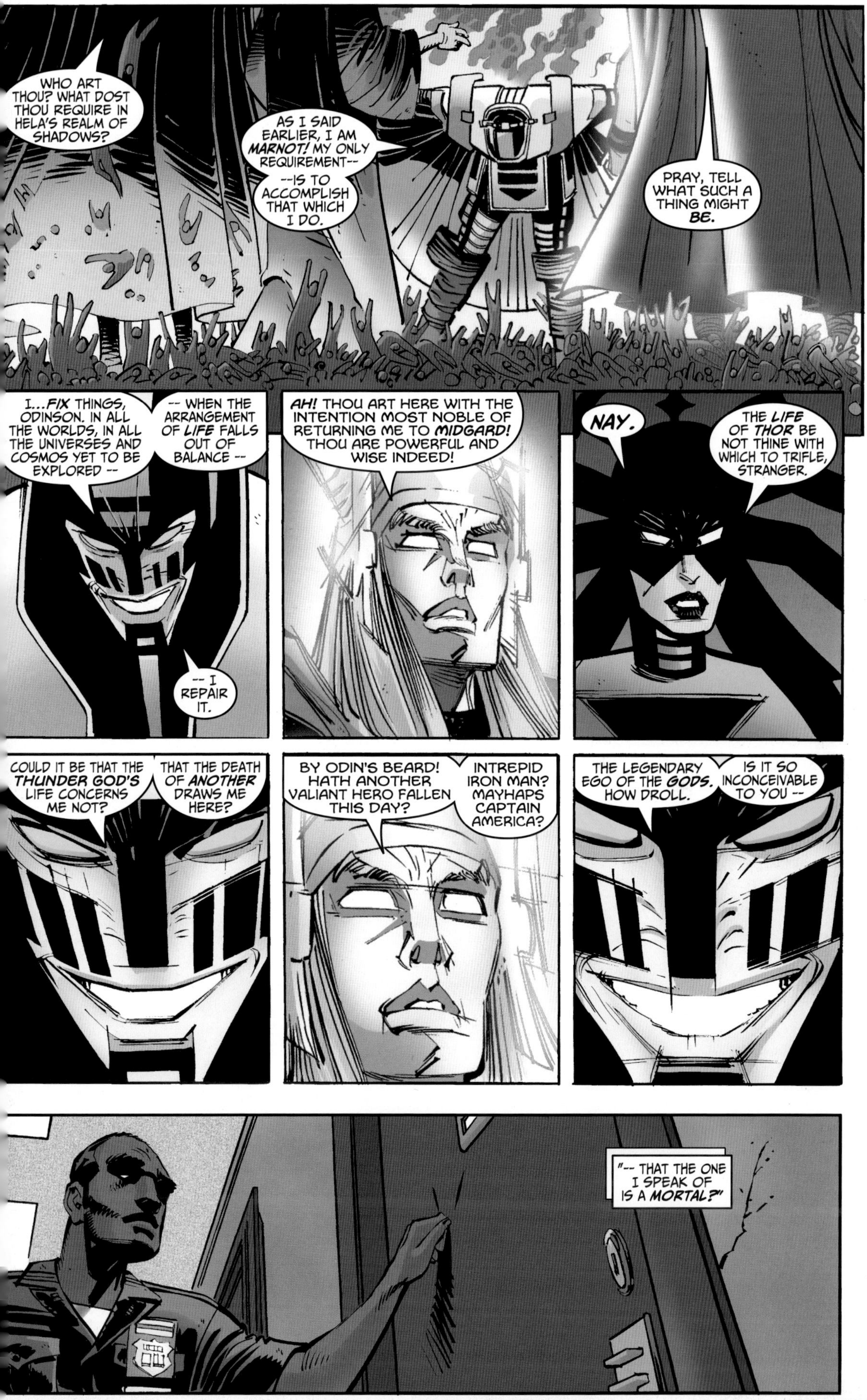
WHO ART THOU? WHAT DOST THOU REQUIRE IN HELA'S REALM OF SHADOWS?
AS I SAID EARLIER, I AM MARNOT! MY ONLY REQUIREMENT--
--IS TO ACCOMPLISH THAT WHICH I DO.
PRAY, TELL WHAT SUCH A THING MIGHT BE.
I...FIX THINGS, ODINSON. IN ALL THE WORLDS, IN ALL THE UNIVERSES AND COSMOS YET TO BE EXPLORED --
-- WHEN THE ARRANGEMENT OF LIFE FALLS OUT OF BALANCE --
-- I REPAIR IT.
AH! THOU ART HERE WITH THE INTENTION MOST NOBLE OF RETURNING ME TO MIDGARD! THOU ARE POWERFUL AND WISE INDEED!
NAY.
THE LIFE OF THOR BE NOT THINE WITH WHICH TO TRIFLE, STRANGER.
COULD IT BE THAT THE THUNDER GOD'S LIFE CONCERNS ME NOT?
THAT THE DEATH OF ANOTHER DRAWS ME HERE?
BY ODIN'S BEARD! HATH ANOTHER VALIANT HERO FALLEN THIS DAY?
INTREPID IRON MAN? MAYHAPS CAPTAIN AMERICA?
THE LEGENDARY EGO OF THE GODS. HOW DROLL.
IS IT SO INCONCEIVABLE TO YOU --
"-- THAT THE ONE I SPEAK OF IS A MORTAL?"

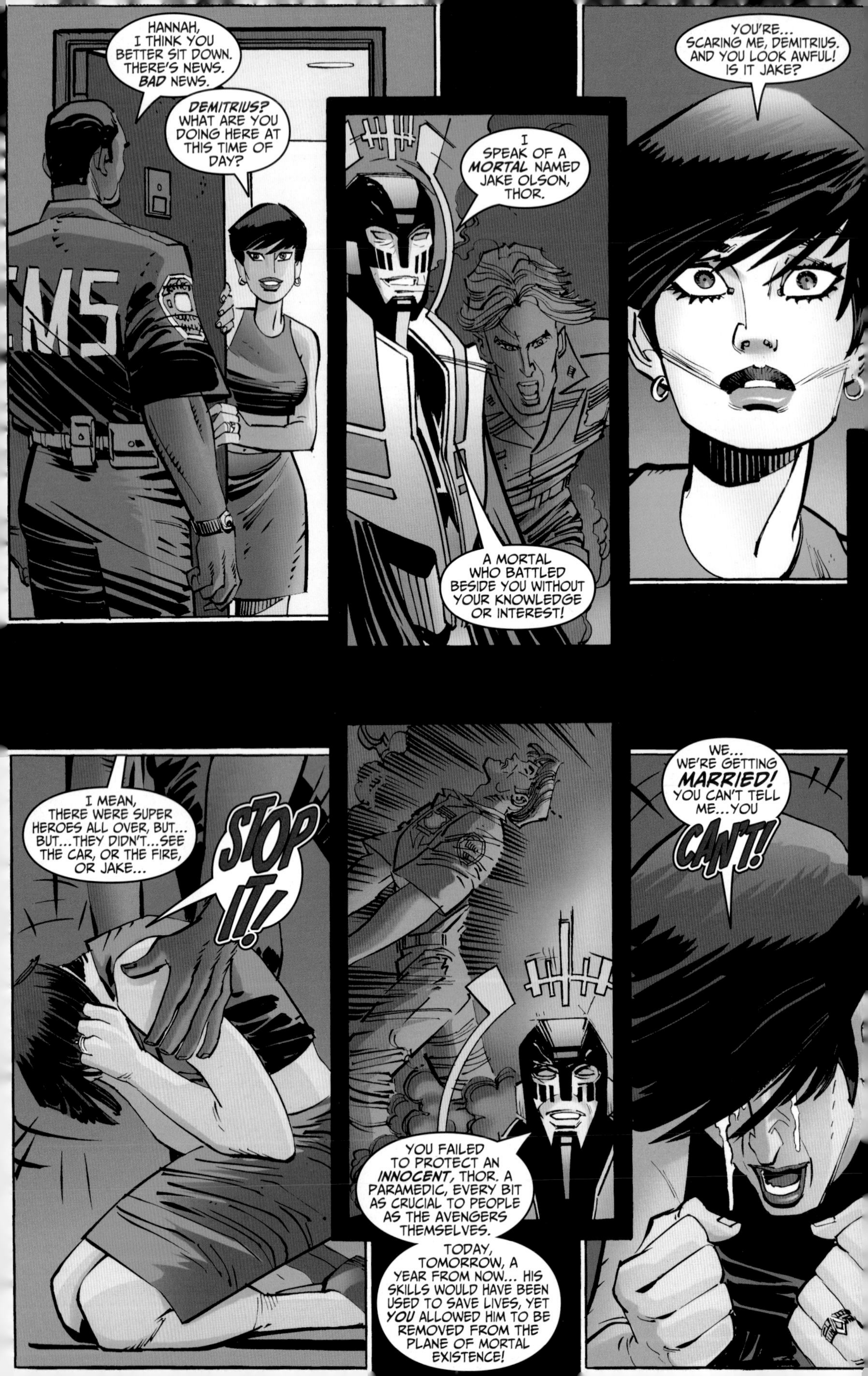
HANNAH, I THINK YOU BETTER SIT DOWN. THERE'S NEWS. BAD NEWS.
DEMITRIUS? WHAT ARE YOU DOING HERE AT THIS TIME OF DAY?
EMS
I SPEAK OF A MORTAL NAMED JAKE OLSON, THOR.
A MORTAL WHO BATTLED BESIDE YOU WITHOUT YOUR KNOWLEDGE OR INTEREST!
YOU'RE... SCARING ME, DEMITRIUS. AND YOU LOOK AWFUL! IS IT JAKE?
I MEAN, THERE WERE SUPER HEROES ALL OVER, BUT... BUT...THEY DIDN'T...SEE THE CAR, OR THE FIRE, OR JAKE...
STOP IT!
YOU FAILED TO PROTECT AN INNOCENT, THOR. A PARAMEDIC, EVERY BIT AS CRUCIAL TO PEOPLE AS THE AVENGERS THEMSELVES.
TODAY, TOMORROW, A YEAR FROM NOW... HIS SKILLS WOULD HAVE BEEN USED TO SAVE LIVES, YET YOU ALLOWED HIM TO BE REMOVED FROM THE PLANE OF MORTAL EXISTENCE!
WE... WE'RE GETTING MARRIED! YOU CAN'T TELL ME...YOU
CAN'T!

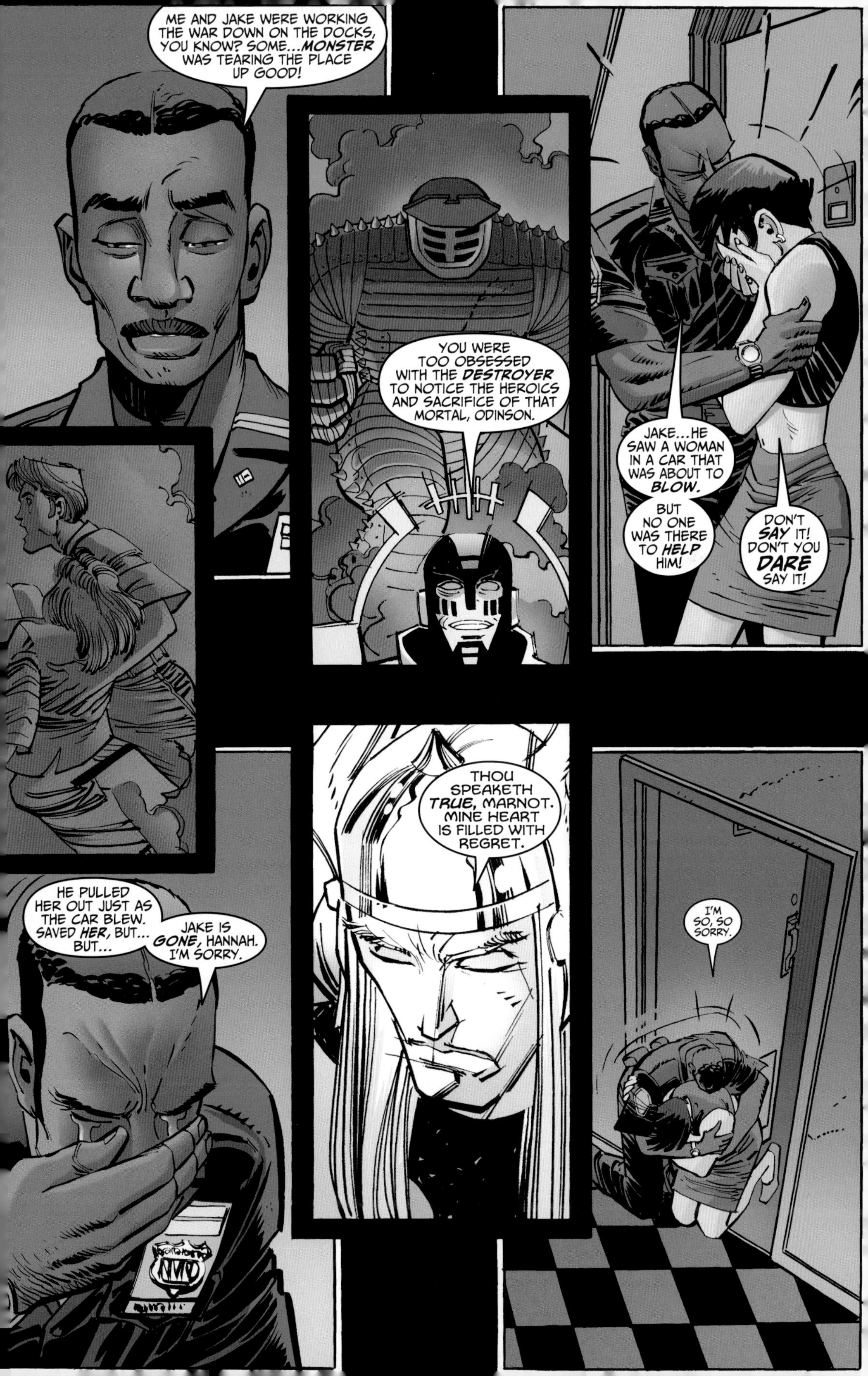
ME AND JAKE WERE WORKING THE WAR DOWN ON THE DOCKS, YOU KNOW? SOME... MONSTER WAS TEARING THE PLACE UP GOOD!
YOU WERE TOO OBSESSED WITH THE DESTROYER TO NOTICE THE HEROICS AND SACRIFICE OF THAT MORTAL, ODINSON.
JAKE... HE SAW A WOMAN IN A CAR THAT WAS ABOUT TO BLOW.
BUT NO ONE WAS THERE TO HELP HIM!
DON'T SAY IT! DON'T YOU DARE SAY IT!
HE PULLED HER OUT JUST AS THE CAR BLEW. SAVED HER, BUT... BUT...
JAKE IS GONE, HANNAH. I'M SORRY.
THOU SPEAKETH TRUE, MARNOT. MINE HEART IS FILLED WITH REGRET.
I'M SO, SO SORRY.

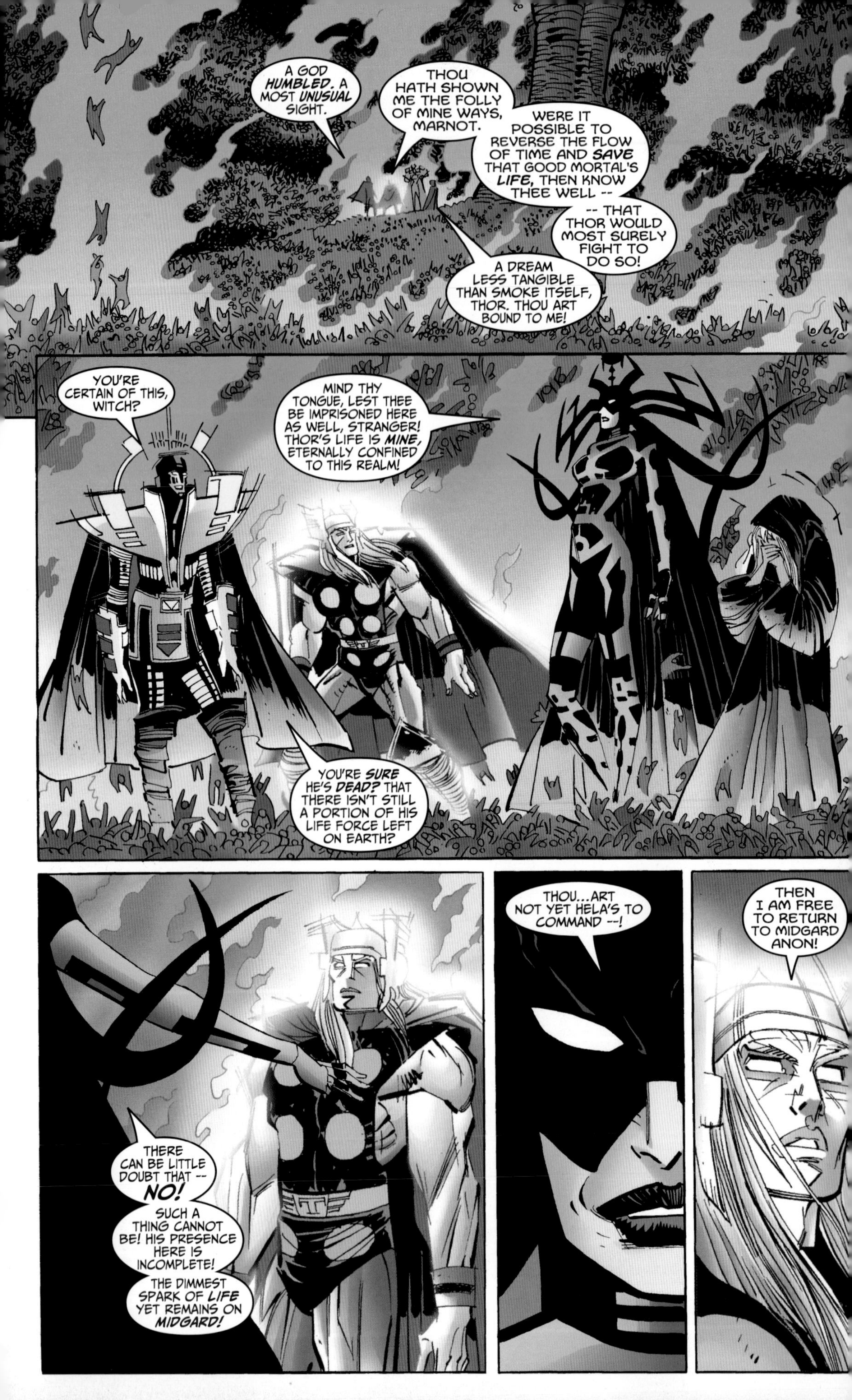
A GOD HUMBLED. A MOST UNUSUAL SIGHT.
THOU HATH SHOWN ME THE FOLLY OF MINE WAYS, MARNOT.
WERE IT POSSIBLE TO REVERSE THE FLOW OF TIME AND SAVE THAT GOOD MORTAL'S LIFE, THEN KNOW THEE WELL --
-- THAT THOR WOULD MOST SURELY FIGHT TO DO SO!
A DREAM LESS TANGIBLE THAN SMOKE ITSELF, THOR. THOU ART BOUND TO ME!
YOU'RE CERTAIN OF THIS, WITCH?
MIND THY TONGUE, LEST THEE BE IMPRISONED HERE AS WELL, STRANGER! THOR'S LIFE IS MINE, ETERNALLY CONFINED TO THIS REALM!
YOU'RE SURE HE'S DEAD? THAT THERE ISN'T STILL A PORTION OF HIS LIFE FORCE LEFT ON EARTH?
THERE CAN BE LITTLE DOUBT THAT -- NO!
SUCH A THING CANNOT BE! HIS PRESENCE HERE IS INCOMPLETE!
THE DIMMEST SPARK OF LIFE YET REMAINS ON MIDGARD!
THOU...ART NOT YET HELA'S TO COMMAND --!
THEN I AM FREE TO RETURN TO MIDGARD ANON!

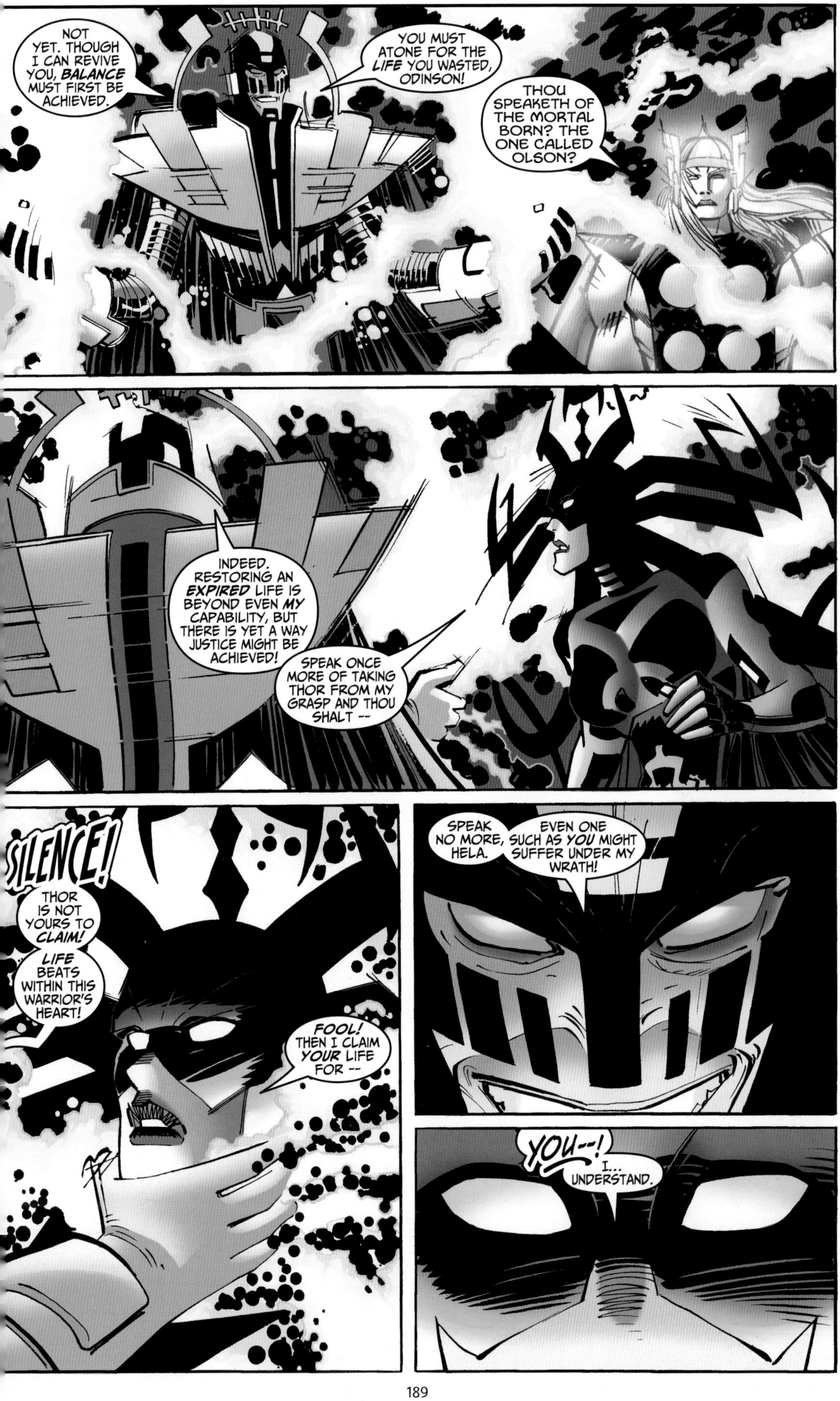
NOT YET. THOUGH I CAN REVIVE YOU, BALANCE MUST FIRST BE ACHIEVED.
YOU MUST ATONE FOR THE LIFE YOU WASTED, ODINSON!
THOU SPEAKETH OF THE MORTAL BORN? THE ONE CALLED OLSON?
INDEED. RESTORING AN EXPIRED LIFE IS BEYOND EVEN MY CAPABILITY, BUT THERE IS YET A WAY JUSTICE MIGHT BE ACHIEVED!
SPEAK ONCE MORE OF TAKING THOR FROM MY GRASP AND THOU SHALT --
SILENCE!
THOR IS NOT YOURS TO CLAIM!
LIFE BEATS WITHIN THIS WARRIOR'S HEART!
FOOL! THEN I CLAIM YOUR LIFE FOR --
SPEAK NO MORE, HELA.
EVEN ONE SUCH AS YOU MIGHT SUFFER UNDER MY WRATH!
YOU--!
I... UNDERSTAND.

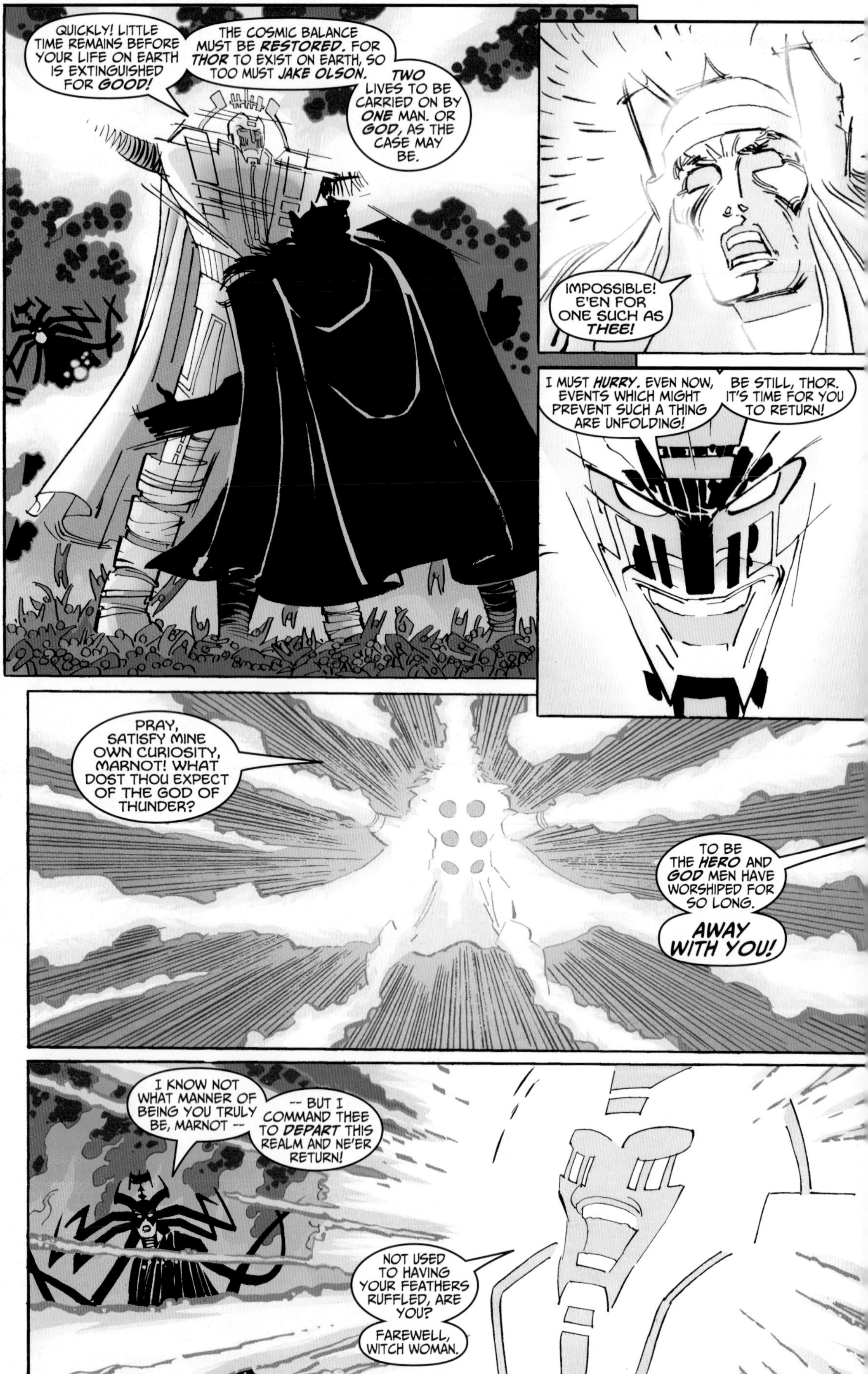
QUICKLY! LITTLE TIME REMAINS BEFORE YOUR LIFE ON EARTH IS EXTINGUISHED FOR **GOOD!**
THE COSMIC BALANCE MUST BE **RESTORED.** FOR **THOR** TO EXIST ON EARTH, SO TOO MUST **JAKE OLSON.**
TWO LIVES TO BE CARRIED ON BY **ONE** MAN. OR **GOD**, AS THE CASE MAY BE.
IMPOSSIBLE! E'EN FOR ONE SUCH AS **THEE!**
I MUST **HURRY.** EVEN NOW, EVENTS WHICH MIGHT PREVENT SUCH A THING ARE UNFOLDING!
BE STILL, THOR. IT'S TIME FOR YOU TO RETURN!
PRAY, SATISFY MINE OWN CURIOSITY, MARNOT! WHAT DOST THOU EXPECT OF THE GOD OF THUNDER?
TO BE THE **HERO** AND **GOD** MEN HAVE WORSHIPED FOR SO LONG.
AWAY WITH YOU!
I KNOW NOT WHAT MANNER OF BEING YOU TRULY BE, MARNOT --
-- BUT I COMMAND THEE TO **DEPART** THIS REALM AND NE'ER RETURN!
NOT USED TO HAVING YOUR FEATHERS RUFFLED, ARE YOU?
FAREWELL, WITCH WOMAN.

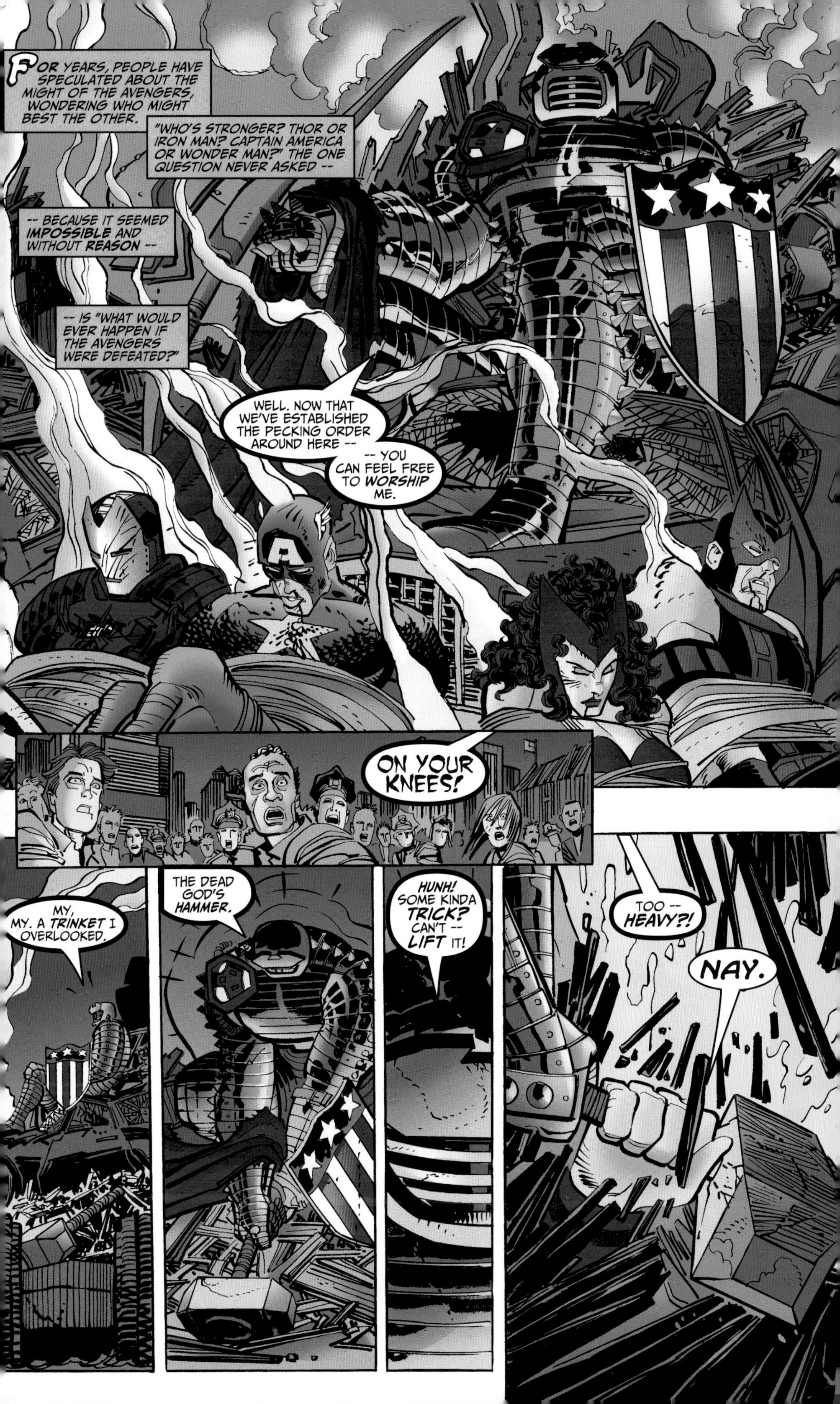
FOR YEARS, PEOPLE HAVE SPECULATED ABOUT THE MIGHT OF THE AVENGERS, WONDERING WHO MIGHT BEST THE OTHER.
"WHO'S STRONGER? THOR OR IRON MAN? CAPTAIN AMERICA OR WONDER MAN?" THE ONE QUESTION NEVER ASKED --
-- BECAUSE IT SEEMED IMPOSSIBLE AND WITHOUT REASON --
-- IS "WHAT WOULD EVER HAPPEN IF THE AVENGERS WERE DEFEATED?"
WELL. NOW THAT WE'VE ESTABLISHED THE PECKING ORDER AROUND HERE --
-- YOU CAN FEEL FREE TO WORSHIP ME.
ON YOUR KNEES!
MY, MY. A TRINKET I OVERLOOKED.
THE DEAD GOD'S HAMMER.
HUNH! SOME KINDA TRICK? CAN'T -- LIFT IT!
TOO -- HEAVY?!
NAY.

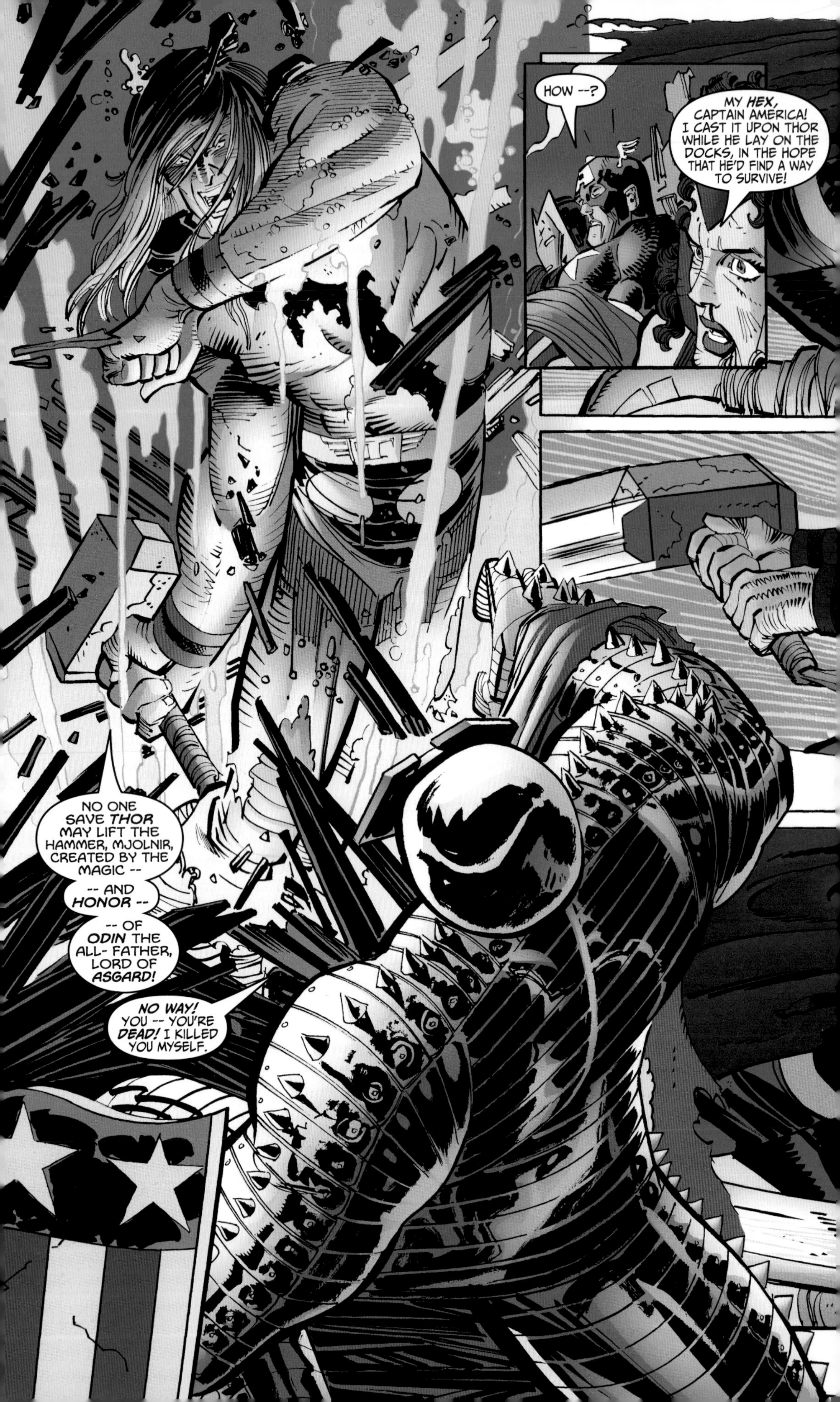

HOW --?
MY *HEX*, CAPTAIN AMERICA! I CAST IT UPON THOR WHILE HE LAY ON THE DOCKS, IN THE HOPE THAT HE'D FIND A WAY TO SURVIVE!
NO ONE SAVE *THOR* MAY LIFT THE HAMMER, MJOLNIR, CREATED BY THE MAGIC --
-- AND *HONOR* --
-- OF *ODIN* THE ALL- FATHER, LORD OF *ASGARD!*
NO WAY! YOU -- YOU'RE *DEAD!* I KILLED YOU MYSELF.

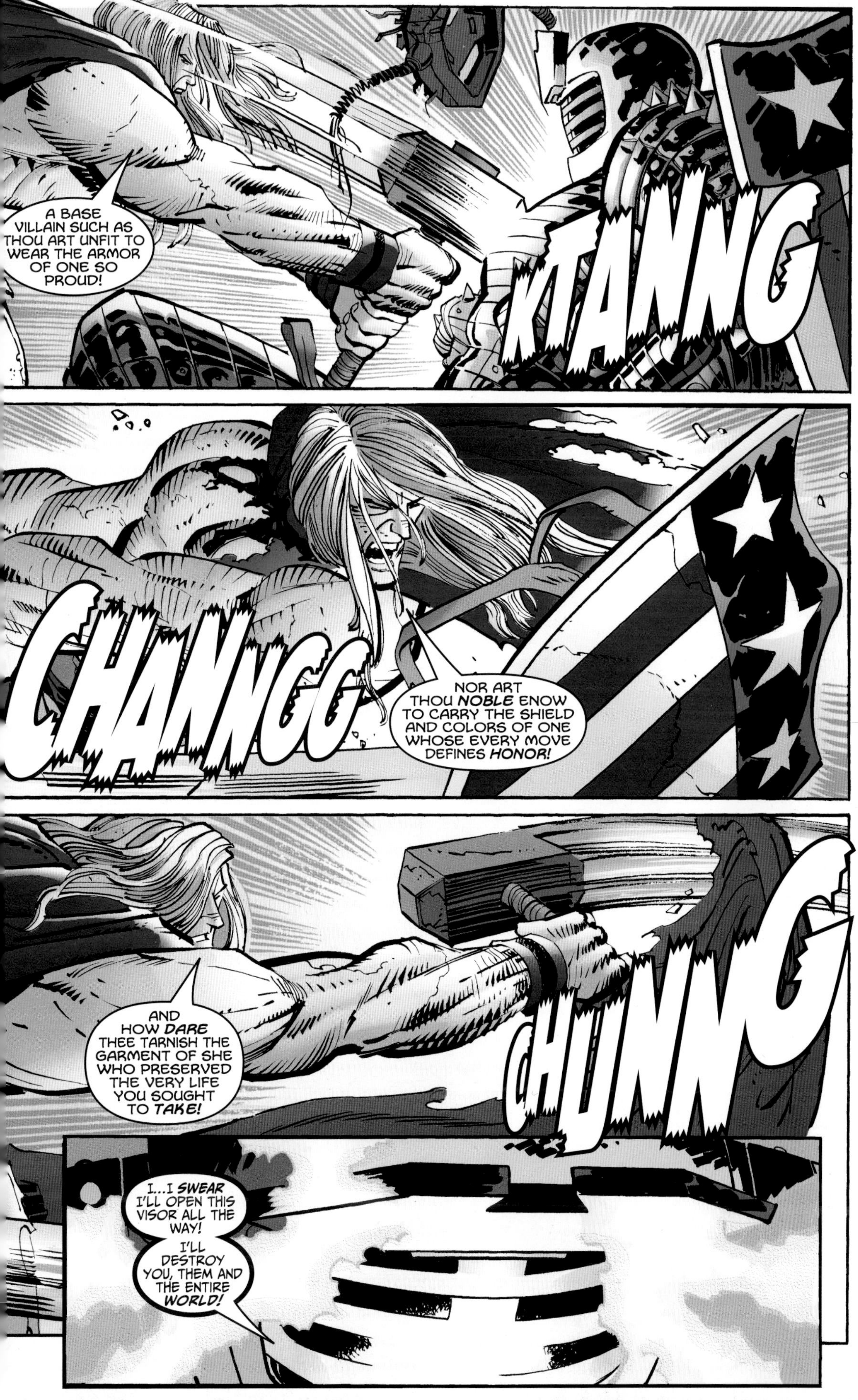
A BASE VILLAIN SUCH AS THOU ART UNFIT TO WEAR THE ARMOR OF ONE SO PROUD!
KTANNG
CHANNGG
NOR ART THOU NOBLE ENOW TO CARRY THE SHIELD AND COLORS OF ONE WHOSE EVERY MOVE DEFINES HONOR!
AND HOW DARE THEE TARNISH THE GARMENT OF SHE WHO PRESERVED THE VERY LIFE YOU SOUGHT TO TAKE!
CHUNNG
I...I SWEAR I'LL OPEN THIS VISOR ALL THE WAY!
I'LL DESTROY YOU, THEM AND THE ENTIRE WORLD!

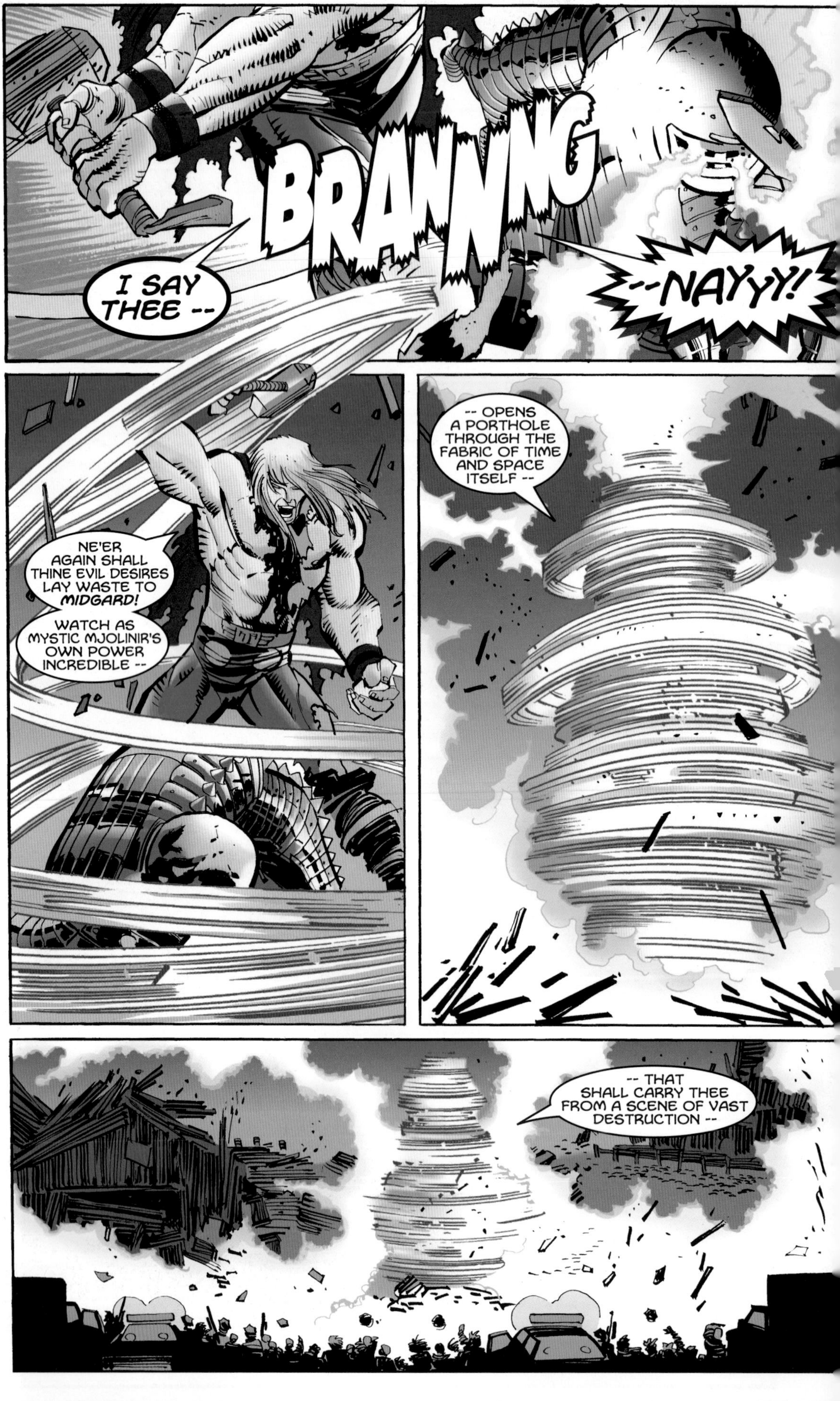
BRANNNG
I SAY THEE --
--NAYYY!
NE'ER AGAIN SHALL THINE EVIL DESIRES LAY WASTE TO MIDGARD!
WATCH AS MYSTIC MJOLINIR'S OWN POWER INCREDIBLE --
-- OPENS A PORTHOLE THROUGH THE FABRIC OF TIME AND SPACE ITSELF --
-- THAT SHALL CARRY THEE FROM A SCENE OF VAST DESTRUCTION --

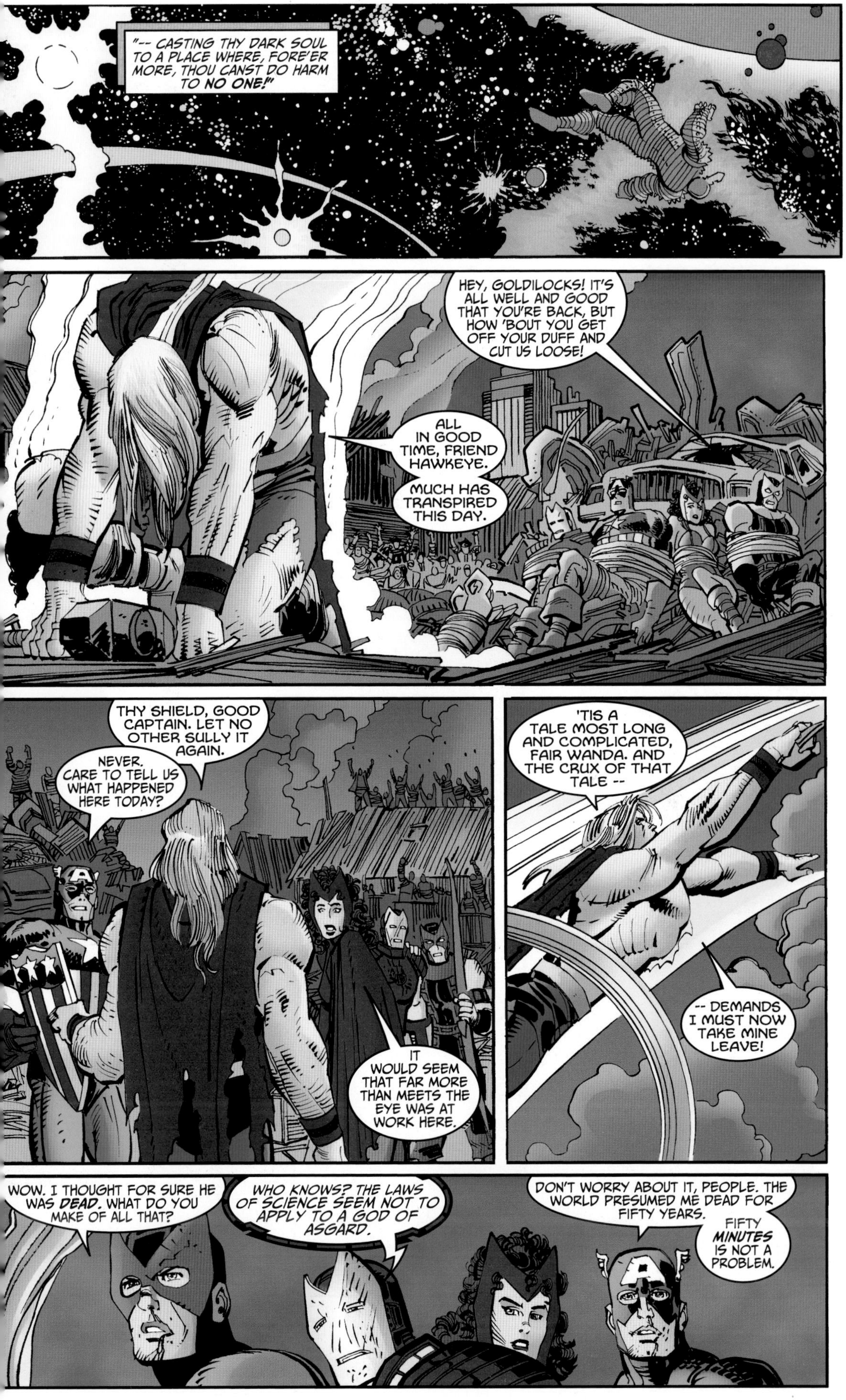
"-- CASTING THY DARK SOUL TO A PLACE WHERE, FORE'ER MORE, THOU CANST DO HARM TO NO ONE!"
HEY, GOLDILOCKS! IT'S ALL WELL AND GOOD THAT YOU'RE BACK, BUT HOW 'BOUT YOU GET OFF YOUR DUFF AND CUT US LOOSE!
ALL IN GOOD TIME, FRIEND HAWKEYE.
MUCH HAS TRANSPIRED THIS DAY.
THY SHIELD, GOOD CAPTAIN. LET NO OTHER SULLY IT AGAIN.
NEVER. CARE TO TELL US WHAT HAPPENED HERE TODAY?
IT WOULD SEEM THAT FAR MORE THAN MEETS THE EYE WAS AT WORK HERE.
'TIS A TALE MOST LONG AND COMPLICATED, FAIR WANDA. AND THE CRUX OF THAT TALE --
-- DEMANDS I MUST NOW TAKE MINE LEAVE!
WOW. I THOUGHT FOR SURE HE WAS DEAD. WHAT DO YOU MAKE OF ALL THAT?
WHO KNOWS? THE LAWS OF SCIENCE SEEM NOT TO APPLY TO A GOD OF ASGARD.
DON'T WORRY ABOUT IT, PEOPLE. THE WORLD PRESUMED ME DEAD FOR FIFTY YEARS.
FIFTY MINUTES IS NOT A PROBLEM.

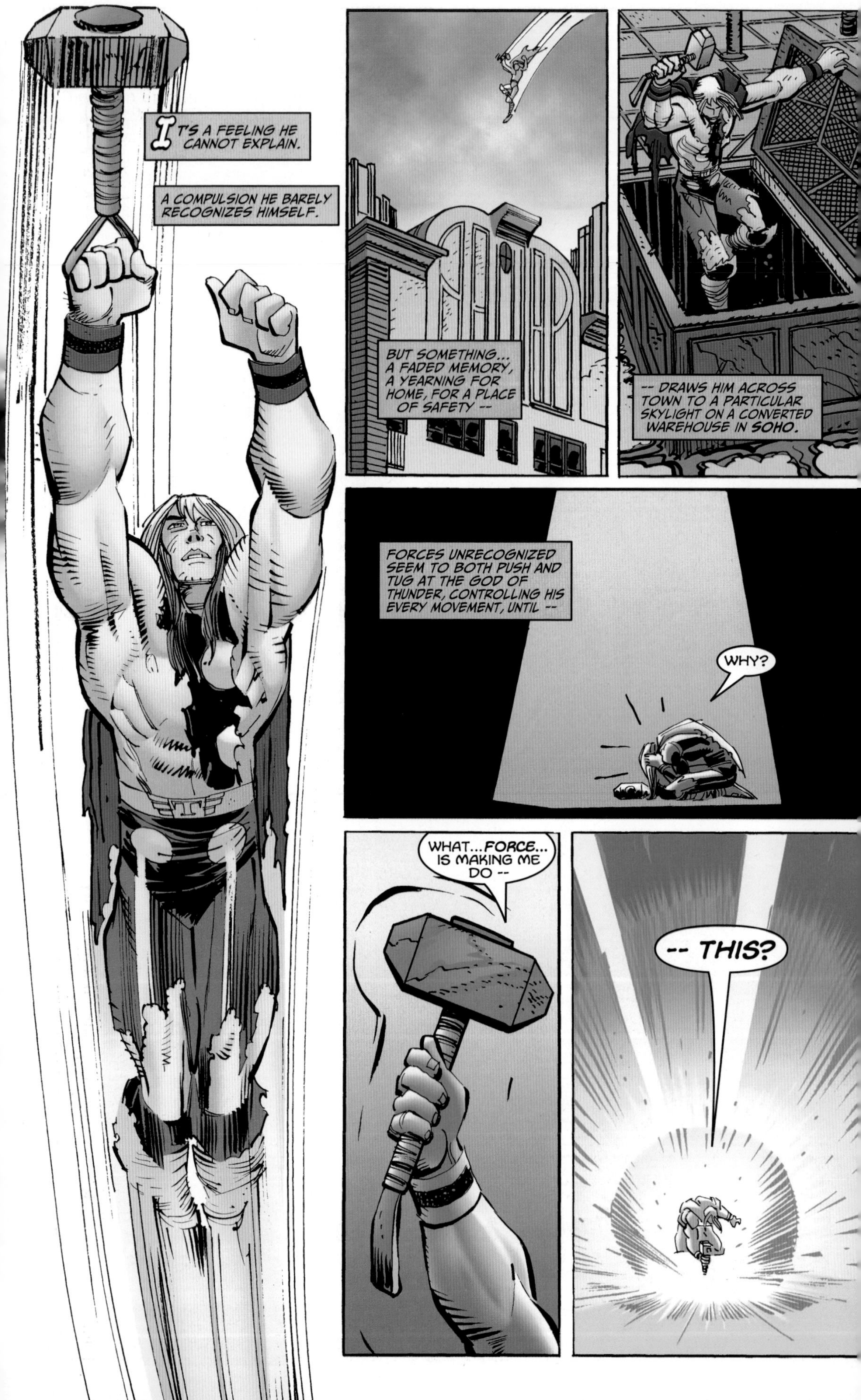
IT'S A FEELING HE CANNOT EXPLAIN.
A COMPULSION HE BARELY RECOGNIZES HIMSELF.
BUT SOMETHING... A FADED MEMORY, A YEARNING FOR HOME, FOR A PLACE OF SAFETY --
-- DRAWS HIM ACROSS TOWN TO A PARTICULAR SKYLIGHT ON A CONVERTED WAREHOUSE IN SOHO.
FORCES UNRECOGNIZED SEEM TO BOTH PUSH AND TUG AT THE GOD OF THUNDER, CONTROLLING HIS EVERY MOVEMENT, UNTIL --
WHY?
WHAT... FORCE... IS MAKING ME DO --
-- THIS?

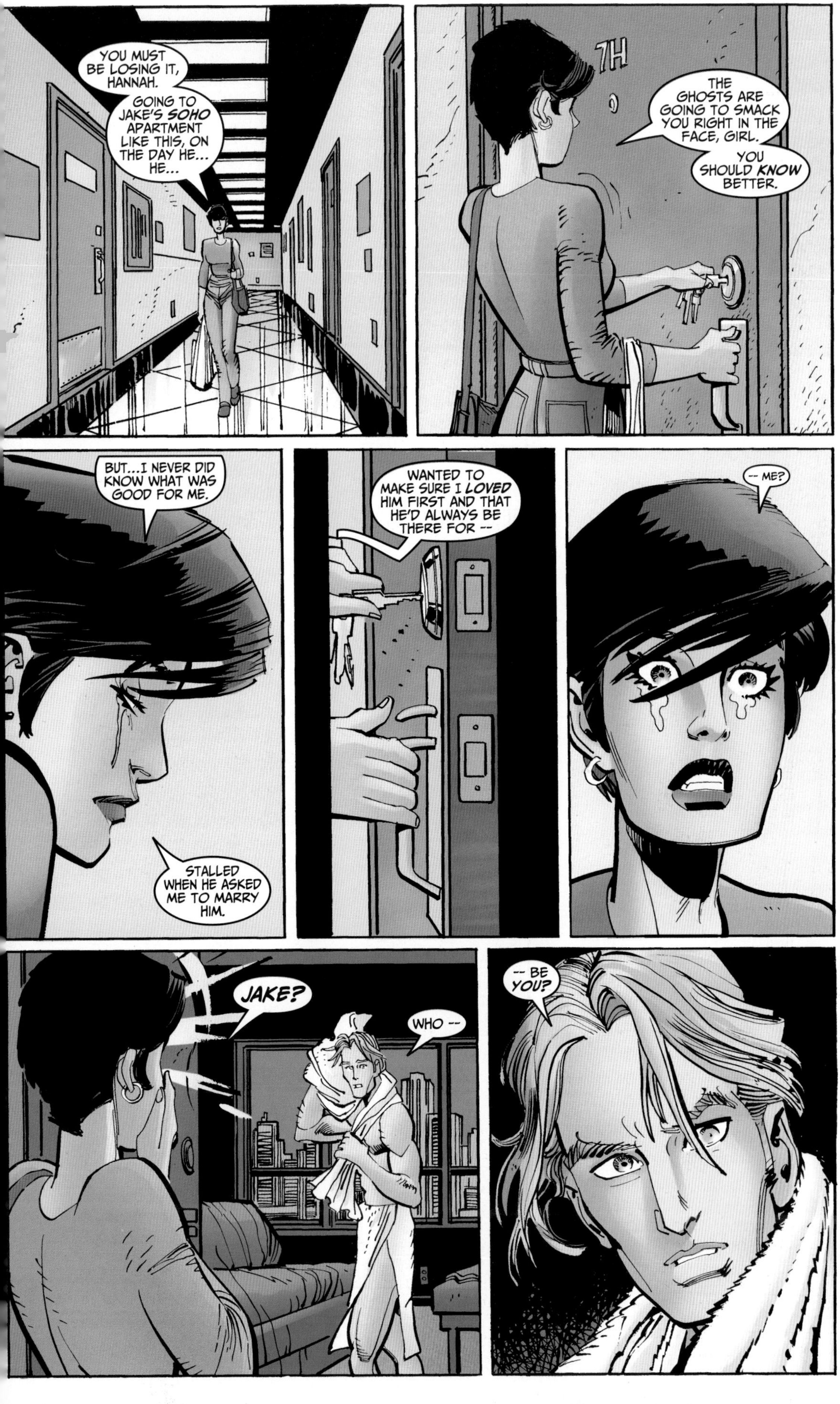
YOU MUST BE LOSING IT, HANNAH.
GOING TO JAKE'S SOHO APARTMENT LIKE THIS, ON THE DAY HE... HE...
THE GHOSTS ARE GOING TO SMACK YOU RIGHT IN THE FACE, GIRL.
YOU SHOULD KNOW BETTER.
BUT...I NEVER DID KNOW WHAT WAS GOOD FOR ME.
STALLED WHEN HE ASKED ME TO MARRY HIM.
WANTED TO MAKE SURE I LOVED HIM FIRST AND THAT HE'D ALWAYS BE THERE FOR --
-- ME?
JAKE?
WHO --
-- BE YOU?
7H

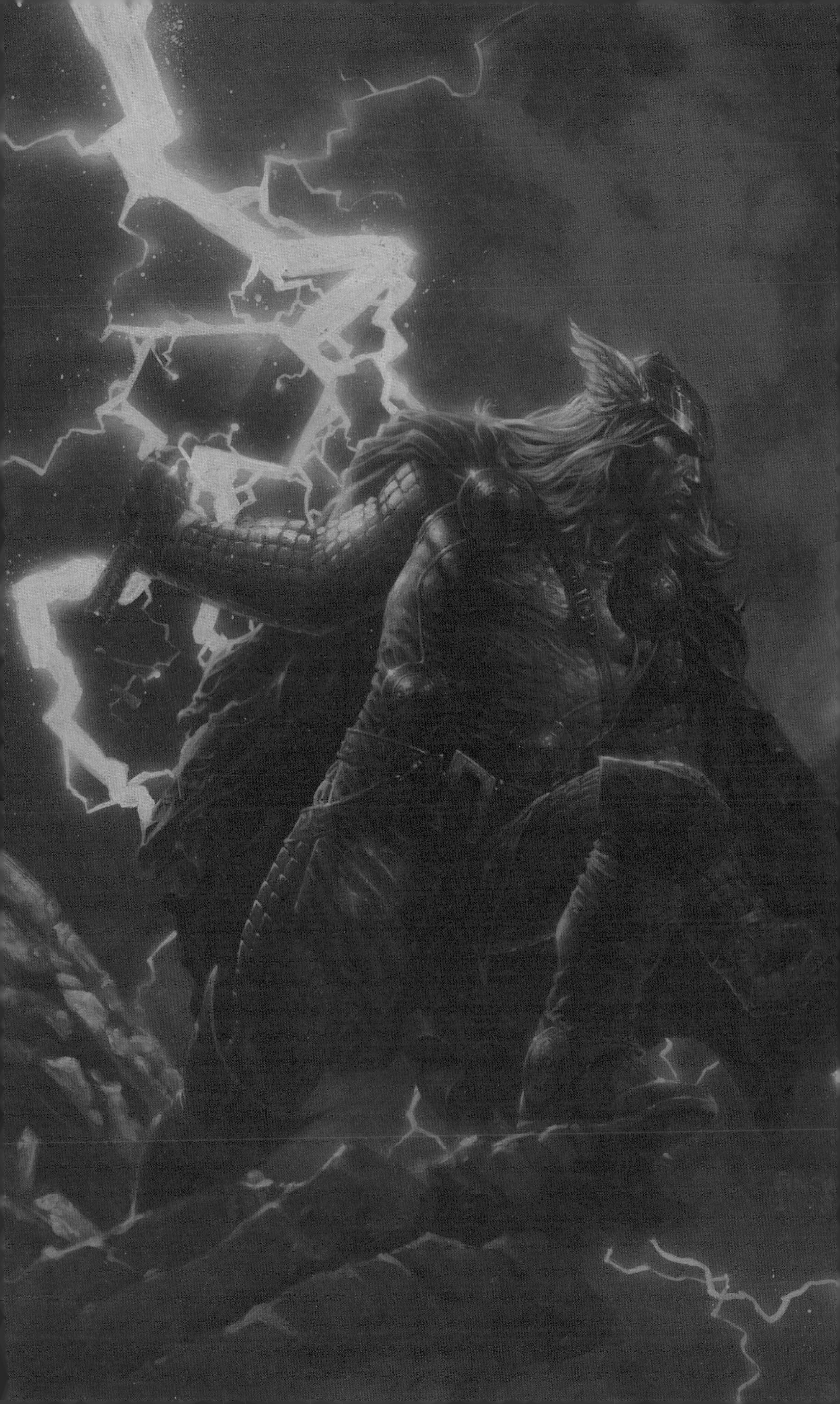

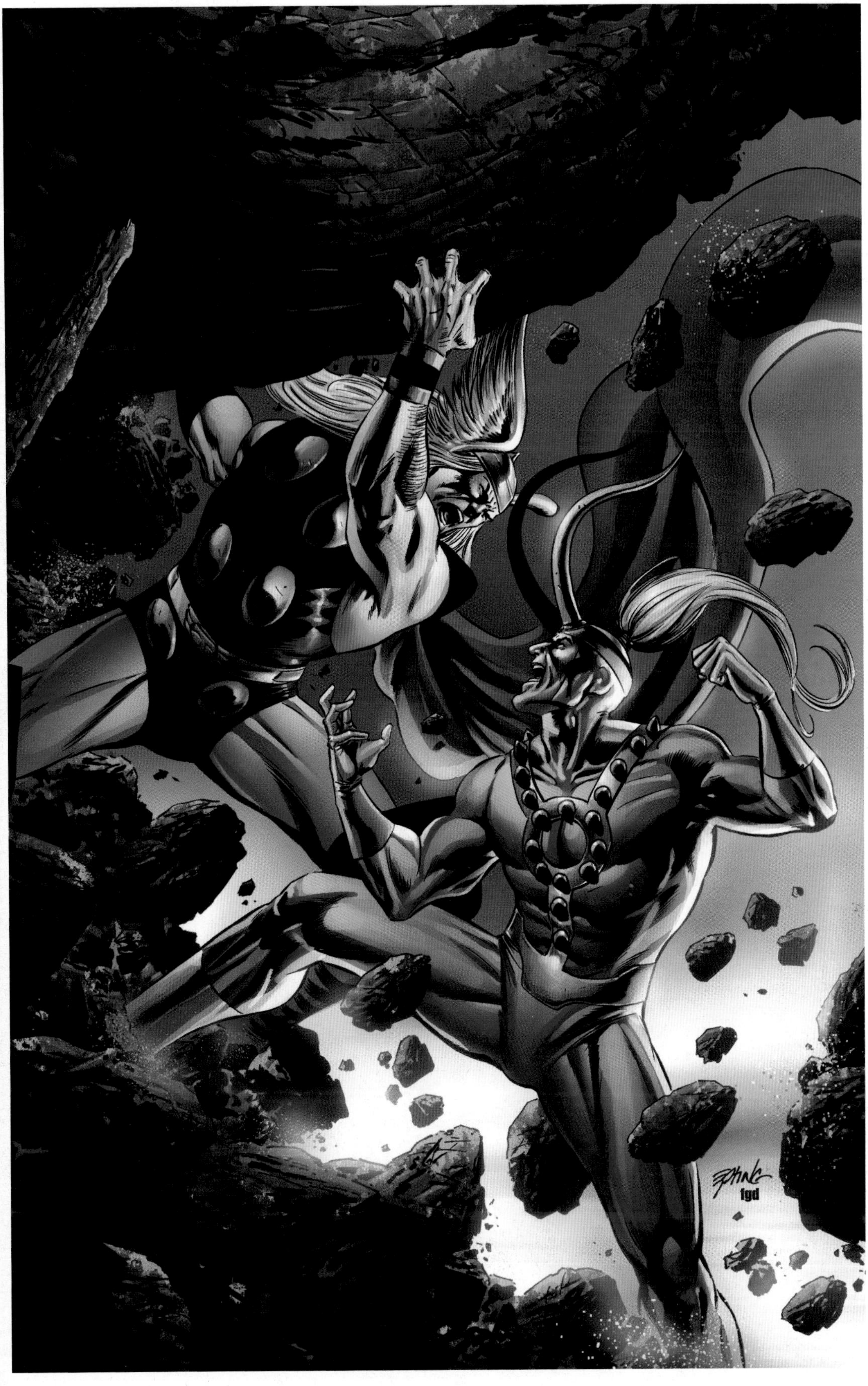

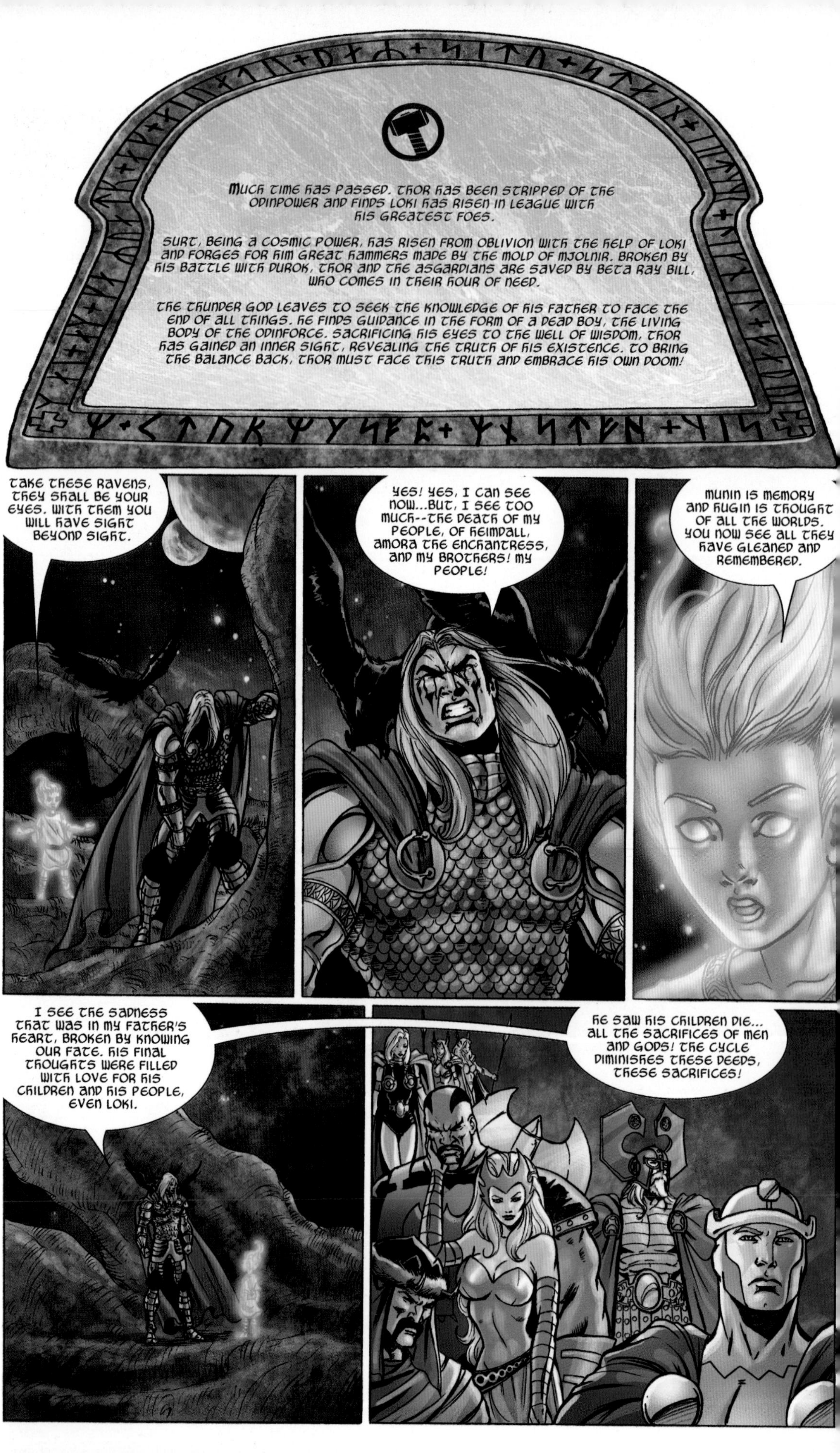

Much time has passed. Thor has been stripped of the Odinpower and finds Loki has risen in league with his greatest foes.
Surt, being a cosmic power, has risen from oblivion with the help of Loki and forges for him great hammers made by the mold of Mjolnir. Broken by his battle with Durok, Thor and the Asgardians are saved by Beta Ray Bill, who comes in their hour of need.
The Thunder God leaves to seek the knowledge of his father to face the end of all things. He finds guidance in the form of a dead boy, the living body of the Odinforce. Sacrificing his eyes to the Well of Wisdom, Thor has gained an inner sight, revealing the truth of his existence. To bring the balance back, Thor must face this truth and embrace his own doom!
Take these ravens, they shall be your eyes. With them you will have sight beyond sight.
Yes! Yes, I can see now...but, I see too much--the death of my people, of Heimdall, Amora the Enchantress, and my brothers! My people!
Munin is memory and Hugin is thought of all the worlds. You now see all they have gleaned and remembered.
I see the sadness that was in my father's heart, broken by knowing our fate. His final thoughts were filled with love for his children and his people, even Loki.
He saw his children die... all the sacrifices of men and gods! The cycle diminishes these deeds, these sacrifices!

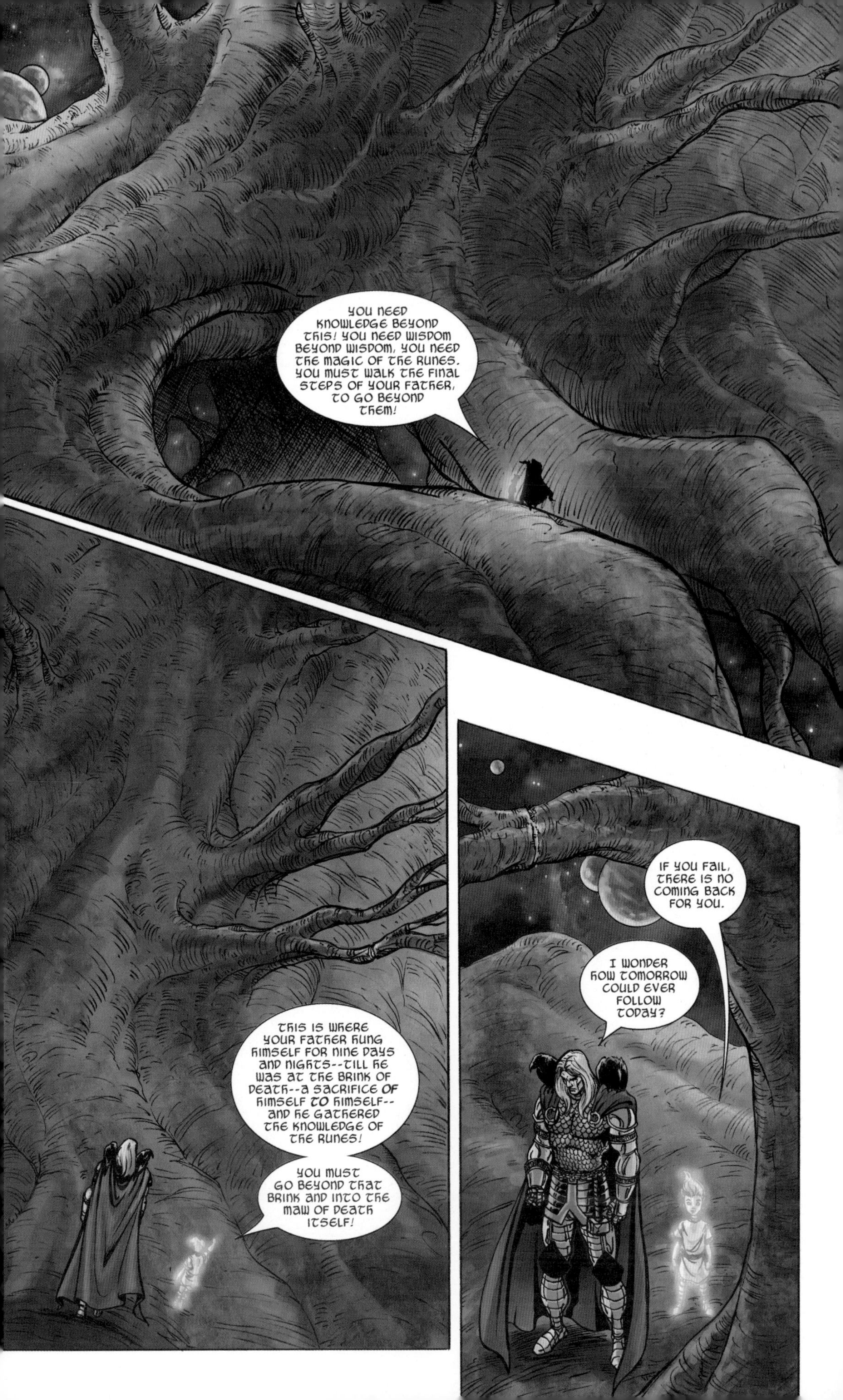
YOU NEED KNOWLEDGE BEYOND THIS! YOU NEED WISDOM BEYOND WISDOM, YOU NEED THE MAGIC OF THE RUNES. YOU MUST WALK THE FINAL STEPS OF YOUR FATHER, TO GO BEYOND THEM!
THIS IS WHERE YOUR FATHER HUNG HIMSELF FOR NINE DAYS AND NIGHTS--TILL HE WAS AT THE BRINK OF DEATH--A SACRIFICE OF HIMSELF TO HIMSELF--AND HE GATHERED THE KNOWLEDGE OF THE RUNES!
YOU MUST GO BEYOND THAT BRINK AND INTO THE MAW OF DEATH ITSELF!
IF YOU FAIL, THERE IS NO COMING BACK FOR YOU.
I WONDER HOW TOMORROW COULD EVER FOLLOW TODAY?

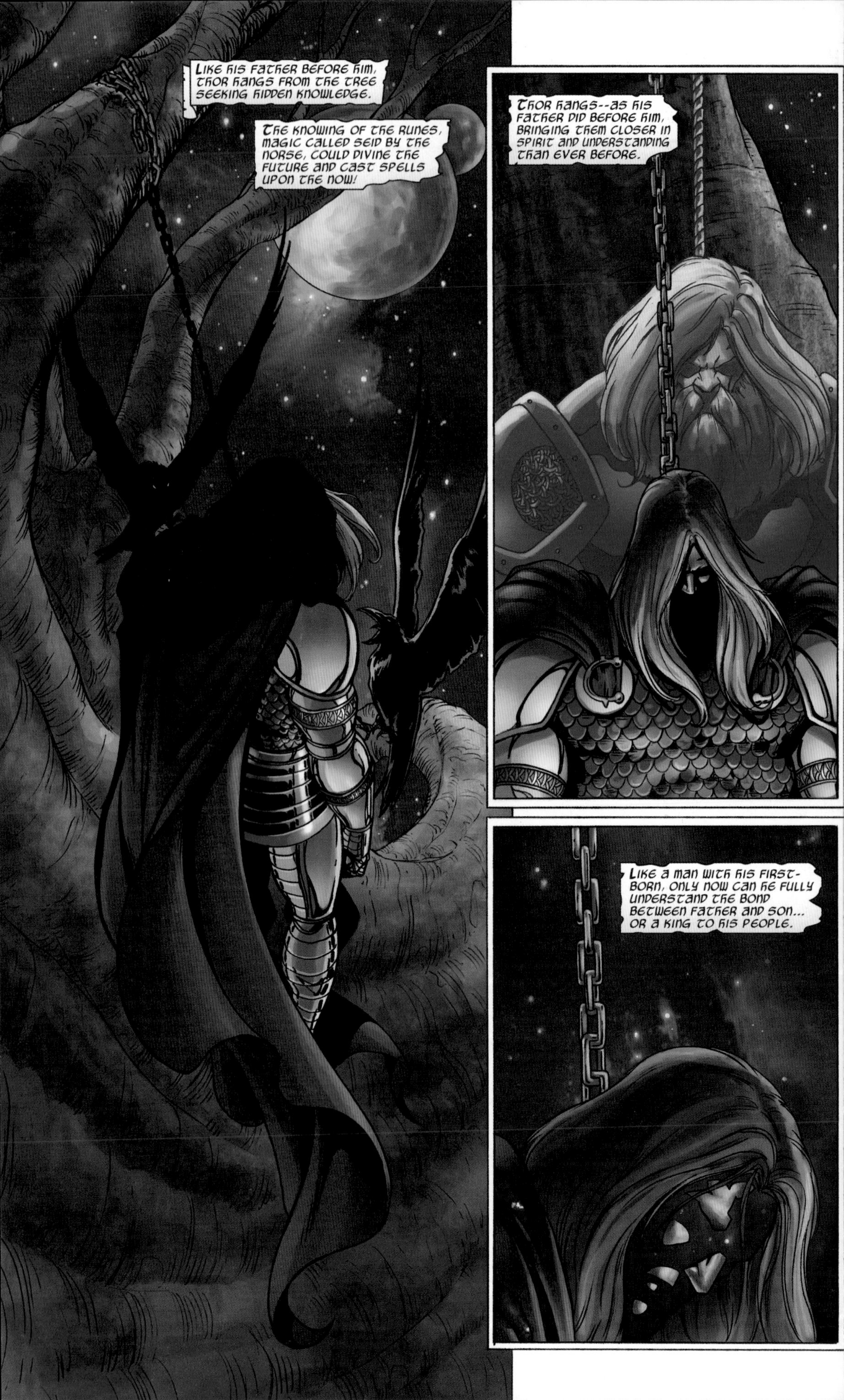
LIKE HIS FATHER BEFORE HIM, THOR HANGS FROM THE TREE SEEKING HIDDEN KNOWLEDGE.
THE KNOWING OF THE RUNES, MAGIC CALLED SEID BY THE NORSE, COULD DIVINE THE FUTURE AND CAST SPELLS UPON THE NOW!
THOR HANGS--AS HIS FATHER DID BEFORE HIM, BRINGING THEM CLOSER IN SPIRIT AND UNDERSTANDING THAN EVER BEFORE.
LIKE A MAN WITH HIS FIRST-BORN, ONLY NOW CAN HE FULLY UNDERSTAND THE BOND BETWEEN FATHER AND SON... OR A KING TO HIS PEOPLE.

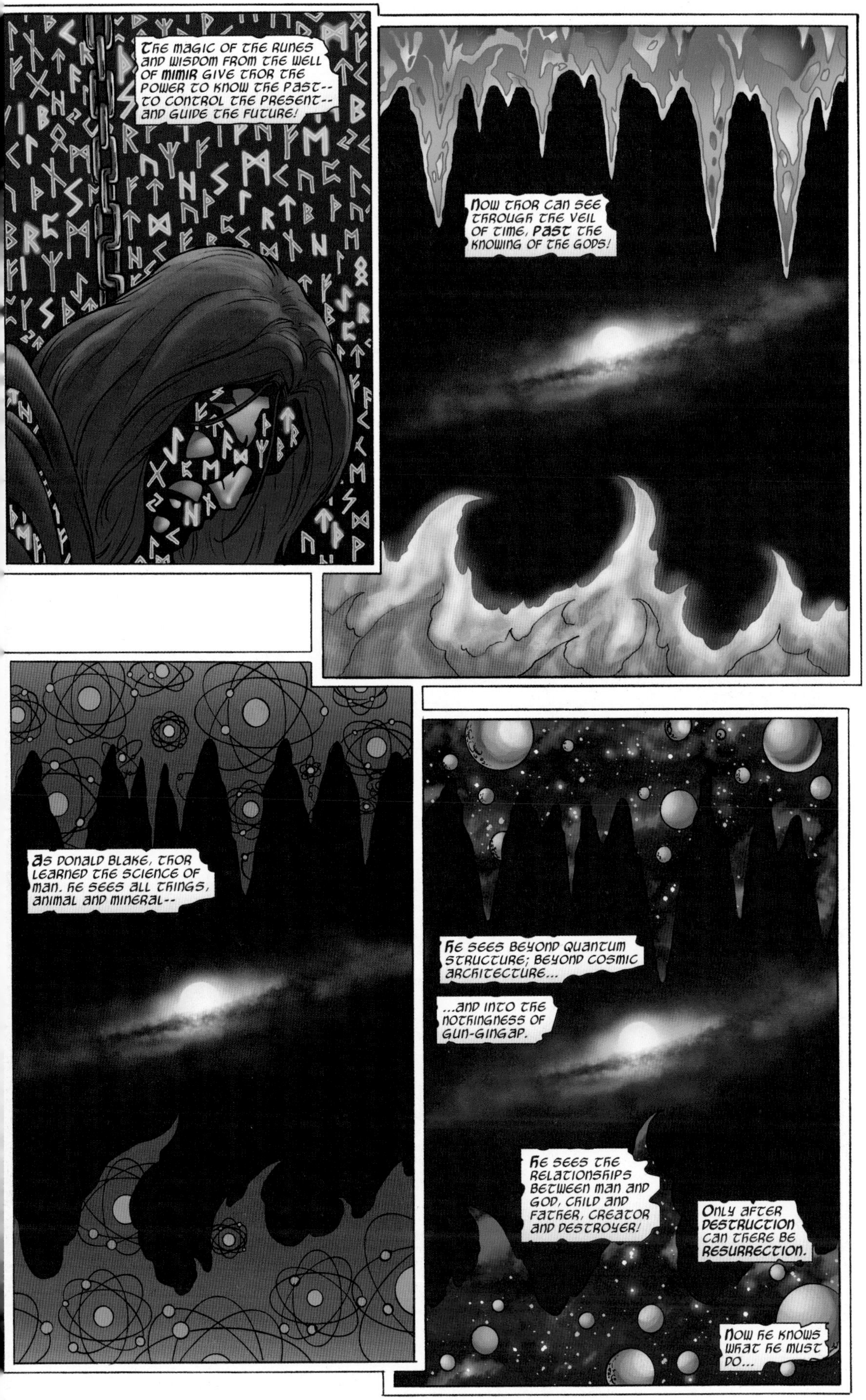
THE MAGIC OF THE RUNES AND WISDOM FROM THE WELL OF MIMIR GIVE THOR THE POWER TO KNOW THE PAST--TO CONTROL THE PRESENT--AND GUIDE THE FUTURE!
NOW THOR CAN SEE THROUGH THE VEIL OF TIME, PAST THE KNOWING OF THE GODS!
AS DONALD BLAKE, THOR LEARNED THE SCIENCE OF MAN. HE SEES ALL THINGS, ANIMAL AND MINERAL--
HE SEES BEYOND QUANTUM STRUCTURE; BEYOND COSMIC ARCHITECTURE...
...AND INTO THE NOTHINGNESS OF GUN-GINGAP.
HE SEES THE RELATIONSHIPS BETWEEN MAN AND GOD, CHILD AND FATHER, CREATOR AND DESTROYER!
ONLY AFTER DESTRUCTION CAN THERE BE RESURRECTION.
NOW HE KNOWS WHAT HE MUST DO...

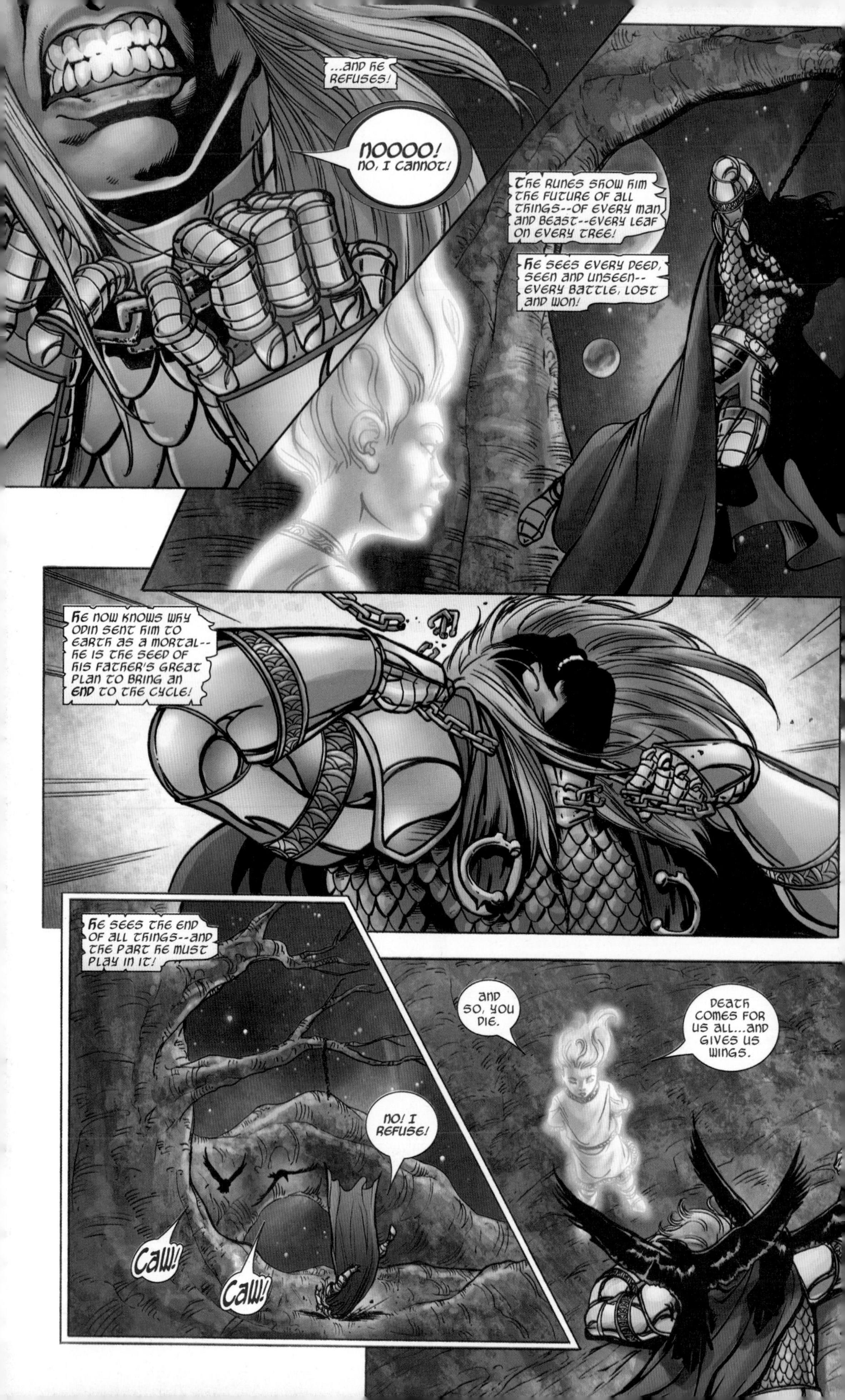
...AND HE REFUSES!
NOOOO! NO, I CANNOT!
THE RUNES SHOW HIM THE FUTURE OF ALL THINGS--OF EVERY MAN AND BEAST--EVERY LEAF ON EVERY TREE!
HE SEES EVERY DEED, SEEN AND UNSEEN-- EVERY BATTLE, LOST AND WON!
HE NOW KNOWS WHY ODIN SENT HIM TO EARTH AS A MORTAL-- HE IS THE SEED OF HIS FATHER'S GREAT PLAN TO BRING AN END TO THE CYCLE!
HE SEES THE END OF ALL THINGS--AND THE PART HE MUST PLAY IN IT!
NO! I REFUSE!
CAW!
CAW!
AND SO, YOU DIE.
DEATH COMES FOR US ALL...AND GIVES US WINGS.

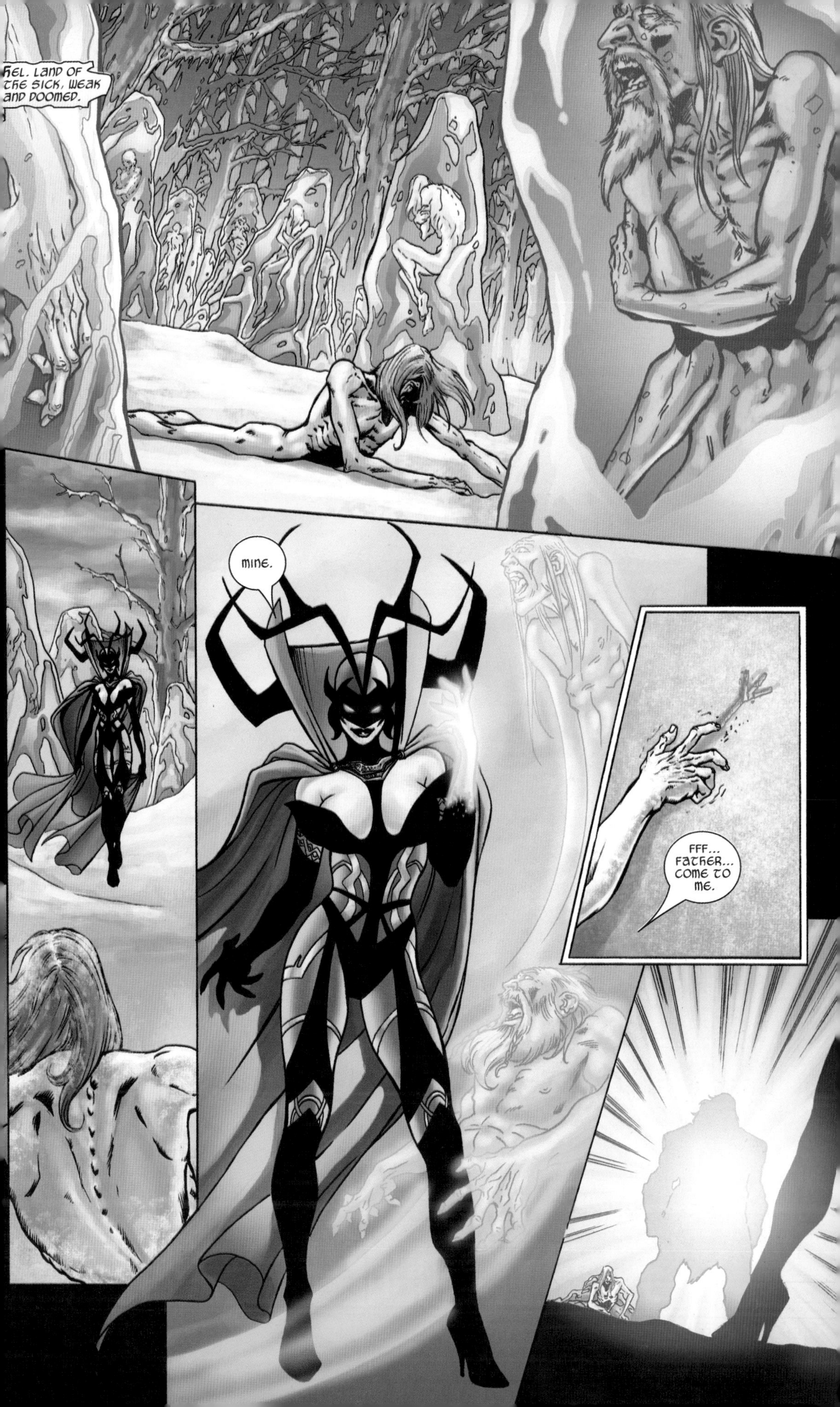
HEL. LAND OF THE SICK, WEAK AND DOOMED.
MINE.
FFF... FATHER... COME TO ME.

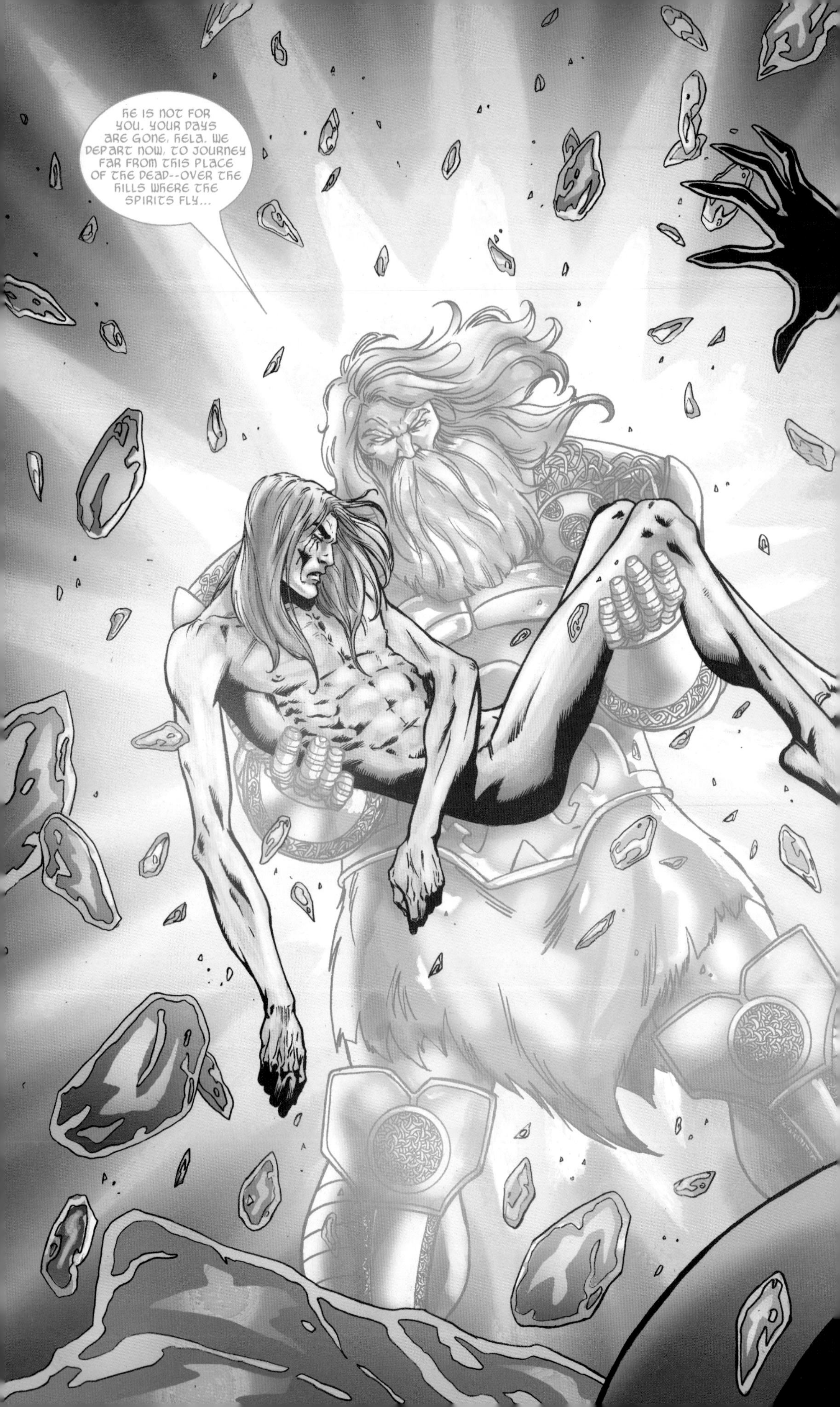
HE IS NOT FOR YOU. YOUR DAYS ARE GONE, HELA. WE DEPART NOW, TO JOURNEY FAR FROM THIS PLACE OF THE DEAD--OVER THE HILLS WHERE THE SPIRITS FLY...

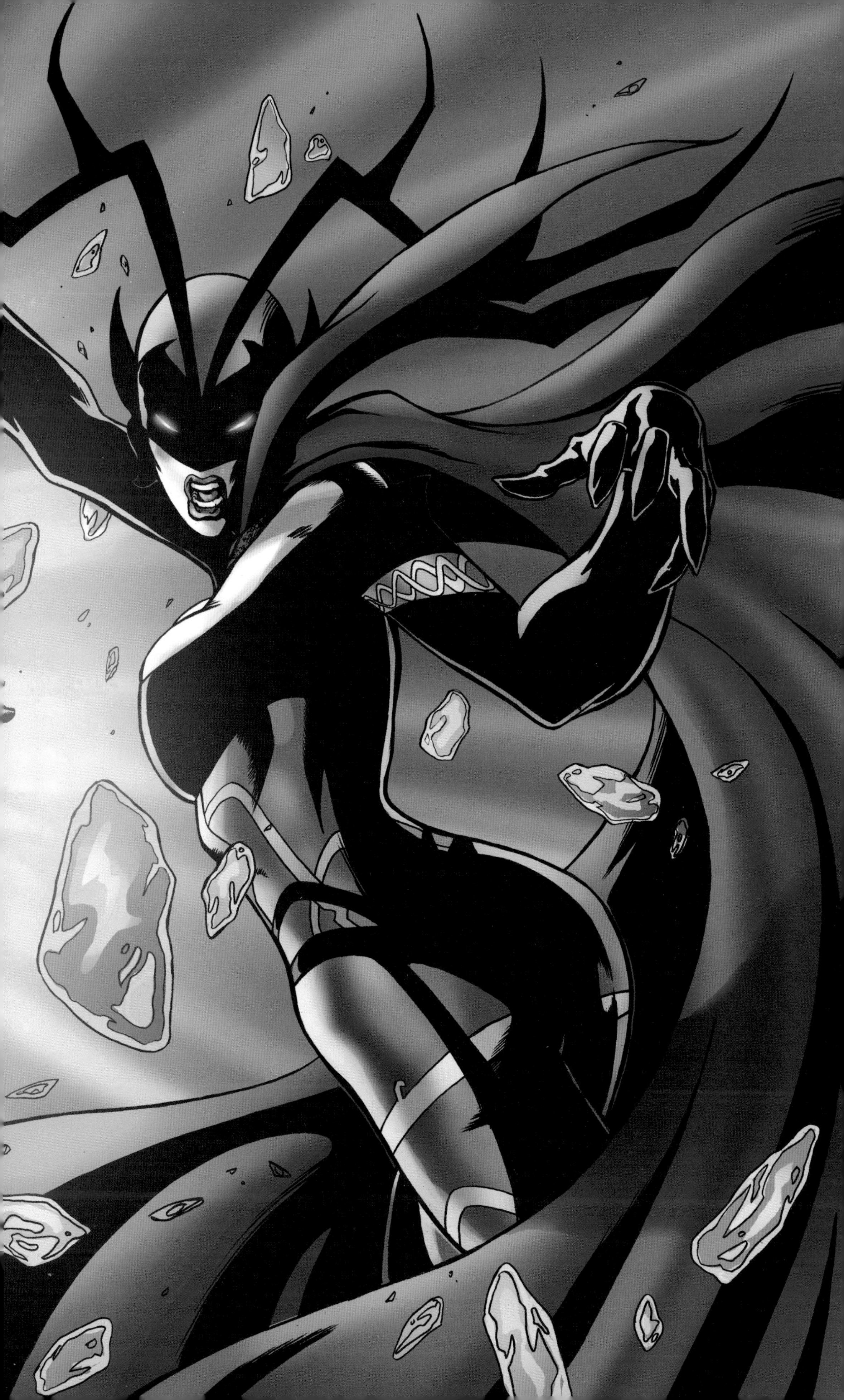

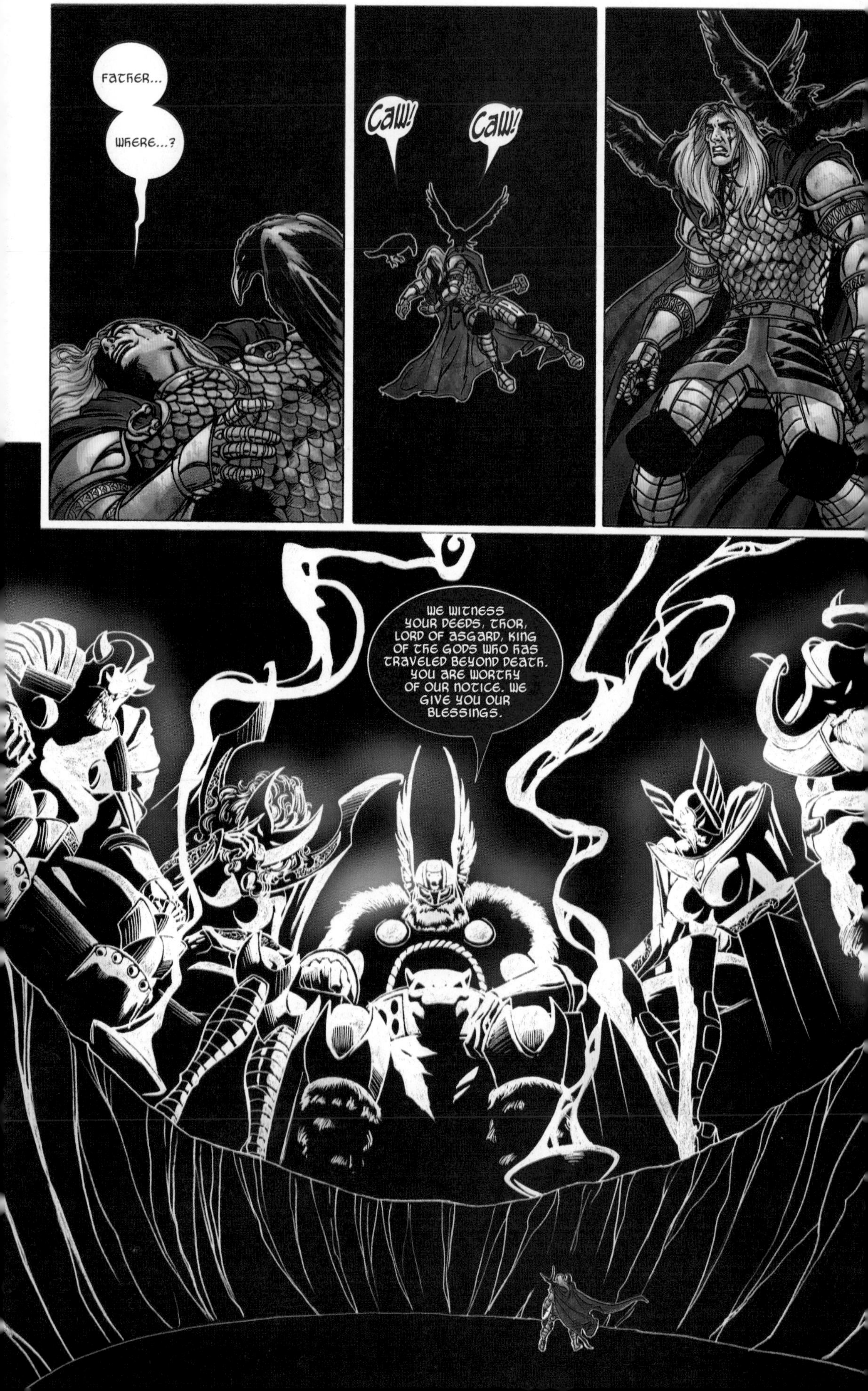
FATHER...
WHERE...?
CAW!
CAW!
WE WITNESS YOUR DEEDS, THOR, LORD OF ASGARD, KING OF THE GODS WHO HAS TRAVELED BEYOND DEATH. YOU ARE WORTHY OF OUR NOTICE. WE GIVE YOU OUR BLESSINGS.

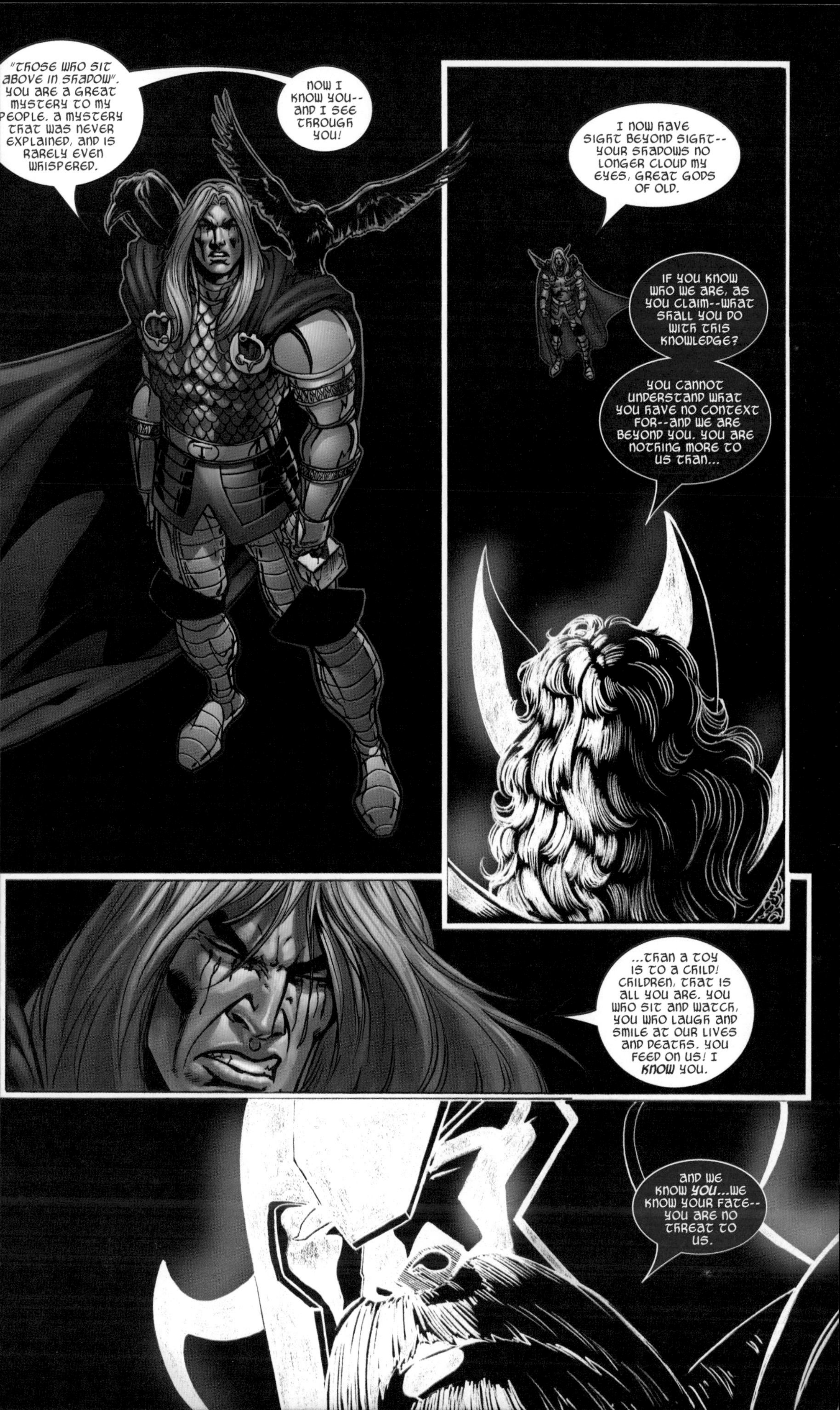
"THOSE WHO SIT ABOVE IN SHADOW". YOU ARE A GREAT MYSTERY TO MY PEOPLE. A MYSTERY THAT WAS NEVER EXPLAINED, AND IS RARELY EVEN WHISPERED.
NOW I KNOW YOU-- AND I SEE THROUGH YOU!
I NOW HAVE SIGHT BEYOND SIGHT-- YOUR SHADOWS NO LONGER CLOUD MY EYES, GREAT GODS OF OLD.
IF YOU KNOW WHO WE ARE, AS YOU CLAIM--WHAT SHALL YOU DO WITH THIS KNOWLEDGE?
YOU CANNOT UNDERSTAND WHAT YOU HAVE NO CONTEXT FOR--AND WE ARE BEYOND YOU. YOU ARE NOTHING MORE TO US THAN...
...THAN A TOY IS TO A CHILD! CHILDREN, THAT IS ALL YOU ARE. YOU WHO SIT AND WATCH, YOU WHO LAUGH AND SMILE AT OUR LIVES AND DEATHS. YOU FEED ON US! I *KNOW* YOU.
AND WE KNOW *YOU*...WE KNOW YOUR FATE-- YOU ARE NO THREAT TO US.

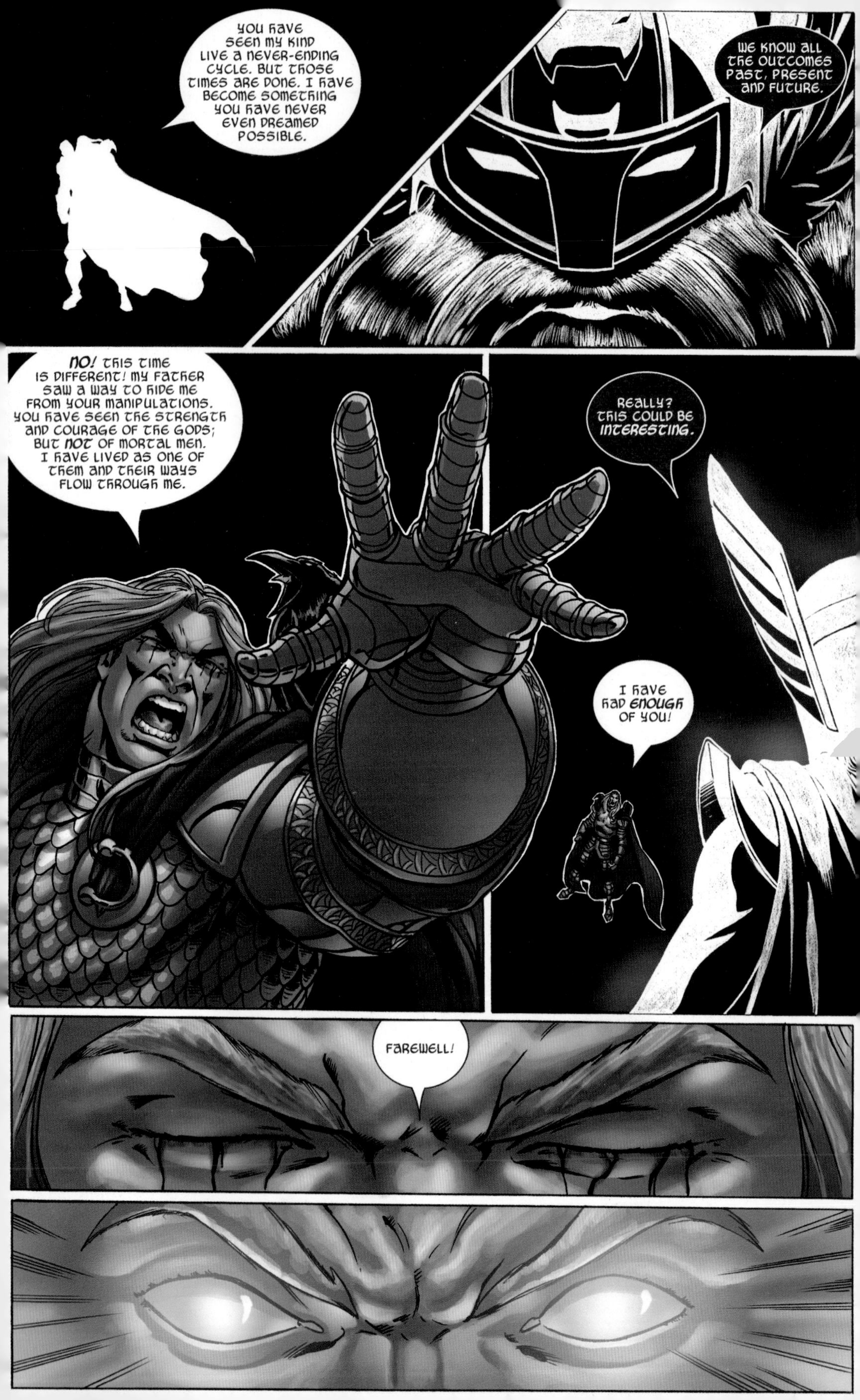
YOU HAVE SEEN MY KIND LIVE A NEVER-ENDING CYCLE. BUT THOSE TIMES ARE DONE. I HAVE BECOME SOMETHING YOU HAVE NEVER EVEN DREAMED POSSIBLE.
WE KNOW ALL THE OUTCOMES PAST, PRESENT AND FUTURE.
NO! THIS TIME IS DIFFERENT! MY FATHER SAW A WAY TO HIDE ME FROM YOUR MANIPULATIONS. YOU HAVE SEEN THE STRENGTH AND COURAGE OF THE GODS; BUT NOT OF MORTAL MEN. I HAVE LIVED AS ONE OF THEM AND THEIR WAYS FLOW THROUGH ME.
REALLY? THIS COULD BE INTERESTING.
I HAVE HAD ENOUGH OF YOU!
FAREWELL!

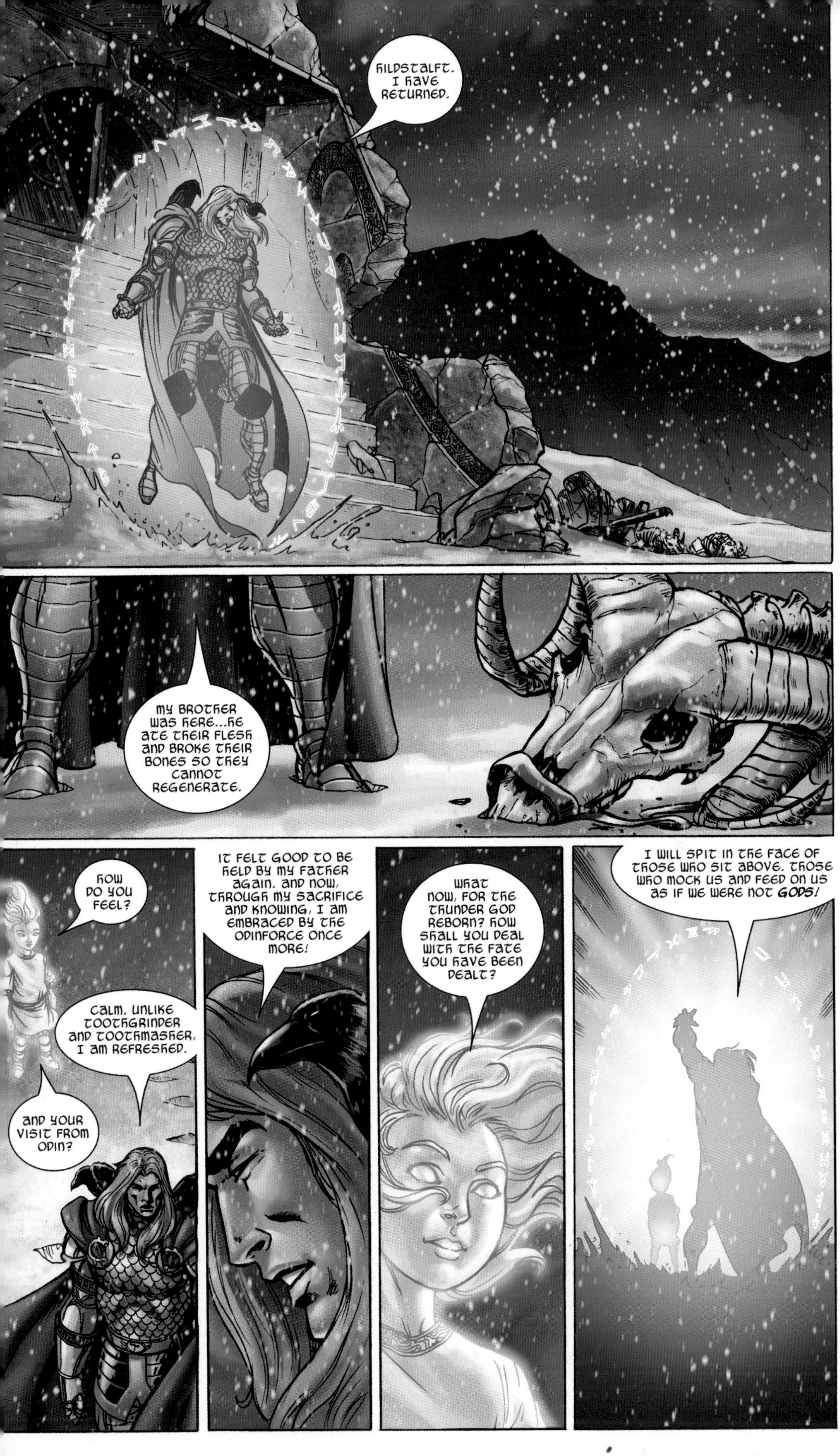
HILDSTALFT. I HAVE RETURNED.
MY BROTHER WAS HERE...HE ATE THEIR FLESH AND BROKE THEIR BONES SO THEY CANNOT REGENERATE.
HOW DO YOU FEEL?
CALM. UNLIKE TOOTHGRINDER AND TOOTHMASHER, I AM REFRESHED.
AND YOUR VISIT FROM ODIN?
IT FELT GOOD TO BE HELD BY MY FATHER AGAIN. AND NOW, THROUGH MY SACRIFICE AND KNOWING, I AM EMBRACED BY THE ODINFORCE ONCE MORE!
WHAT NOW, FOR THE THUNDER GOD REBORN? HOW SHALL YOU DEAL WITH THE FATE YOU HAVE BEEN DEALT?
I WILL SPIT IN THE FACE OF THOSE WHO SIT ABOVE. THOSE WHO MOCK US AND FEED ON US AS IF WE WERE NOT *GODS!*

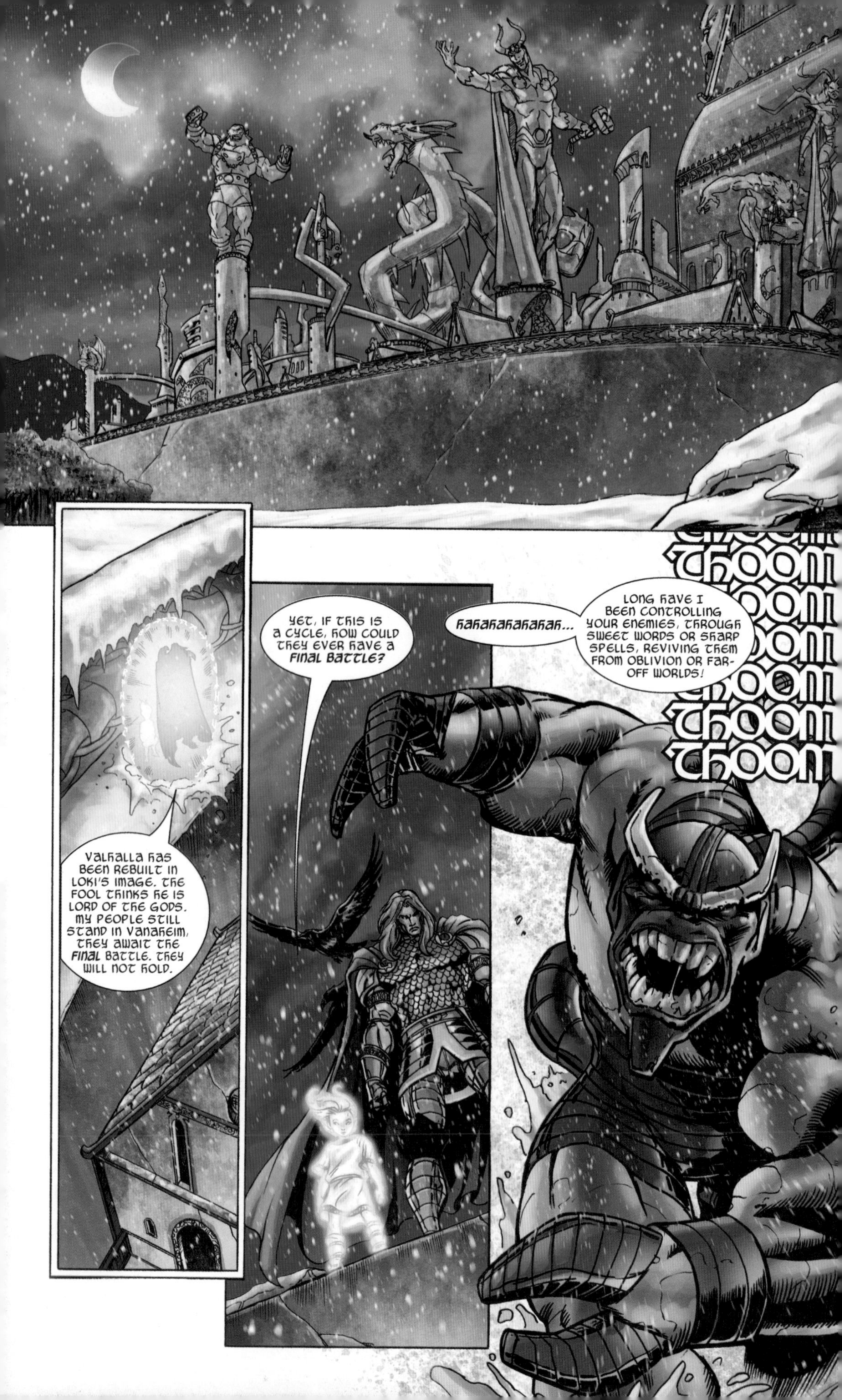
VALHALLA HAS BEEN REBUILT IN LOKI'S IMAGE. THE FOOL THINKS HE IS LORD OF THE GODS. MY PEOPLE STILL STAND IN VANAHEIM, THEY AWAIT THE FINAL BATTLE. THEY WILL NOT HOLD.
YET, IF THIS IS A CYCLE, HOW COULD THEY EVER HAVE A FINAL BATTLE?
THOOM THOOM THOOM THOOM THOOM THOOM THOOM
HAHAHAHAHAHAH...
LONG HAVE I BEEN CONTROLLING YOUR ENEMIES, THROUGH SWEET WORDS OR SHARP SPELLS, REVIVING THEM FROM OBLIVION OR FAR-OFF WORLDS!

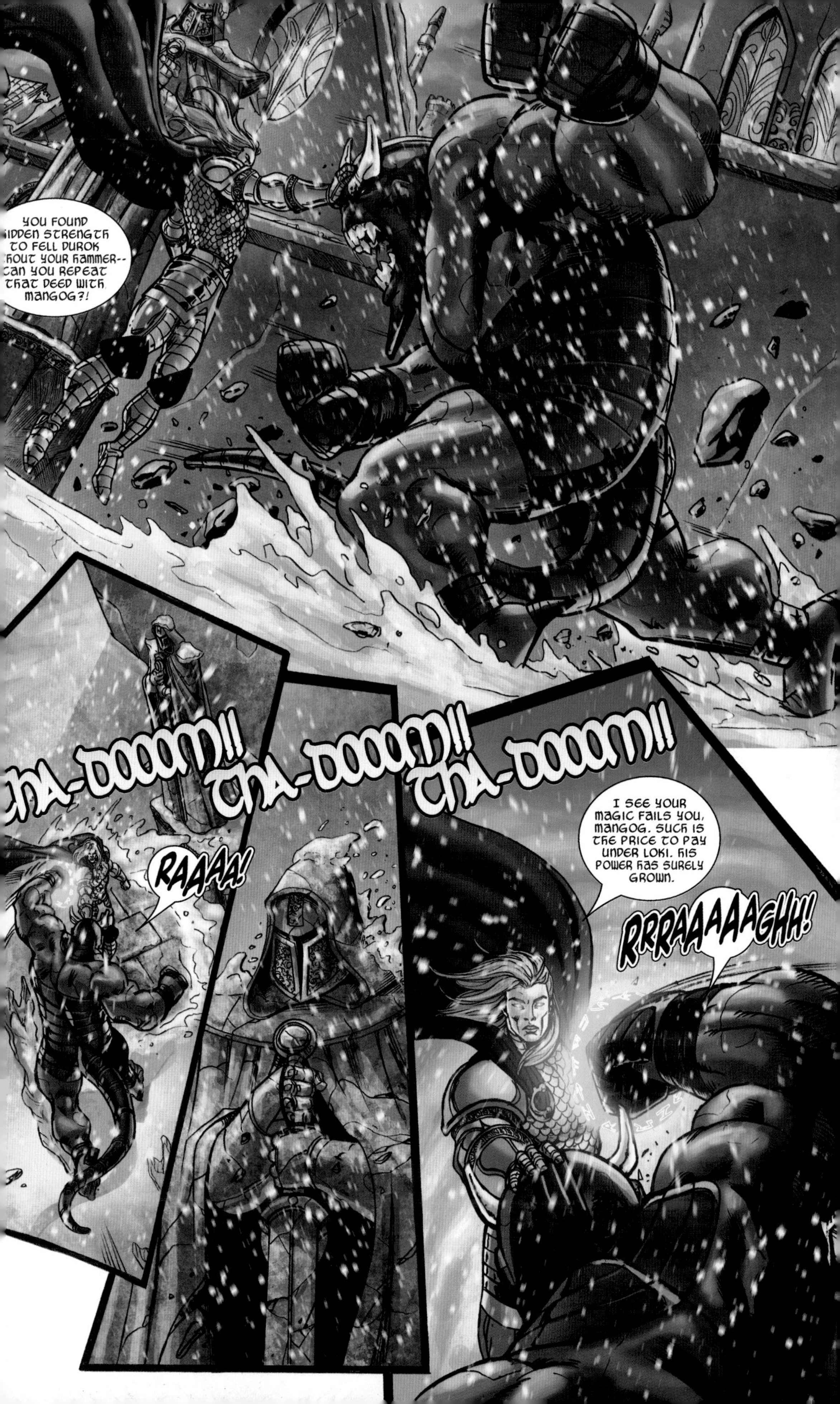

YOU FOUND
IDDEN STRENGTH
TO FELL DUROK
THOUT YOUR HAMMER--
CAN YOU REPEAT
THAT DEED WITH
MANGOG?!
HA-DOOOM!!
THA-DOOOM!!
THA-DOOOM!!
RAAAA!
I SEE YOUR MAGIC FAILS YOU, MANGOG. SUCH IS THE PRICE TO PAY UNDER LOKI. HIS POWER HAS SURELY GROWN.
RRRAAAAAGHH!

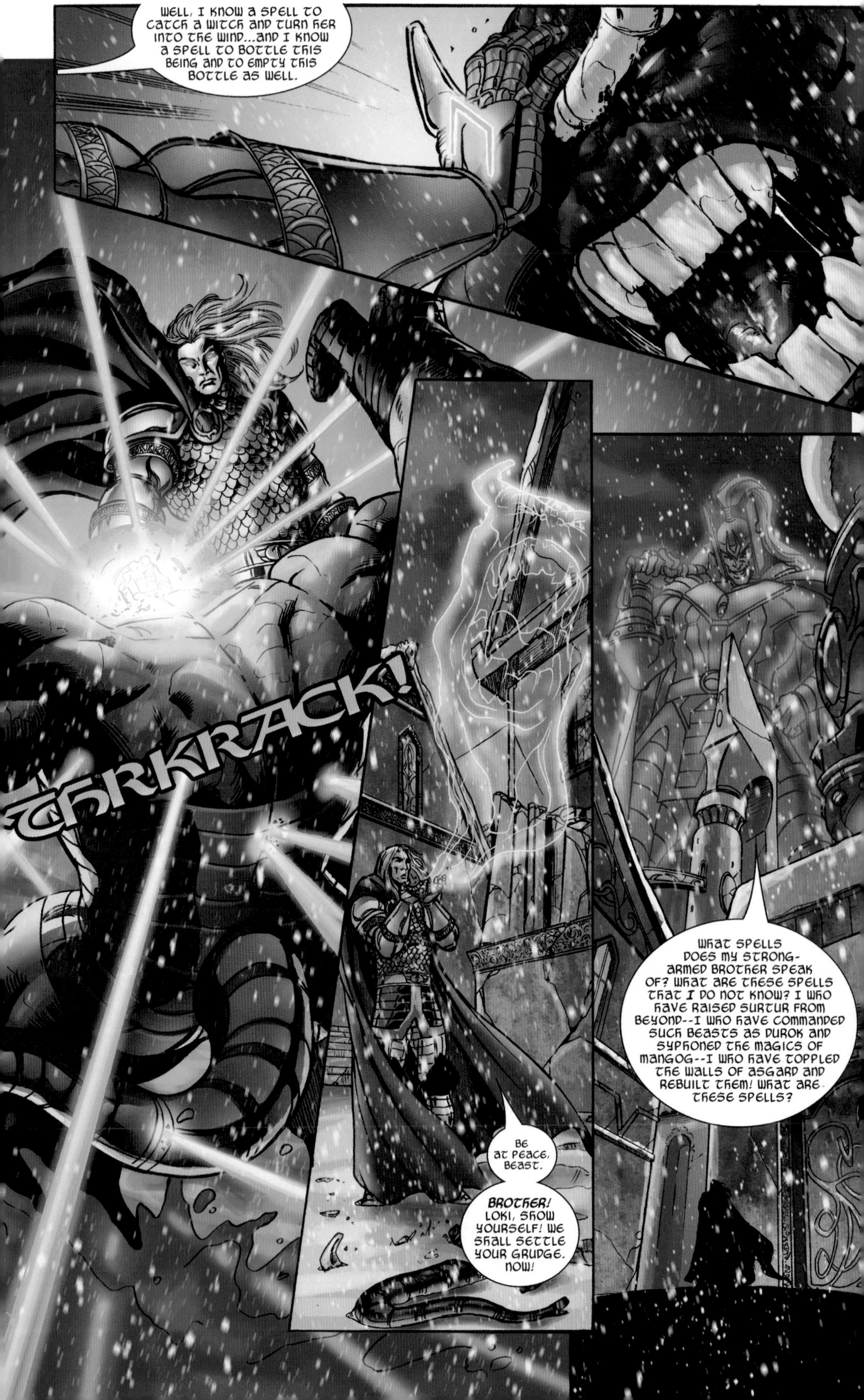
WELL, I KNOW A SPELL TO CATCH A WITCH AND TURN HER INTO THE WIND...AND I KNOW A SPELL TO BOTTLE THIS BEING AND TO EMPTY THIS BOTTLE AS WELL.
THRKRACK!
BE AT PEACE, BEAST.
BROTHER! LOKI, SHOW YOURSELF! WE SHALL SETTLE YOUR GRUDGE. NOW!
WHAT SPELLS DOES MY STRONG-ARMED BROTHER SPEAK OF? WHAT ARE THESE SPELLS THAT I DO NOT KNOW? I WHO HAVE RAISED SURTUR FROM BEYOND--I WHO HAVE COMMANDED SUCH BEASTS AS DUROK AND SYPHONED THE MAGICS OF MANGOG--I WHO HAVE TOPPLED THE WALLS OF ASGARD AND REBUILT THEM! WHAT ARE THESE SPELLS?

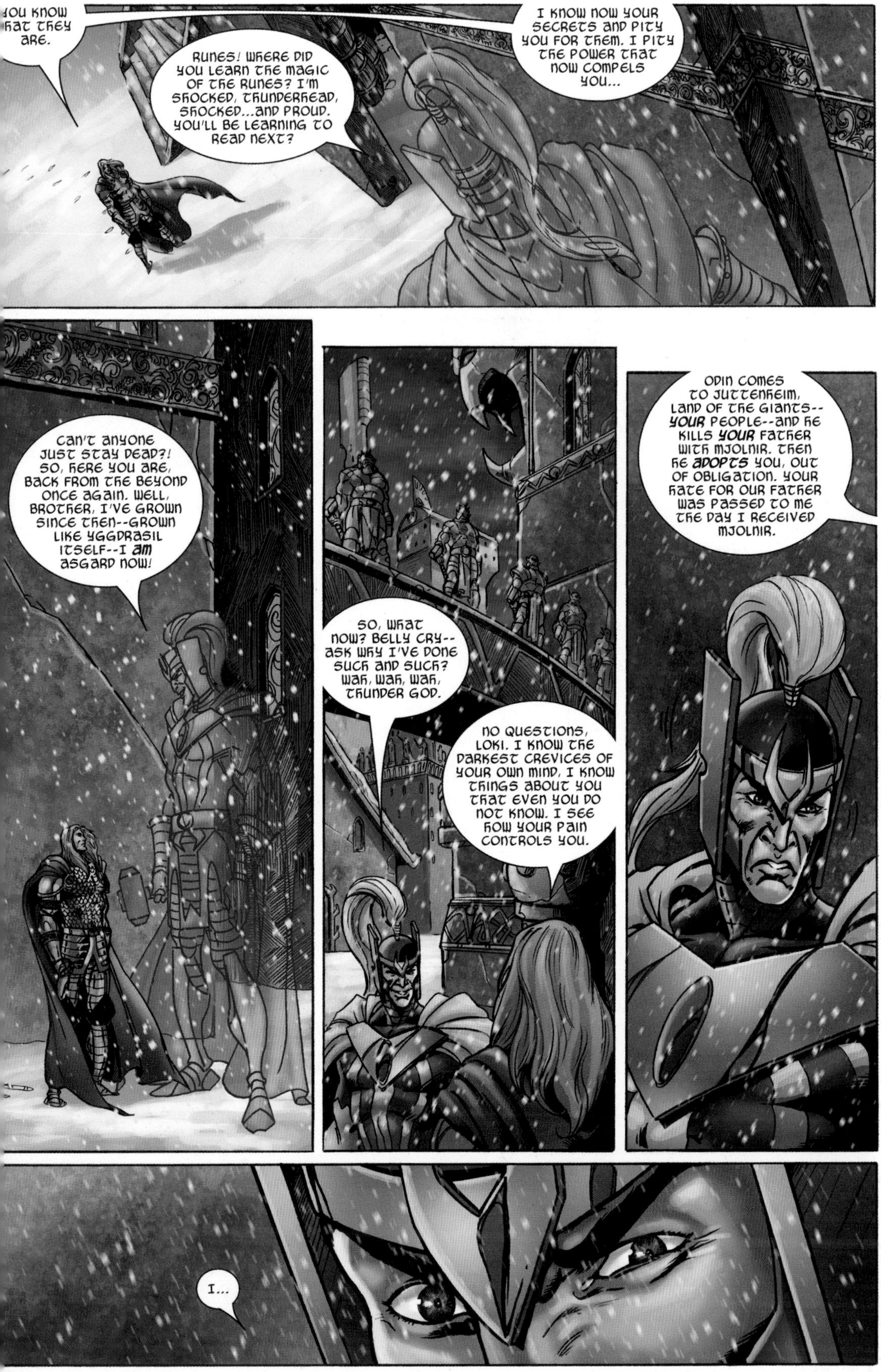
YOU KNOW
HAT THEY ARE.
RUNES! WHERE DID YOU LEARN THE MAGIC OF THE RUNES? I'M SHOCKED, THUNDERHEAD, SHOCKED...AND PROUD. YOU'LL BE LEARNING TO READ NEXT?
I KNOW NOW YOUR SECRETS AND PITY YOU FOR THEM. I PITY THE POWER THAT NOW COMPELS YOU...
CAN'T ANYONE JUST STAY DEAD?! SO, HERE YOU ARE, BACK FROM THE BEYOND ONCE AGAIN. WELL, BROTHER, I'VE GROWN SINCE THEN--GROWN LIKE YGGDRASIL ITSELF--I AM ASGARD NOW!
SO, WHAT NOW? BELLY CRY--ASK WHY I'VE DONE SUCH AND SUCH? WAH, WAH, WAH, THUNDER GOD.
NO QUESTIONS, LOKI. I KNOW THE DARKEST CREVICES OF YOUR OWN MIND, I KNOW THINGS ABOUT YOU THAT EVEN YOU DO NOT KNOW. I SEE HOW YOUR PAIN CONTROLS YOU.
ODIN COMES TO JUTTENHEIM, LAND OF THE GIANTS--YOUR PEOPLE--AND HE KILLS YOUR FATHER WITH MJOLNIR. THEN HE ADOPTS YOU, OUT OF OBLIGATION. YOUR HATE FOR OUR FATHER WAS PASSED TO ME THE DAY I RECEIVED MJOLNIR.
I...

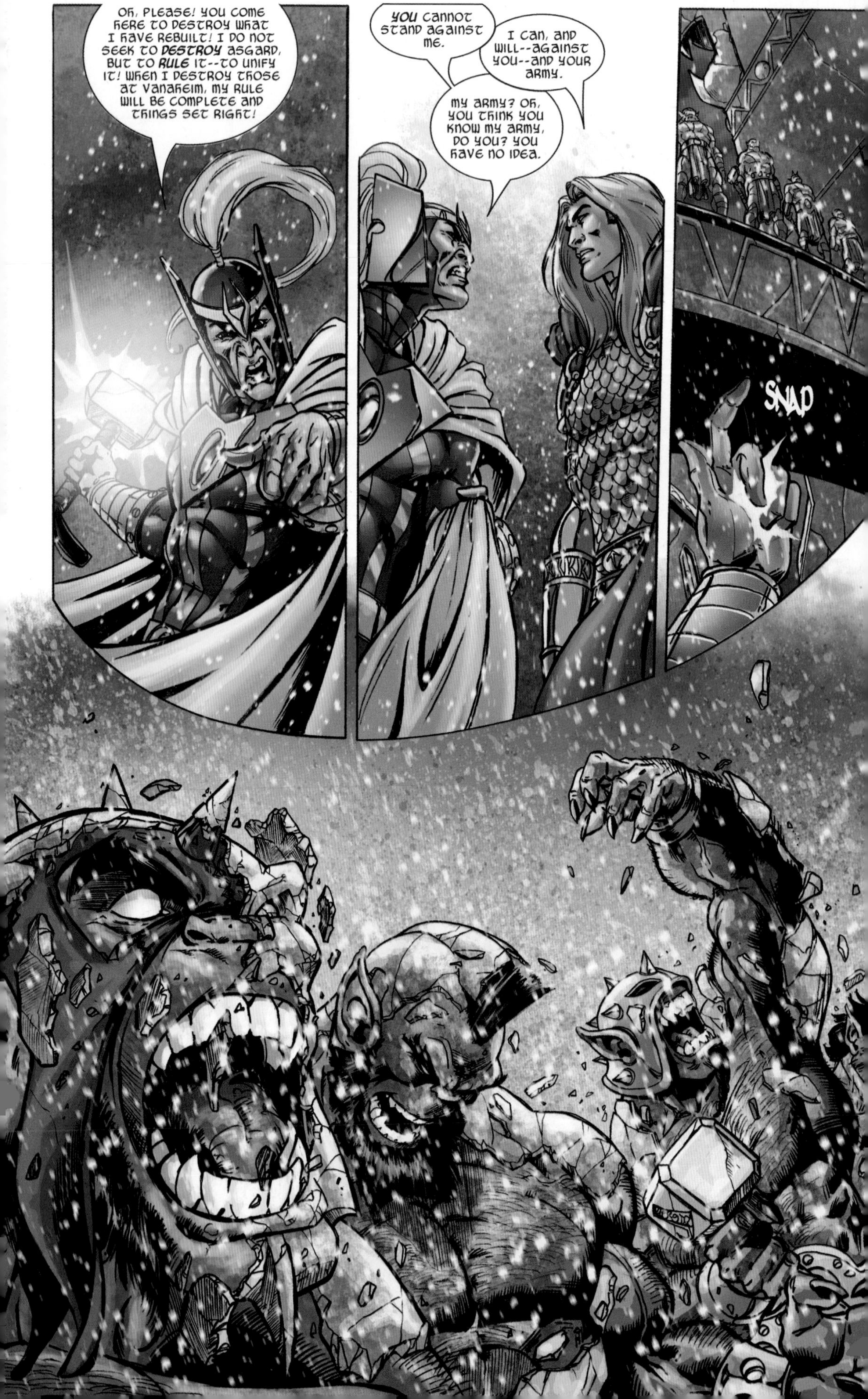
OH, PLEASE! YOU COME HERE TO DESTROY WHAT I HAVE REBUILT! I DO NOT SEEK TO DESTROY ASGARD, BUT TO RULE IT--TO UNIFY IT! WHEN I DESTROY THOSE AT VANAHEIM, MY RULE WILL BE COMPLETE AND THINGS SET RIGHT!
YOU CANNOT STAND AGAINST ME.
I CAN, AND WILL--AGAINST YOU--AND YOUR ARMY.
MY ARMY? OH, YOU THINK YOU KNOW MY ARMY, DO YOU? YOU HAVE NO IDEA.
SNAP

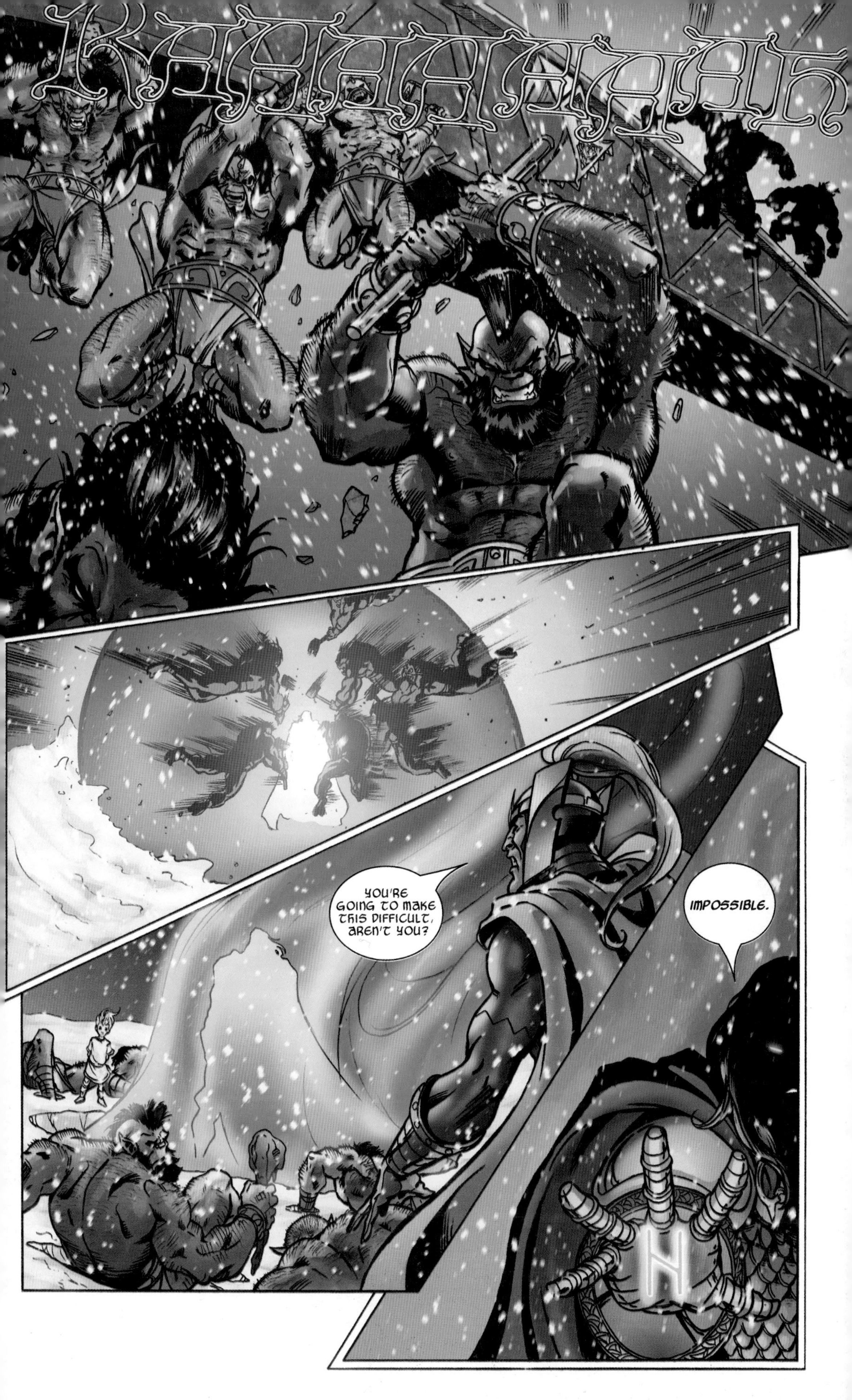
YOU'RE GOING TO MAKE THIS DIFFICULT, AREN'T YOU?
IMPOSSIBLE.

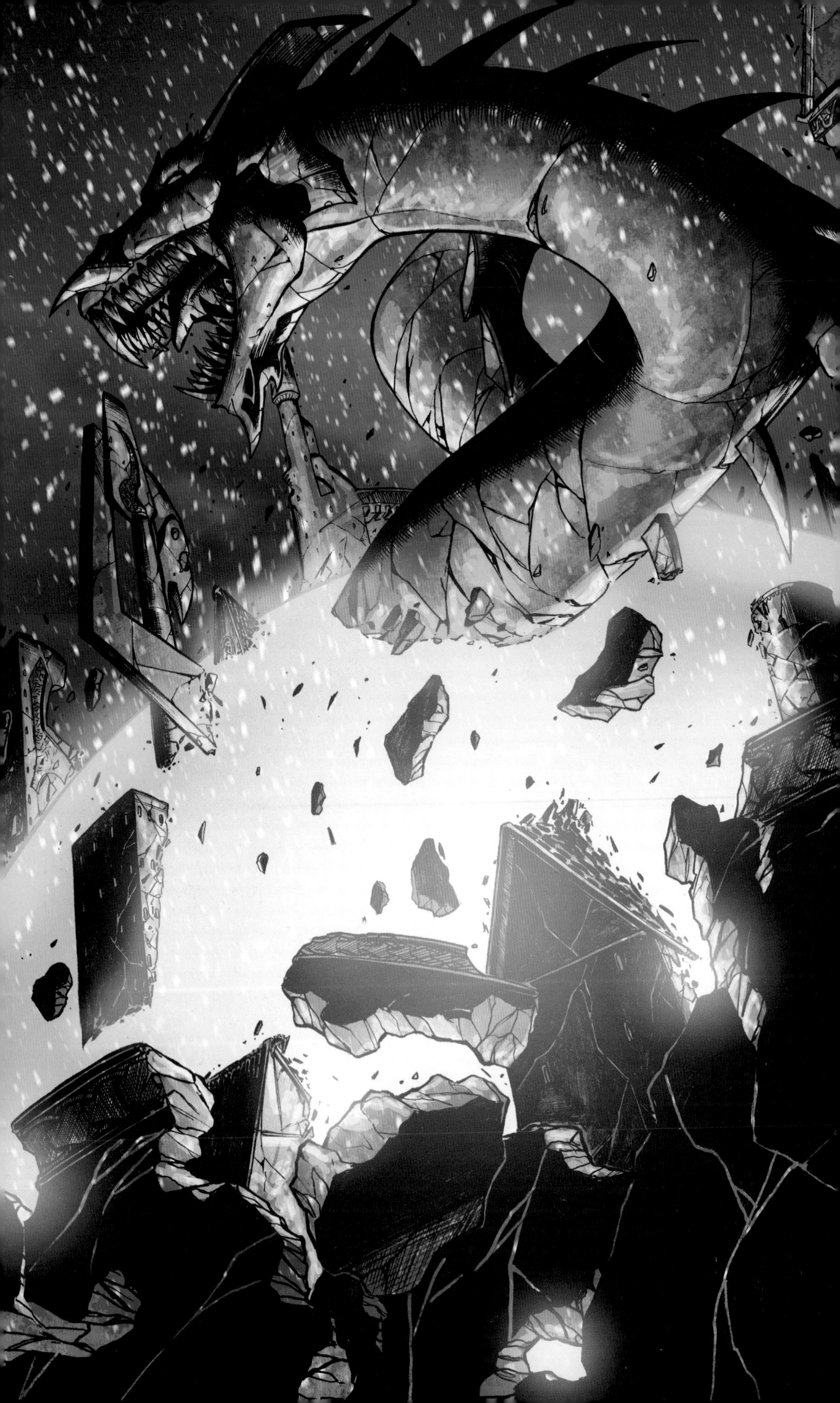

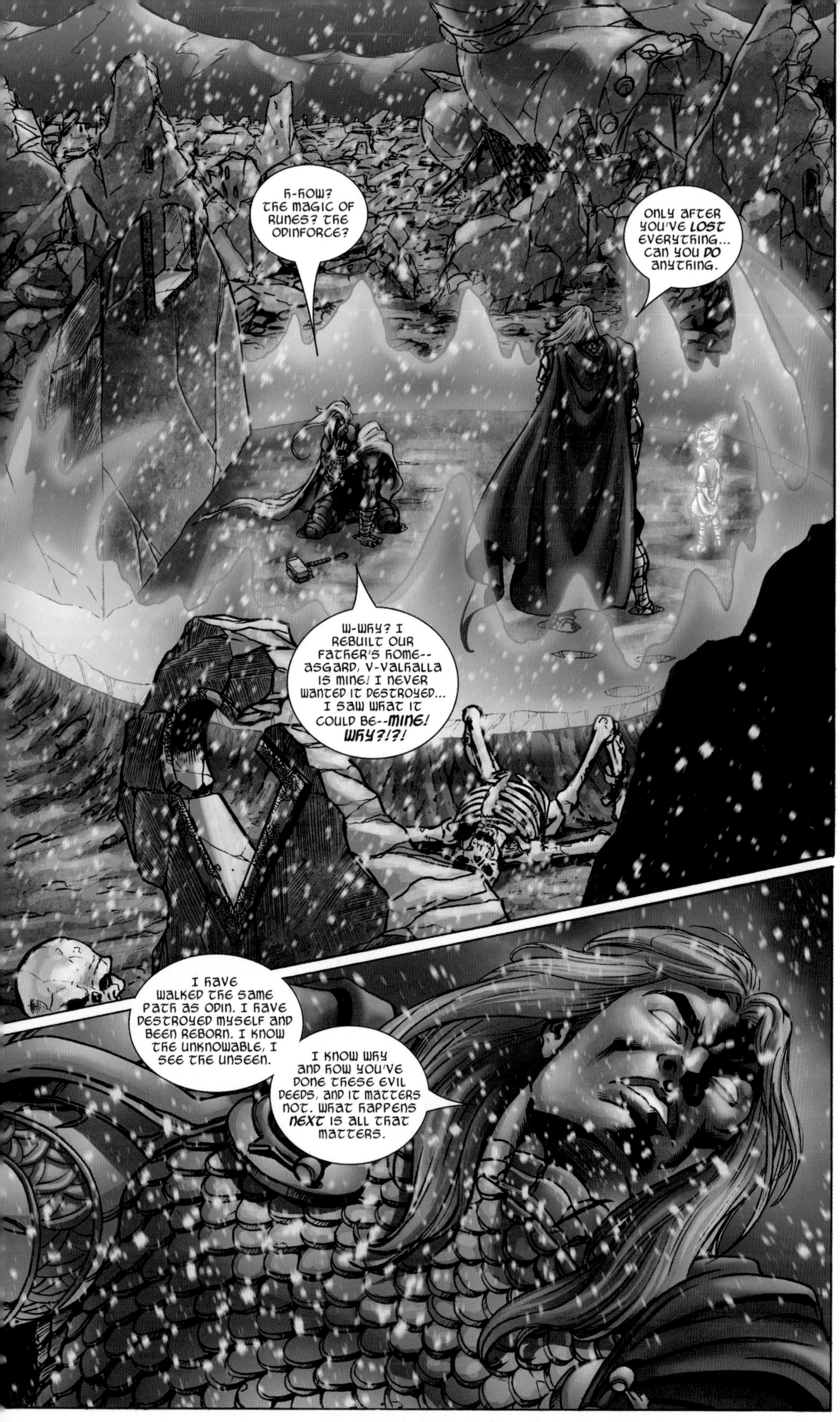
H-HOW? THE MAGIC OF RUNES? THE ODINFORCE?
ONLY AFTER YOU'VE LOST EVERYTHING... CAN YOU DO ANYTHING.
W-WHY? I REBUILT OUR FATHER'S HOME--ASGARD, V-VALHALLA IS MINE! I NEVER WANTED IT DESTROYED... I SAW WHAT IT COULD BE--MINE! WHY?!?!
I HAVE WALKED THE SAME PATH AS ODIN. I HAVE DESTROYED MYSELF AND BEEN REBORN. I KNOW THE UNKNOWABLE, I SEE THE UNSEEN.
I KNOW WHY AND HOW YOU'VE DONE THESE EVIL DEEDS, AND IT MATTERS NOT. WHAT HAPPENS NEXT IS ALL THAT MATTERS.

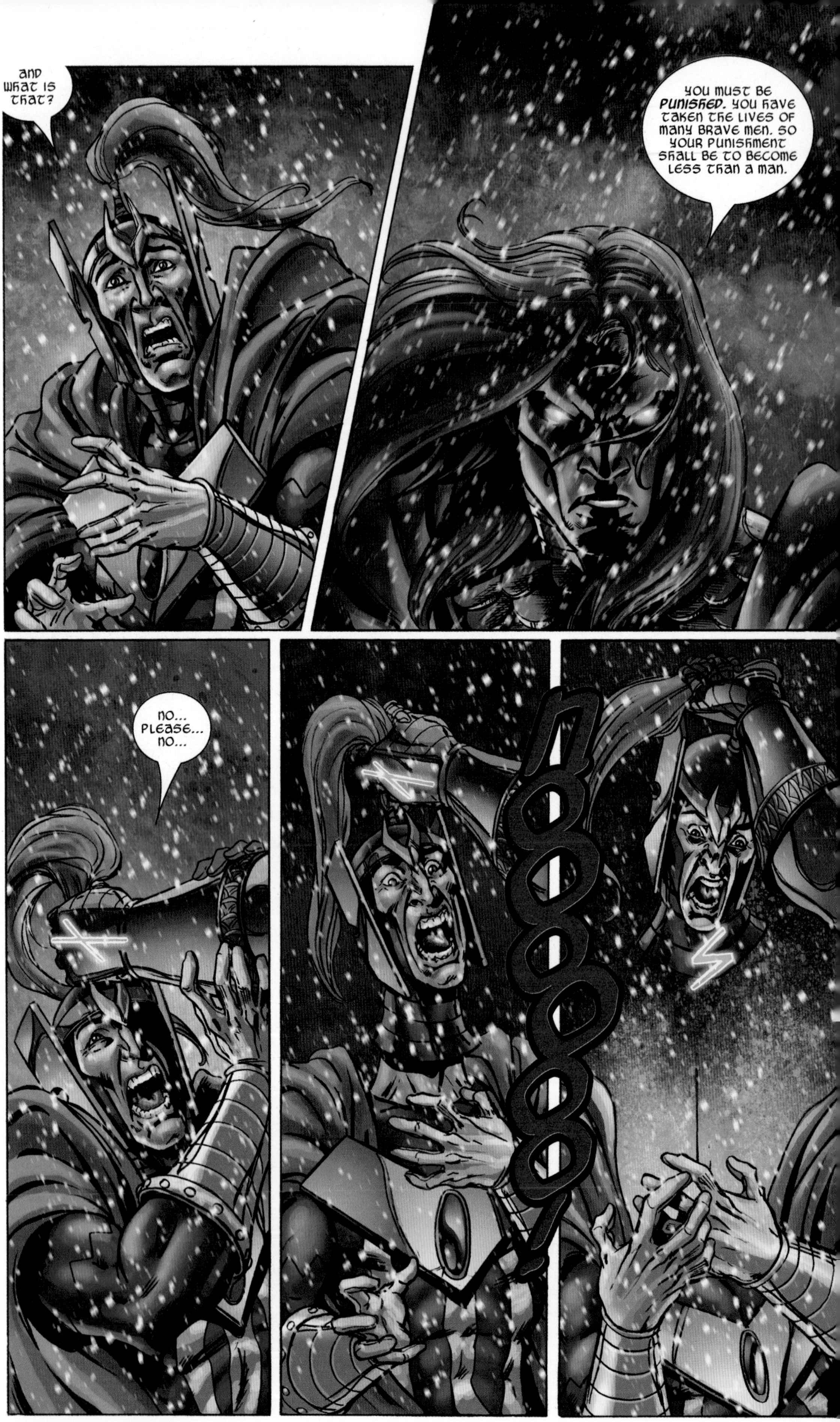
AND WHAT IS THAT?
YOU MUST BE PUNISHED. YOU HAVE TAKEN THE LIVES OF MANY BRAVE MEN. SO YOUR PUNISHMENT SHALL BE TO BECOME LESS THAN A MAN.
NO... PLEASE... NO...

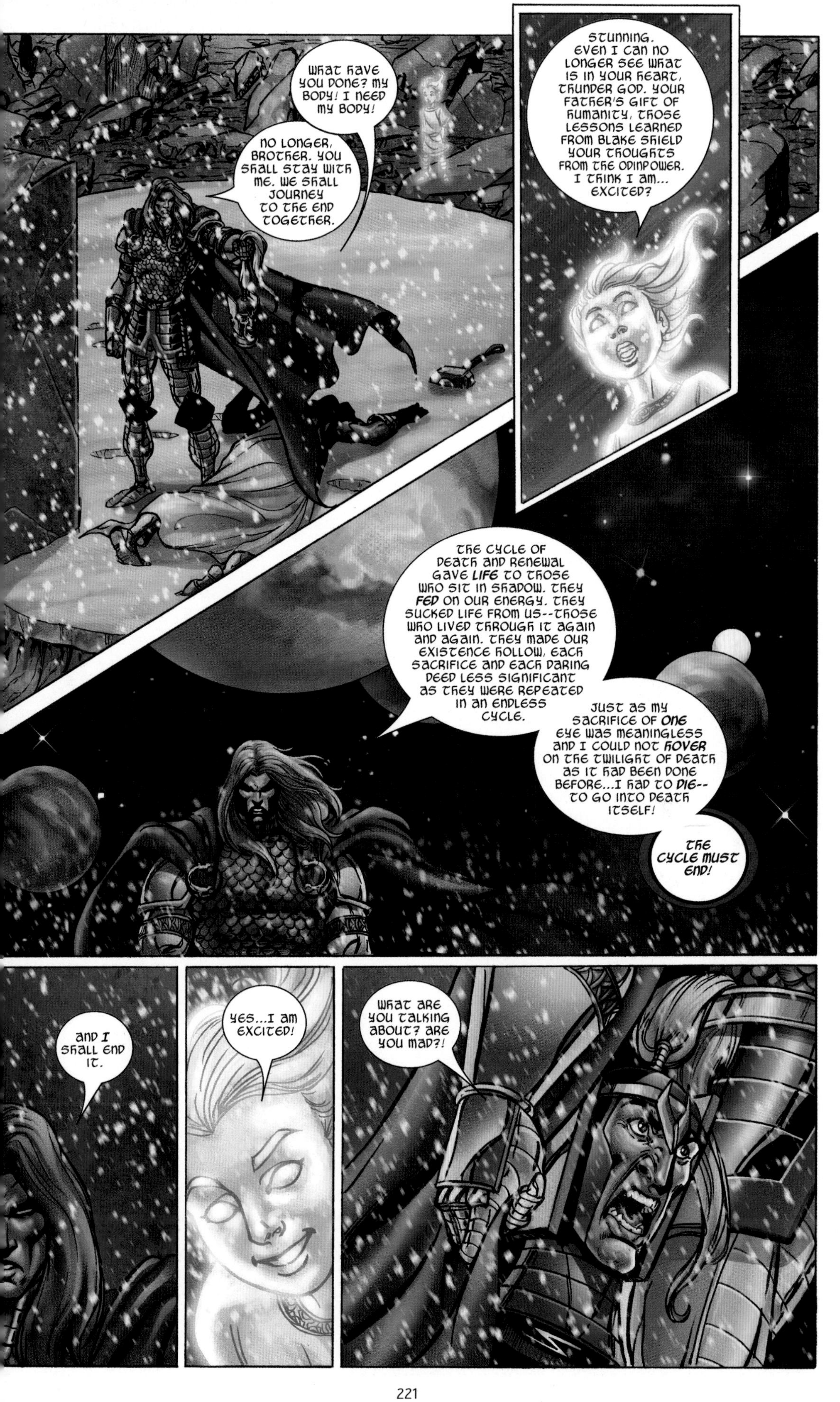
WHAT HAVE YOU DONE? MY BODY! I NEED MY BODY!
NO LONGER, BROTHER. YOU SHALL STAY WITH ME. WE SHALL JOURNEY TO THE END TOGETHER.
STUNNING. EVEN I CAN NO LONGER SEE WHAT IS IN YOUR HEART, THUNDER GOD. YOUR FATHER'S GIFT OF HUMANITY, THOSE LESSONS LEARNED FROM BLAKE SHIELD YOUR THOUGHTS FROM THE ODINPOWER. I THINK I AM... EXCITED?
THE CYCLE OF DEATH AND RENEWAL GAVE LIFE TO THOSE WHO SIT IN SHADOW. THEY FED ON OUR ENERGY. THEY SUCKED LIFE FROM US--THOSE WHO LIVED THROUGH IT AGAIN AND AGAIN. THEY MADE OUR EXISTENCE HOLLOW, EACH SACRIFICE AND EACH DARING DEED LESS SIGNIFICANT AS THEY WERE REPEATED IN AN ENDLESS CYCLE.
JUST AS MY SACRIFICE OF ONE EYE WAS MEANINGLESS AND I COULD NOT HOVER ON THE TWILIGHT OF DEATH AS IT HAD BEEN DONE BEFORE...I HAD TO DIE--TO GO INTO DEATH ITSELF!
THE CYCLE MUST END!
AND I SHALL END IT.
YES...I AM EXCITED!
WHAT ARE YOU TALKING ABOUT? ARE YOU MAD?!

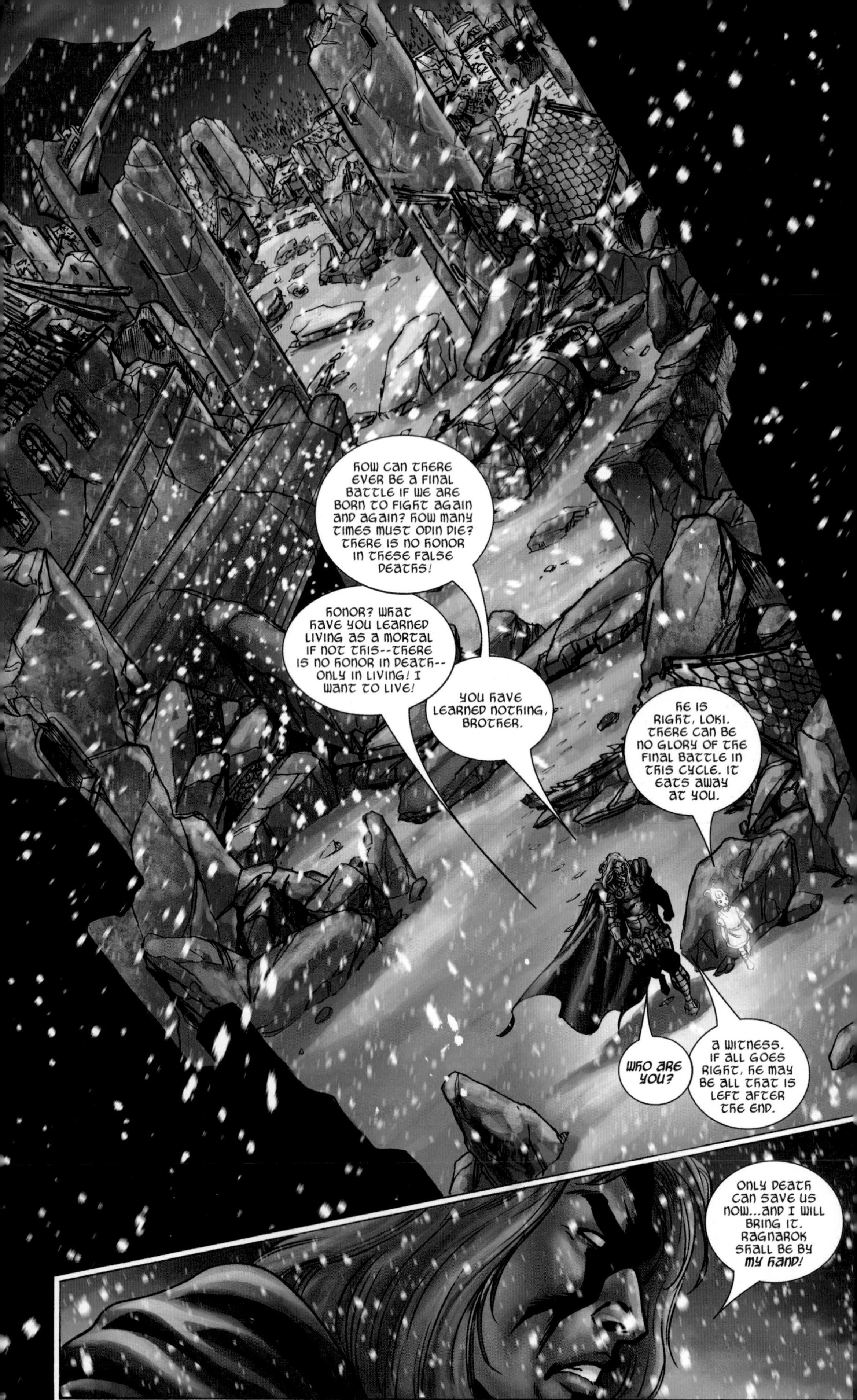

HOW CAN THERE EVER BE A FINAL BATTLE IF WE ARE BORN TO FIGHT AGAIN AND AGAIN? HOW MANY TIMES MUST ODIN DIE? THERE IS NO HONOR IN THESE FALSE DEATHS!
HONOR? WHAT HAVE YOU LEARNED LIVING AS A MORTAL IF NOT THIS--THERE IS NO HONOR IN DEATH--ONLY IN LIVING! I WANT TO LIVE!
YOU HAVE LEARNED NOTHING, BROTHER.
HE IS RIGHT, LOKI. THERE CAN BE NO GLORY OF THE FINAL BATTLE IN THIS CYCLE. IT EATS AWAY AT YOU.
WHO ARE YOU?
A WITNESS. IF ALL GOES RIGHT, HE MAY BE ALL THAT IS LEFT AFTER THE END.
ONLY DEATH CAN SAVE US NOW...AND I WILL BRING IT. RAGNAROK SHALL BE BY MY HAND!

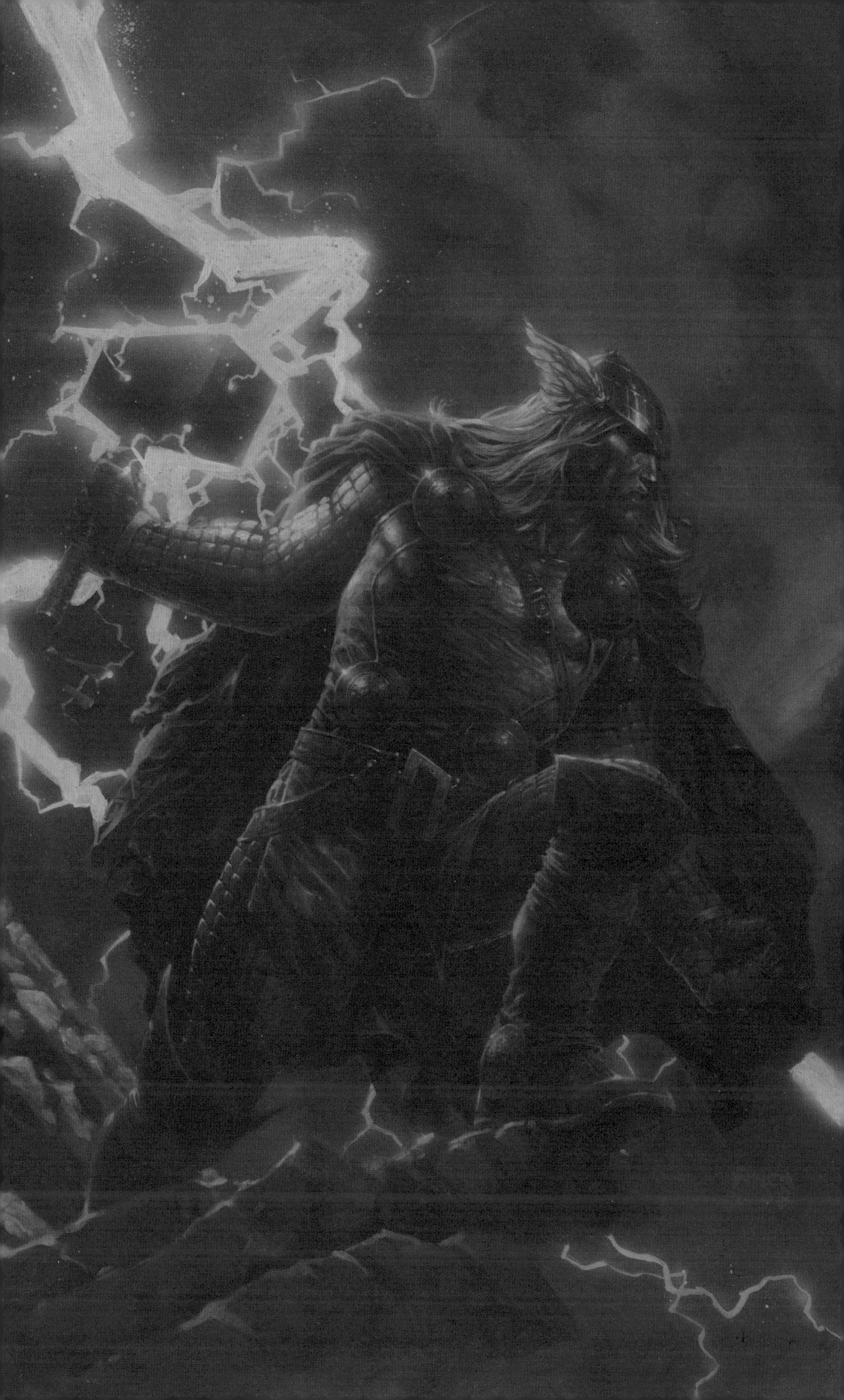

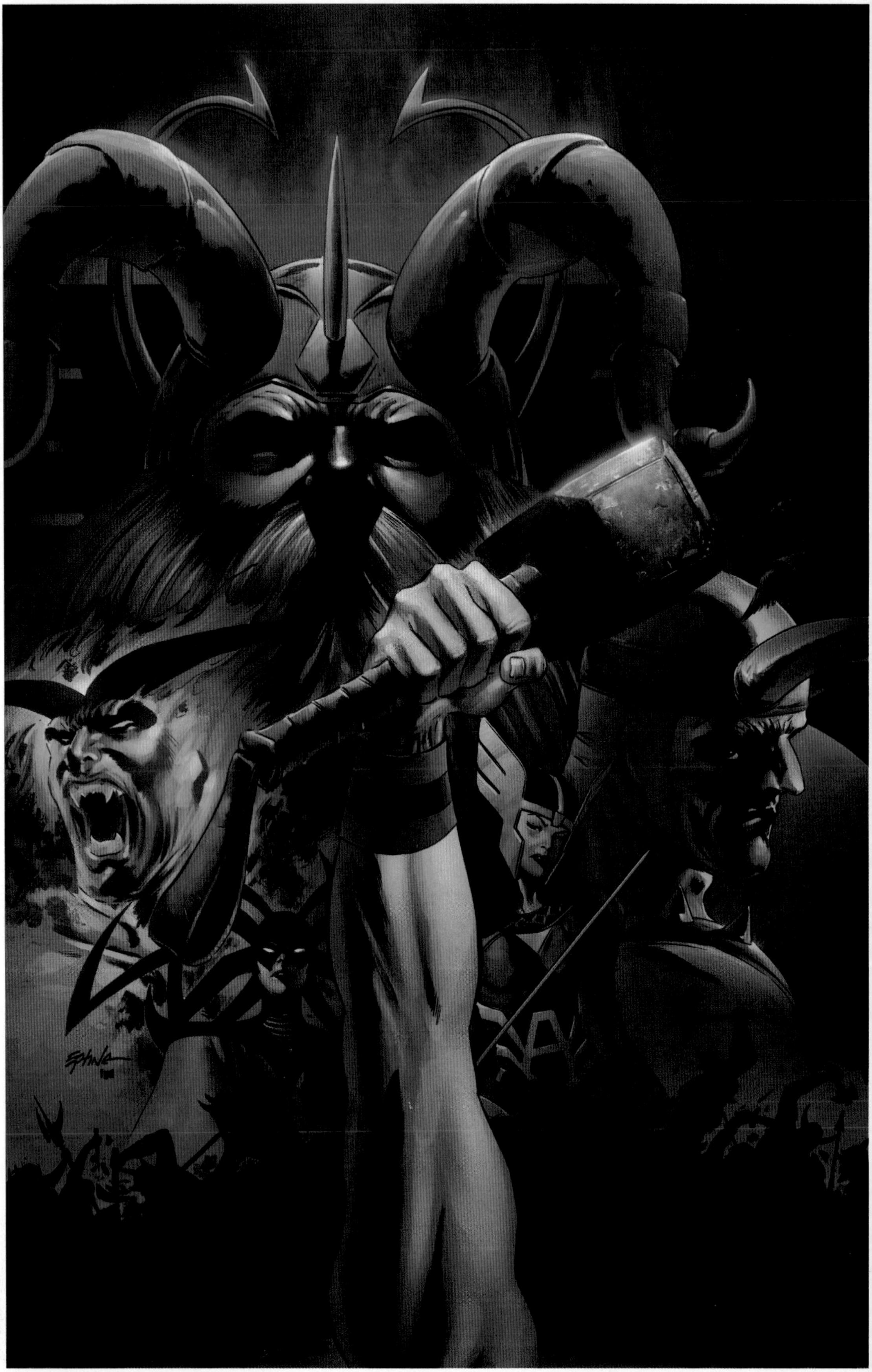

RAGNAROK
IS ONCE AGAIN UNLEASHED UPON
THE GODS. AS KING OF ASGARD, THOR MUST
LEAD HIS PEOPLE. HE FINDS NEITHER STRENGTH NOR
WEAPON TO BE OF ANY USE AT THE END OF ALL THINGS...
HE MUST SEEK THE KNOWLEDGE OF ODIN, HIS FATHER.

GUIDED BY THE ODINPOWER INCARNATED AS AN ORPHANED BOY,
THOR MUST WALK THE PATH TO WISDOM AND MUST SACRIFICE
MORE OF HIMSELF THAN EVEN HIS FATHER DID.

THOR LEARNS THAT RAGNAROK IS A COSMIC CYCLE WHICH GENERATES LIFE
ENERGY FOR THE OLD GODS, **THOSE WHO SIT ABOVE IN SHADOW**. EACH CYCLE
REDUCES THE WORTH OF THOSE WHO LIVE THROUGH THEM. FOR THE
ASGARDIANS, WHO LIVE EACH DAY IN ANTICIPATION OF A FINAL GLORIOUS
BATTLE THAT WILL END ALL THINGS, IT IS AN EVEN CRUELER FATE.

ODIN SAW A WAY TO BREAK THE CYCLE. HE PLANTED THE
SEEDS IN THOR, WHO DRAWS HIS STRENGTH FROM BOTH
GOD AND MAN--WHOSE WAYS **THOSE WHO SIT
ABOVE IN SHADOW** COULD NOT PREDICT
WOULD BE THEIR UNDOING.

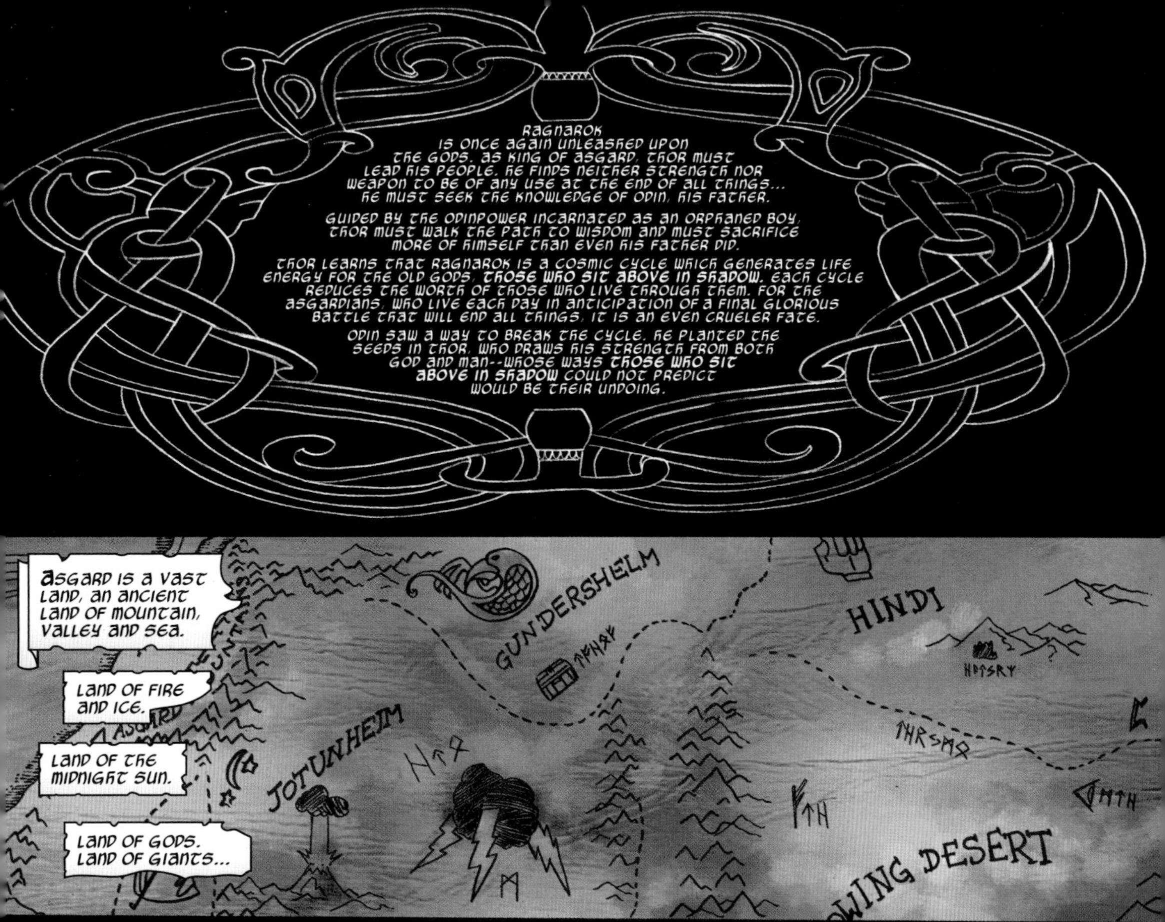

ASGARD IS A VAST LAND, AN ANCIENT LAND OF MOUNTAIN, VALLEY AND SEA.
LAND OF FIRE AND ICE.
LAND OF THE MIDNIGHT SUN.
LAND OF GODS. LAND OF GIANTS...
GUNDERSHELM
HINDI
JOTUNHEIM
WING DESERT

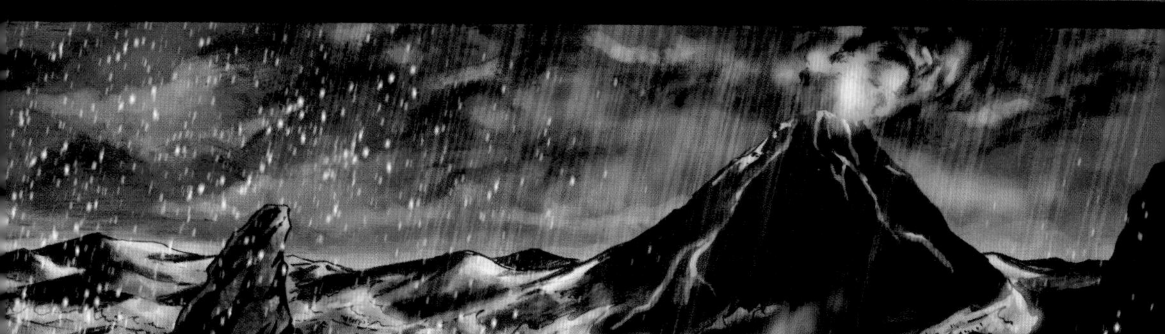

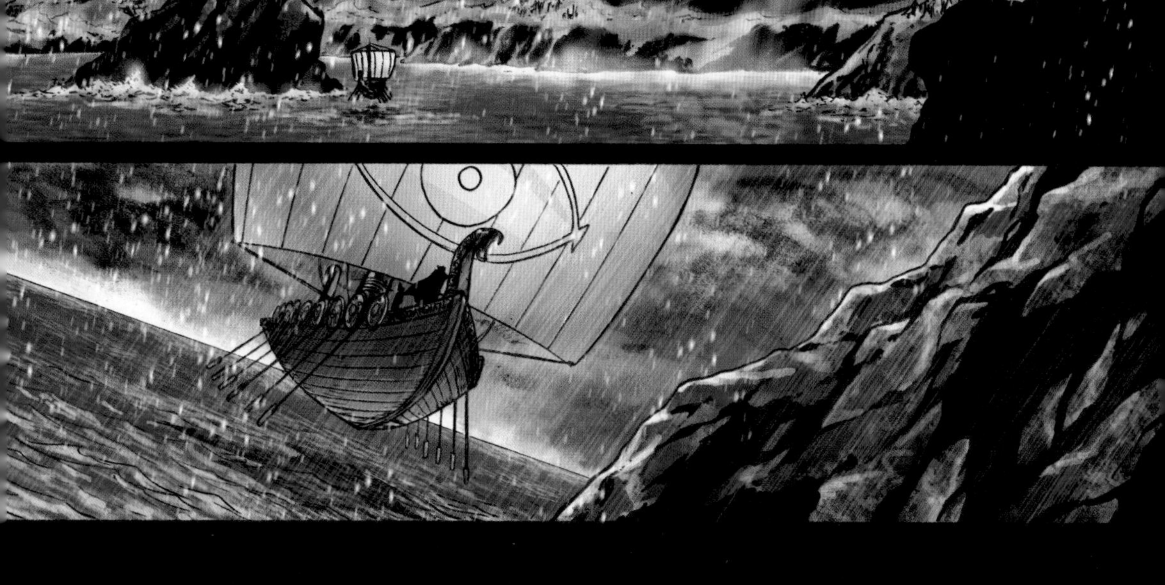

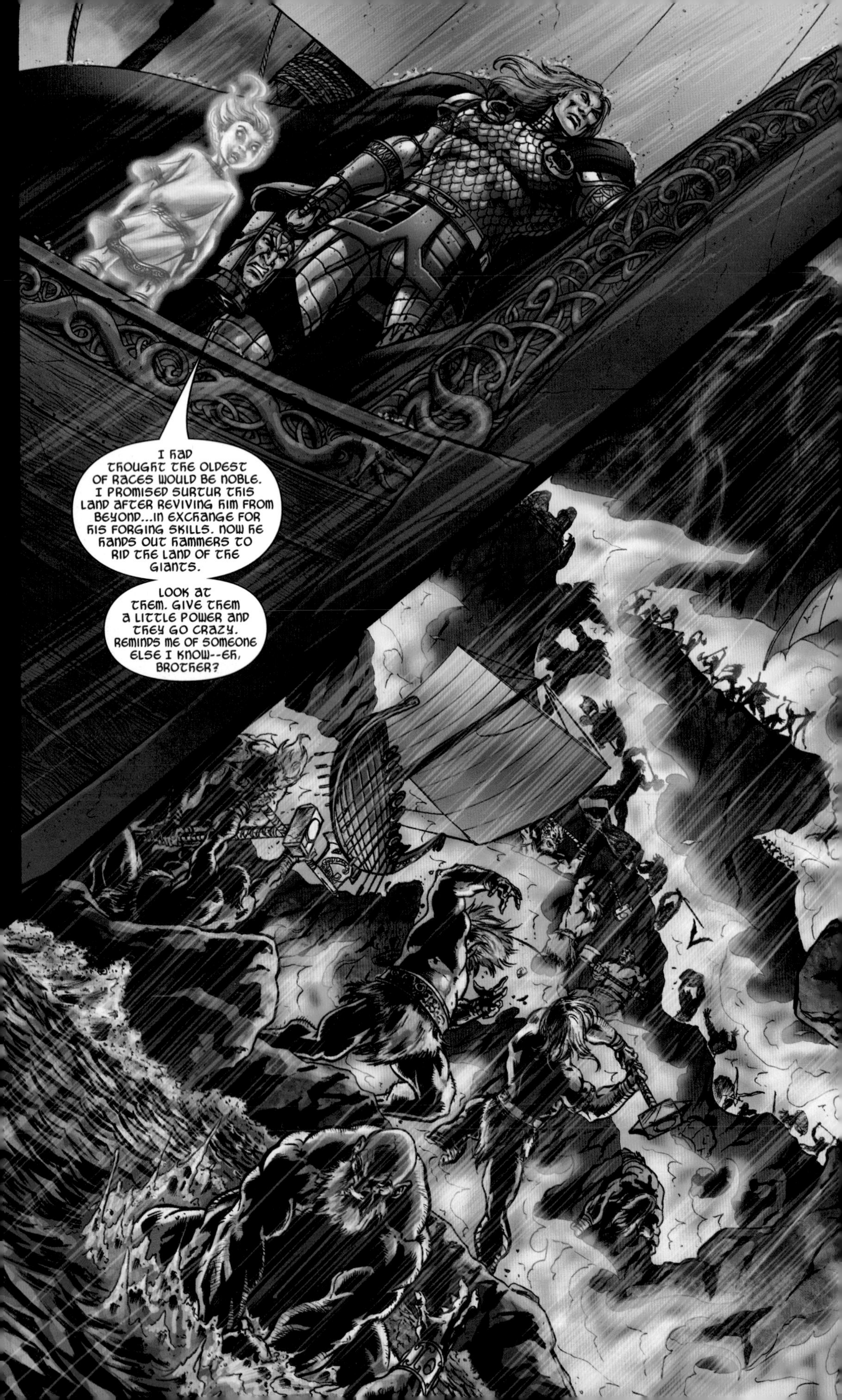
I HAD THOUGHT THE OLDEST OF RACES WOULD BE NOBLE. I PROMISED SURTUR THIS LAND AFTER REVIVING HIM FROM BEYOND...IN EXCHANGE FOR HIS FORGING SKILLS. NOW HE HANDS OUT HAMMERS TO RID THE LAND OF THE GIANTS.
LOOK AT THEM. GIVE THEM A LITTLE POWER AND THEY GO CRAZY. REMINDS ME OF SOMEONE ELSE I KNOW--EH, BROTHER?

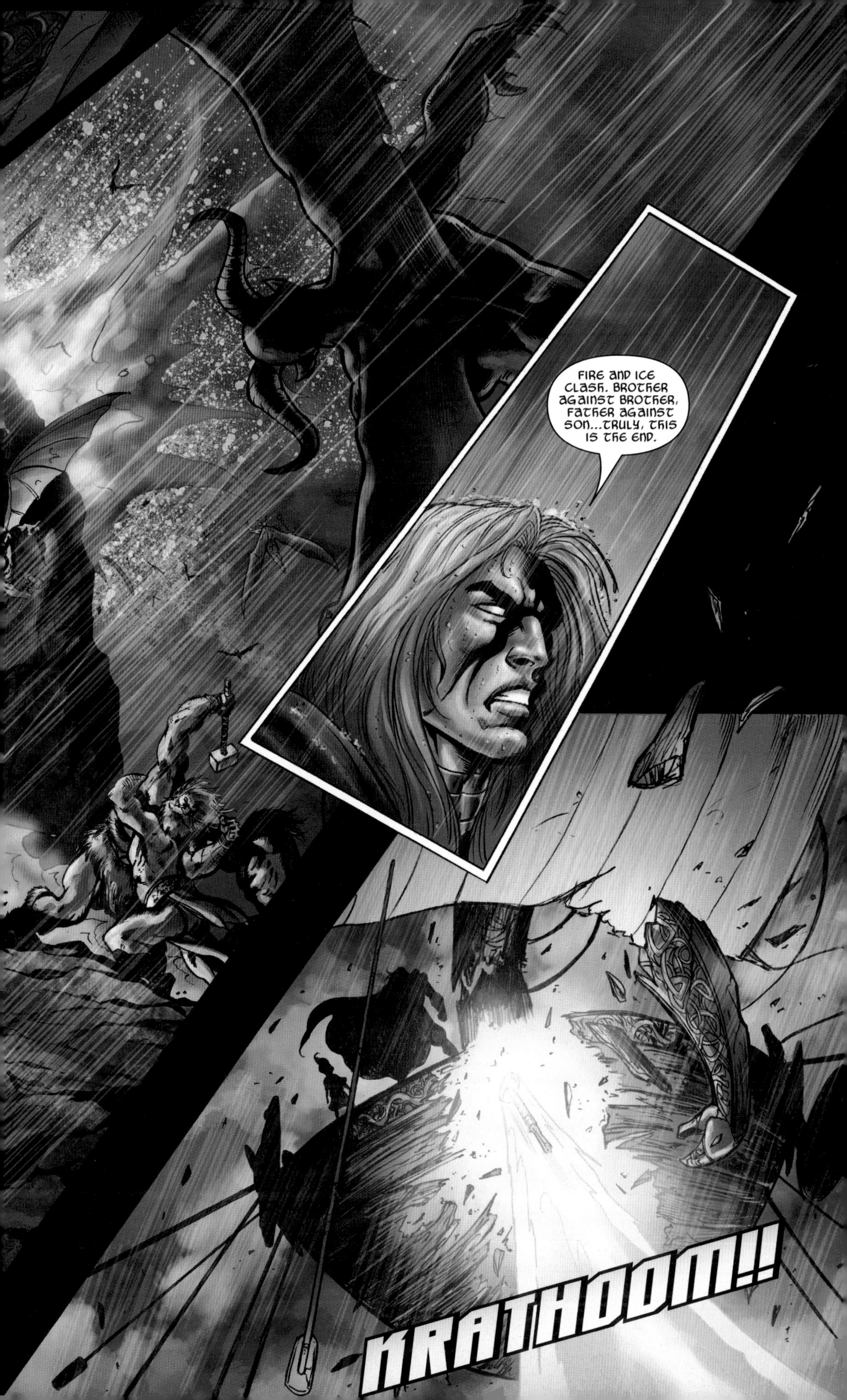
FIRE AND ICE CLASH. BROTHER AGAINST BROTHER, FATHER AGAINST SON...TRULY, THIS IS THE END.
KRATHOOM!!

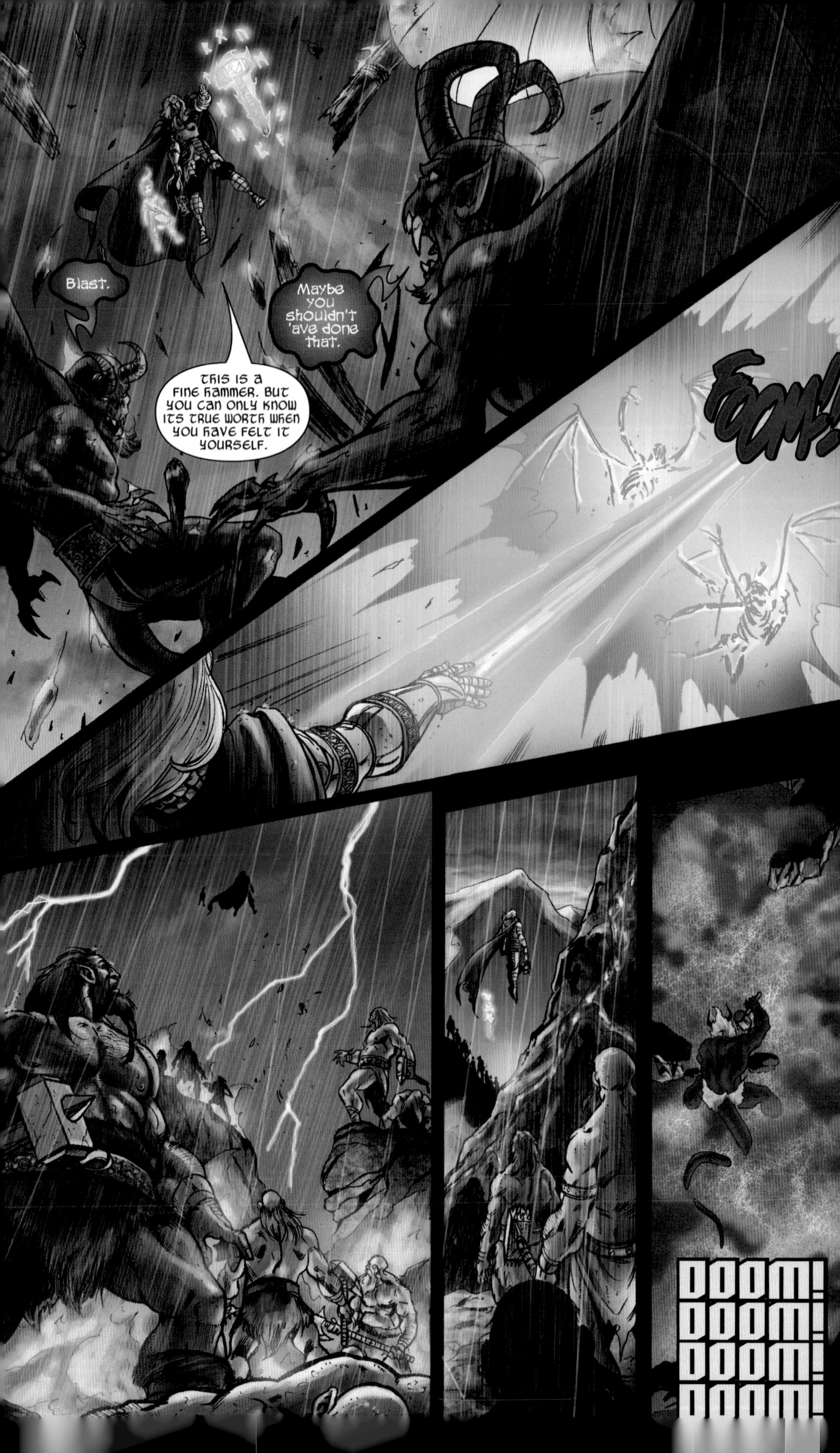
Blast.
Maybe you shouldn't 'ave done that.
THIS IS A FINE HAMMER. BUT YOU CAN ONLY KNOW ITS TRUE WORTH WHEN YOU HAVE FELT IT YOURSELF.
FOOM!!
DOOM!
DOOM!
DOOM!
DOOM!

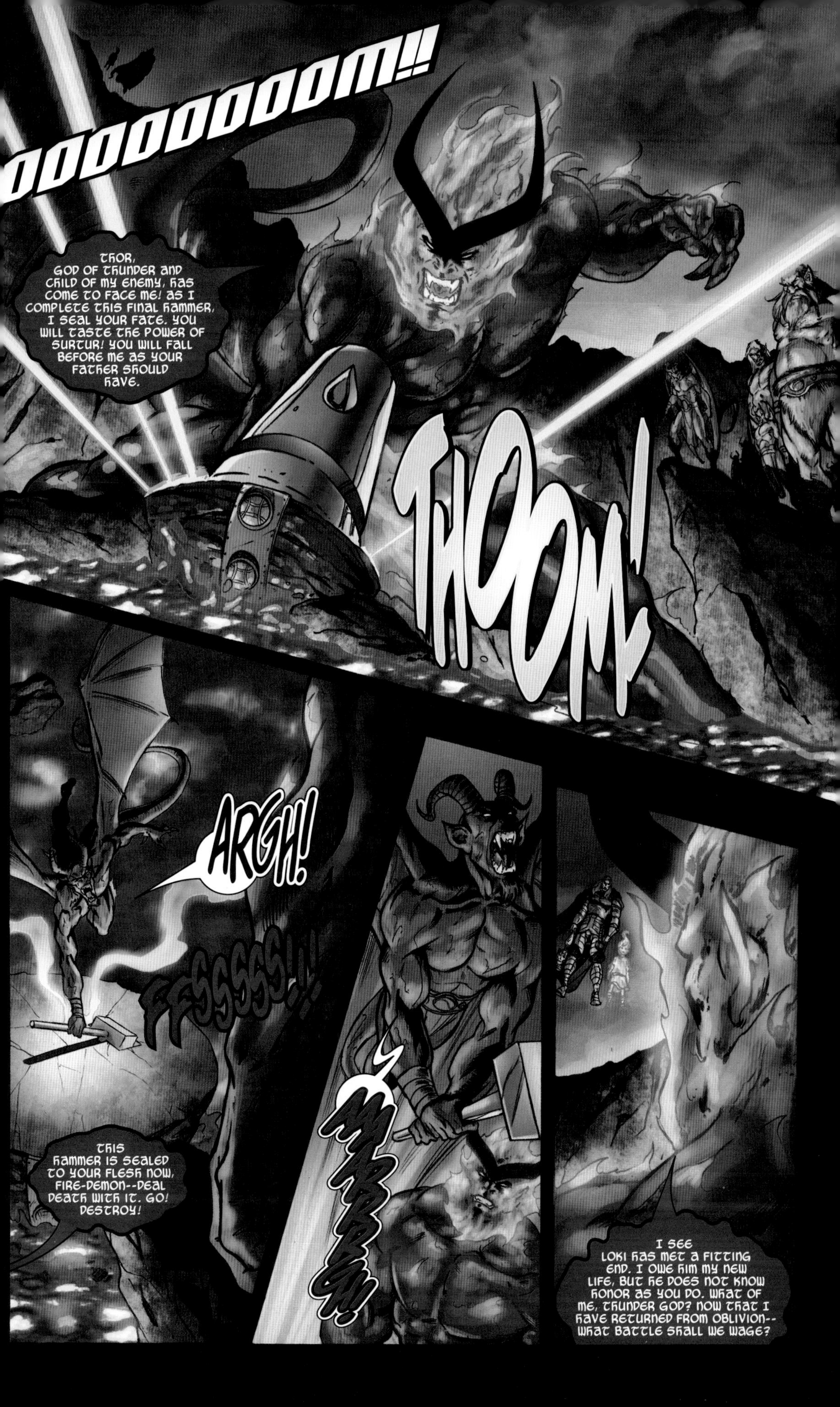
OOOOOOOOOM!!
THOR, GOD OF THUNDER AND CHILD OF MY ENEMY, HAS COME TO FACE ME! AS I COMPLETE THIS FINAL HAMMER, I SEAL YOUR FATE. YOU WILL TASTE THE POWER OF SURTUR! YOU WILL FALL BEFORE ME AS YOUR FATHER SHOULD HAVE.
THOOM!
ARGH!
FFSSSSS!!
THIS HAMMER IS SEALED TO YOUR FLESH NOW, FIRE-DEMON--DEAL DEATH WITH IT. GO! DESTROY!
I SEE LOKI HAS MET A FITTING END. I OWE HIM MY NEW LIFE, BUT HE DOES NOT KNOW HONOR AS YOU DO. WHAT OF ME, THUNDER GOD? NOW THAT I HAVE RETURNED FROM OBLIVION--WHAT BATTLE SHALL WE WAGE?

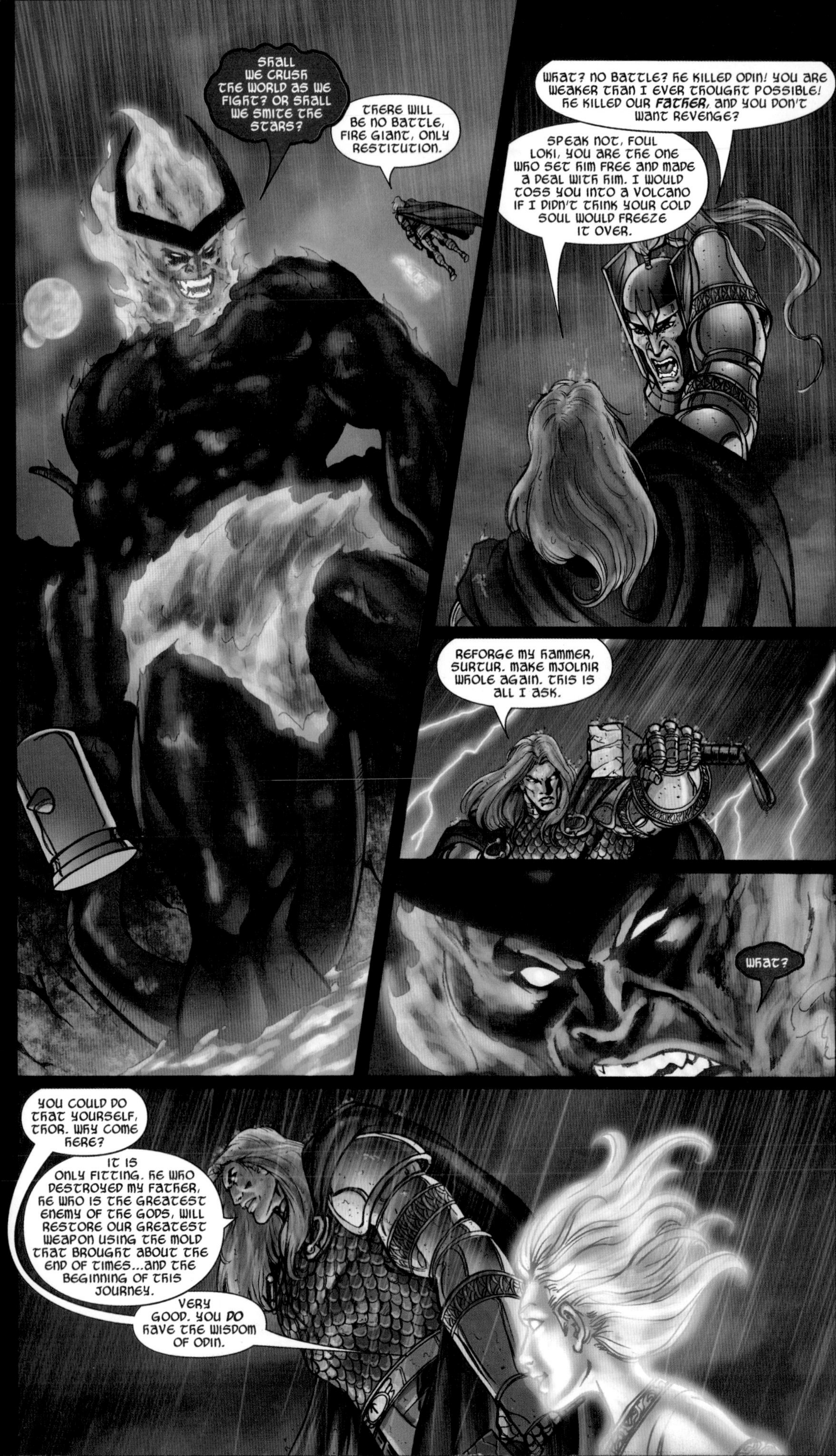
SHALL WE CRUSH THE WORLD AS WE FIGHT? OR SHALL WE SMITE THE STARS?
THERE WILL BE NO BATTLE, FIRE GIANT, ONLY RESTITUTION.
WHAT? NO BATTLE? HE KILLED ODIN! YOU ARE WEAKER THAN I EVER THOUGHT POSSIBLE! HE KILLED OUR FATHER, AND YOU DON'T WANT REVENGE?
SPEAK NOT, FOUL LOKI, YOU ARE THE ONE WHO SET HIM FREE AND MADE A DEAL WITH HIM. I WOULD TOSS YOU INTO A VOLCANO IF I DIDN'T THINK YOUR COLD SOUL WOULD FREEZE IT OVER.
REFORGE MY HAMMER, SURTUR. MAKE MJOLNIR WHOLE AGAIN. THIS IS ALL I ASK.
WHAT?
YOU COULD DO THAT YOURSELF, THOR. WHY COME HERE?
IT IS ONLY FITTING. HE WHO DESTROYED MY FATHER, HE WHO IS THE GREATEST ENEMY OF THE GODS, WILL RESTORE OUR GREATEST WEAPON USING THE MOLD THAT BROUGHT ABOUT THE END OF TIMES...AND THE BEGINNING OF THIS JOURNEY.
VERY GOOD. YOU DO HAVE THE WISDOM OF ODIN.

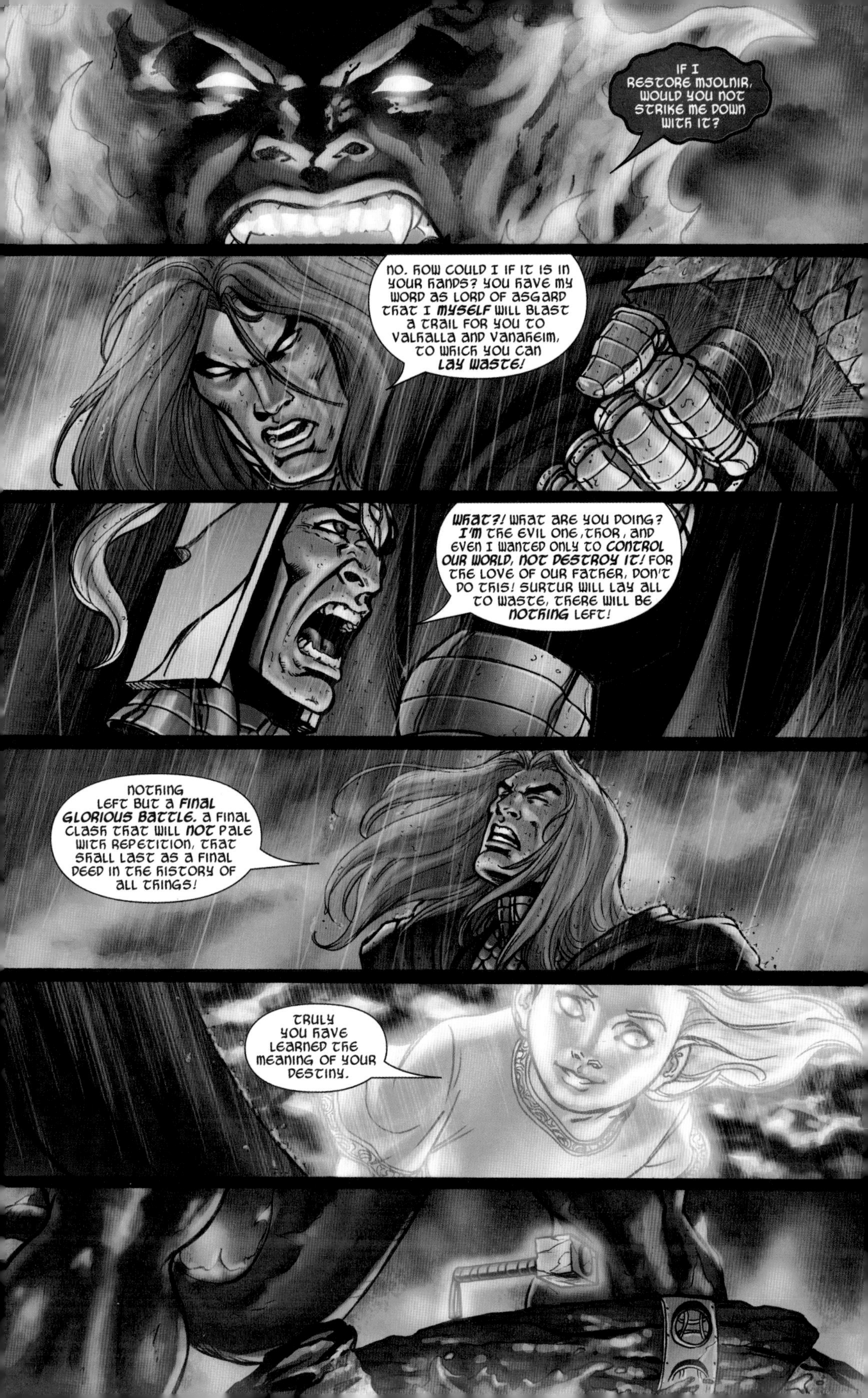
IF I RESTORE MJOLNIR, WOULD YOU NOT STRIKE ME DOWN WITH IT?
NO. HOW COULD I IF IT IS IN YOUR HANDS? YOU HAVE MY WORD AS LORD OF ASGARD THAT I MYSELF WILL BLAST A TRAIL FOR YOU TO VALHALLA AND VANAHEIM, TO WHICH YOU CAN LAY WASTE!
WHAT?! WHAT ARE YOU DOING? I'M THE EVIL ONE, THOR, AND EVEN I WANTED ONLY TO CONTROL OUR WORLD, NOT DESTROY IT! FOR THE LOVE OF OUR FATHER, DON'T DO THIS! SURTUR WILL LAY ALL TO WASTE, THERE WILL BE NOTHING LEFT!
NOTHING LEFT BUT A FINAL GLORIOUS BATTLE. A FINAL CLASH THAT WILL NOT PALE WITH REPETITION, THAT SHALL LAST AS A FINAL DEED IN THE HISTORY OF ALL THINGS!
TRULY YOU HAVE LEARNED THE MEANING OF YOUR DESTINY.

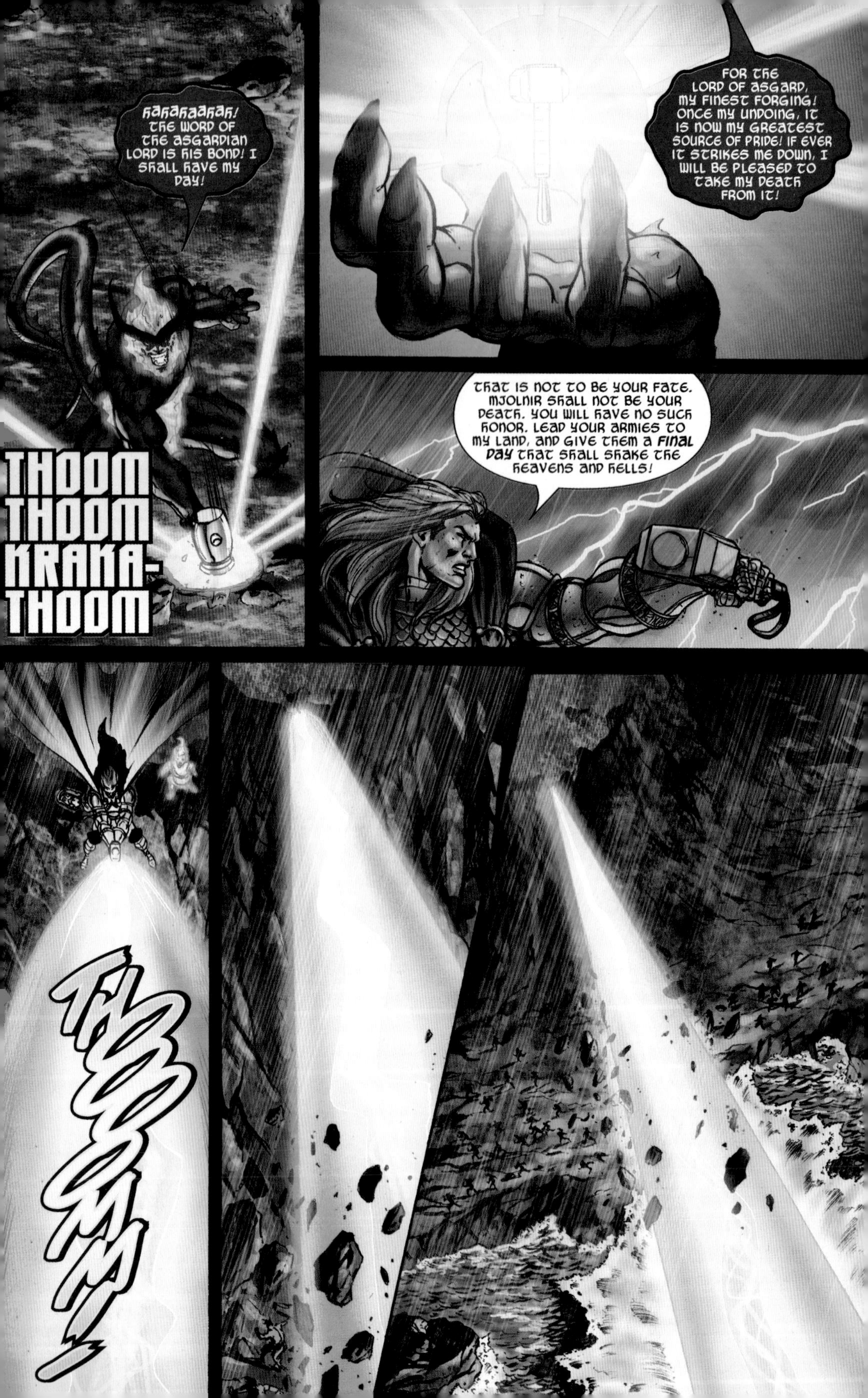
HAHAHAAHAH! THE WORD OF THE ASGARDIAN LORD IS HIS BOND! I SHALL HAVE MY DAY!
FOR THE LORD OF ASGARD, MY FINEST FORGING! ONCE MY UNDOING, IT IS NOW MY GREATEST SOURCE OF PRIDE! IF EVER IT STRIKES ME DOWN, I WILL BE PLEASED TO TAKE MY DEATH FROM IT!
THOOM THOOM KRAKA-THOOM
THAT IS NOT TO BE YOUR FATE. MJOLNIR SHALL NOT BE YOUR DEATH. YOU WILL HAVE NO SUCH HONOR. LEAD YOUR ARMIES TO MY LAND, AND GIVE THEM A *FINAL DAY* THAT SHALL SHAKE THE HEAVENS AND HELLS!
THOOOMMM!

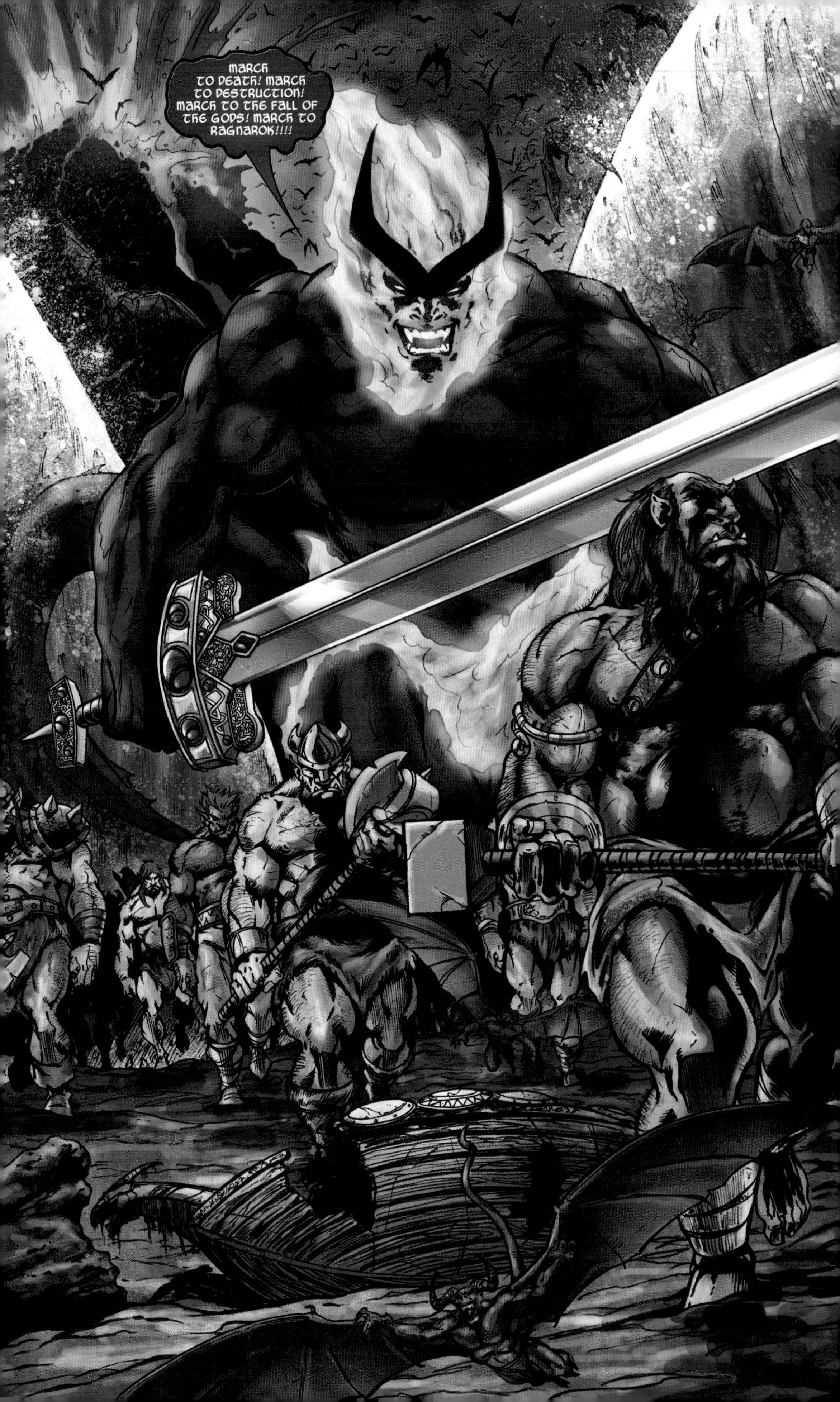
MARCH TO DEATH! MARCH TO DESTRUCTION! MARCH TO THE FALL OF THE GODS! MARCH TO RAGNAROK!!!!

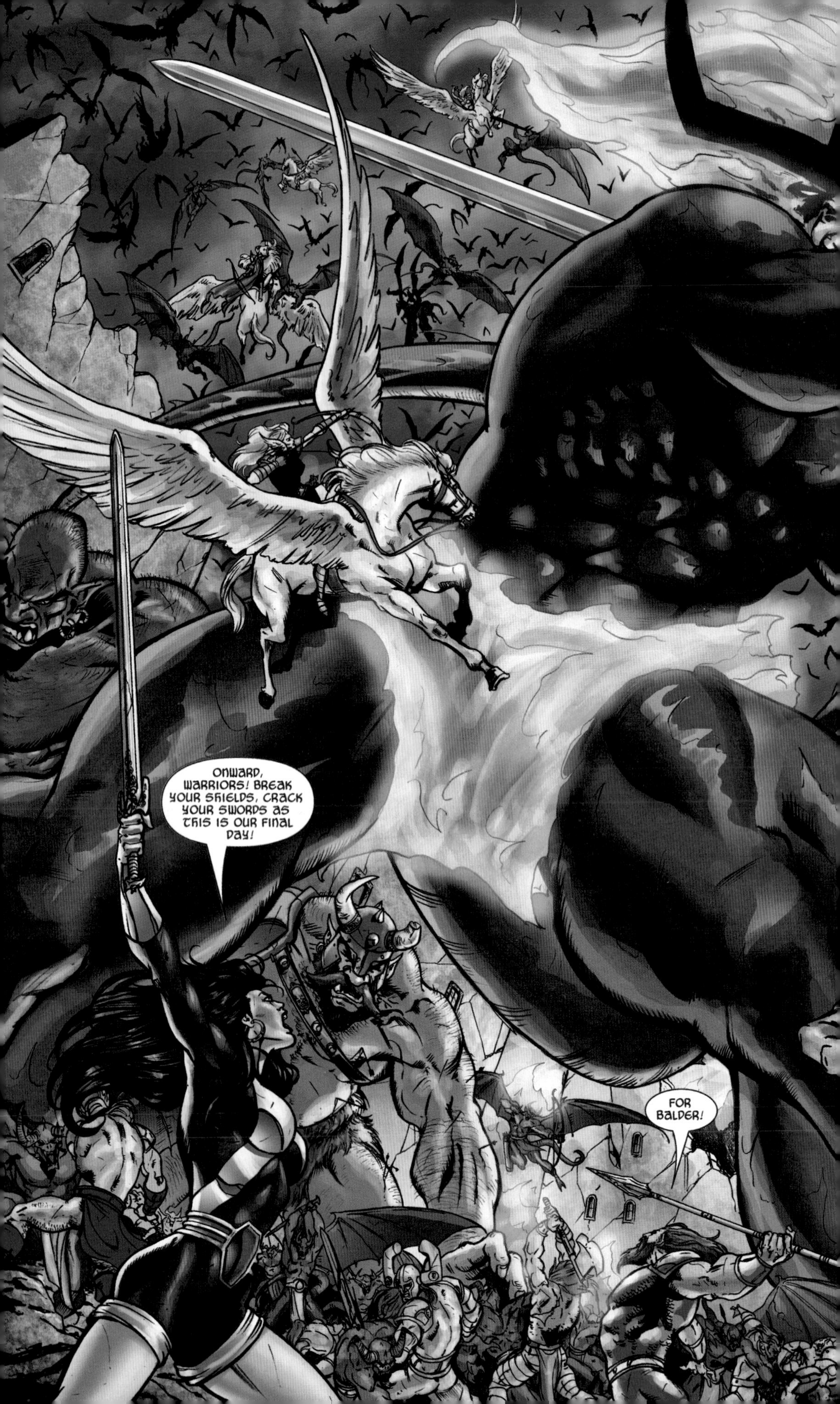
ONWARD, WARRIORS! BREAK YOUR SHIELDS, CRACK YOUR SWORDS AS THIS IS OUR FINAL DAY!
FOR BALDER!

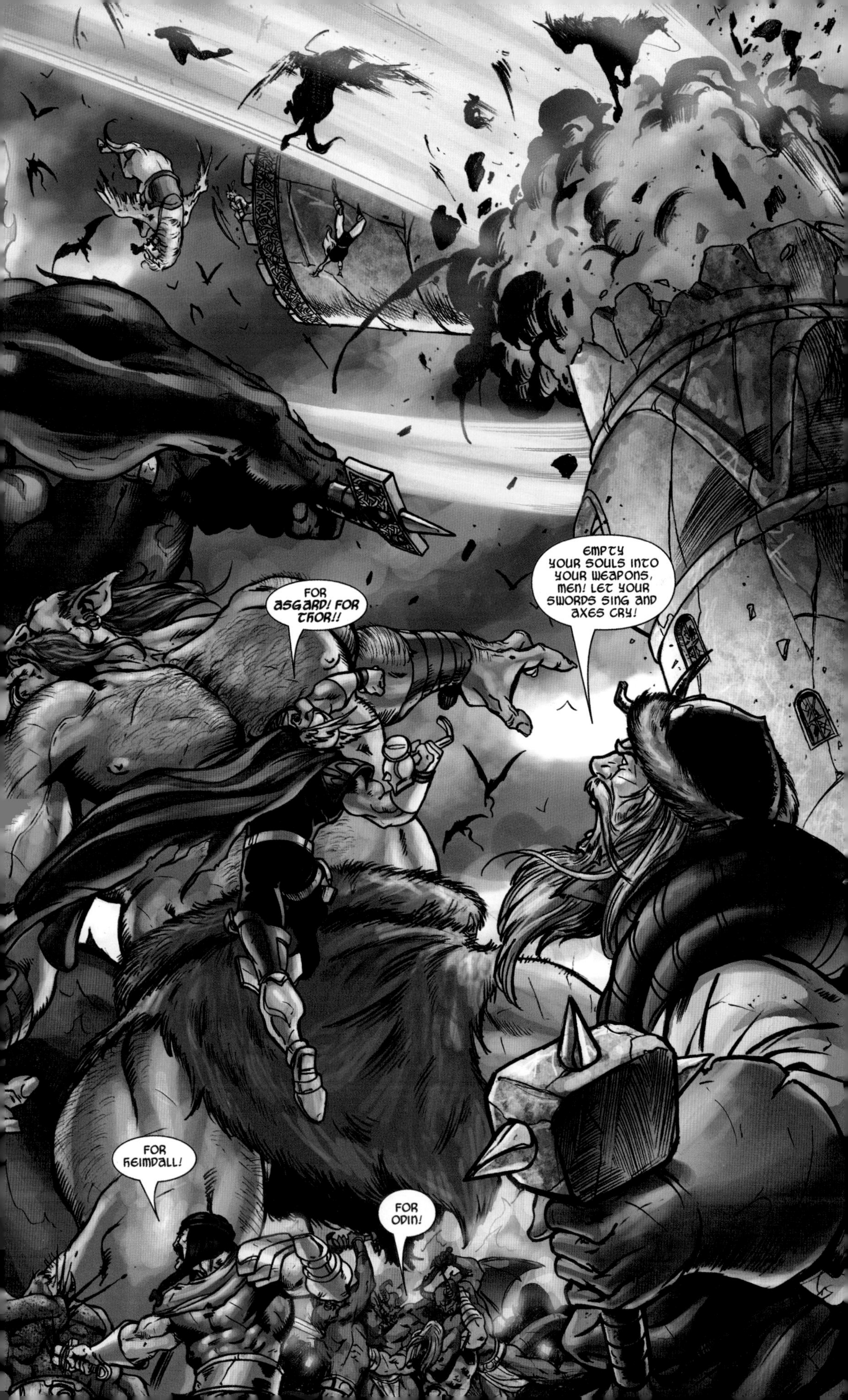
EMPTY YOUR SOULS INTO YOUR WEAPONS, MEN! LET YOUR SWORDS SING AND AXES CRY!
FOR ASGARD! FOR THOR!!
FOR HEIMDALL!
FOR ODIN!

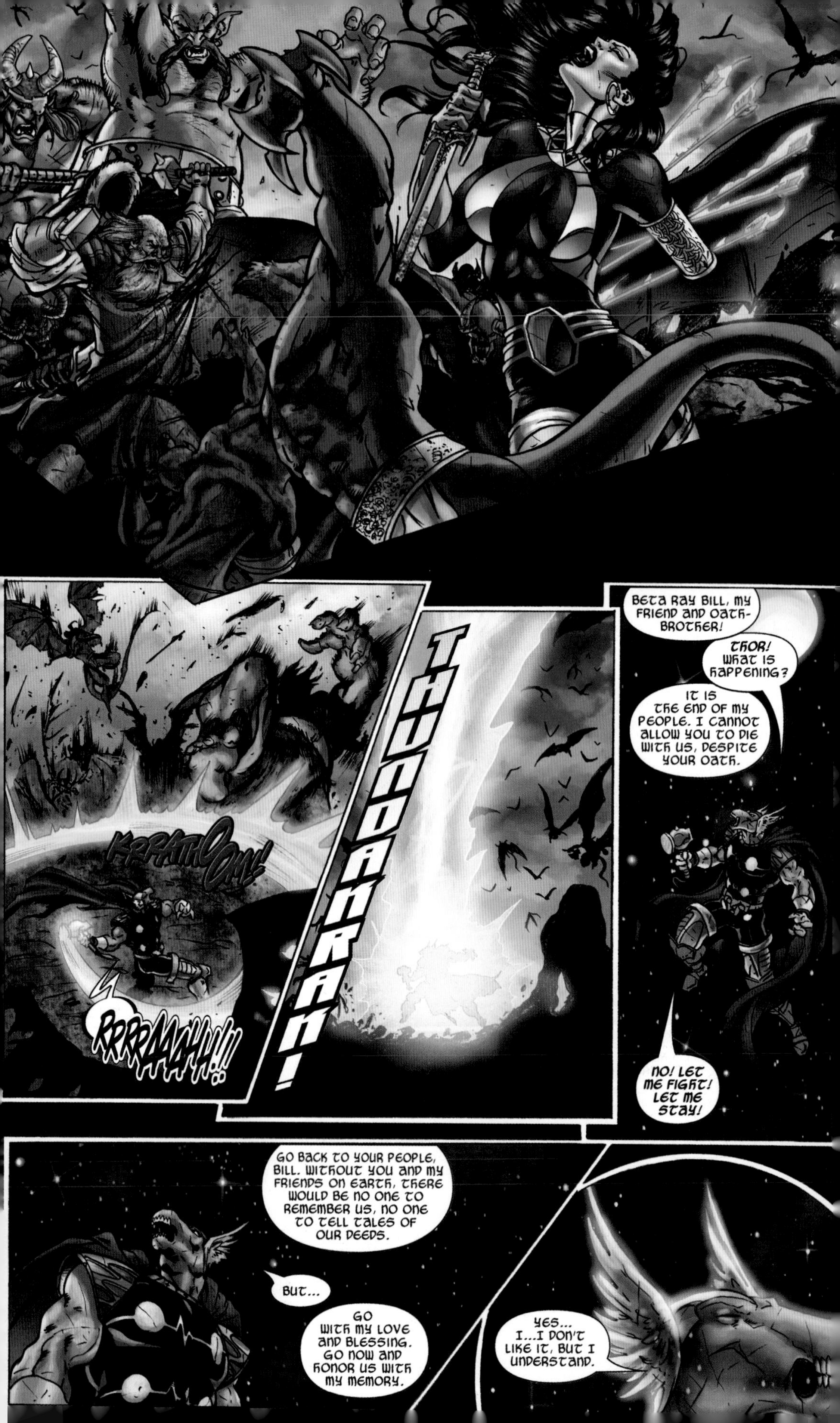
KRRATHOOM!
RRRRAAAHH!!!
THUNDAAARRAM!
BETA RAY BILL, MY FRIEND AND OATH-BROTHER!
THOR! WHAT IS HAPPENING?
IT IS THE END OF MY PEOPLE. I CANNOT ALLOW YOU TO DIE WITH US, DESPITE YOUR OATH.
NO! LET ME FIGHT! LET ME STAY!
GO BACK TO YOUR PEOPLE, BILL. WITHOUT YOU AND MY FRIENDS ON EARTH, THERE WOULD BE NO ONE TO REMEMBER US, NO ONE TO TELL TALES OF OUR DEEDS.
BUT...
GO WITH MY LOVE AND BLESSING. GO NOW AND HONOR US WITH MY MEMORY.
YES... I...I DON'T LIKE IT, BUT I UNDERSTAND.

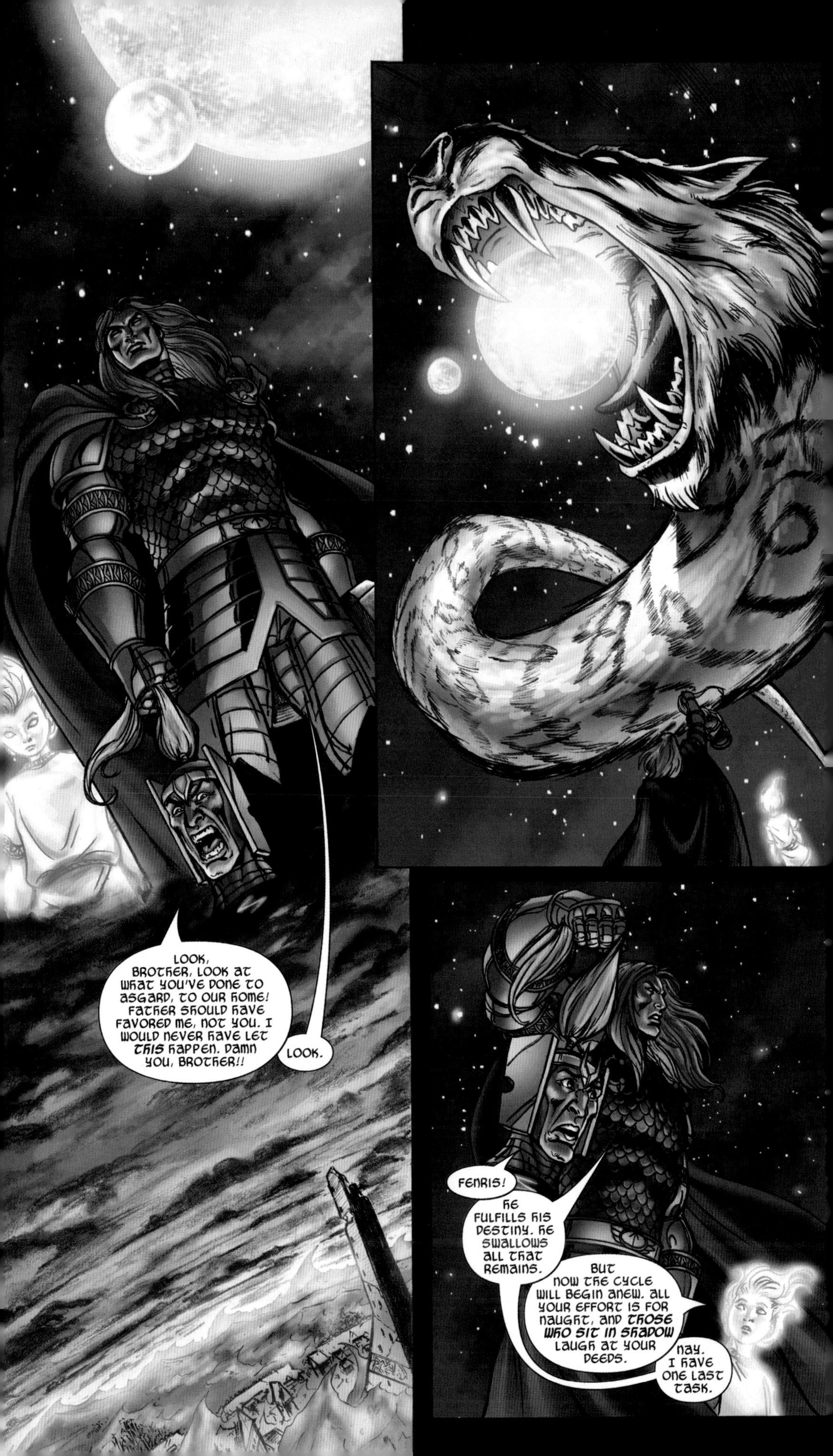
LOOK, BROTHER, LOOK AT WHAT YOU'VE DONE TO ASGARD, TO OUR HOME! FATHER SHOULD HAVE FAVORED ME, NOT YOU. I WOULD NEVER HAVE LET THIS HAPPEN. DAMN YOU, BROTHER!!
LOOK.
FENRIS!
HE FULFILLS HIS DESTINY. HE SWALLOWS ALL THAT REMAINS.
BUT NOW THE CYCLE WILL BEGIN ANEW. ALL YOUR EFFORT IS FOR NAUGHT, AND THOSE WHO SIT IN SHADOW LAUGH AT YOUR DEEDS.
NAY. I HAVE ONE LAST TASK.

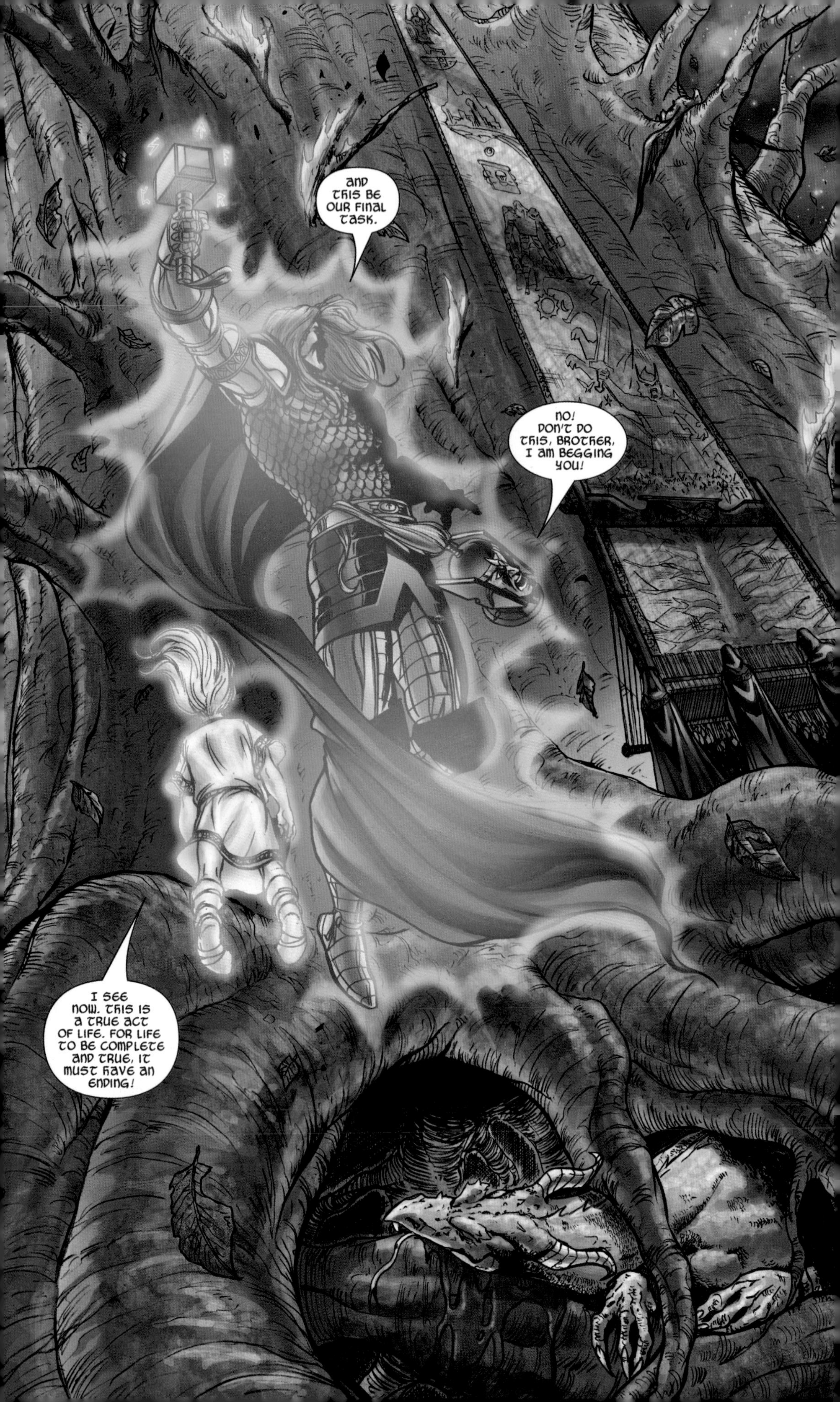
AND THIS BE OUR FINAL TASK.
NO! DON'T DO THIS, BROTHER, I AM BEGGING YOU!
I SEE NOW. THIS IS A TRUE ACT OF LIFE. FOR LIFE TO BE COMPLETE AND TRUE, IT MUST HAVE AN ENDING!

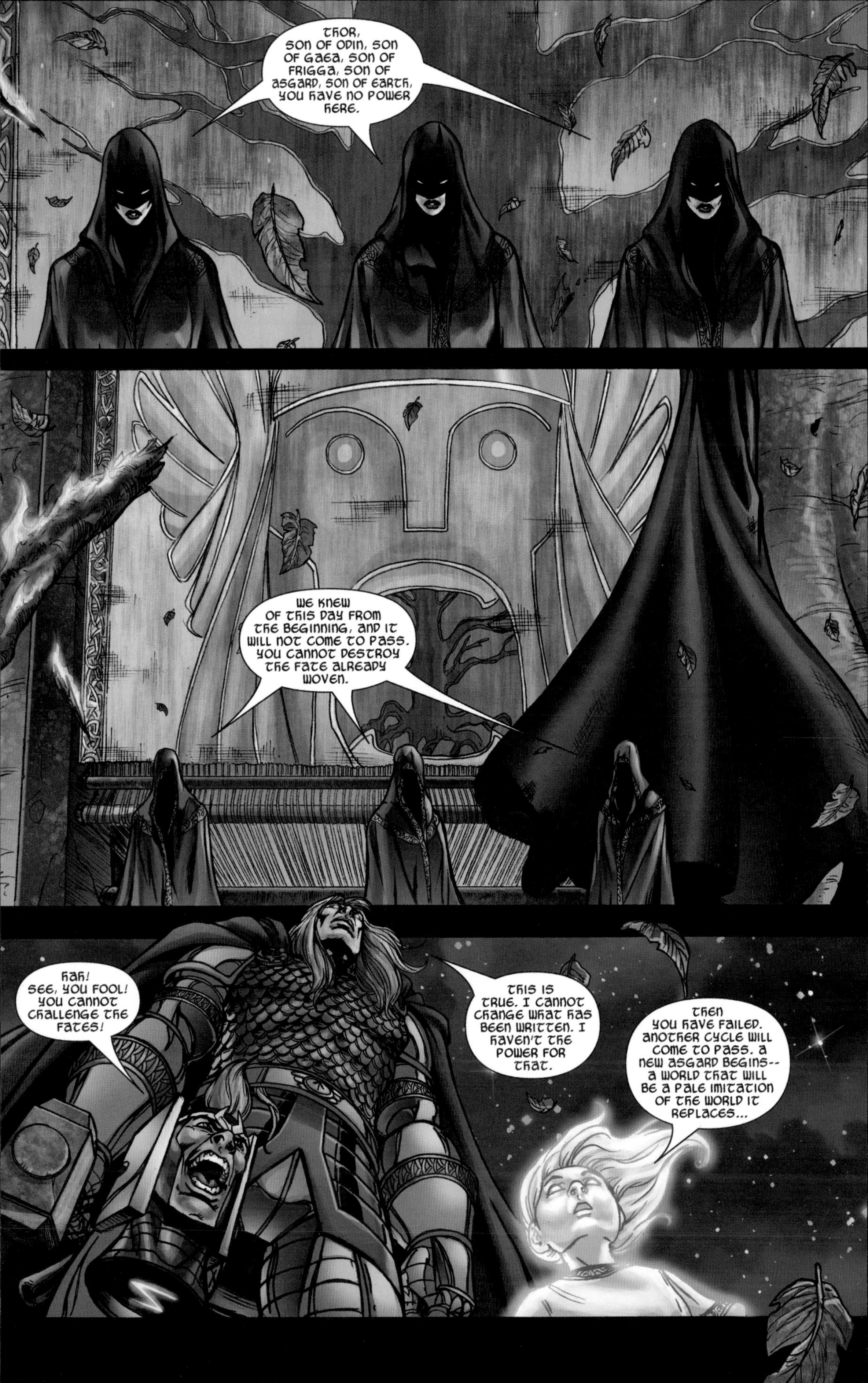
THOR, SON OF ODIN, SON OF GAEA, SON OF FRIGGA, SON OF ASGARD, SON OF EARTH, YOU HAVE NO POWER HERE.
WE KNEW OF THIS DAY FROM THE BEGINNING, AND IT WILL NOT COME TO PASS. YOU CANNOT DESTROY THE FATE ALREADY WOVEN.
HAH! SEE, YOU FOOL! YOU CANNOT CHALLENGE THE FATES!
THIS IS TRUE. I CANNOT CHANGE WHAT HAS BEEN WRITTEN. I HAVEN'T THE POWER FOR THAT.
THEN YOU HAVE FAILED. ANOTHER CYCLE WILL COME TO PASS. A NEW ASGARD BEGINS-- A WORLD THAT WILL BE A PALE IMITATION OF THE WORLD IT REPLACES...

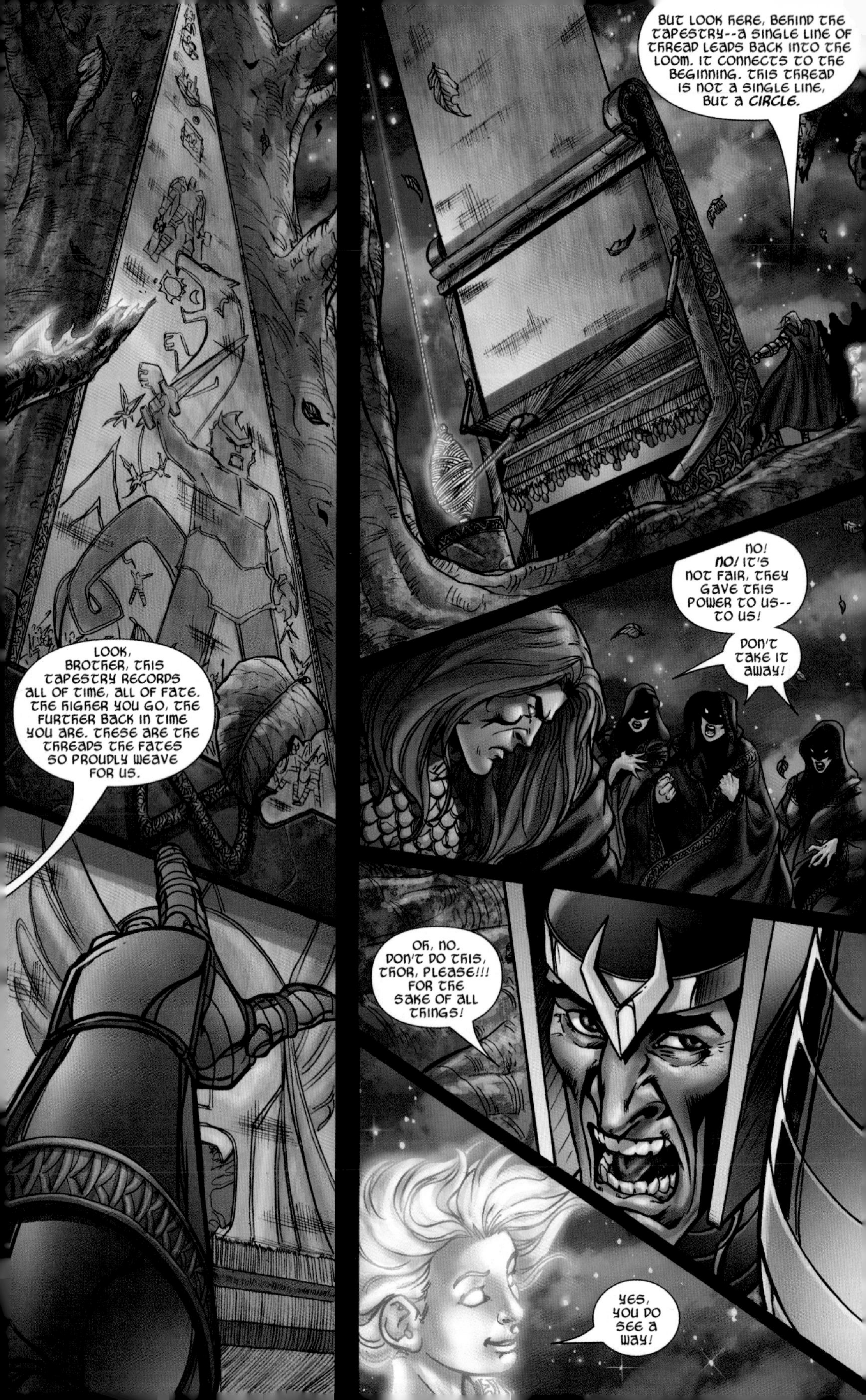
LOOK, BROTHER, THIS TAPESTRY RECORDS ALL OF TIME, ALL OF FATE. THE HIGHER YOU GO, THE FURTHER BACK IN TIME YOU ARE. THESE ARE THE THREADS THE FATES SO PROUDLY WEAVE FOR US.
BUT LOOK HERE, BEHIND THE TAPESTRY--A SINGLE LINE OF THREAD LEADS BACK INTO THE LOOM. IT CONNECTS TO THE BEGINNING. THIS THREAD IS NOT A SINGLE LINE, BUT A ***CIRCLE.***
NO! ***NO!*** IT'S NOT FAIR, THEY GAVE THIS POWER TO US-- TO US!
DON'T TAKE IT AWAY!
OH, NO. DON'T DO THIS, THOR, PLEASE!!! FOR THE SAKE OF ALL THINGS!
YES, YOU DO SEE A WAY!

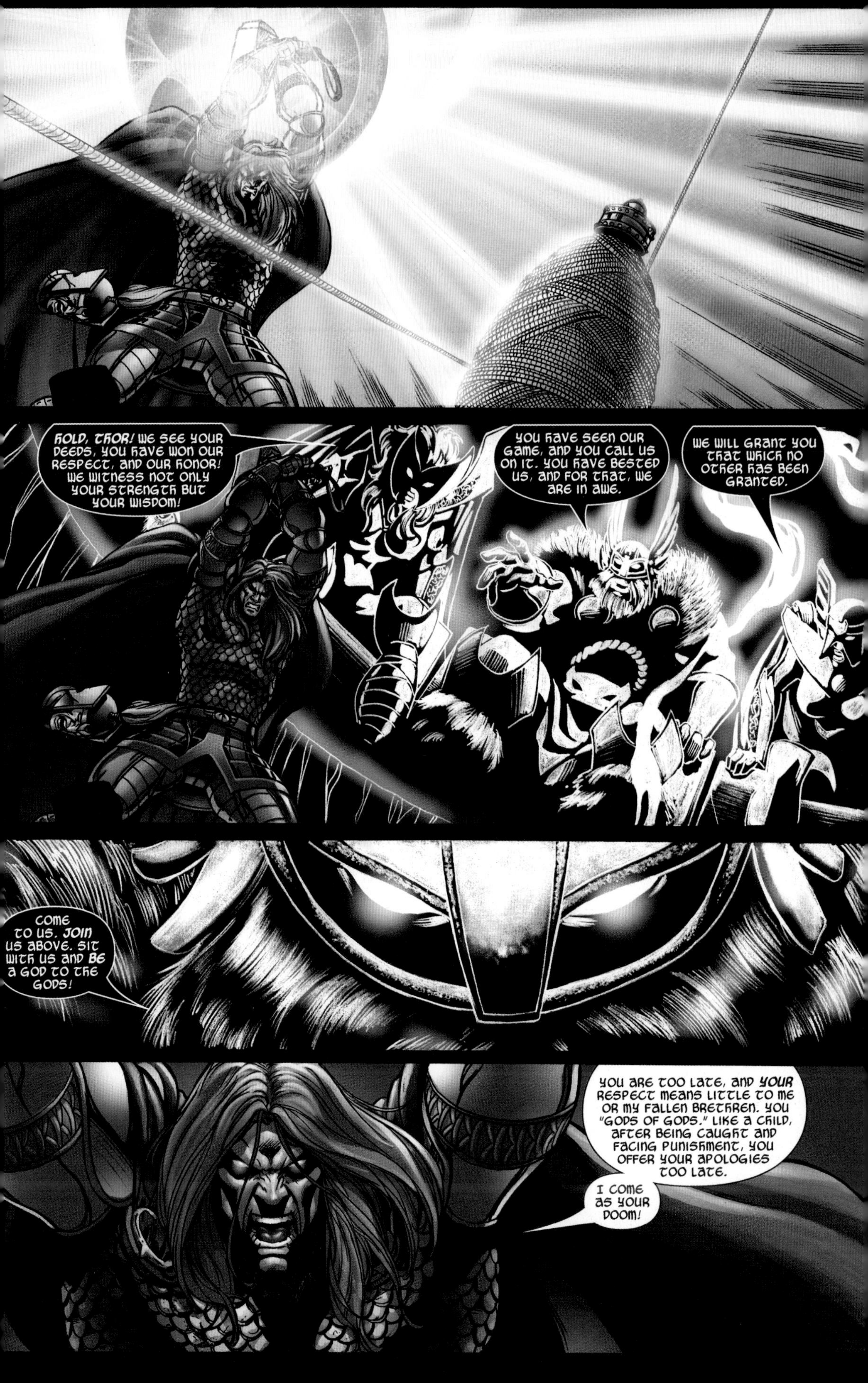
HOLD, THOR! WE SEE YOUR DEEDS, YOU HAVE WON OUR RESPECT, AND OUR HONOR! WE WITNESS NOT ONLY YOUR STRENGTH BUT YOUR WISDOM!
YOU HAVE SEEN OUR GAME, AND YOU CALL US ON IT. YOU HAVE BESTED US, AND FOR THAT, WE ARE IN AWE.
WE WILL GRANT YOU THAT WHICH NO OTHER HAS BEEN GRANTED.
COME TO US. JOIN US ABOVE. SIT WITH US AND BE A GOD TO THE GODS!
YOU ARE TOO LATE, AND YOUR RESPECT MEANS LITTLE TO ME OR MY FALLEN BRETHREN. YOU "GODS OF GODS." LIKE A CHILD, AFTER BEING CAUGHT AND FACING PUNISHMENT, YOU OFFER YOUR APOLOGIES TOO LATE.
I COME AS YOUR DOOM!

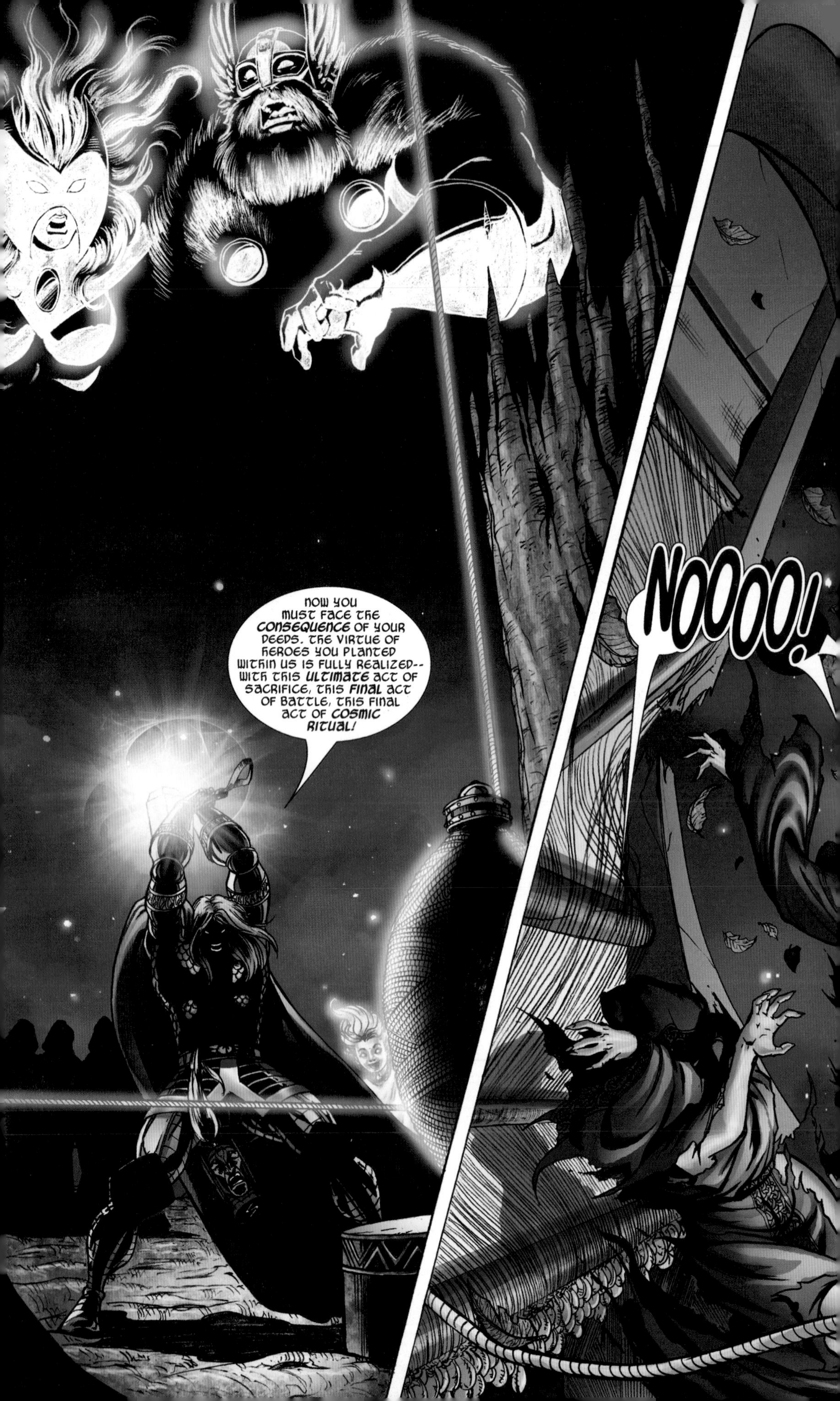
NOW YOU MUST FACE THE CONSEQUENCE OF YOUR DEEDS. THE VIRTUE OF HEROES YOU PLANTED WITHIN US IS FULLY REALIZED-- WITH THIS ULTIMATE ACT OF SACRIFICE, THIS FINAL ACT OF BATTLE, THIS FINAL ACT OF COSMIC RITUAL!
NOOOO!

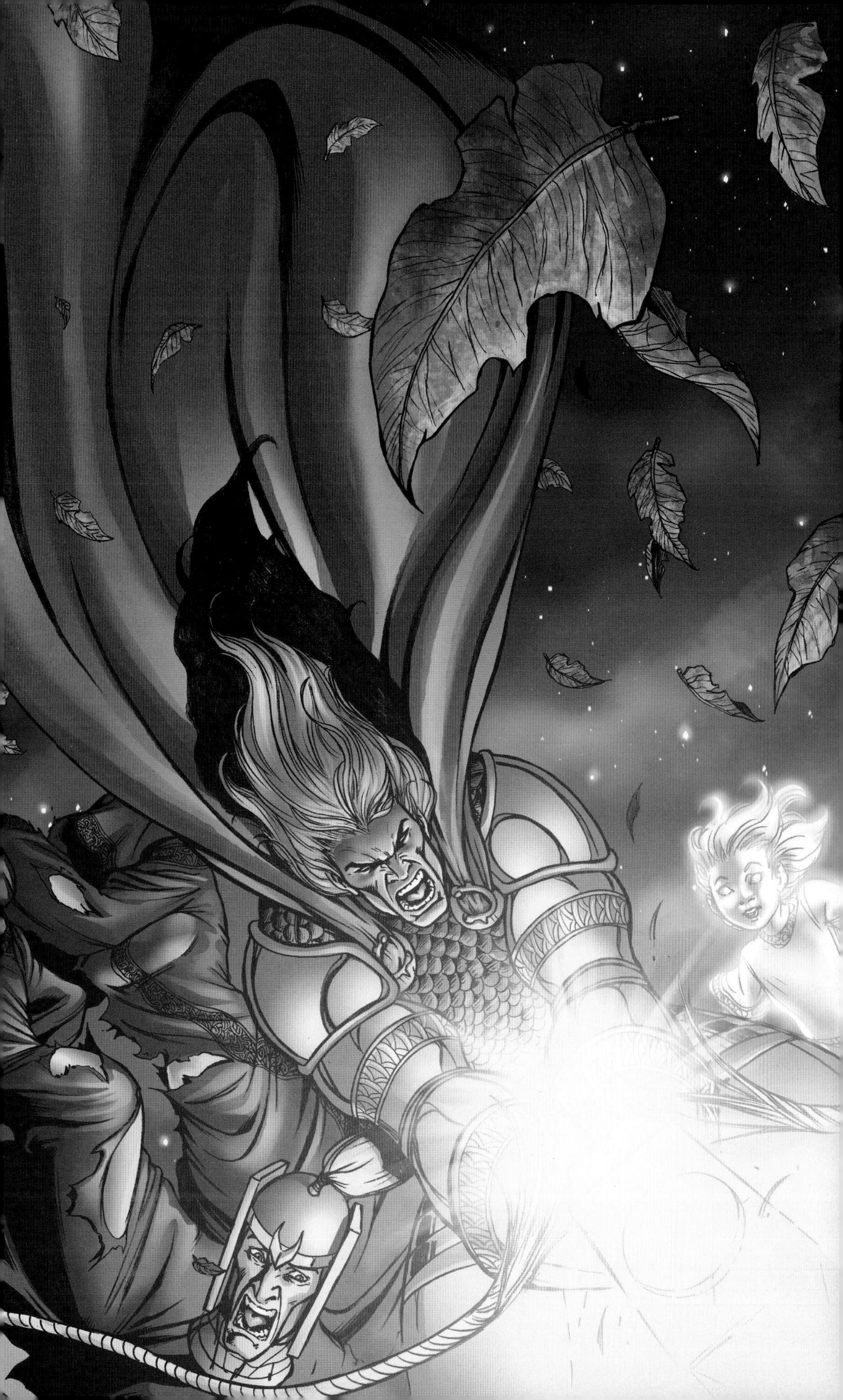

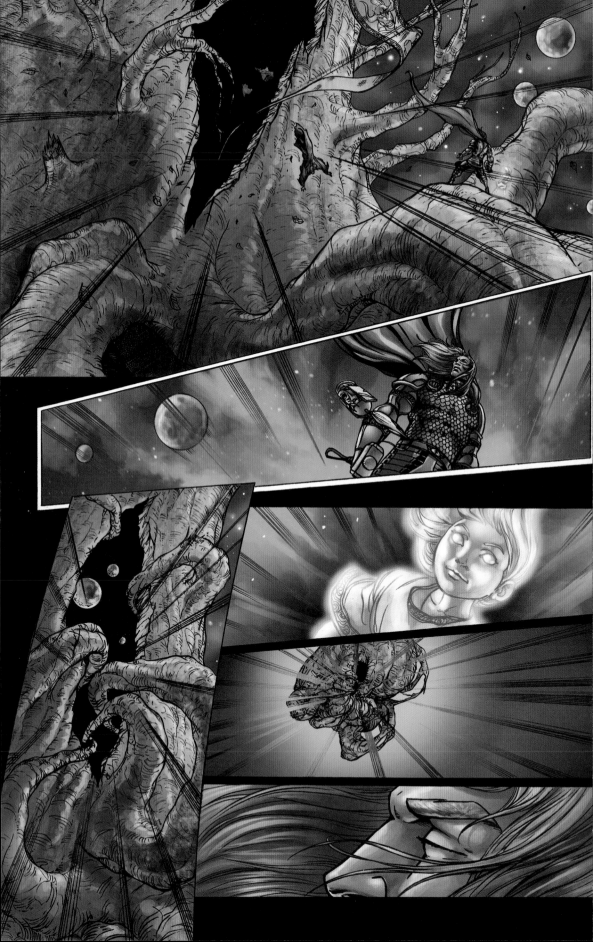

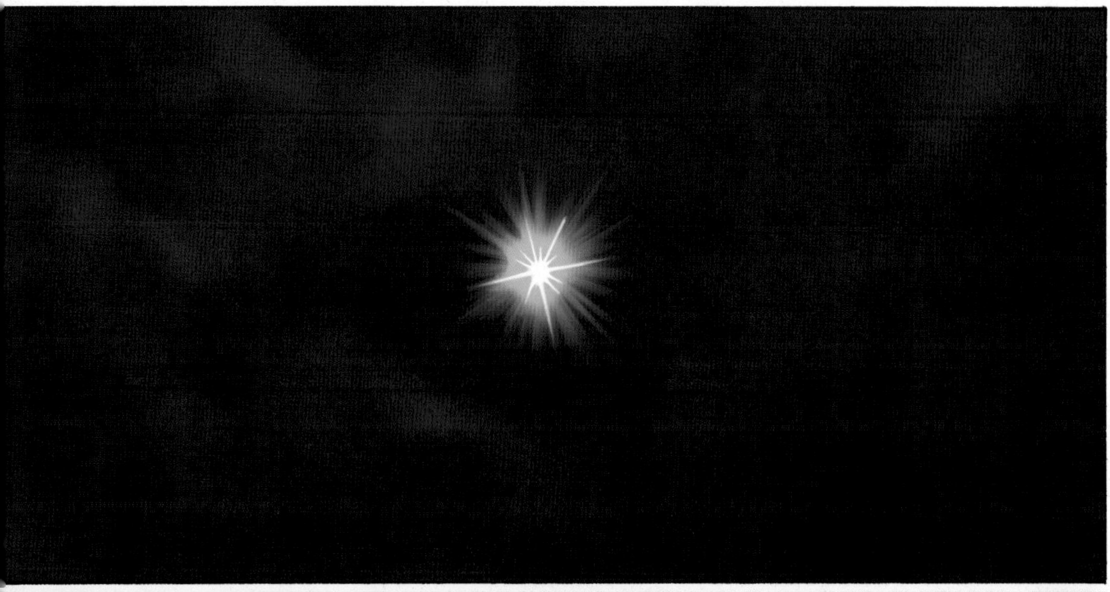

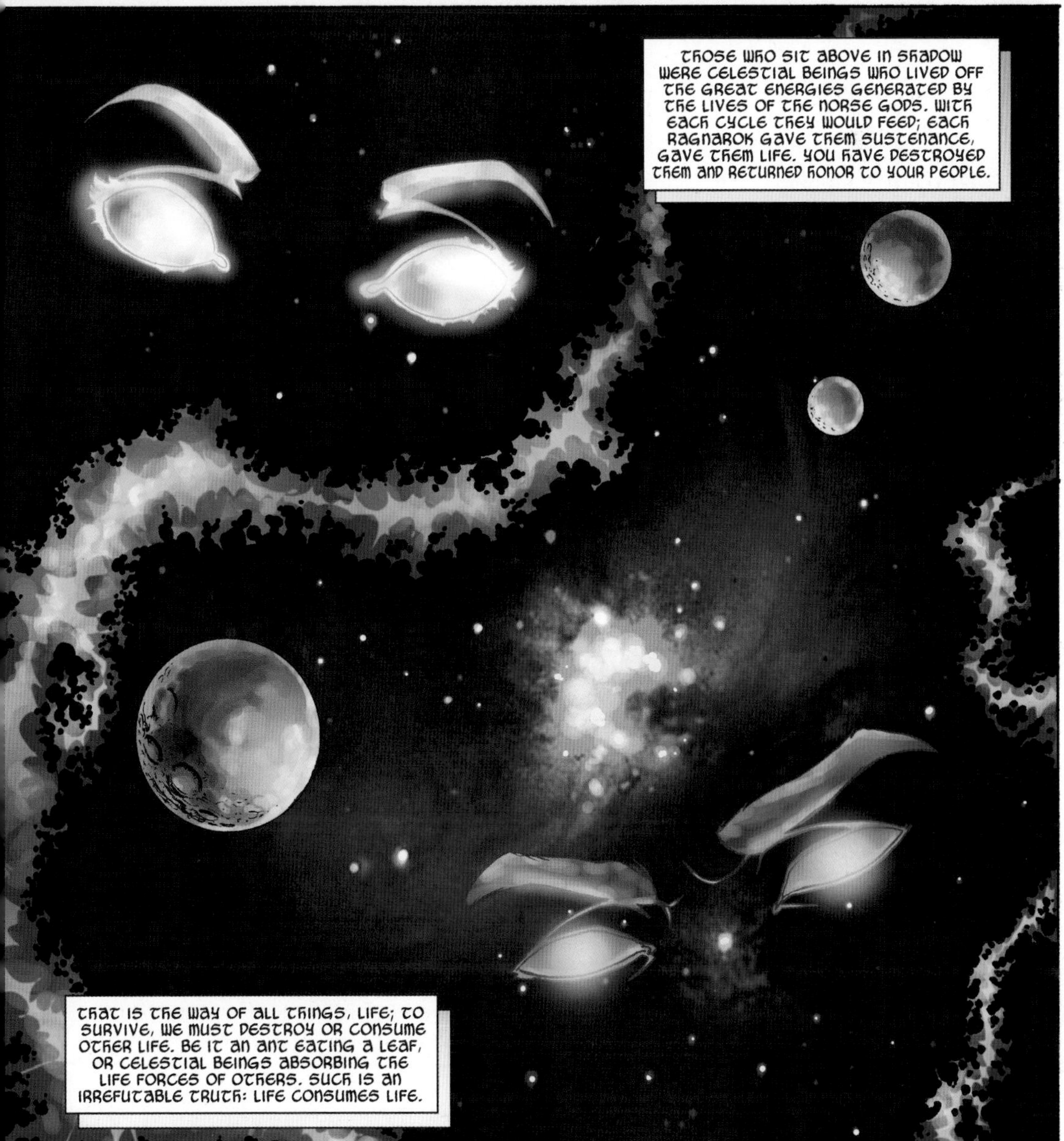
THOSE WHO SIT ABOVE IN SHADOW WERE CELESTIAL BEINGS WHO LIVED OFF THE GREAT ENERGIES GENERATED BY THE LIVES OF THE NORSE GODS. WITH EACH CYCLE THEY WOULD FEED; EACH RAGNAROK GAVE THEM SUSTENANCE, GAVE THEM LIFE. YOU HAVE DESTROYED THEM AND RETURNED HONOR TO YOUR PEOPLE.
THAT IS THE WAY OF ALL THINGS, LIFE; TO SURVIVE, WE MUST DESTROY OR CONSUME OTHER LIFE. BE IT AN ANT EATING A LEAF, OR CELESTIAL BEINGS ABSORBING THE LIFE FORCES OF OTHERS. SUCH IS AN IRREFUTABLE TRUTH: LIFE CONSUMES LIFE.

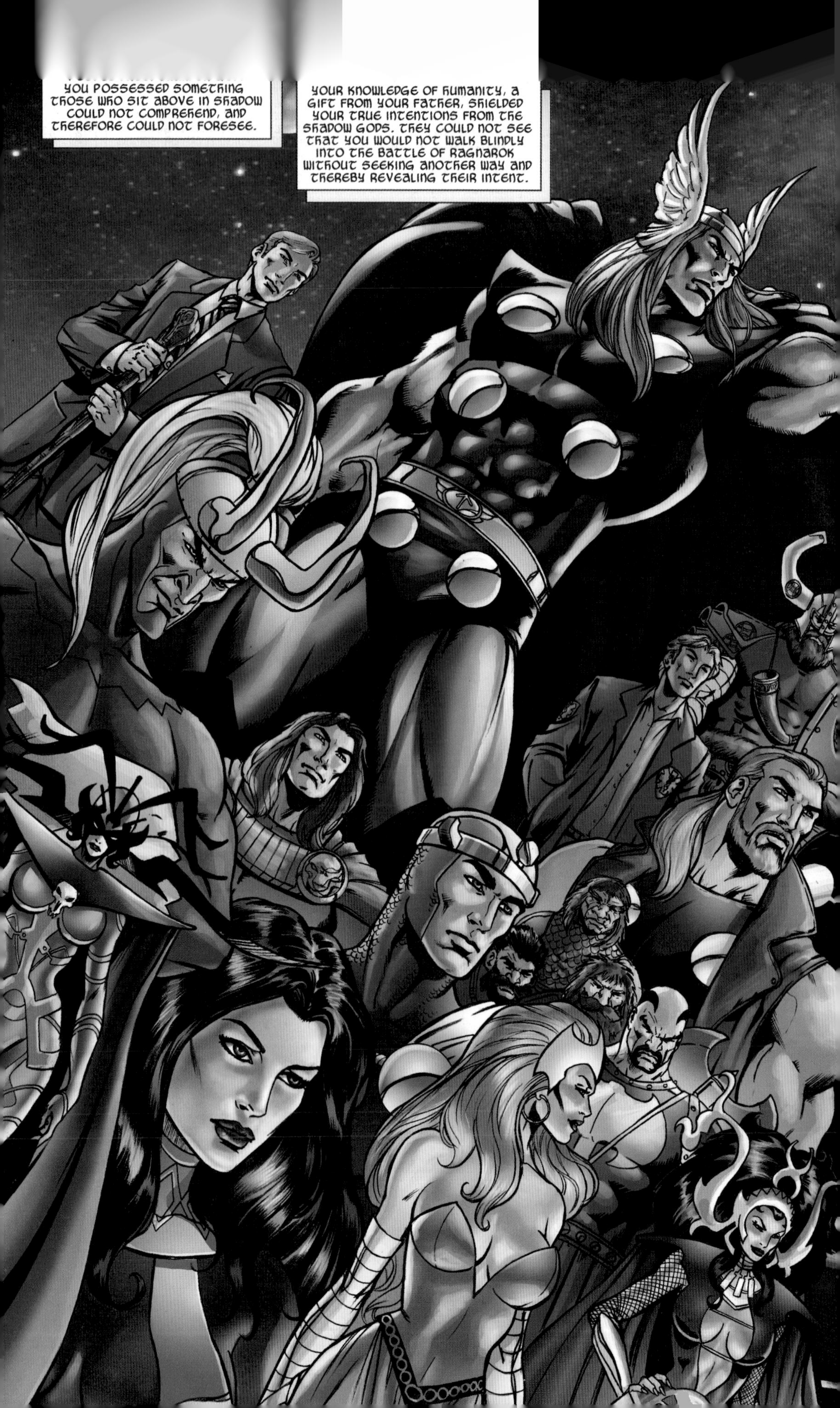
YOU POSSESSED SOMETHING THOSE WHO SIT ABOVE IN SHADOW COULD NOT COMPREHEND, AND THEREFORE COULD NOT FORESEE.
YOUR KNOWLEDGE OF HUMANITY, A GIFT FROM YOUR FATHER, SHIELDED YOUR TRUE INTENTIONS FROM THE SHADOW GODS. THEY COULD NOT SEE THAT YOU WOULD NOT WALK BLINDLY INTO THE BATTLE OF RAGNAROK WITHOUT SEEKING ANOTHER WAY AND THEREBY REVEALING THEIR INTENT.

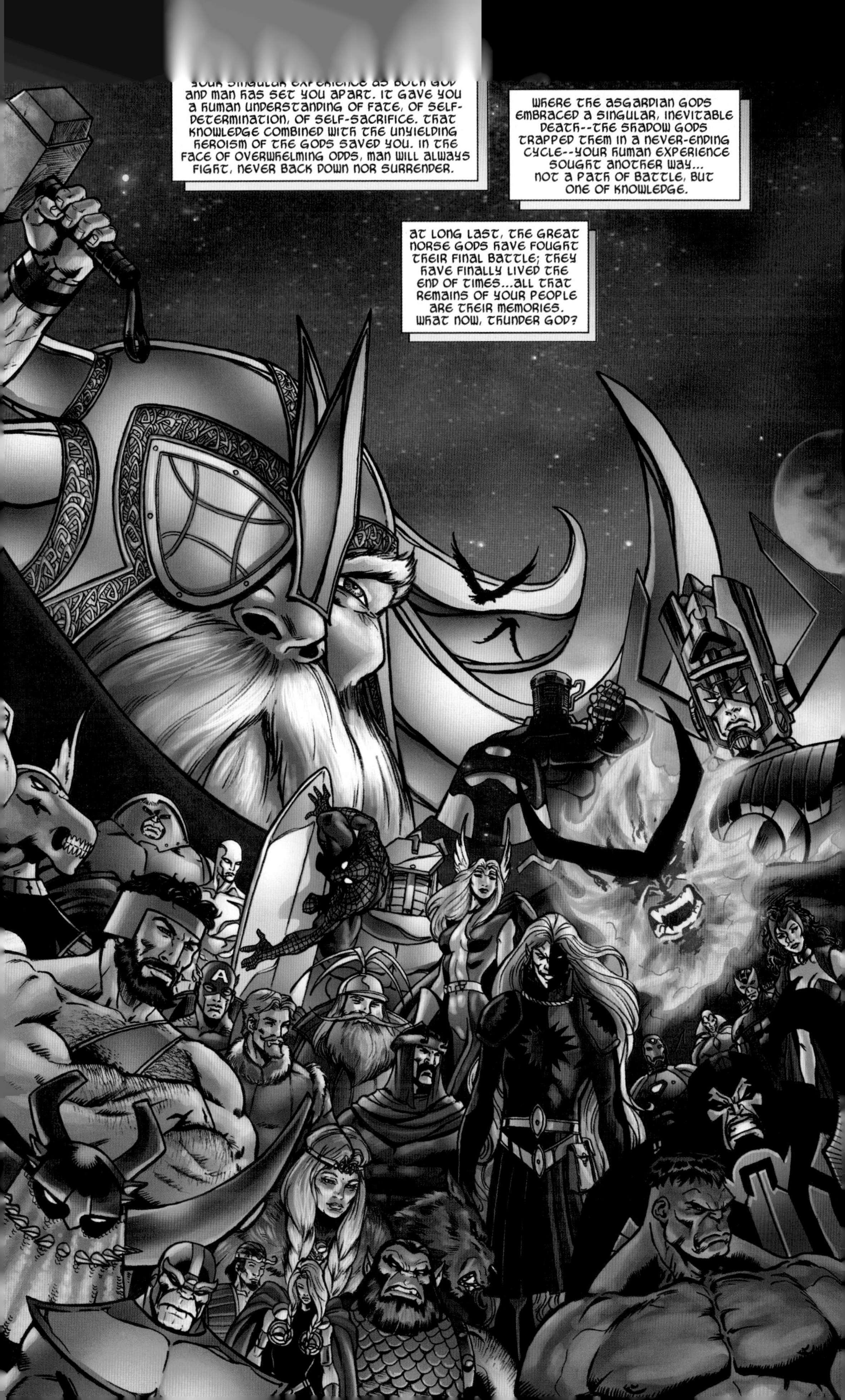
AND MAN HAS SET YOU APART. IT GAVE YOU A HUMAN UNDERSTANDING OF FATE, OF SELF-DETERMINATION, OF SELF-SACRIFICE. THAT KNOWLEDGE COMBINED WITH THE UNYIELDING HEROISM OF THE GODS SAVED YOU. IN THE FACE OF OVERWHELMING ODDS, MAN WILL ALWAYS FIGHT, NEVER BACK DOWN NOR SURRENDER.
WHERE THE ASGARDIAN GODS EMBRACED A SINGULAR, INEVITABLE DEATH--THE SHADOW GODS TRAPPED THEM IN A NEVER-ENDING CYCLE--YOUR HUMAN EXPERIENCE SOUGHT ANOTHER WAY... NOT A PATH OF BATTLE, BUT ONE OF KNOWLEDGE.
AT LONG LAST, THE GREAT NORSE GODS HAVE FOUGHT THEIR FINAL BATTLE; THEY HAVE FINALLY LIVED THE END OF TIMES...ALL THAT REMAINS OF YOUR PEOPLE ARE THEIR MEMORIES. WHAT NOW, THUNDER GOD?

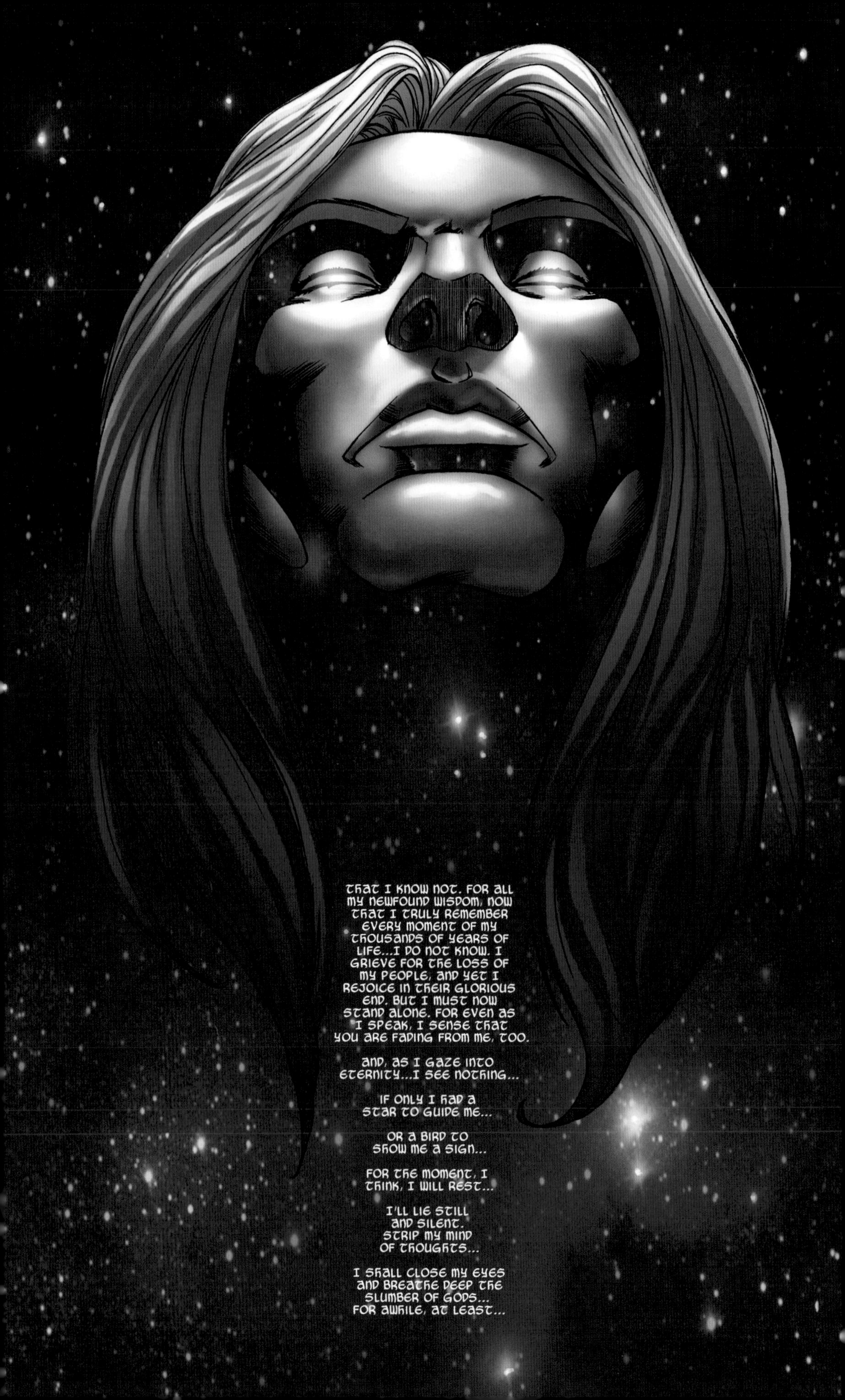
THAT I KNOW NOT. FOR ALL MY NEWFOUND WISDOM, NOW THAT I TRULY REMEMBER EVERY MOMENT OF MY THOUSANDS OF YEARS OF LIFE...I DO NOT KNOW. I GRIEVE FOR THE LOSS OF MY PEOPLE, AND YET I REJOICE IN THEIR GLORIOUS END. BUT I MUST NOW STAND ALONE. FOR EVEN AS I SPEAK, I SENSE THAT YOU ARE FADING FROM ME, TOO.
AND, AS I GAZE INTO ETERNITY...I SEE NOTHING...
IF ONLY I HAD A STAR TO GUIDE ME...
OR A BIRD TO SHOW ME A SIGN...
FOR THE MOMENT, I THINK, I WILL REST...
I'LL LIE STILL AND SILENT. STRIP MY MIND OF THOUGHTS...
I SHALL CLOSE MY EYES AND BREATHE DEEP THE SLUMBER OF GODS... FOR AWHILE, AT LEAST...

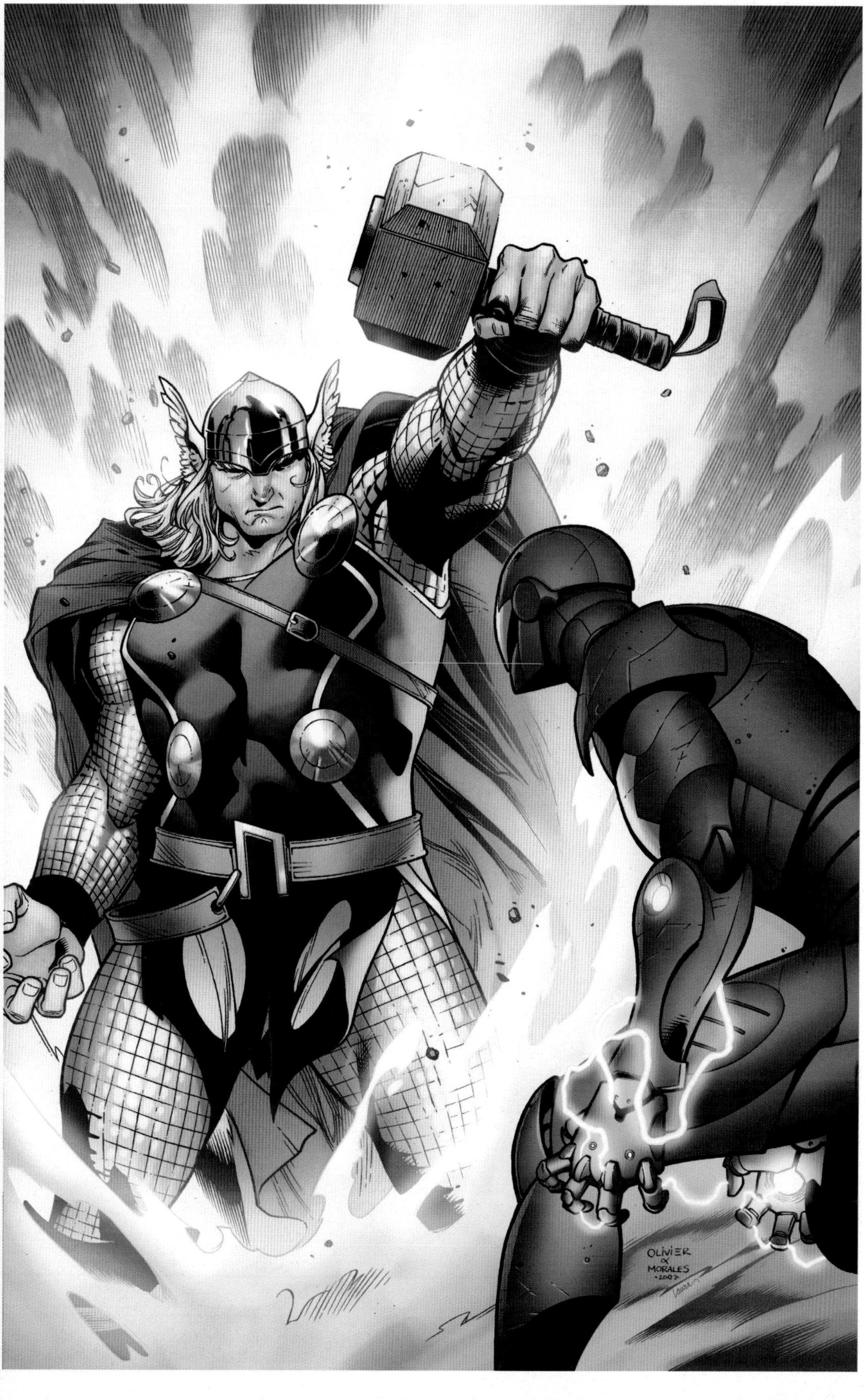
OLIVIER
&
MORALES
2007

...WAS CHRISTENED WITH THAT NAME IN 275 A.D. BY THE ROMAN EMPEROR AURELIAN.

THE PEOPLE OF OLD ORLÉANS DROVE BACK THE INVADING TIDE OF BARBARIANS LED BY ATTILA THE HUN, AND SURVIVED THE SIEGE OF ORLÉANS IN 1429 THROUGH THE INTERCESSION OF JOAN OF ARC.

welcome

to

EW ORLEANS

THE PEOPLE OF NEW ORLEANS HAVE NOT BEEN QUITE AS FORTUNATE IN THEIR DEALINGS WITH TIDES AND SIEGES.

WHAT BETTER PLACE, THEN, FOR THE GOD OF STORMS TO START HIS OWN SEARCH FOR THE LOST...THE LOST GODS OF ASGARD, WHO HAVE DESCENDED INTO THE FORMS OF MEN?

WHAT BETTER PLACE FOR ONE WHO WALKED THE EARTH WHEN THE NAME ORLÉANS WAS FIRST SPOKEN...WHO HEARD TALES OF ATTILA'S BATTLES FROM HIS OWN SECOND IN COMMAND...AND WHO SAW IN JEANNE D'ARC A WARRIOR QUEEN BORN, TOUCHED BY GRACE, POWER, AND MADNESS?

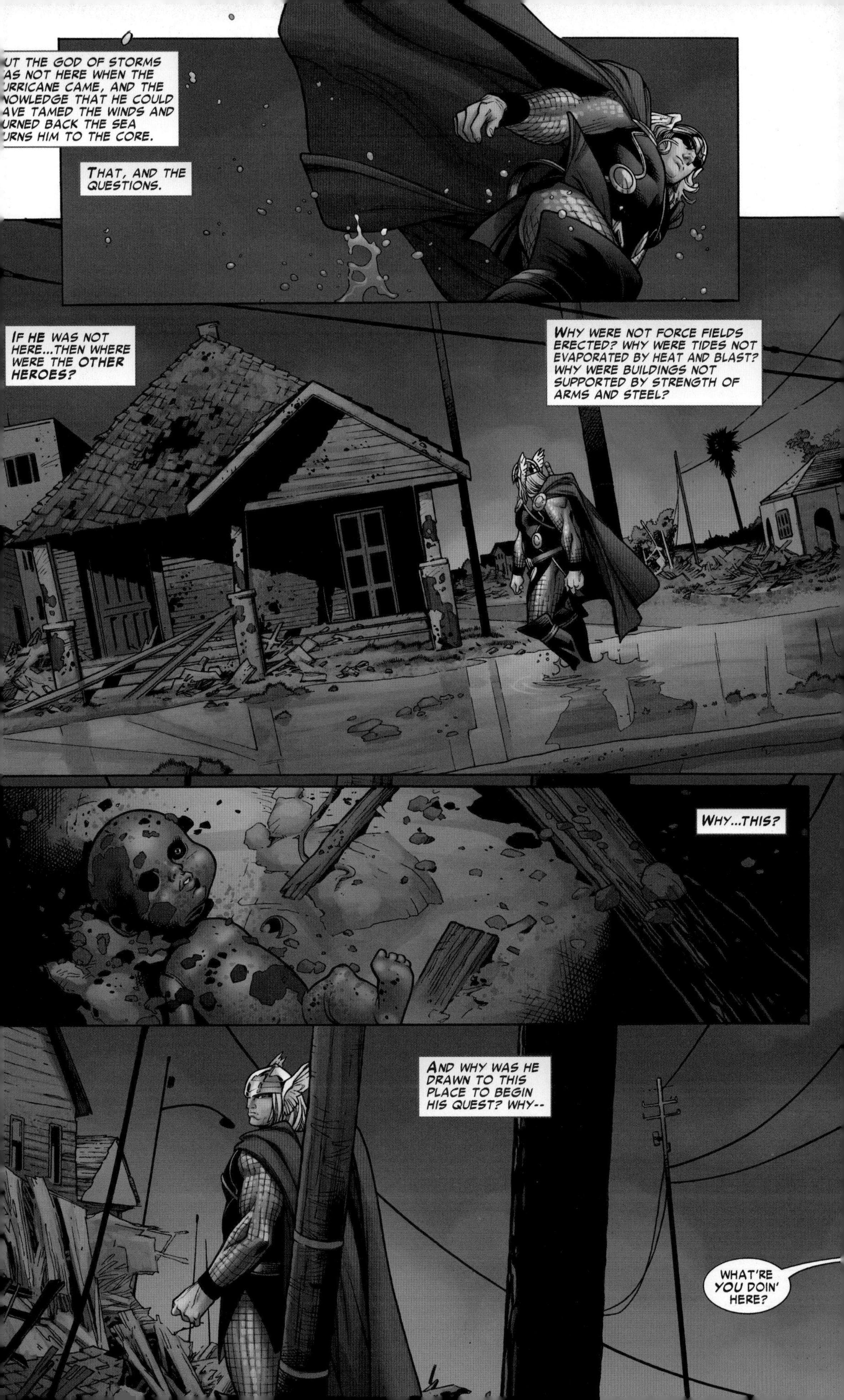
UT THE GOD OF STORMS AS NOT HERE WHEN THE URRICANE CAME, AND THE NOWLEDGE THAT HE COULD AVE TAMED THE WINDS AND URNED BACK THE SEA URNS HIM TO THE CORE.
THAT, AND THE QUESTIONS.
IF HE WAS NOT HERE...THEN WHERE WERE THE OTHER HEROES?
WHY WERE NOT FORCE FIELDS ERECTED? WHY WERE TIDES NOT EVAPORATED BY HEAT AND BLAST? WHY WERE BUILDINGS NOT SUPPORTED BY STRENGTH OF ARMS AND STEEL?
WHY...THIS?
AND WHY WAS HE DRAWN TO THIS PLACE TO BEGIN HIS QUEST? WHY--
WHAT'RE YOU DOIN' HERE?

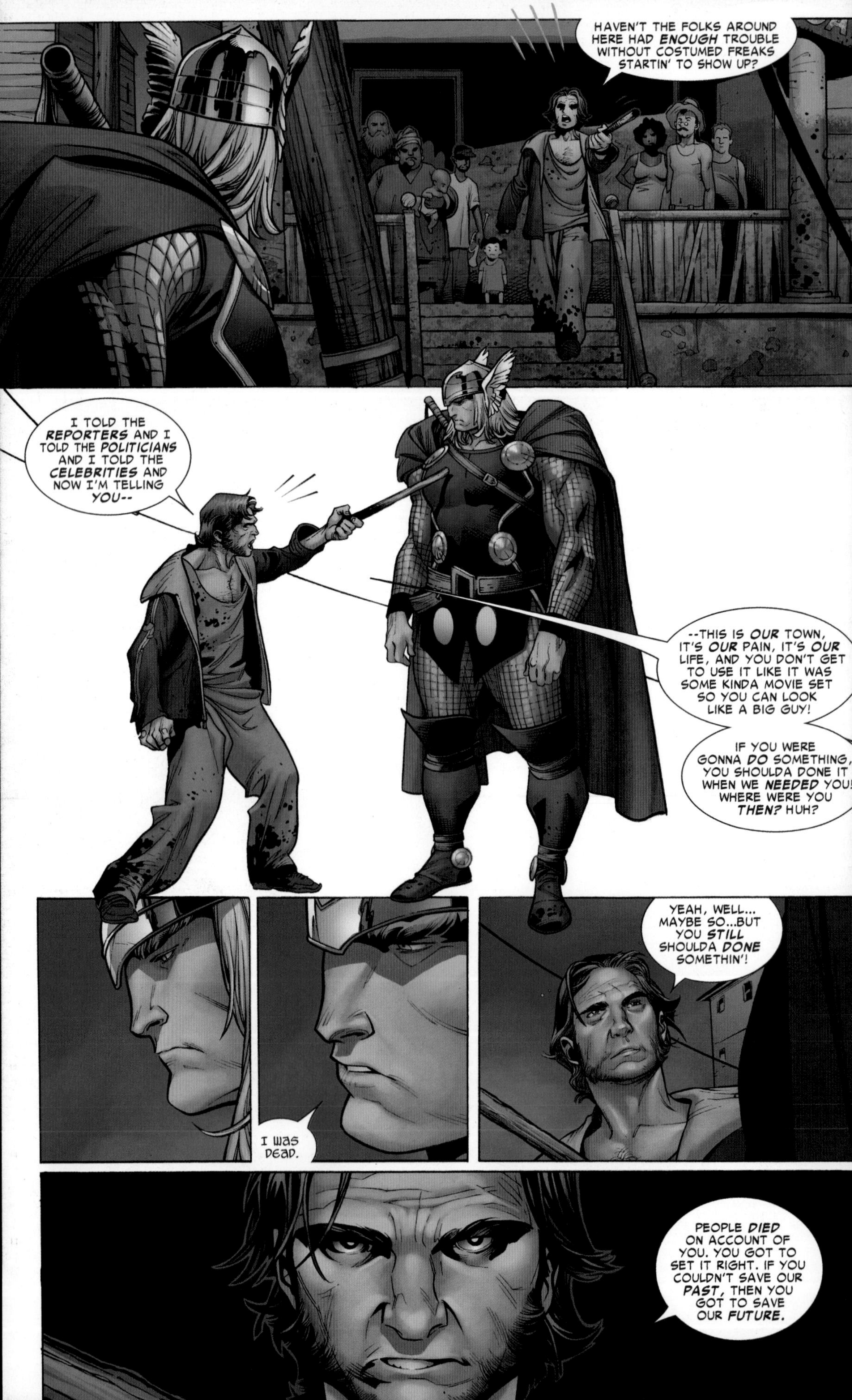
HAVEN'T THE FOLKS AROUND HERE HAD ENOUGH TROUBLE WITHOUT COSTUMED FREAKS STARTIN' TO SHOW UP?
I TOLD THE REPORTERS AND I TOLD THE POLITICIANS AND I TOLD THE CELEBRITIES AND NOW I'M TELLING YOU--
--THIS IS OUR TOWN, IT'S OUR PAIN, IT'S OUR LIFE, AND YOU DON'T GET TO USE IT LIKE IT WAS SOME KINDA MOVIE SET SO YOU CAN LOOK LIKE A BIG GUY!
IF YOU WERE GONNA DO SOMETHING, YOU SHOULDA DONE IT WHEN WE NEEDED YOU! WHERE WERE YOU THEN? HUH?
I WAS DEAD.
YEAH, WELL... MAYBE SO...BUT YOU STILL SHOULDA DONE SOMETHIN'!
PEOPLE DIED ON ACCOUNT OF YOU. YOU GOT TO SET IT RIGHT. IF YOU COULDN'T SAVE OUR PAST, THEN YOU GOT TO SAVE OUR FUTURE.

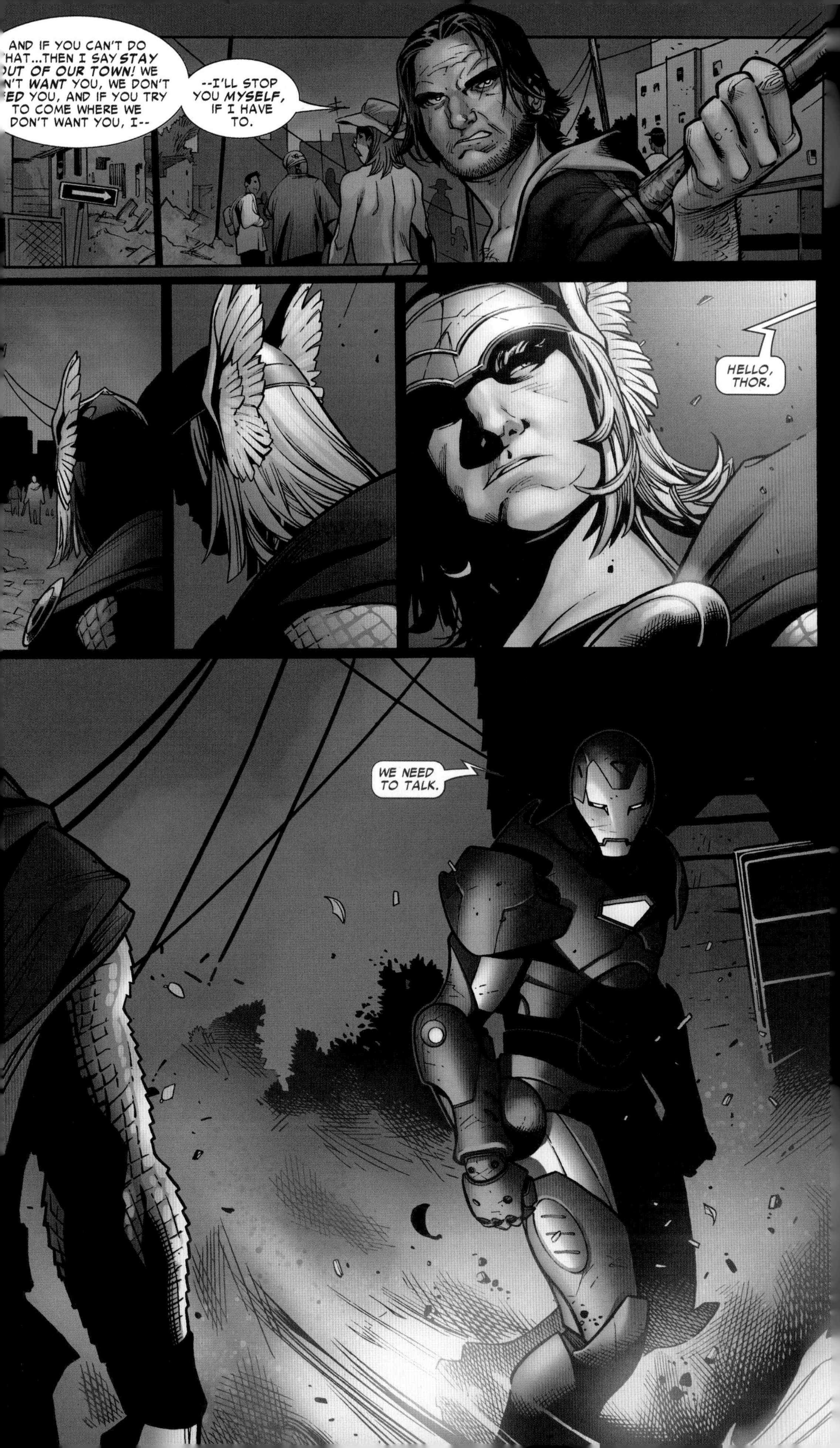
AND IF YOU CAN'T DO HAT...THEN I SAY STAY UT OF OUR TOWN! WE N'T WANT YOU, WE DON'T ED YOU, AND IF YOU TRY TO COME WHERE WE DON'T WANT YOU, I--
--I'LL STOP YOU MYSELF, IF I HAVE TO.
HELLO, THOR.
WE NEED TO TALK.

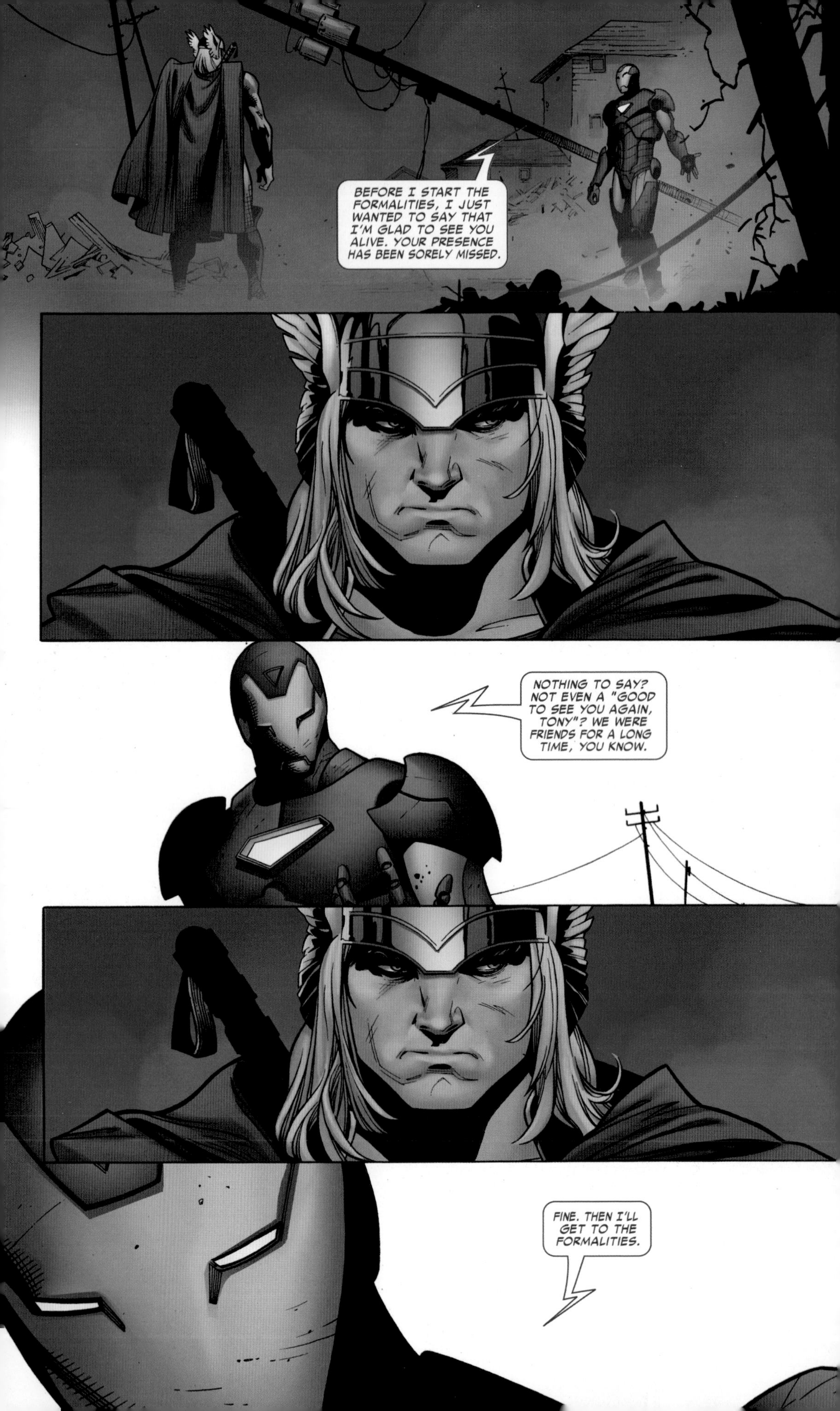
BEFORE I START THE FORMALITIES, I JUST WANTED TO SAY THAT I'M GLAD TO SEE YOU ALIVE. YOUR PRESENCE HAS BEEN SORELY MISSED.
NOTHING TO SAY? NOT EVEN A "GOOD TO SEE YOU AGAIN, TONY"? WE WERE FRIENDS FOR A LONG TIME, YOU KNOW.
FINE. THEN I'LL GET TO THE FORMALITIES.

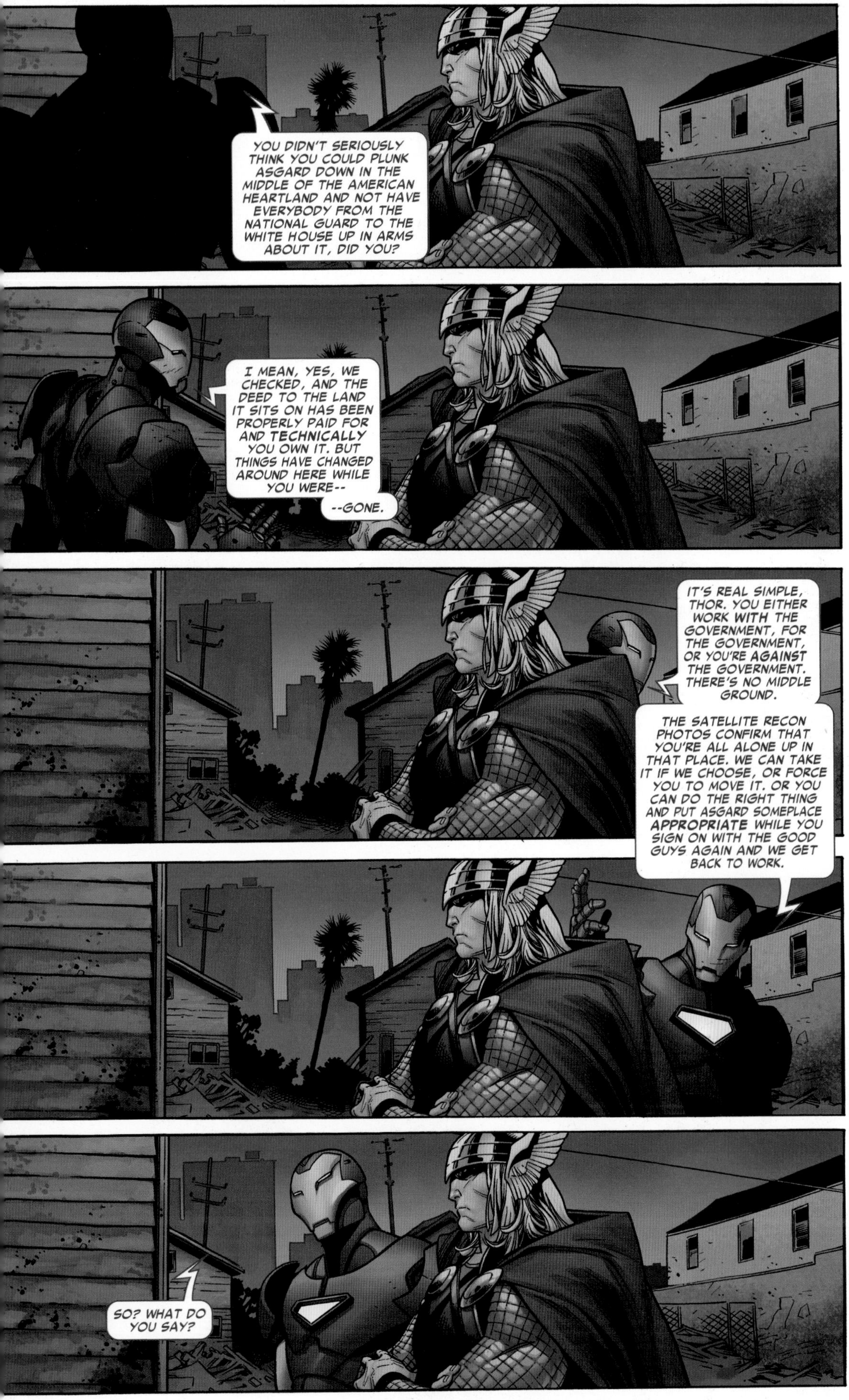
YOU DIDN'T SERIOUSLY THINK YOU COULD PLUNK ASGARD DOWN IN THE MIDDLE OF THE AMERICAN HEARTLAND AND NOT HAVE EVERYBODY FROM THE NATIONAL GUARD TO THE WHITE HOUSE UP IN ARMS ABOUT IT, DID YOU?
I MEAN, YES, WE CHECKED, AND THE DEED TO THE LAND IT SITS ON HAS BEEN PROPERLY PAID FOR AND TECHNICALLY YOU OWN IT. BUT THINGS HAVE CHANGED AROUND HERE WHILE YOU WERE--
--GONE.
IT'S REAL SIMPLE, THOR. YOU EITHER WORK WITH THE GOVERNMENT, FOR THE GOVERNMENT, OR YOU'RE AGAINST THE GOVERNMENT. THERE'S NO MIDDLE GROUND.
THE SATELLITE RECON PHOTOS CONFIRM THAT YOU'RE ALL ALONE UP IN THAT PLACE. WE CAN TAKE IT IF WE CHOOSE, OR FORCE YOU TO MOVE IT. OR YOU CAN DO THE RIGHT THING AND PUT ASGARD SOMEPLACE APPROPRIATE WHILE YOU SIGN ON WITH THE GOOD GUYS AGAIN AND WE GET BACK TO WORK.
SO? WHAT DO YOU SAY?

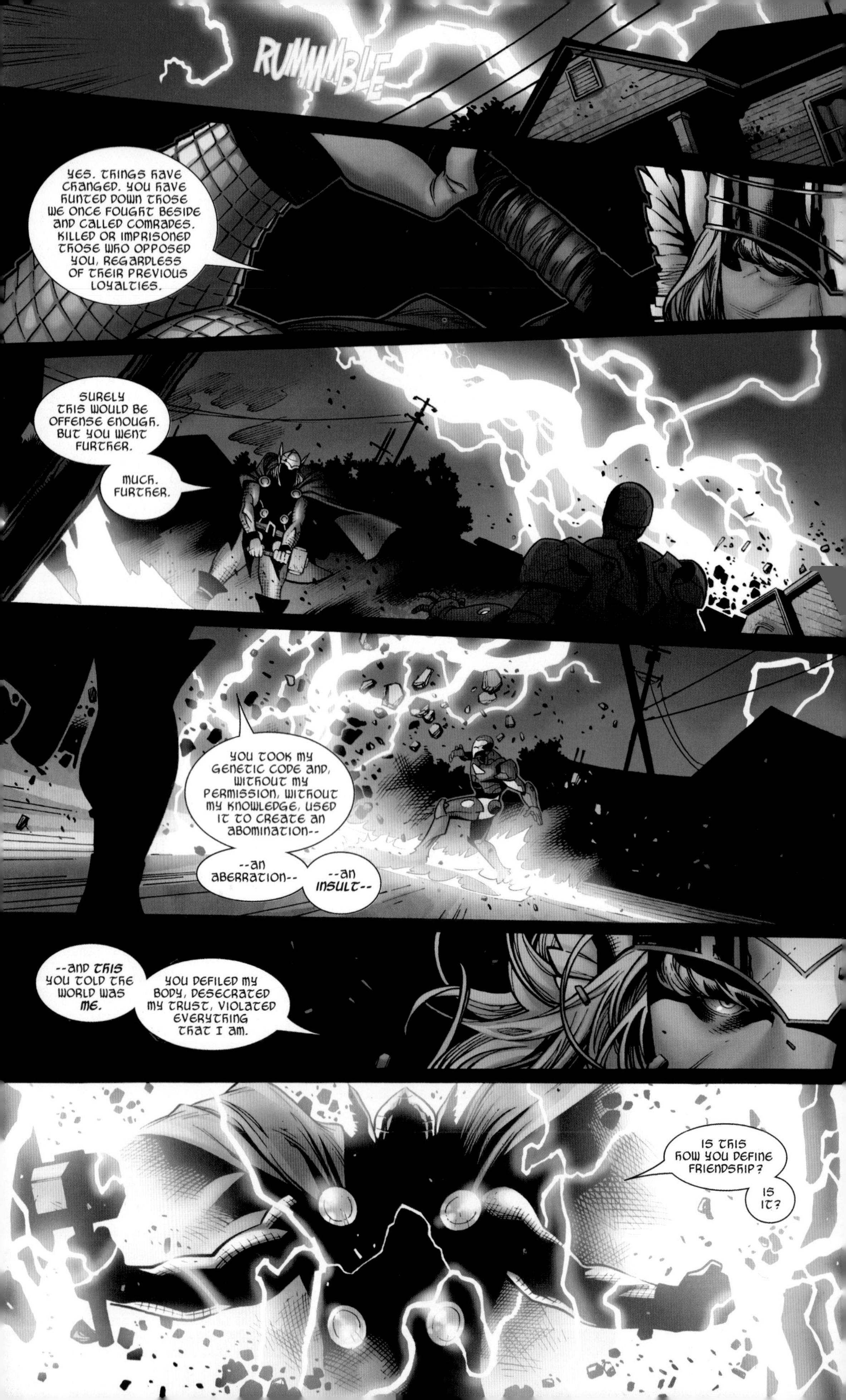
RUMMMBLE
YES. THINGS HAVE CHANGED. YOU HAVE HUNTED DOWN THOSE WE ONCE FOUGHT BESIDE AND CALLED COMRADES. KILLED OR IMPRISONED THOSE WHO OPPOSED YOU, REGARDLESS OF THEIR PREVIOUS LOYALTIES.
SURELY THIS WOULD BE OFFENSE ENOUGH. BUT YOU WENT FURTHER.
MUCH. FURTHER.
YOU TOOK MY GENETIC CODE AND, WITHOUT MY PERMISSION, WITHOUT MY KNOWLEDGE, USED IT TO CREATE AN ABOMINATION--
--AN ABERRATION--
--AN INSULT--
--AND THIS YOU TOLD THE WORLD WAS ME.
YOU DEFILED MY BODY, DESECRATED MY TRUST, VIOLATED EVERYTHING THAT I AM.
IS THIS HOW YOU DEFINE FRIENDSHIP?
IS IT?

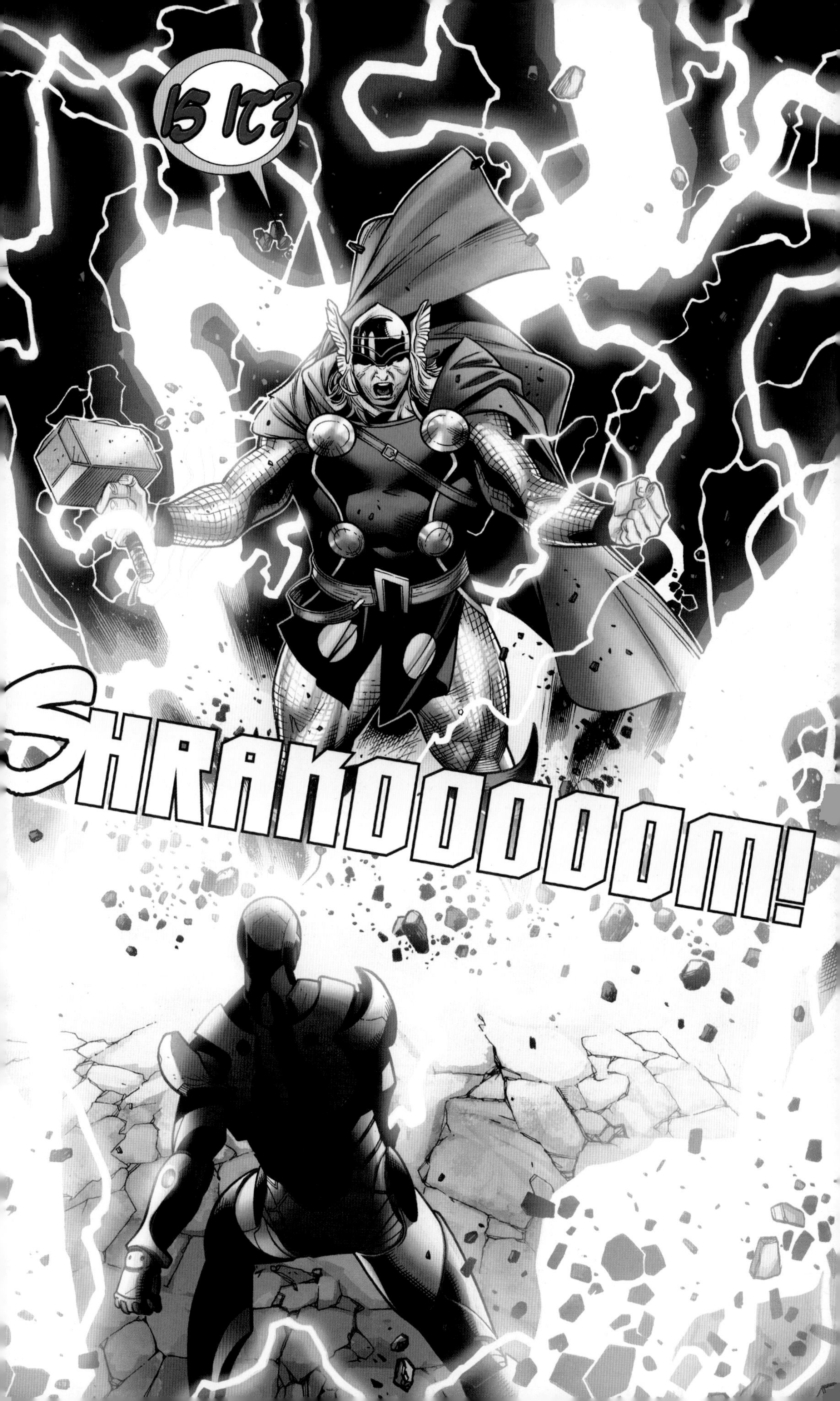
IS IT?
SHRAKOOOOOM!

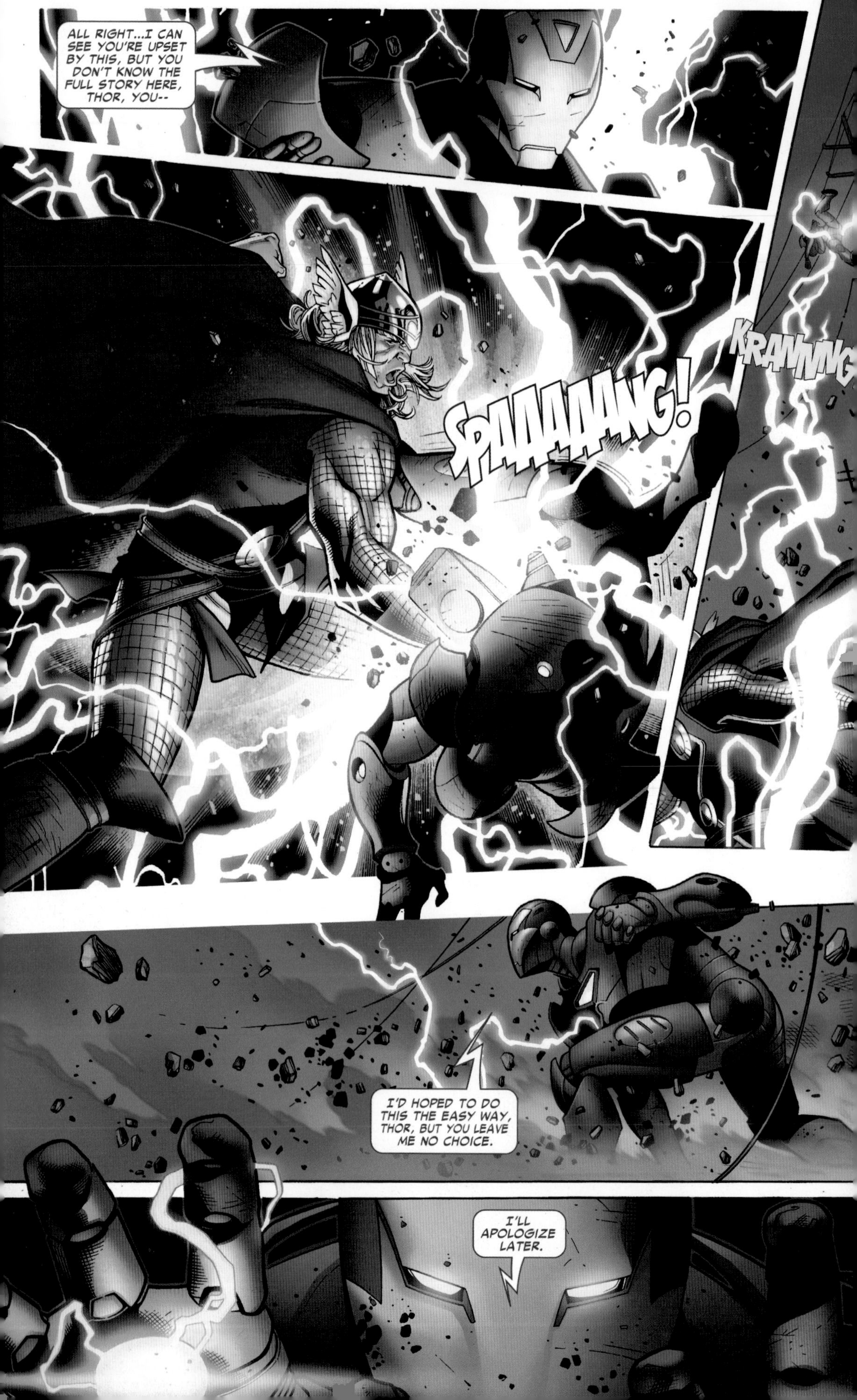
ALL RIGHT...I CAN SEE YOU'RE UPSET BY THIS, BUT YOU DON'T KNOW THE FULL STORY HERE, THOR, YOU--
SPAAAAAANG!
KRANNNG
I'D HOPED TO DO THIS THE EASY WAY, THOR, BUT YOU LEAVE ME NO CHOICE.
I'LL APOLOGIZE LATER.

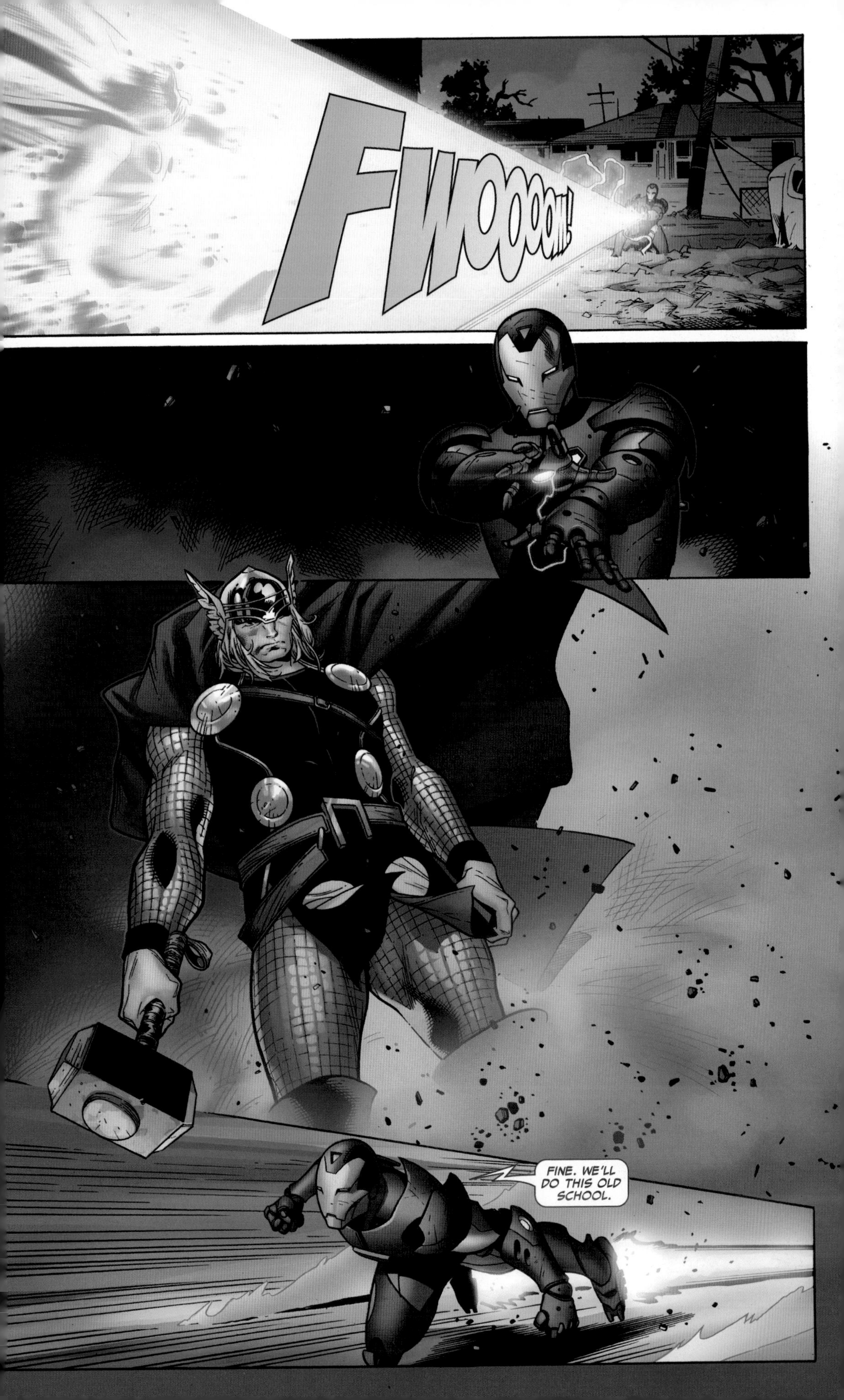
FWOOOOM!
FINE. WE'LL DO THIS OLD SCHOOL.

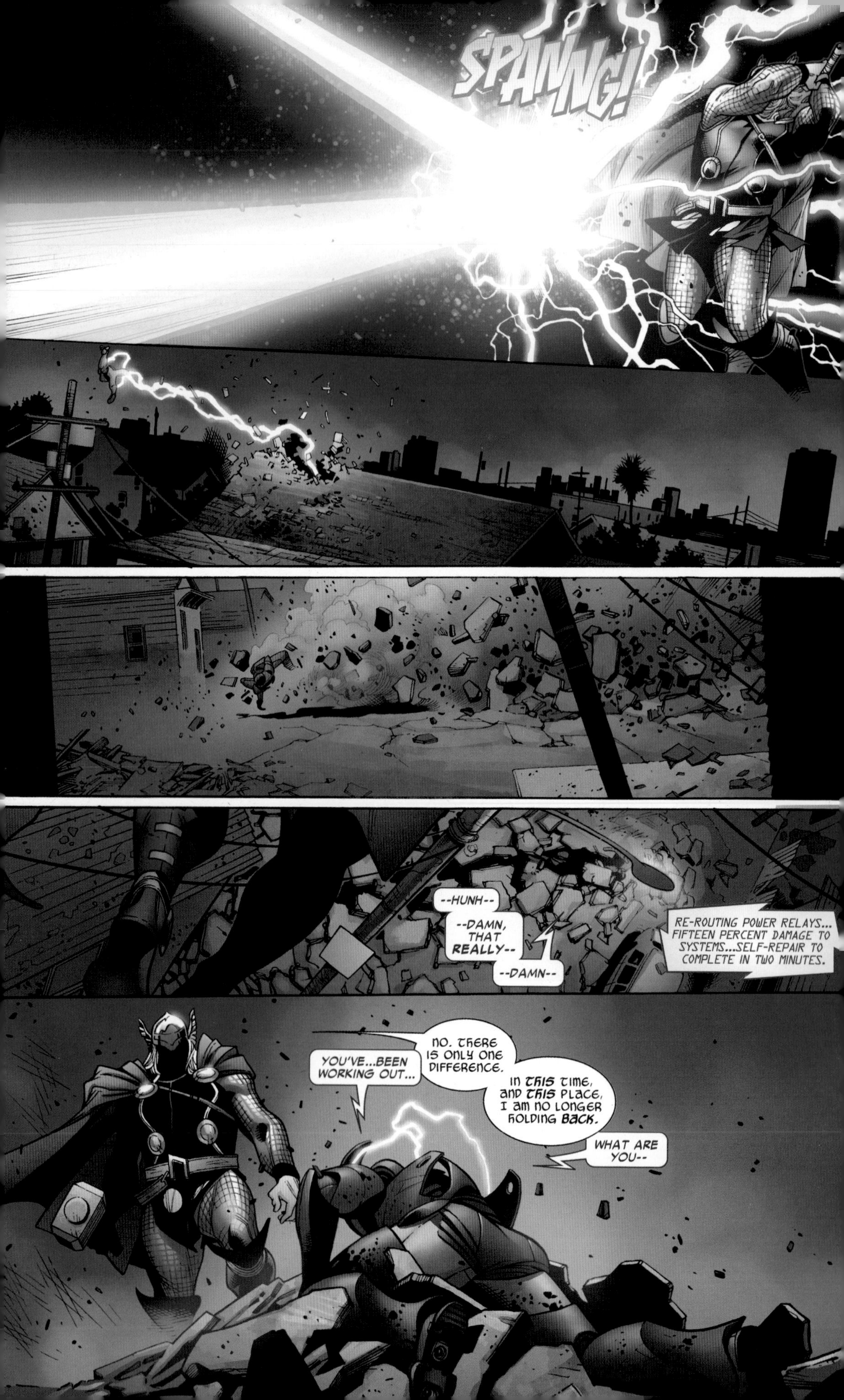
SPANNG!
--HUNH--
--DAMN, THAT REALLY--
--DAMN--
RE-ROUTING POWER RELAYS... FIFTEEN PERCENT DAMAGE TO SYSTEMS...SELF-REPAIR TO COMPLETE IN TWO MINUTES.
YOU'VE...BEEN WORKING OUT...
NO. THERE IS ONLY ONE DIFFERENCE.
IN THIS TIME, AND THIS PLACE, I AM NO LONGER HOLDING BACK.
WHAT ARE YOU--

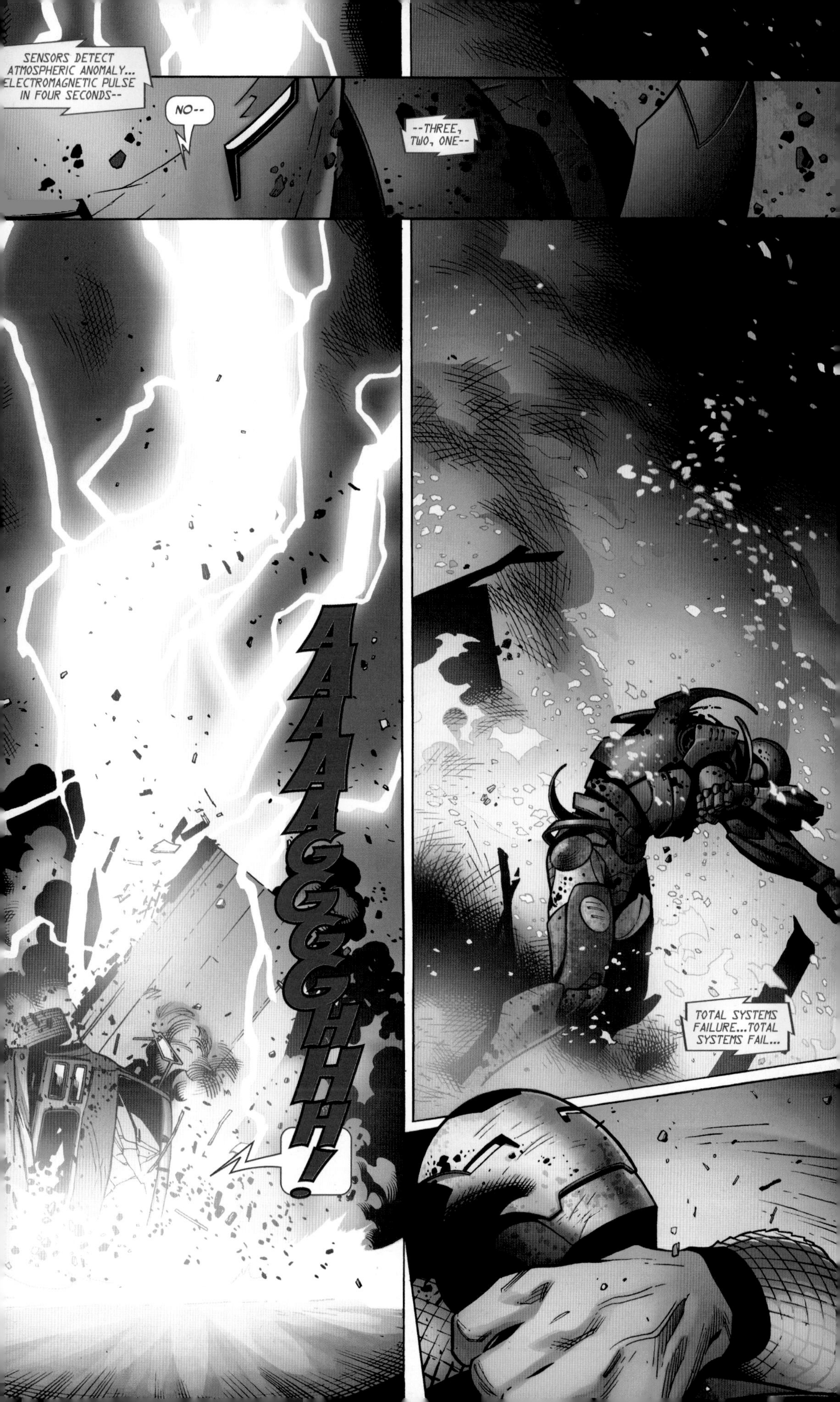
SENSORS DETECT ATMOSPHERIC ANOMALY... ELECTROMAGNETIC PULSE IN FOUR SECONDS--
NO--
--THREE, TWO, ONE--
AAAAAAGGGGHHHH!
TOTAL SYSTEMS FAILURE...TOTAL SYSTEMS FAIL...

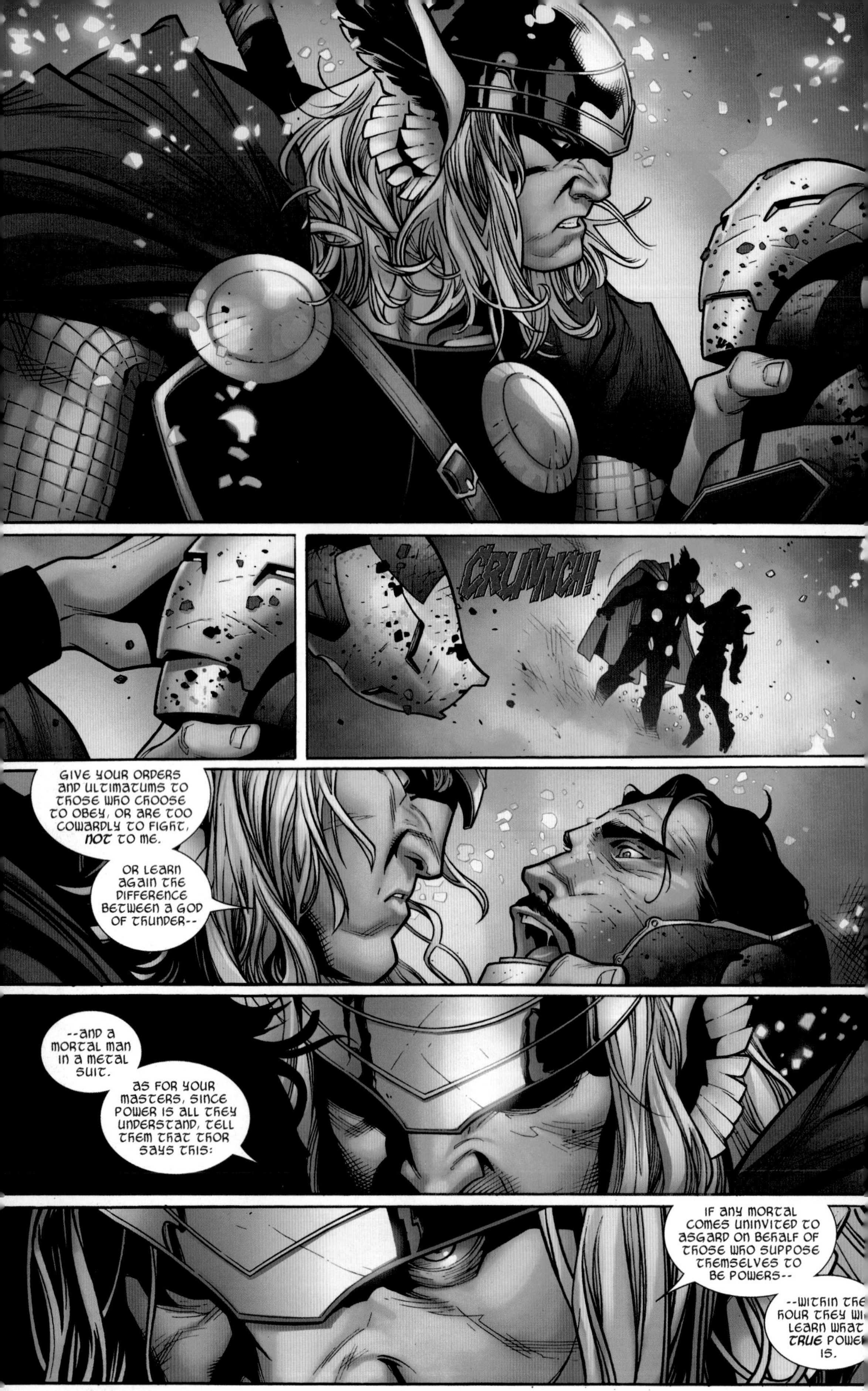
CRUNNCH!
GIVE YOUR ORDERS AND ULTIMATUMS TO THOSE WHO CHOOSE TO OBEY, OR ARE TOO COWARDLY TO FIGHT, NOT TO ME.
OR LEARN AGAIN THE DIFFERENCE BETWEEN A GOD OF THUNDER--
--AND A MORTAL MAN IN A METAL SUIT.
AS FOR YOUR MASTERS, SINCE POWER IS ALL THEY UNDERSTAND, TELL THEM THAT THOR SAYS THIS:
IF ANY MORTAL COMES UNINVITED TO ASGARD ON BEHALF OF THOSE WHO SUPPOSE THEMSELVES TO BE POWERS--
--WITHIN THE HOUR THEY WI LEARN WHAT TRUE POWE IS.

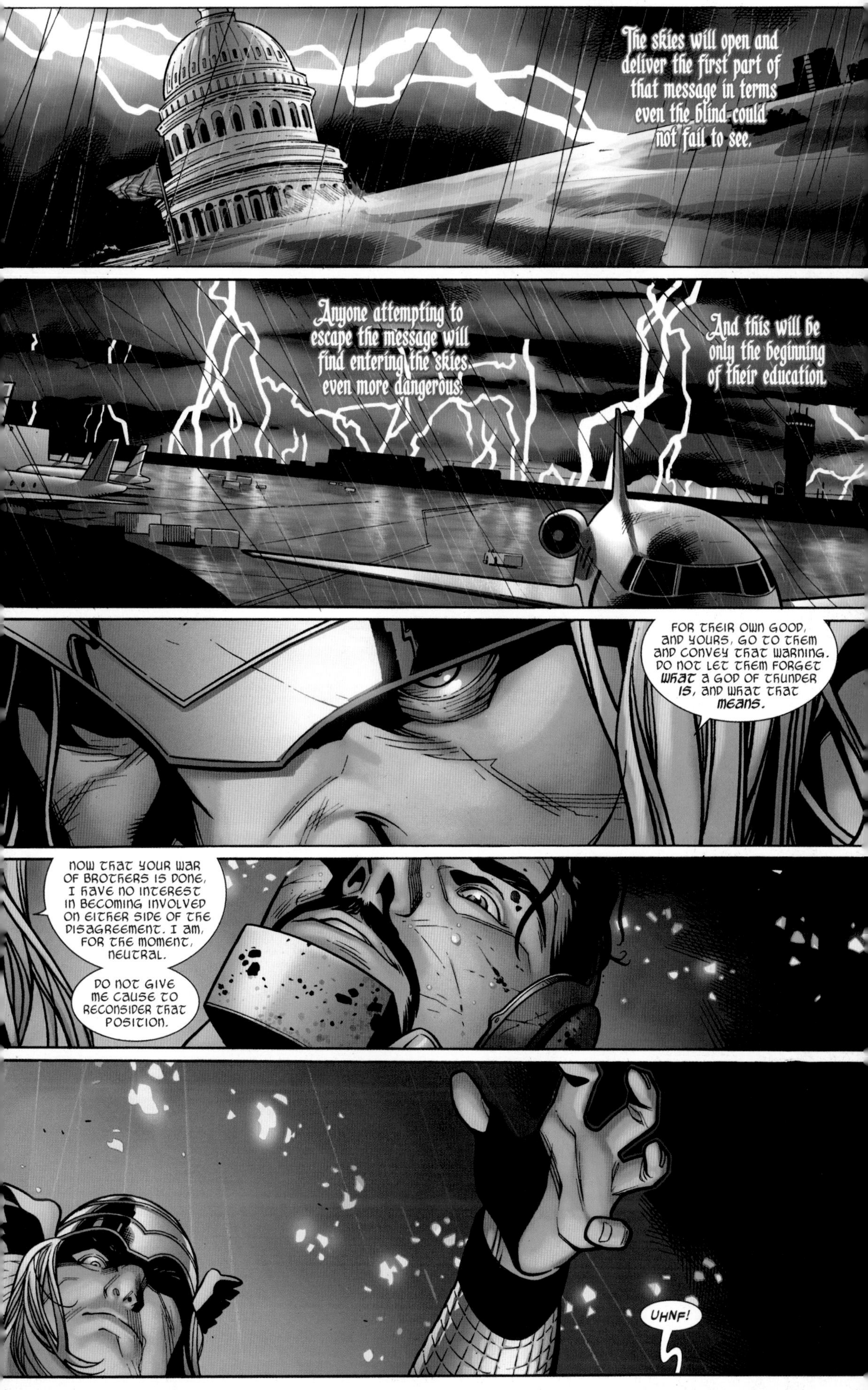

The skies will open and deliver the first part of that message in terms even the blind could not fail to see.
Anyone attempting to escape the message will find entering the skies even more dangerous.
And this will be only the beginning of their education.
FOR THEIR OWN GOOD, AND YOURS, GO TO THEM AND CONVEY THAT WARNING. DO NOT LET THEM FORGET WHAT A GOD OF THUNDER IS, AND WHAT THAT MEANS.
NOW THAT YOUR WAR OF BROTHERS IS DONE, I HAVE NO INTEREST IN BECOMING INVOLVED ON EITHER SIDE OF THE DISAGREEMENT. I AM, FOR THE MOMENT, NEUTRAL.
DO NOT GIVE ME CAUSE TO RECONSIDER THAT POSITION.
UHNF!

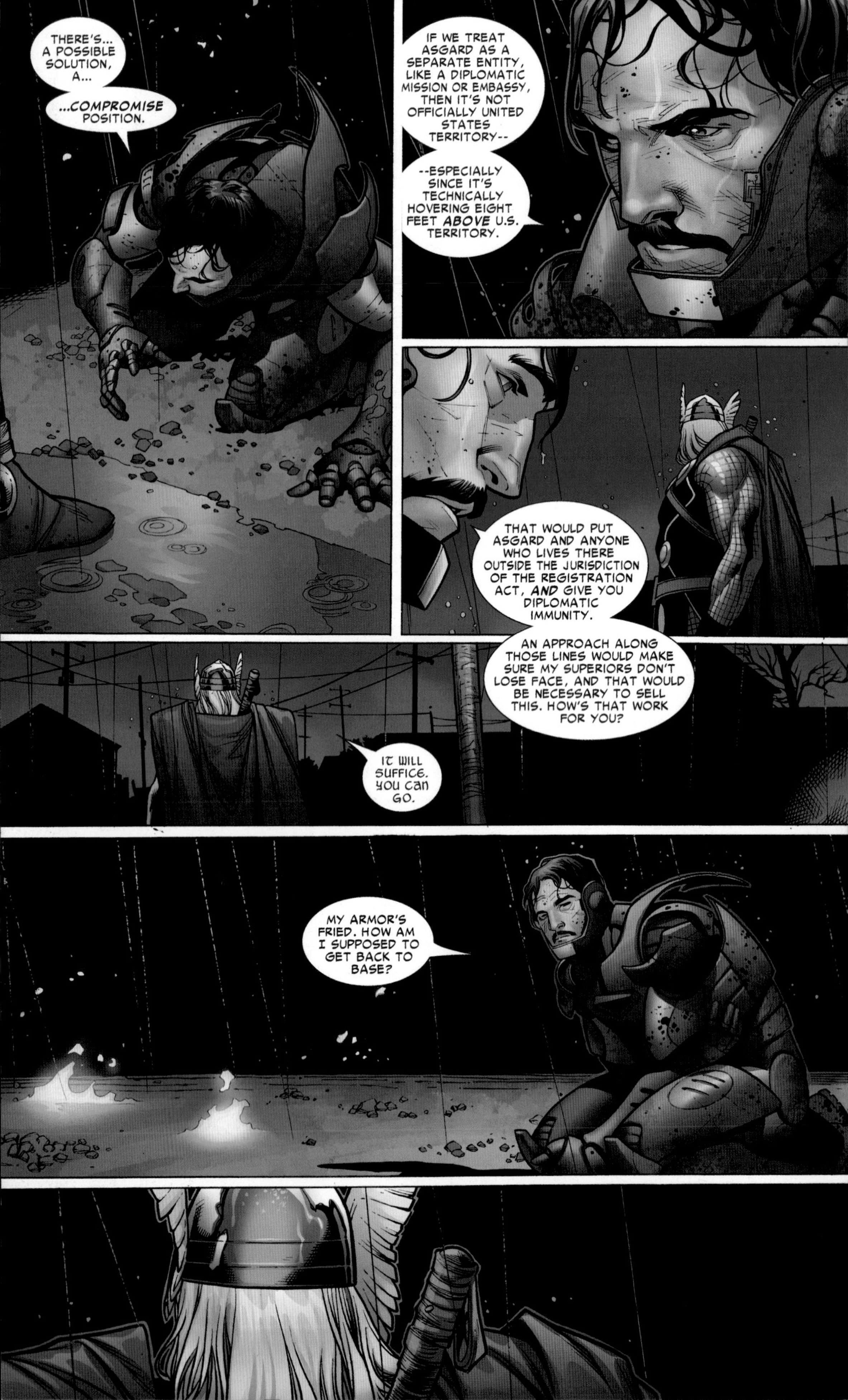
THERE'S... A POSSIBLE SOLUTION, A...
...COMPROMISE POSITION.
IF WE TREAT ASGARD AS A SEPARATE ENTITY, LIKE A DIPLOMATIC MISSION OR EMBASSY, THEN IT'S NOT OFFICIALLY UNITED STATES TERRITORY--
--ESPECIALLY SINCE IT'S TECHNICALLY HOVERING EIGHT FEET ABOVE U.S. TERRITORY.
THAT WOULD PUT ASGARD AND ANYONE WHO LIVES THERE OUTSIDE THE JURISDICTION OF THE REGISTRATION ACT, AND GIVE YOU DIPLOMATIC IMMUNITY.
AN APPROACH ALONG THOSE LINES WOULD MAKE SURE MY SUPERIORS DON'T LOSE FACE, AND THAT WOULD BE NECESSARY TO SELL THIS. HOW'S THAT WORK FOR YOU?
IT WILL SUFFICE. YOU CAN GO.
MY ARMOR'S FRIED. HOW AM I SUPPOSED TO GET BACK TO BASE?

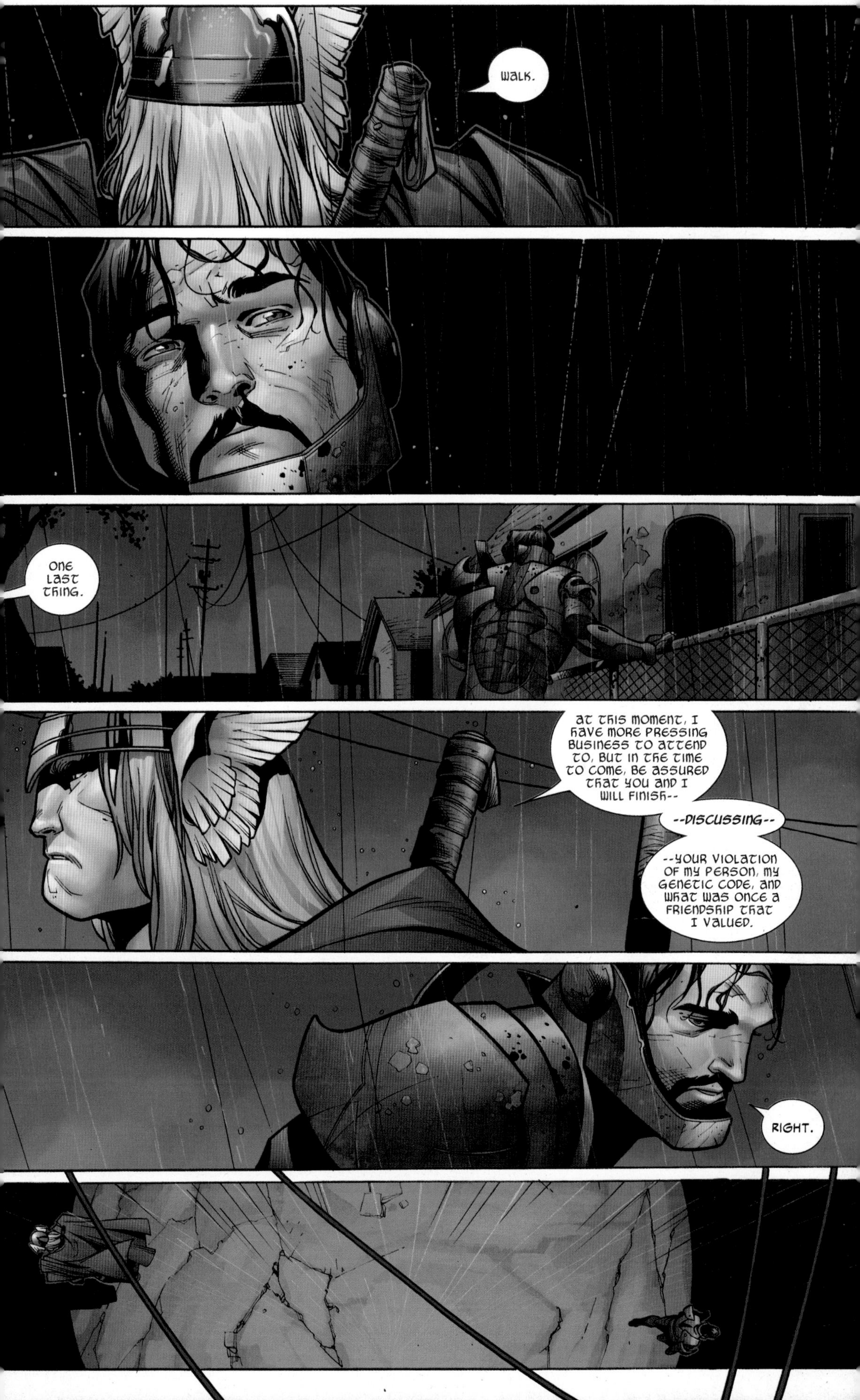

WALK.
ONE LAST THING.
AT THIS MOMENT, I HAVE MORE PRESSING BUSINESS TO ATTEND TO, BUT IN THE TIME TO COME, BE ASSURED THAT YOU AND I WILL FINISH--
--DISCUSSING--
--YOUR VIOLATION OF MY PERSON, MY GENETIC CODE, AND WHAT WAS ONCE A FRIENDSHIP THAT I VALUED.
RIGHT.

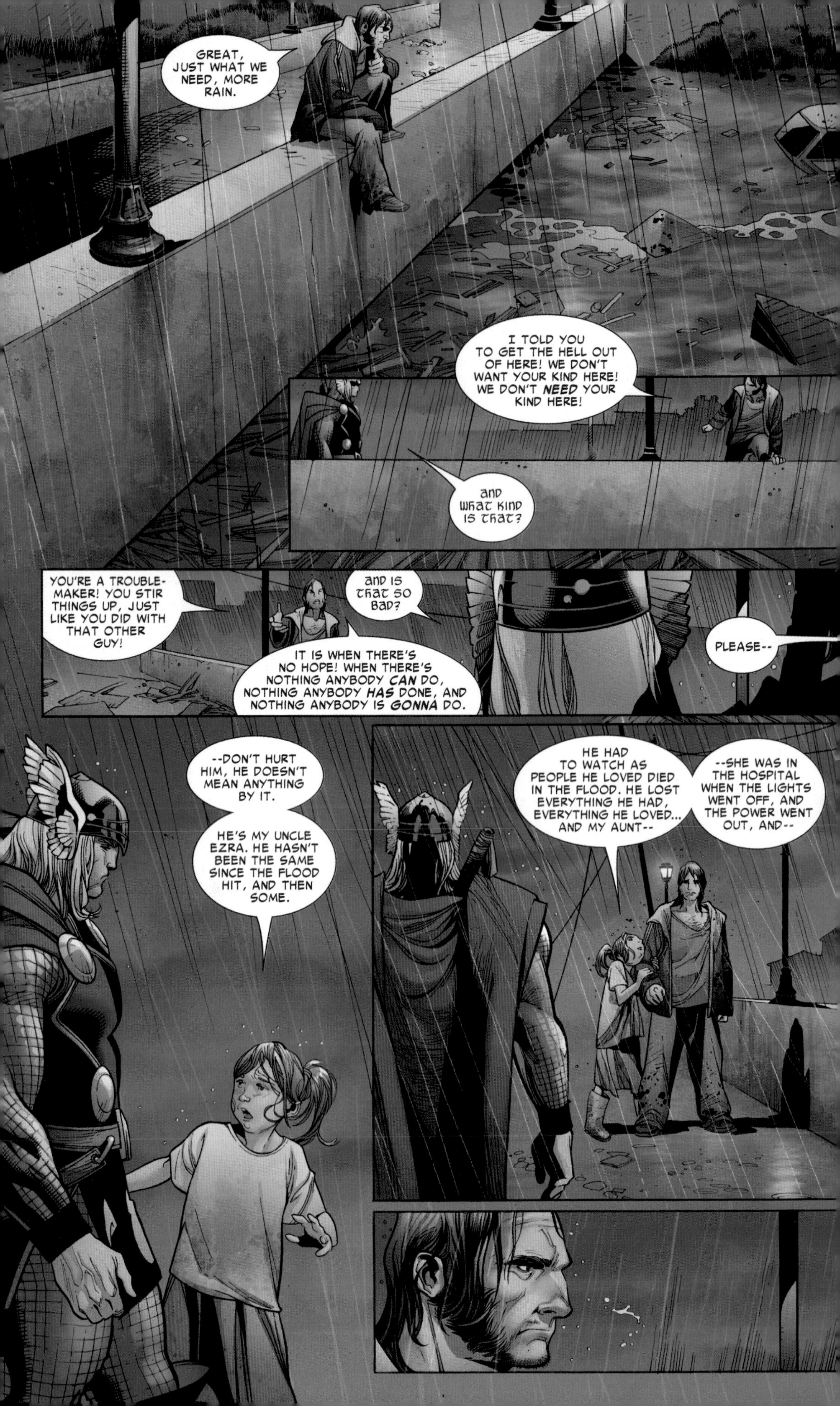
GREAT, JUST WHAT WE NEED, MORE RAIN.
I TOLD YOU TO GET THE HELL OUT OF HERE! WE DON'T WANT YOUR KIND HERE! WE DON'T NEED YOUR KIND HERE!
AND WHAT KIND IS THAT?
YOU'RE A TROUBLE-MAKER! YOU STIR THINGS UP, JUST LIKE YOU DID WITH THAT OTHER GUY!
AND IS THAT SO BAD?
IT IS WHEN THERE'S NO HOPE! WHEN THERE'S NOTHING ANYBODY CAN DO, NOTHING ANYBODY HAS DONE, AND NOTHING ANYBODY IS GONNA DO.
PLEASE--
--DON'T HURT HIM, HE DOESN'T MEAN ANYTHING BY IT.
HE'S MY UNCLE EZRA. HE HASN'T BEEN THE SAME SINCE THE FLOOD HIT, AND THEN SOME.
HE HAD TO WATCH AS PEOPLE HE LOVED DIED IN THE FLOOD. HE LOST EVERYTHING HE HAD, EVERYTHING HE LOVED... AND MY AUNT--
--SHE WAS IN THE HOSPITAL WHEN THE LIGHTS WENT OFF, AND THE POWER WENT OUT, AND--

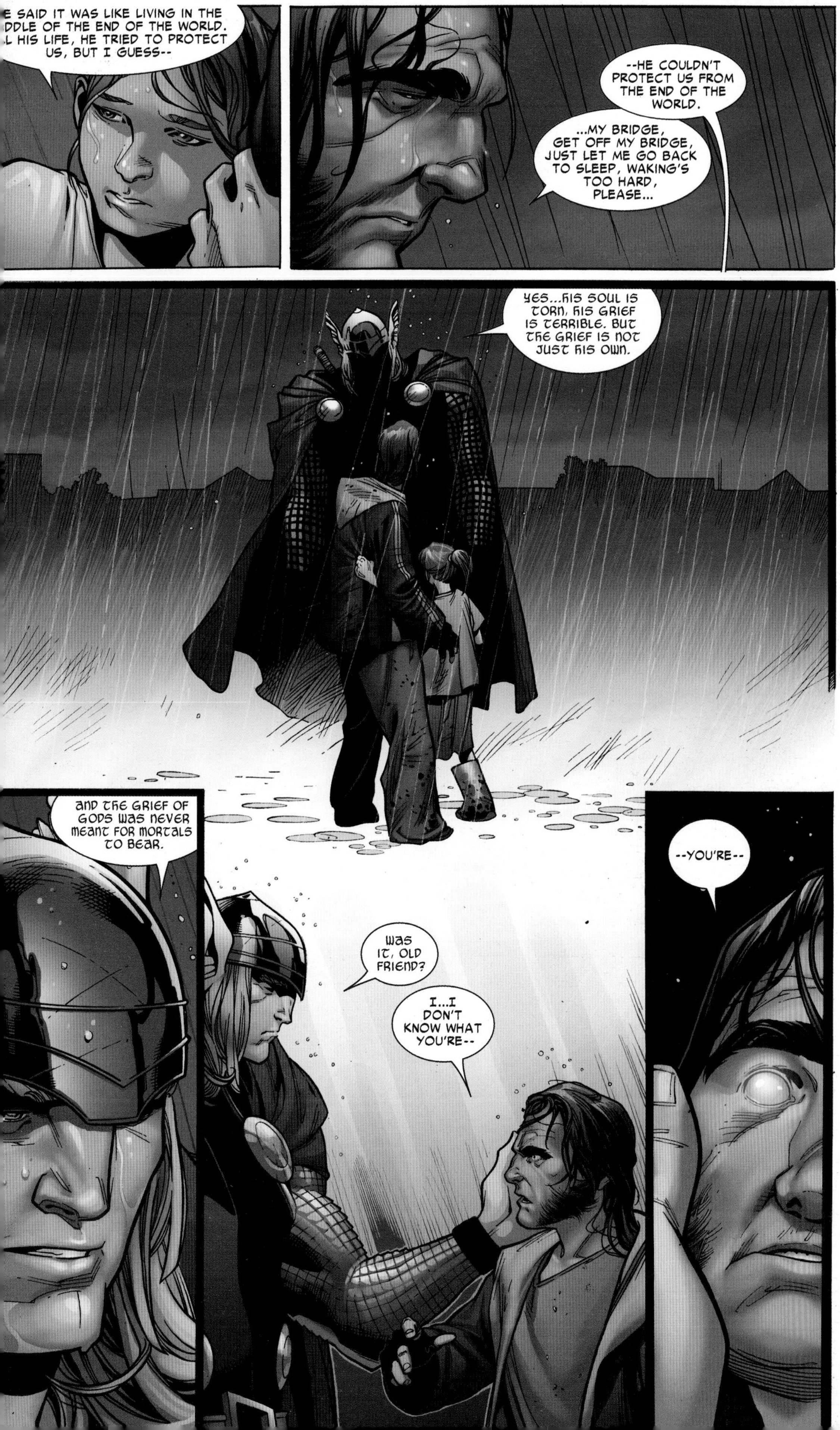
E SAID IT WAS LIKE LIVING IN THE DDLE OF THE END OF THE WORLD. L HIS LIFE, HE TRIED TO PROTECT US, BUT I GUESS--
--HE COULDN'T PROTECT US FROM THE END OF THE WORLD.
...MY BRIDGE, GET OFF MY BRIDGE, JUST LET ME GO BACK TO SLEEP, WAKING'S TOO HARD, PLEASE...
YES...HIS SOUL IS TORN, HIS GRIEF IS TERRIBLE. BUT THE GRIEF IS NOT JUST HIS OWN.
AND THE GRIEF OF GODS WAS NEVER MEANT FOR MORTALS TO BEAR.
WAS IT, OLD FRIEND?
I...I DON'T KNOW WHAT YOU'RE--
--YOU'RE--

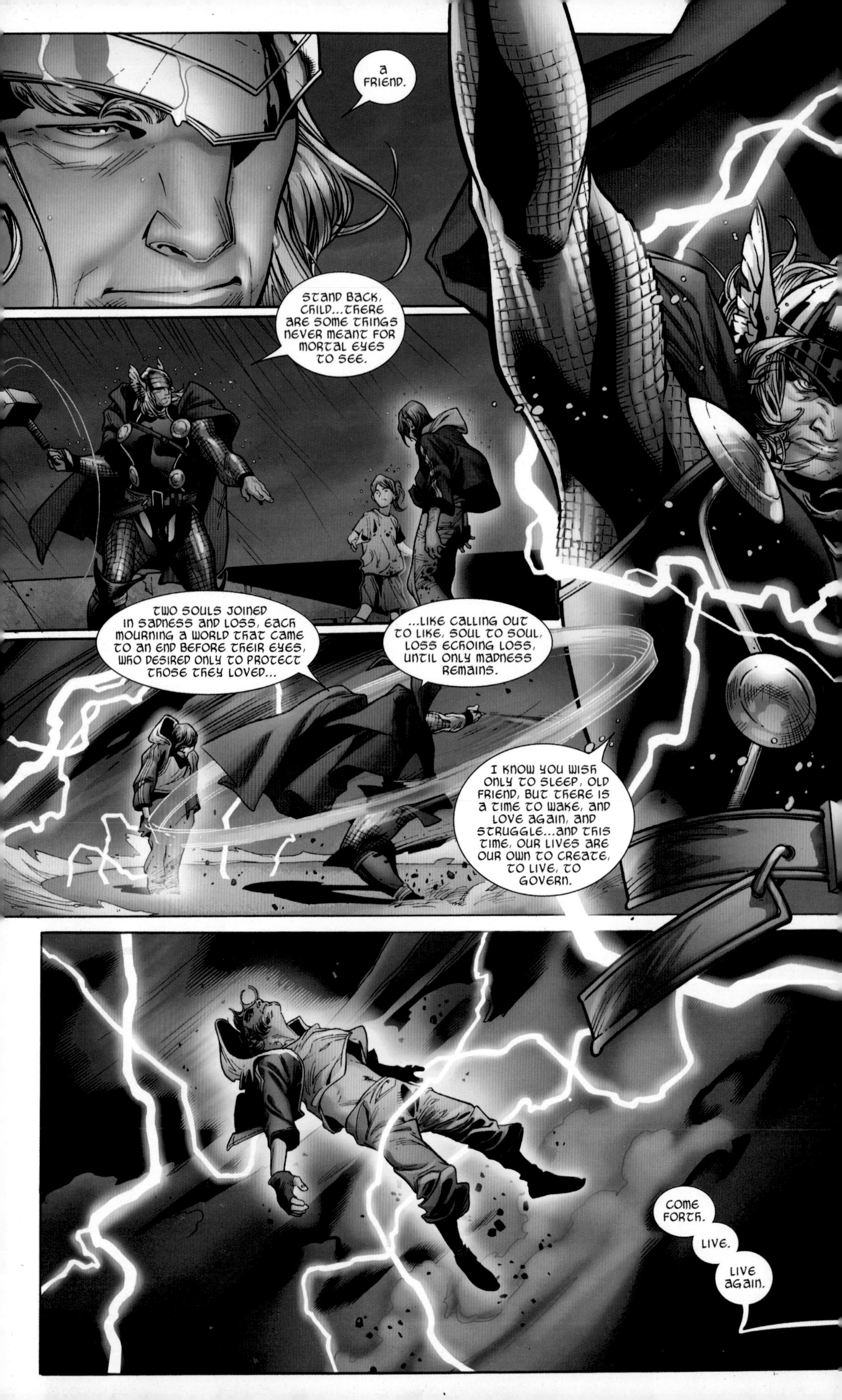
A FRIEND.
STAND BACK, CHILD...THERE ARE SOME THINGS NEVER MEANT FOR MORTAL EYES TO SEE.
TWO SOULS JOINED IN SADNESS AND LOSS, EACH MOURNING A WORLD THAT CAME TO AN END BEFORE THEIR EYES, WHO DESIRED ONLY TO PROTECT THOSE THEY LOVED...
...LIKE CALLING OUT TO LIKE, SOUL TO SOUL, LOSS ECHOING LOSS, UNTIL ONLY MADNESS REMAINS.
I KNOW YOU WISH ONLY TO SLEEP, OLD FRIEND, BUT THERE IS A TIME TO WAKE, AND LOVE AGAIN, AND STRUGGLE...AND THIS TIME, OUR LIVES ARE OUR OWN TO CREATE, TO LIVE, TO GOVERN.
COME FORTH.
LIVE.
LIVE AGAIN.

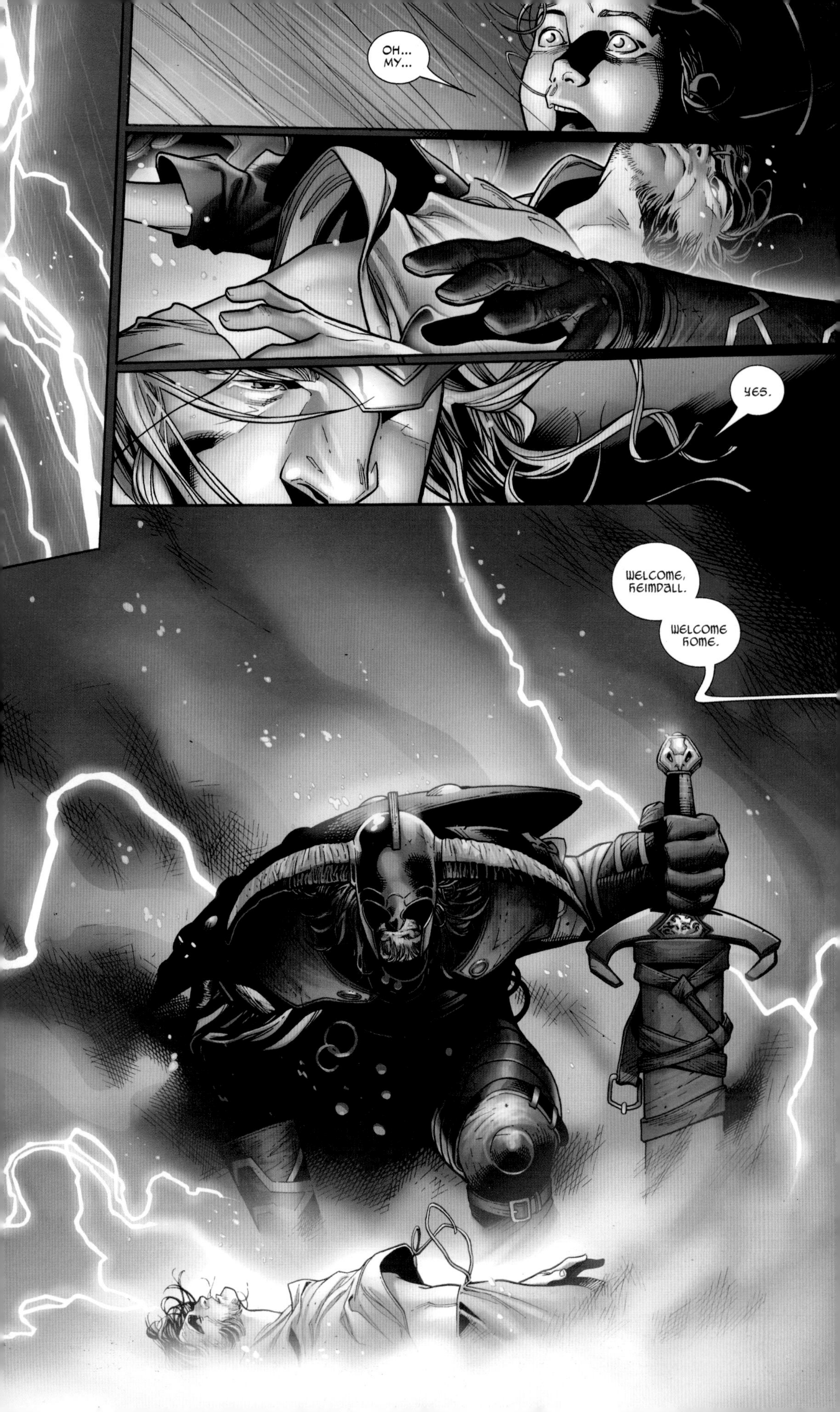
OH... MY...
YES.
WELCOME, HEIMDALL.
WELCOME HOME.

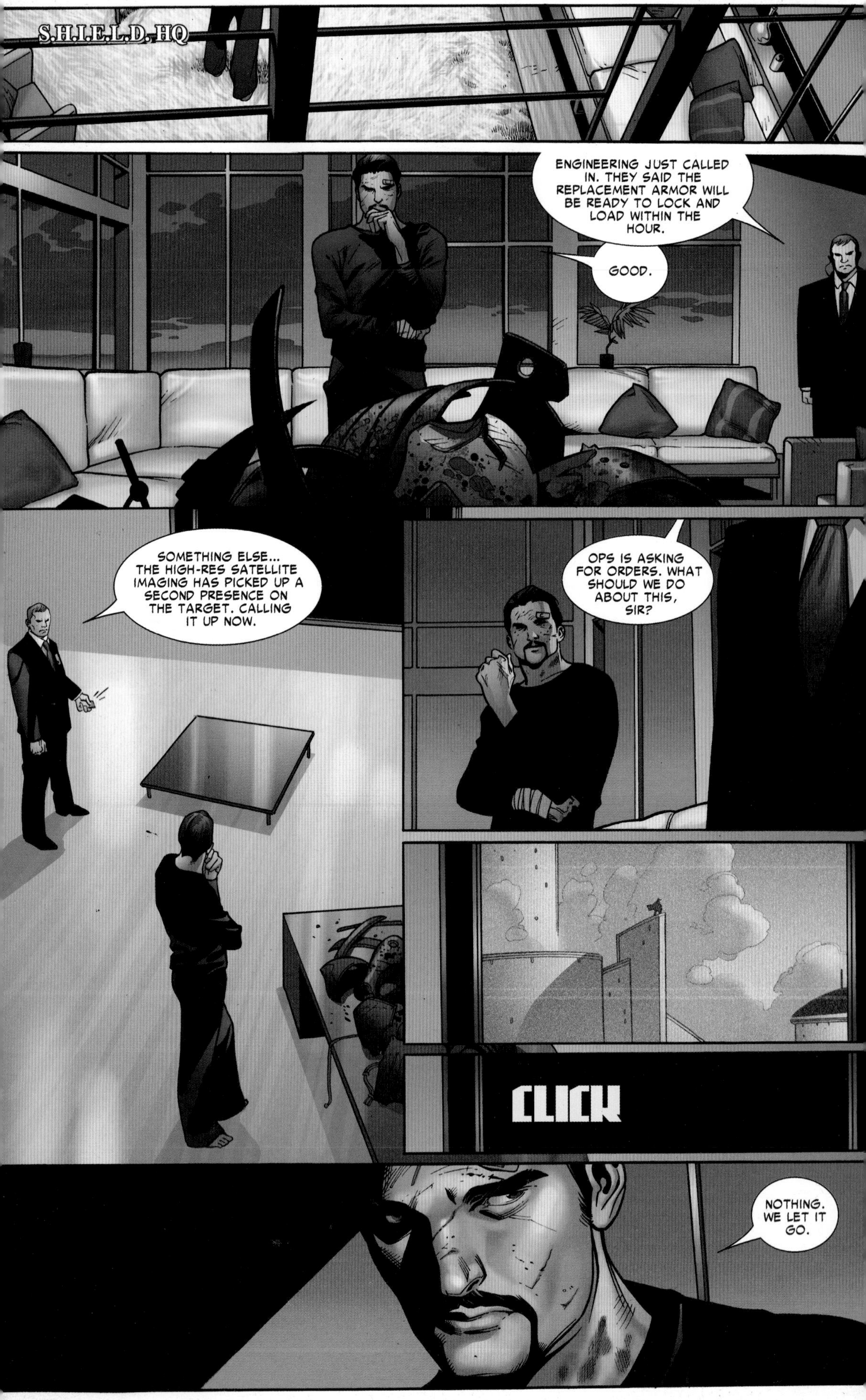
S.H.I.E.L.D. HQ
ENGINEERING JUST CALLED IN. THEY SAID THE REPLACEMENT ARMOR WILL BE READY TO LOCK AND LOAD WITHIN THE HOUR.
GOOD.
SOMETHING ELSE... THE HIGH-RES SATELLITE IMAGING HAS PICKED UP A SECOND PRESENCE ON THE TARGET. CALLING IT UP NOW.
OPS IS ASKING FOR ORDERS. WHAT SHOULD WE DO ABOUT THIS, SIR?
CLICK
NOTHING. WE LET IT GO.

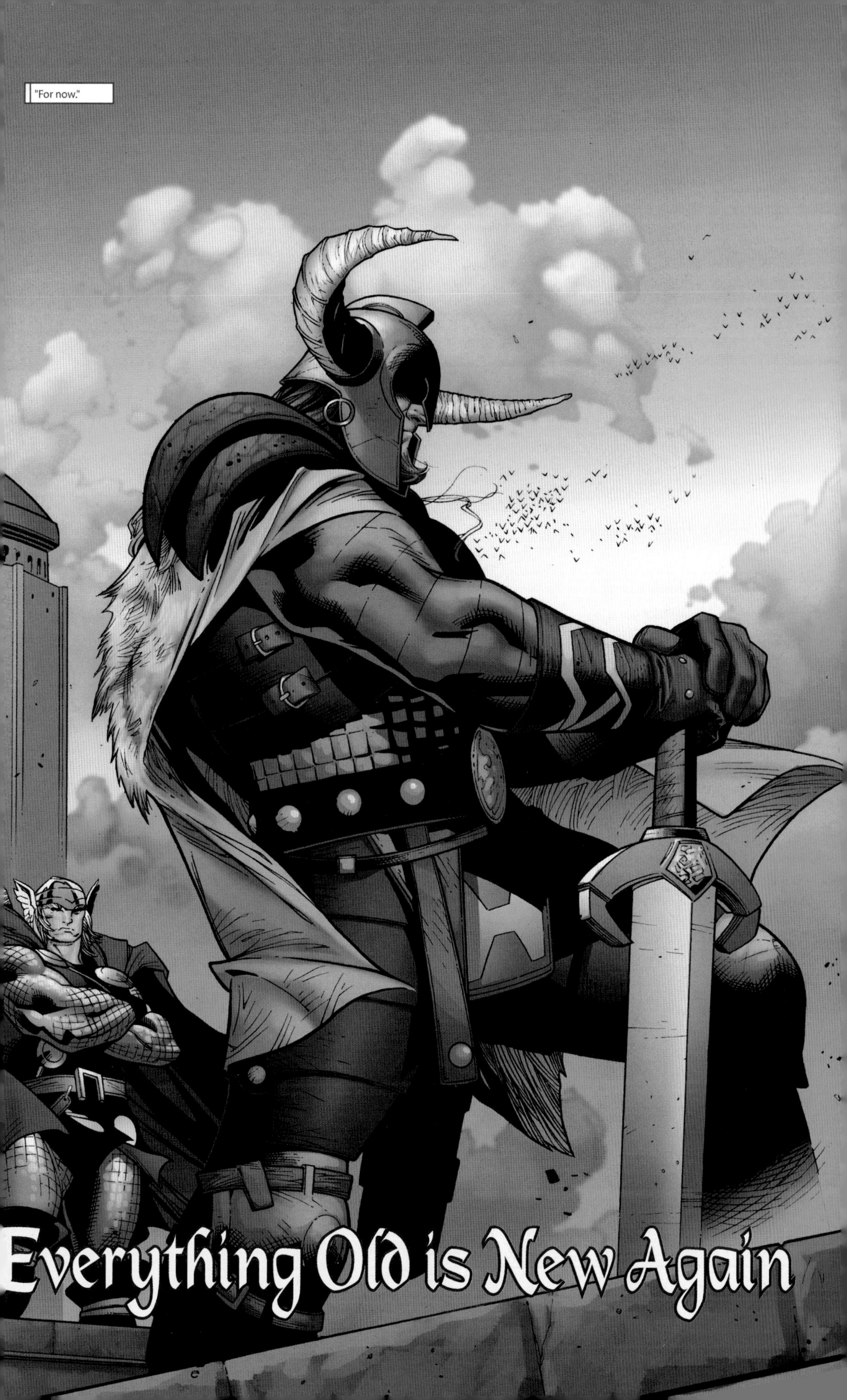
"For now."
Everything Old is New Again

THOR

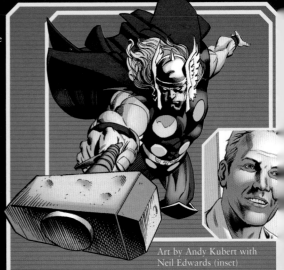

Art by Andy Kubert with Neil Edwards (inset)

TORY: Thor is one of several powerful ancient beings who
ll in a magical realm called Asgard. Through history, these
gs have been revered and worshiped as gods. Ages ago,
n, lord of the Asgardian gods, desired a child who would one
exceed him in power. Odin wooed Gaea, the earth goddess,
from their union Thor was born in a small cave in Norway
Earth. Odin took him to be raised in Asgard by his wife,
ga.

he young Thor grew up alongside his adopted brother Loki,
trickster, who was always jealous of his more favoured
ng. Thor grew in power and popularity and on his eighth
nday, Odin had the hammer Mjolnir created for him,
nanting it with powerful magic. Odin decreed that Mjolnir
ld be presented to Thor when his son had been proven a
thy warrior. After spending the next eight years training
performing heroic deeds, Thor was given the hammer and
ared the greatest warrior in Asgard.

While Thor continued to engage in many heroic battles and
entures through the years, he grew headstrong and proud.
one occasion, Thor broke a truce between the Asgardians
their enemies, the brutal Frost Giants, nearly starting a war.
each his son a lesson in humility, Odin sent Thor to Earth
he mortal body of a crippled medical student, Donald Blake.
ped of his hammer, his powers and memories of being an
ardian, Thor, as Blake, graduated medical school with top
ors, gained a reputation as a caring family doctor and a
iant surgeon, and opened a private practice in New York
. He worked beside a caring and skillful nurse, Jane Foster,
the two fell in love.

fter 10 years on Earth, Blake received a subconscious
lding from Odin to vacation in Norway where alien Kronans
e preparing to invade Earth. Fleeing into a cave (which,
eknownst to him, was also his birthplace) Blake discovered
in walking cane in a secret chamber. When Blake struck
cane against a boulder, he transformed into Thor while the
became Mjolnir. Thor fought against the Kronans and their
sion was thwarted. Tapping the ground with Mjolnir, Thor
able to transform back into Don Blake, holding the simple
den cane once again.

lake returned to New York, using his secret identity of
r to fight crime, defend Earth and contend with the jealous
hateful Loki, who plagued Thor with many devious tricks
outright confrontation. One such trick led Thor and other
es, including Ant-Man (Hank Pym), the Wasp (Janet van
e), and Iron Man (Tony Stark) to fight the Hulk (Bruce
ner). Learning of Loki's manipulations, the heroes, along
n the Hulk, bested Loki and agreed to continue their
nership, forming the Avengers.

While Thor faced many struggles as an Avenger, his personal
as a human was also tumultuous. Despite the sincere
between Blake and Foster, Odin was displeased by the

REAL NAME: Thor Odinson
ALIASES: Donald M. Blake, God of Thunder, Son of Odin, the
Thunderer, Lord of Asgard, Jake Olson, Sigurd Jarlson, Donar,
Donner, Hloriddi, Unhappy Hrungnir's Playmate, Veur, Hrodr's
Foe-Man, Longbeard's Son, Vingthor the Hurler, Siegfried,
Siegmund, "Woe-King"; impersonated Hercules, Harokin, Freya;
formerly bound to Eric Masterson
IDENTITY: (As Donald Blake) secret
CITIZENSHIP: Asgard; honorary US citizen
PLACE OF BIRTH: A cave in Norway
OCCUPATION: Warrior, adventurer; former monarch, paramedic,
construction worker; (as Donald Blake) physician, surgeon
KNOWN RELATIVES: Odin Borson (father, deceased), Gaea
(mother), Frigga (adoptive mother), Loki (adoptive brother,
deceased), Balder, Hermod, Tyr, Vidar (half-brothers), Buri
(Tiwaz, paternal great-grandfather), Bolthorn (maternal great
grandfather), Bor Burison (grandfather, deceased), Bestia (paternal
grandmother, presumed deceased), Vili, Ve (paternal uncles,
deceased), Sigyn (sister-in-law),Solveig (sister-in-law, deceased),
Jormungand (Midgard Serpent), Fenris Wolf (nephews), Hela
(niece), large extended family via Gaea and others
GROUP AFFILIATION: Gods of Asgard, Avengers; formerly
Queen's Vengeance, Godpack, Thor Corps
EDUCATION: Tutored by scholars of Asgard; (Blake) M.D.
HEIGHT: 6'6"; (Blake) 5'9"
WEIGHT: 640 lbs; (Blake) 150 lbs.
EYES: Blue
HAIR: Blond
FIRST APPEARANCE: Journey Into Mystery #83 (1962)
ORIGIN: The Mighty Thor #159 (1968)

relationship between a god and a mortal. He forbade Blake
from revealing his identity to her, creating a strange love triangle
between Foster, Thor and Thor's alter-ego, Blake.

Even though Donald Blake knew he was the legendary Thor,
he still lacked his full memories from his former life as an
Asgardian. However, over time his memories slowly returned,
until one day Odin finally revealed himself and restored Thor's
complete memory. Odin also admitted his role orchestrating
Blake's trip to Norway to discover his Asgardian alter-ego. Thor
was reintroduced to his childhood friend and former lover, the
Asgardian warrior Sif, further complicating Thor's love life on
Earth

The love affair between Thor and Jane Foster eventually nded when Foster fell in love with a mortal man, Dr. Keith Kincaid. Resuming their ancient romance, Sif and Thor were betrothed, and Sif lived on Earth posing as Donald Blake's cousin. Foster and Kincaid married, but wedding plans were cancelled for Thor, as Sif grew bored with his time spent as Blake, and returned to Asgard.

The fire demon Surtur, enemy of the Asgardian gods, ravaged distant galaxy (the "Burning Galaxy") for the sake of forging his Twilight Sword, the "Sword of Doom." A fleet of survivors of the galactic massacre from the planet Korbin traveled the cosmos in search of a new home, under the protection of their noble guardian, Beta Ray Bill. As the fleet ventured close to Earth, Thor mistook them for a threat and attacked the Korbinites. Separated from Mjolnir, Thor reverted into Donald Blake, while Beta Ray Bill retrieved and wielded the hammer, magically unliftable to all but the most worthy. With Donald Blake helpless and defeated, Bill made a claim to keep the hammer to help him fight back against Surtur's demons. Odin had Thor and Beta Ray Bill compete for the right to use the hammer and Beta Ray Bill won, but Odin awarded him with a similar weapon, Stormbreaker, rather than disarm his son. Once Thor, Bill, and Sif defeated Surtur's demons, Odin transferred the enchantment that changed Thor into Donald Blake onto Stormbreaker, so that Bill could revert to his mortal form. Thor, therefore, abandoned his Donald Blake identity, and resided in Asgard. He and Bill still successfully teamed together to vanquish Surtur when the demon led an assault against Asgard and Earth. Afterward, Bill departed with his people to find a new home.

After commuting back and forth from Asgard to Earth to continue his heroic adventures with humans, Thor sought help from Nick Fury, director of the spy agency S.H.I.E.L.D., to create another human identity to enable him to live among humans. A new alias was created, that of construction worker Sigurd Jarlson. However, Thor infrequently used the guise, consumed by his adventures as Thor.

After being defeated by Thor and Beta Ray Bill, the vengeful Surtur made an alliance with the Dark Elves of Svartalfheim (one of the realms of Asgard) to war against the Asgardian gods. Thor, Loki, and Odin protected Asgard by merging their spiritual essences together, thereby increasing their powers. However, the battle could not be won until Odin sacrificed himself for Asgard, seemingly dying as he grappled Surtur and plummeted into a huge chasm. With Asgard left without a leader, Loki schemed for ways to assume power. Working in collusion with Loki, the Asgardian goddess Lorelei (a notorious seductress like her sister Amora the Enchantress), cast a spell on Thor causing him to fall in love with her in hopes that he would then help Loki become the new ruler. Thor broke free of the enchantment, but the incident strained Thor's relationship with Sif, who still loved the thunder-god.

As the gods of Asgard performed the "Great Althing," a ceremony to choose a new leader to replace Odin, Loki continued to scheme to seize Asgard's throne for himself. He incapacitated Thor by turning him into a frog on Earth. As a heroic amphibian, Thor became embroiled in a battle between the frogs and the rats of Central Park, New York, until he turned into a frog-like humanoid upon finding his hammer. Meanwhile in Asgard, Harokin, an Asgardian warrior, pretended to be Thor so as to cast his vote for Loki. Thor captured Loki and Thor's friend Volstagg returned him to his normal form. Thor was offered his father's seat, but declined the throne, nominating Balder as Asgard's new leader.

A Dark Elf named Algrim the Strong defended his ruler, Malekith the Accursed, from Thor when the thunder-god attempted to rescue Lorelei from capture. Malekith dropped both Thor and Algrim into a chasm towards molten lava. While Thor escaped, Algrim was badly burned and left an amnesiac with nothing but vengeance against Thor on his mind. The near-omnipotent being called the Beyonder, curious about human desires, transformed Algrim into Kurse, healing his injuries, augmented his strength, and remodeling his armor. Kurse wreaked havoc searching for Thor in Manhattan. Assisted by the junior super-team Power Pack, Thor defeated Kurse, reawakening his memories in the process. Kurse realized it was Malekith, not Thor, who caused his fall, and redirected his anger. At Thor's request, the Beyonder sent Kurse to Hel to find Malektih, where Hela, the Asgardian death goddess, grew furious with Kurse's rampage through her realm. Kurse eventually found Malekith in Asgard and slew him. In retaliation, Hela cursed Thor such that his bones became brittle, yet he was prevented from dying from his injuries. Humiliated but determined to remain a warrior to the end, Thor donned a suit of battle armor to support his fragile body.

Loki took this opportunity to release the Midgard Serpent, the beast prophesized to kill Thor and start Ragnarok, the apocalyptic end of the Asgardians. Despite his weakened condition, Thor was able to kill the Midgard Serpent and, thanks to Hela's curse, Thor survived the battle although his body was completely broken and battered. Loki then sent the enchanted Destroyer, an animated indestructible suit of armor, to torment Thor but instead, Thor managed to send his spirit into the Destroyer armor and take command of it. He traveled to Hel in the Destroyer and

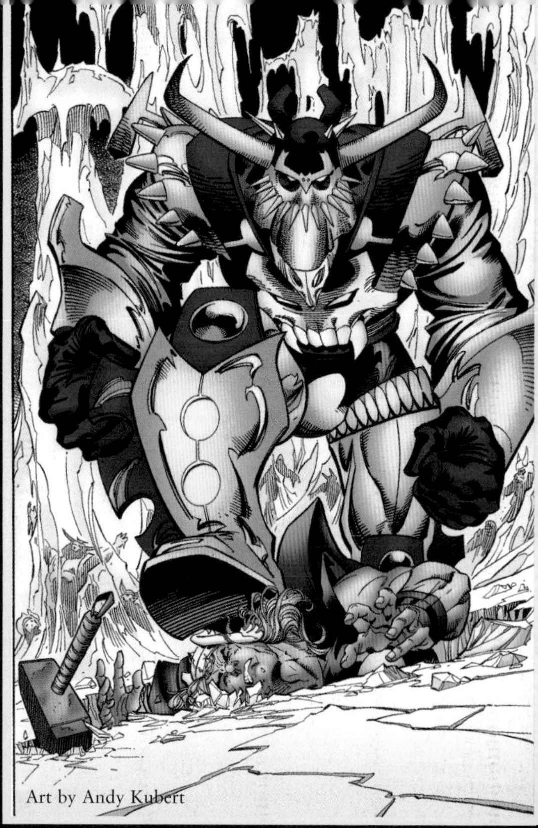
Art by Andy Kubert

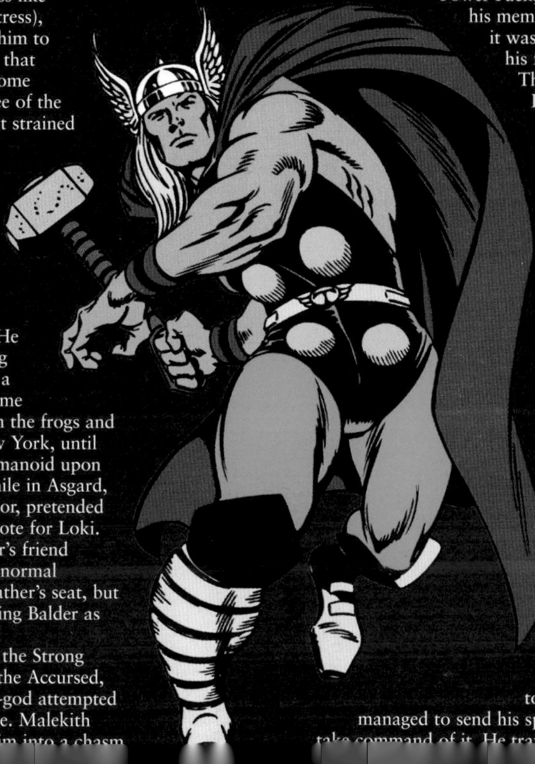

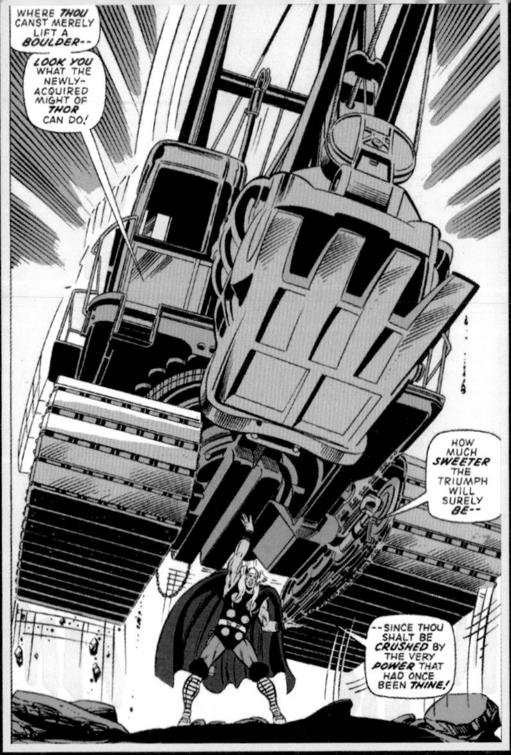
WHERE THOU CANST MERELY LIFT A BOULDER--
LOOK YOU WHAT THE NEWLY-ACQUIRED MIGHT OF THOR CAN DO!
HOW MUCH SWEETER THE TRIUMPH WILL SURELY BE--
--SINCE THOU SHALT BE CRUSHED BY THE VERY POWER THAT HAD ONCE BEEN THINE!
Art by Neal Adams

began wreaking havoc. The desperate Hela had no choice but to fully restore Thor's original body and release him from her curse.

After a battle between Asgard and the Egyptian god of death, Seth, which resulted in Odin triumphantly returned to the throne of Asgard, Thor began to suffer sudden and momentary bouts of weakness during times of stress. Travelling within Thor's mind, Doctor Stephen Strange the Sorcerer Supreme, discovered an evil version of Thor present, derived from Loki's evil residue which had manifested when Thor, Loki, and Odin had mingled their essences to battle Surtur. Thor defeated his evil alternate version within himself.

Thor, in his civilian identity of Jarlson, had become friends with the architect Eric Masterson and his son, Kevin. Eric was kidnapped by Mongoose (a superhuman agent of the powerful scientist, the High Evolutionary) who had previously attacked Thor, attempting to gain a cell sample. Thor tracked Eric to the High Evolutionary's European base at Mount Wundagore, wher Mongoose led the animalistic residents to attack. Freeing Eric, Thor learned that the High Evolutionary and the Greek demigo Hercules were missing. Accompanied by Eric, Thor rescued Hercules and the High Evolutionary from the ancient galactic entities, the Celestials, in the Black Galaxy. Upon returning to Earth, they were again attacked by the Mongoose, and Eric blocked a blast of energy meant for Thor, giving Thor and Hercules a chance to defeat Mongoose.

With Eric dying from Mongoose's attack, Thor pleaded with Odin for aid on Eric's behalf. Odin reluctantly agreed to save him, but did so by merging Thor and Masterson together, body and soul.

Thor and Eric shared a body in the same manner in which Donald Blake and Thor had, although the latter two were never truly separate beings. They dealt with their new condition, despite the problems it caused for Eric's private life and custody of his son. Thor continued his adventures, plagued by Loki. Eventually, the two's bodies were separated by a Celestial while they were involved in the birth of a new Celestial in the Black Galaxy. During a tremendous battle between the fiery Surtur and the frost giant Ymir, a battle that signaled Ragnarok and th end of the Asgardians, Thor recovered Surtur's powerful sword from the Sea of Eternal Night to oppose the elemental giants. Weakened by his separation from Masterson, Thor was easily stopped by Surtur and Ymir, but Masterson willingly merged with Thor again, even though it meant giving up part of his life. While Ymir and Surtur fought over the sword, Thor opened a dimensional rift that sucked them both into the Sea of Eternal Night, ending the threat of Ragnarok.

When Thor returned to Earth, he quickly found himself in battle with Loki over the fate of Kevin Masterson. Although Thor defeated Loki, the trickster fired one last blast at Kevin and his mother Marcy, but it was blocked by Eric' secretary, Susan Austin, killing her. Angered as never before, Thor absorbed all of Loki's lifeforce with his hammer, seemingly destroying the evil god forever, despit breaking Odin's sacred rule forbidding Asgardian gods from killing each other.

However, this was all according to Loki's plan with the Hell-lord Mephisto. Loki's spirit was able to possess Odin while Odin's spirit was sent to Mephisto's realm in exchange. Posing as Odin, Loki exiled Thor into Eric's subconscious mind, though Eric could still assume Thor' form after striking his cane. Loki's decrees while in Odin body became increasingly irrational and oppressive. Eric, Balder and Sif discovered Loki's deception and rescued Odin and reclaimed his body from Loki. Mephisto seize Loki's soul, allegedly his true goal. Eric then freed Thor's spirit from within himself. For Eric's courageous efforts, Odin granted him an enchanted uru mace. Still able to transform into a version of Thor, Eric adopted a new separate heroic identity, Thunderstrike.

With the frequent shifting of identities between godly and human forms, and the sharing of his power, Thor was left mentally unbalanced for a time. Sif began to suspect Thor was falling prey to the incurable "Warrior' Madness" and, along with Beta Ray Bill, Silver Surfer, and the self-appointed guardians of the universe, the Infinity Watch, she confronted Thor. During the conflict, Thor stole one of the most powerful artifacts in the universe, the Power Gem, becoming power incarnate. Th heroes elicited the help of the wicked mad titan, Thanos, believing only he could stop Thor. Restrained, Thor was taken to Odin, who discovered the truth behind the malady after a spiritual journey through his son's mind. Thor fought the personification of his own madness, that of a beautiful Valkyrie (handmaiden of Odin), and destroyed it.

This experience sparked Thor's anger at his father regarding his discipline of humility. He left Asgard, allying with the High Evolutionary and his newly createc godlike beings, the Godpack. In the meantime, Odin

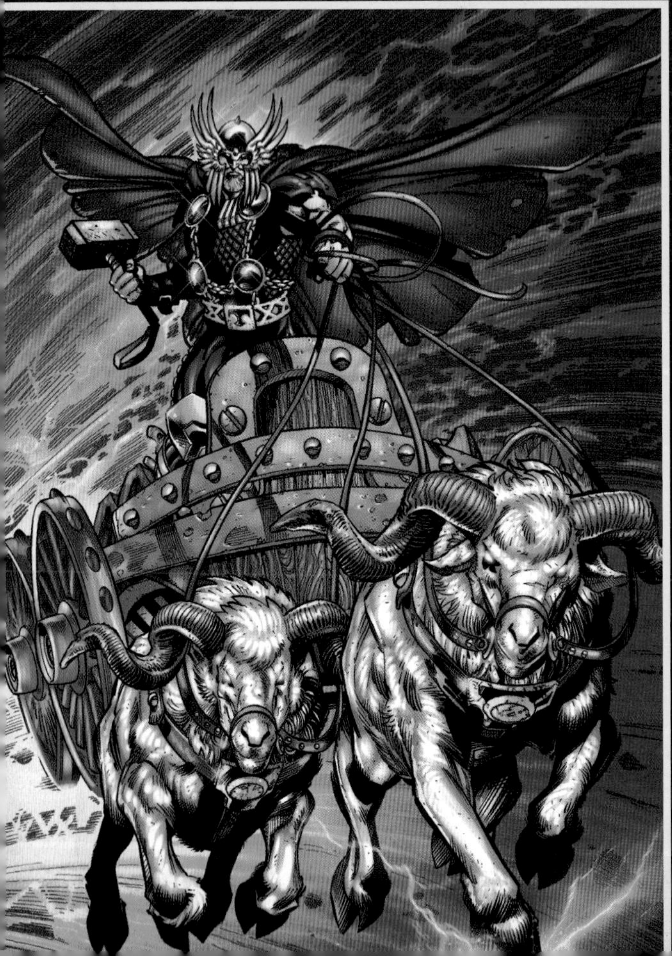
Art by Scott Eaton

ecided that the time had come for Ragnarok to begin, and he
needed Thor. Disowning Thor, Odin resurrected Red Norvell,
who once held the mantle of thunder god but had died in battle,
and re-made him into a new "Thor." Odin also divulged the
ruth to his son about Donald Blake, that he and Thor were
never separate beings. Thor became enraged and severed his ties
with Asgard.

Odin hoped to bypass Ragnarok by transforming the
Asgardian gods into mortals, but his plan was hijacked by the
Egyptian god Seth, and put it into action prematurely. Asgard
ell, and its gods were banished to Earth. Odin hoped Thor
would restore the gods to power, but before he could, Thor
ell in battle with the psychic entity, Onslaught. Thor vanished,
along with the Avengers and other heroes, but, was merely
reborn to another dimension, Counter-Earth. He eventually
returned through the reality altering power of the boy Franklin
Richards, son of the Fantastic Four's Mr. Fantastic and the
nvisible Woman.

When Thor returned, he discovered Asgard had been
destroyed by the cruel Dark Gods (beings formerly banished
by the Asgardians to the farthest reaches of the universe). They
ent the Destroyer to Earth on a rampage, leaving the Avengers
defeated and Thor nearly dead. The mysterious being named
Marnot (secretly Hescamar, one of Odin's magical ravens)
offered to restore Thor in exchange for taking the place of
ake Olsen, a paramedic who died during the battle. Thor
agreed, fighting the Destroyer again and banishing it to another
dimension. Thor found he could transform between himself and
Olsen, although he had none of Olsen's memories, making it
difficult to maintain two identities.

The Dark Gods, in the guise of Asgardians, attacked Olympus
and left it in ruins. Thor and Hercules uncovered the truth and
ed the battle against the Dark Gods, eventually freeing both
Asgard and Olympus, restoring them to glory. Marnot revealed
hat the Dark Gods had once invaded Asgard ages ago, and
Odin had prepared an enchantment on Hescamar to seek out
a way to defeat the Dark Gods should they return. The raven
ulfilled this by transforming into Marnot and helping Thor.
Afterwards, Thor remained on Earth with his dual identity of
ake Olsen.

Among his subsequent adventures, Thor rescued a woman
named Tarene, a cosmic being also known as the Designate.
She later took on the identity of Thor Girl out of admiration of
Thor. Thor and Thor Girl battled the time-travelling Gladiator
Kallark), who vowed to destroy Thor in a preemptive strike to
prevent a terrible horror that he believed Thor would inflict in
he future.

Soon after, Thor failed to defend Asgard against an army of
monstrous Asgardian trolls during one of Odin's "Odinsleeps"
a time when Odin recharges his energy and is left vulnerable),
Odin punished Thor, stripping him of his immortality and
eft him on Earth. Shortly afterward, Loki (who had escaped
Mephisto's captivity) brought the Destroyer back to Earth,
animating it with the soul of Tarene. Ultimately, the Destroyer
was thwarted and Tarene was restored, but during the battle,
Thor was severely wounded. Dr. Jane Foster tended to Jake

Olsen's wounds but was unable to treat Thor's. Odin brought
Thor to Asgard and physically separated Thor from his alter ego
to allow Thor to heal while Jake Olsen was returned to his life
on Earth.

Later on, Surtur appeared on Earth and an assemblage of
Asgardian heroes and allies confronted the demon and its
hordes. Tarene used her powers to restore Thor to full health,
joining with Odin and the Asgardian warriors against Surtur.
In the end, Odin tapped into both Thor and Tarene's powers to
deliver a fatal blow against Surtur, but sacrificed himself in the
process.

In mourning the loss of his father, Thor initially refused
to take Odin's place. Eventually a discussion with Jake Olsen
convinced Thor to accept the responsibilities of the new

monarch of Asgard. Thor did so, gaining his father's might, the "Odinpower," as a right of rule.

Thor decided to restore the gods of Asgard to their former role on Earth, guiding humanity's affairs. He did this by bringing Asgard directly into the Earth dimension. Worship of the Asgardians flourished, with many branches of the Church of Thor established around the world. Defending his followers, Thor was pitted against the Avengers, and broke ties with the team of heroes. Later on, Earth's citizens became wary of Thor and launched an assault upon Asgard, reducing it to rubble. Thor then devoted himself to conquering Earth and for nearly two hundred years, he ruled the planet. Eventually, he recognized how unjust he had become, and travelled back in time to prevent his younger self from becoming a despot, merging him with Jake Olson to ensure he retained some humanity. Thus, his future as a tyrant was prevented (diverged into a separate timeline called Reality-3515, "the Reigning").

Almost immediately after restoring Asgard to its own realm away from Earth, Thor was attacked by Loki and his armies, who had teamed with Surtur to create weapons for Thor's enemies, forged in the same way as Mjolnir. The fight for Asgard escalated into Ragnarok. Although Thor managed to defeat Loki, severing his head, the war left many of Thor's allies dead, including Sif and his friends "the Warriors Three." Thor forced Surtur to re-forge Mjolnir, which had shattered during the battle. While Asgard succumbed to Ragnarok, effectively wiping the Asgardian world from existence, Thor sought out the gods known as Those Who Sit Above In Shadow, who gained power from repeating Ragnarok and Asgardian rebirth throughout history. Thor refused an offer to join them. Confronting them in battle, Thor destroyed Those Who Sit Above In Shadow as Asgard died. The Odinpower congratulated Thor on succeeding at his greatest mission. Thor then closed his eyes, apparently joining his people in death.

Sometime later after Ragnarok, Mjolnir sped through the cosmos and landed on Earth, releasing a blast of light. This signaled the return of Thor and the Asgardians. Thor had been residing in a limbo-like dimension since Ragnarok where he was visited by his Donald Blake aspect. Blake encouraged Thor to return to life and recreate Asgard, observing that with Those Who Sit Above in Shadow vanquished, the Asgardians could finally chart their own destiny rather than repeatedly be caught in the life, death and rebirth cycle that was Ragnarok. Thor agreed and used the Odinpower to restore Asgard as a floating city hovering near the town of Broxton, Oklahoma. Once again, Thor and Blake shared their existence and Blake resumed his work as a physician. The rest of the gods were reborn in mortal guises, but Thor quickly located them and restored them to normal. Unfortunately, Thor was tricked into releasing Loki and other villainous Asgardians as well. Loki again sowed discord, revealing Balder was Odin's son, a secret kept from Balder himself. He also manipulated Thor into slaying his own grandfather, Bor, and spurred Balder into claiming the throne of Asgard and exiling Thor. However, when Norman Osborn (the crafty but mentally unstable criminal known as the Green Goblin), then leader of the US peace-keeping forces, schemed with Loki to invade Asgard with his Avengers team and super-human armies, Thor defended Asgard. Loki switched sides after Osborn's supremely powerful pawn, the Sentry (Robert Reynolds), threatened to destroy both Earth and Asgard. The mad Sentry slew Loki but was ultimately defeated by Thor, and Osborn's forces were also defeated with the aid of Thor's comrades from the true Avengers. Under the leadership of Steve Rogers (formerly Captain America), Osborn's Avengers were disbanded, and a new Avengers team, including Thor, was forged.

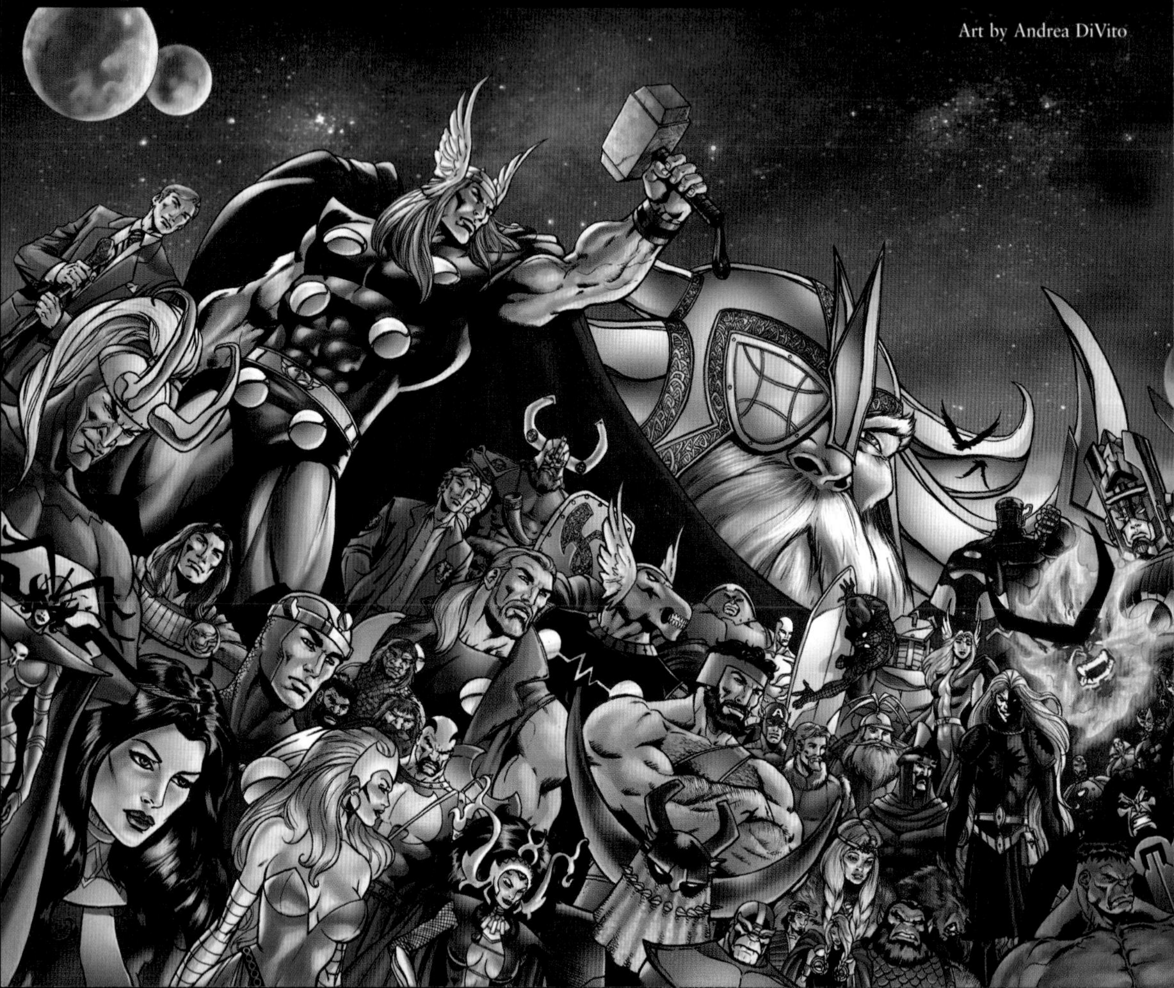

Art by Andrea DiVito

HEIGHT: 6'6"; (Blake) 5'9"
WEIGHT: 640 lbs; (Blake) 150 lbs.
EYES: Blue
HAIR: Blond
DISTINGUISHING FEATURES: Animal-like canine teeth, hirsute physique, unique hairstyle

SUPERHUMAN POWERS:
As the son of Odin and Gaea, Thor's strength, endurance and resistance to injury are greater than the vast majority of his superhuman race. He is extremely long-lived (though not completely immune to aging), immune to conventional disease and highly resistant to injury. His flesh and bones are several times denser than a human's.
As Lord of Asgard, Thor possessed the Odinforce, which enabled him to tap into the near-infinite resources of cosmic and mystical energies, enhancing all of his abilities. With the vast magical power of the Odinforce, Thor was even able to dent Captain America's virtually indestructible shield with Mjolnir.
Thor possesses physical powers superior to those of normal Asgardian gods. He has an extended lifespan augmented (although not immortal) by the Golden Apples of Idunn, immunity to conventional diseases, enhanced endurance (Thor's Asgardian metabolism is far greater than a human), superhuman strength ([lifting 100 tons]), which increases further when he succumbs to "warrior's madness," a berserker rage, the mindless battle passion that increases a warriors strength tenfold. By chanting and performing an ancient ritual, Thor can also invoke the berserker rage to increase his strength. His skin and bones are several times denser than those of mortals, granting him extreme resistance to injury.
Thor shares a unique bond [1] and affinity with Mjolnir, which has been increased further after Dr. Stephen Strange bound Thor's lifeforce to Mjolnir to repair the hammer [2]. Via this bond, Thor has a strong affinity with the forces of weather and acting as a conduct can channel Mjolnir's powers through himself allowing him to summon lighting from his hands. Thor's affinity with Mjolnir is so strong that even when damaged, as long as there is a significant piece remaining intact, Thor can use Mjolnir's powers. However due to the increased bond via Thor's lifeforce, if Mjolnir were to be damaged, Thor himself would perish. Thor can channel his godly energies/lifeforce through Mjolnir into blasts called "Godforce" so powerful that they can slay even immortals, although it leaves him in a weakened state afterwards.
Thor wears a full body hauberk composed of Asgardian steel. It belt has the Norse symbol of physical health as a belt buckle along with the Norse symbol of Gemini most likely to symbolize his bond with Dr. Donald Blake. [3]
While empowered with the Odinforce, or more accurately called Thorforce since the Asgardian lifeforce resided within Thor, Thor was able to tap into a near-infinite resource of cosmic and mystical power, enhancing all of his powers. With the Odinforce's vast power, Thor was even able to dent Captain America's Vibranium/steel alloy shield. At regular intervals (usually occurring once per year) or when using the Thorpower too greatly, Thor would be required to enter the "Thorsleep." Learning from his father's mistakes, Thor had Falki, Odin's metalsmith, create a casket that contains enchantments that create a coma-like state to replenish and retain mastery over the Thorpower in order to heal more quickly. Once closed, it can only be opened from within. When Thor entered this casket of Thorsleep and into the Thorsleep, Donald Blake emerged from the Void until Thor awoke once again. Thor briefly had mastery of the Norse runes and could use them to break any Asgardian enchantment.

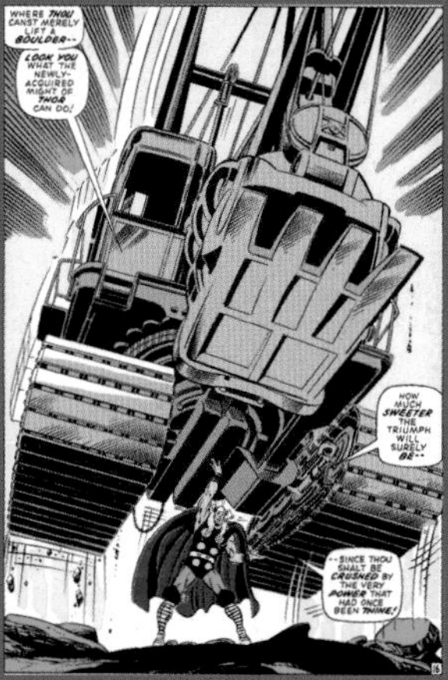
WHERE THOU CANST MERELY LIFT A BOULDER--
LOOK YOU WHAT THE NEWLY-ACQUIRED MIGHT OF THOR CAN DO!
HOW MUCH SWEETER THE TRIUMPH WILL SURELY BE--
--SINCE THOU SHALT BE CRUSHED BY THE VERY POWER THAT HAD ONCE BEEN THINE!
16

Art by Neal Adams

During the period when he was cursed by Hela with brittle bones that would not heal, Thor wore a full body suit of armor composed of Asgardian steel for protection. This armor possessed ancient rune symbols of power emblazoned by lightning upon the armor along with an exoskeleton complete with circuits connected to a series of feedback microcomputers programed to respond to minute changes in electrical conductivity of the nerves to prevent the broken bones from shifting, while allowing Thor to use his arm.

PARAPHERNALIA: Thor occasionally dons a Belt of Strength, which doubles his strength but weakens him after its use. He also possesses a pair of iron gauntlets to protect him when unleashing Mjolnir's most potent powers. For extended periods of travel, Thor rides a chariot drawn by the Asgardian goats Toothgnasher and Toothgrinder.

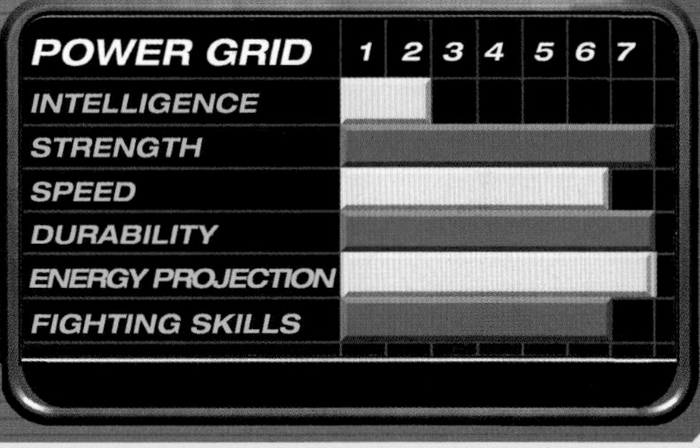
POWER GRID
1 2 3 4 5 6 7
INTELLIGENCE
STRENGTH
SPEED
DURABILITY
ENERGY PROJECTION
FIGHTING SKILLS

POWER RATINGS

INTELLIGENCE
Ability to think and process information
1 Slow/impaired
2 Normal
3 Learned
4 Gifted
5 Genius
6 Super-Genius
7 Ominiscient

STRENGTH
Ability to lift weight
1 Weak: cannot lift own body weight
2 Normal: able to lift own body weight
3 Peak human: able to lift twice own body weight
4 Superhuman: 800lbs-25 ton range
5 Superhuman: 26-75 ton range
6 Superhuman: 76-100 ton range
7 Incalculable: in excess of 100 tons

SPEED
Ability to move over land by running or flight
1 Below normal
2 Normal
3 Superhuman: Peak range: 700 MPH
4 Speed of Sound: Mach-1
5 Supersonic: Mach-2 through orbital velocity
6 Speed of light: 186,000 miles per second
7 Warp speed: transcending light speed

DURABILITY
Ability to resist or recover from bodily injury
1 Weak
2 Normal
3 Enhanced
4 Regenerative
5 bulletproof
6 Superhuman
7 Virtually indestructible

ENERGY PROJECTION
Ability to discharge energy
1 None
2 Ability to discharge energy on contact
3 Short range, short duration, single energy type
4 Medium range, duration, single energy type
5 Long range, long duration, single energy type
6 Able to discharge multiple forms of energy
7 Virtually unlimited command of all forms of energy

FIGHTING SKILLS
Proficiency in hand-to-hand combat
1 Poor
2 Normal
3 Some training
4 Experienced fighter
5 Master of a single form of combat
6 Master of several forms of combat
7 Master of all forms of combat

MJOLNIR – THOR'S HAMMER

Mjolnir is a virtually unbreakable hammer enchanted by Odin with various spells that augment its physical qualities via the Odinforce, the life essence of the Asgardian gods. It is forged from mystical uru metal, whose chief properties are durability, the ability to maintain enchantments, and absorb energies. Thor shares a unique bond and affinity with Mjolnir, which has been increased further after Doctor Stephen Strange, Earth's Sorcerer Supreme, bound Thor's lifeforce to Mjolnir to repair the hammer. Via this bond, Thor has a strong affinity with the forces of weather and, acting as a conduct, can channel Mjolnir's powers through himself allowing him to summon lighting from his hands. Thor's affinity with Mjolnir is so strong that even when damaged, as long as there is a significant piece remaining intact, Thor can use Mjolnir's powers. However due to this increased bond, if Mjolnir were to be damaged again, Thor himself would perish. Thor can channel his godly energies/lifeforce through Mjolnir into blasts called "Godforce" so powerful that they can slay even immortals, although this leaves him in a weakened state afterward.

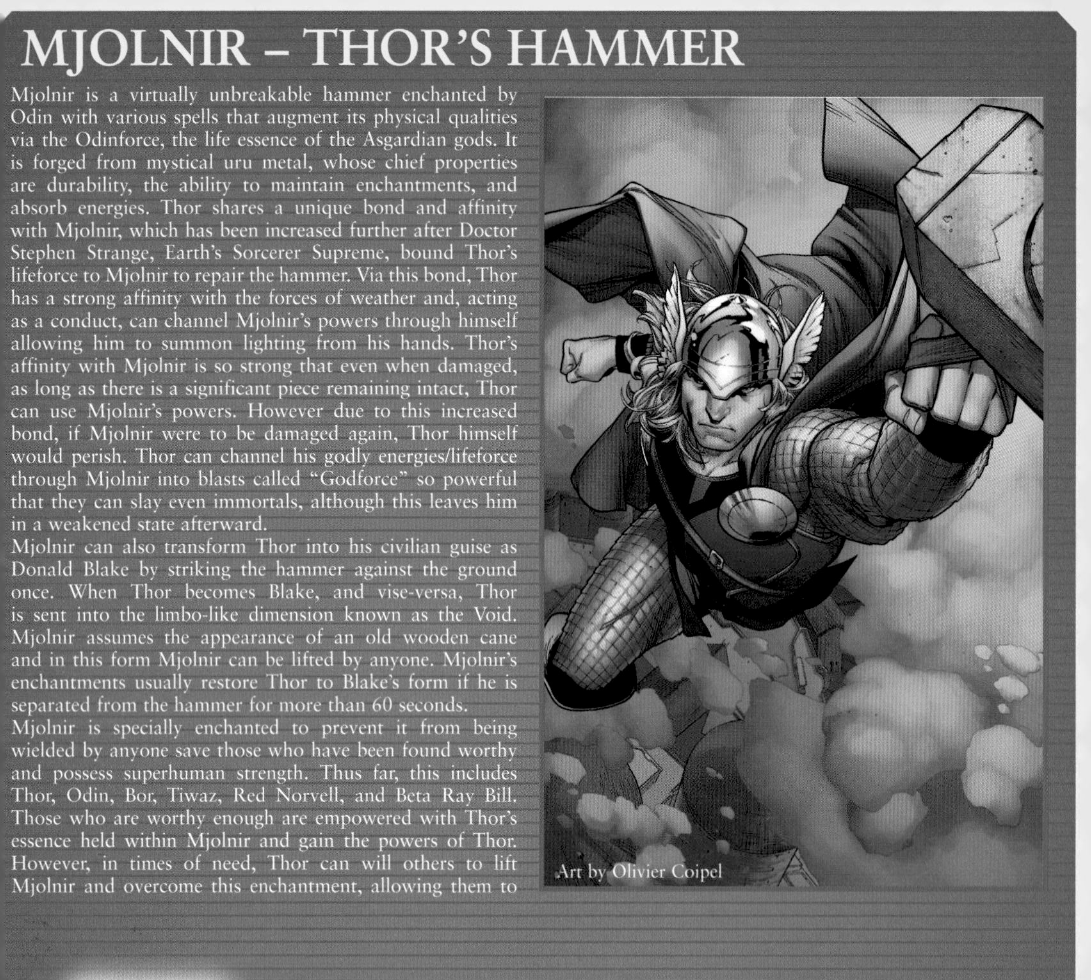
Art by Olivier Coipel

Mjolnir can also transform Thor into his civilian guise as Donald Blake by striking the hammer against the ground once. When Thor becomes Blake, and vise-versa, Thor is sent into the limbo-like dimension known as the Void. Mjolnir assumes the appearance of an old wooden cane and in this form Mjolnir can be lifted by anyone. Mjolnir's enchantments usually restore Thor to Blake's form if he is separated from the hammer for more than 60 seconds.

Mjolnir is specially enchanted to prevent it from being wielded by anyone save those who have been found worthy and possess superhuman strength. Thus far, this includes Thor, Odin, Bor, Tiwaz, Red Norvell, and Beta Ray Bill. Those who are worthy enough are empowered with Thor's essence held within Mjolnir and gain the powers of Thor. However, in times of need, Thor can will others to lift Mjolnir and overcome this enchantment, allowing them to

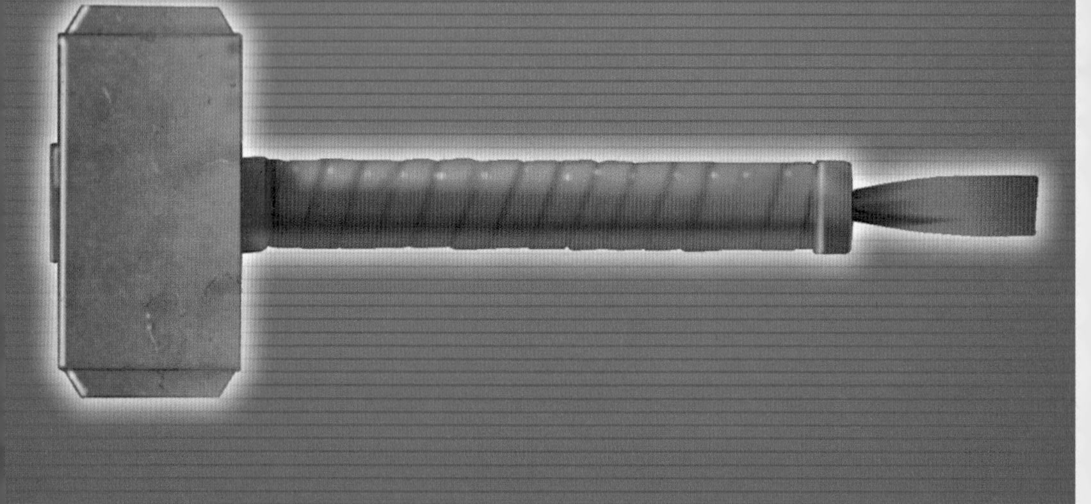

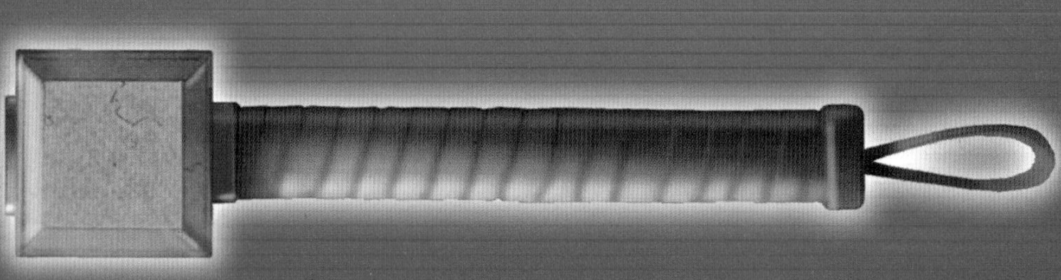

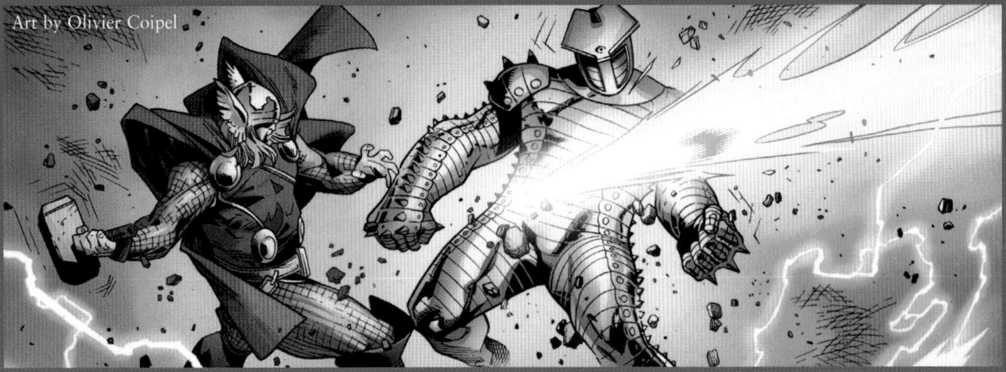
Art by Olivier Coipel

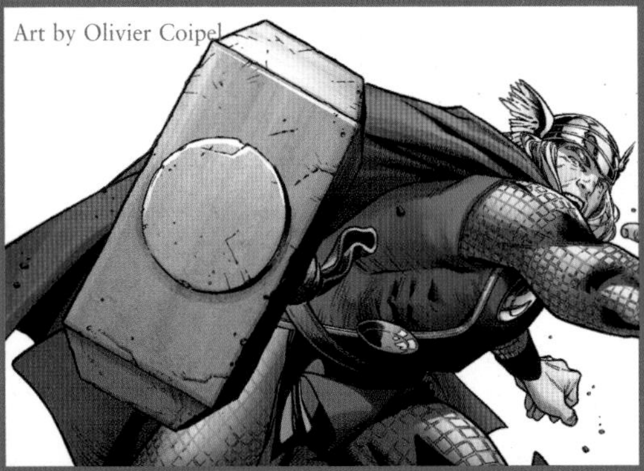
Art by Olivier Coipel

Thus far, Eric Masterson has been the only one to receive this enchantment. To anyone else, Mjolnir cannot be lifted from the ground nor wrested from Thor's grip. This enchantment does not affect non-sentient beings (such as robot drones), but even non-sentient forces must possess some level of superhuman strength to lift Mjolnir. However, without the presence of gravity, anyone can overcome this enchantment and lift, or more accurately "push," and hold Mjolnir. However, they cannot access or use the enchantments within the hammer.

Wielding Mjolnir, Thor can summon and control the powers of the storm, causing rain, wind, thunder and lightning. Thor can channel the storm's fury into devastating energy blasts that can destroy even secondary Adamantium. Mjolnir can also generate energy blasts called "Anti-Force." Due to its uru metal composite, Mjolnir can absorb other energies into itself, which Thor can then release.

lift the hammer. Thus far, this includes Steve Rogers, Eric Masterson, and a red and blue costumed adventurer from another universe. While holding Mjolnir together, Thor can empower others with his essence to gain the powers of Thor.

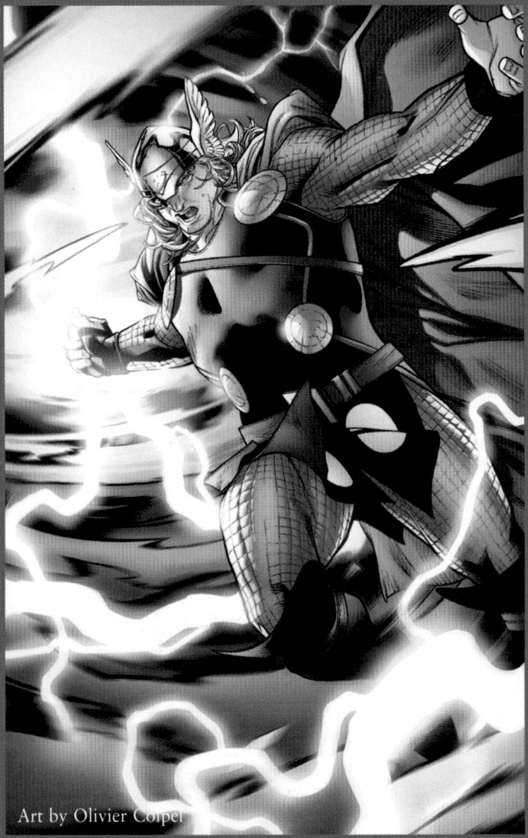
Art by Olivier Coipel

By throwing Mjolnir while grasping its leather thong, Thor can simulate flight at speeds up to Mach 32 (over 24,000 mph). Thor can steer Mjolnir's path via his mental control over Mjolnir while traveling and can "hover" in place by spinning Mjolnir in his hand. While throwing Mjolnir when "hovering," Thor can use winds to keep himself afloat allowing him to appear to be in flight. Mjolnir obeys Thor's mental commands, via his bond with the hammer, as though it was alive and, if Thor's will is strong enough, the hammer can pass through nearly any barrier to reach his hand should he so desire. Once thrown, Mjolnir returns to Thor's grasp when he mystically calls upon it to return to him.

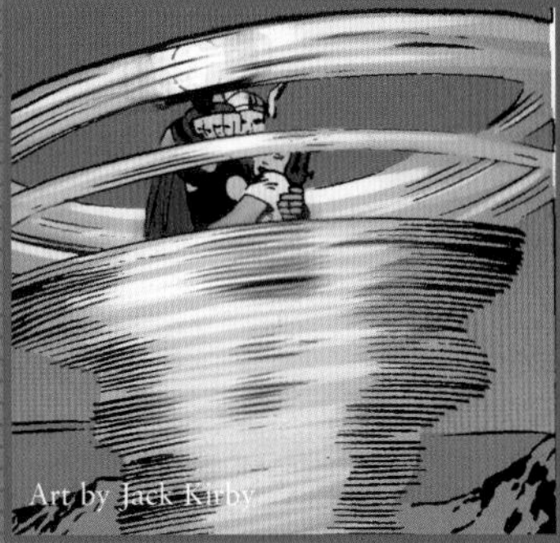
Art by Jack Kirby

Thor often uses Mjolnir defensively to deflect attacks by spinning it around his body at terrific speeds.

By spinning Mjolnir in a circle, Thor can open interdimensional portals, allowing him to travel to other dimensions. Formerly, it could also allow him to travel through time, but Immortus removed this power.

Mjolnir has occasionally served as a power source for the Avengers' Quinjets, enabling them to attain faster-than-light travel.

In addition, Mjolnir enables Thor to sense the use of magic, particularly Asgardian enchantments. Thor has also used Mjolnir to break spells such as the one that allows the Wrecker to share his power with the Wrecking Crew.

THE TRUE ORIGIN OF THOR

by Mike Conroy

In early1962 the Marvel Universe was mere months old and still in its embryonic state with only the **Fantastic Four** and **the Hulk** making their presence felt.

At the same time **Journey into Mystery** was just one of a handful of Marvel's surviving horror-cum-monster-cum-fantasy-cum-science fiction anthologies sitting alongside such companion titles as **Strange Tales, Tales of Suspense** and **Tales to Astonish,** where **Hank Pym** had recently made his first (pre-**Ant-Man**) appearance. Also on the roster was **Amazing Adult Fantasy**, the former **Amazing Adventures**, which was retitled one last time, becoming **Amazing Fantasy** for the title's landmark final issue introducing a certain wall-crawling web-slinger.

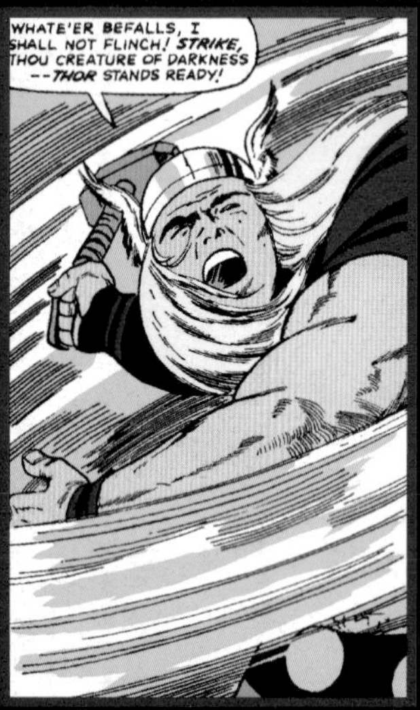
WHATE'ER BEFALLS, I SHALL NOT FLINCH! STRIKE, THOU CREATURE OF DARKNESS --THOR STANDS READY!

While **Spider-Man** was making his historic entrance in **Amazing Fantasy #15, Stan Lee** and artist **Jack Kirby** were concurrently inserting their version of a certain Norse Thunder God into Marvel's fledgling superhero cosmos.

As is so often the case when, years after the event, a once inconsequential matter grows to become a subject of relative importance, the principals involved often differ over the detail. Such is unquestionably the case with many of the concepts Lee and Kirby developed together.

On the subject of **Thor**, the creative duo often referred to as the Lennon and McCartney of comics cannot even agree which of them brought the Thunder God and all his Asgardian trappings to the table.

At one point Kirby referred to Lee as "the type of guy who would never know about Balder and who would never know about the rest of the characters," a comment that does not gel with Lee's remembrance of Thor's genesis...

With the Fantastic Four and the Hulk already under his (and Kirby's) belt, the editor/writer was working to expand Marvel's fledgling line of superheroes. With Spider-Man – drawn by **Steve Ditko** – waiting in the wings, he was looking for someone who could eclipse those heroes; someone who was superior in every way... and in particular more powerful.

He concluded that what he needed was a Super-God, but realised that the world of the early 1960s really wasn't ready for a comicbook hero with such palpable religious undertones. Even so he was constantly drawn back to that same concept until he recalled a radio interview during which the host had referred to Marvel stories as 20th century mythology. Lee had his solution... if he couldn't use God, he'd use a god.

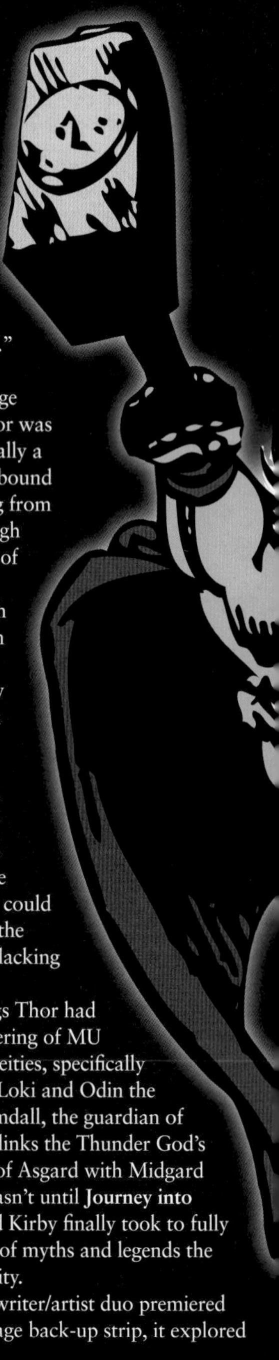

Norse mythology, he claimed, had always inspired him so that's where he looked for inspiration. "There was something about those mighty, horn-helmeted Vikings and their tales of Valhalla, of Ragnorak, of the Aesir, the Fire Demons and immortal, eternal Asgard home of the gods."

First seen in **Journey into Mystery #83**'s 13-page *Stone Men of Saturn*, Thor was the star of what was initially a somewhat aimless Earth-bound series with stories ranging from his SF-tinged debut through clashes with a succession of nonentities among them the pro-Communist South American warlord known as the Executioner, the time-travelling Tomorrow Man, the mobster known as Thug Thatcher, the alien Carbon Copy Man and Sandu, Master of the Supernatural. Admittedly the Radioactive Man and Mr Hyde were a tad more memorable but even they could not negate the sense that the Thunder God's saga was lacking in direction.

During his early outings Thor had also encountered a smattering of MU versions of other Norse deities, specifically his trickster half-brother Loki and Odin the All-Father as well as Heimdall, the guardian of the Rainbow Bridge that links the Thunder God's other-dimensional home of Asgard with Midgard (aka Earth). Even so it wasn't until **Journey into Mystery #97** that Lee and Kirby finally took to fully utilising the rich tapestry of myths and legends the Vikings had left to posterity.

In that 1963 issue the writer/artist duo premiered *Tales of Asgard.* A five-page back-up strip, it explored

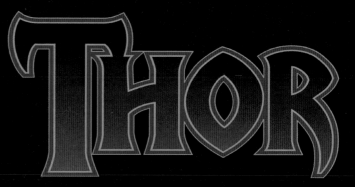

the history and world of the Norse gods integrating such elements as the Ice Giants, Surtur the Fire Demon, the Storm Giants and Hela, Goddess of Death (a character based loosely on the Viking goddess Hel) into the Marvel Universe. The decision to blend the ancient Norse legends with the nascent mythology of the MU was exactly the boost the series needed: it gave Thor a mythic backdrop that not only expanded on and complemented the fledgling superhero cosmos but also gave the Thunder God an identity and history that made him unique among his peers.

While originally developing the concept of a superhero "Super-God", Lee had to overcome a number of hurdles, among them how Thor should be armed. "Then, another thought hit me. I wanted him to be able to fly. I wanted him to be able to zip around the sky and make the trip between heaven and Earth without waiting for Pan Am. The Hulk simulated flight by leaping into the air; the Human Torch did it by bursting into flame; Spidey had his webbing and swung around like Tarzan. God only knows how Superman manages it… I never figured that out. I didn't want to merely say, 'There goes our hero, flying off again.' I wanted it to be somehow more believable. And then I realised I could solve both problems at once – with a hammer!"

Lee – who was then reserving his real name, Stanley Lieber, for when he authored the great American novel… or the great American motion picture – was

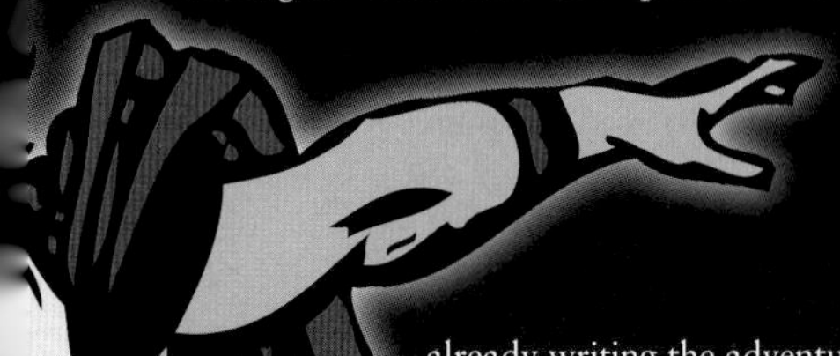

already writing the adventures of the Fantastic Four, Hulk and Spider-Man [who, as mentioned earlier, debuted all-but simultaneously with Marvel's Thunder God] as well as Western, humour, romance, mystery and monster/fantasy strips. Needing someone else to script the first appearance of Thor in 1962's **Journey into Mystery #83**, he handed his plot to his younger brother (as he would later do again when needing someone to introduce **Iron Man** in 1963's **Tales of Suspense #39**).

Larry Lieber's contribution to the Thunder God's legend was limited to that inaugural 13-pager but it did give him the opportunity to add one important element to the Marvel mythos, he established that Mjolnir, the hammer carried by Thor is manufactured from an asgardian metal known as uru.

Commenting on his sibling's embellishment, Lee said; "When I read that I figured the kid had done a lot of research and unearthed the name of some ancient metal. I was proud of him. It wasn't until we were discussing it years later that he casually mentioned that he'd made the name up. He liked the sound of it. Well, I have to admit that an Uru hammer sounds a lot more impressive than a plain, ordinary carpenter's hammer. I'm still proud of him."

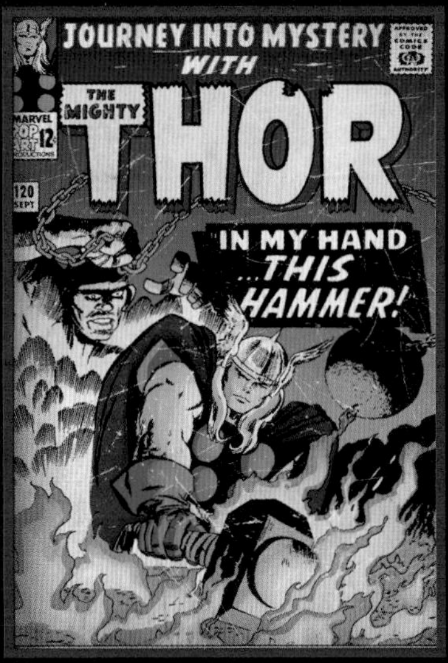
JOURNEY INTO MYSTERY
WITH
THE MIGHTY
THOR
MARVEL POP ART PRODUCTIONS 12¢
120 SEPT
IN MY HAND ...THIS HAMMER!

Kirby had often sourced his stories from the myths and legends of old, with gods a recurrent presence in his work. Recalling his work on Thor, the artist, acclaimed as the King of Comics, declared he did much to build the mythic setting for the series. "I built up Loki. I simply read Loki as the classic villain and, of course, all the rest of them. I even threw in the Three Musketeers… I drew them from Shakespearean figures… I combined Shakespearean figures with the Three Musketeers and came up with these three friends [Fandral the Dashing, Hogun the Grim and the implausibly corpulent Volstagg the Voluminous aka the Warriors Three; first seen 1965's **Journey into Mystery #119**] who supplemented Thor and his company."

And speaking of Shakespeare, Lee, who became both plotter and scripter of the series as of 1963's **Journey Into Mystery #87**, explained, "When I began writing the strip, which means actually putting the words in all their pink mouths. I decided I wanted the hammer holder to speak more like a god. And everyone knows that gods speak with biblical and Shakespearean phraseology. So I slowly and deliberately changed the entire style of the strip, filling it with 'thou shalts' and 'thou shalt nots' and 'so be its' and 'get thee gones' and the like."

"I've always been a nut about the poetic flavour of the Bible and the sentence structure and lilt of Elizabethan writing and this was my chance to play with it," added Lee, who was frequently warned that no superhero strip could succeed if the writing were too archaic or too stylised or too lyrical.

Forsooth the passage of time hath proven the one they dub Stan the Man to hath called it rightly. Verily should those doubters who cried nay hangeth their heads in shame.

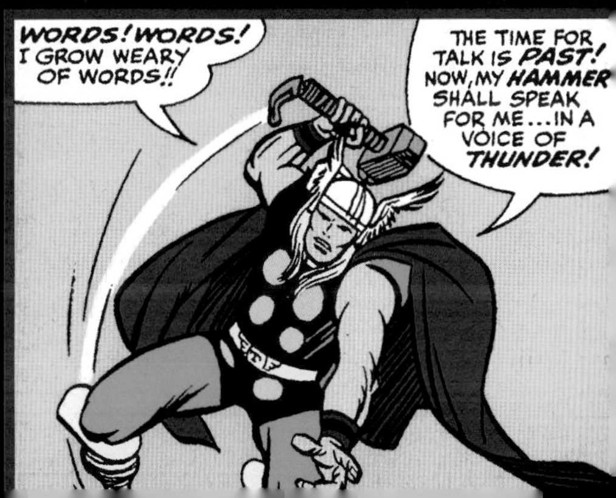
WORDS! WORDS! I GROW WEARY OF WORDS!!
THE TIME FOR TALK IS PAST! NOW, MY HAMMER SHALL SPEAK FOR ME... IN A VOICE OF THUNDER!

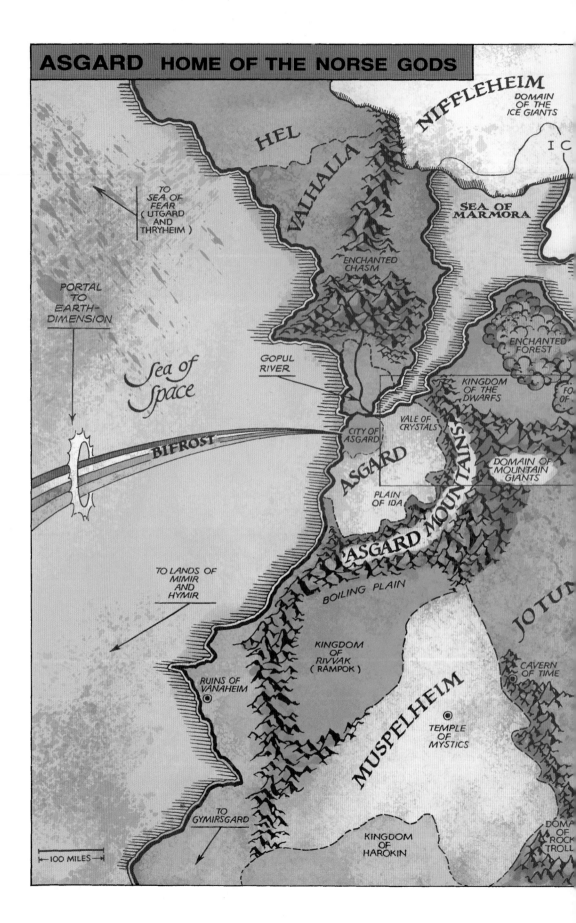

ASGARD HOME OF THE NORSE GODS

NIFFLEHEIM

DOMAIN
OF THE
ICE GIANTS

IC

HEL

VALHALLA

SEA OF
MARMORA

TO
SEA OF
FEAR
(UTGARD
AND
THRYHEIM)

ENCHANTED
CHASM

PORTAL
TO
EARTH-
DIMENSION

Sea of
Space

ENCHANTED
FOREST

GOPUL
RIVER

KINGDOM
OF THE
DWARFS

FO
OF

BIFROST

VALE OF
CRYSTALS

CITY OF
ASGARD

ASGARD

DOMAIN OF
MOUNTAIN
GIANTS

PLAIN
OF IDA

ASGARD MOUNTAINS

TO LANDS OF
MIMIR
AND
HYMIR

BOILING PLAIN

JOTUN

CAVERN
OF TIME

RUINS OF
VANAHEIM

KINGDOM
OF
RIVVAK
(RAMPOK)

MUSPELHEIM

TEMPLE
OF
MYSTICS

TO
GYMIRSGARD

DOMA
OF
ROCK
TROLL

100 MILES

KINGDOM
OF
HAROKIN

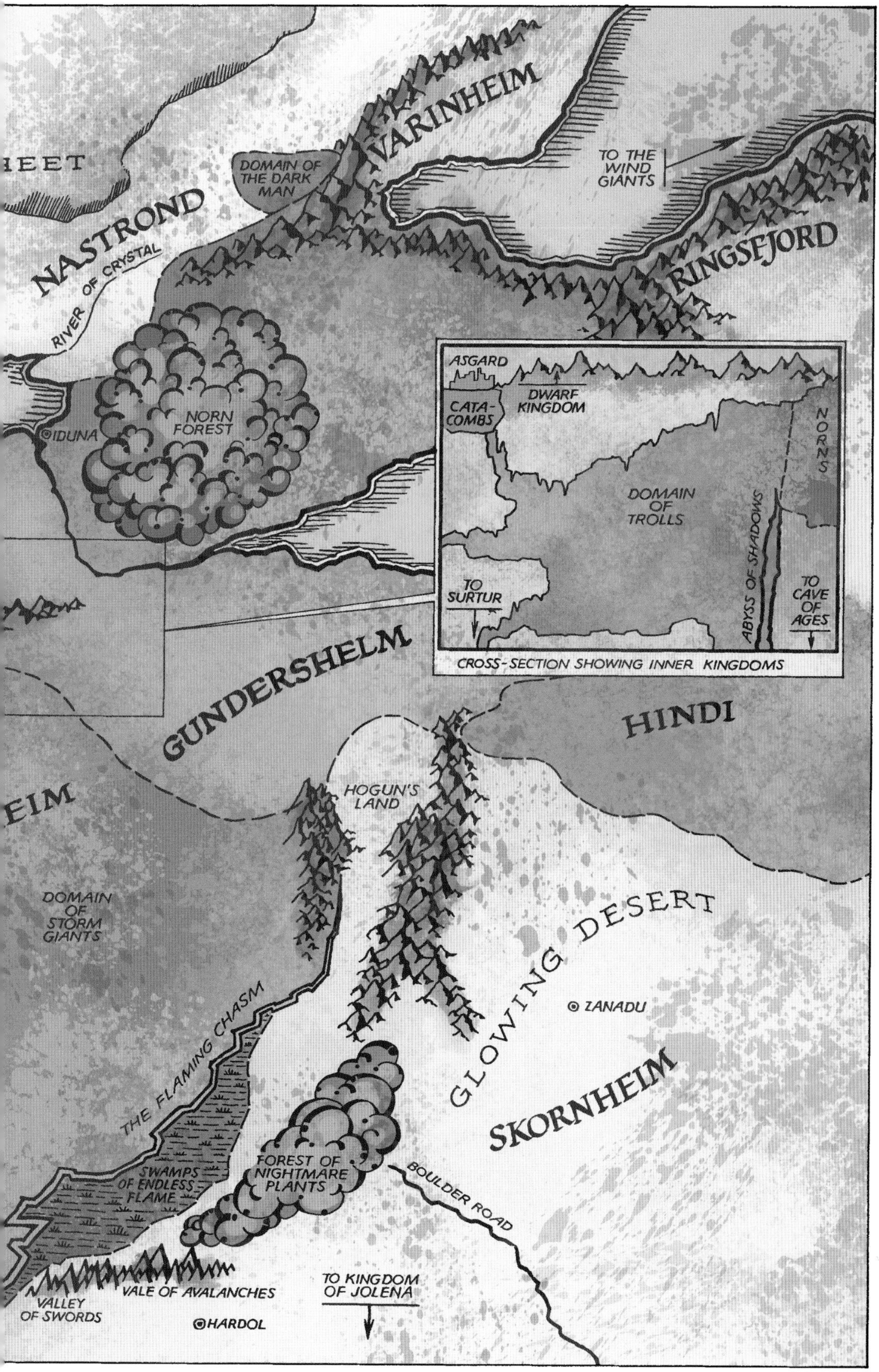

NASTROND
RIVER OF CRYSTAL
DOMAIN OF THE DARK MAN
VARINHEIM
TO THE WIND GIANTS
RINGSFJORD
NORN FOREST
IDUNA
ASGARD
DWARF KINGDOM
CATA-COMBS
NORNS
DOMAIN OF TROLLS
ABYSS OF SHADOWS
TO SURTUR
TO CAVE OF AGES
CROSS-SECTION SHOWING INNER KINGDOMS
GUNDERSHELM
HINDI
HOGUN'S LAND
DOMAIN OF STORM GIANTS
GLOWING DESERT
ZANADU
THE FLAMING CHASM
SKORNHEIM
SWAMPS OF ENDLESS FLAME
FOREST OF NIGHTMARE PLANTS
BOULDER ROAD
VALE OF AVALANCHES
VALLEY OF SWORDS
HARDOL
TO KINGDOM OF JOLENA

ASGARD: THE NINE WORLDS

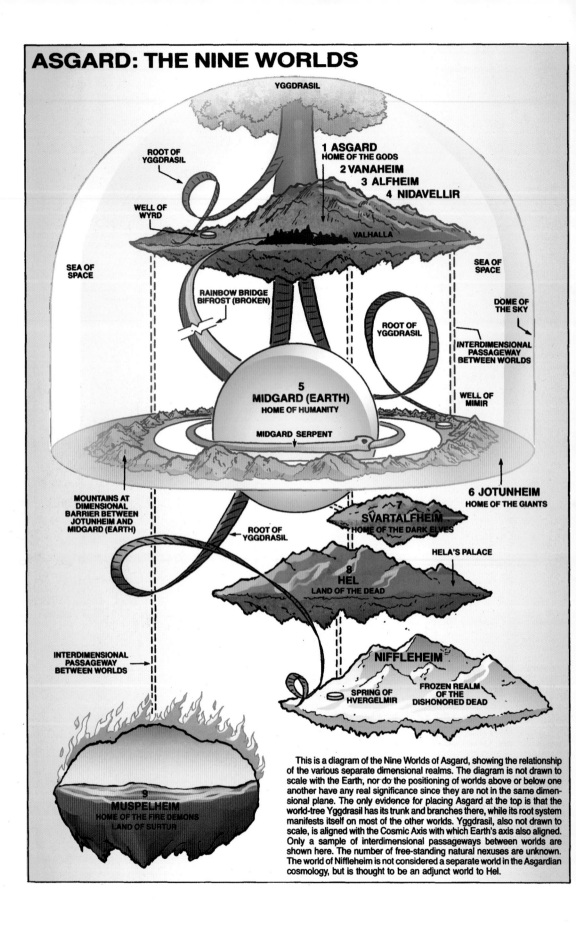

YGGDRASIL

ROOT OF YGGDRASIL

1 ASGARD
HOME OF THE GODS

2 VANAHEIM

3 ALFHEIM

4 NIDAVELLIR

WELL OF WYRD

VALHALLA

SEA OF SPACE

SEA OF SPACE

DOME OF THE SKY

RAINBOW BRIDGE BIFROST (BROKEN)

ROOT OF YGGDRASIL

INTERDIMENSIONAL PASSAGEWAY BETWEEN WORLDS

WELL OF MIMIR

5
MIDGARD (EARTH)
HOME OF HUMANITY

MIDGARD SERPENT

6 JOTUNHEIM
HOME OF THE GIANTS

MOUNTAINS AT DIMENSIONAL BARRIER BETWEEN JOTUNHEIM AND MIDGARD (EARTH)

ROOT OF YGGDRASIL

7
SVARTALFHEIM
HOME OF THE DARK ELVES

HELA'S PALACE

8
HEL
LAND OF THE DEAD

INTERDIMENSIONAL PASSAGEWAY BETWEEN WORLDS

NIFFLEHEIM

SPRING OF HVERGELMIR

FROZEN REALM OF THE DISHONORED DEAD

9
MUSPELHEIM
HOME OF THE FIRE DEMONS
LAND OF SURTUR

This is a diagram of the Nine Worlds of Asgard, showing the relationship of the various separate dimensional realms. The diagram is not drawn to scale with the Earth, nor do the positioning of worlds above or below one another have any real significance since they are not in the same dimensional plane. The only evidence for placing Asgard at the top is that the world-tree Yggdrasil has its trunk and branches there, while its root system manifests itself on most of the other worlds. Yggdrasil, also not drawn to scale, is aligned with the Cosmic Axis with which Earth's axis also aligned. Only a sample of interdimensional passageways between worlds are shown here. The number of free-standing natural nexuses are unknown. The world of Niffleheim is not considered a separate world in the Asgardian cosmology, but is thought to be an adjunct world to Hel.

ODIN

Real Name: Odin
Occupation: Lord of Asgard
Identity: Publicly known to the citizens of Asgard, regarded by the citizens of Earth as mere myth
Legal status: Citizen of Asgard
Other current aliases: All-Father
Former aliases: Woden, Wotan, Atum-Re
Place of birth: Unknown
Marital status: Married
Known relatives: Frigga (wife), Thor (son), Loki (adopted son)
Group affiliation: Gods of Asgard
Base of operations: Dimension of Asgard
First appearance: JOURNEY INTO MYSTERY #85
Origin: Odin was born ages ago as a member of the race of gods who would one day be called Asgardians. Although the precise circumstances of his birth are lost in antiquity, Odin is believed to be the son of Buri, one of the first great Asgardians, and Bestla, a frost giantess. Odin's parents produced two other sons as well, Vili and Ve. The three brothers eventually assumed leadership of the fledgling tribe of gods and helped them establish themselves in the dimension now known as Asgard. As ages passed and the gods rose and fell and rose again stronger than before, Odin gradually achieved ascendancy within the tribe. Finally at the twilight of the last age, it was Odin who mystically redistributed the Asgardians' life-forces into their current physical incarnations. Having done so, Odin was given the name All-Father, and has ruled Asgard as its absolute sovereign ever since. Though he took Frigga as his wife, Odin chose to mate with the non-Asgardian Earth-goddess Gaea (whom he knew as Jord) to produce a son who would have qualities beyond those of any Asgardian. This son was named Thor.

In recent years, Odin sacrificed his right eye to Mimir the All-Knowing Well of Wisdom in order to learn how to thwart Ragnarok, the cyclic cataclysm that brings a fiery end to the age. With the help of his son Thor, Odin managed to avert the natural coming of Ragnarok, perhaps indefinitely. Odin is attended by two mystical ravens, Hugin and Munin (whose names mean "Thought" and "Memory," respectively), who help him to survey the realm. Odin dwells in his royal palace at the center of Asgard's capital city, but also has a palace in Valhalla, overlooking the Land of the Honored Dead.

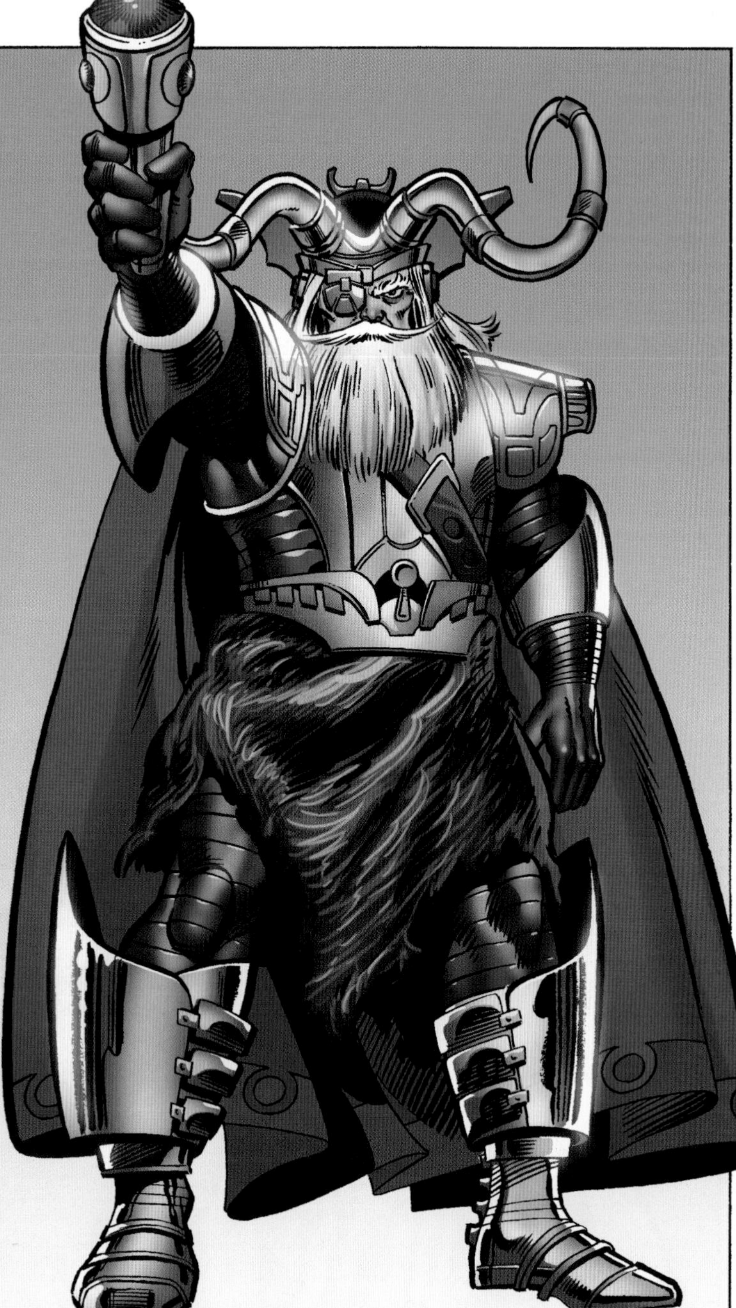

Height: 6' 9" **Weight:** 650 lbs
Eyes: Blue **Hair:** White
Powers: Odin possesses the conventional physical attributes of an Asgardian male ("god"), as well as the greatest single share of power in all Asgard. Like all Asgardians, he is extremely long-lived (though not immortal in the same sense as the Olympians), superhumanly strong (the average Asgardian male can lift about 30 tons; Odin can lift 60), is immune to all diseases, and resistant to conventional injury. (Asgardian flesh and bone is about 3 time as dense as similar human tissue, contributing to the Asgardians' superhuman strength and weight.) His Asgardian metabolism gives him far greater than human endurance at all physical activities.

Odin possesses vast energy powers of an unknown nature. Magical in their apparent form and function, these powers can be employed for numerous purposes, among which are: the augmentation of physical strength and endurance, the enchantment of beings or objects, and the projection of energy bolts. Odin's enchantments (such as the one he placed on Thor's hammer, Mjolnir, to return to the thrower's hand) last until he rescinds them or they are overpowered by a superior enchantment. Odin can also create interdimensional apertures with a gesture and project a 3-dimensional, audio-visual image of his visage, visible to only those he wishes, across space or dimensions. Odin commands the life energies of the entire race of Asgardians, and can absorb any or all of their life energies into his person at will, or in certain instances, restore life to an Asgardian whose life energies are ebbing. (He cannot resurrect the dead once they have passed into the dominion of Hela the Death Goddess.

At periodical intervals, approximately once every Earth year, Odin is required to sleep for about a week to renew his godly energies. If Odin misses the "Odinsleep," or is awakened before it is through, his power level begins to diminish. (Once while in such a state, his power diminished to the point that he could be drugged and kidnapped by aliens.) Odin's power is also dependent upon the dimension of Asgard itself. Unlike his son Thor, Odin's power wanes when he is on Earth or another dimension.

Odin is not omniscient, nor can he create life from nothingness, travel through time unaided, read thoughts, teleport (except interdimensionally), or move worlds. He is, however, perhaps the most powerful mythological god still active today.
Weapons: Odin wields the trident Gungnir (the "spear of heaven") and the power scepter Thrudstok, a small mace. Both of these weapons are made of uru metal and are objects through which he can channel his power. He also wears Draupnir (the "Odinring") as a symbol of supremacy. The specific properties of the ring are yet unknown.
Transportation: Odin rides the eight-legged steed Sleipnir, who can fly through the air at incalculable speeds. He sometimes employs Skipbladnir, a Viking longboat whose enchanted sails and oars enable it to navigate the "sea of space." Skipbladnir can be mystically shrunk to the size of a fist.

BALDER

Real Name: Balder
Occupation: Warrior-god, Asgardian god of light
Identity: Publicly known on Earth, although the general public of Earth does not believe him to be the god of Norse mythology.
Legal status: Citizen of Asgard
Other current aliases: Balder the Brave
Place of birth: Asgard
Marital status: Single
Known relatives: None
Group affiliation: Gods of Asgard, frequent personal ally of Thor and the Warriors Three
Base of operations: Asgard
First appearance: JOURNEY INTO MYSTERY #85

History: Due to his many heroic deeds over the ages, Balder has long been regarded as Asgard's noblest god and its greatest warrior next to the thunder god Thor, who has long been Balder's closest friend (see *Asgard*). Balder has been unsuccessfully sought as a lover by the sorceress Karnilla the Norn Queen (see *Karnilla*).

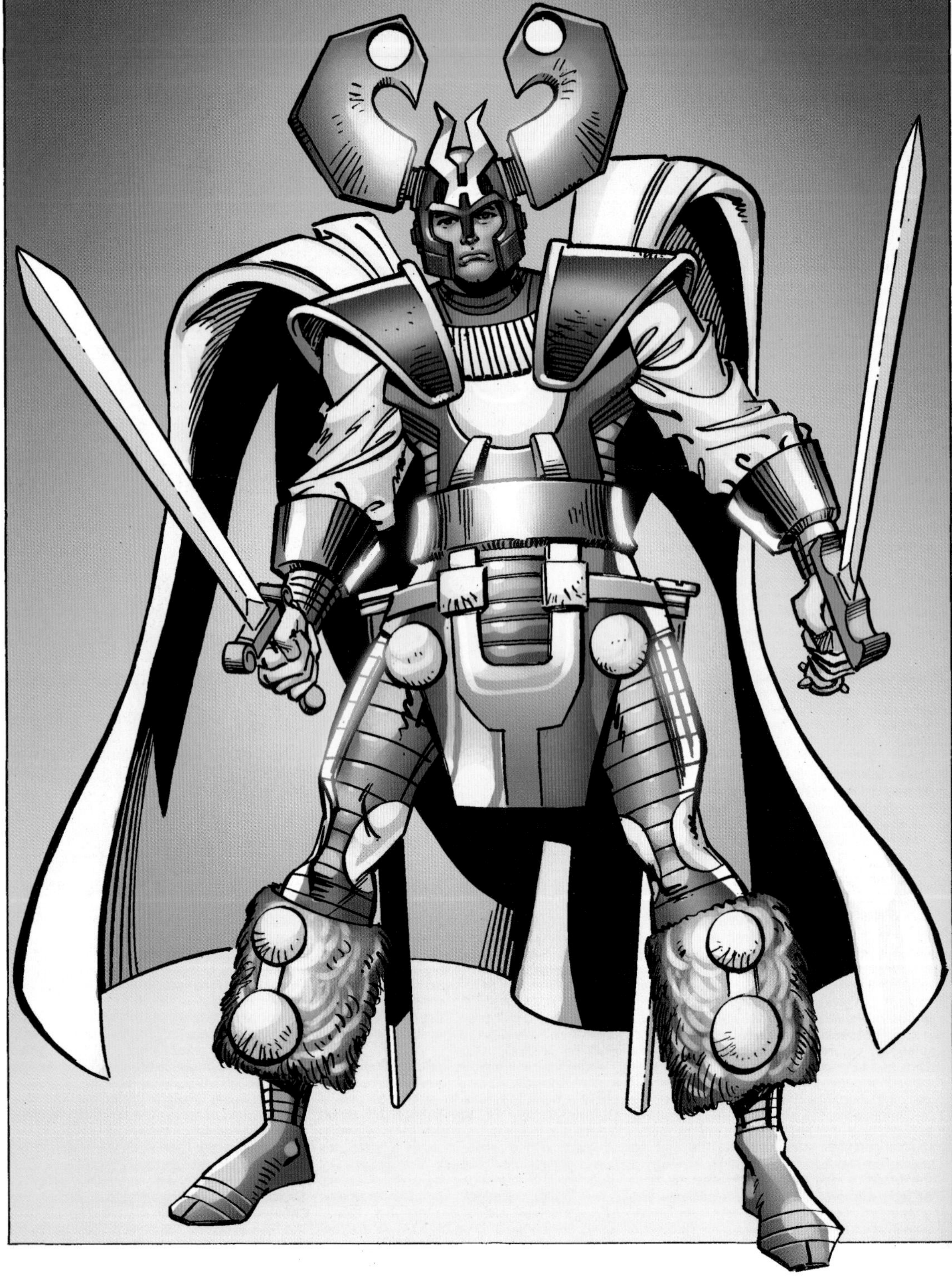

Because of prophecies that Balder's death would help trigger the coming of Ragnarok, the destruction of Asgard and its inhabitants, Odin, ruler of Asgard, commanded his wife Frigga to make Balder invulnerable to harm. Frigga cast spells that would protect Balder from harm by any living or inanimate thing while he was in the Asgardian dimension. (The legends describe her as extracting promises from all of these things not to harm Balder, as if they were all sentient and capable of speech.) The sole exception was mistletoe. This omission is probably not due to forgetfulness on Frigga's part, since she has not made him invulnerable to harm from mistletoe since his vulnerability to it became known. It is more likely that his vulnerability to mistletoe is a necessary side effect of the spells making him invulnerable to harm from other things.

Loki, the god of mischief, learned of the prophecies tying Balder's death to the coming of Ragnarok, and also learned of Balder's vulnerability to mistletoe (see *Loki*). Seeking to bring about Ragnarok, Loki tricked the blind god Hoder into firing an arrow tipped with mistletoe wood at Balder. Balder was fatally wounded, but Odin's power prevented him from actually dying and instead kept him in a state resembling suspended animation (see *Odin*). Nevertheless, Balder's spirit journeyed to Hel, one of the Asgardian realms of the dead. There Balder was appalled at seeing the horrors endured by the spirits of so many of those whom he had slain in battle.

Odin finally restored Balder fully to life, but Balder's hair turned white as a result of his experiences in Hel. His beloved, Nanna, sacrificed her life to save him from entrapment in marriage by Karnilla, and Balder was so distraught that he has resolved never to speak of this incident or of her again. Anguished by Nanna's death and by what he had seen in the land of the dead, Balder forswore the life of a warrior, attempted unsuccessfully to forget his misery through eating, gainining considerable weight in the process, and finally rode out into the desert, hoping to die there. Instead, Balder encountered the Norns, the three goddesses who oversee the workings of destiny. The Norns gave Balder a vision that restored his faith in the value of life and in the need for him to continue living. Balder rode back to Asgard and was sent by Odin to Karnilla to seek her aid in the Asgardians' battle against Surtur and the legions of Muspelheim (see *Surtur*). Balder was successful in this mission, and his relationship appears to have changed in the process. Balder has also returned to his normal weight through vigorous exercise.

Height: 6′ 4″
Weight: 320 lbs.
Eyes: Blue
Hair: White, formerly brown
Strength level: Balder is somewhat stronger than the average Asgardian male, and can lift (press) about 35 tons. (The average Asgardian male can lift about 30 tons.)
Known superhuman powers: Balder possesses the conventional superhuman physical attributes of an Asgardian. Like all Asgardians, Balder is extremely long-lived (though not immortal like the Olympians), superhumanly strong, and immune to all diseases. (Asgardian flesh and bone is about three times denser than similar human tissue, contributing to the Asgardians' superhuman strength and weight.) His Asgardian metabolism gives him superhuman endurance in all physical activities.

Because of spells placed on him by Frigga, queen of Asgard, Balder cannot suffer injury by any living or non-living thing while he is in the Asgardian dimension. Any projectile hurled at Balder which is capable of killing or injuring an Asgardian will be magically deflected from its path before it can strike him. However, Balder can be injured or killed by weapons made of mistletoe wood. Presumably he can also be harmed by the power of Odin, and possibly by the spells and magical energies used by others. Balder could also die in the Asgardian dimension through means that do not involve weaponry: for example, he could starve to death or be asphixiated. Moreover, Frigga's spells do not protect Balder when he is in the Earth dimension. It is not known whether Balder also becomes vulnerable when he is in dimensions other than those of Asgard and Earth.

Abilities: Balder is a brilliant warrior, greatly skilled in hand-to-hand combat, swordsmanship, and horsemanship. ■

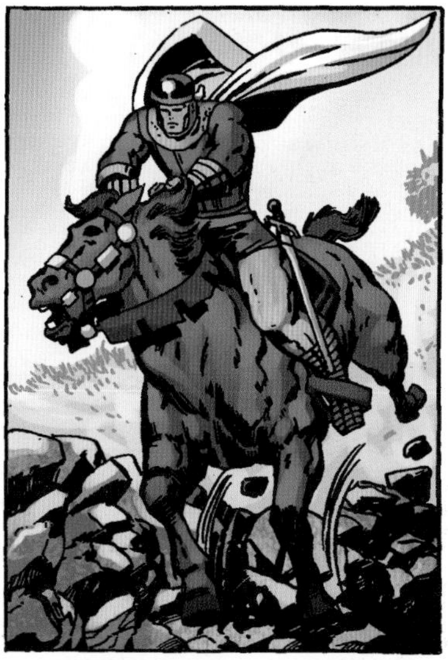

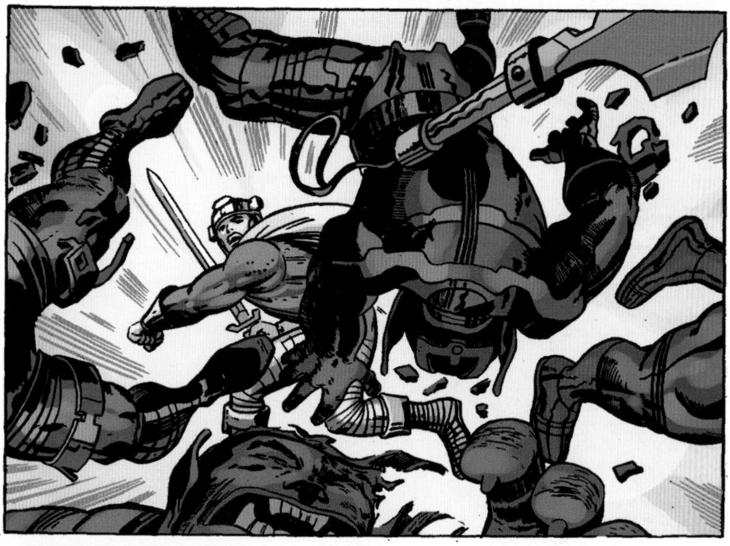

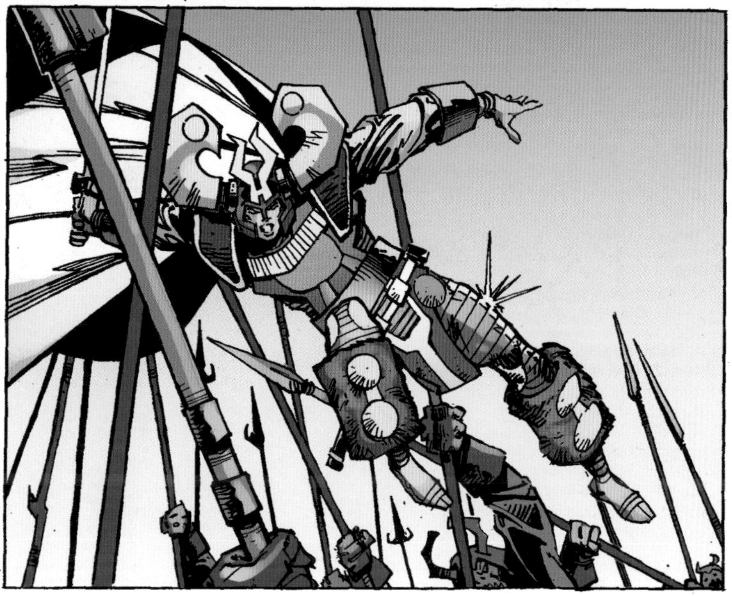

WARRIORS THREE

The Warriors Three are three of Asgard's most celebrated heroes, Hogun, Fandral, and Volstagg, longtime friends who usually work together as a team (see *Asgard*). Their first known mission together took place at an unknown time in the past when they joined the quest by sea led by the prince of Asgard, Thor, to discover the reason why a crack had appeared in the Odinsword (also called Oversword) of Asgard, a power object that could bring about Asgard's destruction (see *Thor, Appendix: Odinsword*). Hogun, Fandral, and Volstagg aided Thor in quelling a mutiny led against Thor, on this mission by his adoptive brother Loki (see *Loki*). Since then Hogun, Fandral, and Volstagg have been Thor's friends, allies, and companions, and have aided him in numerous exploits.

Hogun the Grim is not a native of Asgard, but originally came from an unnamed land elsewhere in the Asgardian dimension. Hogun's homeland was conquered by Mogul of the Mystic Mountain, but together Thor and the Warriors Three defeated Mogul and liberated Hogun's homeland (see *Appendix: Mogul of the Mystic Mountain*).

In contrast with Hogun, who bears a somber demeanor, Fandral the Dashing is known for his humor, high spirits, and love of displaying his prowess with the sword in battle.

Volstagg is older than his two companions, and is rumored to have been one of Asgard's greatest warriors in his youth. Volstagg and his wife Gudrun are raising an enormous family, of whom the best-known member is their spirited daughter Gunnhild ("Hildy"). Recently Volstagg has adopted two children from Earth, Kevin and Mick, the orphaned sons of a woman named Ruby, who was killed by Thor's enemy, the Zaniac (see *Appendix: Zaniac*). Volstagg is motivated to join Hogun and Fandral in exploits both by a love of adventure and by a need to get away from his large family (whom he nonetheless deeply loves) from time to time. Although Volstagg's boastfulness about his battle prowess is sometimes belied by his occasional clumsiness, he remains a far more formidable opponent than his appearance would suggest.

Like other Asgardians, the Warriors Three are extremely long-lived (although not immortal like the Olympian gods), superhumanly strong, immune to all terrestrial diseases, resistant to conventional injury, and in possession of superhuman endurance (see *Asgardians*).

VOLSTAGG

Real name: Volstagg
Occupation: Warrior, father, adventurer
Identity: The general populace of Earth knows of Volstagg but does not acknowledge his godhood
Legal status: Citizen of Asgard
Other aliases: Volstagg the Enormous, the Lion of Asgard
Place of birth: Asgard
Marital status: Married
Known relatives: Gudrun (wife), Alaric, Rolfe (sons), Flosi, Gudrun, Gunnhild ("Hildy") (daughters), Kevin, Mick (adopted sons)
Base of operation: Asgard
First appearance: JOURNEY INTO MYSTERY #119
Height: 6' 8"
Weight: Unknown
Eyes: Blue
Hair: Red
Strength level: In his prime Volstagg could lift (press) about 40 tons. Now he can lift about 35.
Known superhuman powers: Volstagg possesses the conventional superhuman physical attributes of an Asgardian god.
Abilities: In his prime Volstagg is said to have been a great warrior. Although no longer as physically fit as he once was, Volstagg can still use his tremendous bulk to his advantage in combat.

HOGUN

Real name: Hogun
Occupation: Warrior
Identity: The general populace of Earth knows of Hogun but does not acknowledge his godhood
Legal status: Naturalized citizen of Asgard
Other aliases: Hogun the Grim
Place of birth: An unnamed land in the Asgardian dimension
Marital status: Single
Known relatives: None
Base of operation: Asgard
First appearance: JOURNEY INTO MYSTERY #119
Height: 6′ 3″
Weight: 590 lbs.
Eyes: Grey blue
Hair: Black
Strength level: Hogun can lift (press) about 35 tons.
Abilities: Hogun is a superb hand-to-hand combatant and horseman.
Weapons: Hogun's preferred weapon is the mace.

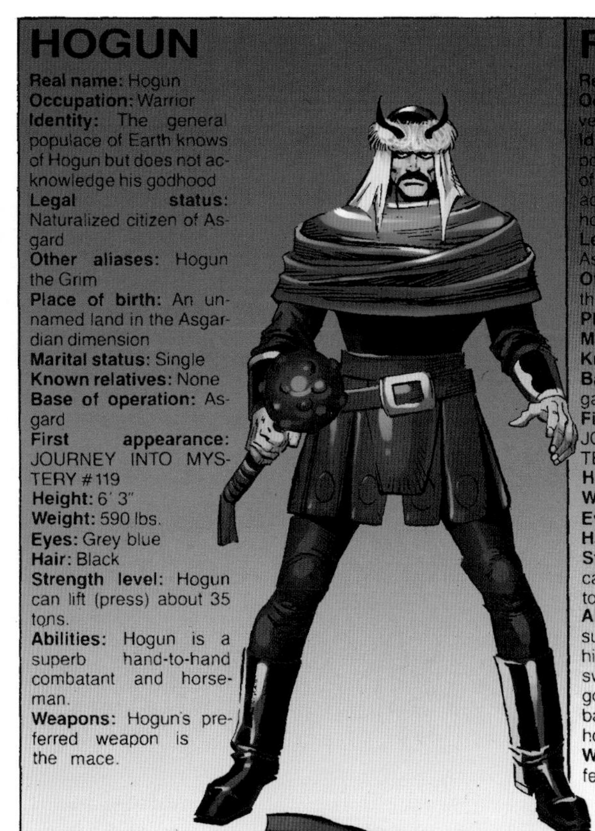

FANDRAL

Real name: Fandral
Occupation: Warrior, adventurer
Identity: The general populace of Earth knows of Fandral but does not acknowledge his godhood
Legal status: Citizen of Asgard
Other aliases: Fandral the Dashing
Place of birth: Asgard
Marital status: Single
Known relatives: None
Base of operation: Asgard
First appearance: JOURNEY INTO MYSTERY #119
Height: 6′ 4″
Weight: 585 lbs.
Eyes: Blue
Hair: Blond
Strength level: Fandral can lift (press) about 30 tons.
Abilities: Fandral is unsurpassed in Asgard in his mastery of swordsmanship. He is good hand-to-hand combatant and an excellent horseman.
Weapons: Fandral's preferred weapon is the sword.

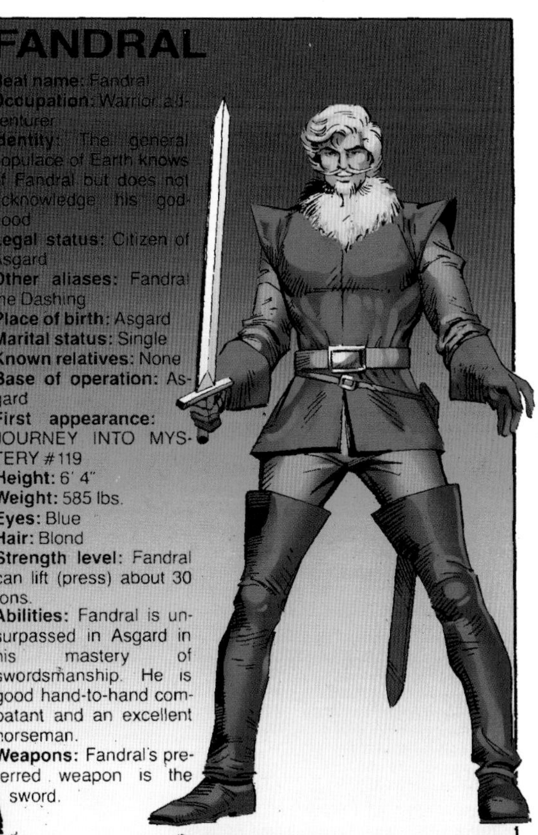

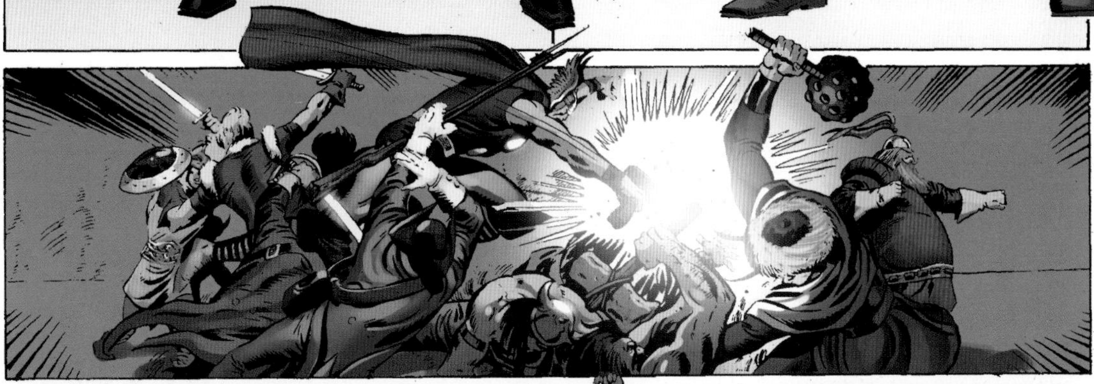

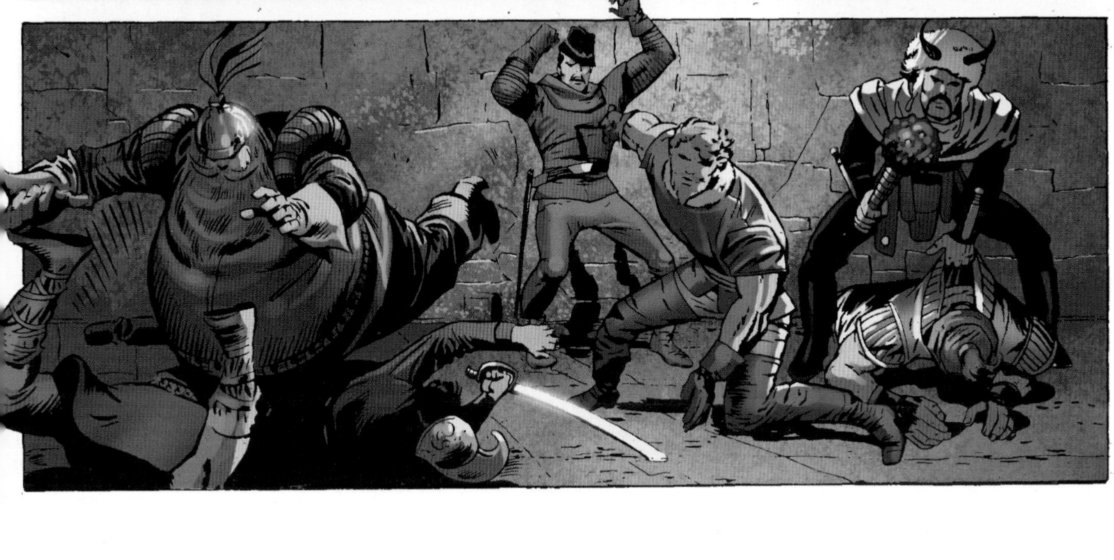

SIF

Real name: Sif
Occupation: Warrior, shield maiden
Identity: Publicly known in Asgard and on Earth, although the general populace of Earth tends not to believe she is a goddess
Legal status: Citizen of Asgard
Other aliases: None
Place of birth: Asgard
Marital status: Single
Known relatives: Heimdall
Group affiliation: Gods of Asgard
Base of operations: Asgard
First appearance: JOURNEY INTO MYSTERY #102
History: Sif is a warrior goddess of Asgard and the sister of Heimdall, the watchman of Asgard (see *Asgard, Asgardians: Heimdall*). As a child she had golden hair and was an occasional playmate of Thor, son of Asgard's ruler Odin, and Thor's adoptive brother Loki (see *Loki, Odin, Thor*).

While Thor and Sif were still adolescents, they fell in love with each other. Determined to ruin his hated adoptive brother's happiness by ending the relationship between Thor and Sif, Loki cut off all of Sif's golden hair while she slept. Realizing Loki must have been responsible, Thor angrily confronted Loki and demanded that he restore Sif's hair. Loki sought out the dwarves Brokk and Eitri and asked that they create new hair for Sif through their arts. However, Loki was either unable or unwilling to pay the dwarves gold for this work. The dwarves decided that for the "price of naught" they would create "strands of naught." They magically created long black hair from the blackness of night. Once set upon Sif's head, the hair magically took root and began to grow. Thor thought Sif was even more beautiful with the black hair than she had been before, and thus Loki's plan to ruin their romance failed.

Eventually Thor and Sif parted when Sif began her training to be a warrior in earnest. Odin, lord of Asgard, had long deemed Sif to be a fitting mate for his son Thor. Just after Thor's relatively brief relationship with the mortal woman Jane Foster came to an end, Odin, hoping to turn Thor's feelings in a different direction, arranged for him to meet Sif once more. Sif was now highly accomplished in the ways of the warrior. Soon after meeting Sif again, Thor and Sif became lovers and companions, as well as allies in numerous battles. Eventually, they decided to marry.

However, Thor's attachment for Earth frequently came between them. Sif much preferred the world of the gods to the mundane world of mortals, and, after attempting to adjust to Earth life on more than one occasion, returned to Asgard to live without Thor. Once, when Thor's mortal paramour Jane Foster was dying, Sif lent her life force to revive the woman, "merging" with her in the process. She did this apparently in an attempt to understand Thor's attraction for this mortal. Jane Foster was separated from Sif shortly thereafter, and sent to the limbo-realm of the Runestaff of the Possessor (see *Possessor*). Sif and Thor have since rescued Foster. Sif and Thor both aided the alien champion Beta Ray Bill in defending his people against the onslaught of the demon armies of Surtur (see *Beta Ray Bill, Surtur*). Sif and Beta Ray Bill found themselves increasingly drawn to each other emotionally. Sif's relationship with Thor was greatly worsened when Thor, who was forced by enchantment to fall in love with the Asgardian Lorelei, struck Sif in anger (see

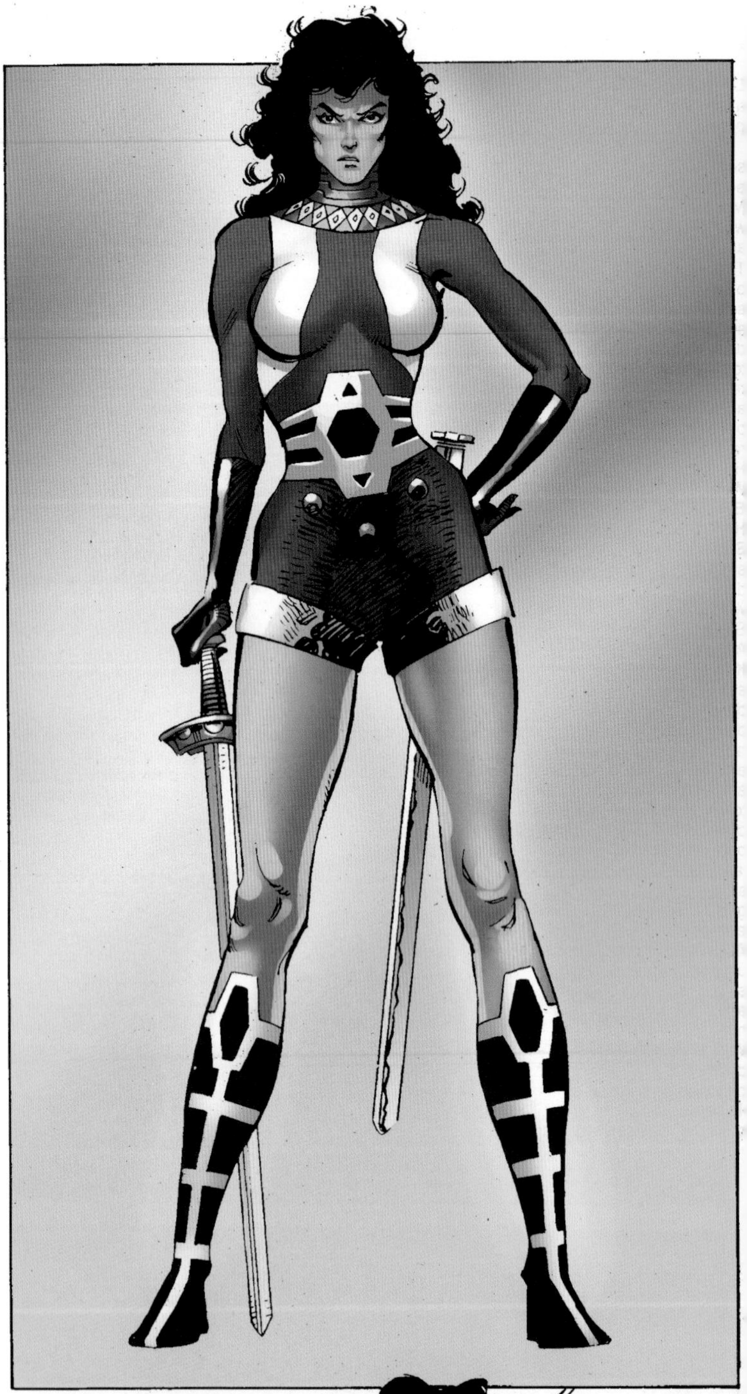

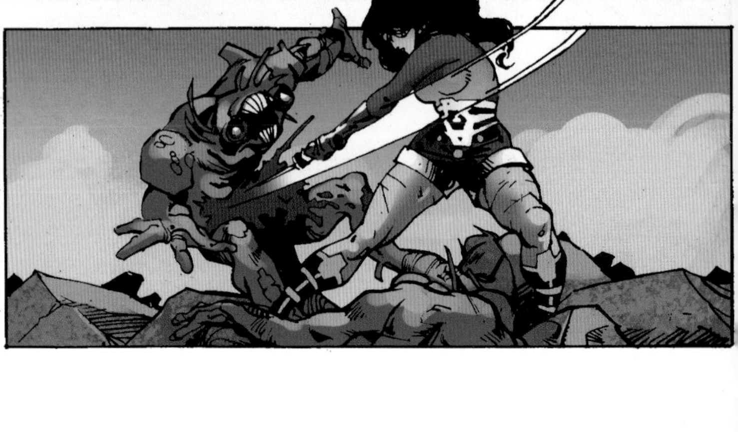

Lorelei). Sif even decided to leave Asgard and accompany Beta Ray Bill back to his people.

However, Sif came to realize how deeply sorry Thor, who had been freed of Lorelei's enchantment, was for having struck her. Moreover, Sif finally fully realized that Lorelei was really to blame for Thor's striking her, and Sif was also greatly impressed by Thor's heroism in descending into the realm of the death goddess Hela to rescue the souls of Earth mortals (see *Hela*). As a result, Sif finally accepted Thor's role as guardian of both Asgard and Earth, and decided to stay behind in Asgard while Beta Ray Bill returned to his people. Sif and Thor are once again linked by strong bonds of affection, but what path their relationship will next take remains to be seen.

Height: 6′ 2″
Weight: 425 lbs.
Eyes: Blue
Hair: Black, originally gold
Strength level: Sif possesses the normal strength of an Asgardian woman ("goddess") of her physical age, height, and build, who engages in intensive regular exercise. Sif can lift (press) 30 tons. (The average Asgardian woman can lift about 25 tons.)
Known superhuman powers: Sif possesses the conventional attributes of an Asgardian woman ("goddess"). Like all Asgardians she is extremely long- lived (though not immortal like the Olympian gods), aging at an extremely slow rate upon reaching adulthood, superhumanly strong, immune to all Earthly diseases, and resistance to conventional injury. Asgardian flesh and bone is about three times denser than similar human tissue, contributing to the gods' superhuman strength and weight. Sif's Asgardian metabolism gives her superhuman endurance at all physical activities.
Abilities: Sif has had extensive training in unarmed combat as well as swordsmanship. Her fighting ability is only surpassed among known Asgardian women by Brunnhilde the Valkyrie (see *Valkyrie*).
Weapons: Sif wields a special sword enchanted by Odin to enable her to "cleave" passageways between dimensions (primarily between Asgard and Earth) by a special pattern of swinging motions. ■

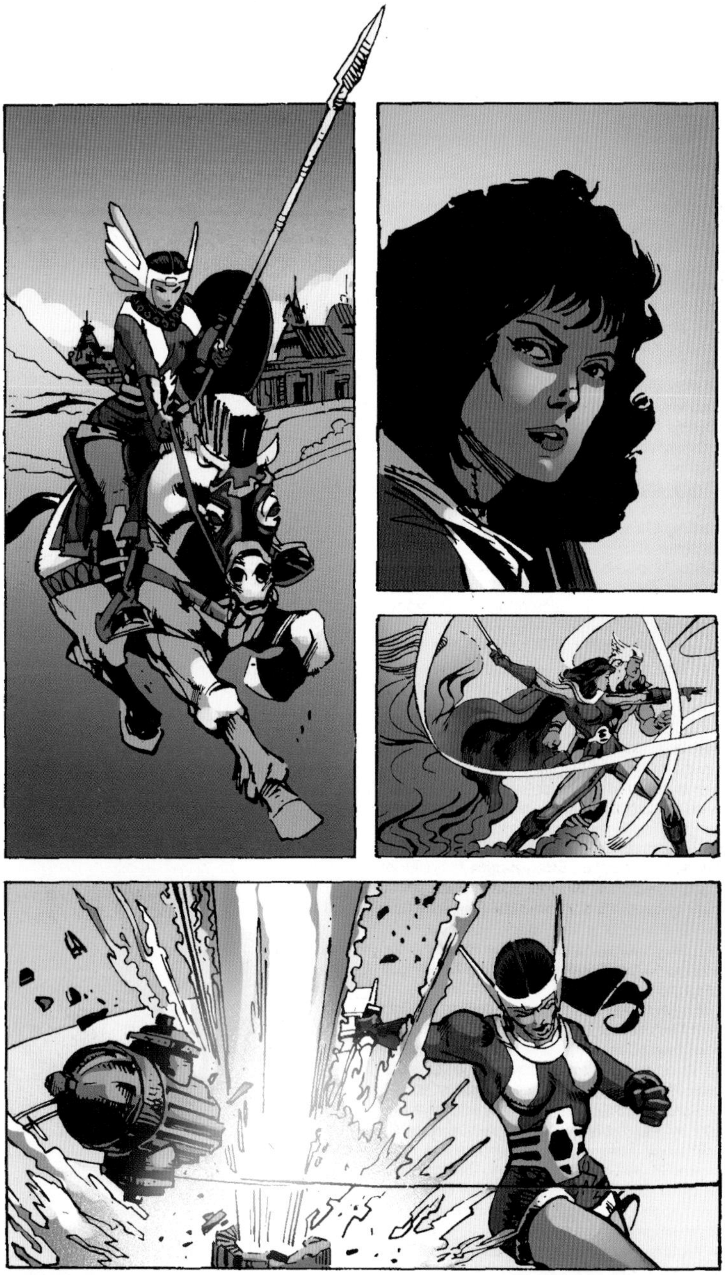

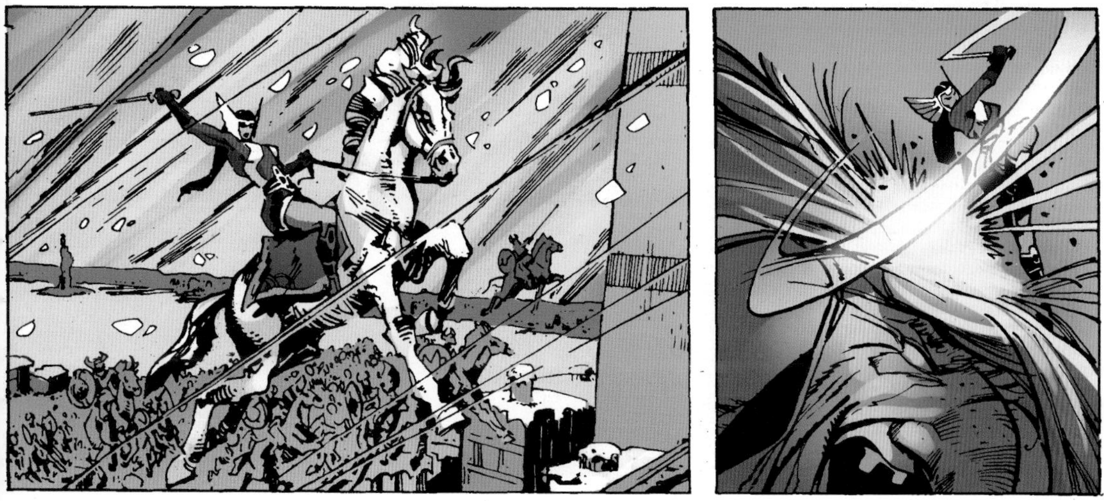

LOKI

Real Name: Loki Laufeyson
Occupation: God of Mischief
Identity: Publicly known to citizens of Asgard. His existence is not known to the general public of Earth.
Legal status: Citizen of Asgard (often in exile)
Former aliases: As a shape-changer, Loki has impersonated a vast number of individuals and things.
Place of birth: Jotunheim
Marital status: Separated
Known relatives: Sigyn (wife, separated), Laufey (father, deceased), Farbauti (mother), Odin (foster father), Frigga (foster mother), Thor (foster brother)
Group affiliation: Sometime ally of Karnilla, the Enchantress, the Executioner, the Absorbing Man, and Lorelei, former ally of Dormammu
Base of operations: A castle on the outskirts of Asgard
First appearance: JOURNEY INTO MYSTERY #85
Origin: JOURNEY INTO MYSTERY #112, 113, 115
History: Loki is the son of Laufey, king of the frost giants of Jotunheim, one of the "Nine Worlds" of the Asgardian cosmology (see *Asgard, Asgardians*). Odin, ruler of Asgard, led his subjects in a war against the giants (see *Odin*). Laufey was slain in battle and the giants were defeated. Surveying the spoils of war, the Asgardians discovered a small god-sized baby hidden at the giants' main fortress. The infant was Loki, whom Laufey had kept hidden due to his shame over his son's diminutive size. Because Loki was the son of a king fallen in battle, Odin elected to adopt him and raise him as a son alongside his bloodson Thor, the future god of thunder (see *Thor*).

In childhood Loki greatly resented the fact that Odin and the other Asgardians favored the young Thor, who already had a nobility of spirit and excelled in all his endeavors, over himself. As a boy Loki began studying the arts of sorcery, for which he had a natural affinity. His hatred of Thor grew, and while still a boy, Loki vowed to become the most powerful god in Asgard and to destroy Thor in order to achieve this end. Ater achieving adulthood Loki began making alliances with other enemies of Asgard.

As Loki grew to adulthood, his inborn propensity for mischief had begun to manifest itself, and he earned the nickname "God of Mischief." But as his deeds grew increasingly malicious, and his lust for power and vengeance became apparent, he became known as the "God of Evil". Loki attempted many times over the centuries to destroy Thor and seize the throne of Asgard for himself. Finally, Odin magically imprisoned him within a tree as punishment for his many crimes. Sometime thereafter, Thor was banished to Earth to learn humility in the mortal form of Dr. Donald Blake.

Shortly after Blake regained the ability to assume the godly form and power of Thor, Loki succeeded in freeding himself from his mystical imprisonment. There followed a long succession of clashes between Loki and Thor. Sometimes Loki battled Thor directly. On other occasions Loki used pawns to fight Thor, some of whom he temporarily endowed with increased superhuman power, such as the Cobra and Mister Hyde (see individual entries). Loki is responsible for transforming "Crusher" Creel into the Absorbing Man and for the revival of the

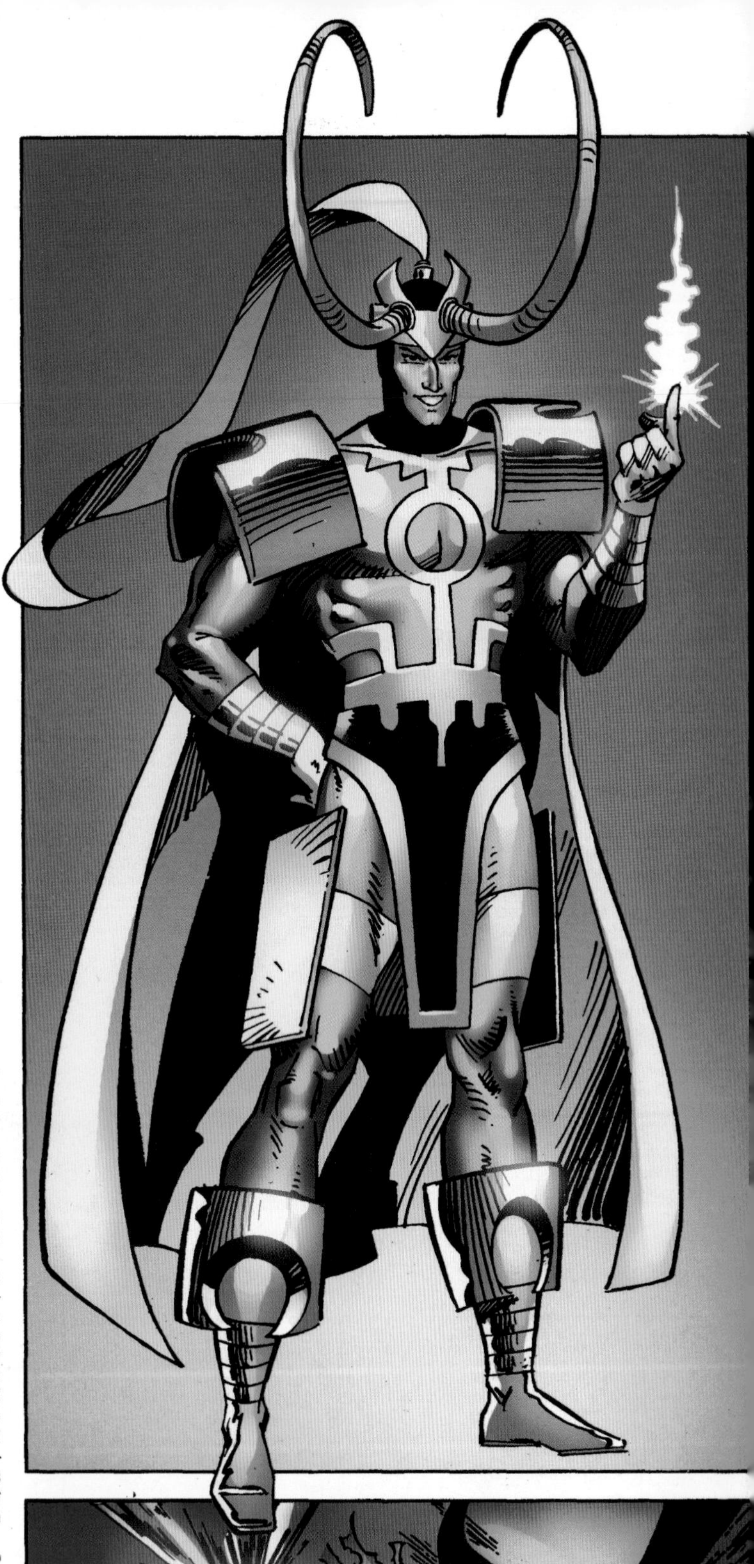

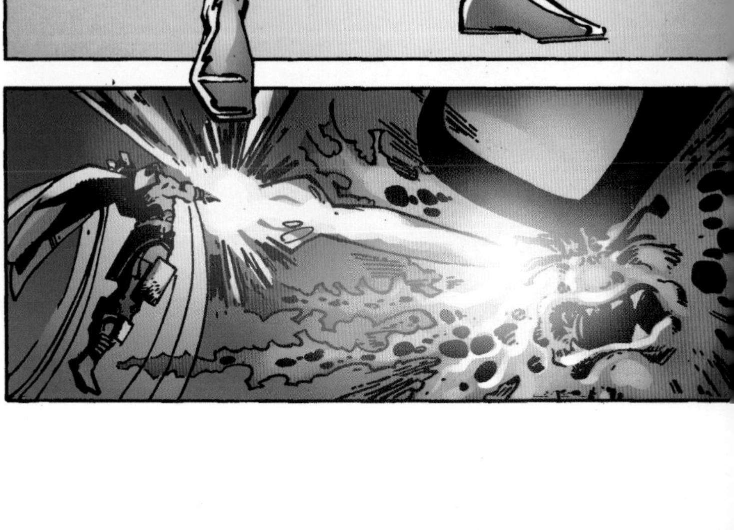

Asgardian Destroyer as an opponent for Thor (see *Absorbing Man, Destroyed: Destroyer*). Loki has attempted to turn Odin against Thor and to steal Thor's enchanted hammer. On one occasion Loki mystically exchanged bodies with Thor. Loki has temporarily seized control of Asgard when Odin was incapacitated. However, Loki has invariably been thwarted in his bids for power and revenge by Thor.

Recently, Loki joined Thor and Odin in their battle against the demonic Surtur (see *Surtur*). Surtur intended to destroy Asgard, and Loki, whose goal is to rule Asgard, therefore felt obliged to stop him. After Odin and Surtur vanished at the end of this battle, Loki began his machinations to be named as the new ruler of Asgard. As part of his plans he magically transformed Thor into a frog, using power drawn from Surtur's abandoned sword. But Thor was returned to his normal form when the Asgardian Volstagg destroyed the engine draining power from the sword (see *Warriors Three*). Loki was unable to prevent the ascension of Balder to the Asgardian throne after Thor refused the throne himself (see *Balder*).

However, Loki is continuing his quest for supreme power in Asgard. It has been said that should the time of Ragnarok, the destruction of the Asgardian gods ever come, Loki will lead the forces of evil against Asgard.

Height: 6' 4"
Weight: 525 lbs
Eyes: Green
Hair: Black-grey
Strength level: Loki possesses the normal strength of an Asgardian male of his age, height, and build. He can lift (press) about 30 tons.

Known superhuman powers: Loki possesses the conventional attributes of an Asgardian, as well as certain innate magical powers. Like all Asgardians, Loki is extremely long-lived (though not immortal like the Olympians), superhumanly strong, immune to all diseases, and resistant to conventional injury. (Asgardian flesh and bone is about 3 times denser than similar human tissue, contributing to the Asgardian's superhuman strength and weight.) His Asgardian metabolism gives him superhuman endurance in all physical activities.

Besides these physical abilities, Loki possesses a host of magical skills. Among these is his ability to transform his shape at will into those of other creatures. He has become such animals as a snake, eagle, mouse, and bee, gaining the basic natural abilities inherent in each form. While he can take on the likeness of another god, giant, or human, he will not necessarily gain the special physical or mental powers of the being he imitates. Loki can also transform external objects into other forms and substances by magic; for instance, he can turn clouds into dragons. He can also bring inanimate objects to life, or mystically imbue objects or beings with specific but temporary powers. He has, for example, augmented the might of such human criminals as the Cobra and Sandu (see *Cobra, Appendix: Sandu*). These magical effects remain only for as long as he maintains the spell that created them.

Loki can project highly powerful concussive bolts of mystical energy. He can also create magical energy fields which serve various purposes. With great concentration, Loki can create a field of sufficient resilience to repel Thor's enchanted hammer (though repeated blows would undoubtedly penetrate it) or physical objects such as large-caliber projectiles. He can also surround objects in mystical energy to levitate them. He once lifted and supported an entire building off the ground for several minutes. He can also mystically levitate himself and thereby fly at great speed. As with his influence over matter, his magical energy feats only last as long as he maintains them.

Loki also has a number of mental and extrasensory powers which are analogous to psionic abilities. He can broadcast his thoughts into other minds as well as plant compelling hypnotic suggestions. These telepathic abilities do not appear to be limited by distance: Loki can even cast his thoughts across dimensions. Loki cannot, however, perceive the thoughts of others. He does have certain extrasensory powers of perception, however, enabling him to see and hear events in distant places simultaneous to their occurrence. He can also mentally project an image of himself, in a manner not unlike astral projection, through which he can communicate with beings in other places.

Loki can also magically create rifts between dimensions, allowing him or other objects passage from one universe to another. Most often this rift is between Asgard and Earth.

Loki also has a vast knowledge of spells which he can use for many magical effects.

Loki has used his magic to enable him to endure injuries with little or no effect which would kill another Asgardian. He has even been beheaded, and yet he continued to live, magically reattached his head to his body, and was in the same condition as he was in before the beheading.

Weapons: Loki occasionally employs certain magical power objects, such as the Norn Stones or rare Asgardian herbs, to augment his own magical powers. These objects or substances are generally used to enhance his immediate personal strength or abilities, or to create a permanent magical transformation, such as that which gave the Absorbing Man his power. He once used the mystical sword of Surtur along with various equipment to transform Thor into a frog while Loki was in Asgard and Thor on Earth (see *Surtur*). The destruction of the engine drawing power from the sword caused Thor to return to his normal form. ∎

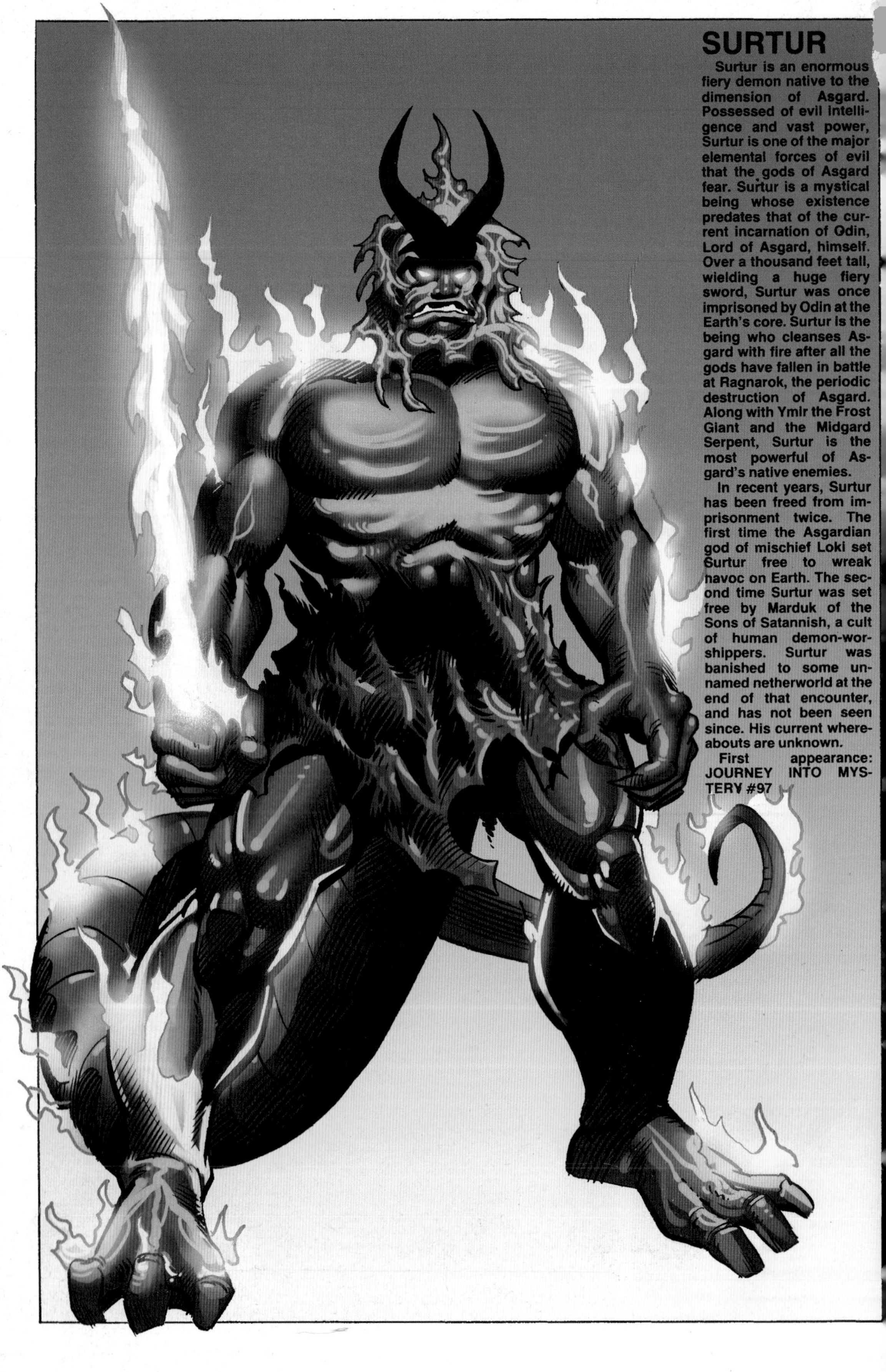

SURTUR

Surtur is an enormous fiery demon native to the dimension of Asgard. Possessed of evil intelligence and vast power, Surtur is one of the major elemental forces of evil that the gods of Asgard fear. Surtur is a mystical being whose existence predates that of the current incarnation of Odin, Lord of Asgard, himself. Over a thousand feet tall, wielding a huge fiery sword, Surtur was once imprisoned by Odin at the Earth's core. Surtur is the being who cleanses Asgard with fire after all the gods have fallen in battle at Ragnarok, the periodic destruction of Asgard. Along with Ymir the Frost Giant and the Midgard Serpent, Surtur is the most powerful of Asgard's native enemies.

In recent years, Surtur has been freed from imprisonment twice. The first time the Asgardian god of mischief Loki set Surtur free to wreak havoc on Earth. The second time Surtur was set free by Marduk of the Sons of Satannish, a cult of human demon-worshippers. Surtur was banished to some unnamed netherworld at the end of that encounter, and has not been seen since. His current whereabouts are unknown.

First appearance: JOURNEY INTO MYSTERY #97